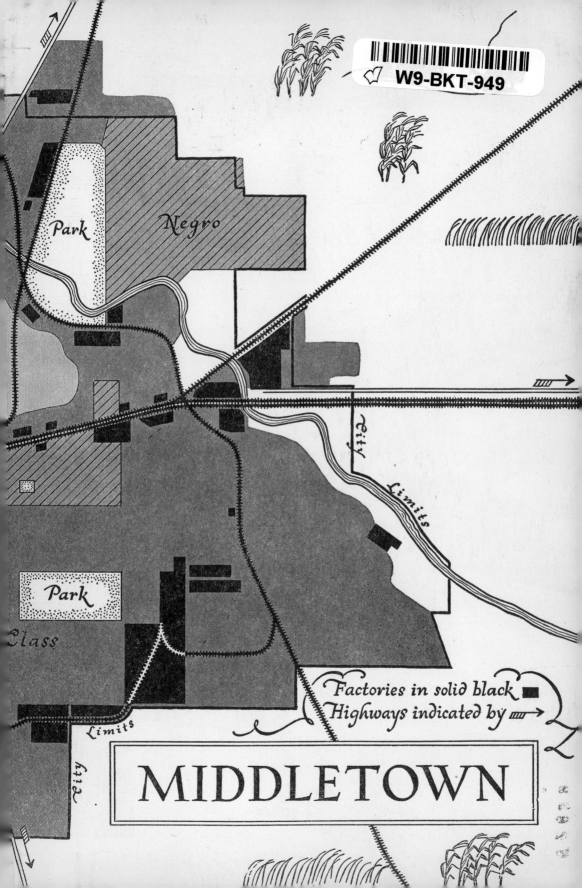

Park

Negro

Park

Class

Factories in solid black
Highways indicated by

City Limits

City Limits

MIDDLETOWN

MIDDLETOWN IN TRANSITION

MIDDLETOWN IN TRANSITION

A Study in Cultural Conflicts

BY

Robert S. Lynd & Helen Merrell Lynd

Harcourt, Brace and Company
New York

20568

CONTENTS

CONTENTS

ACKNOWLEDGMENTS

The field staff for this study included, in addition to the director, the following persons, the first three graduate students at Columbia University and the last two graduates of Sarah Lawrence College:

> Bela Gold
> Katharine Hogle
> Mary Frances Holter
> Hannah Cheney
> Edna Albers Stewart

Without their keen and untiring assistance it would have been impossible to gather the wealth of material which makes this restudy possible. The director is particularly indebted to Mr. Gold, who, in addition to sharing in the field work, has also given helpful criticisms in the writing of the manuscript and contributed particularly to the statistical analysis in Chapter II.

Most of all, this report is indebted to the people of Middletown. Not only did they cooperate generously during the period of the field work, but in the subsequent period of adding to and checking the data, many individuals have been endlessly helpful in assembling material, making special studies at certain points, and in reading and criticizing sections of the report. It is the hope of the writers that Middletown will not regard this study as an attempt to single out Middletown, or groups or individuals in the city, for praise or blame. The reason for undertaking such a study as this lies in the assumption that there is so much that is common to tendencies in the broader culture of the nation in a Middletown that a detailed interwoven analysis of the single community will throw light on the situation we all face at this stage of our American civilization.

Helen Merrell Lynd did not take part in the 1935 field work, but, from her background of the earlier study and continued contacts with the city, she has shared in the analysis of the material and in the writing of the report.

PREFACE

O NE turns back with misgiving in the midst of other urgent concerns of later growth to the restudy of a problem once familiar. Life does not live itself backward, nor does one willingly linger over one's own earlier footprints.

Then, too, every extended piece of painstaking research leaves a kind of emotional scar tissue in the investigator. The field work is strenuous but exciting. In the case of the original *Middletown* study it lasted a year and a half. Thereafter one lives for an equal time or longer—in the case of *Middletown* it was three years and a half—in a mood alternating between enthusiasm and weary disgust as the job worms its exhausting course through rough draft, revision, checking and cross-checking, and compression for publication.

In the present instance there has been the additional deterrent that the investigator is critical of the type of research that throws its net too broadly, as does the general "survey." By and large, social research seems to him to make larger gains by digging vertically rather than by raking together the top-soil horizontally; and a disproportionate amount of energy in current social research appears to him to be going into the latter sort of work. There are, to be sure, certain situations in which the broader procedure is in order: where, as in the study of many primitive societies, the object of investigation is changing so rapidly under contact with more advanced cultures that the best that can be hoped for is the sketching in of the wider aspects of these remote cultures before they are lost; or where a new field, like that of child development, is emerging, and certain broadly integrative studies are useful to define problems; and, finally, in cases where many separate vertical borings have been going forward in older fields and an effort is made periodically by a horizontal study to re-view these current findings as a single pattern. In the last two cases the survey justifies itself only as it invites attention to new problems, and not by simply throwing another chunk of miscellaneous data onto the research pile.

The original *Middletown* study of 1924-25 may perhaps qualify under the third of the above exceptions, *i.e.,* as integrating many

ix

scattered vertical research borings, not without some useful redefinition of focus at certain points.

The point made in all of the above is not that social science needs to put on blinders or to narrow its range of vision. Quite the contrary. The most hopeful tendency in contemporary research in the social sciences is the viewing of sharply defined problems against the widest possible setting in the entire institutional world in which they operate. But this type of research looks at the broad field *with a single problem as its focus.* This is quite a different procedure from approaching a broad field with a number of very general hypotheses and seeking to get a "general picture."

The social scientist as an impersonal worker selecting problems and analyzing them with bloodless concern only for science exists no more than does the "economic man." Subjective factors inevitably intrude, and the community survey tends to be peculiarly vulnerable in this regard. Its very scope and informality, combined with the necessity of protecting individuals by scrupulous anonymity, tends to throw undue weight upon detached comments by inadequately identifiable persons, and upon the use of such bits of data as supporting evidence for a generalized conclusion. The reliance upon the subjective processes of the investigator which the use of such evidence entails goes far beyond the normal tolerances of scientific accuracy. If the inferences drawn from such episodic material are correct, they owe this to sensitive insights of the investigator rather than to their being scientifically based conclusions. The attempt to apply such labels as "superior" and "inferior" to insight *as over against* the careful marshaling of data seems to the investigator irrelevant and misleading; for knowledge cannot advance without both insight and data, and the need is obviously for the maximum admixture of both, the one constantly checking the other in the endless game of leapfrog between hypothesis and evidence as understanding grows.

In view of all the preceding, the reluctance of the investigator to return to Middletown for what had of necessity, in view of other heavy research commitments, to be a brief and inadequate "restudy" will be understandable. The suggestion for such a restudy had been made repeatedly by various persons and agencies. The investigator was immersed in another study dealing with the impact of the depression upon a small, relatively homogeneous group of families. The opportunity to use the 1925 study of Middletown as a base line against which to analyze the broad changes of the dramatic ten years of boom and depression as they affected a familiar community finally tempted him to undertake what in anticipation was to be at most one or two chapters added as a postscript to a new edition of the original volume. What was to have been an exciting summer interlude has turned into an intensive analysis of more than a year. That this was the case testifies to the vitality of the problem which Middletown presented in 1935.

Middletown naturally has varied reactions to the original 1925 study. A question asked of people of all sorts in connection with the 1935 re-study was: "What statements in the study of ten years ago do you Middletown people feel to have been distorted or inadequate?" Such of these sins of omission and commission as could be discovered are noted in the appropriate places throughout the pages that follow. The local attitude toward the book is fairly well summarized in the following editorial comment by the editor of the afternoon paper:

MIDDLETOWN

If you have not read *Middletown,* you have not taken proper stock of yourself. I scanned through it when it was first issued and lately have been reading it in detail, comparing [the author's] notations with my own knowledge of the town—a knowledge that encompasses most of a lifetime, whereas Lynd's observations cover only a few months.

And I was startled to discover that in a rather large way his conclusions, or what may be taken for conclusions since he never renders a definite opinion, were the things that had occurred to me time after time. I was startled because, being a citizen of the community, I was fearful of facing the facts which he, as a nonresident, could face with utter nonchalance.

Of course, Lynd has the provincial view of the highly trained specialist in humanology, if there is such a word which I doubt greatly. He likes to take a mind apart, especially a rather inferior mind, to see what makes it tick, if it does. But one reading his story, in spite of the fact that it has been highly acclaimed by H. L. Mencken, must admit that it largely rings true.

Lynd endeavors to take the bunk out of our social conditions, not as meaning [Middletown] but meaning America, and he does it rather thoroughly by quotations instead of assertion of opinions. . . .

Still it is well to have such a critic. The body politic needs an overhauling at certain intervals just as the physical body needs it. Lynd has done a distinct service for [Middletown] or he would have done it if everybody here were to read his book, for it would awaken us all out of our contented, quiescent attitude.

The words that Middletown inclines to apply to the earlier study are "cold," "cynical," and "mechanical." (On the other hand, a research seminar engaged on the book at the University of Vienna envisaged the author as a bewhiskered elderly gentleman because of the benign conservatism which the book appeared to them to exhibit!) The dean of the local college, addressing clubwomen on the book, told them:

"It is no longer fashionable to take the cynical view of life, and the survey of the city grew out of an era of criticism. . . . The era of cynicism in which the book was written is waning."

A speaker at the great "recovery" dinner of the Chamber of Commerce in June, 1935, said of the book:

"One thing that was resented in the book *Middletown* was that, with all the dispassionate laboratory analysis and all the microscopic study of Middletown and its people, the Lynds used everything but a stethoscope. Had they used a stethoscope, they would have had a far different report to write. They would have depicted the influences that made it vital—[Middletown's] heart."

The central criticism of *Middletown* by the Middletown people is, then, that, while true, it tends to be cold, an aggregation of facts lacking some of the vital tissue that makes the city live. The writer doubts whether one hundred individuals in Middletown (other than students at the college) have actually read the book through, though many more than that have taken it from the library. The vagueness of the answers to the request for specific criticisms suggested that many local people knew the book chiefly by hearsay. Most South Side people had apparently not even heard of the book. Local regard for the book has actually had its ups and downs: When it first appeared, many people were immediately proud of the fact that the city "had been written up in a book"; the Chamber of Commerce used on its literature, "Selected as the Ideal American City," and this phrase was widely used locally. Shortly after its publication, the book was placed in the cornerstone of the handsome new downtown Methodist Church, and this elicited from the editor of Middletown's Democratic weekly the gleeful jibe: "If any of you people had taken the trouble to read *Middletown* and had read what it says about your Methodist Church instead of accepting it as a fine book on the world's say-so, that book would never have been placed in that cornerstone. I am looking forward to the day when you people will read it and rush to tear down your 'cathedral' in order to get that damned book out of the cornerstone. Just because it *is* a wonderful book that tells the truth." When Mencken reviewed *Middletown* in the *American Mercury* under the title "A City in Moronia," with the text of the review stressing the "unbelievable stupidities" of the people, the review hurt, and it made Middletown mad. As the book gained recognition, however, the earlier positive mood returned.

When the research staff arrived in 1935, the city was friendly and cordial, with perhaps just a note of caution. There were bantering reproachful remarks that "you sorta made us out as a town of hicks," but everywhere the cooperation was marked and spontaneous. While the investigator was confronted on every hand by the general statement that "we have made big changes since you were here before," other persons remarked as did one business man, "Generally speaking, [Middletown] is sitting on about the same spot as it was when the survey was made." As one editor put it: "[Lynd in 1935] may be seeking some decisive change he will not find. His story of the [Middletown] of 1925 does not need any important revision. People's minds and habits do not change much in a decade."

In view of the difficulties in being completely "objective" in any study of this sort, as noted above, and of Middletown's friendly strictures on the earlier book, it is perhaps not out of order to seek to appraise briefly the basic attitudes with which investigator and community look out on the world.

Although reared during his first eighteen years in a city of 18,000 population in the same state as Middletown, the investigator came to Middletown in 1924 after fourteen years spent in the East. Accordingly, he may have had an outlook somewhat different from the modal outlook of Middletown, even though the cultures of the East North Central and Middle Atlantic States are fundamentally overwhelmingly alike. The fact that he came from ten years of residence in New York City to a city of 36,000 in 1924 may have emphasized latent differences. The fact that, despite several years of business experience, he came as an "academic" person undoubtedly made a difference. Middletown, immersed in the immediacies of getting a living with its current coinage of techniques and symbols, naturally finds it hard to understand a person who spends his working life appraising rather than manipulating the going system, and particularly one who habitually uses as part of his professional equipment unfamiliar ways of looking at familiar things. If to all of these potentials of difference is added a rather fundamental difference in the way investigator and community view cultural processes, the likelihood of mutual divergence in opinion as to what are "the essentials" becomes precariously great. For every people tends to regard its own culture as superior, not perfect, perhaps, but essentially admirable. In such an emotional outlook there is no place for the possibility that one's culture may be employing at certain points stone-age axes side by side with its modern industrial machines. The commonplace assumptions of the student of comparative culture— such assumptions as that no cultural form is ultimate, inevitable, divinely or otherwise ordained, and that every culture is a congeries of institutional habits representing marked differences in modernity and functional adaptation—lie in the main over the horizon from everyday Middletown thought. In such matters an inescapable gulf separates the points of view of Middletown and of an investigator who comes in from outside to study it, for the latter is under no emotional compulsion to defend Middletown. He is not a permanent part of its life, his future is not its future, his hopes need not be its hopes. In this difference in emotional need to emphasize local integrity lies the genesis of many of the criticisms of "superficiality" and "unfairness" that are leveled by the people observed against the outside observer.

An analysis of a community may be attempted either in terms of how the community views itself, or of how it appears when its symbols are viewed *as symbols,* its rationalizations *as rationalizations,* with the aid of hypotheses as to how human nature functions and how cultural processes occur. The first type of picture tends to err on the side of the optimism of a Chamber of Commerce brochure, and the second may err on the side of an apparent cynicism—the "I-am-wise-enough-to-see-what's-the-matter-with-you" attitude. The object of a penetrating study is to combine both procedures; to understand through intimate participation how the persons who carry the culture within their skins feel toward it, and yet to avoid the contagion of local enthusiasm enough to be able to analyze the how's and why's of the local scene against the generalized knowledge of comparative cultures. Obviously, no study achieves such Jovian prescience and impartiality. (And fictitional treatments, likewise, seeking to walk the same narrow fence, tend to fall off to one side or the other—with the Booth Tarkingtons on the one hand and the Sinclair Lewises on the other; and it is probable that the insights of a writer like Ruth Suckow are more appreciated by Iowa folk who have "escaped" to large cities than by those who continue to reside in Iowa.)

This complex problem was summed up simply by a local editor in the following paragraph in his daily column of "Comment" in June, 1935:

Elbert Scoggins [a local successful fiction writer of whom Middletown is proud and who has removed from Middletown since 1925] once told me that he would like to write a story that would depict the life of [Middletown], but he thought he was unable to do so, although he is famous as a writer of fiction. "If I were able to tell the story of [Middletown]," he said, "I am pretty sure I could not do it without offending somebody." The story of [Middletown], if truthfully told, would reflect the same kind of tale that could be told anywhere—of miserliness, of generosity, of wealth, of pauperism, of bitterness and hatreds, of love and loyalty, of beauty and utter ugliness.

Even so-called "scientific" description of social phenomena is inevitably selective, the field being strained, as suggested above, through the awareness of the observer as sensitized by his past experience. If to this "mere description"—which is thus never "mere"—is added analysis, the element of selection, and the role of the describer-analyst's values assume critical importance. No social scientist works without "values" in the *selection* of his problems—though the "good" scientist seeks to test his hypotheses rather than to prove his values. What he tries to do is to make his values with which he approaches and selects problems internally coherent and as close as possible to reality as he sees it, to curb those values that are in his judgment inappropriate to a given research situation, and, where his values diverge from those commonly held, to make his point of view explicit. In line with this last and in at least partial illumination of the difference in outlook of the investigator from the outlook of Middletown, the following points of view of the investigator pertinent to the earlier study as well as to the present one are listed briefly:

Middletown tends to regard human nature as "rational," "free," and "responsible," and there is large precedent for so doing. On the other hand, the emphasis of recent psychology is that actions of human beings are only to a limited extent rational, while to a far greater extent they are colored by individual emotional needs and responsive to previous cultural conditioning.

People tend, therefore, to act as cultural agents, and society shares responsibility with the individual for his actions. A given culture tends to select out and to emphasize personality types that are viable in it.

Middletown tends to read into social change, particularly in the development of the United States, a fairly consistent and ultimately inevitable movement toward "betterment." It thus takes for granted, for the United States and for itself, "progress." The student of cultural change, however, tends to regard the process as neutral, not loaded permanently in either direction, with future eventualities wide open.

Again, Middletown tends to regard its institutions—its capitalist economy, its religion, its education, its form of government—as substantially final products of "progress" and as the "best in the world." This imparts a certain sacrosanct quality to them in the mind of Middletown. But, again, the student of comparative culture takes the view that any institutional form in a given setting is simply a product of a given set of conditions, to be scrutinized candidly in the light of the rest of the culture, including its values, with the question: "How does it operate?"

With such a view of progress and of its social institutions, Middletown regards foreign intrusions involving criticisms of its institutions and invitations to cultural change with initial antagonism. It tends to regard all cultural change uneasily and to reject the idea of sudden change altogether as contrary to that "slow progress dictated by the order of nature." The student of culture recognizes here a tendency common to human beings everywhere and to the cultures which their habits constitute; for the habit systems of human beings tend to resist change and only to make small minimum adaptations by a process of "inching along." This resistance to change tends to be maintained long after the demands of inner coherence and smooth functioning of individual and of culture demand more forthright adaptation; and this tolerance of disparities is the psychological accompaniment of the cultural phenomenon known as "cultural lag." According to this point of view, which the present investigator shares, the "goodness" or "badness" of slow or sudden, large or small, cultural change is relative and not absolute, and relative only to the values which a given culture wishes to achieve and the conditions controlling its achievement of them. But in a culture that values, as Middletown does, "progress" and having "the best in the world," particularly when this culture is involved in an era of rapid and irregular cultural change, the investigator believes that the realization of these very values depends at many points upon the cultivation of an attitude of hospitality, rather than of resistance, to change. In view of the

rapidity of some cultural changes in Middletown in recent decades, its resistance to change, its failure to embrace change as an opportunity to lessen
its frictions, may constitute a liability to its own values.

The role of habit and of the familiar in so prompting Middletown to resist change is heavily supplemented at all critical points by the existence of
pressure groups with vested interests of property and status in the maintenance of past procedures favorable to them.

Middletown believes that *laissez-faire* individualism is the best road to
"progress." The present investigator holds the view, on the other hand, that
our modern institutional world has become too big and too interdependent
to rely indiscriminately upon the accidents of *laissez faire;* and that this
fact has been tacitly recognized by various interested groups in the culture in their sporadic substitution of other procedures at certain points.
In this situation, he believes that either an undiscriminating adherence to
the symbols of *"laissez faire,"* "individual freedom," and "free competition" or sporadic and privately controlled abandonment of *laissez faire*
operates not to realize others of Middletown's central values such as "progress" and "making the city a better place to live in," but to increase the
confusion and friction within the culture.

The recognition by the investigator of these differences in point of
view means that he has tried constantly to correct for any bias they
might introduce. On the other hand, research without a point of view
is impossible. If research were mere photography science would stand
still, swamped in the mass of undifferentiated and unoriented detail.
Science depends upon sensitized, coherent points of view orientated
around reality. This outlook of the investigator influences directly the
selection and formulation of the questions he thinks it important to
ask (*e.g.,* the decision to *include* in the present study such a question
as the relevance of Middletown's present political symbols to the tasks
its political institutions are actually seeking to cope with, but to *exclude*
such a thing as how many stones went into the south wall of the new
Methodist church). His point of view thus performs the indispensable
function of operating as a screen sifting out what seem, in his view of
the field as a scientific problem area, the relevant and significant from
the irrelevant and insignificant questions. Thereafter, if he is honest
and self-critical, he does not seek to bolster his own intellectual position but rather to marshal all relevant data, pro and con, around these
questions.

No such inventory of one's own orientation as that given in the
items listed in the pages above is exhaustive, as one can peel down

layer after layer of tentatively held specific conclusions under each such general heading. The above listing of the investigator's tentatively held assumptions in approaching the study of Middletown should suffice, however, to give to the reader and to Middletown some of the sources of the "cold analytical cynicism" of which the investigator himself is unconscious. If he has missed the "great warm heart" of Middletown, he is nevertheless not unaware of a deep emotional kinship with these open-hearted folk so many of whom he thinks of as his friends. On more than one late evening in June, 1935, he refused his hospitable host's offer to drive him back to his hotel, in order to walk back alone along the quiet, shaded streets pondering the birthright that he, along with other midland boys migrated to large cities, has relinquished for the debatable advantages of the metropolis.

Needless to say, the present investigation does not in any sense supplant the earlier study covering the years 1885-1925. It is built upon the earlier work, and brings down to date that record of forty years of change. Many of its elaborations can be understood only when viewed from the base line of the earlier study. The format of six sections and twenty-nine chapters of the earlier study is here compressed to thirteen chapters. All six areas are brought down to date, and in general the earlier method of building the chapters around persistent institutional functions is followed.

One additional point regarding method might well be added to the Note on Method appended to the original study, in view of the large use made of quoted statements of individuals. In many cases it was impossible to write down a statement in the midst of an interview or informal conversation. In all such cases it was the practice of the staff to note the sequence and phraseology of the statement carefully and to record it as literally as possible immediately after the interview. There is an element of error lurking in such a procedure; it is believed that with this method of immediate recording it is reduced to an unimportant minimum.

R. S. L.

New York City

MIDDLETOWN IN TRANSITION

CHAPTER I

Middletown Revisited

THE YEAR and a half of field work that preceded the original Middletown study ended in June, 1925. The Middletown of the mid-1920's was viewed as a culture rooted in custom and yielding unevenly to the pressure of changes in its technologies and beliefs. A forty-year time span extending back to the placid little county seat of the 1880's was employed in presenting this turgid process of change and lag. The industrial revolution came to Middletown in this period and the county seat of 6,000 grew into a city of six times that size. One was viewing the intertwined processes of industrialization and of urbanization in a contemporary culture.

Since 1925 the city of 36,500 has grown under the prodigal hand of prosperity to almost 50,000 [1] and has experienced momentous impetus to social change. During the greater part of these ten years it has not been primarily the familiar concomitants of growing size and of the further mechanization of its industrial processes that have forced the pace of social change. The major impetus has come, rather, from events outside the control of this immediate local culture, resulting in the shock of sharp and sudden institutional breakdown. This type of situation is one of the most emphatic invitations to social change which a culture can experience. During the first half of the decade, the good years of the late 1920's, men were talking of the arrival of "permanent prosperity"; here it seemed was America's "manifest destiny" come to stay, the culminating vindication of the goodness of being alive and an American. Middletown busily turned its wishes into horses—and then abruptly and helplessly rode them over a precipice.

It is the constant lament of the social sciences that the subjects of their study can never be analyzed under exact experimental conditions. There is no escape from this, but it becomes the more important to exploit as far as possible anything approaching an experimental situ-

[1] See Appendix I for population estimates for each of the years since 1925. The city's population rose to 48,000 in 1931-32 and stood at 47,000 in 1935.

ation wherever it presents itself. Here is an American city which had been the subject of eighteen months of close study in 1924-25. During the following decade the conditions of its existence had been unexpectedly altered in a way which affected every aspect of its life. Its growing population had been tossed from prosperity beyond any experienced prior to 1925 to an equally unprecedented depression. The opportunity thus presented to analyze its life under the stress of specific interrupting stimuli, whose course can be traced, offered something analogous to an experimental situation.

Inevitably certain questions urgently invited further study: How much has the city actually changed through the experiences of boom and depression? Has the basic texture of this culture been tough enough to resist change and to remain intact? Have the different rates of change in different areas of living pointed out in the earlier study been maintained during this critical period? How has the deep faith of this people in the value of standing unaided on one's own feet withstood the experience of unprecedented public relief? Is their confident outlook on the future altered? Are people returning sharply to the old faiths, or are they moving out to embrace new ways of thought? What changes are being wrought in the young as compared with their elders, and in the various groups in the community? Has the depression created more sense of community, or new cleavages? Have the latent conflicts observed in 1925 within this culture pattern been sharpened or modified?

Despite a natural reluctance to seek answers to questions of such subtlety and moment in the unavoidably limited time available, it was decided to make a try. In June, 1935, the director of the original study returned to Middletown with a staff of five assistants.

The appraisal which follows does not pretend to be a restudy comparable in scope and thoroughness to the original 1925 study. The study involved less than a tenth of the man-days of research time spent in Middletown on the 1924-25 study; but this disparity in time was lessened somewhat by the fact that in the restudy it was possible to make a running start without the usual loss of time in fumbling for local sources and personal contacts. Brief visits to the city had been made during the ten years, and through personal friends and the local press the writers had kept in touch with the main events in the city's life.

The research yield was further enhanced by the cordial cooperation of local people; for no finer evidence of the spirit of these open-hearted people of the American midland could be cited than this fact that, after enduring once the not wholly pleasant process of sitting for a portrait that had avoided the flattering manipulation of lights and screens dear to booster philosophy and had painted "wart and all," they again cooperated wholeheartedly with the research staff.

The brevity of the field work made the use of refined research techniques and measurements impossible. Existing records of all kinds were combed, scores of interviews both formal and informal were made and recorded, the research assistants lived in homes scattered throughout the city and participated in a variety of the normal social affairs of the city; and newspaper files from January, 1929, through November, 1936, have been searched systematically, with a coverage of six to twelve months in each year. Since the field work came to an end, many additional data have been secured from national and local sources, again with the assistance of Middletown people.

Field workers are not cameras snapshotting uncritically whatever they are aimed at, and the different members of the staff came to Middletown with varying tentative hypotheses as to what they might find. On the one hand, there were some who were ready to believe that the city must differ radically from its earlier self, since no population could go through the things the United States has experienced in the past ten years without changes in both the overt and the intangible aspects of its life so profound as to alter that life fundamentally and permanently. As over against this tentative position was another held by other members of the staff. These persons, deeply impressed by the retarding undertow of habit, particularly habits of thought and sentiment, were curious as to whether Middletown had changed at all in any fundamental respects; whether, in other words, the boom of the late 1920's had been essentially but a further extension of the old midland American gospel of "progress," and the succeeding depression, however drastically felt at the moment, little more than an external depression in a ball ready to spring back the moment the outside pressure was released. In between these two extremes was the possibility, always to be looked for in the study of a culture presenting a social organization as elaborate and tolerating such wide extremes as are to be found in a Middletown, that the decade 1925-35 might not have affected all elements of the city alike. Thus, for instance, the impact of these changing years upon business class and upon working class might conceivably have been different; [2] or some sectors of living might have changed radically and permanently for all the people in Middletown, while other areas of living remained much as they were in 1925. Yet another possibility was that seeds of change might have been sown whose growth, scarcely apparent as yet in the familiar institutional thicket of the culture, portends significant alterations in the Middletown of a not too distant future.

It was with such questions that the research staff stepped off the train at Middletown early in June, 1935. The fact that answers to its questions might open windows into the future of our larger American culture imparted a mood of especial seriousness but also of exhilaration to the venture.

[2] See *Middletown,* pp. 22-24, for the basis of this division of Middletown's population into "business class" and "working class."

CHAPTER II

Getting a Living

O NE's job is the watershed down which the rest of one's life tends to flow in Middletown. Who one is, whom one knows, how one lives, what one aspires to be,[1]—these and many other urgent realities of living are patterned for one by what one does to get a living and the amount of living this allows one to buy.

The activities of Middletown in getting its living were treated first in the earlier study because of the pervasiveness of those activities throughout the life of the city. Since the most marked social changes of the decade 1925-35 have occurred in or been generated by this central complex of the city's life, it is appropriate again to begin with "the long arm of the job" in Middletown.

After nearly six years of depression Middletown was in June, 1935, in the first flush of reviving business. Some hardy businessmen, when asked about the depression, responded jocularly, "What depression? We haven't had a depression here." One got the impression that by 1935 it was regarded as part of the reviving civic spirit to minimize the effects of the depression in one's public comments. But, as more than one businessman put it, "We may be smiling and perking up on the outside now, but down under our vests we're still pretty much scared to death."

Owing to the facts that Middletown's industries are so heavily weighted on the side of producers' and consumers' durable goods—automobile and machine parts, foundry products, wire, glass fruit jars, table silverware, and metal household furniture—and that it was the durable goods industries that led the forward surge of American industry in the 1920's,[2] Middletown was skimming in the 1920's a dis-

---

[1] See *Middletown,* pp. 22-24.

[2] As F. C. Mills shows in his thorough analysis of *Economic Tendencies in the United States,* during the period 1922-29, "Our productive energies, in excess of those necessary to maintain existing standards of food consumption and of dress for a constantly expanding population, were devoted in the main to augmenting the aggregate supply of durable goods—capital equipment and durable articles of consumption. If we lump together all durable goods we secure a group which increased 59 per cent in volume of output between 1922 and 1929,

proportionate share of the cream from an economy bulging with optimism. Nor was the optimism without tangible support, for over the years 1922-29 the physical income of the theoretically average American citizen was growing at more than double the pre-war rate.[3] Middletown took its winnings joyously while they came—and then the tide turned, slowly at first in Middletown, and later catastrophically.

The amplitude of the giant swing which Middletown underwent between 1925 and the bottom of the depression in 1933 is sharply apparent in the Federal Census figures summarizing employment and the dollar volume of its industrial and retail business presented in Table 1.[4] Briefly, the industrial figures, when translated into index numbers, show the following marked rises and abrupt declines in the magnitude of the industrial sector of Middletown's living:

Year	Number of manufacturing establishments [5]	Wholesale value of manufactured products [6]	Average number of wage earners [7]	Total wages
1925......	100	100	100	100
1929......	106	159	150	147
1933......	81	69	80	49

at an average annual rate of 5.9 per cent. Semi-durable and perishable goods together constitute a group which increased in aggregate volume by approximately 23 per cent over the same period, at an average rate of 2.8 per cent. The current flow of goods which had a useful life, either procreative or for consumption purposes, well in excess of two years was increasing at a rate more than twice that at which perishable and semi-durable goods were increasing." (New York; National Bureau of Economic Research, 1932, pp. 312-13.)

[3] To quote again from Mills: "Over an eight year period the American economy was moving forward at a rate perhaps never surpassed, a rate which represented a potential doubling of the physical income of the average citizen once every 29 years. [Whereas ". . . at the pre-war rate, 63 years would have been required for a doubling of the individual's share in the annual output of the country."] For a period of almost a decade a rate of advance was achieved which gave promise of material comforts for the citizens at large on a broader scale than had ever before been attained." (Op. cit., p. 310.)

It is worth while to note in passing that, as Mills implies by his use of the word "potential," this "potential doubling of the physical income of the average citizen" applies only to a very theoretical "average citizen." No serious student of the situation pretends that under the pattern of income distribution maintaining in the United States the average employed American worker's income rose in the 1920's pari passu with the rise in the national income.

[4] See Appendix III for this table.

[5] These include all industries doing $5,000 or more of business.

[6] All dollar figures for industrial and retail volume of business and payroll are distorted, particularly after 1929, by changes in the price level. Table 1, n. b., shows changes in the price level by year.

[7] A closer view of the swing of industrial employment in Middletown is presented in Table 2 in Appendix III.

Here one sees the build-up of the late 1920's which many men thought would go on permanently, and then an abrupt withering back of the city's industrial life to a point well below even that of the locally poor business year 1925, when the city was a quarter smaller in size. If the heavy concentration of Middletown's industrial production in the durable-goods industries was a decided asset in the good years that preceded the crash, this fair-weather asset became a liability when the weather changed. Durable goods constitute the highly variable elements in the aggregate production of economic goods. Middletown's vulnerability is reflected in the more erratic fluctuation of its industrial employment than of that of the United States as a whole and in its longer continuance in the trough of the depression.[8]

Such changes in the amount of Middletown's industrial activity affect directly the amount of living the city is able to buy. Figures on Middletown's retail business are not available prior to 1929, but the immense sideslip revealed by the totals for 1929 and 1933 [9] parallels that in local industry. Against a rise of 6 per cent in the number of stores, total net retail sales in dollars fell off by 57 per cent, the average number of full-time retail employees by 42 per cent, and the city's retail payroll by 53 per cent.

An idea of precisely where Middletown pulled in its belt between 1929 and 1933 is afforded by Table 3,[10] which sets forth the shifts in retail sales by types of stores. There is a hypnotic quality attached to economic statistics that inclines one to view them merely as indices of business activity. Actually, however, dollar totals of retail sales by kinds of commodities represent a vivid index to the pattern of people's values. Particularly in a period of rapid expansion or sharp enforced curtailment, they represent in their order and relative amplitude of movement the urgencies and tenacities of a people's wants. While a short-run view comprising only four crisis years distorts the basic weighting assigned by people to durable goods like houses and furniture, one can nevertheless glimpse here the depression-intensified drama of Middletown's competing values.

[8] See Table 2 in Appendix III.

Middletown had one alleviating bit of sheer good fortune, however, in that one of the city's largest industries makes glass fruit jars for home preserving. Not only was this durable commodity depression-proof, but it throve on the depression, as will be noted later.

[9] See Table 1 in Appendix III.

[10] See Appendix III for this table.

With one exception, the declines in retail dollar volume [11] between 1929 and 1933, as shown by Table 3, range from 38 per cent to 85 per cent. The exception is filling stations, whose sales fell by only 4 per cent,[12] affording eloquent testimony to the extent to which Middletown has clung to the use of its automobiles as a "necessity" in the depression. Meanwhile, the number of filling stations almost doubled over the four years. Jewelry stores have been hardest hit, with a drop from ten to only four in the number of stores and a decrease of 85 per cent in dollar sales.[13] Close after jewelry come the sales of retail

[11] See n. 6 above and also the last paragraph of n. *a* under Table 3 for changes in the price level.

[12] There has been some tendency to increase the number of items sold by filling stations, but this factor has probably been offset to a considerable extent by sales of gas by garages and others of the many motor-vehicle establishments not included under filling stations.

It is of interest in this connection to note that gasoline consumption in Middletown's state actually advanced to an all-time high for the first four months of 1932, standing at 137,697,383 gallons. For the same four-month period of 1934, consumption in the state was down 5 per cent from this 1932 peak, and for the same months in 1935 it rose to only 0.1 per cent under the 1932 figure. (From [*State*] *Business Review*, published by the Bureau of Business Research of the State University, June 20, 1935.)

See Ch. VII and Table 43 for figures on automobile registrations, reflecting little or no decline in cars registered annually during the depression. While fluctuations in the price of gas and also its use in trucks are here involved, the totals suggest that cars have not been laid up out of use to any great extent during the depression.

[13] The decline in jewelry sales is not merely a depression phenomenon. A marked change in American folkways over the past generation, and especially since the World War, has occurred in the popular shift away from expensive jewelry. Good jewelry used to be regarded both as an investment and as a mark of financial status. As an investment it has been surpassed by the stock market as, since the World War, a wider share of the American public went into the market. Likewise, the marked rise of other competing commodities, notably expensive automobiles and fur coats, as objects giving both status and other more obvious utilities has offered many optional ways of showing that one "belongs." The rise of "ensembling" in the women's field, with its concurrent emphasis upon a whole new type of smartly designed inexpensive jewelry which one varies with one's costume, has lessened the vogue of the diamond pins which women of earlier generations coveted. This last is a part of the new American emphasis upon color, design, and personal "type," as over against the earlier emphasis upon more rigidly fixed types of ornament. In this connection see the treatment of this point by the investigator in his chapter on "The People as Consumers" in *Recent Social Trends* (1933, Vol. II, p. 904).

It is also significant that, according to a well-informed local insurance man, there has been a heavy drop in insurance on jewelry in Middletown during the depression: "People have put their jewelry away in their bank safety boxes, as they haven't felt it was wise to flash expensive jewelry about in times like these."

outlets dealing in lumber and building materials, with a drop in dollar volume between 1929 and 1933 of 82 per cent. Next in descending order of magnitude of cut in sales come stores selling motor vehicles, with a drop of 78 per cent as Middletown clung to its automobiles but rode in old cars and shunned new models; candy and confectionery stores, with a decline of 70 per cent; furniture, household, and radio stores, whose sales fell off by 69 per cent; and commercial eating places, with a drop of 63 per cent. All of the above suggest that it was luxuries such as jewelry, candy, and "eating out" and the replacement of durable goods such as houses, furniture, and automobiles which Middletown curtailed most sharply. Food, as might be expected, fell off less, with only a 49 per cent drop, while it is the "Five-and-tens" that registered the smallest drop, after gasoline, only 38 per cent.

The differential rate of decline in sales of men's and women's clothes suggests an interesting commentary on the extent to which the status of the two sexes is felt to be related to the factor of dress: [14] "men's and boys' clothing and furnishings" stores declined between 1929 and 1933 from fifteen to eleven and dropped in sales by 67 per cent, whereas "women's ready to wear specialty stores (apparel and accessories)" actually increased from nine to ten in number and their sales dropped by only 47 per cent. This differential vulnerability confirms the index numbers for national production from 1919 through 1931 in *Recent Social Trends,* there summarized in the statement: "Men's clothing is apparently more responsive to business declines than women's." [15]

An important commentary on Middletown's culture is afforded, in passing, by the fact that by 1933, with its retail dollar volume more than halved, and after a considerable shuffling of retail stores into and out of business, Middletown actually was supporting the overhead costs of 6 per cent more retail stores than in 1929, and 9 per cent more

[14] The comparison here is not exact, since stores are reported by general Census type, *e.g.,* the two types here cited, whereas stores in such a third classification as "Department stores" may sell both men's and women's clothing.

[15] Vol. II, pp. 906 and 897-98. The figures there presented show, for instance, a rise in the index (in deflated dollars) for the national output of "Men's suits" from a base of 100 in 1925 to 115 in 1927, a fall to 103 in 1929, and thereafter a sharp fall of 25 per cent in 1930; whereas the index for "Women's and children's dresses" rose (again in deflated dollars) from 100 in 1925 to 119 in 1927, then sharply up to 165 in 1929, and fell off only by 13 per cent in 1930.

These differences involve a long list of factors—from the respective status and roles of the two sexes in our culture to the much greater and not unrelated grip which fashion (whipped up by a wide and adroit array of current commercial devices) has upon women's clothing.

proprietors and firm members were riding the back of the purchasing power of the community. No one has yet attempted to sift out and to assign dollar totals to the elements of necessary and of socially super-fluous cost to a city involved in maintaining a free-for-all merchandising system under a *laissez-faire* economy. It has been suggested [16] that a portion of the cost of such a system—including a level of retail markups necessary to keep the marginal retailer in business, the costs of the very high failure rate in certain fields like the grocery field, and a long list of related overhead factors—may be viewed as a "processing tax" habitually carried by the culture as a "normal" deduction from its standard of living.[17]

A further view of the giant arc through which the city has swung in these ten years may be had from the figures for bank deposits and debits and for building construction.[18] Local bank deposits rose from $16,200,000 on January 1, 1925, to $23,000,000 on January 1, 1929, and then fell off to $17,400,000, or substantially the 1926 level, in 1933-34. Bank debits dropped much more spectacularly in the depression—after

[16] We are indebted to an unpublished paper by Lawrence K. Frank on "The Cost of Competition" for this point.

[17] The retailing system of the small American community represents one of the more lagging phases of the economic aspects of the culture—only surpassed perhaps by "the backward art of spending money" within the individual family.

Middletown retailers felt the pressure of chain-store efficiency increasingly as the 1920's wore on and the number of chain units increased. The depression brought some recession in chain-store growth. Both the Atlantic and Pacific and Kroeger closed some local units. Schulte, which had bought a location, never came in with a store, and United Cigar reduced its stores to a single unit. Local independents, with their backs to the wall in the depression, took advantage of this lull in the pressure, organized, promoted a city-wide lottery to bring in trade, and generally whipped up the sentiment against the impersonal, "unneighborly" chain run by "outside capital" and "taking money out of the community." It is significant of the animus engendered that in 1935 a leading retailer, referring to the lengthening of retail hours (to 8:30 to 5:30 on week-days and 9 to 9 on Saturday) since October, 1933, blamed it on "the Jews and the chain stores."

Since the turn of the tide in 1934-35, chain stores are again opening new units. Woolworth moved in 1936 into the entire street floor of the leading office building, and now offers Middletown "the widest assortment of Woolworth's merchandise that has ever been offered" the eastern part of Middletown's state. Grocery chains have invaded the region "south of the tracks" and women's dress units and chain filling stations are increasing. A local real-estate man claims that his company has "averaged three or four requests a month from chain gas companies for filling station sites since January, 1934."

[18] See Table 4 in Appendix III. See, also, the treatment of saving in Ch. XII and Appendix II.

climbing steadily from $147,000,000 in 1925 to $201,000,000 in 1929—to $75,000,000 in 1933. And local building construction, after mounting to a peak of almost $2,500,000 before the depression, shriveled in 1933 to only one-twentieth of that sum, or $111,000.

What does it feel like to a city to have its mainspring speed up and then go dead in this fashion? Neither boom times nor depressions are a novelty in this culture; the long-term trend has been toward increasing prosperity, but depression, like a recurrent infection, is endemic in its system. The city's prevailing mood of optimism makes it view prosperity as normal, while each recurrent setback tends to come as a surprise which local sentiment views as "merely temporary." Shifts in local industry and business of the amplitude of those summarized above, however, involved eventually a staggering traumatic effect. The pages which follow depict the interplay of shock, Middletown's native optimism, and fear as they wove the restless pattern of the years 1929-35.

The week the research staff returned to Middletown in June, 1935, the city had just celebrated the return of good times by an exuberant outpouring of 450 businessmen for a dinner "in recognition of the city's recent industrial and civic progress." It was the first time Middletown's businessmen had had the heart to renew the annual Chamber of Commerce dinner since 1931; this dinner had been allowed to lapse during the depression, along with the meetings of the Dynamo Club,[19] and other manifestations of earlier business vigor. The immediate occasion for the dinner was the fact that General Motors was coming back to Middletown after having stripped its floors of machines and moved away three years before.[20] The effect of the return of this major industry was electric: "A new spirit of optimism and progressiveness has prevailed since the announcement," proclaimed the press. "An indication of [Middletown's] industrial future . . . 500 men already at work and 1,200 within a few weeks." One felt the optimism

[19] See *Middletown,* pp. 303 and 374. The Dynamo Club, a weekly gathering of the "live-wire" young businessmen, was revived in the fall of 1935.

[20] This refers to the large General Motors unit manufacturing Chevrolet transmissions. A second General Motors subsidiary, a branch of the Delco-Remy plant in a neighboring city manufacturing automotive ignitions, was opened in Middletown in 1928 and had continued to operate in the depression. The latter is smaller than the great transmissions unit. Throughout the following pages, when reference is made to the moving away and return of General Motors, the reference is to this major transmissions unit, known locally as "the Products" ([Middletown] Products Division of General Motors).

like a thing physically present on the streets. A member of the research staff, a New Yorker new to the friendly, resilient Middle West, exclaimed after a first glimpse of the business section: "What kind of city *is* this, anyway? I've just seen more people smiling on the streets in an hour than you can see in New York in a day." There were, as further inquiry revealed, misgivings—plenty of them; but the command was "Forward!" after nearly six years of depression, and the response was immediate and boisterous. One felt, one suspected, something akin to the gas boom optimism of forty-five years before.

If not so self-consciously buoyant, the mood of early 1929 had been none the less exuberant and, moreover, free from the acid undertone of misgiving present in 1935. Week after week the local press had noted in 1929: "B—— Co. Plans Growth. Stock Increased Today"; "The D—— plant, not here a year ago, now has 500 on the payroll and is turning out 5,000 batteries a day"; "The prospects for general industry in [Middletown] never were brighter"; "Hoover Plans Big Projects. Engineering Era Now Faced by Nation. 'Constructive Prosperity' Will Now Replace the Famous 'Economy' Slogan of the Coolidge Administration. Looking Forward to Continued Peace and Prosperity": "'Good Jobs Are Hunting Men,' Executive Says. 'If a Man Is Any Good at All, He Can't Help Progressing'"; "W—— Plant in Big Expansion"; "G—— Plant Plans New Addition . . . Expanded Production." It was a prosperous time to be alive and in business—and, along with the rest of American business, Middletown wore its gains jauntily as a part of its birthright.

When the stock market faltered in March, an editorial, followed by another in like vein the next day, neatly dissociated the "gamblers' finance" of Wall Street from the respectable business of Middletown: "Let it be understood that none of this [Wall Street gambling] has anything to do with legitimate business. There was a time when such a crash in the stock market would have produced a panic, but today so stable are our financial institutions and so prosperous is business generally that what the Wall Street gamblers do has no effect of importance upon anybody else."

Middletown did not ship much water in the fall of 1929. The papers did not stress the depression. All through November and December they reported: "[Middletown's] clouded industrial skies may clear within the next few weeks. Factory heads are optimistic"; "Employment Is Normal Here: Employment conditions in [Middletown] dur-

ing November were almost normal, it is revealed by the monthly report of the United States Department of Labor"; "[Middletown] today
closes a generally successful year. It is estimated that the population
in 1930 will be 62,000"; "The 1930 outlook for [Middletown] is bright.
A boom is expected."

Middletown entered 1930 prepared for the best. There had been a
stock-market crash, to be sure, but that was not popularly regarded as
having much relation to the smooth-running cams of Middletown's
factories and the Saturday-night crowds in the downtown shopping
section. Local bankers were predicting a boom "in the spring." "The
steadiness of American Business in the face of the recent debacle in
the stock market," commented the evening paper, "is the most remark-
able evidence it would be possible to adduce of the soundness of the
American commercial structure. . . . It proves that, while American
prosperity can be made to lag or hesitate, it cannot be made to stop."
And in February Middletown was reassured that "It is becoming more
and more evident that the much feared 'depression' that was to have
followed the stock-market debacle is not going to materialize." At the
end of March "a slight surplus of workers" was reported, "but indications are for normal operating and employment within thirty days."

One of the most illuminating aspects of this early period of the
depression was the reluctance of Middletown's habits of thought to
accept the fact of "bad times." This reluctance was related to the tough
emotional weighting of the concept of "the future" in this culture.[21]
Then, too, one does not like to admit that the techniques and institutions which one uses with seeming familiarity and nice control are
really little-understood things capable of rising up and smiting one.[22]
A very few of the more astute businessmen were from the first somewhat apprehensive, but in the main hopes prevailed, urged on in part
by the recognized need for "maintaining public confidence." The local
press, living as it does primarily off business hopes (more commonly
known as "advertising") became even more than usually under these
conditions a reflection of business-class psychology and a conscious
and unconscious suppressor of unpleasant evidence.[23] Hopeful statements by local bankers and industrialists, increases in local work forces,
and similar items tended to make the front page, while shrinkages in

[21] This is discussed in Ch. XII.   [23] See Ch. X.
[22] See *Middletown*, p. 89.

plant forces and related unhappy news commanded small space on inside pages or were omitted entirely.

Actually Middletown's business class had better reason to feel hopeful than did the working class. The years 1930 and 1931 meant slow business and many worries, but in the main business-class jobs continued. According to the head of the local trust company, one of the best informed men in the city, "Retail business in Middletown was good to the end of 1931." Businessmen tell one that "The depression did not strike [Middletown] till 1932"; that "[Middletown] was going good till the end of 1931"; and that "Till 1932 the depression was mainly something we read about in the newspapers." Among the working class, however, factory employment fell off sharply in 1930, the index for a representative group of local industries [24] slumping from 109 in 1929 to 77 in 1930; though even here a slender element of hope was introduced by the fact that in 1931 the index actually advanced slightly to 82. This differing appraisal of when "bad times" exist, whereby Middletown businessmen, applying their own yardstick to a situation, can say, "Till 1932 the depression was mainly something we read about in the newspapers," while at the same time every fourth factory worker had lost his job by 1930, affords an interesting commentary on the class basis of many judgments by Middletown people.[25]

It was near the end of April, 1930, that the first appreciable breaks in the confident optimism of Middletown's public attitude, as reflected

[24] See Table 2 in Appendix III.

[25] In particular, this affords insight into the way in which businessmen and laborers of Middletown look out upon their economic activities: To the former, "good times" mean "profits"; to the latter, "a steady job." The economic ideologies of the culture have been built up from the point of view of the businessman entrepreneur. Thus "profits" and "risks" are regarded as having a complementary relation, morally and in fact. "Risks" are customarily thought of as money risks and "profits" as money profit—and business-class psychology customarily swings back and forth between these two poles. This business-class view of the economic scene habitually leaves out of consideration the facts that profits are primarily a perquisite of the business class, and that other risks than the capitalist's money risk—e.g., the laborer's risk of unemployment—are chronically involved as concomitants of the capitalist's money risk without the same chance to acquire an extra reward in the form of profits. Thus the business-class press of Middletown was thinking within this type of outlook in April, 1930, when an editorial about the Van Sweringen brothers of Cleveland stated, under the caption, "Day of Opportunity Still Here": "Don't let any pessimist tell you that the age of opportunity has passed. . . . It is here just as much today as it was in 1916."

See the discussion of class differences in Ch. XII.

in the evening paper,[26] began to appear. The first admission of a "bad slump" locally appeared under the still hopeful caption: "[Middletown] Factories Are Recovering from Bad Slump." The report went on to speak of the past "hard winter for workers" and to express the hope of "eventual absorption of the city's unemployed." A month later, near the end of May, the paper reported, "Recovery Is Slower than Predicted."

Meanwhile, the local press still viewed the "causes" of the depression as essentially extrinsic to business and essentially due to politicians' wrong ideas. In April, 1930, an editorial in the afternoon paper on "The Cause and Its Remedy" spoke of "the industrial depression which began to develop last summer, reached its peak in '29, and has begun to diminish": The "cause," it asserted, "cannot be blamed on the Hoover administration," but "the fault lies with a hostile Senate, with an anti-business majority" in the Senate whose "chief aim was to hit and hamstring American business enterprise. It did not believe in the policy of giving to American productive enterprise the benefit of tariff protection. . . . In other words, it was for throwing American workmen out of jobs. . . . Except for President Hoover's prompt action . . . in the fulfillment of his prosperity program, the country would not now be on the way to industrial recovery." Again the same note in this paper a month later: "The difference between good times and bad times in the United States, so far as history indicates, is the difference between an adequate protective tariff for the products of our farms and our factories and an inadequate tariff."

By June, with the dawning realization that Middletown was not in for immediate recovery, the "cause" was discovered by this paper to lie elsewhere: "This whole depression business is largely mental," said an editorial entitled "Loosen Up!" "If tomorrow morning everybody should wake up with a resolve to unwind the red yarn that is wound about his old leather purse, and then would carry his resolve into effect, by August first, at the latest, the whole country could join in singing, 'Happy Days Are Here Again.'"

This "underconsumption" note—alternately wheedling and belaboring the individual citizen overboard in midocean for not throwing away his life belt—went on year after year through the depression, linked with the argument that depressions are "merely psychological."

[26] This paper is editorially more outspoken on local affairs than the morning paper and its files were therefore scanned more closely.

In January, 1931, the city was told that "the 1930 slump" had been due to "hoarding." "Advertising Is Business Cure: [It] can stabilize business if we will use it." And the paper announced: "American Legion Plans National War against Depression in Collaboration with A. F. of L. and National Association of Advertisers."

Occasionally individuals injected other causes into the picture. A professor from the local college told Kiwanis of the international "causes"; while the president of the State Chamber of Commerce made the statement to Rotary that the depression was due to "the vicious principles of business," including the "lack of interest in the consumer. . . . If production is increased, the employee must be given the ability to consume more. . . . In the future, business will take more interest in the consumer, because of its own self-interest, for its prosperity depends upon the payroll. . . . It will do no good to build schools and churches if people do not have the fundamental needs of life." The president of a local bank likewise attributed the depression to business, itself, seeing the cause in "Speculation, overproduction, and the wide use of installment-plan buying." But the owner of the evening paper, a national politician in the Hoover entourage and former Secretary of the Republican National Committee, told Middletown: "There is extensive overproduction of talk about overproduction. . . . The depression was caused by underconsumption."

Middletown's automotive-parts plants, though showing decided decreases in employment, still helped hold the city up during 1930, and a large fruit-jar plant (a leader in this industry), blessed with capacity production by the depression's impetus to home preserving, helped to sustain local business morale in 1931. In the summer of 1931, also, local enterprise developed a home-modernization, job-creating campaign which attracted wide national attention as the "[Middletown] plan to end the depression," and the éclat of this campaign helped to keep up local hopes. But from the fall of 1931 the local trend was more steadily downward. Vacant stores became more noticeable along the main business street,[27] two-page bankruptcy-sale advertisements appeared in the papers, and failures and mergers of local industries began to occur more frequently. The papers during these days were carrying more and more small ads in the "Miscellaneous Sale" column: "Hoover sweeper in first-class condition—$15"; "Pair lady's white Enna Jettick

[27] Middletown was hailing in June, 1935, the renting of the last vacant store on this street as a symbol of recovery.

shoes, size 7"; "For sale for less than ½ price: 2 men's suits for short stout man; also Red Fox neckpiece"—always with a discreet telephone number or address but no name attached. Other ads featured "Quick loans on household goods up to $300," while the local Credit Bureau admonished: "Credit is your best friend. Protect it. Always pay promptly."

The first definite intimation of what was to give the coup de grâce to local confidence came in April, 1932, when a four-inch article on an inner page of the afternoon paper announced that the local branch of General Motors would "be affected by changes proposed," followed in a day or so by the announcement that part of the plant might be moved away to another city. Now a latent tendency to apprehension appeared in renewed strength. As a businessman described it: "People would go around saying in low tones, 'Have you heard that they're boarding up the so-and-so plant?' And a few days later, 'Have you heard that so-and-so-many trucks of machinery were moved out of town today? They say that half the floor at the plant is stripped already.' It got on our nerves as this went on!" And by late summer General Motors had stripped its floors and moved away, lock, stock, and barrel. A delegation of local businessmen went to Detroit and persuaded the company not to board up the empty plant because of the bad publicity it would give the city owing to the plant's prominent location on the through railroad line that crosses the city.

By this time, despite the running in the paper of a "Bright Spots in Business" department every few days citing hopeful signs over the United States, editorial optimism was becoming sobered to the grim and more cautious reassurance that "The pendulum cannot swing forever in one direction. It must swing back." And the editor of the evening paper so far let himself slip from the officially correct attitude of Middletown papers as to qualify his congratulation of Middletown banks for their sound condition by the acid comment: "Far be it from this column to laud banks unduly. In general its opinion of them is not so high." This remark literally could not have appeared in either of Middletown's dailies in 1925.

Among the casualties of the black days of 1932-33 were some of the small factories of younger businessmen. These men, fighting ahead under the American formula of "a little credit and a lot of hard work," included some of the growing business leaders of the city. As will be pointed out in Chapter III, the unseating of these potential independent leaders has operated to tighten the grip of the central group of elder businessmen, who in 1935 appeared so markedly to control the city.

Over against this loss of struggling young factories must be set the widespread inventiveness in earning money in small ways that cropped up. All over town, with the exception of the more exclusive residential neighborhoods, one sees evidences of this ingenuity. Little signs in yards announce the presence of household beauty parlors and cleaning and pressing businesses; grocery stores have been opened in cottage front rooms or in additions to residences built out flush with the street; some houses on prominent corners have installed on the corner of the lot little ice-cream and soft-drink booths in the form of spotless ice-cream freezers twelve feet high and eight feet in diameter; others have cashed in on the forced sales of old farms in this section of the state by opening household antique shops; while one woman whose husband's flourishing meat market went under is serving well-appointed dinners in her home to local women's clubs and sororities.

During the dark days of 1933 the city wrestled with the unprecedented problem of relief which was costing in excess of $1,000 a day.[28] Radicalism was in the wind, though it never attained any large proportions locally.[29] The substantial businessfolk were envisioning the possibility of a general collapse of their world. As one of these people laughingly remarked in 1935:

"We all laugh about it now, but it was no joke then! At the time of the national bank crisis in 1933, when it seemed for a while that everything might collapse, many of us bought a great deal of canned food and stored it in our cellars, fearing a possible siege. One family I know bought enough for more than five years. People in our set were talking to each other about how long the city could get along on its available food supply if transportation and communication broke down, where we'd buy candles, and all that sort of thing."

There was no revival of business until late in 1934, and even then the city's mood was that of grasping at straws of hope rather than the welcoming of large reality. Middletown's leading department store went under in April, 1934.[30] But from late 1933 on, Federal farm sub-

---

[28] See Ch. IV.

[29] See Chs. IV and XII.

[30] This store did not in 1925 have either strong management or strong local support. The coming of a concrete road between Middletown and the state capital since 1925, making the latter an easy hour-and-a-half's drive away, handi-

sidies, for wheat acreage reduction at the beginning [31] and later for corn and hogs, began to give a lift to the constricted flow of money as the farmers from the rich counties around Middletown brought in their Federal checks and took away clothing, home furnishings, and farm supplies. The return of legal beer is regarded by one banker as having had a symbolic value operating to cheer people up, though other local persons doubt that this significance attached to the end of prohibition. Federal relief helped some, and the city grasped all it could get. During 1934, moreover, one local plant secured new capital and moved to larger quarters; an automotive-parts plant had a big year; fruit jars continued to boom; and two local glass plants added the production of beer bottles to their schedules. The industrial gears were beginning to catch again.

But the turn in the tide came psychologically in 1935. One of the city's largest plants, manufacturing automotive parts, passed its all-time employment peak early in the year. And then, in April, came the heady news that put Middletown "over the top" emotionally: General Motors was moving back to Middletown! And, as, with the lifting of the smallpox quarantine in 1893, local morale had surged back with "General jollification, assemblies of people on streets, blowing of horns, burning of red fire," [32] so in June, 1935, Middletown called in the governor of the state and celebrated the return of good times with a great public dinner. As one businessman said: "We were joking earlier this year when we talked about the 'past' depression, but now we mean it!" Later in 1935, heavy production in the city's automo-

capped the store, although the extension of other surfaced roads has helped to draw in to Middletown rural and small-town shoppers from four surrounding counties. But this department store tended more and more to lose the best trade to the state capital, while two cheaper stores offered strong competition for the less well-to-do trade.

[31] In November, 1933, the press announced the arrival of wheat reduction checks from Washington for 180 farmers in the county, the checks aggregating $6,890. In June, 1935, an editorial summarized the total receipts to date from the Federal Government by farmers in Middletown's county as totaling $510,145, adding dryly, "If you didn't get your share, don't worry; you will now help pay those who did."

During the depression an effort was made to cultivate this farm trade by the opening of a Farmers' Market in a vacant storeroom on the Court House Square. This market, still operating in 1935, brought in on two days each week the produce, including bread, cakes, and other home products, from miles around; an inexpensive country dinner was served; and much of this money tended to go back into local retail stores.

[32] See *Middletown*, p. 447.

tive-parts plants kept the big drum booming. The Borg-Warner unit broke ground for an enlargement of its plant and in November announced its "all-time high" in local employment; while the Delco-Remy plant manufacturing motor batteries reached in November "the highest daily production in the history of the [Middletown] unit, or four times its daily output in 1928 when Plant No. 9 moved to [Middletown]." Early in October the National Retail Credit Association reported that Middletown had led the country in September with its 30 per cent increase in its retail credit collections.

A factor in this business-class jollification was "the end of N.R.A." Local businessmen do not like to recall now the eagerness with which they turned to the Federal Government in the crisis of 1933, and little is said of the now inconsistent fact that they still utilize all the Federal relief money the city can get.[33] Since the first flush of emotional relief in the late spring of 1933, Middletown's reaction to the Roosevelt administration and its New Deal have been uneven and sharply marked by class differences. As noted elsewhere,[34] the New Deal legislation has driven a wedge between business- and working-class attitudes toward the national governmental machinery. A local banker commented in 1935: "Our local workingmen are for the New Deal and our businessmen are against it. While our workingmen are beginning to feel that Roosevelt has let them down in his promises to further labor organization, their attitude has been and still is that the people in Washington had a pretty good idea and they knew what they were doing. But our businessmen hate Roosevelt's guts and his whole New Deal!" "[Middletown] is so rock-ribbed Republican," commented another businessman, "that our best people around here are unwilling to give the New Deal type of thinking and planning an even and candid break."

But the political label of an administration has been of trivial concern as compared with the possibility of the return of prosperity, so Middletown's businessmen ate political crow during 1933-34 in the hope of eating economic turkey. After insisting to Middletown before the 1932 election that ruin would be the only possible outcome of electing a Democratic president, the local press expressed the hope after the election that "the public, regardless of partisan politics, [would] give the new administration a 'break.'" When the business leaders met

[33] See Ch. IV.
[34] See Chs. IV and XII.

at the Chamber of Commerce to organize the local code authorities, an officer of the Chamber is reported to have expressed the prevailing sentiment in opening the proceedings by exclaiming, "God damn Roosevelt and the N.R.A.!"—but Middletown's businessmen drove ahead with as much of the N.R.A. as they could stomach. In October, 1933, they actually staged an enthusiastic N.R.A. parade which the press described as "the greatest peacetime parade in Middletown's history: distinctly big-town stuff!" Simultaneously, "a permanent [Middletown] National Recovery Crusade Board" was organized, composed chiefly of the presidents of local civic clubs, "to convince people that there is a way out"; and the public was urged to "Get behind the N.R.A. until something better comes along."

But as the fall and winter wore on, N.R.A. became troublesome to one group or another to the extent that it really began to operate. Labor began to organize under Section 7a of the Recovery Act. Some local plants eagerly took advantage of N.R.A. wage rates to drive down Middletown's always relatively low wages.[35] Where local business could, it did what big business was doing widely elsewhere under the codes, and the headlines read: "Bids for School Coal Are Same; [School] Board Is Irate." Attached to each of the nine bids by local coal dealers, according to the press report, was "the usual affidavit stating that there had been no collusion among dealers, but to each form affidavit had been added the words, 'except as required by the compliance agreement of the retail solid-fuel industry.'"

As the halo around the New Deal wore off with the non-appearance of prosperity, local protest over these complications mounted. While the local business leaders and their newspapers set the direction and dictated the slogans, much of the sustaining weight of the thrust behind this local protest came from that section of Middletown's business largely outside the great industrial codes. Aside from the heads of half-a-dozen major industries, Middletown's businessmen regard themselves proudly as "small businessmen," who, their traditions have taught them, are the purest strain of our American democratic economy. One cannot understand the reaction of Middletown to the N.R.A.,

[35] An editorial in the afternoon paper for March 2, 1934, on "When N.R.A. Sends Wages Down" states: "Here in [Middletown] could be cited examples by the hundreds of men who had comfortable living wages before N.R.A. codes went into effect, but who now are having a struggle for existence. . . . Wonder whether these people are receiving consideration from Gen. Johnson's conference of kickers?" (See *Middletown,* p. 84 f.; also "Wages" in index to present volume.)

"bureaucracy," "organized labor," and to Middletown's other political
and economic devils apart from the American conception of the "small
businessman." Perched on his toe hold of advantage in the economic
system, intent on climbing higher, he believes with the intensity of
single-track conviction that Western economy was made "of, by, and
for" individual strivers such as he. To this "small-businessman" culture—a culture stressing "Every tub on its own bottom," "You win
if you're any good and your winnings are caused by you and belong
to you," and "If a man doesn't make good it's his own fault"—one
must look for much of the sustaining support for the outspoken, bitter
resentment of bureaucracy and social legislation by Middletown businessmen in 1935. As the owner of a small non-manufacturing business
remarked, "We small businessmen resent the way we've been soaked
in the New Deal." A businessman went dramatically to his file and
held up a folder: "See that? It's a pension plan for our two [Middle-
town businesses], all worked out. Now"—with a disgusted gesture—
"it's just shelved, with the Wagner bill passed!" A banker, a man of
great ability and breadth of outlook, voiced the same disgusted protest when he said: "We object to our bank's being taxed to pay for
industrial security when we don't have any unemployment at the
bank. We actually take on extra help in the summer so that our people
can have their vacations."

Middletown banks are reported to have quietly sabotaged the Federal Home Owners' Loan Corporation, after unloading some of their
poorer risks on it; while N.R.A., A.A.A., C.W.A., the Securities Act,
and social-security legislation are all now looked upon by many businessmen as unwarranted interferences with "the normal functioning of
business."

Everywhere in Middletown one sees these small businessmen looking
out at social change with the personal resentment of one who by long
defensive training asks first of every innovation, "What will it do for
(or to) me?" The resulting tendency is to stress the negative aspects
of new proposals and for local opinion to dwell upon and to crystallize
around extremes of possible abuse which might occur. It is typical of
this tendency that a local banker warned Middletown regarding the
proposed child-labor amendment to the Federal Constitution that: "If
it is carried to the logical extremes now discussed, it may not only dis-
turb us economically but throw a very serious social problem on our
hands in the activities of the young people not allowed to work."

The tendency noted here is not so much a commentary upon the kinds of people Middletown's businessmen are as upon the kind of culture in which they have grown up and to which they must largely conform if they are to survive. They live in a culture built around competition, the private acquisition of property, and the necessity for eternal vigilance in holding on to what one has. In such an exposed situation, rife with threats and occasions for personal tension, human beings tend to react primitively in the direction of warding off threats and seeking to conserve whatever stability they have personally been able to wrest from their environment.

Across the railroad tracks from this world of businessmen is the other world of wage earners—constituting a majority of the city's population,[36] nurtured largely in the same habits of thought as the North Side, but with less coherence, leadership, and morale.

Among these people the New Deal fanned briskly for a brief period the faintly smoldering ashes of local labor organization. Middletown was in the 1890's "one of the best organized cities in the United States." [37] The new workers pouring into the city with the gas boom had come heavily from already industrialized areas rather than off the farm, and they had brought a faith in labor organization. By 1925 this earlier fabric of organization had long since largely raveled away, and the lethargy as regards labor organization observed in 1925 [38] not only continued but was even increased by the early years of the depression. Middletown entered the depression as an industrially open-shop town. Seven of its sixteen active unions affiliated with the Central Labor Union were in the building trades, and one more in the printing trades; six of the remaining eight were in a straggling group of barbers, musicians, motion-picture operators, postal carriers, and two groups of railway workers. The great metal-working industries comprising Middletown's leading group of factories—the automotive-parts plants and foundries—were unrepresented save for small molders' and pattern-makers' unions. The glass industry, the second group of industries in local importance, was totally unorganized.[39]

The significance of the wave of labor organization encouraged by

[36] The working class constitute roughly seven out of ten of the city's gainfully employed. (See *Middletown*, p. 22.)

[37] See *Middletown*, p. 76.

[38] See *Middletown*, pp. 77-80.

[39] See n. 67 below for a complete list of Middletown's unions in 1929 and in January, 1936.

the N.R.A. lies not so much in the number of new unions it brought as in the momentary vitality it gave to the whole local labor movement by reason of the fact that it advanced straight on the two central strongholds of the open shop in Middletown: the automotive machine shops and the glass plants. Four of the ten new unions organized in 1933-34 aimed at the metal-working industries, while a fifth sought to awaken the moribund glass unions, once strong in Middletown, and to organize the X plant.[40]

Middletown's working class in recent years has been heavily recruited from first- and second-generation farm stock. These men share the prevailing philosophy of individual competence. Working in an open-shop city with its public opinion set by the business class, and fascinated by a rising standard of living offered them on every hand on the installment plan, they do not readily segregate themselves from the rest of the city. They want what Middletown wants, so long as it gives them their great symbol of advancement—an automobile. Car ownership stands to them for a large share of the "American dream"; they cling to it as they cling to self-respect, and it was not unusual to see a family drive up to the relief commissary in 1935 to stand in line for its four- or five-dollar weekly food dole. "It's easy to see why our workers don't think much about joining unions," remarked a union official in 1935. He then went on to use almost the same words heard so often in 1925: [41] "So long as they have a car and can borrow or steal a gallon of gas, they'll ride around and pay no attention to labor organization; and if they can't get gas, they're busy trying to figure out some way to get it."

To men in this mood, the depression came as an individual calamity. Like the businessmen across the tracks, their attention was focused on the place where the shoe pinched and they were initially disinclined to take either a broad or a long-term view of the situation. As one looks at the upsurge and abrupt subsidence of union activity under the New Deal—the "newness" of which to Middletown's working class as to its business class lay in its being a personal life line rather than a commitment to social change—one must bear constantly in mind the

[40] The symbol X is used throughout this study to refer to a leading family of industrialists whose position in the community is described in detail in Ch. III. In order to simplify reading, brackets will be omitted from X in quotations throughout.

[41] See *Middletown*, p. 254, n. 6.

personal and institutional frictions against which labor organization in Middletown operated. The opposition of employers and the press to organized labor was of long standing and without subtlety in its expression and operation.[42] To which should be added the following four deterrents to local labor organization, as listed by an officer of the local Central Labor Union in 1935:

1. Men who have jobs are afraid of losing them if they organize.

2. They can't pay union dues in bad times, for some of them are unemployed; and, while some are employed, they are on wages of only $10-$12 a week part time, or $16-$17 a week full time.

3. Some plants are still importing Kentucky and Tennessee hillbillies. These hillbillies can be educated into joining the union, but as soon as they do, they lose their jobs and drift off.[43]

4. As long as a man has any morale left he will do anything, even leave his union and accept any wages and hours, in order to stay off the relief rolls.[44]

And to this list should be added yet another factor stressed by a local carpenter and probably widely operating: "Men's families press them hard from behind to work for anything they can get, regardless of union rates." [45]

Middletown had in 1929 roughly 900 union members out of a total of approximately 13,000 persons of both sexes gainfully employed in working-class occupations. Early in 1933, before the advent of the New Deal, the total of union members had shrunk by "a couple of hundred." At the peak in 1934 the total stood at 2,800, and by the end of 1935 it had wasted back to 1,000.

When Section 7a descended on Middletown it plunged the meager forces of local organized labor into a welter of problems that they

[42] One plant in 1925 had had for years a prominent sign at its gate threatening union men with prosecution as trespassers under a permanent court injunction granted to the company years before.

[43] See *Middletown,* p. 58, n. 13.

[44] The Middletown building-trades unions were especially hard hit during the depression, as, with a virtual cessation of local construction (see Table 4), these men had to scatter to find any employment they could.

[45] This statement suggests a widespread aspect of the depression bearing sharply on morale: In our culture the husband's and father's role has become increasingly that of being a "good provider." Thus when a man is unemployed and his wife and children bring pressure upon him to work on any terms, they are at one and the same time stressing the failure-of-role over which he may be most sensitive and, at the same time, offering him the obvious and easy path to reinstatement of lost prestige. See Ch. V.

were unequipped to handle. The Central Labor Union elected an organizing committee which reflected the largely nonindustrial character of local union membership: of the eight members only two, both of them molders, were in industrial plants, while the other six were two printers from the shop of the morning newspaper, two barbers, and two carpenters. These men set out in their spare time to build— against the traditions of the local culture and the will of the business class control mechanisms—a large and powerful labor organization able, in the words of the preamble to the National Recovery Act, to "induce and maintain united action of labor and management under adequate governmental sanction and supervision . . . [and] to improve standards of labor." It was a chaotic venture, marked by hasty decisions, jurisdictional disputes, and much fumbling and bad feeling even within labor's ranks; and also by some alleged "double-crossing" by organizers, both local and those sent in from outside by some of the international unions.

If organization was to go in Middletown, it must tackle the X glass plant, an old industry employing largely unskilled labor and with a reputedly long record of union opposition; the city's automotive-parts plants, owned by great motor corporations with an even more definite anti-union policy; a large wire plant; and various smaller industries. The following record of what ensued is set down from the written account prepared for this study by an officer of the Central Labor Union who participated actively in the organization drive, checked as to its main facts by the independent statement of another official of the Central Labor Union:

We started out to enroll all new men in a Federal labor union, which we looked on as just a recruiting union until the new craft unions could be organized. Men were coming in faster than we could handle them and we soon rolled up a total of 1,800 to 1,900 new men.

Then along came a Mr. ——, sent in by the Amalgamated Iron, Steel and Tin Workers, who helped us line up the men at the K—— wire plant and the M—— bed-spring plant. But each time just about when things looked all set, he would pull some dumb stunt—we could never tell whether accidentally or on purpose. He would call premature elections at a plant to select our N.R.A. negotiators; or he would encourage hotheads to make fools of themselves and get fired, and then he would hale the firm before the Labor Board, tell hazy stories, and put all our hard work on the rocks. The upshot of bum tactics like these was that all our people would get scared. The union at the wire plant struggled along for six or eight months and then went under. It didn't collapse because of any direct company intimidation, but because the organizer was no good and because the men lost interest when nothing big happened. This shows one of our problems in organizing these men, who have lived all their lives in an open-shop town. The men wanted spectacular gains all at once, and when they paid their dues and there wasn't a strike and big achievements immediately they lost interest and began to kick. It's no cinch trying to organize a town like this!

Then we tried the [company manufacturing table silverware],[46] and were going good till the Metal Polishers' Union finally sent in an organizer; he was a typical windy labor faker and such a poor man on the job that the men and women out there at the plant got disgusted and quit the campaign cold.

The effort to organize the X Brothers' glass plant was the worst blow of all.[47] Organization enthusiasm was hitting toward its peak in 1933, and some of the X employees asked the Central Labor Union to organize their plant. We enrolled these first people in our recruiting union, held a mass meeting with about 150 of the 960 workers at the X plant present, and they signed up for the Glass Bottle Blowers' Association. We then sent a letter to the international union's central office asking that an organizer be sent to [Middletown]. To the surprise of us officers of the Central Labor Union, the answer came back that an official organizer named —— was already stationed in [Middletown] and that there was a chartered local already. Neither this man nor delegates of this local had attended any of our labor meetings or sought affiliation with the Central Labor Union. So you see why we were surprised to learn that we had a chartered local and official organizer all the time right here in town!

When a delegation looked this organizer up, he seemed uninterested in the progress we had made, and claimed that the X plant couldn't be organized. He finally said he was willing to cooperate, but he sure moved slowly. It was a time when men were being enrolled in other unions as many as 125 in a single afternoon, and the X workers grew restless at ——'s stalling. Letters were again sent by us on to the Glass Bottle Blowers' Association asking them for another organizer; and, when we got no answer, a letter was sent to William Green, the president of the A. F. of L.

[46] This plant has operated on a heavy production schedule in the depression and is said locally to have been highly profitable. Considerable business is said to have been switched to it from the East because of its low labor costs.

[47] The local union men interviewed feel that the Glass Bottle Blowers' Association "gummed up" the efforts to organize this plant.

It is obviously difficult to unscramble a situation of this sort, in which disappointment leads on easily to charges of double-dealing.

Meanwhile, in January, 1934, we got fed up and invited the American Flint Glass Workers to come and take on the job. They sent in Mr. —— who did fine work, and by March we had organized about 900 of the plant's total of 960 workingmen. This was done by working out through groups of six to ten men from the 150 who had signed up at the first organizing meeting in the high school.

When everything was ready to present demands to the X plant, the Glass Bottle Blowers' Association came to life and their president and vice-president came to town. They did not come to the Central Labor Union to see us, so we went to the hotel to look them up. They were abusive because we had gone over their heads to William Green, and they demanded that the Flint Glass Union hand over the men it had organized.

There was a lot of bicker between the two unions, and finally the two presidents agreed that the men should join the Glass Bottle Union, but that both the Glass Bottle and Flint Glass Unions would join in working for the workers' demands and in presenting them to the X company. On the afternoon set, the representative of the Flint Glass Union presented to the X company the demands agreed upon for recognition of the union and other steps to be taken. The company said they were willing to accept unionization of the skilled operatives,[48] but refused point-blank to allow organization of the unskilled and semiskilled workers, who constitute the great bulk of their force.

Here we were square up against the issue between industrial and craft unions. The Flint Glass people were an industrial union including all the unskilled workers as well as the skilled, and they favored the same type of organization for the X plant. The Glass Bottle representative told us later that his union did not want industrial unionism because these unskilled people would not have any craft to protect and if they sent delegates to any of the annual conventions they would swamp the old-time craft union men.

But the spokesman from the Flint Glass Union stuck to his demands for an organization to include the unskilled labor, in his conference with the X company officials. Then at this point the company spokesmen took another tack and asked what right a Flint Glass man had to represent the Bottle Blowers' Association to which their men should belong if they organized. They said that a representative of the Glass Bottle Blowers' Association had called on them that morning and had warned them that the president of the American Flint Glass Workers did not represent the Glass Bottle Blowers' Association.

[48] Skilled men are said to comprise only about one in twenty of the X plant's force, including about ten brick masons who build the glass tanks, ten to fifteen Owens machine operators, twenty-five to thirty machinists, about twelve mold-makers, and a small group of zinc-mill rollers. See the discussion of the decline in skilled workers below.

This jolted our negotiator back onto his heels because the two union heads had agreed jointly to back his negotiations. So he ended the interview in order to go back and consult with the Glass Bottle people before pushing the demands further.

It was decided to hold another mass meeting to discuss a course of action. This time the high-school auditorium was refused to us. After our Central Labor Union threatened to air the situation to local taxpayers, the ruling was modified to permit use of the auditorium with payment of a $35 fee.

At the mass meeting of workers that followed, the various organizers spoke and had the crowd aroused and ready for action. Then Mr. ——, still the official Middletown district organizer for the Glass Bottle Blowers' Association, spoke, and the longer he spoke the more his pessimism antagonized the men and dampened their enthusiasm, until men began to get up and leave.[49] That killed the effort to organize the X plant, and another meeting was never held. Company union "tools" got busy about this time, too, and pushed the company Benefit Association. All that's left now of the effort to organize the X plant, aside from the union bricklayers and carpenters, is the little group of moldmakers who hold their charter in the Flint Glass Workers' Union.

While the international unions were stepping all over each other, the X company was busy all the time—never missed a trick. Early in 1934, before the unions had fumbled the ball completely, some of the plant's employees asked that the Labor Board supervise an election at the plant so that the employees could express their preferences concerning collective bargaining. The company opposed this demand and threatened court action. During this period cautious firing and black-listing were being employed by the company.[50] In one instance, a group of unskilled women workers engaged in punching rubber rings to fit under fruit-jar caps were dismissed. The women secured a hearing before the Regional Labor Board, and at the hearing the company maintained that the women had not been dropped because of union activity but because it had been decided to change the organiza-

[49] Middletown labor leaders are angry about this organizer's role in the effort to organize the X plant. One man characterized him as "a former X employee and a member of the old craft-union school who never forget and never learn."

[50] The visibility of life in the small community operates to increase the ease of control of labor by employers and municipal authorities. When a lieutenant of Francis Dillon's was secretly sent to Middletown by the A. F. of L. after the Toledo General Motors strike, the police began the day he arrived to trail him continuously, and workmen were afraid to be seen talking with him. One picks up references in Middletown talk to "stool pigeons"—loyal sub-foremen brought from Toledo by General Motors, "stools" of the police within local unions, etc. The sharp competition among local labor leaders for small-time political jobs facilitates the penetration of official Middletown into the loosely knit ranks of organized labor.

tion of the department in which they worked [51] and the process employed. This process, involving the pulling of a lever on a punch machine, was never changed in any important respect. When the required affidavits would be submitted on contested points, the company's affidavits would flatly deny the charges of the employees—and there the matter would usually stop. In a few cases where an investigation was ordered, notice of investigation usually came long enough in advance so that before the investigator came, the matter could be brought temporarily into line with the N.R.A. ruling. When the men threatened a strike, the owners of the plant responded with the threat to move the plant to another city.[52] Don't forget, too, that all through these years the company was making some of the largest earnings in its history.

Finally a sense of futility and disillusionment with N.R.A. settled down over the workers when they realized how ineffective their long-distance letters and telegrams to Washington were as compared with what the Xs' representatives in Washington were able to do on the spot. So the men were licked both by the unions and by their employers, and they just gave up.

The whole mess at the X plant was a body blow to local organization. Our people began to sense the lack of harmony in the A. F. of L.; and, after a few months, those who had paid in dues when enthusiasm was running high began to ask for the return of their money since no union had been formed. The money had gone to the International Union and was not re-

[51] This process of quiet readjustment of a troublesome department is succinctly described in a paragraph from the steel industry's trade press in 1935: "Ford continues the envy of other manufacturers in handling labor. It appears that recently a number of malcontents were detected in various departments at the Rouge [Detroit River Rouge plant]. Quietly they were all transferred to one department, then this department's work was farmed out, the department was closed, and the malcontents were automatically out of a job." (*Steel,* June 3, 1935, p. 16.)

[52] The psychological urgency of such a threat should be viewed against the enormous reality of the fact that only two years before General Motors had stripped its large local plant of machinery and moved out of Middletown. If such action had involved a jolt to business-class pride, it had meant calamity to the families of upwards of a thousand workers, the neighbors of these workers now threatened by the X company.

The situation of labor was well expressed by the minister of a working-class church in an interview with a member of the research staff: "One of my parishioners who works down there came to me when they were trying to organize the X plant and asked whether I advised him to join up. He said he was sick of the low wages and the uncertainty even of that. I just couldn't do anything but tell him not to organize for the sake of his family, as he could not afford the risk of losing his job or being black-listed locally—as some of the X employees subsequently were. Since their threat to move the plant away from [Middletown], labor has been very careful not to stir there again."

turned. The men just can't understand this. And the upshot is that a lot of these fellows now think the unions are a racket, and they are not interested in trying again to organize. We local officers have got pretty thoroughly fed up with international union officers, too. They're all fiery and for planning big things—and then they prove windbags or—worse—they double-cross you!

Of course we fellows that did stick after the whole drive broke up kept right on working and eating a lot of dirt, too, in the process. We did accomplish some things. In one plant, a foundry that had been granted a permanent injunction against union activities fifteen years ago, the molders organized and conducted a successful strike as late as March, 1935, and got in a closed shop. In other plants we organized successfully and won some concessions, but things would then peter out under inertia, intimidation, or ineffective leadership. At K——'s [a large meat-packing plant] with a record of a sixty hour week for its butchers, bad working conditions, and an anti-union policy, we not only organized it, but actually won a case before the Regional Labor Board, forcing the company to rehire dismissed union men and to pay them $6,000 in back pay. But, after it had lasted about a year, an organizer for the Butchers' Union called our local men out on a sympathetic strike he was conducting against the same company in [another city in the state]. We weren't well enough organized to pull the whole plant, and the company fired the union officers—so another union went haywire. The organizer was just another labor skate.

The automotive and machine-shop plants were, of course, always one of our toughest nuts to try to crack. The men were pretty well scared to begin with, since General Motors had moved out of town and another auto-parts plant had closed. We tackled them anyway. We organized a bunch of men at the A—— plant, where they'd paid their machinists as low as twenty cents an hour before N.R.A. And then hell cut loose in the plant! The ax was swung right and left by the company and those who weren't dismissed were scared to death. Finally, the men appealed to the Regional Labor Board for an election in 1934. The company fought against an election, carried the fight up to the top Labor Board through all kinds of appeals, until when the vote came in the spring of 1935, N.R.A. was so weak and the men so intimidated that they were afraid to vote. They're still unorganized out there, and the plant remains a lousy place where men work only to keep from having to go on relief.

At the Borg-Warner plant the company developed its Welfare Association into a company union for the time being—and they've now gone back to a mere welfare organization. Our organizers just couldn't stir up any large interest among the workers out there. Some of the employees have been with the company a long time and were afraid that if they lost that connection they'd never get anything else to do. Others are still able to jingle a couple of dollars in their pocket and can buy gas and just aren't interested.

I guess that's about the picture. There's not a hell of a lot left of all of our big hopes of 1933!

In the days of still high hopes of April, 1934, Middletown's Central Labor Union began the publication of an eight-page weekly labor newspaper. It is symbolic of the flash-in-the-pan quality of the effort to organize local labor under N.R.A. that the paper lasted five issues— and then died.[53]

The local confusion under N.R.A., depicted above, involves no personal devils on either side, but in the main men of good will fumbling to make an awkward and uncoordinated institutional system work. Middletown is a friendly city, a heavily Christian city, whose dominant mood is a tolerant, neighborly live-and-let-live. But money income is its personal and community blood stream. In its *laissez-faire* economy this blood stream flows irregularly, subject to institutional conditions beyond any local citizen's control. And when this economy contracts under the pressure of its maladjustments and the blood stream diminishes, people simply do what any strangling man does—they fight for life.

The city's economic and associated institutions operate by long tradition on the theory of each man for himself; but the theory assumes that all are engaged in a common enterprise; and, from untold centuries of struggle with man's oldest enemy, Scarcity, this local culture and its predecessors from which it derives have seen in the maintenance and increase of Production the keystone of this common enterprise.[54] As Middletown has grown from the highly localized village culture of the middle of the nineteenth century, there has been an increasing tendency for the managers of its productive resources to organize for united effort through such agencies as the Chamber of Commerce. Operating under such a set of traditional assumptions and backed financially by the owners and managers of the city's productive resources, the Chamber of Commerce and its business-class members have thrown their weight increasingly on the side of more organization

[53] The platform for Middletown labor printed at the masthead of this paper is given in Ch. X.

[54] For an elaboration of this point see the investigator's paper, "Democracy's Third Estate: The Consumer," *Political Science Quarterly,* December, 1936.

among management and less organization among labor. Based on the assumption that profitable production is the keystone of local welfare, an "open-shop town" and an "easy labor market" have come to be regarded locally as common civic concerns enhancing the welfare of the entire city.[55]

To a business class schooled to think in these terms and frightened by the incipient radicalism of 1933, the spectacle of mounting union enrollment in the spring of 1934 came as a challenge to their deepest sources of security. Business-class thinking alternated between bitterness toward labor and some candid speculation as to "What will happen if—?" The following editorial on "The Rising Tide of Labor" from the afternoon paper late in March, 1934, reflects the excitement of the latter mood:

We see now a deep underlying movement that is the trend behind each day's news. It is inevitably with us, as changeless and relentless as the passing of the years. It is the rise of Labor. It is the time when Labor strides to the front and shouts for its rights in a voice that kings and counselors must hear. Whether the "rights" are real or imagined, there is the power to enforce them. That is the irresistible trend. It is the ripening of a seed that was planted as long ago as 1840 in the so-called Industrial Revolution. It is the concomitant of teeming cities, mighty industrial empires. Power shifts. The masses push and strive and grow strong. Labor sits in the high place— and wherever Labor may take us, we might as well go along peaceably. Because we have no other choice.

How Middletown's well-intended but apprehensive civic spirit operates is well seen in the events surrounding the moving back of General Motors in 1935. The plant moved back after, and because of, the bitter Toledo strike, and the central issue in its return was the fact that Middletown is an open-shop town and its controlling businessmen were prepared to pledge its continuance as an open-shop town. Alfred P. Sloan, the president of General Motors, stated in his report on his company's operations in the first half of 1935 that "In the second quarter of the year a strike at one of the company's plants at Toledo, manufacturing parts for the Chevrolet Motor division, reduced the

[55] The *General Commercial, Civic and Industrial Survey of* [*Middletown*] issued by the Chamber of Commerce in 1935 to attract industries to the city states in the section on "Labor" that "Strikes and wage disputes are practically unknown. . . . The [labor] supply usually exceeds the demand."

output and earnings of the corporation. To meet this threat, the company opened a new factory at [Middletown]." [56]

Middletown's controlling businessmen have always realized that
such competitive advantage as their city possesses in the national
market is traceable to its lower living cost and to its ability to mop
up an "easy labor market" of corn-fed, unorganized American workers, willing to work for relatively low wages, and a substantial marginal
number of them able to live on the farm during slack periods in the
industrial year.[57] But the return of General Motors has had an incal-
culably great symbolic effect in crystallizing this awareness of the city's
asset. Middletown businessmen are coming out of the depression with
their asset of being an "open-shop town" nailed to the city's masthead—and they mean to keep it there. At the great public welcoming
dinner to General Motors at the Chamber of Commerce in June, 1935,
the mayor stated that "Our people are in no mood for outsiders to
come into [Middletown] to agitate," and he assured the company that

[56] Quoted from the summary in the New York *Times,* August 12, 1935.
It is pertinent to note that, in this rough-and-tumble scramble of the cities to
maintain their livelihood, the city of Toledo promptly hit back in defense of its
threatened prestige with a three-column advertisement in the press of leading
cities in June, 1935, as follows:

"WHERE STANDS TOLEDO?

"Toledo is a rare combination; a city of teeming industry, and a city of art
and culture. The art museum, sixth largest in the country, housing many price-
less collections, attracts nearly 400,000 visitors annually.
"Industry in Toledo is greatly diversified. In 1934 there were 1,110 individual
business establishments. In 1920 the number was 896, and at the peak of 1929
the number was but 1,042. The recent strikes in Toledo have been limited
to but one or two industries and lasted only a very short time. Few cities in the
country have had so few labor disturbances.
"Do you know that Toledo is the third largest railroad center in the United
States? And that more families own their own homes in proportion to its population than in any other city in the United States?" [Here followed sixteen paragraphs itemizing Toledo's industrial assets: "the world's principal center in the
glass industry"; "the third city in the United States in the auto industry";
"largest nickel-plating plant for auto bumpers in the world," etc., etc.]
"But Toledo is not only a thriving city of diversified industry; it is also a
fine place to live in, with its boulevards, wide avenues, famous old trees—third
largest zoological gardens in the country—attractive parks—and magnificent
schools and colleges. . . ." (Printed in New York *Times,* June 28, 1935.)
[57] "Our men from our local district here, born and bred on the farms near
here, knowing the use of machinery of some sort from their boyhood, reliable,
steady, we call 'corn-feds.'" (Remark of a local manufacturer, quoted in *Middle
town,* p. 58, n. 18.)

such agitators would not be tolerated. A leading businessman re-marked to a member of the research staff in a tone of quiet determina-tion: "We're not going to have any labor trouble here. We're not going to let it happen. Our mayor was pretty radical back years ago in his first term, but he is more cooperative now.[58] During the Toledo automobile strike this spring the mayor had policemen stationed out on roads leading into town, and they'd stop cars, look men over, and those that didn't look desirable they'd tell to keep right on going through town and not stop."

When in June, 1935, the A. F. of L., following the Toledo strike, sent in Francis J. Dillon to initiate the organization of Middletown's automotive workers, all the business-controlled local agencies worked with smooth precision.

A worker distributing handbills on a downtown street announcing the meeting was picked up by the police.

Middletown's commercial radio station, which had concluded an agreement and received advance payment for the proposed broad-casting of Dillon's speech on Saturday afternoon, interrupted the in-stallation of the necessary telephone wires and microphone late Friday afternoon by a message apologizing for its inability to broadcast the speech, and returned the money paid for the broadcast.

The afternoon paper, though accepting an advertisement announcing the meeting, ran at the top of its front page four days before the meet-ing a large picture of an Oregon strike picket being dragged along the ground by three policemen. The picture did not accompany a news story and the timing and motif of the picture seemed to the research staff too extraordinary to have been a mere coincidence. The caption read:

This Picket Had Real "Drag" with Cops: Lumberjacks, famed for their "nothing-barred" style of warfare, learned of a new one in this clash be-tween Oregon State Police and pickets stationed at a Forest Grove, Ore.,

[58] In his earlier campaigns and in 1934 this mayor electioneered as "a friend of the workingman." According to a prominent fellow politician: "He told me that his conviction and sentence to the Federal penitentiary when he was mayor before was due to his having antagonized local financial circles. He added that he has learned his lesson. Consequently, in his 1934 campaign, though he ran on the old platform, declaring himself to be a friend of the workingman and labor unions to catch the big South Side vote, he was also playing ball with the businessmen." The more militant fringe of Middletown's labor movement now regards the mayor as having "double-crossed" labor. (See Ch. III at n. 22, and also Ch. IX and the note on p. 73.)

sawmill in the long-drawn-out strike in the northwest. Police introduced the "dragout" to remove this militant picket from the scene en route to the patrol wagon, with the trooper bringing up the rear carrying a formidable shillalah for emphasis.

Dillon stated (probably incorrectly) in his address that the X family had donated large sums for the building of the Masonic Temple with the understanding that non-union labor be employed, and that as a result non-union iron workers were imported for the job. Four days later an advertisement in the morning paper, in which the X family has an interest, called attention to Dillon's remark and stated that union bricklayers were employed on the Masonic Temple, are employed in the X factory,[59] and have always been treated fairly. The advertisement appeared over the name of the Bricklayers' Union, whose head is a brother-in-law of the contractor who does the X construction work.

Meanwhile, with the advent of the General Motors plant, the local police force was heavily increased, a local police officer was taken over as head of the General Motors police force, and a close relation established between the company's police and the city police force.[60] Great secrecy surrounded this augmenting of the local police force.[61] According to a responsible labor-union official, when General Motors decided to move from organized Toledo to Middletown, Chevrolet contracts were awarded to the two other large Middletown automotive machine shops in order to spread the pressure for city protection of the plants. It was not possible to discover the nature of the deal that was alleged to have been made. Nobody in Middletown bothered about the matter until August, 1935, when the city budget came up for consideration. The real-estate men, threatened personally by the high tax rate, then demanded loudly to know why the police force had been increased

[59] The X factory employs union labor in certain minor groups of skilled workers in its force. See n. 48 above.

[60] The following paragraph from the automotive section of *Steel,* a trade paper, suggests a condition probably little known to the workers in the Middletown plant: "General Motors boasted up to the time of its recent Toledo strike that it had no undercover men in its plants. This situation is being remedied, and henceforth General Motors will have a close check on sentiment in its plants." (*Steel,* June 3, 1935, p. 16.)

The statement was made by a speaker at the Dillon organization meeting in Middletown that General Motors now has a tie-up with the Pinkerton detective agency. (Cf. U. S. Senate committee hearings on labor espionage, Feb., 1937.)

[61] See Ch. IX.

and pointed out that the force was actually in excess of the per capita quota of police allowed by State law. No answer was forthcoming from the city administration. The situation perplexed even persons wise in local political folkways. "How in hell are the new cops being paid?" exclaimed the former mayor, defeated for reelection in 1934. "They are being paid with city warrants. The regular police budget is too small. If General Motors is paying these warrants, how is it doing it? The mayor requires that 2 per cent of all city employees' salaries be taken from them for a 'welfare fund,' though nobody has shown what the money is used for. Is it being used to pay the special police?" By the early fall of 1935 the city policemen and firemen missed their September 6 pay for the last half of August, and on October 2 the editor of the afternoon paper commented in his column: "City officers had to pass up their payroll checks, yesterday, as did the police and firemen a few days ago, for the ample reason that there is no money in the treasury with which to pay them. But the budgets made out last year were supposed to be sufficient to cover all expenses of the city government this year. What has become of the money?" [62]

Here again, in this tightening of business controls over labor incident to the return of General Motors and the renewed activity of organizers, one may not read personal malevolence on the part of the inner control group. Middletown's inner group of powerful businessmen are fighting to keep the city alive. They take the position they do on the high and obvious ground of "public interest": "It is the public that suffers in the long run," according to a local editorial, "through strikes, lockouts, and other interferences with industry." When labor trouble occurs, the papers are wont to call for "an immediate settlement of the present difficulties before they threaten the town's progress and its consequent prosperity further." The press calls upon the workers to arbitrate on the obviously sensible grounds that "As a general rule, one who fears to submit his case to arbitration has a losing cause; and if the workers' demands are just, there is no reason to think that the

---

[62] It is significant that the "deal" alleged to have been made with the plant was so secret that not even the press knew (or admitted that it knew) what had happened. It is also a commentary on the hierarchy of business-class controls and also on the latent lines of division within the business class itself that the real-estate group fought hard and openly to force the facts into the open, while the non-X-controlled afternoon paper sided with local taxpayers rather than maintaining the solid, official, business-class front. See Ch. IX, n. 10 and Ch. XII for further discussion of this.

employers will not be just." But always this "justice" must operate within the margin of competitive advantage which a Middletown plant must maintain in order to get that Ford contract away not only from Detroit but from the other Middletowns. If plants equip them-selves, as at least one Middletown plant is reported to have done under the threat of N.R.A. unionization, with tear gas; if, as a local profes-sional man in touch with labor conditions asserts, "Even in the stronger Middletown unions many of the key men are controlled by business interests"; if the press constantly features such threatening headlines as "Ohio Union Chief Sent to Prison" or "National Guardsmen Rout Strikers with Tear-Gas Attack" or "Bloodshed and Rioting Mark Cali-fornia Strike"; none of these steps is taken out of "pure cussedness," but, as one of the advertisements in the special forty-four-page edition of the afternoon paper celebrating the return of General Motors phrased it, to keep Middletown "a good town to live in! A good town to work in!" Within this "iron law" of competitive advantage, the several harassed parties struggle among themselves to maintain their several conceptions of what constitutes "local prosperity."

The whole picture of industrial morale in Middletown is full of apparent contradictions. One sat in the crowded little labor hall listen-ing to Dillon as he whipped up enthusiasm with the declaration: "The A. F. of L. is in [Middletown] and it is here to stay. We are going to organize the [Middletown] General Motors plant and the X plant first, and they haven't jails big enough to hold all the Detroit staff I'll send down here to do it." [63] One talked with the minister of a working-class church who said: "[Middletown] labor realizes that its pay is low and a lot of the men are bitter underneath and their families are com-plaining. But they're all afraid to start anything." Personal conversa-tions with individual workers brought out fear, resentment, great in-security, much disillusionment: "Our people are nervous about their jobs and don't dare kick about working conditions"; "I've been work-ing fairly steadily at the D—— plant for seven years, but I have been and still am afraid to let out my belt and buy anything beyond im-mediate necessities, for I might get canned any day. There's no security in seniority when a man is thrown out and when a kid just out of school is willing to do the job for less"; "We auto workers aren't get-ting too excited about the return of General Motors. It means a job,

[63] The local General Motors plant is still (February, 1937) completely unor ganized. See p. 73, n. The situation at the X plant also is unchanged.

and that's important—for the months in the year they're willing to
hire you. Only the Chamber of Commerce crowd are optimistic, and
they're trying to fool us workers." Newly rehired General Motors men
confided that they were afraid to go to the Dillon meeting for fear
they would be spotted.

And yet, as noted above, this fear, resentment, insecurity, and disillusionment has been to Middletown's workers largely an *individual*
experience for each worker, and not a thing generalized by him into
a *"class"* experience.[64] Such militancy as it generates tends to be sporadic, personal, and flaccid; an expression primarily of personal resentment rather than an act of self-identification with the continuities of
a movement or of rebellion against an economic status regarded as
permanently fixed. The militancy of Middletown labor tends, therefore,
to be easily manipulated, and to be diverted into all manner of incidental issues. The Ku Klux Klan movement of the early 1920's is a case
in point, for, to quote an editorial in the weekly Democratic paper,
"The [Ku Klux] Klan,[65] a distinctly antisocial arrangement, split the
workmen of Middletown and elsewhere into two armed camps, and
the exploiters of labor took charge of things." It is highly typical of
the blurred outlook of even organized labor in Middletown that when
the news leaked out that the mayor was going to expand the police
force to see that the General Motors plant got protection, the local
Central Labor Union first demanded that the mayor call his plan off,
and then, failing in this demand, insisted that some of their own unemployed union members be hired as policemen. This last demand
was granted and union workers became, in effect, company police.
This easy diversion of the aims of labor bobs up again and again.
Local businessmen now thank the abortive flurry of labor organization under N.R.A. for diverting the mounting radicalism of 1933. A
typical remark of this sort is quoted in *Business Week's* study of "Middletown—Ten Years After," [66] as follows: "Not many people know
how desperate workmen were. The agitators were making real headway. You've got to give the A. F. of L. credit for turning that trend.
It's an unwritten chapter of history."

Labor organization in Middletown, in the opinion of the present

[64] This is elaborated further in the discussion of awareness of class differences
in Ch. XII.
[65] See *Middletown*, pp. 481-84.
[66] June 9, 1934.

investigator, is emerging from the pit of the depression and from its experience under N.R.A. weaker than it was in the 1920's. The original sixteen active unions holding local charters in 1929 [67] were still extant on January 1, 1936, and their number had been increased by the addition of five other small locals. But, as noted above, these are mainly negligible minority groups in the industrial life of the city. It is, perhaps, not too much to say that they are tolerated only because of their small size and inconsequential power and for their saving evidence that Middletown is not officially completely opposed to organized labor.[68] The central fact in Middletown's labor situation in 1935 was that an effort had been made to organize Middletown's really important labor majority, outranking in number these minor trades by perhaps ten to one, and had failed dismally. Here is the record for 1933-35:

New Unions Organized in 1933-1935	Status as of January 1, 1936
Machinists	Dead
Metal Polishers	Dead
Foundry Workers	Dead
Amalgamated Iron and Steel Workers	Dead
Butchers and Meat Cutters	Dead
Teamsters and Chauffeurs	Continuing
Fire Fighters	Dead
Flint Glass	Continuing (Membership of fifty skilled moldmakers only)
Printing Pressmen	Continuing
Bartenders, Cooks, and Waiters	Continuing

The depression and subsequent events have strengthened greatly the determination of the industrial business class to maintain an open-shop town; and one must contrast the halting local labor leadership

[67] These sixteen unions are as follows: Brick Masons, Plasterers and Cement Finishers, Carpenters, Lathers, Painters and Decorators, Electricians, Plumbers and Steam Fitters, Molders, Patternmakers, Railway Maintenance of Way Workers, Railway Clerks, Typographers, Motion-picture Operators, Musicians, Postal Carriers, and Barbers.

In addition to these sixteen, the Building Laborers held a charter but had been defunct for five years; the Green Bottle Blowers maintained a charter and an "official organizer," but, as noted above, were not known to exist by the Central Labor Union and had no active members; and the Postal Clerks were organized but not affiliated with the A. F. of L.

Some idea of their size may be gained from the following total memberships of those unions for which memberships could be secured for early 1936: Molders, 175; Patternmakers, 19; Typographers, 110; Carpenters, 89; Painters, 31; Electricians, 9; Plumbers, 7.

[68] The advertisement by the Bricklayers' Union at the time of the Dillon meeting noted above seems to bear out this latter point.

and the bickerings among the rival officers of the international unions of the A. F. of L. with this greater clarity of business-class organization.

And yet, if one takes a long view of the local situation, the very disillusionment of the labor rank and file, its doubts as to the honesty of the A. F. of L. "higher-ups," and its tendency to look on labor unions as "just another racket" may be significant. Middletown factory labor is discouraged and "fed up" as regards organization, but it also appears to be slowly and vaguely taking somewhat more of a view of itself as a group over against the businessmen than it did in 1925. Another tendency that may also be significant appears in the fact that the depression has decreased somewhat the insularity of the various crafts. Some of the workers, at least, have been brought face to face with the craft- *vs*. industrial-union issue, and a few of the city's automotive workers are watching their better-organized fellow workers in a city a hundred miles to the north of them with keen interest.[69] All of these things—the disillusionment as well as a more matter-of-fact sense of the issues involved—may, over the long pull, be the stuff out of which working-class explosions occur.

Organization membership is already, in 1936, picking up in the strongly established nonindustrial unions such as the building trades; for instance, the local Carpenters' Union, which fell to sixty-three in the depression, is again nearing 100 and will in time probably return again to the 300 of 1929 as its members become employed and are again able to pay union dues. That reviving good times will bring marked organization among the mass of machinists and similar workers in Middletown's major industries appears doubtful. Any extensive effort

[69] The state A. F. of L. met in Middletown in September, 1935, and industrial unions from two larger cities came in militant force and succeeded in carrying a resolution endorsing industrial unions. They also proposed resolutions condemning the method of election of state A. F. of L. officers, requesting a new election and the conducting of elections at the conventions; and, also, two resolutions barring their state officers from holding political appointments and endorsing the formation of a labor party. "But," as a veteran local labor man summed up the convention, "these new industrial union men were amateurs as compared to the smooth-running parliamentary machine of the old guard A. F. of L. crowd. They left town feeling they had been steam-rollered, but the facts of the case are that they didn't know how to operate as cleverly as the A. F. of L. boys. At that, though, such resolutions as we did get through at the convention, such as the one condemning the governor's use of martial law in the general strike at Terre Haute in July, would have been enough twenty years ago to have brought in the Department of Justice with its sword and scales to put us down as 'anarchists'!"

at organization is likely to be met by a prompt threat to livelihood such as is described in the following news item of mid-October, 1936:

[MIDDLETOWN] PLANT TO BE CLOSED
LABOR DIFFICULTIES RESPONSIBLE

Closing of the American Lawn Mower Company plant . . . where work-ers went on strike last Friday was announced today by ——, secretary and treasurer.

"It is with deep regret that with a 35-year record of continuity of employ-ment and freedom from any serious labor difficulties, we are now compelled to announce the closing of the American Lawn Mower Company plant. A few months ago, when the company re-opened its foundry which had been closed since 1930, an effort was made to unionize this department. Unusual and unwarranted disturbances have followed. . . .

"In the face of these facts, our only alternative is to close the plant."

That some minor groups of workers are still militant enough to go out on strike suggests that the present disillusionment is not complete. As this goes to press, it is reported that a veteran local labor man is again setting out to try to organize the glass workers under the Flint Glass Union. The fact that, as one worker describes it, "We workers licked the big bosses here in [Middletown] by our majority for Roose-velt [in 1936]" may foreshadow some increase in South Side morale. For the immediate future, however, it seems likely that Middletown labor in the city's dominant automotive and glass industries will have neither the stomach nor adequate leadership for testing its strength soon again. One suspects that, even over the long pull, militant work-ing-class organization, a thing so basically foreign to the present popu-lation of Middletown, will not come through local initiative. If and when it comes to this population, it will probably be as a lagging phase of a movement diffused from larger industrial centers.

Other changes, less spectacular than these clashes over labor organi-zation under N.R.A., have been happening since 1925 in the ways in which Middletown gets its living. These shifts include apparent changes in the opportunity for men and women to be employed at all, in the kinds of work they may get, in the balance of "skilled" and "un-skilled" jobs, in the chance to be "promoted" and to launch out "on one's own,"—subtle changes for the most part not even generally recog-nized by Middletown itself, but of major significance over time in those regions of status and hope where men's morale struggles to live.

There has been a significant shift in recent years in the relative concentration of Middletown's workers in different types of work. The increments [70] in the 1920's ranged all the way from a gain of 8.0 per cent between 1920 and 1930 in the number employed in the Manufacturing and Mechanical Industries to one of 55.6 per cent in the Professional Services. Each of the "service industries" [71]—including Professional Service which grew during the decade of the 1920's by 55.6 per cent, Transportation and Communication which grew by 44.6 per cent, Public Service which added 44.0 per cent, Trade which added 27.1 per cent, and Domestic and Personal Service with an increment of 26.1 per cent—increased its share of Middletown's gainfully employed personnel at several times the rate of gain of the industries manufacturing physical commodities. What one is witnessing here is the relative slowing up of the traditionally heavy concentration of jobs in Middletown's factories, as machine technology decreases the necessary ratio of human working units to volume of output, and, on the other hand, a relative increase in the number of jobs available in a wide group of occupations involved in the mechanisms of living more comfortably. Or stated another way, in terms of the share of the net increment of new workers during the 1920's going to each class of occupations, while the activities involving the production of physical commodities absorbed 26.0 per cent of the new working personnel of the city, the service occupations absorbed 65.7 per cent.[72]

The rapid increase which this suggests in the share of Middletown's overhead carried in these services of welfare, luxury, and comfort should be viewed along with the heavy concentration of the city's manufacturing industries, noted earlier in this chapter, in the "feast or famine" industries producing producers' and consumers' durable goods. Together these meant that, when the wave crashed over in 1929, the local economy was probably more vulnerable than it had been at any time since the gas-boom growth that preceded the crash of 1893.

[70] See Table 5 in Appendix III.

[71] This term follows the usage of F. C. Mills, *op. cit.*, p. 245, n. 2.

[72] The Census groups Agriculture and Extraction of Minerals are here grouped with Manufacturing and Mechanical Industries to secure the above 26.0; and, following Mills (*op. cit.*), the Clerical group, which absorbed 8.3 per cent of the new workers, is omitted since they "cannot readily be classified either under service or nonservice industries."

Theoretically, getting a job in Middletown's culture is assumed to depend only upon one's "willingness" to work. Competition, under the prevailing system of *laissez-faire* capitalism, is assumed to provide automatically in a world of rational men all needed goods and services in due proportion to their social utility. And the array of available jobs at any given time is assumed to be in symmetrical, rational accord with the array of socially useful functions to be performed, due allowance being made for the stage of development of the culture's technologies for handling a given function. If one brushes aside this mist of official assumptions, however, and looks at the realities of the situation, one sees in Middletown a raggedly shifting array of opportunities for work, with the changes dictated not so much by a rational appraisal and balancing of socially useful functions and available manpower as by the accidents of the main chances to make money at any given time out of various areas of human need and susceptibility. The moment one begins to ask the rationale of a culture's having only 278 of its working personnel in Public Service (nearly all of them policemen, firemen, park laborers, and similarly employed persons) and 1,714 in Domestic and Personal Service and 2,776 in Trade, one is stopped short by the presence of the assumptions at the beginning of this paragraph. Here is a culture suckled on the lion's milk of getting ahead by personal exploitative prowess; a culture which believes that things order themselves best under this scrambling private struggle for pecuniary gain, and that the society as a unit should plan and do as little as possible so as not to interfere with this beneficent private scramble; a culture hypnotized by the gorged stream of new things to buy—automobiles, electrical equipment for the home, radios, automatic refrigeration, and all but automatic ways to live; a culture in which private business tempts the population in its every waking minute with adroitly phrased invitations to apply the solvent remedy of more and newer possessions and socially distinguishing goods and comforts to all the ills that flesh is heir to—to loneliness, insecurity, deferred hope, and frustration.[73]

[73] Paul Mazur, himself a businessman, describes in his *American Prosperity* the sharp, self-interested tactics of merchandising that have dominated the "progress" of the American people in recent years: "The community that can be trained to desire change, to want new things even before the old have been entirely consumed, yields a market to be measured more by desires than by needs. And man's desires can be developed so that they will greatly overshadow his needs. . . . Human nature very conveniently presented a variety of strings upon which an appreciative sales manager could play fortissimo. . . . Advertis-

From the point of view of the individual who must find a continuing livelihood, the erratic shifts in chances to work in such an unstable world spell uncertainty in deciding what field of work to enter, in finding a job, and in maintaining oneself in a job.

Even during the prosperous 1920's, there was a diminution in the total share of Middletown's population who "usually" worked. This decrease involved not only those under twenty years of age, many of whom, as shown in Chapter VI, were prolonging their education, but also those twenty and over; and even in the case of the latter it probably involved an increasing inability to get work rather than increased disinclination to work due to affluence leading to early retirement and similar voluntary choices. It probably involved, also, increased competition for such jobs as were available. In the case of the male part of the population these tendencies seem fairly clear; and in that of the females, though the absolute figures do not reveal it, the same tendencies were very probably operating if one takes into account the increased psychological drive toward women's working.

The basis for the above generalizations lies in the close analysis of the Federal Census figures for Middletown in 1920 and 1930.[74] While Middletown's population ten years old and over increased by 26.2 per cent between 1920 and 1930, its group of "usually" gainfully employed grew by only 18.5 per cent. A breakdown of these figures for the two age groups, ten and under twenty years old, and twenty years old and over, reveals some striking differences. Not only did the number of persons in the younger of these two groups grow at a rate less than half as rapid as that of the older group,[75] but the proportion of even

ing became a force in American life. Threats, fear, beauty, sparkle, persuasion and careful as well as wild-cat exaggeration were thrown at the American buying public as a continuous and terrifying barrage. . . . And so desire was enthroned in the minds of the American consumer, and was served abjectly by the industries that had enthroned it." (New York; Viking Press, 1928, p. 24 ff.)

[74] See Table 6 in Appendix III.

It should be borne constantly in mind that all judgments based upon a comparison simply of the two ends of a single decade must be used only tentatively.

The Federal Census, taken on January 1, 1920, and April 1, 1930, does not take account of temporary unemployment at the time of enumeration: "The term 'gainful workers' in Census usage," according to the Census, "includes all persons who usually follow a gainful occupation, although they may not have been employed when the Census was taken."

[75] Table 6 shows that between 1920 and 1930 the city's population between the ages of ten and twenty increased by only 13.2 per cent, while those twenty and over increased by 29.9 per cent. The expansion of this older group involved

this relatively reduced younger group that continued to engage in re munerative employment was cut in half.

The implications of this development for those under the age of twenty deserve further examination. Table 7 [76] shows the distribution of Middletown's gainfully employed by sex and by narrow age groups in 1920 and in 1930. In the case of both boys and girls it reveals a marked diminution in employed persons under twenty years of age. The declines in persons of both sexes under eighteen are especially marked. In the lower ages—ten to fifteen—the better enforcement of the school attendance and child-labor laws has influenced this trend; [77] and in all ages under twenty, the drive toward higher education has undoubtedly been a significant factor.

The diminution in employment of persons under twenty may not, however, be passed over as due entirely to such factors as child-labor laws and education. The child-labor law drops out as a factor when the child completes the eighth grade; and yet Middletown had at the time of the 1930 Census roughly 6 per cent of its children fourteen and fifteen years of age, 18 per cent of its children of ages sixteen and seventeen, and 21 per cent of the eighteen- and nineteen-year-olds who were neither in school nor employed.[78] What we appear to be seeing here is the slow emergence of a social problem likely to be momentous in the future, namely, the presence in Middletown even in the pros-

the slow secular trend in the population to the older side, but even more the migration of adult workers into Middletown in the big years in search of jobs.

[76] See Appendix III for this table.

[77] The State law requires that "No minor under the age of fourteen years shall be employed or permitted to work in any gainful occupation other than farm labor, domestic service or caddy"; and that "Any child over fourteen and under sixteen years of age who has completed the work of the first eight grades of the public school or its equivalent may be permitted to withdraw from school upon the issuing to such child of a lawful employment certificate." Employers require the showing of a work certificate before hiring a person under eighteen. An amendment in 1933 to the workmen's compensation law provides for double compensation in the case of accidents to minors working in violation of the child labor laws. Only in this last respect have the laws regarding the schooling and employment of minors changed since 1925.

The sharp inroads of the depression upon the work of children needing work certificates is shown by the following totals of certificates issued by Middletown's State:

1925 14,179	1930 10,942	1933 3,833
1929 15,752	1931 7,435	1934 5,884
	1932 4,467	

[78] See Table 8 in Appendix III.

perous 1920's of a jobless and schoolless population, an idle in-between age group commencing in the mid-teens and culminating in the after-high-school age of nineteen. Table 7 shows that the gainfully employed fell between 1920 and 1930 in all ages up to twenty and began to increase only in the age group 20-24. With the growing pressure for available jobs from the steadier workers past their teens, Middletown's industries may be absorbing less and less of the population under twenty,[79] leaving a helpless group too old for school and too young to get jobs. Under the circumstances, the prolonging of schooling through high school and into college in the 1920's may represent not only a desire for more education but a slowly growing necessity to choose between school and idleness.[80]

The problem of idle youth was emphatically present in Middletown in 1935. Middletown blamed this entirely on the depression and regarded the preference being given to married heads of families in local reemployment as but a temporary necessity. It may be, however, that, with tighter competition for jobs as a more or less permanent aspect of the economy from now on, Middletown may have to face the continuing social problem of the too-old-for-school-and-too-young-to-work.

The dropping out of these workers under twenty during the decade of the 1920's tended to ease materially the competition for jobs by those twenty and over. The latter group was thereby enabled to increase its share of the total gainfully employed by 7.4 per cent—from 87.7 per cent of the total to 94.2 per cent [81]—while the proportion which the group twenty and over constituted of the total population rose by only 2.0 per cent—from 64.9 per cent of the total to 66.2 per cent. The easement of competition among this group twenty years old and older, which these figures seem to demonstrate, was offset, however, by the fact that the number of persons gainfully employed grew less rapidly over the decade than did the population; and so, despite their increased share in whatever jobs were available, the proportion of this twenty-and-over group who were "usually" gainfully employed fell from 59.7 per cent to 58.5 per cent.[82] A smaller share of the people twenty

[79] See *Middletown*, pp. 30-35.

[80] The high-school teachers complain of the poor work of many of the South Side children who have been crowding into the high school. An explanation of this may lie in the fact that, in view of their inability to get work, they are merely marking time in school. See Ch. VI.

[81] See Table 7.

[82] See Table 6.

and over were "usually" working by the end of the 1920's, and it seems likely that this is due primarily to the fact that fewer of them could get work. The actual change was small but probably significant for the future.

A minute fraction of this decline may be accounted for by the in-- crease in the number of persons of ages twenty and over attending college. Very little of it, if any, may be attributed to an increase in the number of persons who "retired," as there was even in the 1920's no pattern of "retiring" in Middletown. Middletown men on all income levels work at something until death or infirmity takes the decision whether or not to work out of their hands.[83] It is difficult to say how much the old-age deadline has been involved in this decline in the share of the total adult population who are gainfully employed.[84] Actually more persons in the older age groups in both sexes were employed in Middletown in 1930 than in 1920.[85]

[83] The 1930 Census shows 750 families (6.0 per cent of all families) in Middletown as having no "usually" gainfully employed member. This suggests the possibility of a sizable group of retired persons—businessmen, farmers, etc. It is, however, the strong belief of the investigator—though based on nothing more definite than his familiarity with the community—that these 750 families are made up of those unable-to-work due to extreme age or infirmity and either possessed of a pittance covering the bare minima of subsistence or supported by relatives, of the widowed similarly situated, of persons living on alimony, and similar cases. Farming in Middletown's county was not sufficiently prosperous in the 1920's to encourage any large increment of retired farmers to move to the county seat. Unfortunately, comparable Census figures for 1920 are not available. Were they available, the investigator does not believe that any significant increase since 1920 would appear—though this again is a largely unsupported judgment.

[84] See *Middletown*, pp. 31-35.
It is not unlikely that the age factor in employment, and particularly in reemployment, operates selectively; that it has continued to be as important as in 1925 in many of the principal groups of industrial jobs open to Middletown workers, despite the fact that in general more older workers were employed in some kind of job in 1930 than in 1920, is believed to be the case by the investigator.

[85] See Table 7.
Mapheus Smith has analyzed the shifts in the gainfully employed in the United States as a whole in "Trends in the Ages of Gainful Workers, by Occupation, 1910-30" (*Journal of the American Statistical Association,* December, 1935):
"A decrease in younger workers, and a corresponding increase of older workers has brought about an increase of 5.9 years in the median age of the gainfully employed male population and an increase of 1.2 years in the age of female workers from 1910 to 1930. . . . Unless the whole system of American democracy is changed to a revolutionary extent, the aging of the working population will continue for some time yet, almost certainly for at least two decades, and probably longer. There has been an unquestioned decline in the number of

Despite the increase in older persons gainfully employed, it appears that it is among the older male workers that the competition for jobs is most acute. The unevenness of the gains in numbers employed registered by males and by females in the age groups over twenty between 1920 and 1930 is noteworthy. While in 1920 the age composition of gainfully employed women over twenty years of age was more heavily weighted to the younger side than was the case among men over twenty, the two sexes moved in the direction of a closer agreement during the ensuing decade. In this decade opposite tendencies operated in the two sex groups, gainfully employed men increasing relatively more rapidly on the younger side and women on the older. This appears in the following relative changes during the decade in the percentage which each age group constituted of the total for each sex gainfully employed: [86]

Age	Males	Females
20-24	+14.8 per cent	+12.3 per cent
25-44	+ 5.3	+17.9
45-64	+ 3.3	+19.0
65 and over	+ 3.2	− 7.3

Thus, while among the males the proportion who were of ages twenty to twenty-four was being increased very much more rapidly than other age groups, the women were shifting their composition in the reverse direction. Among the women the greatest relative growth was actually achieved by the group forty-five to sixty-four years of age. Judging from conversations with some of these older men in June, 1935, the

young persons in the population. The population pyramid is actually smaller at the bottom than formerly and this condition of affairs will automatically spread to the older group as the years pass. By 1940 it will already be affecting the youngest working groups. The increased length of schooling, child labor agitation, and the probable loss of interest in gainful employment following a history of emergency relief and a large amount of chronic unemployment will serve to reduce drastically the number of workers below 20 at that time. By 1950, the effects of the declining number of births may be expected to reach the 20 to 30 year group, and the result will be further aging of workers in all occupations in which workers are not already as old as they can be and retain their efficiency. But by 1960, or 1970 at the latest, the decline in the birth rate will probably have had its greatest effect on the age of the working population—at least its greatest effect during the present phase of our national development. By the latter date the age of gainful workers in each occupation will be somewhat closer to the upper age limit of productive efficiency than now unless an interruption of recent trends occurs."

[86] Based on Table 7 in Appendix III.

pressure upon them has become particularly severe during the depression. Some of Middletown's older, locally owned plants—notably the X plant—try to "look out for" their older workers, and, as reemployment was occurring in 1935, formerly-hired men with families were tending to be taken on first in these plants. The preference of the large machine shops for young men was, however, markedly apparent as one stood at the gate of the newly opened General Motors unit at closing time. These men as they streamed out past one, newly hired under a hiring policy involving little compunction to "take care of anybody," were overwhelmingly in their twenties and thirties—the pick of the crop. Older men now unemployed and not having strong local job ties face a decidedly chancy future, which may involve slipping down the job scale to "anything they can get."

Against Middletown's marginal male workers, whether those under twenty or those above the mid-forties, presses continually the stream of available vigorous young labor in the surrounding rural region. The threat of this out-of-town labor pool may have increased since 1929 and almost certainly has not decreased. The Federal Farm Census, taken on April 1, 1930, and again on January 1, 1935, and covering the years 1929 and 1934, respectively, reveals an increase by 1934 of 10.8 per cent in the number of farmers in Middletown's county reporting work for pay not connected with their farms, and an increase of 20.5 per cent in the total number of days so worked.[87] The comparison is confused, however, by the fact that relief work was included in 1934. The back-to-the-farm movement during the depression probably involves a net increase in the competition for industrial jobs in Middletown. There were 1,761 persons living on 609 farms in the county on January 1, 1935, who had been living in non-farm residences at the beginning of 1930. Most of these new farmers were probably men who had previous industrial employment in Middletown, and most of them probably continue to maintain at least seasonal ties with Middletown factories. Since Middletown's own population actually increased slightly during the depression, despite this farm exodus, and since the actual number of available jobs had not increased, this sug-

[87] The number of farmers working for pay off their farms rose from 888 in 1929 to 984 in 1934, and their total days so worked totalled 129,860 in 1929 and 156,432 in 1934. During 1934, 80 per cent of these farmers worked fifty or more days off their farms, 57 per cent of them 150 or more days, and 29 per cent 250 days or more.

gests enhanced competition for such jobs as were available in 1935.[88]

There is obvious need for detailed study of what happens to older workers in a place like Middletown—what they do, whether getting old means for the factory worker the chance to work only in the seasonal peaks of employment, and how their kinds of jobs change as their speed and endurance wane and they are shifted from machines to being timekeepers and watchmen, and to such jobs as sweeping up. Between 1929 and 1934 the number of farms in Middletown's county rose by 8.9 per cent and tenant farmers by 19.5 per cent. These figures, combined with the preceding ones, suggest that there may be a tendency for the farms around Middletown to lose their young and vigorous workers to Middletown, while Middletown's less successful workers, including many men who are "getting along in years," may be taking small tenant farms where they can raise winter subsistence crops like potatoes and still look for work in Middletown's factories during seasonal peaks of industrial employment.

The brackish pool of unemployment which was slowly growing in Middletown during the 1920's corresponds to a similar development throughout the nation. For as F. C. Mills said in 1932: [89]

Even before the period of expansion was terminated in 1929, a widening margin of unemployed was accumulating. The turn-over of men, the shifting of labor among industries, the enforced displacement of labor [90]—these

[88] The net farm population of the county rose by only seven persons during these five years. This indicates that there was an exodus *from* the county's farms almost precisely balancing the numbers returning to the farms. As shown in Appendix I, Middletown's population rose by 1,500 in 1931-32 over 1929, and in 1935 stood at 500 above 1929. That it was not the same group of families who moved to Middletown early in the depression and back to the farms by 1935 is revealed by the fact that the 1,761 persons added to the county's farm population by January 1, 1935, had been living in *non-farm* residences in 1930. There is no way of telling how many of the migrants from the farm came to Middletown, though it is likely that a large number of them did.

[89] *Op. cit.,* p. 481.

[90] Mills summarizes these heavy gains in output per worker in recent decades in the United States as follows: "With a steadily advancing volume of production, the number of wage-earners and the number of manufacturing establishments declined, while output per wage-earner and output per establishment showed notable gains. Most impressive of these changes is the gain in productivity per worker. Over the fifteen years from 1899 to 1914 output per wage-earner increased approximately 30 per cent—notable evidence of the growing efficiency of both the human and mechanical factors of production. Great as this gain was, it was exceeded during the decade from 1919 to 1929. Output per worker increased no less than 43 per cent during these ten years." (*Op. cit.,* p. 314.)

were becoming more prominent features of industrial progress than they had ever been before. Security of tenure was declining, a condition particularly true as regards men past the prime of life. The rewards for employed men were high, but mechanical improvements and a faster pace were making it harder to hold on.

This compression of job opportunity apparently affected both males and females. The percentage of Middletown's males aged twenty and over who were "usually" gainfully employed fell from 94.7 in 1920 to 92.8 in 1930.[91] If, as seems entirely likely, we can assume a constant desire in Middletown's male population to work, this suggests, as noted above, a small though real decrease in the relative number of available jobs. Contrary to this situation among the males, the percentage of females twenty and over who were "usually" gainfully occupied actually showed a small gain over the decade, from 22.8 per cent of all women of these ages in 1920 to 23.3 per cent in 1930.[92]

While women thus seem superficially to have had less shrinkage in job opportunity than men, it should be borne in mind that we are dealing with different situations as regards the propensity of Middletown's two sexes to work. Virtually all adult males in Middletown worked in 1930, as in 1920, for an able-bodied male who is "idle" loses caste in this culture;[93] but as over against this unchanging situation for the males, the sentiment regarding women's working has grown steadily more favorable during recent years. Among the working class, the psychological standard of living of the 1920's so far outran any actual increase in male earnings that there was apparently no tendency for women of this group, whether married or single, to cease working;[94] while, among the business class, working at something between school and marriage has become more and more "the thing to do." Even in 1925 there was still something of the "fad" about the vague expectation of Middletown girls of the business class that they would "work" after leaving school,[95] but the sentiment in favor of working was spreading steadily among them. The following statement by a young businessman in 1935, typical of several comments on this point, reflects the continued growth of this sentiment: "The girls I knew here

[91] See Table 6 in Appendix III.
[92] Ibid.
[93] See Middletown, p. 25.
[94] See the discussion of married women workers in Middletown later in this chapter and in Ch. V.
[95] See Middletown, p. 26, including n. 2.

ten years ago took up careers largely as a protection against failure to marry and similar contingencies. Now those who plan to work are nothing like so much confined to the hopeless." In view of this apparently steadily growing pressure of Middletown's females toward working, the diminutive increase in the proportion of them actually working shown above probably reflects an actual sharp increment in competition for such jobs as were available.

With the competition for jobs among members of each sex apparently tightening even in a decade of "good times," a more aggressive competitive jockeying for jobs between the two sexes is an almost inevitable consequence. This development is hardly apparent when only the total figures are consulted, for women constituted 21.1 per cent of all usually gainfully occupied persons in 1920 and 20.6 per cent in 1930.[96] Yet behind this seemingly stoutly held front significant changes were in process. While Middletown's women workers became relatively more strongly entrenched in some occupations, they have been forced to retreat in others. Women's gains[97] have come largely from more intensive cultivation of work traditionally done by women, and their chief losses have been felt in those fields traditionally men's which they had entered. The chief shifts between 1920 and 1930 in the number of each sex employed in each major type of work are as follows:

	Males	Females
Manufacturing and mechanical industries ..	+10 per cent	— 9 per cent
Transportation and communication	+49	+11
Trade	+32	+ 9
Professional service	+52	+61
Domestic and personal service	+43	+17
Clerical occupations	+ 8	+31

Women have gained more rapidly than men in only two job areas, Clerical and Professional.

The decrease in number of women in the central field of Manufacturing and Mechanical Industries which the above figures show is apparently part of a larger trend, for in the United States as a whole the percentage of the total employees in this group of activities who have been women has fallen from 17.1 in 1910 to 15.0 in 1920, and to

[96] The fact that the number of females ten years old and over in Middletown increased more rapidly than did the corresponding male population (26.9 per cent for the former and 25.6 per cent for the latter) augments the importance of the above relative drop from 1920 to 1930.

[97] See Table 9 in Appendix III.

13.4 in 1930. This recession in Middletown did not occur in a single type of industry, but in driblets all along the line, save for operatives in the glass and silverware plants and a few smaller industries where small gains were recorded. What may be happening in this factory type of occupation for women is that, whereas such factors as the introduction of power and materials-handling equipment, their tolerance of routine types of work and of a wage below male wages, and their greater disinclination to unionization originally gave women their chance and established them in factories, other counter factors are now crowding them out. Among these latter may be the fact that the wage differential in favor of women is apparently declining somewhat; and also that the emergence of a new emphasis upon the relation of labor to physical plant overhead, which stresses the economies to be derived from more continuous use of plant under the "speed-up," is tending to reinstate the earlier predominance of male strength and endurance.

In the group of occupations under Trade, women registered a small net increase, but this was entirely confined to a rise from 303 to 358 in Saleswomen and a rise of from four to eight in the number of Insurance Agents. In all other branches of Trade women lost in numbers over the decade. Their net increase of 9 per cent in this group of occupations is only a little over one-quarter of the 32 per cent gain of men in Trade.[98]

That women bettered slightly their relative position in Professional Services is due largely to their sizable gains as Teachers and Trained Nurses, with smaller gains as Actresses. They lost slightly in number of Artists and Teachers of Art, dropping from five to four, while men rose from five to fourteen.[99] Women likewise declined by more than a quarter in their number of Musicians and Teachers of Music, while men increased by more than a quarter. All eight of Middletown's women Physicians and Surgeons in 1920 had disappeared by 1930, as had also the two women Osteopaths.[100] The only woman Dentist dis-

[98] In the classification Bankers, Brokers, and Moneylenders women dropped from four to one; in Real-estate Agents and Officials, from seven to three (while men dropped only from 80 to 66); in Retail Dealers they showed a slight loss, while men gained by nearly one-fifth in numbers.

[99] These men do not represent a body of local male artists in the fine-arts sense, but rather commercial illustrators, poster designers, etc.

[100] Middletown's Physicians and Surgeons declined by one-fifth over the decade—from 87 in 1920 to 68 in 1930. This probably represents a transfer of

appeared, while male Dentists increased from twenty to twenty-six in number. The lone woman Lawyer continued, while male Lawyers increased from sixty to seventy-three. The three women in the classification Designers, Draftsmen, and Inventors dropped to two, while men rose from forty-two to eighty-five. Middletown had in neither period any women Chemists or Technical Engineers, while the men in the former rose from three to thirty and in the latter from forty-three to ninety-eight.

This relative crowding of women from other professional fields and the heavy concentration of their professional activities in teaching and nursing is significant in view of the fact that professional work offers one of the few chances for the able woman to break through to a position of relative independence in the job world of Middletown.[101] In 1930, 62 per cent of the 368 Middletown women in the professional fields were teachers or trained nurses. And it is significant, perhaps, for their future status in even school teaching (the larger of these two main professional strongholds) that men were overhauling them even here in the 1920's; for male teachers increased over the decade by 157 per cent while female teachers increased by only 74 per cent.

In the group of Domestic and Personal Services, such increases as women showed between 1920 and 1930 were only 40 per cent as great as those made by men. The women in this group of occupations were heavily concentrated among Servants, Waiters, and Hairdressers and Manicurists, with smaller gains among Laundry Operatives, Restaurant, Café and Lunchroom Keepers, and Midwives and Nurses (Other than Trained Nurses). Even in such a field as that of Waiters, women's rate of gain was outstripped by that of men. Their losses in the stay-at-home jobs of Laundresses (Not in Laundry) and Boarding and

certain meagerly trained marginal types of therapists from this category to such general classifications as "Other Professional Pursuits."

By 1935 there were again two women physicians in Middletown.

[101] See the further discussion below in this chapter and in Ch. V of the meagerness of the work outlets open to women in Middletown.

It is significant for the quality of Middletown's life that the small and locally little-recognized Business and Professional Women's Club has become since 1925 perhaps the most thoughtful of all Middletown's civic clubs. As yet Middletown has developed no imaginative ways of utilizing a strong group of this sort in the city's life. Such a group, like everything else in Middletown's life, tends to be allowed to run along its course as best it can under the general local philosophy that all things mysteriously but surely work together for good. Middletown also has an Altrusa Club, composed of business and professional women.

Lodging House Keepers were heavy, and represent (like their losses as Dressmakers and Seamstresses, Not in Factories, and as Milliners, under the Manufacturing and Mechanical group above) a closing of the door on the stay-at-home type of job followed particularly by married women.

The gains made by women between 1920 and 1930 in employment in the Clerical Occupations were at four times the rate of gain registered by men. This represents, however, a gain in a field carrying little or no status, and it marks another stage in the concentration of Middletown's women workers into the "women's fields."

If one combines the above strands of analysis of this uneasy scene of competition between the two sexes for jobs in this small city, the total picture appears in its larger outlines to be somewhat as follows:

Even during the "good" decade of the 1920's, a decreasing proportion of Middletown's men was able to find employment. There was accordingly increased competition among them and with women workers for such jobs as the city had to offer.

Women managed almost to hold their own in the total share of the city's jobs which they held. But they did this only at the cost of diminishing their hold upon the types of jobs in which male competition is most acute, and concentrating more within a narrowed group of "women's jobs."

It is unlikely, unless there is a marked change in Middletown's types of industry, that women will regain the ground they have lost in the city's factories. Nor is it at all likely that the rate of transfer to nursing and teaching, made possible in the 1920's by the two nonrecurrent phenomena of the opening of the new hospital and the postwar influx of children into the schools, will be maintained in future. In certain niches—nursing, teaching, clerical work, household servants, hairdressers and manicurists, and telephone operators (until manual dial instruments are introduced into Middletown)—they occupy a fairly secure position. But elsewhere, and in fact as just noted even in teaching, the pressure of men for women's jobs apparent even in the 1920's is likely to increase, particularly if business continues more or less chronically "down" from the 1929 level. With Middletown's male heads of families the most rigid element in the city's labor supply, and even this preferred group under augmented competition to get and to hold jobs, the less preferred elements down the line from them are being forced to "fit in" where they can: married women workers are doing monotonous hand jobs in factories that can be done more cheaply by pieceworkers who do not have to support themselves but merely supplement a husband's income; unmarried women in business and the professions are doing either extremely poorly paid work as retail clerks and teachers,[102] or manifestly "women's work" like stenography and typing, or helping professional men as assistants; while those under twenty years of age are accepting prolonged schooling as an alternative to enforced idleness.

In the face of this situation, it is of interest to note that married women [103] actually bulked noticeably larger among Middletown's workers in 1930 than in 1920. They rose from 27.9 per cent of all "usually" employed females in 1920 to 37.7 per cent in 1930, and their ratio to total gainfully employed persons of both sexes rose from one to seventeen to one to thirteen. A number of factors were probably involved in this increase: With females under twenty years of age holding only 10.4 per cent of the positions held by women in 1930, as against 22.5 per cent in 1920, there would be more jobs held by the share of the female population twenty and over, among whom marriage is heaviest. The tendency toward earlier marriage during the decade noted in Chapter V [104] was also a factor, not only because it increased the share of the population married, but also because there is a strong tendency for these young couples to marry "on a shoestring" and for the wife to continue to work in order to make marriage possible on their joint income. A third factor is probably the ability of married women to work at piecework for wages of $7 to $10 a week in the small furniture and related marginal plants of the city, whereas wages so low enforce very much more severe privations upon the woman who does not have another source of income from a husband.

The 1930 Census makes available data not to be had from the 1920 Census on Middletown's homemakers. Of the 12,128 families having a homemaker in April, 1930, 14 per cent had a homemaker who was "usually" gainfully employed. Some rough idea of what these married women do is gained from the following: [105]

[102] See Ch. VI.
[103] The term "married women" as here used does not include widowed and divorced women. The latter are grouped here with single women.
[104] Chapter V shows that between 1920 and 1930 the percentage of Middletown's males of ages fifteen to twenty-four who were married rose from 21.7 to 24.9, and of its females of the same ages from 40.5 to 46.2.
Over the decade the percentage of all females fifteen years of age and over who were married rose from 66.0 to 67.5.
[105] Unfortunately for our purposes, the Census does not separate out here the 220 gainfully employed homemakers who are not married from the 1,490 who are married. The total of 1,710 here used necessarily, therefore, includes both groups. The "homemaker" is defined by the Census (*Families*, p. 9; Vol. VI, of

Homemakers by Type of Employment	Number	Per cent
Homemakers gainfully employed at home........	131	7.7
Homemakers gainfully employed away from home	1,578	92.3
Industrial workers	488	28.5
Saleswomen	196	11.5
Professional workers	179	10.5
Servants, waitresses, etc.	355	20.7
Office workers	286	16.7
Other occupations away from home..........	74	4.3
Homemakers gainfully employed, place not specified	1	...
Total	1,710	100.0

A comparison of these figures with the distribution of all Middletown's women workers in 1930 shows that only in the Industrial and possibly [106] in the Domestic and Personal Service fields do married women run ahead of their sex in the distribution of their services among the various lines of work. There were 28.5 per cent of these gainfully employed homemakers in industrial work, as over against only 22.2 per cent of all female workers, and this difference would even be augmented slightly if that share of the 131 homemakers employed at home who are dressmakers, milliners, etc., were added to the above 28.5 per cent. Homemakers in the Trade Occupations run about 10 per cent behind the share of all women workers who are in Trade; those in the Professional field 30 per cent behind; [107] and those in the Clerical Occupations 20 per cent behind. The fact that the share of homemakers who are in industry outstrips so clearly the corresponding share of all women workers so employed may confirm the point suggested above that married workers are heavily used for sporadic jobs or piece-

Population) as "that woman member of the family who was responsible for the care of the home and family." She is not, therefore, necessarily the wife of the male head of the family, nor is her husband necessarily living. Since homemakers, as thus defined, are in 87 per cent of the cases wives living with their husbands, the term is here used as roughly synonymous with "married women."

[106] This contingent statement is necessitated by the fact that the categories in the two Census classifications do not entirely overlap. The percentage of the gainfully employed homemakers working away from home who are Servants, Waitresses, etc., is 20.7 and the total percentage of all employed women in Domestic and Personal Service is 25.9. But many of the 7.7 per cent of the homemakers who are employed at home are boarding- and lodging-house keepers and women doing other work in the Domestic and Personal Service classification.

[107] Middletown, according to a recently adopted policy, will no longer hire married women schoolteachers.

work that is too cheaply paid to invite women who must support themselves. It also suggests the likelihood that Middletown's industries favor the stable, mature woman worker who has "got over any flightiness" and is available year after year without involving each time she is hired the cost which would be involved in breaking in green girl hands. The rise in the relative number of these married women workers probably accounts for a not inconsiderable part of the tendency noted above for women workers, contrary to men workers, to have added to their numbers between 1920 and 1930 at an accelerating rate in each age group above twenty, up to age sixty-five.

Though married women thus seem, on the basis of the trend during the 1920's, to occupy a fairly secure niche in the job world, this security may be illusory. While no figures are available since 1930, it is probable that married women workers have not only lost ground heavily but have received a possibly permanent check due to the depression. By 1935 the sentiment was growing in Middletown against the employment of married women so long as male heads of families remained unemployed. During the depression, men's rates of pay have fallen more heavily than women's, for the simple reason that women's were already close to or below the subsistence minimum. Women's earlier wage and salary differential has accordingly been heavily decreased. Not only are men competing more directly for women's jobs, but so great has been the burden of local relief that a strong, though still scattered, sentiment has developed, as already noted, in favor of filling new jobs with unemployed men first, especially married men—and only after that with women, and, save for intermittent piecework at wages too low to support a single woman, with needy single women before married women. It seems not unlikely that Middletown, in common with the rest of the United States, is facing a future including the prospect of a permanently augmented burden of unemployment— aggravated by the new awareness that it is no longer possible to tell the person who cannot find a job "here" to "go to the next town." If this proves to be the case, there seems a real likelihood that the, at present scattered and unorganized, sentiment in favor of giving priority to male workers will crystallize into an official sentiment resembling the discrimination against women job holders officially propagated in a country like Germany today. The more rapid increase of males than

females in such a field as schoolteaching during the 1920's may foreshadow a condition in the United States in which, as in Europe, fields
like teaching, nursing, bookkeeping, and stenography will be more
heavily overrun by males. And as males move over into more and
more direct competition with females, it will not be surprising if we
see workingmen agitating increasingly for minimum-wage laws for
women in the effort to put a legal floor under their own depressed
earnings.

In Chapter V the pressure of the commercially encouraged psychological standard of living is cited as a strong contributing cause to the
increase of Middletown's married women workers in a decade of
prosperity like the 1920's. The 1930 Census gives for the first time
data on the extent of supplementary earning by other family members
than the family head in Middletown, as each family scrambles for
more security and more things in a culture in which one is largely
judged by the things one has.[108] The following figures are for Middletown's central group of native white families [109] who comprise 92.4
per cent of all the city's families:

[108] It is characteristic of urban life, with its large jumbled populations that
include many strangers, to bridge the gap between anonymity and "belonging"
by the device of overt material possessions that "place" one. As a Middletown
citizen remarked in 1925, "People know money, and they don't know you."
Thorstein Veblen has described this process in *The Theory of the Leisure Class*.
He has also described the "creative psychiatry" employed by American business
to make profit from this tendency in human beings, as follows: "The production
of customers by sales-publicity is evidently the same thing as a production of
systematized illusions, organized into serviceable 'action patterns'—serviceable,
that is, for the use of the seller on whose account and for whose profit the
customer is being produced. It follows, therefore, that the technicians in charge
of this work, as also the skilled personnel of the working-force, are by way of
being experts and experimenters in applied psychology, with a workmanlike
bent in the direction of what may be called creative psychiatry. Their day's work
will necessarily run on the creative guidance of habit and bias, by recourse to
shock effects, tropismatic reactions, animal orientation, forced movements, fixa-
tion of ideas, verbal intoxication." (*Absentee Ownership*, New York; Viking
Press, 1923, p. 306.)

As this is being written, the Federal Bureau of Labor Statistics is making an
elaborate study of family income and expenditure on all income levels in Middletown as a part of a series of comparable studies in all sections of the country.
When these materials are available one will have a better basis than ever before
for appraising the balance of income and possessions in Middletown families.

[109] Figures for all Middletown families, including foreign-born and Negro,
are as follows: Families with no gainful workers, 750; with one, 7,933; with
two, 2,857; with three or more, 934.

	Number	Per cent
Total native white families in Middletown in 1930....	11,521	100.00
Families with 0 gainful workers................	694	6.02
Families with 1 gainful worker.................	7,326	63.59
Families with 2 gainful workers................	2,651	23.01
Families with 3 or more gainful workers........	850	7.38

The dominant pattern here is clear; nearly two-thirds of the families operate in the way Middletown's central traditions regard as "right" and "normal," *i.e.,* with a single person "supporting" the family. But it is significant that, even in an era of "good times" like the 1920's, nearly a third of Middletown's families had two or more persons working to support the family's standard of living.[110]

As one looks over the array of jobs open to Middletown's people in a city in which there are at one and the same time too few jobs for all the people who want to work and yet many socially useful functions beckoning to be attended to, one is struck by the fact that the small city apparently has a distinctive pattern of jobs. This is more varied than the pattern of the village and small town and less varied than that of the large city. The whole problem of the patterning of ways of getting a living in communities of different sizes invites analysis.

The prevailing assumption in any given community is that, true to the *laissez-faire* tradition, competition everywhere insures everything's being done that literally *can* be done. This leads in turn to a kind of "iron law of occupations," similar to the "iron law of wages" of the classical economists which assumed a fixed "wage fund." Everywhere, accordingly, each single community assumes that "There are only so many kinds of things people can do in this community. There are no 'things to do' other than those that people are doing." Each community operates, therefore, with a frozen local pattern of things to do, and it is, as a result, normal to each local culture to have a larger array of potential talent in its men and especially in its women than this rigid pattern of conventionalized jobs is able to set to work.

It is particularly as regards jobs for its women, including married women, of education and intelligence that, as noted in Chapter V, this "iron law of jobs" operates negatively in Middletown. It is important to note that in Middletown's business class the woman's world largely lacks an institutionalized counterpart to the business enterprise which affords an outlet for a restless, energetic, venturesome male. The near-

[110] See n. 83 above regarding the families having no gainful workers.

est a business-class wife can come to the same type of psychological release through risk and courage are competitive social life and the brief experiences of childbirth. Middletown's small-city culture is set up to provide for the more urgent needs of the commoner personality types and functions; and it presents a deterring conservative front to the type of woman who would explore unusual vocational opportunities. The small community tends to be a place of usual personalities, usual jobs, usual recreations. Many of the odd personalities—the political or economic radical, the artistic individual, the person with a flair for the unusual—migrate to larger cities where the cultural pattern is less rigid, the diversity of personal interests and types wider, and the chance to develop selective personal associations or vocational clienteles is correspondingly greater. Those unsatisfied souls who remain in Middletown tend often to carry on difficult lives of outward conformity and unhappy underlying rebellion.[111]

Along with the tightening competition for jobs in the 1920's, subtle changes were taking place in the aspects of work that have to do with skill, promotion, and the chance to launch out and be one's own boss.

By 1925 machine "operating" and "tending" had so far displaced the earlier hand skills that the line between skilled and unskilled worker had "become so blurred as to be in some shops almost non-existent." [112] Even by 1920 the apprenticeship system had so far fallen into disuse, in favor of such equivalent machine-process terms as "machine tender" and "semiskilled operative," [113] that Census figures

[111] See n. 10 in Ch. X for an example of this.

One of the new phenomena in Middletown in 1935 was a coherent group of some two dozen of these somewhat atypical young people of both sexes, interested in literature and radical economic and political doctrines. These young people are largely sons and daughters of the abler group of working class or of the lower groups of the business class. They have graduated from the local college and have acquired there, despite the conservative emphasis of the college, fuel for their moods of protest, plus the all-important resource of a real though extremely limited sense of fellowship in their revolt. Prior to the 1929 depression, the centrifugal tendency of Middletown's culture toward the aberrant personality threw off individuals of this sort more or less automatically to Chicago, New York, and other more hospitable centers.

[112] See *Middletown*, pp. 74-75; also p. 73, n. 1.

[113] See the 1920 Census (*Occupations*, p. 14; Vol. IV of *Population*) regarding the difficulty of classifying "apprentices" under modern industrial conditions. The 1930 Census carries a standard footnote to all its entries, "Apprentices to building and hand trades," as follows: "Many of the machinists' apprentices here included are machine tenders."

for industrial apprentices were no longer an index to changing demands for skill. During the succeeding ten years, the Middletown apprentices listed under that category in the Census fell from 52 in the building and hand trades in 1920 to 10 in 1930, and in all other industrial and mechanical trades from 32 to 9. Of the new workers added in Middletown's dominant occupational group, its Manufacturing and Mechanical Industries, during the decade of the 1920's, the types of workers who may today be classified as "skilled" have increased only approximately two-thirds as fast as have the "semiskilled." [114] While "laborers" have decreased, the semiskilled worker is but a short step above labor. What we appear to be witnessing in Middletown is an industrial scene, particularly in the predominating larger plants, consisting increasingly of a small group of highly skilled mechanics, a heavily numerically dominant group of semiskilled operatives, and a small group of laborers.

This growth in the number of quickly interchangeable semiskilled human machine parts in Middletown's industrial process carries along with it a number of significant changes. It involves for the individual worker the somewhat dubious asset of an enhanced ability to move from plant to plant as the tides of work in a given plant recede, and for the employer a highly convenient increase in the fluidity of the labor pool from which he sucks labor, if, when, and as he needs it. By reducing the equity of the individual semiskilled worker in his unique skill, it turns him into a competitor for a wider group of other men's jobs, and this cityful of other men, in turn, into competitors for his job, with a resulting downward pressure on all their wages. By diminishing the worker's continuing identification with any single craft group, it lessens his inclination to look to the existing type of craft union [115] for a strengthening of his morale and bargaining power.

[114] Among the "skilled" are here included carpenters, masons, and similar workers in the building trades; in industry, machinists, millwrights, toolmakers, blacksmiths, mechanics, patternmakers, moldmakers, founders, casters, molders, forgemen, sawyers, glassblowers, stationery engineers, and cranemen; and so on. Among the "semiskilled" are operatives, filers and grinders, buffers, etc.

That the skilled group has held up as well as indicated above in comparison with the semiskilled is probably due to Middletown's small shops rather than to its central group of large-scale plants. The small plant in the capital-goods industries, turning out special products in a series of short-run orders, tends to have a relatively higher ratio of skilled to semiskilled workers.

[115] It is this absence of definite tie between the increasing number of these semiskilled human machine parts and the old type of rigid craft union that the current drive toward industrial unions seeks to counteract. The apparent

And, finally, this loss of unique skills by the individual worker tends to do to Middletown as a city precisely what it is doing to the individual worker: Middletown itself, as it becomes a city of semiskilled machine workers, is losing any advantage of differentness it may have had in competition with other cities save the differentness of a lower standard of living; it is becoming less the sort of place it was in the 1890's when it was nationally known as a "glass town" and its skilled glass workers gave it an advantage other than cheapness of labor over other cities. Middletown itself, like its individual semiskilled workers, is being subjected to a hammering competition. Confronted by this situation, the uneasy city is following the most obvious and easiest course of elevating its sole remaining asset of a wage differential into a civic slogan—and passing the cost on to its citizens in the form of a lowered standard of living. That this wage differential based on the open shop should thus be widely accepted and approved as a civic asset is understandable in the light of the increase noted earlier in the present chapter in Middletown's service occupations (trade, finance, transportation, etc.); for these service agencies are heavily dependent upon the volume of local industrial activity, and their resulting stake in helping General Motors, Borg-Warner, Owens-Illinois, and other national corporations with branches in Middletown to maintain the low-wage, open-shop conditions that brought them to Middletown is too patent to most local businessmen to require arguing. The resulting interlocking of arms by producers, trading and service people, and city officials to "keep down labor trouble" looks toward government-reenforced strikebreaking; which is precisely what Middletown is today doing on a small scale and what its State has been doing on a large scale in Terre Haute, where the city was still under martial law in 1936, following the general strike of the early summer of 1935.

With such changes in process in the status of skill even in the 1920's, this status has been further jeopardized by the depression. Under its prolonged pounding, skilled men have taken "anything" to keep employed. Even the highly organized building trades have lost members heavily as these men have broken away from their craft to sink or swim at any job they could get. As a result the frail differential be-

sabotaging by the craft-union officials of the A. F. of L. of the effort to organize the various workers in the X glass plant along industrial-union lines in 1934, described earlier in the present chapter, and the open break nationally in the summer of 1936 between the industrial-union group headed by John L. Lewis and the craft-union "old guard" in the A. F. of L. throw light on the confusion that exists even within labor as regards the trend suggested above.

tween skilled and unskilled has been further whittled down until in June, 1935, the general hourly wage rate for skilled men in industry was only 45 cents, as against 43 cents for the unskilled.

With this blurring of skill has come a further blocking of the chance for the individual to "rise" from the "bottom" in the long series of inevitable steps to "bossing oneself" which the American theory holds out as the reward to the "good workman." For the industrial worker the step up to a foremanship is usually the first step up—but this step is becoming higher. In the 1925 study [116] the results of an actual count showed that only one man in every fifty-three of the 531 men (among the 4,240 workers in six Middletown plants) regarded as eligible for promotion to a foremanship had been so promoted in the preceding twenty-one months. The work of management engineers like Frederick Taylor in the early years of the present century inaugurated a trend toward functionalized management, including an increased ratio of specialized foremen to total wage earners. As a result of this tendency, the ratio of foremen to working force was somewhat higher in Middletown plants in 1925 than in 1890.[117] But in recent years this specialization of managerial function has tended to move up into the higher altitudes of training and thereby to clip the foreman's function by introducing specialized departments—technical staff, scheduling and routing department, personnel and training department, and so on—increasingly staffed by technically trained personnel rather than by men who have come up from operating machines and punching the time clock. The following condensed summary from Census figures shows the increases over the 1920's in these technical men and managers as compared with foremen in Middletown's manufacturing plants:

	1920	1930	Change in number	Per cent change 1920-30
1. Number of wage earners employed in those manufacturing and mechanical industries involving foremen [118]	6,809	7,464	+655	+ 9.6
2. Number of foremen and overseers	329	346	+ 17	+ 5.2
3. Number of technical engineers	43	98	+ 55	+128.0
4. Number of chemists, assayers, and metallurgists [119]	3	30	+ 27	+900.0
5. Number of managers and officials [120]	147	193	+ 46	+ 31.3
6. Number of manufacturers [121]	142	126	− 16	− 11.3
7. Total of groups 3, 4, 5, 6	355	447	+112	+ 33.4

[116] See *Middletown*, pp. 65-66.   [118-21] See bottom of p. 69.
[117] See *Middletown*, pp. 70-71.

Here one sees in dramatic concreteness the march of promotion away from the force on the floor of the plant. With only seventeen foremen added over the decade, there were eighty-two trained technicians inserted into the working force, plus a net increase of thirty more owners, managers, and officials; and foremen increased only a little more than half as fast as the wage-earning forces of industries utilizing foremen, while the technical engineers and chemists pulled away from both the preceding groups at rapid velocities.

In other aspects of Middletown's getting a living, the chance for the individual to break away from the ruck and to become independent has also been undergoing quiet change. The industrial march in Middletown is going forward on bigger and bigger feet; in fact, during the decade 1919-29 this concentration of industry into plants of a larger average size occurred in Middletown more markedly than in the industrial United States as a whole, as shown by the following figures:

| | Per cent change, 1919-29 | |
	Middletown	United States
Number of manufacturing establishments [122]....	+ 5.0	− 6.1
Average number of wage earners employed during year per establishment	+49.3	+ 4.0
Wholesale value of output per establishment ...	+89.7	+20.5

---

[118] The totals of 9,086 and 9,811 reported by the Census as "usually" gainfully employed in the Manufacturing and Mechanical Industries in 1920 and 1930 respectively have been reduced by the exclusion of Manufacturers, Managers and Officials, Foremen, Technical Engineers, Chemists, all building-trades workers except Laborers (since the building operations in Middletown are small-scale and do not employ large crews of plasterers, etc., requiring a foreman), and various classes of workers not working in Middletown under foremen, including Dressmakers and Seamstresses (not in factories), Jewelers, Watchmakers, Milliners and Millinery Dealers, Paper Hangers, Piano and Organ Tuners, Shoemakers and Cobblers, Tailors, Upholsterers, etc.

[119] These men are tending increasingly to supplant with their technically exact formulas for mixing ingredients in the metal and glass industries the earlier rule-of-thumb mixing by the foreman.

[120] Some of these men have simply replaced local owners as general managers, but others are specialized overseers of functionalized parts of a plant's process.

[121] Middletown lost no industries through failures in the six months between the beginning of the depression and the date of taking the Census, April 1, 1930.

[122] These include only plants with an output of $5,000 and over.

A minor element of error is involved in the comparison here in both cases. The 1929 Census omits in its summaries of industries by number of employees and value of output all establishments classified in the "automobile repairing" industry, whereas these were included in 1919. The Census for 1929 (*General Report*, p. 63; Vol. I, of *Manufactures*) presents also a revised figure for the

In other words, each of Middletown's 5 per cent more plants was employing in 1929 an average of 49 per cent more wage earners than in 1919 and turning out goods of an average value 90 per cent greater.[123] This slow growth in number and rapid growth in size of plants suggests a reason for the concentration of the "running of the town" in an inner business-class control group, noted elsewhere, and, more pertinent to our immediate point here, a narrowing of the chance for the individual in Middletown's central field of work, industry, to achieve independence. The relative prominence of the large, established plant in Middletown's economy has been increased by the depression; for, with the number of plants having an output of $5,000 or more depleted to eighty by 1933 (a shrinkage of 24 per cent below 1929), such names as X Brothers, General Motors, Borg-Warner, and Owens-Illinois bulked larger in the city's industrial life.

If it was true in 1925 that "The sharp increase in size, complexity, and cost of the modern machine-equipped shop makes the process of launching out for oneself as a small manufacturer somewhat more difficult than a generation ago," [124] the depression and its emphasis upon the over-expansion of productive capacity has sharply augmented this obstacle to the development of new infant manufacturing plants. The Middletown tradition is all in favor of an enterprising man with an idea and a shoestring of capital. But it is this type of small enterprise that has gone under in Middletown in the depression. Though

United States in 1919 which omits for this earlier year these "automobile repairing" plants. (This involves a reduction in the total number of plants in the United States having $5,000 and more of output from 224,620, the figure used in the tabulation above, to 214,383, and also negligible decreases in number of employees and value of output. This revised number of plants for 1919 involves a 4.6 per cent decrease in number, and, had these revised and entirely comparable totals been used in the table presented above, the decline in number of plants in the United States would be one of 1.6 per cent, rather than one of 6.1 per cent as here given.) Unfortunately, the later Census does not also present a similarly corrected figure for Middletown which excludes the "automobile repairing" plants. The procedure has accordingly been followed of utilizing both for the United States and for Middletown the 1919 figure which *includes* "automobile repairing" plants and the 1929 figure which *excludes* them.

[123] The depression has strengthened the position of the large corporate unit in American industry and business relative to the small unit. See the statement by Robert H. Jackson, Special Counsel to the United States Internal Revenue Bureau, made before the Senate Finance Committee in 1935. This is reprinted in slightly condensed form under the title "The Big Corporations Rule" in the *New Republic* for September 4, 1935.

[124] *Middletown*, p. 67.

Middletown banks are full of money clamoring to be put to work, and though this money will again undoubtedly be loaned to help launch new businesses, it will be harder to get these loans. Loans will be made in a new financial climate of opinion. The old buoyant faith that America and an avid foreign market will absorb the products of all the industries the Middletowns of the country can launch has vanished, perhaps for good. Personal savings have been eaten up by the depression, and plain John Smith will have to have a stronger proposition than in the past to pry loose bank credit on his unsecured name.

When one turns from industry to the professions, where the numbers employed rose spectacularly from 892 to 1,388—an increase of 56 per cent—there appears superficially to be in these professional services an enhanced chance for the enterprising individual to win through to the coveted American dream of "bossing oneself." Actually, however, the number of self-employed professionals remained practically unchanged, and the heavy gain of 56 per cent was made in the type of job which professionals are hired to fill—*i.e.*, more than 95 per cent of the gain was made up of such people as industrial chemists, technical engineers and draftsmen, teachers, nurses, semi-professional people, assistants, and helpers. Jobs of this type nearly doubled in number over the decade.

The 16 per cent increase in independent retail dealers between 1920 and 1930 represents a real increase in nominal independence in this growingly hazardous area of independent small trade. If chain-store managers be added to the independent retailers, to make one group of retail dealers and managers, the increase in the combined group over the 1920's becomes 17.5 per cent. These are the bossing, employing retail jobs in Middletown. But over against their 17.5 per cent increase must be placed a gain of 46.4 per cent in the number of hired retail clerks and salespeople. This means bigger retail units with more clerks on the average, and here again in this retail field the man with little or no capital who aimed to "rise" in the world faced more formidable and elaborate competition at the close of the 1920's than at the beginning.

When one brings together all of the above trends as to the likelihood of becoming one's own boss in the Middletown of the 1920's, the central point that emerges is that in every major field of work the share of the population employed was growing more rapidly than the share of the population self-employed or employing others.[125] And the depression has increased this helpless commitment of a growing share of the population to the state of working for others with a diminished chance to "get ahead." The situation in Middletown's industries roughly epitomizes the general situation in all occupations. What one seems to be witnessing here is a fundamental alteration in the vaunted American ladder of opportunity by which one has traditionally been supposed to "go up in the world," "get ahead," "improve oneself," "arrive." Even in the 1920's it was apparently becoming slightly harder even to get a job on the factory floor from which the ladder of opportunity rises. And once on the floor, the old single ladder reaching from the dead-level of the working floor to the factory owner's comfortable chair has been changing:

The ladder has lost some lower rungs, with the disappearance of apprenticeship and the large measure of blurring of the distinction between unskilled and skilled labor.

The step up to the first rung where the foremen stand appears to be getting higher and therefore harder for the mass on the floor to make.

Above the foreman's rung the whole aspect of the ladder has changed in three notable respects since 1890 and especially since the World War:

It is more difficult for the enterprising mechanic to find an alternative way up the ladder by launching out with a plant of his own in competition with the existing productive structure of large-unit plants.

Above the foreman's rung, the ladder is ceasing to be one ladder: there have virtually ceased to be rungs between the foreman and a higher section of the ladder beyond his reach where an entirely new set of personnel usually not recruited from working-class personnel begins.

And, finally, the ladder has lengthened with the relative increase of "absentee ownership" of local plants as units of national corporations, and the increasing absorption of formerly independent local manufacturers into the payrolls of these national corporations.

In other words, Andrew Carnegie's advice to enterprising young men to begin at the bottom appears no longer to be sound advice. Men of his type are advising young men today to get a toe hold in one

[125] The exception of building contractors, who rose in number from 72 to 101 in the 1920's, should perhaps be mentioned; though it is notoriously true of contractors as a group, in Middletown as elsewhere, that they are a highly unstable group. In times of housing shortage, like that which followed the World War, carpenters and real-estate salesmen mushroom out as "contractors," only to sink back again to their former status when the housing boom subsides.

of the managerial or technical departments halfway up the ladder. What appears increasingly in Middletown industries is not one unbroken ladder but two: the one becoming shorter, harder to climb, and leading nowhere in particular; the other a long and repaying one but beginning a long jump above the plant floor. Middletown's industries consist more than ever before of a large, crowded floor of little-differentiated "hands," and a different class of individuals (businessmen and engineers) doing all the "going up" in a world of their own largely beyond the reach of the working class. And this situation has been aggravated by the depression.

There are probably far-reaching social implications in these changes in the American ladder of opportunity. Our American culture has founded its exuberant boast of a classless society upon the two facts of universal suffrage and of vertical mobility up the pecuniary ladder. In the past reality and the alleged permanent continuance of this universally accessible ladder lies the popular justification of the reigning *laissez-faire* philosophy—as regards the present predatory practices of business enterprise, the pattern of uneven distribution of the national income, and the virtue of self-help in contrast to the alleged "immorality" of many types of social legislation, from public "doles" and unemployment insurance to old-age security. As symbol and reality draw thus apart, the scene would seem to be set for the emergence of class consciousness and possible eventual conflict.[126] But dreams, when they express urgent hopes and are heavily supported by the agencies of public opinion, have a habit of living on in long diminuendo into an era bristling with palpably contradictory realities. Middletown labor is not markedly aware of any crystallizing class status or of the tenuous basis for its dreams. So it tends to be oblivious of the apparently fundamental alterations in the American ladder of opportunity; it continues, for the most part, to view its disabilities as unfortunate temporary setbacks in a naturally ordained forward movement. Should the long-term trend actually prove to be toward the contracting of working-class hopes to the permanent boundaries of nineteen-dollar suits, $2.50 shoes, and a secondhand "Chevie," while "raises," "promotions"—all the things associated with "going up in the world"—are largely confined to the three in each ten of Middletown's income earners who fall in the business class, then, with the eventual realization of this

[126] See Ch. XII for fuller discussion of the extent to which this is taking place in Middletown today.

profound difference, one of the most characteristic elements of social cohesion in Middletown's culture may be supplanted by a system of social organization which no one in Middletown is today ready to call "American." It would usher in an era of urgent overhauling of conventional American symbols and incentives.

[*Note, February 1, 1937.* The attempt of the Committee for Industrial Organization to organize General Motors workers has met with the following results in Middletown: No serious effort has been made to organize the two Middletown plants, though workers in a large plant in a city twenty miles away have struck. On January 8, 1937, the Chevrolet transmission plant in Middletown, employing 1,500 people, was forced to close because of the strike in the Fisher Body plant in Cleveland. The local branch of Delco-Remy has continued in production without interruption. On January 12 the city's mayor wired the General Motors offices in Detroit: "I, as mayor of [Middletown], invited General Motors to locate here with a promise of cooperation and freedom from labor disturbance. It is our proud boast that we have cooperated with your local organization. . . . Permit me to again invite you to locate General Motors units here for mutual benefit, a profitable operation of plant with employment for our people, and a continuation of good will and cooperation from a community that appreciates industry." When thirty members of the United Automobile Workers of America from the neighboring city where workers were striking came to Middletown, the police promptly ordered them out of town "so that no trouble would develop." Meanwhile, even before the enforced shutdown, a workers' committee of thirty-six men was set up within the local Chevrolet plant. Within a day after the shutdown, the committee had secured the signatures of all of the 1,500 employees, and it wired the president of General Motors: "We, the representatives of the 1,500 employees of the Chevrolet-[Middletown] Division, wish to assure you of our loyal support in the present labor crisis." The mayor arranged with the governor of the State for a delegation of workers to visit him. The workers declared: "We are bitterly opposed to having anyone come in and try to tell us what we need; we know what we need. . . . We will go to any necessary extreme to get back to work."

Middletown regards the loyalty of the workers, according to the press, as "a demonstration of loyalty unparalleled in [Middletown's] industrial history. . . . Prominent businessmen and civic leaders were outspoken in their belief that the present attitude taken by the workers will result in a greater business and industrial future for the city." On January 19 the press reported: "Stories that new industries are about to be located here are common." On January 23 the arrival was heralded of "a new metal products factory employing 650 men, seventy per cent of whose output is absorbed by the automobile industry." On January 30 Borg-Warner announced the opening of a local foundry.

In all of the above Middletown ran true to the form indicated in this chapter.

It is worth noting that the indignation of local workers over their enforced idleness derives in part from the fact that the return of General Motors actually forced up wages in some local plants. Middletown workers do not take a long view of the seasonal character of automotive production. It is the hourly rate that counts with them. Hence the prevailing mood of local Chevrolet workers in January, 1937, was reported to be: "Why pick on General Motors, which treats its men better than any other outfit in town."]

CHAPTER III

The X Family: A Pattern of Business-class Control

"If I'm out of work I go to the X plant; if I need money I go to the X bank, and if they don't like me I don't get it; my children go to the X college; when I get sick I go to the X hospital; I buy a building lot or house in an X subdivision; my wife goes downtown to buy clothes at the X department store; if my dog stays away he is put in the X pound; I buy X milk; I drink X beer, vote for X political parties, and get help from X charities; my boy goes to the X Y.M.C.A. and my girl to their Y.W.C.A.; I listen to the word of God in X-subsidized churches; if I'm a Mason I go to the X Masonic Temple; I read the news from the X morning newspaper; and, if I am rich enough, I travel via the X airport." (*Comment by a Middletown man, 1935.*) [1]

S INCE *Middletown* was published, some local people have criticized it for underplaying the role of the X family in the city's life.[2] This group of wealthy families, along with four or five others, was not characterized as an "upper class" in 1925, because "these families are not a group apart but are merged in the life of the mass of the businessfolk."[3] Whether or not the earlier study was entirely right in so largely grouping them with the rest of the business class, certainly no local prompting was necessary in 1935 to call attention to their overshadowing position. For, after ten years' absence from the city, one thing struck the returning observer again and again: the increasingly large public benefactions and the increasing pervasiveness of the power of this wealthy family of manufacturers, whose local posi-

[1] As indicated in n. 40 in Ch. II, the symbol X refers to a leading Middletown family of industrialists, and brackets are omitted in its use in quotations.

[2] One such comment in writing from a local source runs as follows: "It doesn't seem to me that the importance of the X family in the city has been adequately portrayed. One must be careful, though, in this criticism, as a considerable portion of the philanthropy bestowed by them on [Middletown] has been done since the 1925 study."

[3] See *Middletown*, p. 23, n. 3.

74

tion since 1925 is becoming hereditary with the emergence of a second generation of sons. Since the ramifying power of this family stems from the economic life of the city, it is appropriate to discuss it here immediately following the city's activities in getting a living.

In and out of the picture of Middletown in 1925 wove the influence of this family of brothers who had come to the city with the gas boom, begun with modest capital and become millionaires, and had ever since held an unostentatious but increasingly influential place in the city's life. The boys had been born on a farm in Ohio, whence the family had migrated during the Civil War by wagon to another farm in western New York State. After receiving a common-school education, the five boys scattered to make their way in the world— one as a farm hand and timber cutter, one to become a doctor, others to develop a small business manufacturing fishing kits. When the latter plant was destroyed by fire, the brothers turned to the glass business. Their original Middletown plant began in 1887 on a $7,000 investment in a plant without foundations perched upon log piers. Now the plant is said to be the largest plant in the world manufacturing fruit jars. All five brothers subsequently lived in Middletown, one of them as a practicing physician and the other four engaged in the management of their glass plant and its extensive subsidiaries.

One of the city's veteran clothing dealers is fond of telling how one of the brothers borrowed a light-weight overcoat for a week-end party of young people in 1889. "He didn't feel he could afford a new coat that year, as he was just starting in business." Middletown prizes these stories about the democracy of these hustling young businessmen "when they were just folks like the rest of us." A newspaper editorial commented at the time of the death in 1925 of the brother who had had charge of the production end of the plant: "He always worked on a level with his employees. He never asked a man to do something that he would not do himself."

Half a dozen other family names in Middletown are associated with the city's industrial development, but none of them so completely symbolizes the city's achievements. Of the original five brothers, four remained in 1924; and when shortly thereafter another died, the entire business of the city stopped during his funeral. Two of the brothers remain today, both men in their seventies, alert, capable, democratic, Christian gentlemen, trained in the school of rugged individualism, patrons of art, education, religion, and of a long list of philanthropies;

men who have never spared themselves in business or civic affairs; high exemplars of the successful, responsible manipulators of the American formulas of business enterprise. In their conscientious and utterly unhypocritical combination of high profits, great philanthropy, and a low wage scale, they embody the hard-headed *ethos* of Protestant capitalism with its identification of Christianity with the doctrine of the goodness to all concerned of unrestricted business enterprise. In their modesty and personal rectitude, combined with their rise from comparative poverty to great wealth, they fit perfectly the American success dream.

Every American city has its successful businessmen, but the American success story has been kaleidoscopic in recent years. Local giants, the boys who have grown up with the town and made good, have shrunk in stature as rapid technological changes, the heavy capital demands of nation-wide distribution, and shifts in the strategic centers for low-cost production in a national market have undercut their earlier advantages of location, priority in the field, or energy; and as Eastern capital has forced them out or bought them out and reduced them to the status of salaried men, or retired them outright in favor of imported managements. One can classify American small manufacturing cities into two groups: those in which the industrial pioneers or their sons still dominate the local business scene, and those in which "new blood" has taken over the leadership; and it is likely that a census would show today a numerical predominance of the second group among cities containing major industries.

Middletown is, therefore, probably a minority city in this respect. The two remaining X brothers, reenforced by the active entry into the family business of four of the sons and two of the sons-in-law of the family, not only still own and control completely their wide business interests, but have become, amidst the local havoc of the depression, far more locally influential than ever before. It so happens that their industry, the making of glass fruit jars, is one that thrived on the depression; the great plant was not only kept busy, often employing night shifts throughout the lean years, but it returned profits reported to have been among the largest in their forty-five years of business. As the general level of the surrounding ground fell away in the depression, their preeminence increased. Their financial liquidity [4]

[4] One of the X brothers was one of the two backers who enabled the Van Sweringen brothers of Cleveland in September, 1935, to rewin control of their

has been such that, with their public spirit, they have been able to cushion the local impact of the depression at a number of points; and a by-product of their strength in the midst of general weakness has been a marked increase in their banking and personal penetration into a number of areas of the city's business life. Both because of their generous help and this resulting increase in control, and because of a very human awe in the presence of a prestidigitator who can make money out of a business depression, the power and prestige of the X family among the business class in Middletown has grown decidedly with the depression. The fact that a local citizen could, late in 1934, characterize as "the one big point about this town" the fact "that the X's dominate the whole town, *are* the town, in fact" suggests the reason for the separate treatment of the family in this chapter.

Middletown has, therefore, at present what amounts to a reigning royal family.[5] The power of this family has become so great as to differentiate the city today somewhat from cities with a more diffuse type of control. If, however, one views the Middletown pattern as simply concentrating and personalizing the type of control which control of capital gives to the business group in our culture, the Middletown situation may be viewed as epitomizing the American business-class control system. It may even foreshadow a pattern which may become increasingly prevalent in the future as the American propertied class strives to preserve its controls.

The business class in Middletown runs the city. The nucleus of business-class control is the X family. What the web of X wires looked like in 1935 may be seen from the following necessarily incomplete

vast railroad and allied properties, with combined assets totalling $3,183,000,000, by a bid of $3,121,000.

With the subsequent death of both Van Sweringen brothers within a year, this member of the X family found himself in November, 1936, the 90 per cent owner of the 23,000-mile "patchwork empire of pyramided railroad interests." Under the original 1935 purchase agreement, the two purchasers had not expected to participate in the operation of the property; the Van Sweringen brothers were to operate the properties and to vote the stock of the two backers, and the Van Sweringens also had an option to purchase at any time within ten years 55 per cent of the common stock at cost plus 5 per cent per year.

What the shifting of this heavy responsibility to the seventy-four-year-old member of the X family means in terms of the future of the other X properties remains to be seen. Taken in connection with the tendencies suggested in the closing paragraph of the present chapter, it may eventually affect profoundly the role of the X family in the local affairs of Middletown.

[5] Only one wealthy business-class family in Middletown lies outside the X court, though at least one other acts with considerable independence.

pattern of activities lying more or less on the surface of the city's life:

1. Getting a Living

(a) *Banking.* Middletown had five banks in 1925. When one spoke of "the banks" one meant the two leading banks and the affiliated trust company of one of them, in all three of which the X family had an interest. The remaining two small banks have gone under in the depression.[6] On February 27, 1933, on the eve of the nation-wide bank "holiday," the local press carried the front-page announcement: "X Brothers Guarantee Sufficient Cash to Meet Needs of 3 [Middletown] Banks," followed by a statement from the X brothers that "We have first-hand knowledge that these three [Middletown] banks are in good condition." A fortnight later, when Middletown's banks reopened after the national bank holiday, there remained only one bank, with its affiliated trust company; Middletown had escaped the banking crisis, thanks to the X family, and the community had avoided a serious loss in the case of one major bank through a "merger."

On the board of directors of the one remaining bank are three members of the X family, with one of them as chairman; while on the board of the trust company are the X member who is chairman of the bank's board, one of the sons, and a son-in-law. In addition to the members of the X family, seven of the remaining eleven members of the board of the trust company are also members of the board of the bank. Middletown's credit facilities are therefore very centrally controlled. In addition, one son is a director in one of the city's building-and-loan associations and two other sons are directors in a small "Morris Plan" loan company.[7]

The ramifications of this banking control of the community's credit resources are wide and subtle. Only the insiders know its details, but one picks up constantly the remark in conversation that "The banks now control the Jones plant"—and the Smith plant and the Brown

[6] See Appendix II for a summary of the banking situation in Middletown since 1925.

[7] Both of the older brothers are interested in a bank in a neighboring city formerly controlled by a brother-in-law, now deceased. This bank failed in the depression and the brothers supplied a considerable amount of capital to reopen it.

One of the brothers was until recently a director of the Chicago Federal Reserve Bank; and the other was a director of the Marine Trust Company of Buffalo, New York, until the recently passed Federal law forced his resignation.

plant. There is probably some measure of truth in the statement by a businessman, who in the earlier study had always proved a reliable source of information, that "If you don't join up with the inner ring, you can't work with them and you can't work against them, and you won't get the credit to run your business if they are not for you." Another member of the business class commented: "It's a one-bank town now. People don't dare complain about the way the Community Fund and other local affairs are run because all of these things stem straight back to the people who control our local credit resources." [8]

Remarks like these must not be taken too literally and sweepingly, and it would be grossly unfair to read into the situation personal malevolence, least of all on the part of the X's at the center of the local control group. This inner financial group is simply the hub of a wheel engaged in running a city.

(*b*) *Legal Talent.* Middletown's best law firms are retained in one or another of the interests of the X family. This renders understandable the comment of a local paper during the depression that "Lawyers and banks get along here. They maintain a happy relationship here as compared with their conflict in other cities." The personal attorney of a leading member of the X family is city attorney.

(*c*) *Industry.* The X family has not followed a policy of deliberately seeking financial control of other industries in the city. While they have an interest, direct or indirect, in some of the city's industrial plants other than their glass plant, paper-board plant, and the city's interconnecting trunk railways (which they own entirely), their power in Middletown industry is otherwise largely banking power and the commanding power of prestige and example.[9] No secretary of the Chamber of Commerce could hold his position against X opposition.

[8] For the ramifications of credit as a coercive institution throughout Middletown's economy, see *Middletown,* pp. 45, 47, 67, 116, 278, and 492.

[9] One of the brothers is a director in the thriving local packing plant which supplies much of the meat to Middletown and to the eastern part of the state, and head of a local metal furniture plant. His out-of-town directorships include the Dictaphone Corporation, Great Lakes Portland Cement, Intertype Corporation, the S. R. Dresser Manufacturing Co. (a Pennsylvania firm making pipe equipment for the oil industry, with a subsidiary in the air-conditioning field), and the Nickel Plate Railroad. See also n. 4 above.

The family glass business now includes five branch factories, a paper mill manufacturing its shipping cartons, and a zinc mill. Other ventures include a brewery, as a bottle outlet; the Amhempco Corporation, of Danville, Ill., making fiber fabrics for the automotive trade; and Texas oil developments.

The statement was repeatedly heard in 1925 and was again heard in 1935 that the X influence had at one time blocked the entry of a Ford plant into Middletown in order to avoid the competition of the higher Ford wage scale. The company's well-known stand in opposition to any considerable organization of local labor, noted in Chapter II, has been the keystone of local opposition to unionization. As a local professional man remarked: "The X's have a long record of pressures against any assertion of claims by Middletown labor. Their philosophy is, 'Keep 'em down—benevolently, but firmly.'" Businessmen quote the X's' alleged threat to move their plant out of Middletown as evidence of the danger to the city of union activity.

The confusion of our current culture as regards the "rights" of employers and employees is well illustrated in the facts that to Middletown's workers the X family epitomizes the sanctimonious oppressions of the employing class and is often even made to stand the brunt of animus generated by the less personalized actions of the absentee owners of other large Middletown plants; while, on the other hand, the X family sincerely regards itself as unusually scrupulous in looking out for its workers. The family knows many of these workers by name. In 1925 the factory had the reputation of being "one of the few places in town that tries to look out for its older workers." [10] During the depression, it is said to have carried occasional unnecessary workers on the payroll when the latter were in especial need. It is quite characteristic of this plant that when a part-time woman worker, dismissed because of a slackening in the work schedule, broke down and wept, saying that her husband hadn't been able to get work for three years and the family had been living on water and five loaves of bread a week, the manager said, "Send your old man around and I'll give him a job." Which he did. The X's are actually following the conventional rules of the game with a margin of conscience to spare, and believe themselves to be looking out for the best interests of all concerned under the traditional business theory that if plants are not run profitably for their owners they will not be run at all and the community will suffer. Some of the X employees are very loyal to the family. In 1936 an item in the press noted that the superintendent of the X plant has "been employed continuously forty-four years by that company and never has missed a day's pay nor ever has had any other employer, nor wanted one." And yet an intelligent working-class

[10] See *Middletown*, p. 332.

minister complained bitterly, though guardedly, to the interviewer about "the low wages paid by the plant, when the company is making so much money and the family can afford to give away so much money." An official of the local F.E.R.A., in citing the hourly rate of forty-five cents for F.E.R.A. work in June, 1935, remarked that "It compares favorably with the average rate of about forty-two cents paid at the X plant."

(d) *Retailing.* During the depression Middletown's largest department store failed. Since it occupied a building owned by the X family, the most conspicuous retail building in the city, the family has reopened it as the "X Store." And, like all X activities, it is a far better store than it was ten years ago under the former management, and a decided asset to the city. The family is reported to have an active interest in at least one other retail business, the leading furniture store in which one of the X brothers is a director, while its indirect banking controls in the retail field are particularly pervasive.[11] Two dairies, run as playthings by younger members of the X family, squeezed the local milk market by pressing X milk into use in local institutions supported in part by X charity, and in 1934 a large independent dealer capitulated and sold out his business to the X's and became the manager for them. This kind of move, again, represents a specific gain to Middletown, as some of the city's milk is bad while the X milk is very superior.[12] The output of a brewery in a neighboring city, in which the X family has a large interest as an outlet for its glass bottles, is said to be heavily pushed against all rivals in the local market.[13]

2. *Making a Home*

Since 1925 the X family has literally moved the residential heart of the city. An outstanding change in these ten years is the development of the northwest section of the city, the section where the X's live and the section most remote from local industrial plants, into the out-

[11] See in Ch. IV the discussion of the alleged use by the banks of relief funds during the depression to salvage a leading wholesale grocery company and a leading men's clothing store, both reported to be "in the hands of the banks."
[12] See Ch. XI.
[13] It was impossible to discover the full ramifications of the X family in the city's business life. A bakery, for instance, is said to have received X funds during the depression. Undoubtedly there are a number of other points at which X money either now reaches, or has reached in the past, into the financial structure of the city's retail business.

standing residential section. This shift has been carefully engineered by members of the X family. As a result, the aristocratic old East End, the fine residential section in the pre-motor period when it was an asset to live "close in" and even in the early 1920's, runs a lame second to the two new X subdivisions in the West End to which the ambitious matrons of the city are removing their families. Here the family has erected the most fashionable apartment building in town; here too it has recently located one of the two socially correct riding clubs (the other is on one of its farms a few miles out of town); and here the city has its first distinguished modern residential section,[14] giving the city the air of what the local newspapers like to call "big-city stuff."

The X residential development in the West End is related to two other major developments engineered by the X's in that section, adjoining the new subdivisions: the purchase and transformation by the X's of the haggard old normal school into a cluster of beautiful buildings now bearing the name "X State Teachers College," with an associated handsome new laboratory grade and high school that is the envy of the rest of the school system; and the location, adjoining the college, of the new million-and-a-half-dollar hospital, an outright gift to the city by the X family. These combined developments give a distinction to Middletown's West End which no section of the city, grimy with soft coal smoke, had in 1925.

And yet, as one watches this flowering forth of the city under the guiding hand of the X family, one must bear in mind the comment of a local man that "The X's are about the only people I know of who have managed to augment their fortune by the art of philanthropy." After five preceding private normal schools had failed on the weedy property in Middletown's Normal City subdivision, the X brothers bought in the property in a receivership sale in 1917. They arranged with the State to donate the property to the State on condition that a strong State Normal School be built out of the moribund institution. In 1922 the X family gave a quarter of a million dollars to

[14] The fine old houses of the first generation of X's have stood for years side by side on a street of their own in this same northwest section, but "closer in" along the river. One other group of about half a dozen well-to-do families live outside the city along the river at the opposite (southeast) end of town. This last suburban development, already begun in 1925, antedated by three or four years the development of the new West End and began with the development of an estate there by a family known locally for its independence.

the school toward its new building program. Meanwhile, through the early 1920's when the normal school was quickening into life, the X real-estate agents were quietly buying up parcel after parcel of residential property in the then socially nondescript Normal School section of town.[15] These houses have subsequently been removed or improved and these extensive operations must have involved a tidy profit to the X family as promoters, offsetting their benevolences to the hospital and college.[16]

3. Training the Young

A member of the X family is president of Middletown's school board, and a prominent X attorney is school attorney. Middletown feels comfortable with a member of this family at the head of its schools. An editorial comment in June, 1936, says: "There is still a feeling among women's organizations that there should be one woman on the [school] board, but that it is not likely to come about until a year hence, if then, or ever. Mr. X's term will expire a year hence *and there is no likelihood of replacing him if he still wants the job. . . .*" (Italics ours.)

The local college, though a State institution, is said to be X controlled both in its larger policies and in occasional small details. From both faculty and students, very guardedly in the former case and more openly in the latter, one heard of the pressure from the X's against radicalism in the college. One of the X's is reported to have been personally responsible for withdrawing certain books such as Bertrand Russell's *Marriage and Morals* and Dos Passos' *1919* from the shelves. The list of outside speakers invited by the student body is said to be scrutinized by the family. And it is freely reported that students with

[15] It is stated by one man who lived in this section that the agent secured one of these properties by suggesting that a pesthouse was to be established in their midst as a part of the new hospital development, and that the X's did not feel that it would be fair to property owners unless they bought up the homes in the neighborhood. Obviously such deceptive pressure methods would not have been authorized by the X family. The statement, as made in writing, lies before the investigator as he writes this, giving the name of the agent and of the person whose house was bought. It is extremely difficult to secure an authoritative check on such a statement, involving a verbal suggestion by the agent in the course of the negotiations. Another man living in the neighborhood said that he had "no direct knowledge of the effort to bully neighbors out of their houses, though I get it by hearsay."

[16] This give-and-take procedure appears to be characteristic of "progress" in Middletown's culture in which "money answereth all things."

radical ideas find it difficult to get recommendations for jobs after graduation.

It is not intended here to suggest that X State Teachers College is under deliberate repressive control. Its student body contains the most politically liberal force in the city. What is here suggested is that the college, though a State institution, is so closely watched by the X family and is so dependent upon their power and influence that it tends to follow officially their intellectual and political emphases. This does not, however, mean that all liberal teaching is stifled.

The family's authority in local educational matters is enhanced by the fact that it has also given $1,000,000 to the State University. One brother is president of the University's board of trustees.

4. Spending Leisure

Both the Y.M.C.A. and the Y.W.C.A. buildings are X philanthropies. The former is reported by the local press to be "the largest and best-equipped Y.M.C.A. building of any town of less than 100,000 population in the United States." The Y.M.C.A. summer camp, a show place in the state, is an outright X gift bearing the name of a member of the family. To it three to four hundred local boys go for a week or two of vacation, some of them on free vacations paid for by the X's. It is characteristic of Middletown and of the X family that free trips to camp are used as rewards for excellence in the Y.M.C.A.-sponsored Bible classes in the schools.[17] While the site for the Y.W.C.A. Camp, new since 1925, was donated by a local civic club, it also is heavily X-subsidized. The local Boy Scout camp is spoken of in the press as the "X Scout Camp." [18]

Personnel and policies in the case of both "Y's" are closely controlled by members of the X family. When a new Y.W.C.A. secretary was needed in 1935, the choice lay directly with one of the X women, who set about looking for "a girl unspoiled by 'Y.W.' training and point of view." Among Middletown's requirements in a "Y.W." secretary are that she shall "reach our industrial girls" but shall not import into

[17] These Bible classes in the public schools flourish today as in 1925, enrolling some 6,000 students. See Middletown, p. 396.

[18] In 1925 the Y.M.C.A. was said to be working quietly to minimize local Boy Scout work, on the theory that the "Y" should handle the boy activities of the city. The Scouts have grown stronger since 1925, but this mutual dependence of both on the same financial source tends to keep their policies in line.

town any of the liberal economic thinking of the progressive group in the national offices in New York.

Among the family's other contributions to the leisure-time activities of the city are the extensive gymnasium at the college, where large local gatherings are held, and the college Arts Building—with its handsome auditorium for public lectures and recitals and galleries housing loan exhibitions of paintings and etchings by old masters and moderns from the family's art treasures. As noted in Chapter VII, under this X sponsorship, the artistic center of the city has shifted to the college. The two riding clubs, out of which have sprung during the depression the present great vogue of riding and the annual horse show attracting entries from all over the Middle West, are recent X projects. The Masons carry on their ancient mystery in a huge Temple, thrusting up above the city's skyline, made possible by X money.[19] Among other things for which the city can thank X philanthropy are the donation of the ground and the equipping of the spacious local airport; the rejuvenation of the local county fair on property owned by the family; the donation of an entire city block containing an old mansion as headquarters for the American Legion; an important contribution toward a community drive to build a large field house and athletic field for high-school sports; a city golf course; assistance in the building of a new armory; and the equipping of a children's recreation center affiliated with a South Side church near the X factory. One of the brothers was for years city park commissioner, and the development of the city's park system as well as of the new riverside boulevard is in no small degree traceable to him.

5. Religion

A number of local churches, including working-class churches, have been helped in their building programs by X generosity. The X family, particularly the older generation, believes in the goodness of religion and in steady churchgoing. The influence of the older generation is, on the whole, theologically conservative.[20] It would be unfair to say

[19] See under Ch. XI the statement that some of these X gifts of large physical plants have outstripped, temporarily at least, the capacity of the city to support them in the absence of adequate endowments.

[20] The following incident, recorded in 1924 as told to the research staff by a member of Rotary but not published in the earlier study, suggests the earnest and conservative temper of the elder generation of X's: "Ed X was just talking

that their aid to local churches—from contributions to building pro-grams to playground equipment—is given in order to influence these churches' teachings. Their gifts are undoubtedly prompted by a de-sire to make Middletown a better place in which to live, and to them as people of long religious tradition the church is an important com-munity civilizing agency. But, though not so intended, their philan-thropy here as elsewhere operates as part of the local business-class control system. All of business-class Middletown, including its min-isters, hesitates to come out in the open against X causes or X points of view. One stubborn "liberal" minister is reported to have been "broken" by the family ten years ago. It is significant that a responsible and informed local citizen expressed the belief that the minister in the prominent church attended by most of the family was "acting under orders" when he flayed from his pulpit incipient political radicalism in X State Teachers College. The significance of this remark lies not in the allegation that the minister did so act "under orders," which is extremely unlikely, but in the realization by at least certain perspica-cious citizens that subtle psychological influences operate in such matters. Ministers express themselves very carefully about the X's. One of them, who must obviously remain completely anonymous, remarked guardedly to the investigator: "If the X's would only plow some of their big profits back into the community by increasing by even two or three dollars a week their low wage scale of fifteen to seventeen dollars a week, instead of giving so much to philanthropy, they would make Middletown a lot more Christian place in which to live."

to me at Rotary about his worry over this jazzy age. 'Where are we going to go to get worth-while young men?' he asked. He then told me how, missing the old Gospel songs he used to sing as a boy, he hunted up the hymnal, bought 200 copies, and sent them to his Sunday School. The Sunday School tried them two or three weeks and then discarded them as too antiquated. Ed jumped on the preacher and told him if those books were too old-fashioned, he guessed he, too, was too old-fashioned for that church."

While the above represents a more reactionary attitude than that held by the family of one of the surviving brothers and, perhaps, by all of the younger generation, it suggests the essentially conservative emphasis of the older gen-eration. It is characteristic of the family that it is reported to have been for years one of the heaviest contributors to the Anti-Saloon League. Largely due to the influence of the X's and a few associated old families, the Middletown Country Club had long been an exception among the country clubs of the state in that it had had no bar even though this involved a financial loss to the club.

6. *Government*

As noted in Chapter IX, Middletown is a Republican stronghold. The business leaders tend to be solidly Republican, and in this the X family sets them a conspicuous model. A member of the family is Republican National Committeeman for the state; the family contributes heavily to Republican campaign funds and to the Liberty League; and they pull a consistently heavy oar financially and personally for the G.O.P. ticket, national, state, and local.

In the face of this established situation, a small sensation was created among Middletown Democrats when, after the turning of the state and nation to the Democratic party in 1932, one of the abler members of the second generation of X's suddenly bobbed up as an influential local Democratic leader and head of the (Democratic) Governor's Commission on Unemployment. The Democratic weekly paper commented in the summer of 1935:

> Young X has done pretty well for a new Democrat who voted the traditional X Republican ticket as late as the last general primary. He has laid himself up a job on the school board, as a Democrat, controls the Democratic mayor and county chairman, is the final word in hiring hands in relief work in ten counties, and the acknowledged boss of the Democratic party hereabouts.

This paper, the erratic personal organ of an old-time swashbuckling editor who was mayor from 1930 through 1934, and the one paper in town that deals baldly with messy local affairs,[21] headlined this situation with characteristic colorfulness:

> Democratic Party Here Now a Possession of the Mighty X Kin: Ruthless in Business and Piratical Forays in Realms of Finance, They Play Both Po-

[21] See *Middletown,* p. 423, n. 10, and p. 475; also Ch. IX, n. 5, and Ch. X of the present study.

It is not here meant to imply that this editor's version of things is always correct. His is a highly personalized type of journalism nourished by many years of direct personal contact with "the boys" in the rank and file of the local political organizations and by many frank prejudices. As stated in the 1925 study, local business people jeer at him publicly but admit privately that "that fellow has the nerve to publish the stuff other papers don't." Typical of his type of journalism is the fact that when the secretary of the Chamber of Commerce was dismissed in 1925 for alleged sex irregularities with a female employee, the other papers simply ran a brief note to the effect that the secretary had accepted a position in a neighboring state, but this editor's paper ran the whole story with the characteristic eight-column headline: "Chamber of Commerce Loses Its Virginity."

litical Parties on Theory That Heads We Win, Tails You Lose; [and again, in a later issue:] Smooth-running Politics Makes New-fledged Democrat President of School Board; Strides Past D—— and Keeps G——, Republican, as School Attorney over Weak Protest of the Mayor; Young X Tells the Democrats Where to Get Off, but His Millions and Influential Family Surround Him With Groveling Servitors.

The present mayor,[22] a Democrat who was reelected in the fall of 1935, after having served as mayor fifteen years earlier, is now sometimes spoken of as "X-controlled." He is said by a political friend to attribute his earlier prison sentence to the opposition of local financial powers, including the X's whom he had antagonized, but now to have remarked that he has "learned his lesson."

It is difficult to get the local values straight in this whole complex of local politics. Undoubtedly, the headlines quoted above exaggerate the situation, and undoubtedly we are not dealing here with the thing popularly called "boss rule." The present mayor is not a mere "tool" of anybody—including the X's and the business group, whose will he has opposed in his efforts to end the relief commissary—but is a well-meaning man, with mellow emotions, a living to make, and, as a local paper remarked, "an inability to say 'no' to his many friends." An acute local observer, whose business involves the close following of such things, submits the following written statement regarding the relations of the X family and the mayor, as of July, 1936:

While there is no apparent working agreement between the mayor and the X's, they are much closer than when he previously was mayor. This arrangement probably came about through [one of the X sons'] close connection with the state Democratic administration. [This X son] was an undercover supporter of the mayor in the 1934 campaign, although it is understood that the X family made contributions to both sides. After the election, the mayor named B—— as his city attorney. B—— is a really high type of man and has long served as personal attorney to [one of the X's]. This appointment also brought the X's and the mayor nearer together. Through [this city attorney] and [the son of the X family interested in politics] there have been no great lasting differences between the mayor and the X families, although there have been some rather sharp disagreements in which the mayor did not bow to the wishes of the X's. [The city attorney] usually has supported the mayor in these matters.

[22] See n. 58 in Ch. II, and also Ch. IX.

On their part, the X family does not seek to exploit Middletown politically in the sense familiar to students of American municipal administration, nor need one read skulduggery, as one local commentator suggested,[23] into the refund of a $52,000 income-tax overpayment by the Hoover administration in December, 1932, to the one of the X's who is a Republican National Committeeman and a heavy contributor to Republican campaign funds. It seems more probable that we are simply confronted here by a situation of conflict between two ostensibly separate but actually interdependent sets of cultural institutions: on the one hand, a set of lagging political institutions fallen into disrepute because of the meager calibre of the men who find it financially worthwhile in this culture to run for municipal office [24] and because of the patent waste and graft incident to their operation; and, on the other hand, a set of economic institutions more ably manned by the best abilities in the male population, somewhat more efficient, and more central to the concern of an industrial community. The operators of the economic institutions do not want to bother with the political institutions; but, on the other hand, they do not want too much interference with their central economic concerns from the political institutions. They, therefore, bother to inject just enough control over the confusion of local politics to insure a tolerable tax rate, support for "sound" municipal cooperation in maintaining an open-shop town, control over the numerically dominant working class, and similar broad policies calculated to enable their central business of money-making to go forward without too much interference. And all of this is done by men like the X's with a strong sense of their actions being "in the public interest."

7. Caring for the Unable

The strong arm of X philanthropies supports all Middletown charities. Year after year the deficit at the close of the Community Fund drive has been anonymously met on the last day and Middletown has gone "over the top." Y.M.C.A. and Y.W.C.A. deficits are quietly

[23] According to this man, a prominent local politician, "The X's have for years backed W—— for the United States Senate, and W—— had always managed to get by on the normally heavy Republican majority in Lake County and [Middletown's] County. The X's contributed heavily to W——'s campaign fund in the fall of 1932, and when W—— lost, he went to Washington and got a big tax refund for one of the X's before the Hoover administration went out of office."

[24] See *Middletown*, p. 421.

met. Company memberships in the latter enable groups of employees to swim and play basketball. An "X Foundation" [25] handles many of these gifts and varied things such as seeing that curable tubercular cases are hospitalized. If funds are needed for seed for community gardens in the depression, a member of the X family provides the funds. A school principal in a working-class district adjacent to the X factory is approached and an arrangement made whereby he is given funds from time to time for incidental welfare aid in his district, and the principal and his family are sent up to the lakes for a three-week summer vacation. Middletown even has a $17,000 animal pound erected in 1930 by one of the X's. The editorial comment in one of the papers in 1934 sums up the pervasiveness of the X's in local good works: "As often has been the case in a civic emergency, the X brothers and their families again have come to the community's rescue, this time by providing," etc. X members are scattered throughout the boards of local charitable institutions and their quiet insistence has been influential in bringing about a centralized administration and some degree of coordination of Federal and local relief in the depression. As noted above, the new million-and-a-half-dollar X Memorial Hospital is an outright gift by the family to the city. Some years ago the family contributed heavily toward the establishment of a hospital for crippled children in the state capital.

8. *Getting Information (the Press)*

The X family has held for some years a powerful stock interest, loosely described locally as "controlling," in Middletown's morning paper. This paper is sometimes spoken of locally as "the X paper." The family also has an interest in a leading daily in the state capital.

In connection with the dissemination of information, one other point deserves note. A local labor man pointed out in 1935 that the X's now control, through their connection with the school board, Masonic Temple, and college, all the large meeting halls in Middletown. Such "control" is at present incidental and inconsequential. This type of situation can, however, assume real significance if, for instance, a labor or radical movement should become marked in Middletown.

[25] This is a nonprofit charitable trust set up by the family in 1929 with assets of $3,500,000 allegedly "to avoid taxes principally on some of the real-estate held by the family."

That this ramifying system of control is not a mere automatic con-comitant of the possession of great wealth in a small community ap-pears in the contrasting position of another pioneer industrial family in Middletown. This family of brothers—whom we shall call the Y family—owns one of the city's major industrial plants and, despite great wealth, is as inconspicuous in Middletown as the X family is conspicuous. A prominent citizen, in close touch with this family, characterizes them as follows:

"The Y's are in many respects just the opposite of the X's. They pay their workers well—even more, I believe, than union wages in other towns. They didn't oppose the organization of their workers under N.R.A. And they have no civic pride whatever. They are a strange, clannish tribe, who are all for themselves and who contribute to Middletown only what they are forced by circumstances to give. They never 'took to l'arnin'' as the X's did. They are good people, and I like them for what they are, but they lead a narrow life, aloof from the local scene here. They aren't mixers at all and still have a feeling they don't quite 'belong' here."

The Y family demonstrates the ability of great wealth to live in Mid-dletown with a large degree of isolation from the city's central inter-ests—if it so elects.

The picture of family-wise control by the X's presented in the pre-ceding pages may have given the impression of close, coordinated planning among the members, old and young, of the family. The situation is actually much more informal than this. Even within the family a considerable degree of rugged individualism exists. There is a common sense of direction, but no family "general staff" mapping the strategy of investment and control. As one local businessman warned:

"Don't make the mistake of lumping 'the X's' all together and treating them as a unit. For all the members of the family—young and old—are in-dividuals. Frequently two or more of them act in concert, or they all act together through the firm, the X Foundation, and so on. Such things as the X Department Store, the hospital, college, Masonic Temple, Y.M.C.A., and Y.W.C.A. are joint or family affairs. Most of the other things are not.

"The two surviving elders of the family are radically different men. The older, the patriarch of the family, is a moneymaker who got rich early and stayed that way. The younger of the two is a plunger—always was and always will be. He has been rich and poor and rich again more than once.

"The men of the younger generation in the family have more money than they know what to do with. The elders won't release the reins of authority at the plant to them, so the second generation spread around with their money and time and interests in various directions."

All the four sons of the X clan and, in addition, two of the five sons-in-law are in Middletown, all primarily employed in various capacities in the offices of the family's plant. In addition, the following partial list suggests some of their other interests:

One son has been particularly interested in the family's real-estate and house-building development in the neighborhood of the college, in the development of medical research at the hospital, and in aviation.[26]

One son has bought control of the brewery in a neighboring city which serves as an outlet for the factory's glass bottles; has various other outside business interests; is a director in the bank; is the new Democratic "boss" in Middletown, and regional director of relief during the depression for twelve counties in the state; and is interested in the American Legion, of which his brother-in-law was a former National Commander.

One son is interested in developing the hospital and the Y.M.C.A. summer camp; and, with the other son noted above, largely supports the local airport; he is a director in the local trust company.

One son is a bank director and, like one or two others of his brothers, has a model farm specializing in Arabian riding horses and fine cattle. The riding clubs, horse show, and dairy activities of the family grow out of these interests.

One of the sons-in-law is a director in the trust company and in a local "Morris Plan" loan bank.

It must, therefore, be borne constantly in mind that "X control" in Middletown is informal and a great deal of it unplanned in any central coordinated sense. The central core of the family's industry and total-family business interests and philanthropies is coherent. Beyond that the outlines become more blurred and depend somewhat upon the whims of individual members. And yet, so far as Middletown is concerned, the important thing is that, at most significant points in the city's life, one of the X's stands at, or close to, the directing center of that particular local movement, thereby throwing about it the protective reassurance that "the X's are interested in it." If the son of a lifetime "dry" and supporter of the Anti-Saloon League buys a brewery,

[26] This is the son who, as noted in une last paragraph of this chapter, died in 1936.

and another son "turns Democrat" (as one businessman remarked, "Of all things, for a member of *that* family!") and is reported not to have opposed personally the organization of labor in the plant under N.R.A., these things do not breed family strife. The family gets along well internally; they have a basically common sense of direction; and it is not surprising that the waters running down these many slopes so often manage to raise the level of the common golden pool by which all the members of the family live.

The important questions in reviewing such a pervasively personal control system are what it feels like to Middletown, and its varied implications for the culture.

It is hazardous to attempt to state what a city of 50,000 "thinks" or "feels" about such a complex situation. It is roughly accurate, however, making due allowance for many individual exceptions, to say that Middletown's working class tends to resent the family and its power, while the business class favors them and covets their friendship. Such gross classifications require refinement. The working-class attitude is probably not so much a reaction to persons as to single incidents: to such things as a neighbor reputedly black-listed; to the new sewer to cleanse the river which runs past the X's handsome row of homes, for which "they" ("the rich people who run the town") want to tax "us" on the South Side; to the anti-labor policy and the wage policy of the X plant, and so on; a reaction to "wealth," to "power," to "being run" on the part of people of independent traditions who are unsure of their jobs and have no particular sense of belonging, of "community." A typical case of this opposition to "rich men's efforts to put things over on the town" occurred in 1930 when the X's are reported to have wanted an outlying road adjoining their real-estate development paved at public expense. The South Side assailed the proposal as "a millionaires' proposal, backed by the rich men's Chamber of Commerce, to improve a street that begins nowhere, goes nowhere, ends nowhere. The whole thing is just a disguised part of a real-estate deal." The road was subsequently paved at public expense. A characteristic comment by a Middletown man is: "Working-class people here pretty generally dislike the X's. They feel they pay scant wages and then give things to Middletown. I ought to know, for I live down among them and I work for the X's." This latent dislike is recognized by local politicians, who "make different speeches to the South Side from those they make to the people here on the North Side"; and by the family itself, which is reported, *e.g.*, to have publicized the statement that it was selling a dairy it owned when this was a gesture involving the change of the name through the taking over of another dairy and the continuance of the sale of milk under a name less vulnerable on the South Side.

On the other hand, the business class, in the main, either embraces or huddles toward the X's because they know that the system through which they earn their salaries, receive dividends, buy new Buicks, and send their children to college depends upon the enterprise of men like these. The X's symbolize security to the Middletown business class. Directly, they mean security through their "safe and conservative" control of the city and their generosity in meeting local needs such as the deficits in the Community Fund, their prevention of local bank losses in the depression, their laying out of a boulevard system for the city, their provision of the new hospital, and their establishment of a college which educates the city's children cheaply and brings much business to the city's stores. And, indirectly, they bolster the business class because "We know that the X's will never let Middletown fail." "Where would we be if it weren't for the X's? They've done everything for the city," commented one business-class woman. A business-man remarked comfortably: "They tell the town during the depression that nobody will lose a dollar in the three big banks, and when an X gets up and says *that,* nobody worries any longer." Middletown's business class tends to look upon the X's as Burke did upon the English nobility, as "The great oaks that shade a country and perpetuate their benefits from generation to generation." [27] To the men in Rotary the ability to say "Hello, Frank" and "Hello, George" to financial royalty carries its own comforting reassurance. Kiwanis awards the family its "star of service" for its supreme community service, and editorially the family is compared to Julius Rosenwald in its willingness to give while its members are yet alive.

One does not hear much criticism of the X's and their control of local affairs from the male part of the business population who are so continuously concerned with business matters. A merchant may grumble confidentially about having to buy advertising space in the special edition of the paper welcoming the opening of the big rival X department store; an occasional younger man with a stubborn streak of in-

[27] In his letter to the Duke of Richmond, Nov 17, 1772.

dependence may resent the teamwork of the local business control group. But in the main the businessmen are content to say, as one did: "The X's are keen, rich, healthy, clean, Christian people, unspoiled by their wealth. They may pay too little to their employees, they may have kept industries out of Middletown, they may control banking, business, and so on, but they contribute generously and do a lot for the town."

The business-class women of Middletown, while sharing the feeling of their husbands that, as one woman expressed it, "the X's are just splendid," have in their women's world a different basis of association with the X's and a correspondingly somewhat different basis for loyalty or its opposite. The women of Middletown have the responsibility not for managing to share in the financial winnings of the business class, but for setting their families in an ever more secure social position,[28] and the coinage in this social market is more subtle than that with which their husbands deal. And, as a Middletown man remarked, "Woman is the most unselfish creature on earth within her family, but with outsiders she is quick to imagine snubs to her family, bristle up, and become unsocial." Hence, there is a trickle of comment of a different currency in circulation among the business-class women of Middletown, that "The X's hold people at arm's length. You never know in your relations with them when the blinds will go down and you will be talking politely to a person you don't really know and who is not really interested in you." And "the X's are very friendly and democratic but they tend to sit off by themselves." Here one witnesses a cleavage between the men's and the women's worlds.[29] In the former the criteria for acceptability are largely impersonal, involving one's business "success," and personal traits such as "coldness" are waived in the face of manifest business achievement. In the women's world the criteria are more directly personal, centering relatively more about the kind of person one is.

From the longer viewpoint, these minutiae drop away and one attempts to gauge the effects of such a manorial control system upon a city. What does it do to a cityful of people to live thus under the benevolent control of a small clan of wealthy and influential related families?

[28] See *Middletown,* pp. 116-17.
[29] See pp. 175 f. and 419 f.

As the sons have taken their places in the family control system in the past ten years and the family's role in the community has thus become hereditary, class lines have apparently stiffened in Middletown. For the midland's freely granted acclaim to the self-made man who wins great success changes when wealth becomes hereditary, when wealth shifts from a matter of personal enterprise and hard-won status to a less personal institutionalized "system" of class, privilege, and taken-for-granted differences. As noted elsewhere, one gained more of an impression of an upper business class as differentiated from a lower business class in Middletown in 1935 than in 1925. The city has grown by 10,000 in the decade, and this in itself would encourage selective differentiation. But the fact that the upper income families of Middletown are today more of "a group apart" and are less "merged in the life of the mass of businessfolk" is not merely a function of the city's size. It appears to be more directly related to the fact that, around the families of the four now grown-up sons and two sons-in-law of the X clan, with their model farms, fine horses, riding clubs, and airplanes, has developed a younger set that is somewhat more coherent, exclusive, and self-consciously upper-class. The physical aggregation of so many of these families in the new X subdivisions in one part of town has helped to pinch off psychologically this upper economic sliver of the population from the mass of business folk. And the pattern of their leisure, symbolized by their riding clubs and annual horse show, tends to augment their difference. The leisure of the older generation of X's was different *away* from Middletown, including such things as trips to Europe and to the opera in Chicago and New York, but *in* Middletown they worked hard like other folk and played, in the little time they had for play, at the same simple things other local people did. Particularly as regards the male members of the older generation, there has always been a continuous preoccupation with business; and they did few of the things associated with a wealthy leisured class. It is the new note of a more self-conscious leisure built upon endowed wealth, and obviously expensive, that the younger generation is bringing to Middletown. They, too, work hard, but they play expensively and at their own sports, with somewhat more definitely their own social set.

The implications for local leadership of the increased ramification of X control, especially during the depression, will bear scrutiny. Two local newspapermen volunteered the statement that "The X's have an unfortunate influence on the community because they make people too dependent upon them." If one aggregates the portions of Middletown's population that are directly or indirectly dependent upon the X's, the total becomes a sizable *bloc* among Middletown's twelve-and-one-half thousand families. It includes the families of the approximately 1,000 employees in the X's factory, five large floors of managerial and sales personnel in their department store, the staffs of the local college, hospital, Community Fund agencies, Y.M.C.A. and Y.W.C.A., of the banks and the leading newspaper, and a long list of political, religious, real-estate, retail, and industrial units which "cannot afford to offend" the X's. It cannot be too often reiterated that the X control of Middletown is for the most part unconscious rather than deliberate. People are not, when one gets beyond the immediate army of direct employees of the family, dictated to. It is rather the sort of control that makes men hesitant about making decisions of importance unless these are in harmony with X policies. Here we are witnessing the pervasiveness of the long fingers of capitalist ownership. Middletown businessmen, in common with their fellows over the country, have suffered a severe setback in the depression; their little corner of the "American dream" has threatened to become a nightmare. They naturally seek cover under any manifestation of confidence, decisiveness, and success, and it requires uncommon courage to lead out in unsanctioned directions. And, in time, such dependence becomes a habit that stifles initiative.

One got an impression in 1935 that there were not many young independent manufacturers in Middletown building up little plants of their own. There were energetic young men working for other people, but one did not get the sense that one did in 1925 of vigorous, diffused young leaders forcing their way up into the directing councils of the elders of the city. "Where are the independent, young, growing leaders such as A—— and B—— were ten years ago?" a businessman was asked.

"They just aren't here," came the reply. "Our younger men fall into three classes: those who've moved away; those who have become good boys and are working for the little group who run the town; and those who are outside that group and blocked. The younger men interested in doing other things than going to work for the old guard here can't get credit easily. I began my business some years ago without a penny, on money borrowed from the bank. Today you can't get credit to start."

This undoubtedly exaggerates the situation and also reflects an obvious banking conservatism bred of the depression. But from other sources one heard the same cautious note: "Every time there's a good job in Middletown, who gets it! Somebody's son or relative. That's why Middletown is a tough place for the young fellow to break through in." Another man, a member of Rotary, still the most sought-after civic club, protested the filling up of Rotary with the sons of members: "Hell! Either our membership classifications mean something or they don't, but if it's the son of a member that's involved, they always can juggle their classifications and get him in." A businessman familiar with other midland cities expressed himself as puzzled over Middletown:

"The city strikes me as curiously conservative and backward. The businessmen here seem to want to lick a problem in advance before they are willing to try anything. I know pretty intimately another city of about this same size. There the city has no rich men supporting it, and as a result it has gone up and down more sharply than Middletown, but its businessmen seem more alert and to have the feeling that they must catch and ride their problems fast. The tighter situation here may be related to the fact that there is less young leadership here, certainly less fresh blood from outside, a less shifting business-management class, fewer new faces. One feels the effect of Middletown's old population in greater social coldness. It's hard to get acquainted here. Even the women's clubs seem less alive."

The remark of another seasoned and observant citizen about yet another aspect of local leadership is perhaps not inapplicable here: "I don't see vigorous young moral leaders here so much as ten years ago; young men of character and bent don't appear." As over against these statements, however, should go that of another local businessman in his early forties, now taking over his father's business:

"I seem to feel a change in the leadership here. There used to be ten years ago a little group of men in their fifties and sixties who ran everything. Young men couldn't get a chance to get in on the city's planning. The Dynamo Club [30] was encouraged by this older group because it kept the younger men out of trouble and busy and enthusiastic, but it was never consulted when any big decisions were to be made. But a lot of these older men have cracked up in the depression—they just seemed to go soggy under the depression, and new blood is coming to the fore. It was the young manager of the H—— Corporation who was given the award a couple of years

[30] See *Middletown,* pp. 303 and 374.

ago for having done most for Middletown, instead of some old banker's getting the award as would have been the case before. The depression has let younger men come into leadership. But"—he added with a grin—"I wonder if the younger men of today feel about me now that I am breezing along on the inside the same way I used to feel?"

We obviously confront here a highly complicated situation regarding which no positive summary judgments are possible. It is the impression of the investigator:

That the lines of leadership and the related controls are highly concentrated today in Middletown.

That this control net has tightened decidedly since 1925 and notably with the depression.

That the control is at very many points unconscious and, where conscious, well-meaning and "public spirited," as businessmen interpret that concept.

That the control system operates at many points to identify public welfare with business-class welfare.

That there is little deliberate effort from above to organize local bankers, businessmen, and leaders of opinion into a self-conscious "we" pressure group; but that this sharply centripetal tendency of Middletown's businessmen is normal behavior in a capitalist, credit-controlled culture where there is a potential control-center in the form of vast personal resources of demonstrated willingness to lend a friendly hand.

That, so long as the owners of such vast personal resources exhibit a public-spirited willingness to help with local problems, leadership and control tend to be forced upon them by circumstances, and their patterns tend to become the official guiding patterns.

That, viewed at any given time as a going concern, this centrally-hubbed control agency both may and does operate in many subtle and even ordinarily unintended ways to "welcome little fishes in with gently smiling jaws," with an accompanying loss to the latter of independent leadership. Those who try to be independent tend to be regarded, as the local phrase puts it, as "gumming the works." As the local Democratic editor, who loves mischievously to pin his victims to the wall not with pins but with broadswords, remarked editorially: "The ownership of banks, factories, colleges, breweries, dog pounds, hospitals, mayors, and county chairmen, centered in this millionaire group, has produced an appalling economic pressure on citizens who find themselves in the house of bondage. However, it is a benevolent protectorate extended over all who come into camp gracefully. But the stuffed club is always at hand, to penalize dissenters. 'Treat 'em right and they'll be good to us' has been preached here long enough."

What the future of this X control system will be is hard to guess. Within another decade the two remaining giants of the first generation will probably be out of active life. At present the policy of the family seems to be that it may as well give away a generous part of its income because it would be taken in taxes anyway. But the family's wealth will pass along fairly intact to the four sons [31] and two sons-in-law now in their early thirties and forties. There is more diversity among these second-generation men, and one gathers that the intentness upon business that characterized the pioneering first generation is finding competition among the second generation from political ambition, activities involved in living as country gentlemen, and other distractions. The second-generation men are in no sense mere "rich men's sons" or "wasters," but are alert, able, and responsible. The fact that they have not removed to larger cities but remain in Middletown, taking their places as wheel horses in the family team, suggests the carrying forward of the *ancien régime*. A local minister expressed the belief that the younger generation of the X's is "even better than the old," though two businessmen concurred in stating that "The younger generation of X's don't stack up in ability with the fading generation." The supporting power of their wealth will remain, but one suspects that the intensity of devotion to local causes will inevitably be somewhat less among these younger families that have not fought shoulder to shoulder with the city's business pioneers to build a city from the boom town of the 1880's. Meanwhile, hereditary, as over against first-generation, wealth offers Middletown the possibility of increasing class stratification and the softening of local fiber that tends to accompany the passage of first-generation wealth into second-generation power.[32]

[31] See the last paragraph of this chapter regarding the death of one of these sons in 1936.

[32] The methodological note should be added to this chapter that such a necessarily impressionistic treatment as this is but a prolegomenon to a type of research too little attempted as yet by American social science. There is definite need for the more exact exploration of a socio-economic control system of this sort through the detailed, systematic charting of the individuals affected, in their specific personal and institutional relationships to the controls. A city is made up of individuals, each presenting a pattern of relationships, individual and organizational.

J. L. Moreno in his book, *Who Shall Survive?* (Washington; Nervous and Mental Disease Publishing Co., 1934), suggests a type of research analysis that needs to be tried on the type of social situation described in this chapter.

Since this chapter was written, the thirty-three-year-old "crown prince" of the X family, the keen young son of the "patriarch" of the family, hailed as Middletown's "first young citizen," has died at the controls of his own airplane in a crash in May, 1936. This may possibly entail a marked shift in the future influence of the family in the city's life. Although brought up in the family pattern, this son had already become an innovating force within the family's sphere of influence. It was characteristic of him that he had given funds both within and outside Middletown for medical research, and the ambitious research unit at Middletown's new hospital in a separate building constructed for it was one of his most substantial achievements. In the loss of this pivotal member of the younger generation, one may conceivably be witnessing an early step in a chain of events which may lead eventually to the absorbing of the family's industrial interests into larger outside corporate holdings and the eventual scattering of the younger members of the family as financially independent men into politics and other interests.

CHAPTER IV

Caring for the Unable During the Depression: Bench Marks for Social Change

NEAR the close of *Middletown* appears a brief chapter on "Caring for the Unable." It was brief because it dealt with an inconspicuous, though chronic, minor aspect of Middletown's culture—the need for provision of minimum charitable help to the fringe of the population who, through some sudden emergency, were in too great want to be disregarded by the public conscience. The chapter described the slow transformation of sporadic private "Christian charity" over the past generation into an increasingly secularized, institutionalized service, culminating in 1925 in the first combined annual Community Fund drive, to which nearly two-thirds of the city's homes contributed. Charity in Middletown in 1925 was still overwhelmingly a private affair, and it was felt to be proper that it remain so. The ratio of public poor-relief expenditures from tax sources to the private Community Fund budget was one to eight.[1] Nobody in Middletown in 1925 dreamed of the extravagant possibility that within seven years tax relief would aggregate three times the entire Community Fund budget, and that the city's major municipal problem would become the financing of tax-supported relief.

It is the tracing of social change in this area, intimately associated with the economic activities of the city, that the present chapter undertakes. Middletown's business class looks upon the plunge into tax-supported relief as a temporary aberration soon to be wiped out by a return to the old private charity. If one believes, however, that social change, even though of an emergency and temporary nature, tends to establish bench marks of precedent to which the future may return repeatedly in the triangulations and plottings of subsequent policy, the course of events connected with the caring for the unable during the

[1] The township trustee paid out $9,720 in poor relief in 1925. In that year a Community Fund budget of $77,610 was subscribed.

depression becomes easily one of the most significant aspects of Middletown in the 1930's.

Middletown has always been used, as an industrial city, to the phenomenon of having marginal families out of work and in need. In May, 1929, a local editorial commented comfortably:

Middletown is prosperous. The indication of this is that there are so many persons one strikes seeking alms. Last Saturday, within a space of three blocks, were five cripples and two blind persons. Those seeking minor aid because of physical defects by soliciting the public don't go to "dead" towns. They go where the money is. So the more "professional" mendicants you see, the more alive is the community.

And Middletown knew what to do with these people. It gave a few pennies when it felt like it, and for its own local people who fell on hard times it raised its annual Community Fund. The philosophy of the Fund was expressed editorially in the press in April, 1929, as follows: "Those in charge have figured out in the matter of dollars and cents approximately what is necessary to preserve the balance in Middletown between those who have and those who haven't."

In the larger matter of why there are "haves" and "have-nots" the local philosophy, derived from some of the clearest and deepest strata of the culture, is equally explicit:

This is a free country of boundless opportunity which guarantees an equal chance to everybody. If people don't get ahead it isn't the fault of society.

Unfortunately there has always been in this and every other society a fringe of "unfortunates." Things like this just happen.

But these things "happen" usually in part at least because the people involved have violated the gospel of "hard work and thrift."

Therefore society should not do too much for them because such extra help "weakens the character" of the recipient.[2]

Roughly half of Middletown's Community Fund total in the years just before the depression went to the three "character-building" agencies: the Y.M.C.A., Y.W.C.A., and Boy Scouts. The remainder was distributed roughly half-and-half between the remaining two groups of services: the health services such as the Anti-Tuberculosis Association and the Visiting Nurse Association, and the miscellaneous charity services such as the Social Service Bureau and the Salvation Army. The machinery for dispensing this health and miscellaneous

[2] See the fuller development of these beliefs in Ch. XII.

aid consisted of nine [3] highly competitive little agencies housed for the most part separately in dingy little offices, staffed by persons without much social standing, and dominated by benevolent society women. The township trustee, whose duties include that of "overseer of the poor," operated entirely independently and doled out his small tax funds in his own inscrutable political way. In 1928 the combined relief resources of the city, private and public, had cared for a "normal" load of only 613 families for brief periods at one time or another throughout the year, less than 6 per cent of the city's families. Around the central core of the Community Fund agencies were various informal charitable services by groups of the "haves" for helping the "have-nots." Social sororities of young business-class women sponsored a day nursery for the children of working mothers, provided automobiles to bring poor mothers and children from the city's outskirts to the monthly child-health clinic, and distributed books and magazines through the wards of the local hospital one day each week. The men's civic clubs gave Christmas parties for "poor kids" and for the inmates of the orphans' home, and their members took turns in doing such things as transporting a crippled boy to school daily.

This whole process of caring for the unable went along without significant change [4] between 1925 and the depression. The city had simply gone on year after year doing its routine bit for charity like other American cities, picking up the least avoidable wreckage of its institutional system, contributing as little as possible help for fear of "pauperizing" free Americans, and sending the wrecks back with momentary reenforcement into the same institutional maze.

When the squall hit in 1929, it is quite characteristic of these generous folk that nobody doubted the social duty to "lend a hand," for "we can't let Americans starve." [5] In January, 1930, local editorials stated:

[3] See *Middletown*, p. 465, n. 8.

[4] The one change worth noting is that the township trustee's poor-relief expenditures rose to $21,214 by 1928, or a little more than double the $9,720 of 1925. The trustee, in a letter to the investigator in May, 1936, attributes the increase to the cumulating cost of human débris thrown on the city by the heavy importation by local industries of "hillbilly" labor from Kentucky, Tennessee, and West Virginia during the World War and after. (See in this connection the footnote on p. 58 of *Middletown*.)

[5] In this same spirit, in the last critical time of unemployment, the winter of 1921-22, local citizens had raised an emergency fund of $40,000 to be distributed among the unemployed. (See *Middletown*, p. 63.)

A good many hundreds of men in Middletown today are out of jobs, and this thing of looking after people who are out of work is sort of your job and mine. A dollar or five dollars go a long way.

It is an open secret that there has been considerable suffering . . . which is likely to continue for several weeks. This situation calls for considerable forbearance on the part of creditors of men out of jobs as well as the continuance of the laudable works of charity by the Social Service Bureau and other agencies. Now is a good time for people who can afford it to have all their odd jobs done to help the unemployed. The best help is helping others to help themselves. That is much better than outright charity, however necessary the latter may be in emergencies.

So Middletown simply took on the job with the equipment and philosophy of the past. "Odd jobs" and "self-help" would do the trick, supplemented by the Community Fund for the more urgent cases. The twelve Community Fund agencies, which had netted $63,000 in the 1928 drive and $71,000 in 1929, pushed up their budget to $101,000 in 1930, and their expenditures for direct poor relief jumped from $21,754 in 1929 to $50,145 in 1930.[6] Local editorials spoke in the spring of 1930 of "the beginning upturn after the sag of last fall" and of the "late depression's" being "forgotten like last summer's straw hat"; and humorous "human-interest" stories were written about the "new fraternity in Middletown" composed of hoboes, "a by-product of present financial conditions," who meet in their "fraternity house" in the basement of the Court House and sleep on the concrete:

Those who arrive first get the softer pallets and one or two wooden doors. Others sleep on papers or cardboard. Still others find the pile of dirt in the northeast corner satisfactory. One ingenious soul fixed up a wire mattress. He found the place so comfortable that he remained too long and the police put him in jail. The white gentlemen claim the Negroes get all the breaks in Middletown for they can get food from grocerymen who refuse it to whites.

As summer came on, free seed and vacant lots were provided for the unemployed to raise vegetables "so that they can profit by self-help."[7]

[6] See n. 19 below and Table 10 in Appendix III.
If the costs for charity nursing by the Visiting Nurse Association and Anti-Tuberculosis Association are deducted, the totals for direct material relief rose between 1929 and 1930 from $7,223 to $33,559.
[7] By the spring of 1933 no less than 2,500 persons were raising these relief vegetable gardens on vacant lots and community land.

Even in June, 1930, the press announced plans for enough minor public improvements to employ 200 men, which, with the activity in a local automobile-gear plant, "should relieve the unemployment situation here to a big extent."

But, meanwhile, charity agencies were being drowned under the flood of requests. The privately supported agencies began reporting the recurrently emphasized condition: "Last month was the heaviest in the history of the organization." A newly organized gospel mission [8] was furnishing, by the late fall of 1930, 4,000 to 5,000 free meals a month, in addition to clothes, sleeping quarters, and other accommodations to transients, and calling for more and more local support. Appeals to the Social Service Bureau for coal in the winter of 1930-31 were four times those of the preceding winter, and the supplying of coal to 4,727 families was but one of the Bureau's many burdens. This "odd-job emergency" was outstripping the resources of private charity, and such news items as "Girls in High School Bake Cookies for Red Cross Relief" were beginning to look a bit foolish. Nor were such spontaneous moves as the opening of a relief soup kitchen at the city barn under the twenty-five-cent-weekly voluntary contribution by the employees of the city street department making headway against the deluge of appeals for relief. And more ominous still to local taxpayers, from the office of the township trustee came the announcement in June, 1930, that every township in the county (including Middletown's township) would exceed its budget in 1930.

Public funds for relief began to run wild as demands, of a magnitude never anticipated when legal controls on the modest office of the township trustee had been established seventy-five years before, began to be met from taxes. Table 10 [9] shows the sharp rise in expenditures from township funds for direct relief, from $21,214 in 1928 to $45,076

---

[8] This gospel mission, opened in November, 1930, by an uneducated evangelist, known throughout Middletown simply as Eddie T——, and his wife, did spectacular relief work all through the depression. Devoted to the principle of "teaching practical religion with relief work," its sturdy work appealed to evangelical Middletown. Supported by pennies and dimes and anonymous contributions, and occupying the basement of an abandoned brick church in the center of town, it packed homeless transients onto the floor to sleep, fed them, begged clothing, shoes, bedding for the poor, and night after night shouted the old-time religion at them. See pp. 141-42 and 306 below.

[9] See Appendix III for this table.

in 1930, $158,604 in 1931, and on to a peak of $293,091 in 1932.[10] By the fall of 1932 tax funds were being expended for relief in the township [11] at the rate of $1,200 a day, and the taxpayers were warned by a committee of responsible citizens that they were facing the prospect of paying out "surely not less than $1,000,000 more before normal conditions are restored." [12] Township expenditures for public relief rose from $57,000 in the third quarter of 1932 to $94,000 in the final quarter.

The harassed council, confronted by a totally unprecedented situation, and under opposite pressures from the taxpaying farmers and articulate business class and from the less articulate but uneasy working class, alternately voted down and then waveringly approved the necessary bond issues for more relief. The administrative system creaked under charges of graft and favoritism. A township trustee had been sentenced in 1931 to from two to twenty-one years for forgeries and misuse of township funds. Some local medical men were charged with exploiting the township by an undue proportion of home visits for which they were paid from public funds at a higher rate than for office visits; there were charges of irregularities in the purchase of relief coal from public funds; and one of the city's 111 grocers was found to be receiving 16 per cent of the township trustee's purchases of relief groceries. That official protested that he had a right to designate

[10] The distribution of expenditures in the year 1932, roughly representative of the years 1931-34, was as follows over the various areas of need:

	Per cent
Food	66.5
Fuel	13.5
Clothing	1.6
Doctors	9.0
Hospital	7.7
Dentists	0.4
Medical Supplies	0.1
Burials	0.8
Miscellaneous	0.4
Total	100.0

[11] 95.1 per cent of the township's population lies within the city of Middletown according to the 1930 Census.

[12] *Report of the Committee Appointed at a Joint Meeting of the Directors of the Community Fund and the Relief Agencies to Study the Problem of Relief of Distress in Center Township.* (February 7, 1933.)

the persons to receive relief business. There were repeated airings of complaints before the council.[13]

The relief system wavered uneasily back and forth from work-slip payment to outright dole, from flat-rate weekly food allowance to sliding scale. The mayor refused to employ laborers on work slips on the ground that he had the right to appoint them. The local press grumbled in April, 1932, that Middletown's "$1,000 a day relief gets nowhere because [the mayor] obstructs the work-slip method of payment. Most of the other communities get a dollar's worth of work for every dollar given out in public and private benefits." Working inside an antiquated legal authorization never expected to bear such a mass load, the city found itself in the familiar institutional jam of having to try to operate a ten-ton truck over a legal road passable only by a horse and buggy. The law required that able-bodied men should receive relief only on the work-slip basis which necessitated the giving by the recipient of the *quid pro quo* of useful labor regarded as so necessary by Middletown's culture; but, the legal jurisdictions of city, township, and county units, coupled with customary ideas as to what may be done as public work and what must be left to private profit-making agencies, rendered it impossible to find enough jobs to keep

[13] One of the minor retail sensations in Middletown during the depression has been the growth of a certain South Side grocery. A letter before the investigator from a responsible Middletown citizen states: "This store is owned by a cousin of the township trustee. [Four sons and other relatives of the owner are among the twenty-five employees of the store.] Situated in the slum district, the grocery has become so prosperous during the depression that it has been enlarged and repainted several times. [The store had a frontage of 100 feet in 1936.] It has an army of clerks who keep their mouths shut. The owner advertises in full-page space in both papers and now goes to Florida each winter while his sons run the business. Meanwhile, other grocers in town can hardly make a living."

A protesting letter to the editor from the head of a small good-government group, printed in the afternoon paper in the spring of 1933, stated: "The organization with which I have been connected has more data concerning the disposition of the poor funds than perhaps any other in the city. . . . The grocers at large are to be pitied, because in general they certainly did not receive their share of the poor-fund business. The figures before me for the last quarter of 1932 and for the first quarter of 1933 show that a few grocers received the big bulk of the township business. One of these, during the last quarter of 1932, was not satisfied to receive better than $11,000 worth of business in three months from the poor fund in one store, but he proceeded to buy another store in another section of the city, and immediately this store proceeded to get practically all of the business in that section of the city from the poor fund. Even the accountants from [the state capital] called this to my attention."

busy all those in need of relief. This dilemma was clearly pointed out in the report of a citizen's committee set up in the fall of 1932 to investigate the relief procedures of the city:

Some form of employment should be provided the able-bodied relief clients. To that principle we believe no responsible thought could object. . . .

The administration of the civil city of [Middletown] does not permit the use of much of this available labor, despite the existence of many projects upon which it could be used to the permanent benefit of the city without displacement of a single regular city employee. No appreciable volume of work can be provided in Center Township under existing laws without the cooperation of the city of [Middletown]. The township roads have been transferred to the county and the law does not permit the use of relief clients outside the township nor upon any but public work. . . .

The County Employment Committee operates as a unit of the Governor's Unemployment Commission in cooperation with the Township Trustee and the Social Service Bureau. . . . All work projects are reported there and men are assigned from the relief clients to perform the work. The employment office, therefore, becomes a clearing house for such work as can be provided. The volume of work provided as compared to the labor available is almost negligible.[14]

From both sides the opposing blades of the shears of local public opinion cut at this confused administrative situation. The farmers of the county, with their strong tradition of fending for themselves and their habit of seeing in "taxes" the major dragon in the path of the farmer, could make no sense of the way public tax funds were being squandered to carry the unthrifty city population. These farmers and their neighbors were not asking the world to support them and the relief claims in their own townships were low.[15] They pointed indignantly to the fact that recipients of relief in Middletown were spending part of the money for "cigarettes, malt, and other non-necessitous things." In the summer of 1932, 137 township taxpayers demanded of the council that it refuse to borrow more money to meet relief claims.

[14] See n. 12 above.
[15] Differences in the relief load in different parts of the county may be glimpsed from the following editorial comment in a Middletown paper in July, 1935: "Let all of us taxpayers move out to Monroe Township where the poor-relief claims last month amounted to $15. In Center Township [Middletown] the total was $8,759.98 and that was a big reduction. And Washington Township, with the good-sized town of Gaston in it, only paid out $83."

As the winter wore on, the farmers repeatedly threatened court action, and in February, 1933, three-column headlines on the front page of the local press announced: "County Council Considers Forcing Township Court Mandate on Poor Relief; Seek Method of Stopping Huge Drain on Public Funds; Legal Procedure Suggested." The farmers hoped that the courts could force the legislature to place legal regulations on the public borrowing of funds for relief. But the pressure of need was too great and apparent, and the council voted four to two in a stormy session against the proposed action.

Both farmers and city businessmen were aided in the decision to tolerate the continuance of relief by the pressure from the other blade of the shears. Rumblings of local working-class radicalism were beginning to make property owners apprehensive. They were small rumblings, but a little radicalism echoes a long way in Middletown, and the way had been amply prepared for such local apprehensions by the copious local newspaper reports of "radicalism" and the "red menace" elsewhere in the country.[16] The business-class sentiment began to be heard: "Full stomachs will battle communist tendencies." Local socialists and communists are so few as to constitute a negligible element. But even in 1931 the papers had announced apprehensively that "[Middletown] communists plan to organize the local unemployed to march on [the state capital]." Nothing happened, however. Early in 1933 the United Veterans "got a bit troublesome. They wanted to bring Coughlin here, and they did bring Patman. They were made up eighty per cent of down-and-outs, and they made organized demands of the city." Also in the spring of 1933, even some of the usually staid farmers showed signs of unruliness: "150 angry farmers in the county . . . caused postponement of a sheriff's sale at the Rinker farm. Rinker's ten-year-old bay mare, two ten-year-old mules, and several pieces of farm machinery were to have been sold to meet a judgment of $380.82 given the Crown City Motor Corporation." In response to local restlessness, the local section of the American Legion had joined with the American Federa-

[16] Middletown's business leaders look back today upon this local radicalism as a very serious menace which the city barely managed to escape in the nick of time. See Ch. II at n. 66. Actually, as suggested elsewhere, Middletown labor has no traditions of or stomach for political radicalism and violence; and, so far as the investigator could discover, there was never at any time during the depression any general radical tendency among Middletown's working class. In a culture as tightly controlled as this from above and with its business leaders reading in their journals of a "red menace," even small marginal groups of radicals can easily manage to set the business control group to "seeing spooks."

tion of Labor in March, 1932, to organize a local section of the "War against Depression Campaign," with the slogan "United Action for Employment"—and no plan to back up the slogan. Even the Negroes of Middletown were organized through the establishment in March, 1933, of a relief unit by the local Negro branch of the American Legion. The unit was ostensibly raised "to serve in time of emergencies such as floods, with a woman's auxiliary to serve as a nurses' corps in an emergency," but its relevance to other types of possible current emergency was patent. Middletown's "red menace" was at its peak in the spring of 1933, with the local press in full cry after it.

If Middletown people were not radical, many of those on relief were certainly restless. Relief payments were being slowly whittled down as the burden of relief mounted. From two dollars a week for two persons they were cut to one dollar for the first family member and fifty cents for each additional person. (In the spring of 1935 the rate was a dollar-and-a-half for a single person; for persons living in a family, the rate for the first person was cut to eighty-five cents, for the second to fifty cents, for the third forty-five, for the fourth thirty-five, and for all additional persons thirty cents each.) [17] A letter printed in the afternoon paper in the dark days, signed by "A Small Town Housewife" and captioned "Living on $1.50 a Week," reveals the desperate mood of many of Middletown's relief recipients:

Our slip called for two dollars a week and [those in charge of relief] thought any woman could prepare forty-two meals a week on a dollar-fifty for two people. So we got fifty cents taken from the two dollars.

Those in charge of relief have never known actual hunger and want, have never lain awake at night worrying about unpaid rent, or how to make a few groceries do for the seemingly endless seven days till the next week's order of groceries. . . . It gives me the nightmare, but I'm used to it.

[17] Payments are not in money but in the form of orders for food on the commissary. These orders are filled on one assigned day each week for each group of families.

No regular provision is made for rent and this item is left to the ingenuity of the family on relief. According to the head of the Social Service Bureau, "Rent is usually cared for by doing odd jobs; those who own cars often use them to earn rent money; others double up with relatives; and some paint and repair the house for the landlord in lieu of rent." For the rest, the landlord "holds the bag," or evicts. When a family is evicted, the Social Service Bureau "helps with a new start by paying the first month's rent in the new house. The Bureau sets no minimum standards, but it likes to see a toilet and running water in the house. Electric lights are unnecessary because coal oil is cheaper."

But we are supposed to have faith in our government. We are told to keep cheerful and smiling. Just what does our government expect us to do when our rent is due? When we need a doctor? When we need clothes? We haven't had a tube of toothpaste in weeks and have to check off some item of needed food when we get soap. I can only do my washing every two weeks, because that is as often as I can get oil for the oil stove to heat wash water and laundry soap with which to do my washing.

But we are supposed to fall down on our knees and worship the golden calf of government when we are in dire need.

It is always the people with full stomachs who tell us poor people to keep happy. I should love to have some new clothes, and I should enjoy a radio the same as anybody. But try to get them!

No work, no hope; just live from one day to the next. Maybe better times are coming. Personally, I doubt it.

Meanwhile, in the face of such confusion and disillusionment, local editorials lamented over the American relief scene:

We have no dole as such, but we have had to disburse charity under other names to several million people . . . and have begun to notice the destruction of morale among many of those that now appear to be more or less constantly on the charity lists. Being forced to accept alms . . . has taken something rather fine out of the life of many men.

There was no possibility of closing one's eyes to the seriousness of the local relief problem in the winter of 1932-33. Families requiring relief had mounted from 613 in 1928 to 1,151 in 1929, to 2,053 in 1930, 2,265 in 1931, 3,036 in 1932—and, with every fourth family in the city on relief, the end was not yet in sight.[18] According to the report of the citizens' committee on relief, issued in February, 1933, "approximately 10,000 persons have been reduced to such dire extremity that they must now be provided with the necessities of life at public expense, and there is another increasingly large group of persons now living on their savings, or on meager part-time employment, who are reaching the end of their ropes and asking for township aid for the first time at the rate of 40 to 60 per week."

The capacity of private charity to hold up its end of the burden was weakening steadily. The Community Fund budget of $80,122 in the spring of 1929 had been oversubscribed. The 1930 budget of $85,762

[18] Families on relief were to increase to 3,506 in 1933, and to decline to 3,073 in 1934 and 2,133 in January, 1935.

was oversubscribed by $1,952.[19] Again in 1931 the unprecedented budget of $115,323 was oversubscribed by $1,000. But in the spring of 1932 the budget of $115,292 fell short by nearly $20,000; and, by December, 1932, pledges aggregating $25,000 out of the pledged total of $96,756 remained unpaid. For the first time Middletown's Community Fund had failed to go over the top.[20]

At this point, in the winter of 1932-33, local businessmen stepped in to enforce greater efficiency in the relief system. There was confusion and wasteful duplication in relief payments between the Community

[19] Subsequent gifts to the Community Fund raised the 1930 total to $101,225. The total budgets in each year included costs involved in the drive. The actual sums received by the twelve Fund agencies from the Fund drive and from all other sources (gifts from wealthy citizens; service charges, *e.g.*, by Visiting Nurse Association; membership fees and dues, *e.g.*, in the Y.M.C.A.; and incidental collections, *e.g.*, by the Salvation Army) may be seen from the following:

	1928	1929	1930	1931	1932
Receipts from Community Fund..	$ 62,672	$ 70,580	$101,225	$ 94,305	$ 82,025
Receipts from all other sources ..	194,048	232,764	132,622	110,911	77,931
Total receipts	$256,720	$303,344	$233,847	$205,216	$159,956

Some idea of the strains thrown upon some of these agencies by the shrinkage in Receipts from All Other Sources (than the Community Fund) may be gained from the following comparative income totals of the indicated agencies from all sources for the years 1928 and 1932:

Agency	1928	1932	Agency	1928	1932
Y.M.C.A.	$120,485	$28,432	Day Nursery	$ 960	$ 704
Y.W.C.A.	44,879	20,367	Tuberculosis		
Boy Scouts	3,600	1,074	Association	3,554	3,720
Red Cross	7,918	5,340	Visiting Nurse		
Social Service			Association	9,480	9,724
Bureau	0	4,590	Humane Society	6	0
Jewish Welfare	0	0	War Mothers	263	217
Salvation Army	2,903	3,763	*Total*	$194,048	$77,931

In the city of 36,500 in 1925 contributions to the Fund Drive were pledged by 6,402 persons, or 18 per cent of the population. (See *Middletown,* p. 464.) In 1929, in the city of 45,500, total contributors numbered 10,500, or 23 per cent of the population. By 1933, with a population of 46,500, those making pledges had fallen off to 5,405, or only 12 per cent of the population. (These figures for 1929 and 1933 are taken from press reports.) The pressure methods employed in collecting these funds are described later in the present chapter.

[20] It is reported informally that the X family deliberately let the drive fail of its goal in that year as a lesson to the community.

In 1933 the budget of $97,277 was still 54 per cent short twenty-four hours before the close of the drive and was only pushed up to $86,589 through heavy last-minute gifts by local wealthy people. In 1934 the budget was dropped still further to $86,610, and was oversubscribed by $593.

Fund agencies and the township trustee's office with its jealously guarded powers as the one political agency able to dispense tax funds for relief. A central clearing house was set up through which appeals must pass for allocation to one or the other source of funds. Local businessmen also caused the appointment of the committee of five, mentioned above,[21] "to study the problem of relief." This committee was charged with recommending further efficiencies best calculated "to give an excellent quality of service to the needy," while at the same time not infringing upon "normal channels of trade" and "preserving as much as possible the character and citizenship of those served."

Out of the committee's report came the following recommendations:

1. Change the present methods of food relief to an arrangement which adequately reduces cost through a Selected Grocers Plan [enabling quantity purchases and, therefore, reduced prices]; or, otherwise, establish a commissary.

2. Study the changes in food prices since the adoption of the present scale to see what revisions in the present scale are justified.

3. Provide printed or mimeographed menus for distribution to families that desire to secure the most food value for their money.

4. Provide employment on public work for able-bodied relief clients to the greatest extent possible.

5. Expand the Home and Community Garden projects.

6. Continue the present plan for providing fuel.

7. Revise the plan of furnishing medical relief. This should include the establishment of a clinic out-patient department for ambulatory patients.[22]

8. Continue the present discount arrangement with the hospital.

9. Gather more detailed and exact information concerning clients, augmenting the clerical and investigating staff of the Social Service Bureau if necessary.

10. Require careful and accurate records of every person rendering business or professional services to indigents.

11. Secure revision by the present General Assembly of the laws relating

[21] See n. 12 above.
[22] See Ch. XI for the detailed recommendations of this committee regarding a health program.

Middletown in 1935, despite its million-and-a-half-dollar hospital, had no general clinical facilities in connection with its hospital. (See Ch. XI, and *Middletown*, Ch. XXV.) The township furnished, in 1932, $22,351 of hospital services to indigents, paying rates varying from a 60 per cent discount for anaesthetics to a 10 per cent discount for ward services, in addition to paying for $27,473 of other medical services. (See n. 10 above.)

to poor relief and its financing.[23] This should include legislation which will permit monthly payment of poor-relief claims.

12. Make available a citizens' committee which would meet with public officials and relief agencies at stated intervals to aid in the coordination of activities and to insure a continual study looking to improvement of the relief program as conditions change.

Here one sees individualism under extreme pressure preparing to take revolutionary steps in the direction of institutionalizing the socialized provision of necessary goods and health services. But, even with this strong sponsorship by the business group, Middletown did not achieve all that its committee desired. A commissary was decided upon as the best way to handle the food-supply problem, but this met with sharp opposition. The county council balked at turning over the township's share of the grocery-relief business, a political plum that in 1932 was aggregating $192,000 of business to the grocers of the township. As late as February, 1933, a grocer who was a relative of the township trustee appeared before the council in opposition to the proposed bilking of the grocers out of this lucrative business,[24] and the councilmen answered him by declaring that they had no intention of allowing a commissary to be set up.[25] But at the same meeting the council wrestled with the problem of how to raise $93,533 owing for relief expenditures in the last quarter of 1932; if the money was to be had, bonds would have to be sold; only the local banks could be looked to as outlets for the bonds; and the banks were owned and operated by the local business control group who wanted the commissary. So in March, 1933, the commissary opened.

But the grocers were easier to override than another vested interest, the medical profession. Local doctors received $11,000 from the town-

[23] "The present laws governing the administration of poor relief," the report states, "are largely three-quarters of a century old and need modernizing."

[24] See n. 13 above.

[25] In all fairness to the grocers it should be borne in mind that they and the landlords of Middletown have borne a heavy burden of bad debts and slow payments throughout the depression. The grocers occupy an exposed position in a *laissez-faire* economy, for they are the people who possess surplus stores of the community's primary commodity—food—and their customers are, to a degree unusual today in urban retailing, their neighbors. Many Middletown grocers refused to subscribe to the Community Fund during the depression. "But," explained one of the Fund canvassers, "we understood their reasons. They were doing their share, carrying some families for two and three months. Our families on relief would have been even larger had it not been for the way these grocers helped."

ship trustee in 1931 and $26,000 in 1932; the medical business was lean, and 1933 bid fair to be a bigger relief year than 1932. The report of the citizens' committee showed that some doctors were making hay cannily. They were being paid from tax funds a higher rate for home visits than for office cases, and, comments the report, "Some physicians are not handling their privileges in the most economical manner, *e.g.*, we find that during the last quarter one physician had 30 home calls and 180 office calls, and another had 192 home calls and 42 office calls." The report also added to its recommendations for the health care of those on relief [26] the following comment:

There is little doubt in the minds of the Committee that the employment of two or three full-time township physicians is the most economical plan possible, but there is so much probability of intangible detrimental effects both to the patients and the morale of the local medical profession that we hesitate to recommend this step.

So strong was the majority bloc in the local Medical Society opposing innovations in relief health care, however, that not only was the idea of "township physicians" discarded, but nothing was done subsequently about setting up the out-patient clinic at the hospital.[27]

When the commissary was set up in March, 1933, it became the target of charges by labor that it was profiteering. An energetic local worker organized a small group under the name of the Council of the Unemployed and it held a turbulent meeting with the county council near the end of March, 1933, at which it presented a fourfold program:

1. To reduce food prices at the commissary, which are in some cases above local retail-store prices.
2. To operate garden plots cooperatively. [This was characterized by the press as "the first attempt to apply socialistic principles to a relief plan here."]
3. To eliminate the Social Service Bureau [and thus throw all relief on tax funds].
4. To inaugurate local public works on a loan from the Reconstruction Finance Corporation.

Businessmen had hoped that the organization of the commissary would deflect some of the restlessness of the unemployed. When the above demands were followed by the announcement that the unemployed

[26] These recommendations are given in full in Ch. XI.
[27] See Ch. XI.

would picket the commissary, business swung into action. One of the drafters of the plan for the commissary describes their line of action as follows: "I had one of my men go to their meetings and get himself appointed chairman of the picketing committee. The day the picketing was to start he walked out on the crowd, didn't go near the pickets, and the thing blew up." The Council of the Unemployed was weak, and in the end nothing came of its demands save that local businessmen noted it as another evidence of "growing radicalism among the workers." The same cry of "radicalism" was raised against the Veterans of Foreign Wars who, in May, 1933, opened a free employment service.

The charge by the Council of Unemployed of high prices at the commissary was met with in a number of quarters during the 1935 field work. The repeated charge was that the inner business group of bankers and businessmen were using relief expenditures to pull certain of their business chestnuts out of the fire. Reference was made particularly to a local wholesale grocery company and to the leading men's clothing store termed "the highest-priced outfitting store in town," both reported to be "in the hands of the bankers" and both utilized as the channels of relief distribution for their respective commodities. According to an officer of the Central Labor Union:

"The [wholesale grocery house] has the exclusive contract to supply the commissary. Its prices to the commissary are higher than regular retail prices, and a $2.50 credit at the commissary will buy only as much food as $2.00 will buy at a retail store. I have compared the official commissary list prices with those charged by my grocer down on the South Side."

From a business-class source came the following written statement:

"I have compared the commissary's daily price lists with those at my own grocer's, one of the best stores in town. Some items on the commissary list are two to five cents higher than at my grocer's. Some are lower, but not lower than prices at stores in the poorer districts. Bad eggs and moldy meat are sometimes sold to commissary patrons and some of them have brought the goods up to the City Hall for all and sundry to see. The middle slices are cut from hams and the two ends sold at the commissary. Clothing merchants who sell serviceable clothing at lower prices than the K—— store haven't a chance to get the relief business. Any bids they make are thrown out. It is all tied up with the fact that Middletown is a one-bank town." [28]

[28] See Ch. III.
The new mayor elected in the fall of 1934 capitalized on the widespread South Side protest against the commissary by running on a platform pledged to

No further direct proof or disproof of these charges was obtained.[29] Business-class Middletown expressed general satisfaction regarding the commissary as the most economical way of handling food relief. The responsible local businessmen supervising relief assert that food is sold in the commissary at current retail prices, the difference between whole-sale and retail prices being turned back to the township. They claim that the taxpayers effected thereby a saving of $20,000 in 1934 through the commissary, as compared with the cost of the same services under the old system of purchase through local retail grocers. From the nature of the various interests involved, the charge that the wholesale grocery and clothing firms mentioned above are favored on other reasons than sheer price seems not unlikely. That recipients of relief are being sys-tematically overcharged to the extent suggested above seems, however, extremely unlikely. It is very unlikely, too, that the businessmen who control relief policies knowingly countenance the sale of any unfit commodities at the commissary. Occasional bad eggs or meat may create a folk prejudice in a period of local stress that grossly misrepre-sents the average situation. A local editor, in January, 1936, threw up his hands over the whole situation, remarking: "Whether the commis-sary plan is a success, this column does not profess to know. It has heard both sides of the story many times." The whole commissary issue was thrown into further confusion by the fact that, after having sup-ported the commissary system, the Governor's Commission on Unem-ployment Relief issued a bulletin in the fall of 1935, directed to all township trustees, urging the abandonment of commissaries and the return to free purchases of private grocers. Whether the shift was in response to business pressure from the retailers of the state is not known. The bulletin pointed to the presence of graft in the administra-tion of commissaries, to their lesser efficiency as compared with private groceries, and to certain obvious humanitarian considerations. Accord-ing to the press summary of the bulletin:

abolish the commissary and to return the relief-food business to the groceries. See in Ch. IX the discussion of the refusal, because of this commissary issue, of the candidate for township trustee on the mayor's ticket to take office in 1935, although he was actually elected.

[29] One is dealing here with an obviously highly complicated and emotionally charged situation, in which well-intended moves by men of the utmost probity and public spirit are easily misunderstood, and in which also the personal and public loyalties of these men can easily become confused.

Families on direct relief in [this state] should be permitted to do their own shopping. The bulletin discredits the so-called "basket" and commissary systems, saying that under these methods families receive about the same kinds of food week after week to the detriment of their health; that these systems cause waste of unusable supplies; that spoiled or inferior food sometimes is sold at the price of good food; that political or personal favoritism toward certain grocers is often shown, and that these methods bring about confusion and waste of time in trustees' offices.

The first rift in the clouds came in May, 1933, when the headlines proclaimed: "Relief Calls in First Drop in Two Years Here." Appeals for aid had, after mounting throughout forty months to a high of 10,821 in March, dropped for the first time in April to 9,603. In the same month seventy-one families went off township relief. But the hard-pressed city found little cause for satisfaction in these oscillations in its relief demands. Some 3,500 of its 12,500 families were still on relief, and even a year later their number was still to stand at only 12 per cent below the 1933 figure.

All through 1933 the local fiscal situation continued chaotic in the extreme. As noted above, the county council in February considered forcing the whole relief issue into the courts by stopping the voting of more bond issues and forcing court action by the township. The voting of funds lagged after their expenditure. Funds for the last three months of 1932 were voted in February, 1933, and when they were voted there were no bidders for the bonds until sometime later when a local bank bid them in after their rate of interest had been raised from 5 to 6 per cent and provision had been made for their early refunding. In March, streamer headlines proclaimed: "County May Seek Federal Loan; Fear Crisis in Sale of Bond Issue; County Relief Bonds Slow in Selling." A month later the papers reported: "The county owes $230,000 for poor relief administered during the last six months, without means of paying the bill, and the costs are continuing to mount." The relief scale was slashed in April. In May came the first Reconstruction Finance Corporation loan of $40,000, but to apply on future expenditures, and a howl went up from the holders of claims for the last three months of 1932 and the first three months of 1933 that remained still unpaid. In July, 1933, fifty-five creditors (local businessmen who had supplied relief materials against township orders) brought suit against the township for $168,000 of unpaid poor-relief debts, covering the period September, 1932, to April, 1933. Even after

Federal funds began to flow in, the bickering and uncertainty continued. At the close of the year the press carried the news: "[Middletown's] C.W.A. program faces a threat as the $100,000 issue of city bonds remains unsold."

When, on November 15, 1933, the blessed rain of Federal C.W.A. funds began to fall upon the parched taxpayers, the straining city brought out projects big and little to catch the golden flood. "County Rushes Projects to Place Unemployed Persons on Government Payrolls" shouted the headlines. It was too good to be true! Thirty hours a week at fifty cents an hour would, the press gloated, bring $22,500 of Federal money every week in place of that amount of local taxpayers' money. And under the C.W.A. the golden stream was not even confined entirely to persons on relief. Good old Uncle Sam! Nobody was talking then about the unbridled waste of Washington spending in the hands of "brainless bureaucrats." It was manna direct from heaven, and Middletown came back for more, and more, and more.

The first week's shower of $6,700 reached less than 500 workers, but by mid-December of 1933 the workers had increased to 1,750, and by mid-January, 1934, $33,500 of Federal funds were pouring in each week to 1,840 workers. The number of workers was forced down to 905 in the spring. Then, after $350,000 of C.W.A. funds had been expended locally, the F.E.R.A. took up the load, and, operating on a more economical basis and hiring only persons on relief, paid in sums ranging up to $16,000 to $17,000 a week. The peak number of men carried under the F.E.R.A. funds was 1,100 in January and February, 1935, and, with increasing employment, this total had dropped to 900 in mid-June, 1935.

In returning to Middletown in 1935 one got an impression of external improvement and sprucing up at a number of points. And, upon inquiry, it developed that many of these changes had actually occurred during the depression. Here was the paradox of a city's largely standing still from the standpoint of civic improvements during the boom years, and actually going in for extensive improvements in the midst of depression. The answer was blithely stated in a local editorial comment in June, 1935, under the caption, "Good Old Santa Claus Comes to Town": "If [Middletown] is not so improved pretty soon that she will not be able to recognize her 'lifted' face, it will not be the fault of good old Uncle Sam." As another press statement expressed it:

Thus far the Federal government apparently has agreed to finance, in part, about everything the city has suggested. [Middletown] now has, or proposes to put through, a list of improvements that probably would not have been considered if the last five years had been "prosperous." It has been said that, had it not been for the "hard times," the city would not have some of these public works twenty-five years from now."

The local projects began as rather obvious jobs such as redecorating public schools and improving their grounds but quickly spread to such things as the following:

A riverside boulevard across the city.

The dredging and cleaning of the river, looking toward its use for recreational purposes when the new sewage system is secured.

New bridges across the river.

A park and $90,000 municipal swimming pool replacing an unsightly city dump near the center of town.

Draining and reclaiming of swamp areas.

Widening, repairing, and paving of streets and construction of traffic signs.

A handsome $350,000 arts building (a P.W.A. project for which the X family contributed the necessary local funds), a swimming pool, and other extensive improvements to buildings and campus at the college.

Drainage and grading of the airport.

Construction of sidewalks, gutters, and back-yard privies (the property owners paying cost of materials only).

An extensive supervised recreational program for adults and children in the city parks.

School athletic fields.

An exhaustive local housing inventory.

The making of mattresses and bedding for the needy.

Provision of plowing and watchmen for community vegetable gardens.

Supplementary staff help for health and welfare agencies, public library, etc.

Remodeling, repairing, redecorating, and in some cases building of additions to public buildings.

The city even received a large Federal grant for the construction of the long-needed modern sewage plant, but local political bickerings, as noted elsewhere,[30] prevented the then mayor, who secured the grant from Washington, from floating the necessary bond issue. As this is

[30] See Ch. IX.

being written, in the summer of 1936, other large improvements are going forward with the help of Federal and State funds:

Part of the long-planned new sewer system is actually under construction, with the W.P.A. paying for the labor and the city supplying the materials and equipment. (The major part of the original program, including a modern sewage disposal plant, which the city fumbled as noted above in 1934, is still pending. This $850,000 additional program, toward which the city would provide 55 per cent of the cost, had in August, 1936, reached the stage of favorable recommendation by the Examining Division of P.W.A.)

A three-state highway through the city, direct to the state capital, is under construction, with the city paying only $125,000 of the $675,000 cost of the construction within its city limits.

Favorable action was also expected on a $500,000 project to build five additional modern bridges over the river that crosses the city.

The city was congratulating itself over the prospect: Middletown, the press reported, "will see in progress the most extensive program of public improvements ever seen here at one time." And, sensing the fact that such a Cinderella existence will not go on forever, a press comment on the new bridges stated: "It is unlikely that ever again will there be an opportunity for the county to build new bridges here at a little more than half of their cost to the local taxpayers."

Here, in the experience of this city in achieving undreamed-of things in the midst of paralyzing bad times and under the guise of "relief," one sees a highly significant commentary on the process of social change in this culture. From an engineering point of view, such things as constructing adequate sewers, streets capable of carrying a given volume of traffic without undue congestion and accidents, and the other physical equipment of urban living present no problem. Middletown has engineers eager to do these things and the nation's warehouses contain materials clamoring for use. As a matter of fact, Middletown was in 1935 threatened with a $35,000 suit by an engineer for a complete survey and set of blueprints for its needed sewer and sewage disposal plant which it had not proceeded to build. It is not, therefore, to the engineering area of the culture that one must look for the checks that make the inauguration of avowedly needed social changes so haphazard and turbulent a process. Given adequate technological skills and raw materials, where do the hindrances lie? They may lie in a lack of ideas, of popular demand, of men, of money, or of social organization. Actually, Middletown has long had many of the ideas that are now being embodied in relief projects; the mangy river, the lack of a modern sewage system, antiquated school equipment, were things people talked about and editors wrote about as old, familiar "local problems" ten years ago. Also, there have always been men unemployed and wanting work. Judging from the amount of local graft and mismanagement habitually tolerated in the spending of the city's budget,[31] there has been money enough to finance the luxury of chronic mismanagement. And in the city government, Chamber of Commerce, and civic clubs there has been a paraphernalia of social organization that even in 1925 was noted as searching for things to "boost." But these human and institutional resources operate in a culture; and that culture by long habituation is patterned. Among these patterns are the following:

1. A tradition of approaching and stating problems negatively rather than positively. The legal structure defining the responsibilities of public officials stresses these negative checks and offsetting balances, and custom and the clamor of vocal minorities representing vested interests see that these legal checks are maintained. The outward *slogans* of Middletown's municipal leaders are "Economy," "We will reduce taxes," "We will give the city a cheap administration," and "Harmony"; and the *animus* of civic administration is: Do as little as is necessary to keep people reasonably satisfied and to get by. Don't start anything you can't finish or that will subject you to criticism from kickers. You can't satisfy everybody, so keep to the middle of the road, keep your neck in, and move only when you are sure of your backing by the right people.[32]

2. A tradition, generated by the concept of Democracy and shaped in civic matters by the tradition immediately preceding, which emphasizes "the average": "We're up to the average," "We're as good as most," "We're no worse than other cities of our size."

3. A tradition of the competence of the untrained common man to direct public affairs effectively. Such training as a Middletown civic official has is training in being a backslapping politician. One is a popular backslapper

[31] See Ch. IX.
[32] Forthrightness is not an asset in Middletown, despite the store it sets upon "honesty." Nor is conspicuous subtlety and adroitness. The blurred, cautious personality that keeps to "the middle of the road" gets along better. Typical of this is the editorial comment in Middletown in 1936, lauding as one of Governor Landon's "advantages as a candidate" the fact that "he has a very short record in public service and, therefore, is little known."

first and foremost, and only incidentally, and according to the wheel of chance, a city controller or councilman.

4. A distrust of "planners," "idealists," "intellectuals," of all men who let their thoughts and imaginations run beyond immediacies. Big steps in a world devoted to gradualness are suspect. It is all right on public occasions of a self-congratulatory type like the Fourth of July or the annual Chamber of Commerce dinner—or even in a pre-election speech—to let oneself go a bit and spin big dreams, but everybody knows that isn't the way to get the world's work done.

5. The tradition of short-term officeholding with the ever-imminent threat of the "next election," which diverts officeholders' attention from all but routine city business, to the crafty business of building personal political fences. Middletown's officeholders are not as a rule engaged in building a city, but in building a personal political organization. One is constantly impressed in going to Middletown city officials by the meagerness and casualness of their records; by the large absence of any conceptualized sailing chart or sense of direction; and by their reliance upon cheap clerks to do the work of the office.[33]

6. A pervasive pride, itself stereotyped, in "how far we've come since ——," whereby the present usually appears good as compared with the past: potholed brick-paved streets are good as compared with the old potholed dusty streets; a dozen dingy grade-school buildings look good as compared with the half-dozen of a generation ago; unpainted cottages with radios look good as compared with the earlier unpainted cottages without radios; running water in 87 per cent of the city's homes looks good as compared with running water three decades or so ago in half the homes; and an epidemic of only 75 cases of scarlet fever looks good as compared with 300 in the old days. The absence of prospective standards makes resort to retrospective comparisons easy and natural. The "fallacy of movement" lulls criticism.

7. A long list of traditions as to what is a proper tax rate; how much salary a mayor or city controller or schoolteacher is worth; what a health officer's duties are; the efficiency of public administration; the relation of administrative units to each other; and so on, indefinitely. Proposals for change in any of these popular stereotypes must work against the set brakes of public custom and private habits.

[33] The padding of Middletown's city payroll with these political henchmen who serve to build up a defensive (and offensive) political machine was remarked in an editorial comment in 1936, headed "No Need of Higher Property Taxes Here": "The number of city employees on the payroll is all out of proportion to the size of the city. If all the city employees were laid end to end, they would reach—for still more jobs. . . . Go into all the departments of the city government and in most of them you will find employees hiding behind doors to keep from running into one another."

In a culture so patterned, the likelihood of the emergence of forth-right civic social change through the city's elected and appointed administrators is curtailed almost to the vanishing point. In good times things inch along; in bad times the city takes in sail. Everything that comes up for consideration as a possible innovation is weighed as a discrete, short-run absolute. A $100,000 expenditure for a new type of civic service is, *ipso facto* and almost regardless of its nature, thrown heavily on the defensive, for the city is not building a city but keeping down the tax rate, and $100,000 is "an awful lot of money." There is no civic frame of reference, no civic design for living, except such rule-of-thumb traditions as those suggested above. People have no idea of what they "have a right to expect," except the average achievement that other cities of similar size and similarly case-hardened institutions near by have. Hair shirts under these circumstances become normal, and Middletown wears its institutional hair shirt willingly.

Now to Middletown, so operating and so equipped with its full quota of rationalizations for so operating, its world made sense even in the early years of the depression; times were hard, but there was no divine Santa Claus to lift the burden off the city, and the only thing to do was to pull in one's belt and meet the civic responsibilities. Then, suddenly, in 1933 the city shifted over, with the interjection of Federal planning into the local scene, and began to move in a non-Euclidian world in which the old civic axioms were suspended and the city was asked to state its civic desires positively, to frame a new series of axioms, and to go ahead and act on them. Having no alternative, the city began to play the new game. Some at least of the conventional institutional checks were removed: here was money and here was a cultural weather in which ideas for civic betterment were not blighted but encouraged to grow.

Never before has this sort of chance to be Cinderella come to Middletown. It may conceivably never happen again. But for a brief span of months Middletown has had the experience of pressing the buttons and pulling the levers to "see how it works." The animus of the city leaders is such that, with the flickering dawn of returning good times, they want to rush headlong back to the old ways. But experiences such as Middletown has been going through tend not to disappear entirely. Precedents have been established and bench marks set, to which the culture may return more and more familiarly in the future.[34]

[34] This lingering, provocative quality in an experience once encountered is suggested by Alfred Whitehead's analysis of how significant ideas enter a

One such bench mark consists in the experience, just described, of stating civic desires positively. Again, a large precedent has been set by the blurring of local administrative autonomy as Federal and State funds and administrative direction have become prominent in local affairs.

Outstanding, too, among these bench marks is the city's experience of assuming corporate responsibility for the support of a quarter of its population during the worst years of the depression, a large share of them able-bodied persons. During the thirty-five years between 1890 and 1925 the local pattern of charitable relief of those in the last extremities of want due to illness and other of the direr exigencies of life had changed from sporadic "passing the hat" to a set of institutionalized services financed by a single, efficient, annual Community Fund drive. But the old ideologies still dominated this organized charity. Implicit in the whole system was the assumption as to the "American way": that able-bodied men should not be demoralized by charity, but should be encouraged to exert themselves to find an inevitably waiting job—at the "next factory" or in the "next town." Charity existed primarily for women, children, and only such men as were physically "unable." Among the 613 families helped by the Social Service Bureau in 1928 were the families of some able-bodied unemployed men, but they constituted the minority, and help to them was brief and accompanied by strong coercion to "find a job at once." Long before the families on relief had climbed to the 3,506 of 1933, Middletown had had to revise its definition of the "unable" to include the families of able-bodied men needing support systematically week after week into an indefinitely long future. The convenient formula of

culture. "We see here," he says, "the first stage of the introduction of great ideas. They start as speculative suggestions in the minds of a small, gifted group. They acquire a limited application to human life at the hands of various sets of leaders with special functions in the social structure. A whole literature arises which explains how inspiring is the general idea, and how slight need be its effect in disturbing a comfortable society. Some transition has been produced by the agency of the new idea. But on the whole the social system has been inoculated against the full infection of the new principle. It takes its place among the interesting notions which have a restricted application.

"But a general idea is always a danger to the existing order. The whole bundle of its conceivable special embodiments in various usages of society constitutes a program of reform. At any moment the smouldering unhappiness of mankind may seize on some such program and initiate a period of rapid change guided by the light of its doctrines." *Adventures of Ideas* (New York; Macmillan, 1933), p. 17 and *passim*.

laissez-faire industrialism, "Go get a job—here or in the next town," had for the time being broken down completely.

While Middletown's business class wants to wipe out public relief at the earliest possible moment, the city's working class, particularly those among them who constitute the city's boasted "easy labor market," have been learning during the depression some, to them, arresting habits. Actually, these working-class people, who constitute roughly seven out of every ten of the city's voters, don't like relief either. Ask almost any Middletown working man what he thinks of relief, and he will reply as those so questioned by the research staff invariably did, "It's lousy!" or "How do they expect two people to live on a dollar-thirty-five a week!" These people are for the most part sturdy mid-landers with the American philosophy of self-help and competent independence. The skilled group formerly employed in industry have, according to the man in immediate charge of assigning relief jobs, resisted relief longest and hardest, preferring to resort to bartering their services, to doing odd jobs, to borrowing—to doing anything else as long as possible rather than to "go on the county." In the face of falling local wages they have tended, where their craft was unionized, to sever connections with the union in order to cling to or to accept a ten- to twelve-dollar-a-week non-relief job.[35] And as they have been forced to accept work-relief jobs, paying from $19 to $70 a month depending upon the size of their family, they have insisted tenaciously upon regarding work relief as "work" and not "relief." Under the F.E.R.A. they have been allowed to supplement their work-relief pay by part-time private employment, using their F.E.R.A. pay as a financial backlog. According to the director of work relief, these formerly skilled workers have tended under this arrangement to keep their initiative and to get better and better jobs, until many of them could leave F.E.R.A. jobs entirely. A policy has been followed of allowing men to try out outside jobs long enough to be reasonably assured of their continuance before the F.E.R.A. door is finally closed to them.

Only half of the relief load could, however, be carried on work relief, and work-relief jobs have been assigned first on the basis of need and only secondarily on the basis of skill and experience. It is among the skilled persons driven down over a long period to direct relief involving humiliation and prolonged abject want, and particularly among families of unskilled workers whose income has always been

[35] See Ch. II.

poor and precarious, that such tendency as exists to rest back inertly on relief appears. Particularly for the latter, those to whom the present has always been mean and chancy and the future meager or non-existent, the assured regularity of relief food represents at worst the swapping of one kind of meanness for another.

Thus, although Middletown's working class does not like the idea of relief, the latter represents to a large portion of them a learned experience they will not easily forget. Both those whose morale is still good and to whom the future is still real, and those who have given up nearly everything except the habit of keeping on living, have lived under a government that has recognized that there are poor people and has done something about it. They feel sold out, many of them, by the failure of the labor section, 7a, under N.R.A., and they hate the idea of being on relief as a personal experience. But these relief dollars are real, and public recognition of the need of the unemployed has to them a symbolic value of great significance. As a class, to the limited extent that they think of themselves as a "class" in Mid-dletown,[36] these people know little of what the depression is all about, and their habits do not include much speculation on the future. They are American bred and "think American"—slogans and all. They want to be "independent" and to "get on in the world," but if the years that lie ahead include relatively heavy un-employment, it is likely that they will return again and again in their thoughts to this depression precedent. What such a slow glacial pres-sure of these seven out of every ten will mean for the other three in ten in Middletown only time can tell.

Related to this extension of local thinking as to who are the "unable" and how they should be cared for is the inauguration by Middletown's State in 1933 of pensions for the indigent aged.[37] Under this plan six dollars a month was being paid on January 1, 1936, to 524 persons

[36] See the discussion of awareness of "class" distinctions in Ch. XII.

[37] See *Middletown,* p. 35, n. 18, regarding the process of social change relating to old-age pensions.

Many, perhaps most, of Middletown's businessmen are still bitterly unrecon-ciled to the idea of old-age pensions. In September, 1936, a leading businessman on the county council moved the appropriation of no funds for old-age pensions for 1937 as a gesture of defiance to the State and Federal governments and in order to force on the State a test case on the State social security law. The mo-tion was carried, but "After a night's sleep, the council discovered a number of reasons why the appropriations should be made," and the action was rescinded the following day.

in Middletown and its county. While this sum hardly represents "social security" for the poor, it is another step in the direction of the acceptance by the community of responsibility for its unable. It was also prompting in June, 1935, some local discussion of the wisdom of abolishing the antiquated county institution, the "poor asylum."

Another innovation in the depression was the better coordination of local relief agencies, public and private. Here again the pressure of the larger-than-local administrative unit forced changes scarcely to have been achieved within the local unit working alone. Commencing in November, 1933, the local Social Service Bureau loaned its staff, supervision, office space, and family records to the Governor's Commission on Unemployment Relief. Not only did this involve the step of looking upon local relief work as part of a larger integral problem not to be efficiently solved by the single local agency or municipality in isolation; [38] but it also brought the trained personnel of the Social Service Bureau and the "under-the-hat" poor relief of the township trustee's office together by an enforced arrangement whereby all cases were investigated by the former prior to the granting of any funds. This reduced duplications in relief [39] and curbed the traditional independence of the trustee's office which, according to local testimony, "is usually filled here by a small-time politician who just doles out funds as he pleases, some of them to his friends." The politically inclined member of the younger generation of X's was chairman of the Governor's Commission on Unemployment Relief and also of the district

[38] The growing local influence of State and Federal agencies is a trend that obviously invites watching. As the recognition of problems too large to be handled locally grows, larger administrative units begin to spend, and spending entails control. In public education, for instance, State financial participation has been growing rapidly. An editorial comment in the Middletown press in 1936 remarked: "In the 1929-30 school year the schools of this State derived only 5.2 per cent of their support from the State, but in 1933-34 the State supplied 27 per cent of the funds, and the prospects are that this kind of help will become even greater." It is significant, too, that the legislatures of the two states adjoining Middletown's state on the east and west took the unprecedented step in 1936 of appropriating State funds to purchase books and periodicals for a number of local public libraries whose funds have been depleted by the depression. As noted in Ch. IX, the adjustment to this lack of ability of "every tub to stand on its own bottom" is one of the major changes slowly taking place today in Middletown.

[39] Under the old uncoordinated system such things occurred as one family's receiving a total of $31 worth of food from no less than eight organizations within two days. The weight of the depression load made such duplication of effort intolerable.

W.P.A. organization, and his efficient administration kept all parties working together fairly smoothly. Such efficiency was, however, contrary to the spirit of local politics, and as soon as State and Federal aid in direct relief was withdrawn, in February, 1936, the township trustee's office took back full handling of relief funds from tax sources, and the Social Service Bureau returned to its old sphere of "strengthening family life" as family consultants on its limited Community Fund budget.

Here again, however, a precedent had been set. And seven months after this return of public and private relief to their pre-depression status of uncoordinated independence, local business-class sentiment was clamoring for a return to centralized coordination. Branding the care of dependents in Middletown and its county as "having all the earmarks of a first-rate 'racket' costing taxpayers more than $1,000,000 [40] this year," and pointing out that "There seems to be no end in sight. The bill for dependents' aid in 1937 will be greater than during 1936," the Chamber of Commerce announced to Middletown through the press in September, 1936:

It has been found that there is no central registration of applicants and no apparent cohesive working arrangement between these various agencies which will eliminate duplication of effort and expense. Also there appears to be overlapping in some instances of relief of various kinds to some people while still a few others do not have needed assistance, all probably due to the increasing number of such agencies.

A listing of all tax-supported and voluntary support agencies and classification of their various fields of work is being attempted, looking toward simplification and coordination of relief to all dependents of every kind.

It is felt that a central agency where all cases of adult and minor dependence can be listed and properly tabulated must be set up in order to avoid

[40] This summary figure for 1936 includes expenditures by all agencies—Federal, county, and city—as follows: *Federal W.P.A. projects,* $604,000, of which only $91,000 was paid directly by the local tax sources and $513,000 by the Federal government; *county direct poor relief* in all townships, $161,700, of which by far the major part was expended in Middletown's township; *other county items,* $153,000 (including $33,000 for the poor farm, $40,000 to the X hospital, $11,000 for expenses for inmates of State institutions, $21,000 for the county orphan asylum, $6,500 for old-age pensions, $5,600 for mothers' aid, $2,000 for the venereal clinic, and a long list of similar small items); *civil city items,* $3,000 (including $1,500 for hospitalization of the indigent, $900 for a police matron, and $600 for nursing care by the Visiting Nurse Association); *school city items,* $6,500 for school health inspections; and *Community Fund,* $50,400.

present apparent confusion. Such an agency saves taxpayers' moneys, whether they be in the form of taxes or voluntary contributions.

Despite the popularly acclaimed "return of prosperity," Middletown was finding itself unable to tolerate the return to the loose-jointed methods of caring for the unable which had been accepted as normal before the depression. Employment in the city's industries and public utilities stood in September, 1936, at a figure which, the Chamber of Commerce claimed, was nearly 1,000 above the 1929 level; but 884 were still on W.P.A. projects, a further 573 on a Federal highway project, and 417 families and 108 single persons still on direct poor relief in Middletown's township. Characteristically, Middletown is not greatly concerned about efficiency in public administration for its own sake, or about its bearing upon the quality of the relief service rendered; such moves as it is making toward increasing the efficiency of its agencies caring for the unable represent, rather, a direct response to the threat which the continuation of past lumbering practices carries to the individual taxpayer's pocketbook.

The present mood may not be satisfied merely by the return to the depression practice of operating a central clearing house for all cases receiving any kind of local relief. The pressure is said to be growing for legislative revision of the office of township trustee. And changes in the traditional definitions of roles of public and private relief may follow in due course. As a matter of fact, the depression has brought the two types of charity, public and private, closer together than ever before, in the sense that contributing to the Community Fund has become almost as obligatory as taxes upon anyone who has property or a job. Modern Community Fund money-raising campaigns in a city the size of Middletown may be regarded as a long halfway step in the shift away from voluntary to compulsory socialized support of local relief. And these pressure techniques have been strained to the limit in the depression. The local press was still speaking in 1930 of the great "soul benefits" to the giver from participating in the work of the Fund agencies, and of the participation of more than 250 volunteer canvassers in "the happy task of carrying the message of Middletown's needy to the people of the city." But for the family waiting for the ring of the doorbell during the week of the drive, its final clang has much the sound of the tax collector. Tentative quotas are systematically assigned by one's banker and others at headquarters who know one's financial status, and "teams" of one's friends and associates descend upon one to collect the quota assignment or as much more as friendly pressure will yield. A paid publicity director is brought in from outside to whip up the pressure by the newest and most efficient methods of the "public opinion manager." For the business class the drive comes pretty close to being a compulsory levy. The city boasts, for instance, that "All of Middletown's schoolteachers gave to the Fund." Factory workers were reached through the device of putting the head of the local division of General Motors at the head of the campaign in 1930-31 to get "100 per cent cooperation" from all stores and factories having more than five employees. The "check-off" was the preferred plan employed, whereby the employer regularly deducted a stated amount each week from the worker's pay. In an open-shop town in which "black lists" are believed by workers to be passed from plant to plant, it is easy to understand why the manufacturer in charge of the Fund drive in one of the early depression years could announce that "Perhaps the finest feature of this campaign is the number of industries that have given 100 per cent." The number of contributors to the Community Fund had been pushed up by 1929 to roughly one person in each four in the city's population, which comes close to being one person per family. The number was nearly halved by 1933, but in 1934 the press again announced "one person in every four" as contributing. The whole job of conducting the annual drive is disliked by the solicitors and dreaded by the solicited. The large experience during the depression in handling relief from taxes, and the possibly permanent heavy increase in the volume of public poor relief, may prompt the city in time to shift the increasingly universal levy for its private charity to the impersonal public tax list. Before this could happen, however, Middletown would have to replace its lingering emotional attitude toward "charity" by a more matter-of-fact attitude toward caring for the unable. This emotional shift has as yet only been begun by the depression.

Basically, Middletown's private welfare agencies have changed little under the depression. One important by-product of the depression, encouraged by the confusion of independent, sometimes overlapping, services in a time of dire strain on the charitable resources of the city, was the bringing together in 1931 of all major welfare agencies[41] in a

[41] These include the Social Service Bureau, the Anti-Tuberculosis Association, Visiting Nurse Association, and Red Cross. The Salvation Army, Day Nursery,

single building, in which is also located the commissary. Most of the welfare agencies still remain, however, essentially tight little vested interests that have grown up in varying periods under the sponsoring interest of some local group,[42] each jockeying for its share of Community Fund money. The status of the Social Service Bureau has probably been permanently enhanced by its central coordinating role in the depression. As against the 2,000 appeals handled by it in 1928, the year 1933 brought a peak total of 91,585, and by 1935 the load was still 46,790. The depression emergency drove the Bureau's share of the total Community Fund up from the roughly one-eighth of the pre-depression years to a little more than half of the total in 1933, though by 1934 the shares of the other agencies were again overtaking that of the Bureau. As noted above, the Social Service Bureau ceased in February, 1936, to handle the investigatory work for the township trustee's office and returned to its work of "strengthening family life . . . where problems of health are involved and where emotional difficulties, serious problems of adolescent boys and girls, unhappy parent-child relationships or other domestic difficulties are threatening family unity."[43] While, therefore, private charity has now returned to the pre-depression pattern of work, the thinking of community leaders is already returning in 1936 to the depression precedent of centralized welfare planning. The status of professional leadership in welfare work has been enhanced by the new realization of the magnitude, complexity, and cost of caring for the city's unable; but Middletown is still too committed to spontaneous charity, too fearful of losing its amateur standing as regards "good works," and too apprehensive of entrusting its affairs to "experts" who might do "socialistic" things, to move strongly in the direction of entrusting its entire welfare program to a single, strong, well-paid, and professionally-trained director. The present system, emphasizing modest, home-grown officials in most of the agencies, facilitates control by the city's leaders and minimizes the danger of large interrupting ideas foreign to local practice.

At yet another point the extreme pressure of the depression, coupled

and the Jewish Welfare (the last too small to have any headquarters) are not located here.

[42] See *Middletown*, pp. 460-61.

[43] It is noteworthy that the Social Service Bureau has made strides since 1925 in the professionalizing of its work. The above positive viewing of its role as that of family counseling is in itself a departure from the earlier conception of its role as primarily that of dispensing private charity.

with pump-priming by Washington, has forced social change in the form of the establishment of a local public employment agency as a part of the State Employment Service. The World War first saw the inauguration of such a public agency in Middletown, but in the bad winter of 1921-22 the city fathers abruptly discontinued the service.[44] Between 1922 and 1933 the city reverted to the old policy of leaving job placement to the haphazard fumbling of the needy applicant wandering unguided from plant to plant. Local businessmen are chary about relinquishing their right to "hire at the gate," and they also tend to regard a central public employment office as just another bit of unnecessary bureaucracy and another dubious departure from traditional ways, inviting "all kinds of socialistic schemes." When the local employment office was opened late in the depression as part of the Federal reemployment program, they did not cooperate with it because, since it was set up to supply workers for C.W.A. projects, they feared men would be sent them on the basis of order of listing at the employment office, or on the basis of need, rather than of skill.[45] When the General Motors plant came to the city in the spring of 1935, it worked through the public employment office, and this gave the latter valuable status as an aid to private industry. But, in June, 1935, the office was again switched back to the job of placing only persons on relief. It is possible that, if moderately fair times continue, the employment office will be again discontinued. But here again precedent is important in the stream of social change, and with a service of this sort each repetition of the experiment under pressure may bring the time nearer when such a service will be regarded as a normal instrument of industrial society in good times as well as bad.

A further wedge has been driven into established public practice in Middletown by the depression through the innovation of a Federal Transient Camp for men, established on the outskirts of the city. Less than fifty of the approximately 330 men in the camp were Middletown men, and less than a third were in June, 1935, even from Middletown's state. In other words, one saw the spectacle of men from some thirty-five other states being fed and sheltered as a part of the social-welfare program—though, of course, on Federal funds. A strik-

[44] See *Middletown*, pp. 63-64 and n. 23.
[45] In the winter of 1933-34 when the office was supplying men for C.W.A. jobs, its maximum registration was 6,000. In June, 1935, it had an active list of 2,305 men and 415 women seeking jobs.

ing aspect of Middletown to the research staff fresh from New York City was the almost total absence of beggars on Middletown's streets. "Where are your beggars?" people were asked. The answer was invariably to point to the transient camp: "Door to door begging got so bad and so many tramps were bothering housewives that it seemed necessary to take care of this dangerous transient class who rob if necessary in order to get food. So we were tickled to death when Uncle Sam gave us a place to refer these people to." This way of providing for needy transient males could literally never have happened in Middletown had it not been for Federal planning and financing; for the same reasoning that made the business control group turn thumbs emphatically down on the proposal to establish a subsistence homestead near the city, "because of its socialistic features," would have caused cries of alarm over the proposal to institutionalize hobo life by establishing a clean and comfortable place to house and feed these men. Middletown could be counted upon not to continue the Transient Camp once Federal funds were withdrawn. The camp was accordingly promptly closed to new enrollments in September, 1935, and later closed entirely. Thrifty Middletown moved the buildings to its Girl Scout Camp. A week after the closing of the Transient Camp the press began again, as before the opening of the camp, to report:

POLICE FACING PROBLEM WITH TRANSIENTS HERE
150 TO 225 SLEEP EACH NIGHT IN CITY HALL

Closing the doors of the [Middletown] Transient Camp as far as new residents are concerned has presented the [Middletown] police department and the [Middletown] Mission with a real problem. If you can imagine yourself confronted with the task of providing for 150 to 225 men every night and the next morning furnishing these men with breakfast, then you will know something of the problem faced by Chief M—— and Mrs. T——, superintendent of the Mission. . . .

"We don't know how we can handle the men under the present arrangement," said [Police] Chief M——. "Every night at least 150 file into headquarters or are brought in by the men on beats or squad cars. . . . Now they can stay two nights, but beginning at once the time will be reduced to one night." The Mission's problem is feeding these men their breakfast and at the same time taking care of all its other duties on the $35 a week that is allotted by the [Middletown] Community Fund. "The Mission can't take care of this number," said Chief M——. "We could send them to jail, but it costs 20 cents a meal for the county to feed them. Should vagrancy

charges be put against those on the streets they might be sent to jail for
10 days, with the county paying board. Our only alternative is not to pick
up the men who are seen wandering about the streets at all hours of the
night. Letting them roam the streets would be foolish, for there is no telling
what some of them would get into. When they are at headquarters we know
where they are."

The significance of the service performed by the Transient Camp has been
realized fully since orders were received to close it to newcomers after mid-
night, September 20. . . .

At the same time such items as the following were appearing in the
press: "A regular 'epidemic' of panhandlers about town this week.
No explanation, for each has a different story, although all of them
profess to be seeking work. . . ." Middletown's traditions teach it in
no uncertain terms that taking care of other cities' transients is not its
responsibility. "Let's Take Care of Our Own"—to quote the title of
a local editorial in the fall of 1935—is as far as Middletown's conscience reaches. Yet, the depression has shown that some problems
cannot be coped with on a basis of self-sufficient local autonomy.
Even in its Transient Camp Middletown may have gained an experience to which future events may force it to revert.

During the depression Middletown also added certain new services
for children: the provision of free milk for babies of the unemployed;
of free crackers and milk to 1,100 to 1,300 needy elementary school
children; of some 150 gallons of free cod liver oil, also to school
children; of warm free lunches to about 900 high-school children,
many of them not from families actually on relief; and of free bus
transportation to the local college to students living too far away to
walk. The community's solicitude for its children also appeared in
the emergency development in 1931 of a Penny Ice Fund whereby
needy families could secure ice in midsummer by calling at designated
depots and carrying home the ice themselves. Later in the depression,
ice manufactured in the state capital sixty miles away under an
F.E.R.A. project began to be shipped in in midsummer and distributed
free to relief families with children.[46] In a culture like this, which is
relatively more sensitive to the health needs of its children than of its

[46] Middletown experimented in a small way during the depression in manufacturing mattresses and clothing on Federal aid in an unused local factory;
but local businessmen felt unhappy over this sort of socialized venture. The
mattresses that were not needed for destitute families began to pile up, nobody
could think of what to do with them, and the whole project petered out.

adults, some of these depression innovations may in time join the school health program[47] as routine socialized services. The larger venture during the depression into widespread public provision of all types of medical services for adults as well as children will probably come into permanence more slowly than extension of child-health services; but the possible shadow of future social change may perhaps be glimpsed from the fact, noted above, that the citizens' committee's report on relief in 1933 envisaged the possibility of the city's hiring doctors on full-time to provide free medical service.[48]

Over against all of the above impetus to social change, which may be viewed as a social plus or minus according to one's point of view, one may not overlook certain negative effects of the depression undoubtedly present. No one can yet estimate the long-term effects of shrunken hopes, dislocated futures, and loss of morale in the case of adults and particularly of persons between eighteen and thirty. Nor can one gauge the costs of the depression in terms of undernourished children.[49] A local editorial comment in 1935 cited the prevalent belief that no one in town was going hungry and added pointedly, "But ask the schoolteachers on the South Side about their undernourished children." And, as noted in the treatment of crime in Chapter IX, the principal of a South Side junior high school stated, "Our boys at the —— Junior High School did a good deal of stealing during this winter [1934-35], and the ominous thing has been the increasing extent to which they seem to feel that it is O.K. if they can get away with it."

One might expect the number of suicides[50] to throw light upon the intensity of cultural pressures on the "unable" individual during the depression. Here one might expect to see in stark outline the havoc of blasted hopes. But, save for the sharp rise in 1930[51] and the abnormally low rate in 1931, there were no marked irregularities in rate during the depression. The rate for Middletown's entire county fluctuated from 1924 through 1929 between one suicide for each 2,500 and one for each 5,000 of population, being above one per 3,000 in all

[47] See Ch. XI and *Middletown*, pp. 448-49.
[48] Fees paid from tax funds to local medical men (exclusive of dentists) for treatment of relief cases in 1932 totalled $26,022. (See n. 10 above.)
[49] See the increase in tubercular cases noted in Ch. XI.
[50] The 1925 study has evoked expressions of surprise from certain European scholars on account of its neglect of this entire problem of suicide.
[51] See Table 11 in Appendix III.

years except 1928. In 1930 it jumped to one per 2,000, only to be followed in 1931 by the lowest rate for the entire twelve-year period —one per 10,000. Thereafter, the rate returned again to the pre-depression level of one per 3,000 to 5,000 of population.[52] We are dealing here with figures too small to be relied upon heavily save for the significant fact of their smallness. The annual totals for Middletown's entire state, also given in Table 11, show a much more even progression: after rising irregularly by a total increment of 118, from the 1924 total of 406, to 524 in 1929, these state totals jump by 125 (24 per cent) in 1930 to 649. They fail to register Middletown's sharp drop in 1931 but, on the contrary, show a slight increase over 1930, while in 1933 they stood at 689, the highest point over the entire twelve years.

One can merely speculate as to what the irregularities in the Middletown totals in 1930 and 1931 mean. It should be recalled that while local businessmen speak of the depression as not having really hit Middletown business until the winter of 1931-32, factory workers felt the drop sharply in 1930.[53] In so far as suicides were caused by unemployment, the sharp drop in local employment in 1930 and the slight betterment in 1931 may be important. The totals for Middletown might seem to warrant the guess that a phenomenon like a great financial depression tends to hit hardest at the outset, when the contrast between recent hopes and present disaster is sharpest, and that human nature thereafter retains some measure of stability in the face of continued pressures; but the figures for the state, which, while also rising sharply in 1930, continue high thereafter, do not bear out this hypothesis.

[52] Local records are very poorly kept as to details of deaths entered as suicides. Any generalizations from them must therefore be rough. A check of those records giving such details, including twenty-three suicides in the years immediately preceding September, 1929, and thirty-eight suicides after September, 1929, suggests the following very tentative conclusions: About one-third of the total in each period were women. (This checks roughly with the Metropolitan Life Insurance Company's national figures, showing that "more than three times" as many white males as white females among its policyholders committed suicide in the twenty years, 1911-30. See its *Statistical Bulletin* for October, 1935.) And roughly one in six to seven of the pre-depression suicides were business-class people (as over against working-class people and farmers lumped together), as compared with one in three who were business-class people during the depression. But generalizations from these figures must be made very tentatively as the groups are small and there is no way to ascertain the representativeness of these sixty-one cases for which the above data could be compiled.

[53] See Table 2 in Appendix III.

A summary view of Middletown's care of the unable in the depression years suggests that Middletown is living simultaneously in two different worlds as regards this problem. It lives in an immediate world in which it must tolerate an unprecedented volume of relief from public funds. But it distrusts this whole process of public relief because of the chronic corruption in local politics;[54] and it cannot take a matter-of-fact attitude toward the continuance of such public aid because of the heavy emotional weighting of its postulates regarding individual self-help on which its institutional system so largely rests. Emotionally, the community still lives in the earlier world of "Christian charity." But, when charity involves large sums, it should be "efficient"—and things that are efficient frequently seem cold and mechanical, and "somebody" must "run" them. And when these somebodies run local charities, other people accuse them of being dictatorial. There is in Middletown a considerable groundswell of resentment, even among many business-class people, over the close-lipped banker control of the Community Fund. Repeated charges have long been heard in Middletown that a local banker "holds the Community Fund agencies under his thumb" and that his central position in control of the city's credit "stifles criticism." This man is in every respect an outstanding type of businessman of exceptional ability and integrity. His interest in the Community Fund is undoubtedly largely motivated by civic spirit. And if with this interest goes a close and pervasive type of control, this is simply one of the most characteristic modern dilemmas of a democratic culture that hates centralized controls and yet worships efficiency.

As noted in Chapter X, an independent woman blasted the local Community Fund situation in 1933 in a three-column indictment of its operations. The investigator has seen some of the letters to her which this statement evoked from local persons he knows to be responsible business-class citizens. They reflect a genuine concern over the local charity situation in such statements as the following:

"Allow me to congratulate you upon your fine and courageous letter to the [afternoon paper] on the administration of our Community Fund. I agree with you heartily."

[54] The following statement in writing from a business-class person lies before the investigator: "——, a former employee in the township trustee's office, says that families on relief were charged with receiving more relief on the trustee's books than they really received [This employee] was fired by a former trustee for refusing to sign falsified statements."

"It took courage to give to the public the facts in your letter last week concerning some of our civic leaders, and I do trust that from that publicity some good may come."

"I, with many other teachers, appreciate your letter to the paper on the Community Fund. You voiced the sentiment of a great number of folks and they glory in your courage."

This printed attack upon the administration of charity raised, among other issues, one that has long made certain more perspicacious citizens uneasy, namely, the "society" tone of the directing boards of the several charitable organizations: [55]

It has always been puzzling to me [the critic said] why certain people are asked to serve as directors [of local charities]. They are all nice people, with whom I have no quarrel, but 60 per cent of those serving on these boards are not even familiar with the situation. Many of them are busy men who never come in contact with the poor at all; others were born with silver spoons in their mouths and have no conception of the problems and needs of the unemployed.

But such objections, under Middletown's type of economy, end precisely where a local editor did in an editorial comment in 1935:

The more I think about the suggestion that nobody who never had experienced poverty should be given the authority to administer relief to those who are in distress, the more I favor it. Maybe that's because I belonged to the patched-pants fraternity. . . . We of the patched-pants cult know more about conditions than those who have had whole garments all their lives. . . . *The only trouble about that is that the persons I would have in such a setup would not be able to raise the necessary money. So I guess I'd better be quiet and string along.* [Italics ours.]

To those absorbed bankers and business leaders who give of their time to local charitable work, these criticisms all seem captious—just efforts, as one of these men expressed it, to "gum the works." These men are running local charity like a business. They regard the Community Fund as a decided improvement upon the old system of multiple campaigns in behalf of each separate charity. With a vested interest in the economy of operation the Fund involves and a realization of the efficiencies of centralized control, these men find themselves in the anomalous position of opposing various sporadic impulses from

[55] See *Middletown*, pp. 461-63.

benevolent persons to set up new philanthropies around some urgent "heart appeal." These things, they argue, involve duplications in service, distract funds from the central charities, and often breed confusion by setting up flash-in-the-pan movements that then collapse back upon the Community Fund for support over the long haul. All of which breeds misunderstanding and some bitterness:

Thus when a small group of neighborhood women began to serve lunches to undernourished children in a South Side school during the depression, an officer of the welfare agencies is reported to have protested the duplication of relief, and the school superintendent stopped the lunches.

A more aggravated source of local misunderstanding has surrounded the relief work of a gospel mission opened in 1930 by an ex-down-and-out, reformed by Billy Sunday. (See n. 8 above.) This mission's relief was conducted throughout the depression with the extreme devotion to the poor that characterizes such organizations at their best. Nobody in town questioned the value of the service the minister was giving in his grimy basement hall to thousands of needy persons. His struggles month after month and day by day to get enough stale bread from bakeries and enough this and that to feed his "boys" were nothing short of heroic. The mission made a large appeal to evangelical Middletown and all kinds of aid—old clothes and dollar bills—trickled in from every quarter of the city. Eddie T——, the evangelist, became an institution. Those to whom this warm, personal, spontaneous sort of charitable upsurge appealed tried to get the evangelist on the board of the Community Fund. The move was sidetracked by those at the top of the latter body. Their reasons were understandable: this devotion was a fine thing, but an organized city-wide welfare program has moved beyond the stage of evangelical mission charity or direction by well-meaning but limited evangelists. There followed a long struggle to add the mission to the list of agencies supported by the Community Fund, to which the Fund officers rejoined that the mission was duplicating existing types of work and intimated that if the door was opened to it, the Fund would shortly find itself with all manner of well-meaning duplicating causes on its hands. Here again was cause for bitterness on the part of the devoted friends of the mission. In 1935 the Community Fund began reluctantly to contribute $140 a month to the mission toward the cost of food. When the Federal Transient Camp was closed to newcomers in the fall of 1935, a greatly augmented load was thrown on the mission as the only remaining agency in Middletown to which the police could send the 150 to 225 wandering men they picked up nightly on the streets to be fed, and the Community Fund allotment was increased to $250 a month.

When the evangelist died in 1934, his wife carried on the struggle; and the wealthy woman quoted above as criticizing the Fund agencies started a movement to establish an "Eddie T—— Memorial Home for Aged Men." This energetic woman contributed heavily to the purchase of an old home on the South Side and personally conducted a publicity campaign in the press to furnish and equip it. The mayor, as noted in Chapter IX, pledged funds from the "welfare fund" raised from city employees by a 2 per cent levy on their salaries to lift the mortgage. This Memorial Home is today the only place in Middletown other than the bare floor of the basement of the Court House where homeless men can find shelter. It is not yet under the Community Fund and the directors of the latter look upon the prospect with very mixed feelings.

In such a complicated setting caring for the unable rests today in Middletown. The community is moving uneasily from its old world of "charity" to a new and feared world of frank recognition of continuing community responsibility for the unable—whoever they may be.

Business-class Middletown is coming out of the depression in a mood of anxious resentment toward those on relief. It has no imagination to spare for, and is prepared to give no quarter to, those whose morale has been broken by long unemployment and the humiliation of relief. The same editor who voiced Middletown's genial mood of charity in 1930 by saying that "Looking after people who are out of work is sort of your job and mine," said in 1936 of those "worthless" local people who "would not work if they had jobs": "—— if some plague were to come along . . . and wipe them all out, that would not be a tragedy but a big relief." The latter editorial reveals the impatience of public opinion in a world in which the needy are no longer the occasional exception that proves the rule but an ever-present body of people too numerous to be ignored or to be disposed of as cases of kindly individual charity:

Who is the "forgotten man" in [Middletown]? I know him as intimately as I know my own undershirt. He is the fellow that is trying to get along without public relief and has been attempting the same thing since the depression cracked down on him. He is too proud to accept relief and yet he deserves it more than three-quarters of those who are getting it. He is the little guy that takes odd jobs when he can get them; . . . he's the one that makes a meal on a quart or two of milk a day rather than ask for charity. . . . He and his kind are of the original spirit that is America.

In the meantime the taxpayers go on supporting many that would not work if they had jobs. . . .

Why not have some one of these ten or so Federal agencies around here devote itself to an investigation of people who should be on relief but are too proud to ask, and to the kicking-off of a lot of them that never were worth feeding for any purpose? Can't let the utterly worthless starve? Maybe not, but if some plague were to come along in [Middletown] and elsewhere and wipe them all out, that would not be a tragedy but a big relief. Too much coddling going on here by too many agencies. . . .

If some authority were to say in [Middletown] tomorrow to all male adults who were physically able to work but who are on relief: "We'll see that your wife and children are cared for, but you either work or starve," you'd be surprised at the local pick-up in employment. Do you know that [Middletown] people find it nearly impossible to find those who will work around their yards and dwellings? . . .

Some place we've got to begin to end this foolishness and the place in which to start a movement of the kind is in your own home town.

CHAPTER V

Making a Home: The Arena of Private Adjustment

IF CLOSING factories, the struggle to raise relief funds, and shaken
civic morale have provided the outward, public drama of recent
years in Middletown, the private struggles behind the doors of
Middletown's homes have been no less intense, though ordinarily less
spectacular.

As one walked Middletown's residential streets in 1935 one felt
overpoweringly the continuities with 1925 that these homes represent.
Whatever changes may have occurred elsewhere in the city's life—in
business, education, or charity—here in these big and little, clean and
cluttered houses in their green yards one gained that sense, always a
bit startling to the returning visitor, of life's having gone on unaltered
in one's absence. "Close in," to use Middletown's own expression, on
the outskirts of the retail section, one became aware of minor notes
of change. There are, here and there, gaps along the streets where
an occasional shiny new filling station sticks up like a gold tooth in
place of an earlier familiar corner dwelling. The once-proud East End,
dethroned by the new West End, seems a bit dingy, the iron lions in
the front yards less challenging to the visitor. And the intrusion of a
pretentious crematorium on the edge of this former exclusive section
dwarfs, by its bright expansive exterior and its businesslike ramps, the
prestige of the former "fine old places" about it. On the South Side
there are more new bungalows scattered among the weathered cottages and boxlike two-story houses. Everywhere the blare of radios
was more pervasive than in 1925. New families were in some of the
houses, and some of the earlier friends were reported to be "living very
quietly just now." But, in the main, one moved along the same shaded
streets, past the same houses, with the family groups talking quietly
on the porches in the twilight and interrupting their talk with occasional ripples of laughter. One could walk these familiar streets blind-
folded!

It was only as one went out to the newly developed "West End" that one felt oneself a stranger. There, in the imposing cluster of expensive brick and wooden Colonial dwellings in two new subdivisions in what were in 1925 cornfields, and in the adjoining handsome college campus, one moved about with a sense of change strong upon one. There, one felt, lives not the world of 1925, but a new world—Middletown's self-conscious emerging "upper class."

As one stood at the emergency commissary watching young and old family members in a long queue waiting for their food doles, one again felt the shock of something new in this enforced mass parading of family extremity. One found oneself speculating as to what this public advertisement of family inadequacy was doing to the face-to-face living of these families in their homes: Who was goading whom to "go down and stand in line—it's *your* turn"? What were the hot retorts from men defending a battered personal status against the sharp words of reproachful wives and children? But even this frayed edge of family living, while more frequent and undisguised, was alike in kind to the bald conditions found by the interviewers in 1925 in many South Side homes. One knew, too, that in the less exposed homes, behind the brave, solid front that local canons of respectable competence require a family to present to its neighbors, difficult problems were being faced in augmented numbers: mortgage foreclosures, the postponement of having children, the shattering of plans for financial security, the crumbling of affection under the hard hand of disappointment and worry, the decision not to send children to college, and the answering low drumbeat of a frustrated younger generation. But, once inside the homes, one got in many of them the same sense as earlier of friendly, somewhat impersonal, tolerant couples, in the same rooms, with the same pictures looking down on them, planning together the big and little immensities of personal living by which people in families in this culture seek to ameliorate the essential loneliness and confusion of life. These homes seem to give the lie to the ricocheting process of social change outside. Actually, they serve as a reminder of the basic sources of human conservatism and resistance to change, but, also, of the stuff of which social change must be made.

It takes time to penetrate to any basic changes in this subtle, intensely guarded inner area of Middletown's living, and the briefness of the field work in the present study largely precluded the gathering of any but the more obvious indices of changing family life.[1]

On the whole, the investigator sensed in Middletown, save in the families on relief where the reaction was usually bitter and unequivocal, a dual attitude toward what the depression has been doing to family life. Each family seems to wish wistfully that the depression had not happened to *it*, while at the same time feeling that the depression has in a vague general way "been good for family life." A local editorial in the spring of 1933 voiced this vague sense of the beneficial effects of the depression on family life:

More families are now acquainted with their constituent members than at any time since the log-cabin days of America. And those who are going back to the farms also are returning to homes and home life in a simpler and more direct way than was possible for them so long as they were city dwellers.

It does no harm for father to look over Johnny's report cards and help him with his homework in the long evenings. Society is not made poorer because mother is now neglecting the encyclopaedia from which sprang full blown the club papers with which she formerly bored her fellow club-women, and is devoting more of her time to cookbooks. . . . City folk had

---

[1] Middletown had demoralized families living in scrawny surroundings in 1925 (see *Middletown*, pp. 99-100), and such families and homes are tolerated constantly as a normal part of this industrial culture. Whole blocks of homes in certain sections appeared run down and discouraged in 1925 and even more blocks appeared so in 1935. But the leaven of families still working was great enough even at the latter time to save the South Side from the complete loss of morale described, for instance, by Lazarsfeld in his study of Marienthal. Marienthal is an Austrian village studied in 1931, two years after the complete removal of its only industry, a textile plant located in the village for nearly a century. By 1931, unemployment gripped 80 per cent of the homes of the 1,486 residents. Here one studied a community unrelieved by the spotty good morale derived from continuing employment of sorts for somewhat over half of the usual number of gainful workers, which held Middletown together even in 1932-33. Lazarsfeld and his associates found, on the basis of close study of a sample of 100 families, that the families in Marienthal fell into the following four groups:

	Per cent
The unbroken families	16
The resigned families	48
The desperate families	11
The apathetic families	25
Total	100

(*Die Arbeitslosen von Marienthal*, Leipzig; Hirzel, 1933, p. 50.)

grown far away from the soil from which their grandparents wrested a living.

All of us are hoping for a quick return of the prosperity we once knew, or thought we knew, but in the meantime some millions of Americans already have a kind of prosperity that includes the strengthening of family ties, better health, and the luxury of simple pleasures and quiet surroundings, although of this they may not be aware.

Here speaks a characteristic mood of these midland folk, living close to the earth, taking good times and bad, like the weather, as natural events to be endured as cheerfully as possible, with a strong conviction that nothing permanently bad can happen to America and that Providence teaches lessons through temporary adversity.

Middletown is a marrying city. The unmarried members of the research staff, coming from New York with its larger proportion of young bachelor men and women, felt the pressure of pairwise activity. One felt it all the way from such simple matters as the dearth of pleasant places to eat if one did not have a home, through the customary activities that constitute "spending the evening" in Middletown. It is a well-known fact that a larger percentage of the rural than of the urban population of the United States of all ages is married, and it has been shown that the percentage who have ever been married falls as one proceeds from rural areas to cities of less than 25,000 inhabitants, falls further in cities of 25,000 to 100,000, and still further in cities of 100,000 and over.[2] Actually, both in 1920 and in 1930 the share of Middletown's population who had never married was substantially smaller than that for the urban United States.[3]

Marriage, under the romantic tradition prevailing in our American culture, nominally depends primarily upon the subtleties of personal response described as "falling in love." [4] Far from being the inscrutably

[2] See Thompson and Whelpton, *Population Trends in the United States* (New York; McGraw-Hill, 1933), p. 214.

[3] The percentages of all persons fifteen years old and older who were single (*i.e.*, excluding married, widowed, and divorced) in the urban United States and in Middletown in 1920 and in 1930, by sex, were as follows:

	MALES		FEMALES	
	Urban U. S.	Middletown	Urban U. S.	Middletown
1920	35.5	28.5	29.0	20.8
1930	33.7	26.6	27.8	19.0

[4] See discussion of rituals governing courtship and marriage in *Middletown*, Ch. X.

personal thing it is popularly supposed to be, however, "falling in love" is a process that is heavily conditioned culturally. Thus the higher marriage rate in the small community is related to such local cultural factors as the standards of desirability and acceptability, financial and otherwise, in a mate and the greater ease of meeting persons of the opposite sex through such democratic media as the single, city-wide, coeducational high school. And it is profoundly affected by differences in the institutionalized availability of satisfactions of the elemental human needs for companionship, sex, and physical sustenance. In most primitive societies one ordinarily has neither status nor the means of day-by-day sustenance and human association unless one belongs to a family. At the other extreme, in a highly urbanized place such as the metropolitan city, status depends not so much upon membership in a family as upon what one can buy, and there have developed in recent decades a variety and completeness of commercial services—providing food, shelter, care of clothing, companionship, recreation, and other needs—which render marriage an optional choice to a probably unprecedented degree. For the personality that fails to find a satisfactory mate of the other sex or that elects personal comfort outside of family life, the modern metropolitan city offers many opportunities and few inescapable penalties. In between these two extremes lies a city like Middletown.

Middletown has developed, as it has grown in the last generation and particularly since the World War, small bachelor apartments, more commercial eating places, and other facilities for living in "single blessedness." But in a city of this size, remote from a metropolitan center, the alternatives are still apparently sufficiently limited to make marriage decidedly "the thing to do," and to do young.

Not only does Middletown have a heavier percentage of its population married than does the urban United States, but, contrary to the experience of the United States as a whole, its population continued to marry younger than formerly right through the decade of the 1920's.[5]

[5] The age at marriage in the United States as a whole rose in the decades immediately preceding the 1890's, and thereafter began to fall. This latter tendency continued through the 1920 Census, when a peak was reached in the proportion of males under twenty-five who were married. By the 1930 Census, however, this national trend toward more and more marriages in the younger age groups had reversed itself, and there was a slight rise in the percentage of men under twenty-five who were single. (See Thompson and Whelpton, *op cit.*, p 204.)

Between 1920 and 1930, the percentage of Middletown's males of ages fifteen to twenty-four who were married rose from 21.7 to 24.9, and of its females of the same ages from 40.5 to 46.2. As noted in Chapter II, this rise is possibly related to the fact that married women among Middletown's gainfully employed women rose during the decade from 27.9 per cent to 37.7 per cent of all employed women.

The depression brought an abrupt decline in marriages.[6] Marriages in Middletown's county dropped off by 207 (27 per cent) in 1930 from the maximum of 753 in 1929; and in the bottom year, 1932, they totaled 275 (37 per cent) under 1929, despite an increase of 5 per cent in total population. Transferred into crude marriage rates per 1,000 of total population, this means that the marriage rate, after fluctuating between 10.2 and 12.1 in the 5 years 1925-29, dropped to 8.1 in 1930, by 1932 it had dropped to 7.0, and it then began to climb again —to 7.6 in 1933, 9.7 in 1934, and by 1935 had recovered again to 10.6. The comparable crude marriage rate for the United States as a whole [7] shows a roughly similar movement, though with a less sharp drop in 1930 and a total decline between 1929 and 1932 at only approximately half the rate experienced by Middletown. The national crude rate of 7.9 in 1932 was the lowest ever recorded for the country. By 1934, the national rate had recovered slightly more rapidly from the 1932 "low" than had Middletown's; and it stood 11 per cent above the national rate of 1929, while Middletown's rate was still 15 per cent below its 1929 rate. These figures suggest that Middletown's high marriage rate in the late 1920's, based in part upon its relatively greater propensity to marry young, as noted above, was more vulnerable under the strain of the depression.

This tendency for marriages to rise and fall with the business cycle is a well-known phenomenon.[8] It is worth noting that Middletown began its march back toward more marriages in a year, 1933, that actually witnessed a further drop of ten points in the index of local employment to the depression "cellar" of 50.2.[9] What one apparently witnesses in Middletown and elsewhere in the country in this upturn in the marriage rate in 1933 is the propensity of people to brook post-

[6] See Table 12 in Appendix III.

[7] *Ibid.*, n. *b*.

[8] See Dorothy S. Thomas: *Social Aspects of the Business Cycle* (New York, Knopf, 1927).

[9] See the index of local industrial employment in the last column of Table 12 in Appendix III.

ponement of marriage only so long, and then to go ahead regardless of adverse circumstances.

One can only speculate as to why Middletown's rate fell off so abruptly in the first year of the depression. The year 1930, as pointed out earlier, was not regarded locally as a catastrophically bad year, and bankers and businessmen speak of Middletown's not having really felt the depression until the end of 1931. Actually, however, although retail and other business employment held up well in 1930, the index of industrial employment fell off from 109 in 1929 to 77 in 1930. Local labor was, as usual, "taking it on the chin" first, and it was probably working-class marriages that were being curtailed disproportionately in this first year of depression. As the depression wore on into 1932, however, there is some slight evidence for believing that the lower income group among Middletown's business class may have become even more conservative than the working class as regards embarking on marriage. It is possible that the very fact of the relatively high marriage rate in Middletown among men under 25 years of age, noted above, may have contributed to the abruptness of this drop in the first year of the depression; for there was some tendency to lay off young unmarried men before married men; and, furthermore, both very young unmarried men and women, the groups particularly apt to embark on marriage on the double "shoestring" of joint employment, may suddenly have found new employment largely blocked to them. While no local figures are available, it is almost certainly the case that Middletown's curve of marriages by men under twenty-five years of age belatedly and precipitately followed in the depression the national curve for marriages in these earlier ages, which, as shown above, had already begun to turn down by the end of the decade of the 1920's.

The problem of marriage postponement in the depression was still vividly enough before Middletown in June, 1935, so that people talked freely of it, many of them as a still present phenomenon. In general, it appears that postponement has been more common among the wide middle band of incomes, the less secure business-class families and the more secure working-class families, than among families at the two extremes. Children from homes where a college education is still a thing to be striven for at all costs, but where the cost represents to the family a real struggle, appear to have shown the most marked tendency to postponement. As a veteran high-school teacher in close

touch with student life remarked: "A top group of business-class children do not seem particularly aware that there has been a depression.
They have gone right on with their social life and their plans to marry.
It is the children from homes with lower incomes that know there is a
depression and worry about it—not just as it affects them but as a
family problem they must help face—and tend to postpone marriage."
The sort of boy who has just barely been able to finance his course at
the local college is the type that is hardest hit. Many in this group
are fearful even of becoming engaged. A typical remark by a boy
of this class, a highly personable young college graduate clerking in
a store at ten dollars a week, was: "Hell! What's the use of my even
thinking of getting married, let alone tying myself up in an engage-
ment. I'm stuck! There's just no future for our generation, and there's
nothing we can do about it. I don't expect to marry—can't hope to on
this sort of job."

Down the economic scale, among the lower working-class income
group, the future is just as full of problems, but these people, including those on relief, are apparently stabilizing their lives more successfully (or resignedly) on the level of a meager and chancy future.
"Those people are going right ahead and marrying," remarked one
man professionally familiar with this group. "They accept their financial difficulties as part of their normal situation. They are increasingly
accepting the inevitability of their station in life and ceasing to struggle." Back of this apparently relatively greater readiness of working-
class children from low-income homes with no clear future to embark
upon marriage in the teeth of the depression lie a number of factors.
They and their families are perforce more used to living in terms of a
very short-run view of the future, for life with them is by long habituation snatched today in the face of tomorrow's hazards; again, habituation has made crowded living, even doubling up with their parents
after marriage, more common and less to be deplored; and, also, the
wife's working outside the home at catch-as-catch-can jobs is more
accepted, there are relatively far more chances for her to work without
losing caste than among the white-collar group, and the couple can
accordingly count on two strings to their economic bow. Furthermore,
the relief system itself has probably encouraged marriage in some cases;
for the provision, since 1933, that only one person in a dwelling unit
can receive relief has operated, according to local real-estate men, to
spread out doubled-up families into formerly vacant houses; and this

has probably meant that some grown sons and daughters, forced un-willingly back into their families by unemployment, have seized upon marriage even upon the scanty relief payments as a means of escape from a troubled family situation. At a time when having someone dependent upon one is a prerequisite to getting a job, even though it be a relief job, marriage offers the unemployed male an easy means of solving two problems at one stroke.

A symptom of this pressure of a blank future upon the very young-est marriageable group, children eighteen and under, is the rise in secret marriages among the high-school population. During the depres-sion the increase in the number of these secret marriages of boys and girls still in high school has emerged as a minor school "problem." This situation has doubtless been influenced by the growing restless-ness of the younger generation and by the relaxation of discipline and lessened contact with their children by harried working-class parents, noted by Middletown's teachers in the depression. But it may also reflect in part the tendency of more reckless couples to plunge ahead in quest of the one thing two people can achieve together even in the face of a blind future—personal intimacy. This willingness to take a chance is strengthened by the reported growing belief among many children of high-school age that marriage need not be final since divorce is no longer a serious disgrace. One of the best informed teach-ers in the high school summed this situation up in the remark, "Our children aren't any longer regarding divorce as a thing to be feared particularly, and in the same way they are breaking with their parents' ideas that marriage is to be regarded as permanent."

If Middletown's marriage rate fell sharply in the depression, its divorce rate also exhibited a marked decline.[10] The solider folk in Middletown incline to regard this drop in divorces as one of the socially "good" aspects of the depression. For, while a local headline could jest in 1935 over the fact that "[Middletown] Beat Hollywood's 1934

[10] See Table 12 in Appendix III.
   Dorothy S. Thomas says of this correlation between number of divorces and the business cycle in the United States as a whole, "The tendency to secure more divorces in prosperity and fewer divorces in business depression is quite marked." (*Op. cit.*, pp. 66-68 and 156.) Alfred Cahen, using a more refined method, sug-gests a smaller degree of correlation than Thomas, though still positive. (*Statis-tical Analysis of American Divorce*, New York; Columbia University Press, 1932, Ch. IX.)

Divorce Rate of 25 per 100 Marriages," responsible opinion in the city is not proud of its record. In 1929, when divorces in the United States [11] reached a peak, with 1.7 divorces for every 1,000 of total population, Middletown and its county had 4.3 per 1,000. One must go back to about 1910, before the wartime jump in divorces, to find an annual crude divorce rate in Middletown's county as low as those of the depression years 1932-33. From a rate of 1.0 per 1,000 of total population in 1890, the rate had risen to 2.9 in 1910, to 4.7 in 1920, to 5.0 in 1925, and to a peak of 5.4 in 1928. The year 1929, which saw the beginning of the depression, also saw the first recession in the divorce rate, to 4.3. There was a further decline to 3.8 in 1930, and an actual rise in 1931 to 4.0,[12] possibly related to the slight rise in the employment index in that year. Thereafter, the rate dropped to 3.2 in 1932 and to 3.1 in 1933. Not until 1934 did the rate begin to rise, reaching 3.8 in that year, and climbing back to 4.8, above the 1929 level (though not above 1928), in 1935. By the end of 1935 total divorces had again risen to within six of Middletown's record total of 336 in 1928. It is likely that a number of deferred old scores were being settled within Middletown homes in 1934, and especially in 1935, when employment was picking up, local people were hailing "the return of prosperity," and more people could afford or, in the case of dependent women, dared to get a divorce.

During the depression, as throughout the 1920's, the ratio of total divorces to total marriages fluctuated from year to year around four to five divorces for every ten marriages.[13] Both marriage rate and divorce rate fell off between 1928, the last full year unscarred by the depression, and their lowest rate in the depression by substantially the same

[11] Divorce rates for the United States are given in n. *d* of Table 12 in Appendix III.

[12] Divorces rose from 255 in 1930 to 276 in 1931, only 5 short of the 1929 total. Marriages also rose from 546 to 549 in the same years. Both marriages and divorces fell sharply again in 1932.

[13] This represents a sharp rise from the roughly one to ten ratio of 1890. (See Table 12.) It is also a much heavier ratio than that which holds for the United States as a whole: Middletown had, for instance, one divorce for every 2.7 marriages in 1929, as against one for every 6.7 marriages in the case of the United States; and in 1932, Middletown had one for every 2.2, as over against one for every 6.1 nationally.

It should, of course, be borne in mind that figures stating the ratio of divorces to marriages in any given year do not mean that, of every ten marriages contracted within a given year, four or five are dissolved within that year. The divorces in any given year involve marriages of varying durations.

amount—by 40.7 per cent in the case of the marriage rate and by 42.6 per cent in the case of the divorce rate. But it is of interest to note that Middletown's divorces did not reach their lowest depression point until 1933, instead of 1932 as in the case of marriages. This means, as shown in Table 12, that divorces did not begin to rise until the year in which the index of local industrial employment actually began again to rise. This lag in the "recovery" of Middletown's divorce rate may, however, be due in part to the element of delay between the filing and the granting of divorces, though Middletown's "divorce mill," as local papers have termed this court process, operates with great celerity. By the close of 1935, the recovery of both marriages and divorces had been almost identical: the marriage rate had risen by 51.4 per cent from its low point in 1932 and the divorce rate by 54.8 from its 1933 low point. The similarities of the amplitudes of the drops and of the recoveries in these rates at which Middletown marries and breaks up its marriages underscore the essentially similar role of the irrelevant factor of money in both the decision to marry and to stay married.

Middletown cannot comfort itself by blaming these broken homes upon its neighbors; its divorces are overwhelmingly a local product, with a year's residence in the state and six months' in the county required before filing suit for divorce, and with only about 3 per cent of its divorces coming from outside its county on a change of venue.[14]

Despite the wistful feeling one encountered in Middletown that the depression has been "good for the family" in that it has "brought family members closer together" and brought some of them "down to earth," one is probably not warranted in inferring less marital friction from the drop of 43 per cent in the local divorce rate per thousand of population between 1928 and 1933. If money makes the marriage go, it also is necessary to get a divorce. Divorces are relatively cheap and easy to secure in Middletown, but even the sixty dollars[15] which is

[14] A State law passed since 1925 lowered the required residence period in the state from two years to one year.

Two local lawyers agreed independently in estimating the number of divorces coming from outside the county on a change of venue at "less than 3 per cent," and a check of the court records for 1934 showed only 8 such cases out of the total of 259—or 3.1 per cent.

[15] See *Middletown*, p. 121. Since the 1925 study, a rule of court has been passed requiring the husband to pay, whether he be plaintiff or defendant in a divorce case, a minimum fee of fifty dollars to the wife's attorney. In addition, court costs are ten dollars. So keen is the competition for this easy divorce business, however, that, today as in 1925, deals are doubtless entered into in some cases whereby a smaller sum is paid.

locally regarded as the minimum cost of a divorce constitutes a formidable barrier when a family is unemployed. As a local lawyer described the resulting situation, "Some of our people who would otherwise have got divorces for 'failure to provide' have just had to sit tight and 'take it' in the depression because they lacked funds for a divorce." No figures are available as to the share of divorces coming respectively from business class and working class. A little over 60 per cent of all families are working class families. (This estimate corrects the 1925 figure of 70 per cent of all gainfully employed *persons* as in working class occupations by allowing for the heavier share of working class families with more than one gainful worker.) [16] Hence the following statement by a veteran judge suggests that the working class may have more than their share of divorces:

"The great majority of divorce cases filed in this county are filed by the laboring class. Of course, there are some divorces sought by people from other classes, but few. I was on the bench for eighteen years, and it was my observation that possibly 85 per cent of the county's divorce cases came from people living in the cities . . . and of this 85 per cent . . . in my opinion more than 80 per cent . . . came from the laboring class."

In other words, the very heavy majority of Middletown's divorces come from the group of people on whom financial cost might be expected to operate most heavily as a deterrent to divorce.

Another financial consideration is said locally to have lessened actual divorces, even among psychologically broken couples, during the depression. Relief tended, even before the coming of Federal relief, to be granted more freely to families than to lone individuals; and, later, the having of dependents became necessary to secure employment on relief projects. This operated to slow up the formal breaking of marital ties, for as the judge quoted above stated, "Many a husband will not sue for divorce if the cost is greater than living with his family." In the case of the women, particularly the majority of Middletown's women not usually gainfully employed, rather than face the blank prospect of hunting a first job in the midst of a labor market unable to absorb even its veteran workers, many of them have preferred to remain in the marital frying pan rather than to jump out into the economic fire.

The percentage of total divorces granted to husbands appears to have fallen slightly in the depression,[17] though the variation from year

[16] See *Middletown*, p. 22 and Table I on p. 511; and also p. 63 above.
[17] See Table 13 in Appendix III.

to year is such as to make generalization difficult, and 1933 presents a thumping exception. While the share of total divorces throughout the nation granted to husbands has moved slowly downward from around a third in 1920 and the three decades preceding to a little over a quarter in the depression years,[18] Middletown's figures have moved much more erratically. In 1925 only 16.8 per cent of all divorces were granted to husbands; the next year, 28.2 per cent; in 1927-28-29, 20.2, 22.6, and 23.1 per cent respectively; then followed a steady drop in the next three years to 15.1 in 1932, followed by a somersaulting rise to 39.6 in 1933, an abrupt return to 17.8 in 1934, and in 1935 a drop to the unprecedented figure of 8.2 per cent.

What these mercurial shifts mean is anybody's guess. Certain factors are fairly clear: Judging by the national figures, there is a slow, long-term trend downwards in the share of divorces granted to husbands. Also, Middletown's charging of the wife's legal fees to the husband encourages collusion in arranging for uncontested divorces to the wife as the most economical plan, especially in hard times. The way this latter system operates is described as follows in the letter from the lawyer and former judge of Middletown's Superior Court, quoted from above:

"Another item which always concerns the man asking for a divorce in [this state] is the fact that the court almost always makes an order requiring the man to pay the expenses of the divorce case, including the fees of his wife's attorney. And there is now and has been for several years a rule of court both in the Superior Court and in the Circuit Court of [this] county that in all divorce cases the court will make a minimum order against the man, whether he be plaintiff or defendant, to pay $50.00 attorney's fees for his wife. That means, of course, that if he brings the suit as plaintiff he has to pay his wife's lawyer $50.00 and his own lawyer $50.00, which is $100.00; so in a great majority of the cases in this county, the woman brings the suit and gets an order against her husband requiring him to pay $50.00 for her attorney. The husband does not appear and is defaulted, and the wife gets the divorce and the husband pays out only $50.00.[19] That is the general rule in practically all uncontested divorce cases, and most divorce cases in this county are not contested, both parties generally wanting a divorce."

[18] See Table 13 in Appendix III, n. a.
[19] In addition there is a charge for court costs of approximately $10.

This helps to explain the downward trend since 1929, though it leaves the heavy rise in the single year 1933 unexplained. As to the general downward movement, one might expect the husband to figure less prominently as the suer for divorce in bad times, since he then occupies the role of major culprit due to his inability to "provide."[20] It may be, too, that the increase in male desertions commonly noted during times of dire unemployment was also an active factor.

As to what the sharp increase in the single year 1933 means, neither the Judge of the Superior Court in that year nor the statistician in the state office charged with compiling the divorce statistics of the state has been able to offer any explanation.[21] The figures for Middletown's state show no such untoward rise in 1933.[22] Likewise, the decline in divorces granted to husbands to only 8.2 per cent of all divorces in 1935 finds no shadow of parallel in the totals for the state.[23]

Since stated grounds for divorce mean little,[24] an effort was made to get a closer view of who these people are who are getting divorces during the depression and why they get them. A responsible local lawyer compiled for this study a summary of the ninety consecutive divorce cases his firm had handled from January 1, 1931, to September 30, 1935. These represent about 8 per cent of the county's total divorces over this four-and-three-quarter-year period. Though names and addresses were not given, for obvious professional reasons, he stated that these cases involve mainly working-class families, with a smaller group from the lower range of business-class families, and a thin sprinkling of wealthier business-class representatives. As such, this probably represents a roughly fair cross-section of Middletown's divorces.

The age of the husband at the time of the divorce was available in eighty-eight of these ninety cases: forty-three of the men were under thirty, twenty-two in their thirties, and twenty-three were forty or

[20] As noted in n. 45 of Ch. II, while economic impotence in time of depression affects the wife as well, it strikes most heavily and directly at the status of the urban husband; for "being a good provider" has become increasingly the narrow apex upon which the entire inverted pyramid of his family status rests.

[21] The latter has rechecked these figures as to their correctness. (See n. *b* to Table 13.)

[22] See n. *b* to Table 13.

[23] One wonders whether an element akin to fashion plays a part in these sharp local shifts and countershifts in the balance of divorces to husbands and wives. It may be that in the small city individual cases sporadically attract attention to certain methods of pleading, thus creating oscillations in the figures that would disappear if the total number of cases were larger.

[24] See *Middletown,* p. 122, especially n. 20 and n. 21; also Table XII, p. 521.

older. Sixty-five of the eighty-eight wives were the same age or not more than four years younger than their husbands, fifteen wives were more than four years younger; and eight wives were older than their husbands.[25] Unfortunately, there are no figures by which to appraise the normality of this distribution.

Forty-seven of the ninety divorces occurred before the fifth year of marriage, nineteen in the next five years, and the remaining twenty-four from ten to twenty-three years after marriage.[26]

Despite the apparent skewing of these Middletown cases to the side of a shorter duration of marriage, there were relatively fewer of them childless than in the state and national totals. Forty of the ninety had no children, twenty-six had one, and the remaining twenty-four had two to four each. As against this figure of roughly 44 per cent childless, 63 per cent of the state total in 1932 and 55 of the national total in 1932 were childless.

It has proved impossible to assign these cases to groups in terms of whether the depression was the direct, immediate cause of the divorce, only an incidental factor, or not involved. The cases run the gamut of marital unhappiness. The lawyer prepared for each case a summary running from 50 to 150 words, characterizing the antecedent elements leading to the divorce as they were known to him. Naturally he was not a psychiatrist; upwards of nine-tenths of Middletown's divorces are uncontested and therefore do not require the lawyer to be ex-

[25] Students of marital adjustment will find significance in the fact that seven of these eight wives who were older than their husbands were included in the group of divorces in which the husband was under thirty years of age.

[26] A comparison of these ninety Middletown cases with all divorces in Middletown's state and in the United States in the year 1932 as regards the duration of the marriage at the time of the divorce affords the following contrasts. Obviously, percentages based upon ninety cases have small reliability as compared with the much larger state and national totals. Perhaps the most significant thing about the comparison, especially with the figures for Middletown's state, is that the Middletown figures are so roughly similar, suggesting thereby the rough representativeness of the Middletown sample:

Duration of marriage at time of divorce	Per cent		
	Middletown (90 cases)	Middletown's state	United States
Less than 5 years	52	42.4	35.7
5-9 years	21	24.2	29.1
10 years and over	27	33.4	35.1
Total	100	100.0	100.0

haustively familiar with the other side of the case; and the routine nature of local court procedure in such cases makes little demand for nicety of understanding by lawyer or judge. With such broad qualifications, these ninety cases may be assigned to the following categories:

	Number of cases
Apparent cause of divorce	
Marked temperamental differences ("nagging," "quarrelsome," "brutal," etc.)	30
Primarily the depression and husband's resulting loss of employment	14
Infidelity	14
Loss of attraction ("She came to think of herself as too good for him," "He began staying away nights," etc.)	13
One or both spouses "shiftless," "no account" ("Husband too lazy to work," "Wife an ex-prostitute," etc.)	11
Drunkenness	6
Husband convicted of crime	2
Total	90

Obviously such classifications overlap heavily; in particular, lack of work seems to have been a contributing factor, even where not a chief factor, in a number of cases. No one can say, perhaps not even the couples involved, just how important each factor was—why the wife grew "nagging and quarrelsome" or the husband "silent and always critical," or what was the relation of unemployment to the husband's "shiftlessness" or "allowing drink to get the better of him."

The following are typical cases in which the depression was directly involved:[27]

Case 5. Husband and wife middle-aged. Married about twenty years. Three children. Husband out of work most of depression, though willing to work. She grew irritable and quarrelsome and made home life unbearable. He sought other female company.

Case 16. Both husband and wife in early twenties. Married a little less than five years. Two children. Husband out of work most of time since marriage, though willing to work. Supported by her relatives. Husband finally ran off; his whereabouts unknown.

Case 18. Both around thirty, though wife four years older than husband.

[27] The summaries are given here substantially as set down by the lawyer, with a few necessary changes and abridgments introduced here to protect anonymity; for instance, only approximate ages and length of marriage are given.

Married about five years. Three children. Husband out of work for some time before divorce filed. They had to break up home and wife went to live with relatives. They drifted apart.

Case 19. Around twenty. Married less than a year. No children. He had no work and they could not establish a home.

Case 22. Both in early thirties, though wife three years older than husband. Married a little more than five years. Three children. Husband has had a streak of hard luck, having been out of work for several years. Her relatives kept them until the relatives tired and urged her to get a divorce. (Lawyer's comment:) "This is purely a depression case."

Case 49. Well along in thirties. Married about eight years. One child. Husband had a prosperous business until the depression hit him. Fine home and family life up to then. Husband began drinking after depression hit him. Business failed and wife went to work to support the family. (Lawyer's comment:) "This is a real depression case."

Case 57. In mid-twenties. Married about three years. One child. Husband got out of work and wife went to work in a factory. She lost attraction for him. They became very bitter toward each other.

Case 63. In early twenties, wife two years older than husband. Married two years. One child. He would not work and support her and she therefore lost all affection for him. (Lawyer's comment:) "He probably would have found some kind of work which he would have liked had it not been for hard times."

Case 67. In mid-twenties. Married about three years. One child. He could not find work and they had to live with her relatives. The latter finally encouraged wife to get divorce.

In sixteen of these ninety cases the record states that the wife had worked outside the home for pay regularly or for long stretches since marriage.

Two local lawyers who handle a considerable number of divorces agreed in the view that, while "non-support" cases have increased relatively in the depression, "Money isn't a very important cause of divorce if everything else is all right." Four lawyers, consulted regarding the role of drinking in divorces, agreed as to its importance; but there was a difference of opinion as to whether it has played a larger role during the depression. Two of the lawyers felt that its significance has been less because, as one of them phrased it, "Back in 1925-29 there were more people who had money and could throw big family parties with unlimited gin." The other two disagreed, one of them saying emphatically:

"Excessive use of liquor has certainly increased as a factor in divorce cases both since the depression and since repeal. During the past year not more than half-a-dozen cases have come through this office in which liquor has not been involved. I think drink has increased 50 per cent as a cause of divorce since repeal. Young married people go out to these drinking parties and get all snarled up. People are drinking during the depression because there's nothing much else to do; they can't have much fun on a few dollars a week and they can get a bottle of whisky for 98 cents—so they booze."

In this whole matter of divorce Middletown shows the kind of ambivalence characteristic of all its cultural change in areas of behavior involving strong moral sanctions. On the one side, the verbal side, Middletown deplores divorce as "bad," "undesirable," a thing to be checked as much as possible. Middletown people are horrified, for instance, by the frank system of "post-card divorce" sanctioned in Soviet Russia prior to 1936. On the other side, the workaday practical side, the community has virtually quit-claimed any responsibility for sifting the cases that come before it. The institution of divorce, like sickness, has largely settled down in Middletown to the status of a means of livelihood for a profession, with the public officials supplying seemly rituals and the official seal. A Middletown lawyer only voiced a well-known local fact when he said, "Judges don't know the real causes in divorce actions." A local judge, with eighteen years of service on the bench, made this quite explicit when he said: "A judge never knows the inside reasons in divorce cases. A divorce case comes up, and it's just another court case to be disposed of. I never look over the records. The lawyers get all those details. *You see, if the judge knew these details, he might not grant the divorce.*" (Italics ours.) [28] This situation was subsequently elaborated by this judge in a letter to the investigator, as follows:

"In our state very little discretion is given the trial judge in divorce cases. The State Statutes set out the grounds for divorce. Each divorce complaint alleges some statutory ground for divorce. Very few divorce cases are contested, the court hears only one side of the case and it is his sworn duty to decide every case on the evidence presented to him; and if he does not, the case can be appealed and he will be reversed by the Appellate Court, so the

[28] This judge protested in an interview with a member of the research staff against the "ministers, parents, and old ladies" who "blame the judge and the court for granting divorces too freely. I, as judge, can't do anything about it after they have muffed the ball and let their messes come into court. It's very seldom that a judge can patch a marriage up in court."

court has very little discretion. Of course, if the case is contested, the court generally does have the right to determine which side is telling the truth. In my opinion, less than 5 per cent of the divorce cases filed in both courts here have been contested, and a very small per cent of even the contested cases were refused, and a still smaller per cent of the uncontested cases were refused. I am not saying this in criticism of our present judges or as an apology or defense of my own record as judge. If there is criticism due at all, it should be directed at the system, not at the judges."

Thus the official responsibility of the community to sift, and in doubtful cases to check, divorces has been largely given up in response to the pressure of the interested parties for easy divorce with no questions asked and the pressure of the lawmen to make more income out of legal cases. Under the above system the meshes of the community's divorce sieve have become steadily wider and wider, until a local lawyer, also a judge, can now remark simply: "I can get anyone a divorce easily any time they want it, and get it through in no time." The court sits passively by while the lawmen juggle the law: "The law requires a two-year period of non-support prior to filing in cases of abandonment or failure to provide," a lawyer explained. "But if a woman comes in to get a divorce on the grounds of failure to provide for only six months, we simply take it under 'cruel and inhuman treatment.'" And the people's surrogate on the bench bows gravely and affixes the seal of the commonwealth to the business.

The truth of the matter appears to be that God-fearing Middletown is afraid of sex as a force in its midst, afraid it might break loose and run wild, and afraid to recognize too openly that those "whom God hath joined together" can be mismated. In theory, therefore, it averts its eyes and talks about marriage as a "sacred institution," while daily in the courtrooms its businessmen lawyers work in the matter-of-fact spirit of their world of personal contractual relations. As one of these lawyers said to a member of the research staff, "I believe that marriage is a contract and that anyone twenty-one years old ought to be able to get out of it just about as easily as he gets into it." [29]

Middletown exhibits the same conflicting system of abhorrent feeling and matter-of-fact acting in the matter of prostitution. The earlier

[29] Needless to add, the writers are not intending to pass a judgment in the above pages as to whether Middletown's divorces should or should not be easy to get. The point under discussion here is the split between local public theory and actual practice.

study of Middletown was in error in underestimating the extent of prostitution in the city.[30] The "openness" of the city fluctuates with the nearness to election time and with periodic waves of local reform when "the lid" is nominally "clamped down." [31] But from many sources the investigator was corrected in 1935 regarding the earlier statement that there were in 1925 "only two or three fly-by-night, furtively conducted houses." In June, 1935, the city had just "cleaned out" houses of prostitution loosely estimated by local people as comprising "five square blocks" just across the tracks from the business section. This was the same location that these houses occupied in 1925. A reinspection of this district after the "clean-up" showed that while many of the ramshackle, weatherbeaten houses had fresh "To let" signs, there were, despite the recent police action, many houses remaining with a woman guardedly extending her invitation from the half-lighted interior behind a protective screen door. In fact, one of the best-known "houses" in the city was said, while the research staff was in the city in 1935 and immediately after the above "clean-up" campaign, to be over the Atlantic & Pacific store on the square facing the Court House.

Middletown is said by a local newspaperman to have had the reputation at one time of being the prostitution center of the eastern part of the state. At one period there were as many as fifty houses. The depression is said to have increased both the number of available girls and women and the ease with which they can be "picked up" along the main business street. And in this informal type of prostitution, the automobile apparently plays a more and more prominent role.[32] A police campaign was in progress in June, 1935, against cars parked without lights in various "lovers' lanes" outside the city. Speaking of the late 1920's, a high-school graduate of that period stated:

"High-school boys fairly commonly picked up girls in their cars rather than going to houses of prostitution.[33] This is easier today than it was even

[30] See *Middletown*, pp. 113-14.
[31] See Ch. IX, including the figures on local arrests.
[32] Albert Blumenthal in his *Small Town Stuff,* a study of a smaller community than Middletown in the Far West, devotes some space to the relation of the automobile to clandestine sexual relations.
[33] Middletown parents are today, as in 1925, very uneasy over this use of the automobile. They do not like to think and talk plainly about it. An incident, unreported in the 1925 study, illustrates this point: The Judge of the Juvenile Court, addressing a women's club on local moral conditions, told them

then. All you have to do is to park on [the leading business street] and you can pick up a girl—often one who won't even charge you anything if you give her a good time. You often can't tell the difference now between professionals and nonprofessionals. The spread of knowledge of contraception has made girls surer of themselves if a fellow looks clean."

Middletown dislikes all these unhappy, "abnormal" things and prefers to think and talk about the normal. Like the chronic corruption of its politics, its bad milk and high infant mortality rate, unemployment, and the smell of its river, Middletown turns away from divorce and prostitution as deplorable aspects of its life. When it talks about "the family" it means "a nice marriage with children." For Middletown keeps its strong belief in children.[34] A marriage without children is regarded, according to the traditions of this culture, as incomplete, and healthy couples who choose to remain childless are alternately sympathized with, gently coerced, or condemned as "selfish." But children in this culture are increasingly mouths and decreasingly "hands"; urban living, a higher standard of living, prolonged education, and other similar factors make "having another baby" an increasingly heavy financial mortgage against a family's income and plans. The era of prosperity emphasized higher standards of living, and the era of depression financial hazards; and each operated as an economic deterrent to childbearing.

The resulting failure of parental nerve is, in part, registered in the continued decline in the average size of Middletown's families during the 1920's. From an average size, as reported by the Federal Census, of 4.6 persons in 1890, 4.2 in 1900, 3.9 in 1910, and 3.8 in 1920, it fell off further by 1930 to 3.7. These average sizes of Census "families" are, however, somewhat unsatisfactory as an index to the changing number of children in Middletown's families because they include persons other than the immediate two-or-three-generation family.[35] The 1930

that "the automobile is becoming a house of prostitution on wheels." The club member who summarized the program on the Women's Club page of the next Sunday's paper stated that "Judge D—— stated that the automobile is becoming a house on wheels."

[34] See *Middletown,* p. 131.

[35] The Federal Census counts households, not biological families, in computing these "average" sizes of families. Included with parents and children are relatives, friends, lodgers, servants living in, as well as inmates of institutions like an orphanage, inmates of hotels and lodging houses, and single persons living alone. Thus, around the ascertainable fact of a slow but steady trend

Census presents for the first time certain additional data on families that throw light both upon the number of children they contain and on the "average" character of Middletown's families. The median size of Middletown's native white [36] "private families" [37] was, in 1930, 3.15 persons, a size identical with that of the median native white family of the urban United States.[38]

Here, then, is a city of small families, quite typical of the present-day American pattern. The heavy share of Middletown's population which

downwards in Middletown's birth rate, we have involved here the increasing number of single persons living alone (as the city's physical facilities for bachelor living grow with an increasing number of small apartments and similar services) and shifts in the number of servants and in-laws living in the home. (See *Middletown,* pp. 169-70 and 110, n. 1.)

[36] These native white families comprised, in 1930, 92.4 per cent of the city's population. Middletown was originally selected for study because, in part, of the relatively very great homogeneity of its population. (See *Middletown,* pp. 7-9.) The composition of the city's population in these respects remained virtually unchanged between the 1920 and the 1930 Censuses.

[37] These "private families," as explained in n. *a* to Table 14, include only related persons and exclude hotels and institutions; they do, however, include single persons maintaining private households alone and unrelated persons sharing quarters as "partners."

[38] See Table 14 in Appendix III.

Middletown's foreign-born white families, on the other hand, have, as shown by this table, a median size nearly a whole person smaller than do the foreign-born white families of the urban United States, while Middletown's median Negro family is decidedly larger than the median Negro family of the urban United States.

It is difficult to say why Middletown's foreign-born white families should have a median size of but 2.80 persons, whereas these families in the urban section of Middletown's state have a median size of 3.74, and, in the urban United States, 3.76. It is quite possible that the fact that there are only 255 of these foreign-born white families in Middletown, only 2 per cent of the city's total families, affords the key to the explanation. Middletown's Census "families" include 763 "families" composed of but a single person; and it is not unlikely that, in a city with as minute a foreign-born population as Middletown's, there tends to be among several minor nationality groups an unduly large number of these one-person families, represented by isolated single males who find it difficult to find a wife. This would tend to lower the median family size. The isolation of the foreign born may be enhanced by the fact that there is no "foreign quarter" in Middletown; the foreign born are scattered through the city, with a sprinkling of foreign-born single men in rooms in the downtown business section.

As regards the relatively large median size of Middletown's Negro families, it may be that the stability of Middletown's Negro population is here a factor. There is little opportunity in Middletown for casual Negro labor, the 5.5 per cent of the city's families who are Negroes are concentrated in two sections of the city, and the percentage married is relatively high.

is married, as noted above, helps to account for the fact that there are fewer one-person families in the city than among the total native white urban families of the United States; but there are more two- and three-person families, fewer four- and five-person families, and more families of six persons and over.[39] Of all Middletown's families of two or more related persons in 1930, nearly a third (30.4 per cent) consisted of only two persons, and three-quarters (75.2 per cent) of two to four persons. At the time of the 1930 Census, 44 per cent of Middletown's families had no children under twenty-one living in the home, 23 per cent more had only one child, 28 per cent had two to four, while a final 4 per cent had five or more.[40]

Middletown's crude birth rate per 1,000 of population was falling slowly, in common with that of the rest of the United States, in the 1920's. The depression speeded up this trend, dropping the rate from 21.9 per 1,000 in 1929 to 18.4 in the low year, 1933.[41] It is significant that the birth rate had fallen off in the depression by only 16 per cent, whereas the marriage rate had dropped by 41 per cent. In other words, "having a baby" was less vulnerable under the prolonged economic pressure than was "getting married."

Like marriages, conceptions apparently started to rise in 1933, against a still falling employment trend, although actual births did not rise until 1934. The recovery of the birth rate in this first year of rise was less than half as rapid as that of the marriage rate; and by the end of 1935 the birth rate had recovered only 34 per cent of the amount it had

---

[39] See Table 15 in Appendix III and especially n. *a* to this table qualifying this comparison.

The presence in Middletown of a considerable minority group of indigent Southern mountain families imported fifteen years ago by local factories may help to account for the presence of a higher percentage of families of six or more persons. These families, as noted elsewhere, constitute one of the "problems" of Middletown's schools and social agencies.

[40] See Table 16 in Appendix III. It should be noted, as pointed out in n. *a* to this table, that "families," as here used by the Census, includes single persons living alone and a small number of "unrelated persons sharing quarters as 'partners.'"

[41] See Table 17 in Appendix III. The index of local employment is given with this table in view of the well-known tendency for the number of births to be affected by the business cycle. Dorothy Thomas (*op. cit.*, p. 75) found a correlation for six states for which satisfactory statistics are available—Connecticut, Massachusetts, Michigan, New Hampshire, Rhode Island and Vermont—of $+0.33 \pm 0.07$ for the fifty years 1870-1920, when the correlation was figured with a one-year lag to care for the pregnancy period.

lost between 1929 and its lowest figure in the depression, while the marriage rate had recovered 75 per cent of its loss.[42]

At least three factors have influenced the movement of births in the depression. The first is the sharp drop in the marriage rate. The fact that so large a share of this decline in marriages occurred in 1930, the first year of the depression,[43] would tend to augment the effect of this change upon the birth rate in all succeeding years. A second factor, operating in the opposite direction, is the local relief policy giving preference to persons with dependents. It has been easier to get both direct relief and work relief if one's wife was pregnant or if one had children, and amount of relief varied directly with number of dependents. Social workers in Middletown report that some couples took full advantage of this situation.

A third factor influencing the movement of births in the depression is the deliberate postponement of children. Here the long-term factor of the growth in local knowledge and ease of purchase of contraceptives is important.[44] A leading downtown druggist reported a steady rise in sales of contraceptives during the last ten years, but was not inclined to feel that the depression has quickened the rate notably. He also reported more frankness on the part of both sexes in asking for various contraceptive aids.[45] The spread of relatively more effective contraceptive practices is said to be particularly rapid among the younger section of Middletown's population, just as it was shown in the 1925 study to be more rapid among the business than among the working class. Such factors as these have probably influenced the incidence of births among different age and income groups during the period of falling births since 1929.[46]

[42] The ground lost by the marriage rate is here figured from 1928, the last year untouched by the depression.

[43] See Table 12 in Appendix III.

[44] See *Middletown*, pp. 123-26.

[45] The local press carries discreet ads of "Dependable products for fastidious women" under the caption "Women's Needs," and drugstores are increasingly open in their window displays. Some filling stations also carry contraceptives. It is of interest in view of Middletown's uneasiness about this whole matter of contraception in relation to its children that the Dean of Women at the local college is said recently to have caused a display of contraceptive materials to be removed from the window of a drugstore near the college.

[46] It proved impossible to get any comparative data on number of abortions before and during the depression. This whole subject is shrouded in silence in Middletown, with a heavy emotional weighting of moral disrepute. Changing mores appear here in the fact that the older physicians tend more often than

Not only have there been fewer children per family during the past ten years, but the gap between the purposes and mutual understanding of parents and children noted in 1925[47] has apparently widened still further. One got the impression in 1935 of a more self-conscious subculture of the young in Middletown.[48] Adult-imposed restraints of obedience to parents, school, and public opinion have weakened further as the adult world has crumbled under the depression. A leading local minister says the disillusionment apparent today among many of the young with the adult world and its values "began early in the depression." "These kids in high school and out at the college know what's going on," remarked a businessman. "They see a lot of the inadequacies in the present setup, and many of them want to buck over the traces." There is even an uneasy trickle of comment in the press to the effect that "In time, today's youngsters, no longer able to be palliated by trite sayings and utterly disrespectful of ancient traditions, may begin spectacularly to make over this thing we have muddled." "Whither are they drifting?" asked a local editorial in 1933 of the "353 graduates coming this spring from Central High School and 350 from the College with no jobs available for them." Most of young Middletown does not know the answer to that question in the large, but in terms of life's immediacies they are going right ahead to rescue from their world more and more of the reassurance that personal intimacy can be made to yield.

Postponement of marriage, coupled with growing frankness as regards sex, is apparently involving an increase in premarital sexual rela-

the younger ones to condemn abortions on moral grounds. According to one informant, not a medical man, "Most people in [Middletown] tend to go out of town for abortions. Those who can afford it go to the state capital, while working-class people tend to go out to dirty hideaways in little towns surrounding [Middletown] where they pay from ten to twenty-five dollars. Antiseptic conditions among these latter are pretty crude, and a common practice among those patronizing these cheap doctors is to rush back to Middletown and place oneself in the hands of a reliable doctor to forestall infection."

[47] See *Middletown*, Ch. XI, and especially pp. 151-52.

[48] It is our impression that no two generations of Americans have ever faced each other across as wide a gap in their customary attitudes and behavior as have American parents and children since the World War. And this disjunction, we believe, has been increased by the depression. The cumulating rapidity of recent social change, including every section of living from industry and business to religion, education, recreation, sex, and family life, is widening in something resembling a geometrical ratio the gap between the things that were "right" yesterday and those that make sense to the new generation of today.

tions.[49] A confidential check-up of one group of more than two dozen young business-class persons in their twenties showed seven out of every ten of them, evenly balanced as to sex, to have had sexual relations prior to marriage. There is no way of knowing whether this represents an increase in rate as over 1925 or earlier years, but one was told positively over and over again that such premarital experience is increasing.[50]

Sex is one of the things Middletown has long been taught to fear. Its institutions—with the important exception of the movies and some of the periodicals it reads, both imported from the outside culture—operate to keep the subject out of sight and out of mind as much as possible. The older matrons say, "Thank goodness, I got my family raised and out of the way before these times came along!" Younger mothers worry and feel inadequate. "Mother, how far shall I go?" asked the daughter of an intelligent business-class family. The mother, conscious of limitations in her own upbringing which had not helped her own adjustment, replied that "One must just use one's judgment"; and, feeling uneasy over the inadequacy of her answer, she sought the advice of a progressive friend, who replied, "But it doesn't help much to tell your daughter *that,* does it? You are just passing the buck back to her." Other parents, retreating behind their authority, tend to adopt some such solution as the one advocated editorially in the local press in connection with a report that "In a certain eighth-grade schoolroom sex is rampant." The solution the editor recommended was "an old-

[49] The advent since 1925 of a larger and growingly "collegiate" student body at the local college, where as in many coeducational collegiate populations at present there is reported to be a considerable amount of direct sex experimentation, may tend to influence somewhat the attitude of local high-school students.

[50] Sex education in Middletown is not in terms of such current practice. On the formal side, the schools still do very little, for the obvious reason that in a city whose adults maintain a position of official silence as regards sex, a public agency tends to play safe. "Our high school does nothing about sex education because we don't dare to," said a well-informed teacher in the high school. The library of the local college took its illustrated books on sex off the open shelves when students were discovered to be looking at the anatomical drawings. The librarian at the Middletown public library was asked where people in Middletown could get information on sex, and the reply was, "Not here!" One grade school, with a relatively progressive group of parents, keeps broods of rabbits and snails in the science room and the science teacher uses such terms as "fertilization" in describing the origin of the young animals, but the school authorities were careful to explain that such a procedure could be employed only in a neighborhood "where we can count on the support of the parents."

fashioned paddle." When in doubt, in such a situation, troubled parents turn for help to teachers or preachers, who are in the unhappy position when they address the children of being criticized by the parents for saying too much and of being laughed at by the children for saying too little.

There is little evidence in Middletown of the conservative reaction among the young to the "Scott Fitzgerald wave" of the early 1920's that some people believe set in in the United States late in the 1920's. The one positive bit of evidence to that effect was the statement by a responsible businessman of forty: "At the 1934 Xmas dances I remarked to my wife that we people of the older generation behaved much less well than the high-school kids. We got tighter and let ourselves go more. I had a sense of the kids' being a bit disgusted with our older crowd." Though this, perhaps, is not so much a comment on the conservatism of the children as upon the relatively greater relaxation of standards by some of their elders. But everywhere else one got in 1935 a sense of sharp, free behavior between the sexes (patterned on the movies), and of less disguise among the young. A high-school graduate of eight years ago, now in close touch professionally with the children of the city, was emphatic as regards the change: "They've been getting more and more knowing and bold. The fellows regard necking as a taken-for-granted part of a date. We fellows used occasionally to get slapped for doing things, but the girls don't do that much any more." A person long in close and sympathetic professional contact with Middletown's high-school students not only denied any signs of a conservative reaction but commented: "Our high-school students of both sexes are increasingly sophisticated. They know everything and do everything—openly. And they aren't ashamed to talk about it." In the early 1930's the situation became so acute, according to one of the city's businessmen, that it "got away from the high-school authorities. There was much drinking and immorality in the high school. One of our leading ministers was called in by the high school to take over the situation in a series of talks to the boys, and a woman talked to the girls."

A striking aspect of this growing adoption of what Middletown's young regard as sophisticated manners is its tendency to reach down to younger and younger children. Rouge and brightly colored fingernails appear on occasional children in the third grade, as do Shirley Temple permanent waves. The age at which one gets one's first "permanent" has become a standard subject of family controversy in Middletown homes.

The driving social pace of the high-school world, set largely by the business-class girls [51] through their illegal sororities (known officially in the schools as "clubs"), appears to have diminished but little in the depression. In fact, one may hazard the generalization that the business-class girls of high-school age have felt the presence of a depression less than any other group over fourteen in the city; surely less than their parents; and probably less than boys of their own age. There has been less money to play with, cars have not been so new, more dresses have been made at home, in fact the whole high school is said to be dressed down somewhat as compared with the pre-depression level,[52] but the social pace has continued. About 1933 the mothers of the most exclusive high-school sorority, quaintly called the Sewing Club, banded together in a drive to curtail the cost of high-school social functions—such things as the importing of a Guy Lombardo orchestra from New York for a sorority dance at a cost of $300-$400. The schools felt themselves unable to act in the matter because the high-school fraternities and sororities are banned by law and therefore officially beyond the reach of the schools. The mothers' protests were met by a united front on the part of their daughters, and the reform movement evaporated. An unsuccessful attempt was made by the schools during the depression to stop pledges to the central core of high-school social "clubs," whose real existence is in their capacity of "sororities" out of school hours, but, according to a school official, "Some mothers with social ambitions encourage social activity by their children—and that upsets everything." In fact, the schools are inclined to trace a number of their problems in the depression back to the parents. A school officer stated that "Perhaps family cooperation and certainly family interest

[51] See *Middletown,* p. 140, n. 17, and p. 215.

[52] The following, from the daily press in February, 1933, however, strikes a high-style note not present in 1925, and exhibits at once the momentum of clothing pressure under commercial sponsoring even at the worst of the depression, and the efforts of the high school to channel it so far as the girls were concerned into the domestic-science classes: "A style show, from which the 'mode' of dress for Central High School's 1933 graduation exercises will be selected, will be staged Thursday at 2:30 P.M. in the high-school auditorium. All seniors and their parents are invited to attend. Sixty seniors will serve as models during the show. Displays will be made of boys' suits, both light and dark, and of girls' dresses in white and pastel colors in sports, semisports, and afternoon styles. Decision as to the vogue for next June's graduating class is being made early so that dresses may be made in the senior sewing classes."

have been more difficult to secure during the depression. Parents have been worried about other things and have had 'no time' for school worries."

A not inconsiderable part of what a Middletown minister termed "the growing irresponsibility of our young people" has been stimulated by changes in adult mores. For a part of Middletown's adult world apparently experienced a shift of its own as regards certain of its traditional moral standards in the boom years and early years of the depression. A local businessman summarized this change succinctly as follows:

"Drinking [53] increased markedly here in '27 and '28, and in '30 was heavy and open. With the depression, there seemed to be a collapse of public morals. I don't know whether it was the depression, but in the winter of '29-'30 and in '30-'31 things were roaring here. There was much drunkenness—people holding these bathtub gin parties. There was a great increase in women's drinking and drunkenness. And there was a lot of sleeping about by married people and a number of divorces resulted."

A newspaperman familiar with local police matters made the following comment to a member of the research staff in June, 1935:

"There is still a great deal of married women's running around with single men here. This is causing no end of embarrassment to the sheriff, and has resulted in the statement by him in the newspapers that he will no longer hold himself responsible for the consequences if people are caught parking on the roads without lights. A farmer sees a strange car parked on the road without lights, and, thinking it may belong to chicken thieves, he phones the sheriff to come out. The sheriff opens the car, sees a couple in a compromising situation, and, too often for his comfort, recognizes one or the other partner as a married person and someone too prominent for him to arrest on such a charge. The farmer insists on the arrest and the sheriff refuses for fear of the consequences to him. Then everybody's in hot water!"

Conversations with lawyers who handle a considerable volume of the divorce cases brought independently such statements as the following:

"Ever since the World War people here have gotten more free and immoral—if you want to call it that. A married man used to slip away for a few nights; but now a married man doesn't mind being seen on our main street with another woman, for nobody minds. Then there are nowadays these parties where a few young married couples get to drinking together;

[53] See Ch. VII for a discussion of drinking in Middletown.

and one husband makes a cryptic remark to another's wife, and one thing leads on to another. Infidelity isn't regarded so seriously as formerly. This past year I had three couples, all friends in the same set, in here getting divorces."

"Moral conditions here are now generally at a low ebb. There is no disgrace attached to divorce and no disgrace attached to the things that cause divorce."

This shift in public morals does not, of course, represent the behavior of everybody or even of most persons in Middletown.[54] Nor

[54] Light is thrown on the tendency to concentration of these changes in certain groups in the community by the following letter to the investigator under date of February, 1929. The letter describes conditions among the business class in Middletown at that time and was written by a businessman (and checked by a second) in answer to specific questions by the investigator regarding the conditions described:

As regards drinking: "There is a circle composed of —— in the upper fringes here [both men and women] who drink hard when they feel like it and have no scruples about liquor or the law; and another circle composed of —— who don't use it at all, less from antagonism than from lack of interest. These last have the backing of the influential X family and represent the sentiment originally responsible for our country club's having no bar and discouraging drinking on the premises. Among the middle group here—people with fair to good salaries or owning medium-sized businesses—there is likewise a group that do and a group that don't. The cost of good liquor and the bad quality of cheaper liquor is a heavy deterrent to these medium-income people. Those who can afford to buy good liquor do so because they think it the smart thing to do. Few of those who don't buy it refrain for ethical reasons. There is still a good deal of wine made, though not so much as immediately after prohibition came in, because many people are tiring of the bother and poor results.

"Don't forget the bone-dry law in force in this state. It is said to be one of the most stringent state enforcement acts in the country, and the penalties are severe. And don't forget the militant dry sentiment of a great many church-going people in [Middletown]. It may be smart to booze but it most distinctly is *not* smart to get caught. We both incline to feel that on the whole there is less heavy drinking here than in other cities of this size we happen to know.

"As regards the young people of high school age and thereabouts, [Middletown] is probably typical—with plenty of boozing and sex, though probably not so much as rumor would have it."

As regards marital infidelity: "Specifically, neither of us knows of a case of any prominence, for years past. We are aware, of course, that there must be some. We've heard rumors, but we are both impressed by the fact that most of our business 'big shots' are so busy making money that they don't have much time for other things, including philandering, here or elsewhere, which takes a lot of time. Then, too, they're a pretty cautious crowd. Of course, down the line from them—the traveling men, etc.—we don't know about them.

"One thing that's pretty important to remember is that this is a relatively small community, and it's not so easy to do things here in violation of the commonly accepted code."

does it represent anything unknown heretofore in Middletown or openly acknowledged standards at the present time. That it does represent, however, a noticeable change in the total pattern of behavior cannot be doubted. It should be borne in mind that in tabooed matters of this sort even slight shifts, or shifts involving only a portion of the population, may have marked repercussions upon the degree of acceptance of formal adult standards by the young. The change in adult behavior noted above is the more significant in that the formally sanctioned standards of this culture remain as rigid as ever with a part of the population. This is still a culture in which some Middletown children in a state denominational college helped to organize a "P.K. [Preachers' Kids] Club," whose members pledged themselves not to "smoke, drink, chew, and neck." This is still a culture in which, when the children in a rural school in Middletown's county organized a card club, the parents confiscated the club dues because, as reported in the press, they "regard card playing as immoral." A local paper, in its "advice-to-the-lovelorn" column, still tells young Middletown that "A girl should never kiss a boy unless they are engaged." The W.C.T.U. passes a resolution against the use of women's pictures on billboards and the use of women radio entertainers to advertise cigarettes; and a high-school pupil, permitted to smoke by his parents, is docked in his school grades when seen by a school official smoking on the street. The Middletown District Epworth League drew up in 1935 regulations for "proper costuming for wear on a Christian beach and on Christian grounds" which, among other things, prohibited "halter-neck" dresses at the League's state summer-camp conference. And a local paper carried in 1935, under the caption "Fit Answer to Unfit Woman," the following retort by one of the state's senators in Washington to a somewhat flippant remark by Lady Astor favoring birth control and the superiority of nursery schools to training by mothers in the home:

"Someone once said that before He could send us a Christ, God first gave us mothers. Certain it is that mother love more nearly approaches all that is holy and divine than all other worldly experiences. It is the hovering angel of our childhood, the inspiration of our youth and the sustaining memory of our old age. Were I to assign all the world of accomplishments in peace and in war, the preservation of all that is clean and dependable and worth while in human affairs, the integrity of nations and the supremacy of wholesome manhood and womanhood, I would lay it all at the shrine of mother love. England is welcome to her unsexed and expatriated Lady Astor and all of her ilk."

Today, in the presence of such rigorous tenacity to the "old, tried ways" by part of the population, the range of sanctioned choices confronting Middletown youth is wider, the definition of the one "right way" less clear. That this is the normal situation in the process we call "social change" does not lessen the confusion it entails, especially in these areas of drinking and sex behavior.

The superficiality of this procedure of talking about "Middletown's doing so and so" becomes here, of course, particularly apparent. There is no single Middletown pattern, but many patterns, loosely aggregated in groups of individuals who come from such a subculture as that of the smart West End, who serve cocktails, and go to the tolerant Presbyterian Church; or from such a subculture as that of East Twelfth Street and membership in the United Brethren Church, where the members of a working-class branch of the Women's Christian Temperance Union pledged themselves in 1930 "to pray for the Eighteenth Amendment that it be not repealed"; and so on through an infinite number of variants.[55] If the child up to high-school age associates, by reason of the assignment of each child to a grade school on the basis of residential propinquity, with other children from somewhat similar subcultural backgrounds, this homogeneity of sorts is lost when the children pour from all quarters into Central High School. Here the whole range of cultural tolerances and intolerances grind against each other; the child of parents who think it "cute" and "attractive" for a daughter to enamel her nails, use rouge, have a crisp "permanent," and "learn to handle boys" sits next to the daughter of a family in which the parents are engaged in a quiet but determined campaign to circumvent the influence of the movies and to keep their daughter "simple," "unaffected," and "healthy-minded." This widening of contact with unevenly sanctioned choices, supported not by outlaw individuals but by groups, means under these circumstances for both parents and children uncertainty and tension.

It is, as noted above, a less uncommon occurrence in these 1930's than it was ten years ago for high-school students to marry and thus to seek to hew a path of freedom out of the cultural conflicts, uncertainties, and stubborn parental restraints in which they find them-

[55] See the discussion of Middletown's values in Ch. XII.

selves. The whole ragged pattern of increasing high-school sophistication may likewise be viewed as an effort on the part of baffled, uncertain individuals to resolve their perplexities by bold, outwardly confident action patterned perhaps not so much upon the lives of their
own cautious parents as upon one or another of these alternative other
worlds about them. And where local patterns are not clear, the sharp
figures on the silver screen of the movies are always authoritatively
present with their gay and confident designs for living.

The worlds of the two sexes constitute something akin to separate
subcultures. Each involves an elaborate assignment of roles to its
members and the development of preferred personality types emphasizing various ones of the more significant role attributes. These two
subcultures, though in general complementary and reciprocal, compete
at certain points. Middletown's culture, in common with the Western
European culture pattern from which it stems, emphasizes difference
in sex on the assumption of contrasting temperamental characteristics
and aptitudes of men and women.[56] Men are expected to perform
certain social functions and to behave in certain ways, and another
set of expectations rules the lives of women. Men get the living, *i.e.,*
earn the money to buy the living for the family; they pay for the children's education and the family's leisure, as well as for food, clothing,
and shelter. They are the representatives of the family in civic affairs,
the government surrogates, the paid religious leaders, the doctors, the
lawyers. They handle certain practical affairs—repairing the car or
buying the tickets to Florida. Women look after affairs within the
household; they care for the small children, and rear and teach the
children, always with male authority in the background in the form
of the father who comes home at night or the male superintendent
of schools. They select the family's social life. They represent the family
in aesthetic activities and in many unpaid civic activities of a refined
or charitable sort.

But this culture says not only that men and women do different

[56] See Margaret Mead, *Sex and Temperament in Three Primitive Societies,*
especially the Introduction and the Conclusion, for its discussion of the way in
which from "the whole arc of human potentialities" each culture selects different sectors for emphasis and on this basis builds the whole fabric of its life,
and of the varying ways in which the facts of biological sex differences are so
selected or ignored. (New York; Morrow, 1935.)

things; they *are* different kinds of people.[57] Men are stronger, bolder, less pure, less refined, more logical, more reasonable, more given to seeing things in the large, but at home needing coddling and reassurance, "like little boys." Women are more delicate, stronger in sympathy, understanding, and insight, less mechanically adept, more immersed in petty detail and in personalities, and given to "getting emotional over things."

Only to state these traditional cultural requirements is to suggest obvious points at which Middletown has departed from them in recent times. But the modifications have been in the kind of behavior sanctioned by the culture, not in the belief that men and women are different in character and temperament, and not in the ways in which they are believed to be different. The modifications of the behavior patterns themselves consist in tolerated exceptions rather than in the development of any clear alternatives meeting with group approval. For the individual, the result is frequently either that he is caught in a chaos of conflicting patterns, none of them wholly condemned, but no one of them clearly approved and free from confusion; or, where the group sanctions are clear in demanding a certain role of man or woman, the individual encounters cultural requirements with no immediate means of meeting them. A man is expected to have a job and provide a home for his family—but how, if he cannot get a job and the bank has, as a result, taken over his home? A woman should marry and rear children, but the community does nothing about providing her with a mate or enabling her to rear children if she must go out to earn the family income.

In general, it is the world of women's roles and personality emphases that has been offering these confusing alternatives in Middletown in recent decades, more than the men's world. The man's path has been the traditional single path of gainful employment. He may have been narrowing his role in the home as a parent, leaving child rearing more and more to his wife. He may have followed his central role of earning the family's living more intensively. He may have been under added strain in the boom years of boasted "killings" on the market and in business if his occupation was a humdrum one that involved no sudden wealth but rather a pedestrian continuance of the old pace. He may even have felt new inadequacies as a husband and lover in these days when grand passions are paraded nightly before Middle-

[57] See *Middletown*, pp. 116-20.

town in the movies. But the things a man is and does have remained fairly clearly and comfortably fixed.

As over against this relative fixity of the male world, the female world has exhibited more change and opened wider chasms of difficult choice. Woman's place has been less exclusively in the home. A large brood of children has become a less easy solution of women's problems in a world of small families and a sharply rising standard of living. Woman's traditional great dependence upon man has been less acceptable and more irksome. Careers for women have opened an alternative path diverging sharply—in its demands for male traits of drive, single-mindedness, the qualities associated with power—from the traditional woman's path in the home with its emphasis upon the feminine traits of gentleness, willingness to be led, and affection. Not only has the alternative path of independence, career, and power beckoned harder, but the traditional world of the affections has become more demanding as the franker modern world has emphasized more openly extreme femininity, including less passivity, more positive allurement, and a richly toned sexual response. The requirement that women remain youthful-looking into middle life is an emphasis on this feminine side that has set up further conflicts even within the traditional feminine path.

During the good years before the depression many of the ragged confusions in the demands of the culture on both sexes were only latent, for prosperity tended to make cultural tolerances wide and alternatives relatively easy, and one could make some sort of pretense at carrying several roles jointly if one chose. The depression, however, brought some of these latent conflicts sharply to the fore. And this sharpening of conflicts heightened for many the already shattering experience of sudden deprivation. The narrowed role of the male, so largely confined to moneymaking, took the brunt of the shock, with the general impairment of financial security and a quarter of the city's families forced onto relief. With the man's failure of role went, as shown above, inability to marry in many cases and the postponement of children. Men's and women's roles have in some cases been reversed, with the woman taking a job at whatever money she could earn and the man caring for household and children; all sorts of temperamental variations have appeared, with women showing perspective and steadfastness under stress and men sometimes dissolving into pettiness and personal rancor. In many cases the wife has had to support not only her own morale but that of her husband as well. One may hazard the guess that it is the world of male roles that has been under most pressure in Middletown in the depression, and that for women the years following 1929 may even in some cases have brought temporary easement of tensions. For an occasional woman the depression may have been almost a relief, akin to a time of serious illness in the family; a time when all worries as to alternative lines of action are laid aside and one does the single, obvious task immediately at hand. For other women, forced to work at earning the family's living, the heightened tolerance of such work on their part in the depression has eased something of the sharp emotional ambivalence often involved in such work in more normal times. It is significant that Lazarsfeld found in his study of Marienthal [58] that the women's world had been disrupted less than the men's world by unemployment: the men, cut adrift from their usual routine, lost much of their sense of time and dawdled helplessly and dully about the streets; while in the homes the women's world remained largely intact and the round of cooking, housecleaning, and mending became if anything more absorbing.

As noted at the outset of this chapter, it is regrettable that a close scrutiny of these subtle aspects of family life lay beyond the range of possibility in the brief scope of the present field work. The analysis of such changes would require a major study in itself.[59] In their outer aspects, the men's world and women's world of Middletown in 1935 were largely unchanged from the picture they had presented in 1925. The men were preoccupied with rebuilding the shaken fences of their job world, and the women were doing the familiar women's work of keeping house, rearing children, and going to clubs, with a modicum of church, charity, or civic work.

High-school girls parade their independence and many of them talk of "working" after they get out of school rather than "just marrying and settling down." As noted above, there has been a slow persistent growth in recognition of the normality of a girl's "wanting to do something with herself," stimulated by the growth of the local college population, by the increasing number of boys and girls "going East to

[58] *Op. cit.*, Ch. 5.
[59] The Middletown study of 1935-36 interrupted a detailed analysis of this problem in another community on which the investigator is engaged. Its findings will be published later.

college," and by the depression. But the cultural pattern dinned into Middletown's girls and women on every hand has no uncertainty as to their different and secondary role, and shows no appreciable change since 1925.[60] The women's pages in both local papers carry syndicated articles telling them: "Women the weaker sex? Yes, and we're glad of it!" "The wise wife takes a minor role and gives her husband the lead." And Dorothy Dix—the same face smiles at Middletown daily that appeared ten years ago—urges her persuasive wiles in "handling men." The old issue in Middletown bobbed up again in 1936 as to whether a woman should go on the school board, and it was again regarded as unnecessary and inexpedient to make such an innovation. Commenting on the suggestion, an editorial said: "It is possible that women will have an inning [two years hence]. But don't bet a nickel on it." "Women," as an editorial in 1932 observed, "accept general standards of values men have set. They take their views of life as a hand-me-down from men and model their demands on life by those of men." And Middletown men carry their superiority easily, and male editors even protest gallantly that "Our prosperity can't be quite all it is cracked up to be if it is placing a constantly increasing economic burden on women." As a matter of fact, Middletown men appear to distrust and not to know what to do with women not reared in the Dorothy Dix tradition, although every generalization of this sort is, of course, particularly hazardous and does not include exceptional individuals of both sexes.

Homemaking continues, as always in this culture, to be women's chief occupation. On April 1, 1930, when the Federal Census was taken, 86 per cent of Middletown's families had homemakers who were not gainfully employed on full- or part-time in or out of the home. Of the 1,710 gainfully employed homemakers, eight in each 100 were employed at work done in their own homes (laundering, sewing, etc.), twenty-nine at industrial jobs, twenty-one as servants and waitresses, seventeen at office work, eleven as saleswomen, ten in professional occupations (nursing, etc.), and four at various other unspecified occupations.[61] The fact that the period of prosperity during the late 1920's resulted nevertheless in a substantial increase in the pro-

[60] See *Middletown*, pp. 117-18.
[61] See the discussion of employed married women in Middletown in Ch. II.

portion of married women gainfully employed in Middletown in relation to the total number of women employed throws interesting light
on the values that go into Middletown's homemaking. Here, among
the very group who, according to Middletown's way of looking at
things, need least to do gainful work, we see in a time of widespread
prosperity the sharpest increase in women's work. If in many cases
the work of married women represents an escape from boredom and
uncongenial home duties, the need to supplement the husband's wage
scale and intermittent opportunities to work, or the sharp increase in
expenses involved in "putting the boy through college," in many other
cases it represents a car, electric refrigerator, a house with a furnace,
and other increments to the material side of living as Middletown's
families race to catch the rear platform of the speeding "American
standard of living."

A change of this sort suggests strongly that Middletown's traditions
regarding its "fundamental institution," the family, are in the grip of
a still stronger cultural pull, namely, a skyrocketing psychological
standard of living. If the single woman in Middletown works for
bread, it appears to be for more than bread alone that its married
women leave their homes to work.[62]

This suggests, in passing, an interesting commentary on the devious
ways of social change. One of the most strongly rooted of Middletown's values is that concerning the goodness of a wife's being a homemaker rather than a toiler in the rough outside world of men.
At every point this value is buttressed against change. The thing that
is changing it most is not changes from within its own coherently knit
ideologies—not changes in awareness of women's individual differences, capacities, and propensities, not changes in the conception as
to what "home" means or what the role of a "wife" or "mother" is—
but the pressure from without of a culturally stimulated rising psychological standard of living. In responding to the latter, wives [63] are
incidentally changing significantly the pattern of "marriage," "family
life," "wife," and "mother" in Middletown.

But in discussing the increase in gainfully employed married women
in Middletown, one point must be kept constantly in mind. When
one speaks of married women's working in Middletown one is talking

[62] See *Middletown,* pp. 27-30, for reasons for women's working.
[63] Like the one quoted on pp. 28-29 of *Middletown.*

almost exclusively of Middletown's working class and the lowest rungs of the business class. Among these last, the most economically inconspicuous members of the business class, the people to whom in a larger and more class-stratified community one might refer as its lower middle class, there is discernible some tendency for a young wife to retain a clerical job until her husband begins to get established. At the other extreme of the business class, there are one or two young wives of men so wealthy that there can be no question locally of their "having to work," and thus no reflection on their husbands' ability to "provide," who do such things as running a dairy with blooded stock as a plaything. But in a decade marked by an increasing independence of American women generally and a more general expectation by the daughters of the business group in this culture that they would work at something if possible in the period between school and marriage, the Middletown business class has stood firm in its deeply grooved habit of thought that the normal thing is for the husband to provide and for the wife to be provided for. There is more indulgent tolerance of a business-class girl's working between school and marriage, but when she marries "all that foolishness stops." Middletown's wives of businessmen are wives and mothers and, over and above these traditional activities, they maintain the local amenities and are endlessly busy with their flower gardens and study clubs, and with such civic and charitable activities as raising money for an oxygen tent to be given to the hospital, serving on charitable boards, and bringing concerts and "the finer things of life" to Middletown.

The routine, subservient nature of most of the occupations open to women in Middletown is a factor which makes it easy for the business-class Middletown husband, backed by the weight of his class culture, to stifle any fugitive aspirations of his wife to get a job, and for the woman herself to allow her restless ambition to "do something" to evaporate. Starting from the position that Middletown's business-class men do not like to have their wives do outside work regularly for pay, the alternative chances for engaging in gainful occupations confronting their wives may be roughly rated, according to the degree of resistance they are apt to evoke from their husbands and from their social class, somewhat as follows. The categories and totals are of necessity those of the Federal Census of Occupations for Middletown in 1920 and 1930, and, as noted below, these Census combinations involve some confusion for our purposes here; *and the totals include all females so engaged, regardless of their marital state:*

Class 1. Occupations not disapproved for a married woman of the business class, and likely even to enhance status:

<table>
<tr><td></td><td colspan="2">*Number of Middletown women so engaged*</td></tr>
<tr><td></td><td>*1920*</td><td>*1930*</td></tr>
<tr><td>Artists, sculptors, and teachers of art [64]............</td><td>5</td><td>4</td></tr>
</table>

Class 2. Occupations slightly disapproved for a married woman of the business class, but which may be engaged in with least loss of caste:

<table>
<tr><td></td><td colspan="2">*Number of Middletown women so engaged*</td></tr>
<tr><td></td><td>*1920*</td><td>*1930*</td></tr>
<tr><td>Authors, editors, and reporters [65]..................</td><td>5</td><td>5</td></tr>
<tr><td>College teachers.................................</td><td>2</td><td>21</td></tr>
<tr><td>Musicians and teachers of music [66]................</td><td>57</td><td>41</td></tr>
</table>

[64] Only "artists" and "sculptors" in Middletown belong in this Class 1. "Teachers of art" would go in Class 2 in Middletown's estimate. On the other hand, "authors," grouped by the Census with Class 2, would be placed by Middletown here in Class 1.

The investigator knows of no professional women sculptors and of only one woman author in Middletown. There may be one, or at most two, women who have sold paintings. So, if one shifts "teachers of art" to Class 2, Class 1 becomes virtually nonexistent in Middletown.

[65] See n. 64 regarding the Census group of "teachers of art," which belongs here, and likewise "authors," which belongs in Class 1. The Census group, "Authors, editors, and reporters," consists in Middletown very largely of only the last two of these three occupations. The "editors" probably are the part-time editors of the women's club pages in each of Middletown's two papers—the remaining two or three women being regularly employed reporters. It is important to note that in Middletown's eyes there is a world of difference between editing a weekly page summarizing the programs of women's clubs and being a "reporter." A married woman may do the former without serious disapproval (though such work is mildly questioned), whereas the latter is much more socially hazardous, belonging more properly in Class 3. There is a strident, knockabout quality in a reporter's life, involving contacts with all kinds of people in their shirt sleeves, that would tend to make this occupation for his wife distinctly distasteful to a Middletown businessman.

[66] A music teacher, if recognized locally as a gifted musician, would belong here by reason of the part-time, artistic-hobby nature of her work. A paid choir singer, harpist, or other occasionally paid musician of recognized ability would also belong here, whereas a musician in a movie theater or dance orchestra would fall below this into Class 3.

Class 3. Occupations which might be engaged in by a married woman of the business class, but which would nevertheless be regarded as queer or unnecessary for a married woman:

	Number of Middletown women so engaged	
	1920	1930
Lawyers, judges, justices........................	1	1
Physicians and surgeons........................	8	0
Public-school teachers [67]........................	178	309
Real-estate agents and officials [68]..............	7	3

Below these three lean groups one runs into a straggling list of occupations that are even more dubious socially for the wife of a businessman, before one comes to the final group of jobs as factory wage earners, hairdressers, servants, and similar occupations that would be completely impossible socially.

Class 4. Occupations highly disapproved for a married woman of the business class:

	Number of Middletown women so engaged	
	1920	1930
Actors and showmen [69]........................	2	15
Bankers, brokers, and moneylenders.............	4	1
Clergymen [70]	3	2
Clerical occupations [71]........................	594	805
Dentists	1	0
Insurance agents, managers, and officials [72].......	4	8
Hotel keepers and managers....................	3	3
Officials and inspectors (City, County, State, or United States)	2	7
Osteopaths	2	0
Photographers	9	7
Owners, managers or officials of trucking business, laundries, etc.	2	2
Restaurant, café, and lunchroom keeper [73].......	8	26
Retail clerks, saleswomen, and floorwalkers [74]....	393	443
Retail dealers [75]	46	44
Trained nurses	48	128
Wholesale dealers, importers, exporters	1	1

[67] Middletown adopted a new policy late in the depression of employing no married women in its public schools.

[68] If a married woman in the real-estate business did simply a straight buying and selling business, her working would fall out of Class 3 into the even less sanctioned group below. Her work would be in Class 3 only if it were done "on the side" as a hobby or were semiprofessional and artistic in that it involved designing, remodeling, and interior decoration. An interior decorator of obviously high ability and select clientele, were there one in Middletown, would go into Class 2.

[69] If a woman were the paid coach of the local little theater, she would fall in Class 1 above on the basis of the sporadic and artistic nature of her work,

Fortunately perhaps for them, most married women of the business class in Middletown, particularly those in their thirties and older, desire no gainful activity and regard themselves as fortunate in being limited to their orthodox pattern of home and social life. A business-class woman with a flair for creating and managing things, however, and either without children or disinclined to let them and the local round of "women's life" monopolize her time, often finds herself in a difficult position. She is chained to Middletown by her husband's job; she is usually compelled to be active and liked locally as an adjunct to her husband's business contacts, and this means in Middletown being "regular," as defined by the central traditions of the business-class mores; if she has no children, she finds an undue load of civic and club work thrown on her shoulders just because she "has more free time"; she often chafes at what she regards as the inconsequential nature of much of the women's routine; and she finds too few of her kind in a city of this size to enable her to develop specialized interest associations.

The depression, as suggested above, has eased somewhat the local business-class rigidity of attitude as regards married women's working. Women's work has received encouragement from the *sauve qui peut*

but women radio performers over the local station and vaudeville performers, who together probably account for the increase indicated above, would fall in this fourth class.

[70] These women are in minor working-class sects, *e.g.*, Spiritualists. The idea of a "lady preacher" is outlandish to Middletown's "nice people."

[71] Here one faces a twilight zone between business class and working class. Actually, a number of wives of business-class men work in offices. They tend, though, either to work in their husbands' small offices as their "helpers," or to be young women continuing to work for a brief period after marriage, or to be persons in the lowest range of the business class where it merges into the working class. In no case would the wife of a businessman over thirty with any pretentions at all to getting ahead socially engage in such work.

[72] This, even more than real estate, is straight "business," and Middletown businessmen dislike their wives to be so engaged.

[73] This again would fall in Class 3 if it were a decidedly "smart" tearoom run by a married woman but in which she did no systematic work other than keep a general oversight over things by dropping in for an hour every day or so.

[74] These occupations are somewhat akin to "Clerical occupations" above, though slightly less desirable because of the exposure of the personnel to a wider contact with the miscellaneous general public.

[75] This type of work would fall in Class 3 above if the shop were an arty specialty shop in the dress, antique, or perhaps confectionery fields and were managed as a part-time plaything with a paid staff doing the actual selling. There are two dress shops of this sort now in Middletown and one small lending library and bookshop.

experience of the depression. These have been no years in which to be too "choosy." Parents have had to struggle to keep their children in college, families have been threatened with losing the home on which they had embarked overexpansively in 1928-29, and similar raw emergencies have had to be faced. Women who "thought I would never go to work" have grasped at small ways of bolstering the family income, and the emergency has made the community temporarily tolerant. While the old pattern will return with even moderate prosperity, more business-class mothers are saying today that they want their daughters "to learn to do something, just in case—" and the idea of a married woman's working is not so completely frowned upon.

Homemaking goes forward in Middletown in houses which are older on the average today than they were in 1925. For, during the six years that followed 1929, new building almost disappeared.[76] New residential construction fell off abruptly in dollar cost at the very outset of the depression in 1930 to only 13 per cent of its volume in 1928; in the three years 1932-34 it fell to between 2 and 3 per cent; and even in 1935 it rose to only about 9 per cent of the 1928 volume. Meanwhile, the city's population increased between 1928 and the peak population of 1931-32 by 14 per cent. The total residential construction for the entire six depression years 1930-35 aggregated only a little more than one-third of the construction in either 1927 or 1928. In view of the fact that a large share of Middletown's families normally are forced to utilize dwellings that would be considered "too old and inconvenient" to be tolerable instruments for modern living by the better-off families of Middletown, this means that this heavy share of equipment, obsolete in terms of Middletown's demands, has grown six years older with practically no offsetting replacement. For, according to the local F.E.R.A. Real Property Inventory,[77] made in January, February,

[76] See Table 18 in Appendix III.
[77] See Table 19 in Appendix III.
All data presented here from this as yet unpublished survey are taken from the tables prepared by the local F.E.R.A. staff. While these Federal-sponsored local housing surveys are subject to some error owing to the inexperienced character of the staffs employed, the Middletown survey is believed to represent the local situation with approximate accuracy.
In the data that follow from this F.E.R.A. survey, the terms "structure" and "unit" are used continually: The first ("structure") refers to entire buildings, while the latter ("units") refers to a separate family's quarters. Thus there are several "units" in a single apartment "structure," two units in a single family house with a second light-housekeeping unit let to strangers, etc.

and March, 1935, less than one in every ten dwellings in Middletown had been built within ten years prior to 1935, despite a 27 per cent growth in the city's population; six in every ten are thirty years old or older, four in ten are forty years old or older, while nearly one in every four antedates the coming of the gas boom to the small town of less than 10,000 persons in 1885.[78]

Eighty per cent of Middletown's families live in single-family detached houses, the characteristic midland house set in its own "yard." Thirteen per cent more live in single-family semidetached or attached houses or in two- to four-family houses; 4 per cent are in flats over stores, and less than 3 per cent in apartments.[79]

When one turns to length of occupancy of these dwellings at the time of the survey early in 1935, one is struck by the fact that Middletown is composed of two sharply different worlds as regards the permanency of this thing called a "home." While one knows in general that renters maintain briefer tenures than owners, and while depression evictions with one family in four on relief had influenced somewhat the mobility even of owners and much more sharply that of tenants, the actual difference between the two groups not only represents a chronic split in the city's population but suggests two patterns of organization of living.[80] Only 3.8 per cent of the owners had been in their homes less than a year, as against 42.2 per cent of the renters; 10.2 per cent of the owners had moved within less than three years, as against 76.2 per cent of the renters; while 82.2 per cent of the owners had been in their homes five or more years, as against only 11.6 per cent of the renters.

A high or a low rate of residential mobility and the existence of such high differentials as the above between two parts of the same com-

[78] As in most small American cities, these residential structures are nearly all built of wood. Over 93 per cent are of wooden construction, another 2 per cent of stucco, 4 per cent (including a heavy percentage of downtown stores with flats above them) are built of brick, while only 22 of the 11,039 structures (one-fifth of one per cent) are of stone.

Even Middletown's apartments are low structures of two and three stories, and the city's residential profile accordingly presents the low sky line characteristic of the small Middle Western city: Sixty in each 100 of the residential buildings are of one story, 39 are two-storied, and only one in each 100 rises to three stories.

[79] See Table 20 in Appendix III.

[80] See Table 21 in Appendix III.

munity suggest deep-lying implications, as yet too little studied, both for the individual personality and for neighborhood and community organization. There may, for instance, be distinct elements of survival value to the individual, living in a culture characterized by rapid change, in his learning to "travel light" and to put on and off the physical paraphernalia of living as readily as he does his coat. But this advantage may be counterweighted by the marked impairment of those elements in social organization in a democratic culture which depend heavily upon the individual's feeling himself to be rooted in the subsoil of neighborhood and community and therefore personally committed to participating in terms of *its* problems and *its* future.[81] Here one might conceivably look for a part of the cause of the "civic indifference" for which Middletown's prosperous, home-owning business and civic leaders so often condemn the working (and heavily renting) class "across the tracks."[82] On the personality side, one of man's deepest emotional needs is for a sense of "belonging." While some adults may lull this need through extreme preoccupation with work or variety of interests, even active adults ordinarily shun the experience of being socially "lost in the shuffle," while with the young and the elderly the need to belong to their world is particularly marked. Dr. James Plant has emphasized the constant and urgent need in the child for an answer to the fundamental question, "Who

[81] One of the major problems of urban living, apparently increasing progressively as one approaches the metropolitan community, is this weakening of personal identification with neighborhood and community ties. At the extreme, in the metropolitan community, one tends to witness a society built of individual bricks largely unbound together by the binding mortar of common community purposes. People are apt to pride themselves on the fact that they have freed themselves from the localisms involved in loyalty to Rotary, to church and Ladies' Aid, to civic drives, and to neighborhood that they regard as characterizing the "small town Babbitt." In so far as this "freedom" reduces the individual to a social atom related to his fellows chiefly by their common pursuit of private gain under the impersonal price system, there is ample basis for questioning whether the freedom may not represent an acute social pathology rather than a gain. The investigator has suggested elsewhere the likeness of New York City in the above respects to a Western boom town, full of the clatter that accompanies physical growth, but socially anarchistic and devoid of the binding mutual loyalties that derive from settled abode and many shared common purposes. See "Manhattan Boom Town," *Survey Graphic,* October 1, 1932.

[82] See *Middletown,* p. 109, for limited but suggestive data on the relatively higher rate of mobility of Middletown's working class than of its business class.

am I?"—an answer patently related to the child's established relationships in the neighborhood and community.[83]

It is difficult to relate to their true antecedents the various manifestations of personality disorganization sometimes found in families
with a more than average degree of residential mobility; for while
some of the causal elements may lie in the sheer fact of the repeated
tearing up of the place roots which the personality continuously seeks
to send down into the social subsoil on which it lives, other causes
are inherent in the fact that the persons and families involved are not
sufficiently integrated as members of their culture to render frequent
moving unnecessary. Obviously, differences in residential mobility
arise both from the kind of person one is and from the culture im-
pinging upon one. American expansion has emphasized mobility; and,
as a frequently necessary accompaniment of "enterprise" and "improving one's lot," mobility itself carries a more honorific connotation than
it does in some other cultures.[84] Among the business class in such a
culture, "moving" is often a natural and highly approved accompaniment of a rising income and expanding opportunity. But this same
American culture presents, notably through its economic institutions,
different opportunities to different parts of its population to engage
in this honorific sort of residential mobility associated with rising income. And the effect upon the individual personality and upon neighborhood and community organization of enforced moves probably

[83] See his paper on "Mental Hygiene Aspects of the Family" in *The Family*
for April, May, and June, 1932.

[84] There is, for instance, in Middletown's culture little of the suspicion of the
stranger as a potentially dangerous person, so frequently met with in primitive
groups—though, as noted in Ch. XII, if the stranger comes from overseas,
particularly if he is an Oriental or does not speak English well, he tends to be
mistrusted in Middletown.

And there is not the clinging place-conservatism characteristic of many old-
world peasant peoples. C. F. Atkinson, for instance, cites, in a footnote accompanying his translation of Spengler's *The Decline of the West,* a French peasant
family that has occupied the same farm since the ninth century. Speaking of
the outlook of such a man, Spengler says: "He has sat on his glebe from
primeval times, or has fastened his clutch in it, to adhere to it with his blood.
He is rooted in it as the descendant of his forbears and as the forbear of future
descendants. *His* house, *his* property, means, here, not the temporary connexion
of person and thing for a brief span of years, but an enduring and inward union
of *eternal* land and *eternal* blood." (Vol. II, p. 104.) The farmers in Middletown's county may feel a weak dilution of this sentiment, but to most Middletown people the French farmer's devotion to the glebe of his ancestors would
seem a fine, loyal sentiment but rather unenterprising.

tends to be markedly different from that of the optional, socially approved removals associated with a family's progress "upwards" in the
world.

The mobility of both renters and owners in Middletown during the
five years preceding early 1935 was markedly increased by the depression. Among the renters, the situation involved simply the old familiar
formula: No job = No money for rent = Eviction. The directness
of operation of this formula was, however, somewhat slowed down by
the lenience of many landlords, in part dictated by their desire to have
their properties occupied by trusted tenants rather than standing idle.[85]
Among the owners mortgage foreclosures increased sharply.[86] A local
real-estate man and the head of a leading building-and-loan company
agreed in estimating that the annual total of foreclosures rose from
"ten or less in 1928 to more than ten times that number" in 1934.[87] The
first properties to go were the homes valued at less than $6,000; these
were the homes bought in the good days by working-class families,
and, as a banker laconically expressed it, "These people had no savings
as shock absorbers: the house had taken all they could scrape together
for initial payments." About 1,000 mortgages were taken over by the
Home Owners' Loan Corporation between January 1, 1934, and June,
1935.[88] The Middletown Real Estate Board estimates that 80 per cent

[85] See n. 17 in Ch. IV.
An editorial captioned "Pass the Hat for Landlords," early in 1933, stated
that "The greatest single class of charity givers in Middletown and in other
cities is the owners of rental dwellings. . . . There are hundreds of occupied
dwellings for which the owners are receiving little or no income. Some owners
have maintained families in these houses for two or three years without receiving anything in the way of rent, or very little."

[86] Only 37 per cent of the owner-occupied dwelling units were owned free of
mortgage at the time of the F.E.R.A. Real Property Inventory in 1935. Some
idea of the pressure of the depression mortgage stringency upon local owners
may be glimpsed from the index numbers for loans on property and total
dollar loans on property by a leading local building-and-loan agency, presented
in Table 22 in Appendix III. This table shows that the number of loans (on a
base of 100 in 1926) stood at 107 in 1928 and fell to 4 in 1932.

[87] The total increased markedly in the early months of 1932, to be checked
on September 1 of that year by an agreement of local loan companies, on request from Washington, to halt foreclosures pending the opening of home-loan
banks. The 1933 total dropped back toward that of 1930 and 1931, only to
rise to over 100 in 1934, when it was reported that "the building and loans
tightened up" in Middletown.

[88] There has been much dissatisfaction in Middletown over the H.O.L.C.
The banks have maintained an ambivalent attitude toward it. Bankers have
resented it as a phase of government interference with private business, because,

of these would have been lost to the owners if this assistance had not been available. Tax delinquencies, particularly on vacant lots originally purchased for speculative purposes, rose steeply in number. By 1933 the local newspapers were carrying two and a half pages of public advertisements of properties with tax delinquencies for sale, aggregating as many as 2,000 parcels in a single year.

These foreclosures and sales for tax delinquencies were in part a result of overextension in the happy days of the 1920's. These people, close to the tradition of farm competence, need little urging to own their homes—if they can manage it. And during the 1920's they were heavily urged to this end, directly by real-estate promoters and indirectly by the pressure of local institutional factors making building for rental purposes a less desirable investment than formerly. Local press editorials quoted in the 1925 study stated that "It is almost impossible to induce anybody to construct rental houses here because it is difficult to obtain a reasonable percentage of profit. . . . It is doubtful if 10 per cent of the new homes erected in [Middletown] last year [1923] were built for rental purposes." [89] Under the pressure of such conditions, the percentage of families renting their homes had dropped from 65 per cent in 1900 to 54 per cent in 1920, according to the Federal Census, and in April, 1930, when the new Census was taken, the percentage had dropped further to 49. Home ownership continued to grow until the peak was reached in July, 1931. Middletown families were overextended as regards home and vacant-lot ownership when the depression storm broke, and many bargain hunters continued in the market even after 1929. "It was our fault," says a real-estate man, "for overselling them, and the banks' fault for overlending. Everybody was buying a better home than he could afford." "Buy lots," had urged an editorial in 1929, pointing to the experience of local buyers who had seen their real estate "rise tenfold in value over the past ten years"; and even in March, 1931, the editor urged, "Now is the time

as one of them expressed it: "It gives people false ideas about their right to get loans. Any loan that's a justifiable risk can be financed through our banks." Middletown's banks are said locally to have sabotaged the H.O.L.C., and yet, as one banker remarked with a smile, "We all tried to palm off our lemons on it." (The operation of the H.O.L.C. in Middletown is reported to have placed a million and three-quarter dollars in the financial institutions of the city.)

Under these circumstances, the difficulty experienced by many hard-pressed home owners in securing H.O.L.C. loans is understandable.

[89] See *Middletown*, pp. 106-09.

to buy real estate because maybe tomorrow prices will go up." By late 1931, houses had depreciated below their purchase price, to their loan value or less, and credit sources for carrying property had diminished to a trickle of about a quarter of the 1928 stream.[90] Repossessions and foreclosures for taxes were mounting, and at the time of the F.E.R.A. housing survey in the early months of 1935, the percentage of renters had climbed again from the low of 49 in April, 1930, to about 54 per cent. This increase in renting was further stimulated by the heavy decline in rents.[91] There was a landslide into the lower-rent brackets during the depression: The median monthly rental was almost halved between 1930 and January, 1935, dropping from $25.27 to $14.45. The share of total rentals under $15 a month rose from 10 per cent to 53 per cent, and rentals of $30 a month and over fell from 32 per cent to 11 per cent. It was this situation, coupled with the fact that, as reported in the local press, "The depression has created a big class of 'dead beat' renters who were shown consideration when they were out of work and who refuse to pay rent when they have work," that led an editorial to characterize the local landlord as "the forgotten man." Rentals in the first three months of 1935 [92] ranged from less than $5 monthly (108 units) to $100 (only one unit), with 71 per cent of the city's rents below $20, and only 3 per cent at $40 a month or more. As over against this rent scale, the 5,511 owner-occupied units ranged in value from under $1,000 (563 units) to $20,000 or over (21 units) with the median value at $2,600. Thirty-six per cent of these owner-occupied dwellings were valued at under $2,000, 59 per cent at under $3,000, 79 per cent at under $4,000, only 6.5 per cent at $6,000 or over, and less than 2 per cent at $10,000 and over.

When the jaws of the depression nutcrackers began to squeeze, some families fled back to the farm. This is a natural move for a population whose working class is habitually heavily recruited from the open country. Part of Middletown's sharp growth in population after 1925 is directly traceable to the mounting totals of farm fore-closures, which reached a high point in 1928 and continued high until

[90] See Table 22 in Appendix III.

[91] See Table 23 in Appendix III.

[92] These rental figures are for the 6,393 occupied rental units. They omit 524 vacant units and 614 light-housekeeping units (576 of the latter being occupied). Eighty-seven per cent of the light-housekeeping units rent for $5 to $24, with the largest single group in the $10 to $14 class; and the remaining 13 per cent include 5 per cent under $5 and 8 per cent in the $25 to $40 class.

popular indignation and Federal aid slowed up foreclosures late in the depression. As early as 1930, the tide began running back toward the farm, and small-farm acreage was in demand. As one real-estate man described this movement: "In 1930 we had a six-months wave of farm enthusiasm. Three per cent of Middletown tried to go, one per cent went, and the bulk of those who went found it an unprofitable venture."[93] The exodus continued throughout the depression. The Federal Farm Census of January 1, 1935, showed 1,761 persons living on farms in Middletown's county who had not been living on farms five years earlier, though the fact that the net farm population of the county had increased over this five-year period by only seven persons suggests a balancing movement of defeated farmers away from the county's farms. In 1934-35 fear of inflation sent business and professional folk in increasing numbers into the depressed farm market, not for residential purposes but as an investment, and by June, 1935, the cream was reported to have been skimmed off the local farm market.

The depression brought a sharp increase in a type of home unnatural to Middletown,[94] namely, light housekeeping. In the main, these units did not appear in the well-to-do or in the very poor sections, but in the medium-priced homes, where people pinched-off part of their homes for a second family in order to avoid enforced moving. The 1935 Real Property Inventory found 614 of these units (thirty-eight of them vacant), or 4.7 per cent of Middletown's total dwelling units, as against a total estimated by the real-estate man who directed the Inventory to have been between one to two hundred in the 1920's.

The doubling up of families in the same quarters reached its peak in 1933, and by early 1935 was considerably reduced. At the latter date, however, in addition to the homes accommodating 576 occupied light-housekeeping units, 544 of Middletown's homes (4.4 per cent of Middletown's 12,480 occupied dwelling units) still had one or more extra

[93] These percentages are very rough, not being based on anything more than the speaker's general impression.

[94] Though Middletown still clings strongly to the idea that a home should be a separate house in its own yard, apartments have become a much more marked, though still minor, feature of the city's housing since 1925. (See *Middletown*, p. 93, n. 2.) In the spring of 1929 alone, two large apartment units of 31 and 35 apartments respectively were completed. There were in all, 338 dwelling units in the city's apartment buildings in 1935, or, as noted above, a total of 2.6 per cent of all dwelling units in the city. All are in low two- and three-story "walk-up" buildings. In addition Middletown had 529 flats over stores in 1935.

families temporarily doubling up with the regular occupants.[95] In-
terestingly enough, the owning families had slightly more extra families in with them than did renters, 5 per cent of the former having
one or more extra families with them, as against 3.7 per cent of the
latter.[96] One reason for this is suggested by Table 24,[97] which shows
more than twice as high a percentage (18.3 per cent) of families in
rented quarters living under "crowded" and "overcrowded" conditions
(more than one person per room) than was the case among families
owning their own homes (8.0 per cent); while nearly three-fourths of
the owners lived in "spacious" or "very spacious" quarters (not more
than three-fourths of a person per room), as over against only a little
more than half of the renters. In other words, there was less spare room
among the renters than among the owners. The tendency toward
smaller houses sacrificing the earlier "parlor" and "spare bedroom"
was noted in the 1925 study.[98] Middletown's median dwelling unit in
1935 had five rooms.[99] The compactness of these homes was augmented
by the fact that the Census of April 1, 1930, revealed eleven in each
hundred Middletown families as having one or more lodgers—seven
in each hundred of them having only one lodger, and four in each
hundred having two or more.

Living in buildings more than 40 per cent of which are forty to
seventy-five years old and another 35 per cent twenty to forty years old,
Middletown carries on the arts and techniques of homemaking in a
wide variety of ways. Middletown houses more than forty years old
date back to the time when a house was simply a box pierced with
doors and windows, heated by a stove, and drawing water from a
pump or cistern.[100] Most of the things that make houses and housekeeping "modern" have come to Middletown's homes since 1890, including such things as central heating, automatic heating with thermo-
static control, electricity, automatic refrigeration, running water, and

[95] Only 25 of the 544 units had two or more of these temporary extra families.
[96] Eighty-eight per cent of the renters having extra families with them were
in houses renting for less than $25 a month, and 95 per cent of the owners
having extra families were in homes valued at less than $5,000.
[97] See Appendix III for this table.
[98] See *Middletown*, pp. 98-99.
[99] This figure is for dwelling units, *not* structures. Of all dwelling units,
1.1 per cent had one room; 4.0 per cent two; 7.4 per cent three; 15.8 per cent
four; 33.8 per cent five; 18.6 per cent six; 10.3 per cent seven; and 9.0 per cent
eight or more.
[100] See *Middletown*, p. 95, n. 7.

modern plumbing. Today, as in 1925,[101] primitive and modern ways jostle each other in the homes along Middletown's streets, and even as regards different processes within the single home. One understands more sharply today than ever "the backward art of spending money" [102] as one lifts off the roofs of Middletown's homes. One looks down upon a ragged array of physical facilities for meeting such basic human needs as keeping clean, sanitation, cooking, keeping warm, and securing artificial light. A detailed analysis of the facilities serving each of these needs is given for owned homes and for rented homes on different income levels in Tables 25-31 in Appendix III. If only that type of facility which Middletown regards as least adequate and modern is selected from these tables one gets the following picture:

Type of facility	Per cent of all Middletown families using	Per cent of all users who own their homes	Per cent of all users who rent their homes	Per cent of all users who rent for less than $15 monthly or live in homes valued under $2,000
No running water in house [103]	13	42	58	92
No bathtub [104]	37	33	67	85
No refrigeration	10	37	63	80
Outdoor privy toilet only [105]	18	40	60	95
Kerosene or candle lighting [106]	4	26	74	96
Kerosene, gasoline, coal or wood for cooking [107]	39	32	68	80
Heating by stove	55	35	65	75

[101] See *Middletown*, pp. 174-79.

[102] See Wesley C. Mitchell's excellent paper under that title in the *American Economic Review* for June, 1912.

[103] Many of these houses not piped for water undoubtedly have a hydrant in the yard.

[104] Fifty-six per cent of all Middletown families have access to one or more baths not shared by other families and 7 per cent more share baths with other families.

[105] Seventy-three per cent of all Middletown families have use of one or more modern flush toilets unshared with other families.

[106] Ninety-six per cent of Middletown families have electric lighting. The index of the number of residential users of electricity in the entire county (of whom Middletown users constitute about nine in every ten) fell off about 5 points from the 1929 level by 1932-33 and then rose sharply by 10 points in 1934 to about 5 points above the 1929 level. The recovery was chiefly in response to a rate reduction of about 20 per cent. The rural rate of recovery paralleled that of the city, due probably in part to Federal crop payments to farmers.

[107] Some indication of the tendency to slide down the convenience scale to

Here the world of the renters—61 per cent of whom had moved within less than two years as against only 7 per cent of the owners—stands out in sharp contrast to the world of the homeowners; for 60-75 per cent of each of these most antiquated homemaking facilities are in rented homes. Likewise, 75-95 per cent of each of these primitive facilities are in the homes of people with low incomes.

None of these items, taken alone, is of commanding importance. Family life has gone on for thousands of years without bathtubs, central heating, and indoor running water; and even the high probability that many of these antiquated facilities overlap in the same under-privileged homes at the bottom of the economic scale need not shock one. The importance of such primitive living side by side in the same city with the most convenient and efficient modern facilities for performing the same functions lies in the fact that it epitomizes Middletown's culture and that culture's theory of social change. The culture is complacent in the face of such widening disparities which exist in every department of its living. If people are without running water and women still must cook over sizzling coal and wood cookstoves with the temperature outside at 90° in the summer, or if they use kerosene or gasoline stoves that occasionally blow up or set the house afire—these things are all ultimately, to Middletown, these people's own fault. The community itself accepts no responsibility for reducing these cultural lags, for in the greatest of all nations everybody will eventually have anything he really wants hard enough to work for. Middletown, like Malthus nearly one hundred and fifty years before, rests back comfortably on such manifest truths as the following:

"To remove the wants of the lower classes of society is indeed an ardu-ous task. The truth is that the pressure of distress on this part of a com-munity is an evil so deeply seated that no human ingenuity can reach it. . . . No possible contributions or sacrifices of the rich, particularly in money, could for any time prevent the recurrence of distress among the lower members of society, whoever they were. . . . Hard as it may appear in individual instances, dependent poverty ought to be held disgraceful. Such a stimulus seems to be absolutely necessary to promote the happiness of the great mass of mankind; and every general attempt to weaken this

---

cheaper cooking fuels in the depression is suggested by the fact that, while the structures served with running water fell off from a base of 100 in 1929 to only 95.2 in 1932 and rose slowly thereafter to 96.0 in 1933 and 97.9 in 1934, dwelling units metered for gas dropped from 100.0 in 1929 to 93.1 in 1932 and on further to 85.1 in 1933, and in 1934 still lagged at 88.7.

stimulus, however benevolent its apparent intention, will always defeat its own purpose. . . . [And finally, the saving loophole for the individual and for the society.] Fortunately for [Middletown—Malthus said "for England"], a spirit of independence still remains among the peasantry.[108]

Meanwhile, as technology adds more and more "improved modern ways," the distance between what different sections of Middletown's population do becomes wider. Multiple choices present themselves where fifty years ago there was often only one "right way" to do a given thing. In a world where everybody heated his house by a stove and nobody had running hot and cold water, the lack of these things prompted no social differences, no sense of inadequacy on the part of the family that could "afford" nothing better, no caustic remarks by wife and children about the husband's meager wages. In such widening disparities in the performance of man's age-old tasks lies one of the most characteristic sources of minor tension in Middletown's culture.[109]

At the time of the F.E.R.A. Real Property Inventory early in 1935, 17 per cent of Middletown's residential structures were listed as "in need of major repairs" and 3 per cent more as "unfit for use." Permits for residential additions, alterations, and repairs fell off by three-fourths between 1929 and 1933. In 1931, in the still hopefully "around-the-corner" days, the local Chamber of Commerce whipped up a home-modernization campaign that attracted national attention as the "[Middletown] plan" for "licking the depression." But deeper economic forces were at work, the building-and-loan companies tightened up to the extent of a virtual cessation of loans in 1932,[110] and repairs thereafter fell off sharply. Building revival started late in 1934 with a slow increase in long overdue repainting, reshingling, and repairs. By June, 1935, there was an actual shortage of painters, new construction was slowly reviving, and since January rents (which had fallen off by a third from 1929) had been increased by 25 per cent.

In these homes of varying degrees of modernity the Middletown housewife customarily does her own work. Only about four homes in every 100 have one or more household servants,[111] and the ratio of

108 *An Essay on the Principle of Population* (1st ed., 1798), Ch. V.
109 See *Middletown,* pp. 174-78.
110 See Table 22 in Appendix III.
111 Based on the "Servants" and "Housekeepers and stewards" classifications in the Federal Census of Occupations, with a deduction of 20 per cent for those

families to total "Servants" and "Housekeepers and stewards" remained identical in 1920 and 1930.[112] The 1925 study suggested a decline in the servant habit.[113] The standstill in Middletown in the 1920's may reflect both prosperity and the pressure of the emerging self-conscious upper class in the expensive new subdivisions in the West End. It is not unlikely that living in a homogeneous community of expensive homes may make the pressure for a servant stronger than when the same people lived scattered throughout the city. During the depression there is reported to have been a marked decrease in the number of families with servants. But the depressing effect of the years 1929-35 upon wages and other available jobs, coupled with the strong sentiment with reviving good times to give men the first chance at jobs, may conceivably mean as business-class incomes increase a reversal of the long-term trend and a rising number of servants.

Middletown apparently "ate out" more during the 1920's, for the number of "Restaurant, café, and lunchroom keepers," according to the Census, rose by 80 per cent (from 49 to 88) between 1920 and 1930, and waiters by 75 per cent (from 85 to 149), while the city's population rose by only 27 per cent. While the growth of a city to close to the 50,000 class is probably normally accompanied by a relative increase in transients, e.g., traveling men, people visiting the city as a shopping center, etc., the above increases in persons engaged in serving commercial meals also reflects undoubtedly a growth in the

employed in these two groups estimated to be employed in hotels and restaurants. (The "Servants" and "Housekeepers and stewards" employed in hotels and restaurants are not separated out by the Census for cities of Middletown's size. The above estimated deduction of 20 per cent covering these hotel and restaurant workers in Middletown has been arbitrarily set by the writers at a somewhat lower per cent than that which maintains in two similar cities of twice Middletown's size in the state, for which Census breakdowns are available. The lower per cent for Middletown is based on the assumption that the share of total persons employed in these occupations in hotels and restaurants increases as the size of cities increases.)

"Charwomen and cleaners" (43 in 1920 and 20 in 1930) and "Launderers and laundresses (not in laundry)" (129 in 1920 and 68 in 1930) are not included here in the number of Middletown's servants.

[112] Actually the number of "Servants" and "Housekeepers and stewards" rose by 39 per cent between the two Censuses, as against only a 27 per cent rise in population. On this basis, the number of families per servant fell from 20.1 in 1920 to 19.0 in 1930, but if one allows but one cook for each of the 39 new restaurants added in the decade, the number of families per servant becomes 20.2.

[113] See Middletown, pp. 169-72, especially n. 21 which shows trends for Middletown's state and for the United States. It should be noted that only the Census classification "Servants" was used in these earlier figures.

eating-out habit by local people. The same factors that have made for the further rise of apartment living in Middletown since 1920 operate also to increase the business of commercial eating places. The restaurant is apparently displacing the boarding house in Middletown, for the number of "Boarding and lodging house keepers" declined in the 1920's from 116 to 43. Middletown is growing up, and along with urban growth in our culture go better facilities for caring for the marginal population of single persons who are not members of families.

Middletown housewives were buying in the 1920's more of their clothes ready-made. The number of "Dressmakers and seamstresses (not in factory)," fell between 1920 and 1930, according to the Census, from 107 to 60, the number of "Tailors and tailoresses" from 40 to 29, and the number of "Milliners and millinery dealers" from 28 to 14.[114] But the local agent for the Singer sewing machine states that, while pre-depression sales involved for the most part the trading in of old machines for new models, current purchases involve relatively more sales to new users: "People are buying machines now who never dreamed of sewing before." [115]

Commercial pressure for "correct" clothing has struggled ahead

[114] These last are classified by the Census under "Manufacturing and Mechanical Industries." As such they represent not retail selling personnel but largely women engaged in stores or in their own homes in *trimming* hats. The coming in the 1920's of the felt cloche has reduced the amount of trimming of hats to order and has tended to encourage the purchase of ready-to-wear hats.

[115] The Singer agent reports the following somewhat fragmentary data on sales through the Middletown agency:

Year	Sales	Repossessions	Net sales
1928	173	0	173
1932	152	31	121
1933	194	86	108
1934	—	"Repossessions low"	115
1935 (to June 20)	90	"Repossessions low"	

These figures for this one agency make a decidedly better showing than do the national totals for all companies. The Census of Manufactures reports the following numbers of complete sewing machines of the household type sold (excluding separate sales of attachments):

Year	Number sold	Index numbers
1929	669,027	100.0
1933	128,008	19.1
1935	284,124	42.5

against the tide of the depression.[116] Each year the leading merchants have given cooperative style shows and, since 1925, these have been extended to include men's clothing. The same crowds of wilted people wearing shoes half-soled for thirty-nine cents were thrilling in 1935 to the parade of Grecian sandals from a local "classy boot shop" and to crisp white mess jackets for men's evening wear; [117] and the completion of the new municipal swimming pool had added to the June, 1935, show as "the treat of the evening" "a parade of bathing beauties in swimming suits of every color with and without backs." The depression is said to have lessened somewhat the competition in clothing. "There has been less pretentiousness in dress," according to a local editor. "Nobody has been buying clothes," remarked a businessman. But remarks like these apply much more to the parental world than they do to the children of high-school and college age. The detailed newspaper descriptions of gowns worn at the sorority dances throughout the depression might have been lifted verbatim, save for certain fashion changes, from the papers of 1925.

Along with the styling up of clothing in the 1920's, went an increase in commercial hairdressing. The Census for 1930 shows a 64 per cent increase in "Barbers, hairdressers, and manicurists" over 1920, as compared with the 27 per cent increase in population. As noted elsewhere, a number of women's hairdressing shops have sprung up in the homes over town during the depression. These little shops advertise "Special permanent waves—75¢" in the classified sections of the newspapers.[118]

While the number of persons occupied as "Launderers and laundresses (not in laundries)" was being halved in the 1920's, falling from 129 to 68, Middletown was also learning to send its washing "out." The dollar volume of business at an old-established, representative, local commercial laundry rose by two-thirds between 1923 and 1929.[119] The index for this company's business, uncorrected for price changes, stood at 82.1 in 1923, at 100.0 in 1926, and at 136.1 in 1929; by 1933 it

[116] See Table 3 and the discussion in Chapter II of the volume of retail sales of clothing in Middletown in 1929 and 1933.

[117] See *Middletown,* p. 82, n. 18.

[118] *Recent Social Trends* (p. 900) shows a sharp rise all through the 1920's in the index (in undeflated dollars) of production of "Perfumes, cosmetics, and toilet preparations": from 49.6 in 1919; to 61.8 in 1921; 80.2 in 1923; 100.0 in 1925; 121.6 in 1927; to 142.3 in 1929. In 1930 the dollar volume of output rose a further 2 per cent.

[119] See Table 32 in Appendix III.

had fallen off to 53.5; it rose 10 points in 1934; and in 1935, according to the manager, was "continuing the trend upward begun in 1934." [120] According to the same source, commercial laundry service was one of the last items of family expenditure affected by the depression and will probably lag behind other items in picking up with better times. The further exit of depression laundering from the home, he stated, will follow upon the reemployment of local women in the city's industrial plants.

It was not possible to secure separate figures for residential telephones since 1925, but the index numbers for all instruments in use in Middletown and a six-mile radius around the city, after rising from a base of 100 in 1926 to 113.3 in 1929, sagged to 82.1 in the bottom year, 1933, and by mid-1936 had recovered only to 97.3.[121] In view of the growth of the city by nearly one-third between 1925 and 1936, this represents a decided shrinkage in ease of social contacts as well as convenience for Middletown families.

When Middletown people are asked whether family life in Middletown has changed since 1925, the answer is in the negative. It is only as one begins to break this broad question into many smaller questions that one begins to elicit even any uncertainty as to whether the old ways still stand unchanged; whether, for instance, any of the depression modifications of men's roles and women's roles will remain, or in what situations the gap between those in middle life and their children in their late teens has widened, with the widespread collapse of adult plans and the undisguised helpless dismay of the parental generation, and where more mutual understanding has resulted. But Middletown is not given to pondering such things. Changes there have been in the material shell of family living—in the houses people live in and how often they move, in the age of the family car, and in such things as the colleges to which people can afford to send their children. But personal relationships, particularly the close relationships within the family, are toughly resistant to change from without. As Lazarsfeld points out in the case of Marienthal,[122] "Personal relations

[120] *Recent Social Trends* (p. 900) shows a steady rise in the power laundry business in the United States between 1925 and 1929. The index (in undeflated dollars) stood at 100.0 in 1925, 122.1 in 1927 and 142.4 in 1929.
[121] See Table 33 in Appendix III.
[122] *Op. cit.,* p. 77.

have exhibited a greater capacity for resistance to disintegration than have relations to one's work and to other social institutions."

In fact, Middletown itself believes, not without some justification, that many families have drawn closer together and "found" themselves in the depression. It is just as certainly true that in yet other families, the depression has precipitated a permanent sediment of disillusionment and bitterness, shown in part by the rapidity with which the divorce rate was climbing back toward its old level in 1935. Where the balance lies as between these two tendencies no one as yet knows. Nor do we know in which familial types the pluses and minuses have been most frequent.

It may be that there are types of families in this culture whose values are sufficiently congruent with dominant group values so that they thrive particularly in the fat years; and others with somewhat deviant values who may gain something from periods of adversity. The depression unquestionably brought an easement of strain to some families who had been frustrated in their ambitions in the gaudy 1920's, by reason of the simple fact that it brought more people down to their level of living. Again the depression experience of a family may depend somewhat on the extent to which its sources of security and cohesion are mainly *external*—amount of money and material possessions, or dependence upon maintaining customary status in the community—or mainly *internal,* bound up with personal intimacy between husband and wife or parents and children. Closer study of the whole concept of "security" and of the capacity of individuals and of the family unit to withstand uncertainty, deprivation, and fear is needed. All of this, however, obviously applies to families to whom the depression has meant something less stark than hunger and grim want.

Nor do we know to which types of families the depression has brought greater isolation and to which a greater sense of kinship with others; whether, on the whole, more families have withdrawn from neighbors and community under the strain of battered hopes and the inability to live up to an accustomed level, or whether, on the contrary, Middletown has experienced an increase in neighborliness and social ease.[123] One may hazard the guess that husbands have suffered more loss of prestige in the depression than have wives, but it seems extremely unlikely that this has changed significantly

[123] See the discussion of friendliness in Ch. XII.

Middletown's conception either of male and female roles or of the attributes it imputes to men and women. Such momentary access of stature in the family as women may have achieved during the depression may be wiped out by the slow relative loss of opportunity which women appear to be suffering in the male-dominated world of business, professions, and industry.[124] It is conceivable that Middletown families are emerging from the pit of the depression into a scene in which the cultural demands upon the individual family for pretentious living have lessened. But there are no evidences of this. Perhaps the remark of a discerning Middletown woman best sums up the situation: "Most of the families I know are after the same things today that they were after before the depression, and they'll get them in the same way—on credit."

[124] See the discussion of women's changing vocational opportunities at the close of Ch. II.

CHAPTER VI

Training the Young

I N A society as heavily oriented towards the future and the next
generation as Middletown, a study of the way it trains its young
offers one of the surest means of penetrating beneath the surface
of life to its dominant values. Middletown cares about its children.
They symbolize to the parent generation a path of release from certain of life's frustrations and a large share of this adult generation's
hope of the future. Some people have exclaimed, "What a crass culture!" after reading the earlier study of Middletown; but one who
knows the city would always insist, "Certainly not in its hopes and
plans and sacrifices for its children!" For Middletown reaches with
eagerness, albeit an eagerness tempered with caution and apprehension over the unfamiliar, for what it conceives to be for its children's
good. If adult Middletown sees its own hope for the immediate future
as lying in hard work and making money, it has been wont to see
in education the Open Sesame that will unlock the world for its
children.

Middletown has accordingly been emotionally ready for change of
a "conservatively progressive" sort in its schools. Whether a community actually effects changes in its institutional habits, and where
the changes occur, depends, however, upon a congeries of factors in
addition to this general emotional receptivity. These factors include a
community's wealth, the relative urgency with which its different
problems press upon it, the tenacity of its traditions, the presence or
absence of strong local personalities with an interest in a particular
change, the rate of change in the larger culture surrounding it, and
the development in this larger culture of clearly defined and easily
transmittable yardsticks by which such relative lags as may exist in
local procedures can be recognized.[1] The principal changes in train-

[1] This rôle of the outside measuring rod in social change is a special phase
of the general rôle of the outside impetus to change, discussed in Ch. IV in
connection with the relation of Federal money and planning to Middletown's

ing the young in Middletown since 1925 have come through shifts in the city's economic welfare as they have affected school attendance; through the presence of great local wealth which has developed the local college rapidly since 1925; through the development of new conflicts as to the role of the schools in relation to other vital institutions; and through the diffusion to Middletown of more of the professionalized practices of the educational boom period of the 1920's.

The 1920's were years of educational "efficiency" in American public education and of yardstick making by which to measure this efficiency, and Middletown was rendered especially conscious of these tendencies by its pride in the rapidly growing X State Teachers College in its midst. Education was becoming "scientific" with a vengeance; "measurement" was in the saddle in all departments, from teaching to administration; and administration ceased to be the business of veteran teachers and became a series of specialties, its offices increasingly filled by specially trained persons. Cities were watching each other's progress and emulating each other in building new "million-dollar high schools" for a future thought to be permanently opulent; administrators were out to make records, because that was the way a superintendent or director of vocational education in a city of 40,000 moved up to a city of 100,000; and the teachers colleges and omnipresent Ph.D.'s were developing the necessary yardsticks which State Departments of Education and Middletown school systems could take over to apply to local problems. The Middletowns added Research Departments which used these yardsticks in the schools and

care for the unable during the depression. Every community's practice in a given respect is a special case attributable to its unique circumstances until certain aspects held in common with other communities are recognized and compared with standards of good practice in these other communities.

Whether such standards of good practice are developed depends in our culture upon a variety of factors. These include the measurability of a given trait (e.g., infant mortality and the rate of pupil retardation, as over against such less ponderable things as the *quality* of the education given); the presence of institutions having a business or professional stake in their development (e.g., the commercial life-insurance companies in the case of mortality and morbidity rates, and the collegiate schools of education in such matters as efficient school administration, as over against the lack of such strong agencies concerned with such matters as the efficiency of politics or the effective spending of private income); and, of course, the biases of the culture.

The whole process of the development of and adherence to standards of effective practice in certain institutionalized sectors of living and their neglect in others offers an interesting line of analytical approach to the understanding of the uneven, waddling gait of cultural change.

issued impressive printed bulletins of comparative charts and tables on "How Much Do Our Schools Cost the Taxpayer?" and "Educational Planning in the [Middletown] Public Schools." [2] Middletown's school system, in step with those of other cities, has been becoming thoroughly "modernized" and "efficient" in its administrative techniques—to the dismay of some of the city's able teachers as they have watched the administrative horse gallop off with the educational cart. Some teachers regarded it as characteristic of the trend toward administrative dominance that in one recent year eight administrators and no teachers had their expenses paid to the National Education Association convention.

In keeping with its own conviction that "the more education any child can get, the better," and with the general forward pressure for more education throughout the nation, Middletown has been sending more and more of its children to school and, at least through the mid-1920's, on into college. Illiterates dropped from 2.5 per cent of the total population in 1920 to 1.3 in 1930. In 1910, 17.6 per cent of the city's population was enrolled in the schools, as against 18.3 per cent in 1920, and 19.0 per cent in 1930. This increase has occurred despite a falling birth rate and the rising average age of the population. [3] It was particularly marked in the high schools and especially in the senior high school (grades 10-12). The percentages of all school enrollments which were in these three final grades show the following movement by five-year intervals since 1907 and by year throughout the depression:

Year [4]	Per cent of all school enrollments which were in grades 10-12 [5]	Year	Per cent of all school enrollments which were in grades 10-12 [5]
1907	7.3	1930	15.2
1912	9.8	1931	17.0
1917	10.8	1932	18.1
1922	14.6	1933	18.7
1927	16.7	1934	18.4
1928	16.6	1935	17.6
1929	15.3		

[2] These are the titles of two bulletins issued by the new Research Department of the Middletown Public Schools in 1932 and 1933 respectively, the first consisting of twenty-five printed pages and the second of 105.

[3] See Table 17 in Appendix III and n. 85 in Ch. II.

[4] Enrollments are taken in the first week of June at the close of the school year. These figures are accordingly for the school years 1906-07, 1911-12, etc.

[5] Kindergarten enrollments are omitted throughout.

These figures, particularly when taken in connection with the decline in high-school graduates from 283 in 1925 to 250 in 1929,[6] suggest that the pressure of children into high school may have reached its pre-depression peak in the mid-1920's and may even have been diminishing somewhat in the boom years of the last half of the decade. It is possible, on the other hand, that the years of heavy population growth between 1926 and 1929 brought to Middletown relatively more mobile small families with young children than older families with children of high-school age; this would have tended to pull down the proportion of school children in high school in those years. In any case, the 1920's exhibited a marked increase in high-school attendance over the years that had gone before, and, as suggested in Chapter II,[7] this increase may have been in part due to a relative shrinkage in available jobs. Middletown's population under twenty may have been experiencing, even before the depression, the growing pressure of the alternatives of keeping on in school—or idleness.

However the fluctuations in high-school enrollment during the 1920's be interpreted, the sharp relative renewal of the rise in high-school enrollment with the coming of the depression years is clear.[8] After a slight further drop in 1929-30, despite a 28 per cent decline in withdrawals from the senior high school in that year,[9] senior high-school enrollments rose uninterruptedly in the three succeeding years. In 1933-34 the tide turned and the relative share of all school enrollments which were in the senior high school began to decline slowly. As Table 34 shows, enrollments in grades 9-12 increased after 1930 at three to four times the rate of enrollments in grades 1-8, and at a

[6] See Table 36 in Appendix III.
[7] See also Tables 7 and 8 in Appendix III.
[8] See Table 34 in Appendix III, and the figures above for the per cent of all school enrollments in grades 10-12.
[9] The withdrawals from the senior high school reflect the struggles of the marginal family to keep its children in school:

Year	Number of withdrawals from grades 10-12	Year	Number of withdrawals from grades 10-12
1928-29	321	1932-33	352
1929-30	230	1933-34	354
1930-31	259	1934-35	223
1931-32	340	1935-36	331

There was apparently a special effort to keep children on in high school in the face of the blank outlook in the first two depression years. Thereafter, the total rose, reflecting not only academic and social failures but also children withdrawn from school when unemployed families moved away from Middletown. No explanation is at hand for the 37 per cent drop in withdrawals in 1934-35.

differential rate even greater when compared with the increase in the city's population. The totals of students continuing on through high school to graduation rose spectacularly during the depression.[10] The class of June, 1929, was the smallest since 1924. That of 1930 rose 20 per cent above 1929, but the class of 1931 fell back towards the 1929 level.[11] The classes of 1932-33-34 rose heavily in numbers, that of 1934 being 56 per cent larger than the class of 1929. The class of 1935 fell off to the level of that of 1930, due possibly to the scramble for jobs with returning good times in the spring of 1935. But the class of 1936 rose again to a record total 61 per cent above the class of 1929. With only a negligible growth in the city's size since 1929, this 1936 figure suggests either a persisting hardy faith in education or simple acceptance of one alternative in a forced choice.

Stepping back from these year-by-year shifts during the depression, the long-term picture of the increasing share of Middletown's population in high school is impressive: Middletown had in 1890 [12] one high-school graduate for each 810 persons in its total population; by 1920, when there were 114 graduates, this ratio had shifted to one to 320; by 1930 the ratio was one to 154; while with the graduating class of 1934 the ratio was one to 120.[13]

No records are kept in Middletown of the total number of its high-school graduates who go on to college. A careful check, made as a part of the earlier study,[14] of the 65 per cent of the graduates of the high-school class of 1924 whose whereabouts was known in October of that year showed about a third (34 per cent) of them already in college. A statement in the local press in May, 1930, attributed to the Guidance Supervisor in the high school and based on a survey made at the time, said that "During the last five years only 30 per cent of the total number of graduates [of the Middletown high school] went

[10] See Table 36 in Appendix III.

[11] This may have been due to the fact that in the second year of depression, as more and more families began to be affected and before it was clearly realized that there just were no jobs for young people, an unusual number of older children may have left high school in their final year in the abortive effort to get work.

[12] See *Middletown*, p. 183.

[13] No effort is made here to carry on the ratio to 1936, with its record graduating class, because no estimate was made of the city's population in that year.

[14] See *Middletown*, p. 183. It was believed by the group of persons who assisted in this check that very few if any of the individuals whose whereabouts was unknown would have been likely to be in college.

to an institution of higher learning." [15] Table 35 [16] gives, from the best available materials, the picture of the movement to college during the depression years. It suggests an increase of roughly two-thirds between the fall of 1929 and the fall of 1930 in the number of Middletown's applicants for college entrance; and while the total for the fall of 1931 registered a loss as compared with 1930, it was still approximately 40 per cent above that for the fall of 1929. These were the years in which to business-class Middletown the depression was "something we read about in the papers"; and college was the logical thing to do in the absence of jobs. But by the fall of 1932, despite a 45 per cent increase in high-school graduates of the preceding June over the total for 1929, those applying for college entrance had dropped back almost to the 1929 level; and by 1934, despite a 56 per cent increase above 1929 in high-school graduates, the college applicants were below the 1929 total. [17]

[15] Unfortunately, the schools could locate no copy of this survey in 1935.

There is a slight bit of evidence that college attendance, like high-school attendance in Middletown, may have reached a peak just past the middle of the 1920's and may have been falling off slightly in 1928-29. Despite the fact that the local college had risen from obscurity in the early 1920's and was in 1928-29 occupying a position of great local prestige, its matriculations from the Middletown high school exhibit the following curve:

Year	Number of graduates from Middletown high school entering Middletown's college	Year	Number of graduates from Middletown high school entering Middletown's college
1924	44	1927	83
1925	54	1928	64
1926	79	1929	63

While the good years may have sent more students to colleges away from home, they also attracted a relatively heavier share of Middletown's college prospects to the local college. The percentage of all college entrants from Middletown who entered the local college increased from roughly 55 to roughly 70 per cent between 1924 and 1929; but, despite this rising percentage, actual enrollments in the local college fell noticeably after 1927. There may, therefore, be a hint here of a real recession in the late 1920's in Middletown's fervor for sending its children to college. The unusually high rate of early marriages in Middletown, shown in Chapter V, may mean that the good employment years, 1928 and 1929, may simply have given to more high-school graduates the choice of marriage rather than of more education.

[16] See Appendix III for this table.

[17] The United States Office of Education has only very fragmentary figures on the national flow of students into colleges. Its figures show a drop of 3.5 per cent between the school years 1931-32 and 1933-34 in the number of freshmen actually entered in all the universities, colleges, and junior colleges of the country; and a drop over the same period of 27.6 per cent in the first year students in teacher-

Undoubtedly Middletown's college attendance will recover somewhat with the easing of the depression. The possibly permanently constricting job opportunities for those in their teens, noted in Chapter II, would favor the continuance of heavy college attendance. As late as June, 1936, Middletown's high-school graduating class broke all previous records by its size, suggesting a strong continuing faith in education, whether as opportunity or sheer stop-gap. Likewise, total enrollments in approved colleges and universities in the United States were 8 per cent above 1934 in the fall of 1935, and again 7.3 per cent above 1935 in the fall of 1936, according to the annual counts published in *School and Society*. Part, though probably by no means all, of these national increases was due to N.Y.A. subsidies.

Over against these evidences of continued or even enhanced interest in higher education, however, should be set the disillusioned attitude of a number of graduates of Middletown's college and of a number of troubled working-class parents with whom the investigators talked in the summer of 1935. As one of these parents remarked: "I think we've been kidding ourselves in breaking our backs to send our children to college. There just aren't enough good jobs to take care of all the college graduates."

The evidence is tenuous and uncertain. Should the movement of Middletown's children toward college have suffered a permanent check, another of the emotional supports to "progress" and "the American dream" may be withering. Middletown's culture has a strong tradition that one's "future" (*i.e.,* one's wealth and happiness) is in one's own hands. But the obstacles in the path of the willing but barehanded individual, particularly in the working class, have been increasing.[18] In this changing world the suspicion has been growing slowly in the minds of some Middletown people that the "American success formula" is a mirage—at least for them. Men still hope, for

training institutions. In view of the fact that 70 per cent of Middletown's college entrants attend the local State Teachers College, the fact that its drop in college applicants over the same years agrees almost precisely with these national figures suggests the representativeness of its experience.

It should, however, be borne in mind that the Middletown figures are only proximate, as explained in n. *a* to Table 36, while the national figures cited above are for actual college entrants.

[18] See the discussion in Ch. II of the increasing difficulties for the workingman in the way of "promotion," "starting up for oneself," and the other traditional ways "up the ladder of success," and the discussion in Ch. XII of the extent of his awareness of this.

the tradition is strong, and the emotional need for hope even stronger. But it is possible that the blind American faith in "a college education" that glutted the American colleges in the 1920's has represented to no small degree the transfer, often unconscious, of the hopes of one generation to the lives of its children. As the prestige of holding a college degree has sagged under this rising tide of graduates, and the miraculous job has failed to materialize in many cases, it may be that this avenue of escape from stalemate has lost prestige which it may not regain. Bit by bit, the process of distinguishing the inescapable realities of a culture from the symbols and traditions that cloak them tends to go forward in times of shock and disappointment; and it may be that the depression is contributing to this development a more sober attitude on the part of both parents and children.

It is Middletown's boys who apparently have lost out most as regards going to college as the depression has worn on. Following are the totals of high-school graduates of each sex in each indicated graduating class who had their high-school records forwarded to a college: [19]

Year	Number of boys	Number of girls	Year	Number of boys	Number of girls
1929	24	24	1932	20	31
1930	40	38	1933	22	27
1931	35	30	1934	14	21

Table 36 [20] suggests that the percentage of boys among total high-school graduates rose during the depression. The above figures show, however, that, whereas the boys were equal in number to the girls or slightly in the lead among those going to college in the three years 1929-31, when the depression began to bite hard in Middletown they dropped off, comprising only two to every three girls in the pinched years, 1932-34. This is probably only a depression phenomenon, but when one recalls that in the 1890's Middletown's college entrants were very largely males, one glimpses here in the greater tenacity of college education for women an index of the changed status of women in Middletown's culture.[21] Can it be that, during the worst of the depression, a college education was a more dispensable perquisite of the

[19] These totals are for only approximately 63 per cent of each year's class. See Table 35.
[20] See Appendix III.
[21] In the year 1890 there were 233 men and only 88 women enrolled in the State University in Middletown's state.

Middletown male than of the female? It is possible that the most direct clew to this situation lies in the limited number of occupations available to Middletown women on the business and professional level and the relatively great importance of teaching among those occupations.[22] Men's choices are much wider, and business (a field virtually closed to Middletown women of the business class) affords an outlet for men even without college training. Teaching, on the other hand, is heavily women's work; only 22 per cent of the persons listed as "Teachers" (not including "College Presidents and Professors") in the 1920 Census were men, and 29 per cent in 1930. The minimum training for a teacher was raised in 1935 to four years beyond high school. All of which means that if a woman is to get any job at all in the most obvious of the few socially accepted fields open to women on the business and professional level, she must go to college. Furthermore, the fact that going to college means to a girl, more than to a boy, an enhanced opportunity to find a mate is an important factor here; for going to college means to the very great majority of Middletown's children attending a coeducational college. It is probable that it is the sons of the working class who have figured most prominently in the drop in college attendance by boys.

Middletown's college attendance has always been allocated heavily to small colleges.[23] A check of roughly 63 per cent of the high-school graduating class for each of the six years, 1929-34, showed from two to six graduates a year among the fifty to eighty annual college applicants in this sample applying for entry to State universities within Middletown's own state; roughly one each year to nationally known State universities outside Middletown's state; about one every other year to prominent endowed Eastern or Midwestern institutions; while the remainder applied to small colleges, for the most part within the state or in adjoining states. As the local college has grown in prestige and particularly as the depression has enforced economy, the share of Middletown's college students attending the local college has increased: from approximately 55 per cent of total college entrants in 1924, the local college came to command by 1929 approximately 70 per cent; in 1930-32 this percentage rose to 80, and in 1933 and 1934 it was in the neighborhood of 75. This high degree of localism in

[22] See the closing pages of Chs. II and V.
[23] See *Middletown*, p. 197, n. 10, for the distribution by location and size of institution in 1924.

college training suggests an increase in cultural inbreeding over the past ten years.

Middletown's college has not stood still, however, in the years since 1925. Some local people call the spectacular growth of the college "the biggest thing of a constructive sort that has happened to the city over the past decade." Middletown has become "a college town." The capital of Middletown's state has for many decades enjoyed referring to itself as "the Athens of the West." A small city not far from Middletown revels in the prestige of its excellent Quaker college. And Middletown, too, has had the fever intermittently since the early 1890's. A newspaper editor who had come to town with the gas boom, noting the presence of a small teacher-training school in an outlying village in the county, began to preach Middletown as "an ideal location for a college or normal school." In 1896 a group of local businessmen promoters bought up a tract of farm land west of town, then "heavily overgrown with a thicket," incorporated The Eastern [State] Normal University, and began a drive to sell building lots at $300 each on part of the site to finance the building of the "university" on the remainder. The campaign failed, was renewed in 1898, succeeded, and the "university" and a new outlying suburb, "Normal City," were born simultaneously.[24] The "University" opened in 1899 under an agreement with the man put in charge of "promoting" the school that "he would conduct an independent normal school, free from all sectarian influence," and that if at the end of a certain number of years he had a stipulated number of bonafide students in attendance,

[24] The long and close connection between the fate of the college and real-estate exploitation should be noted. How the X family reaped from real estate in this section as it sowed philanthropy in the 1920's is described in Chapter III. A description of the flotation of this real estate twenty-five years before, contained in Middletown's afternoon paper for February 27, 1922, states: "Normal City at that time experienced a boom. Lots sold for high prices in comparison with other values at that time, and an old plat of that suburb shows lots sold for prices which could not now be obtained, despite the increase of real-estate values."

The early promoters were evidently not entirely philanthropically inclined, for the ten-acre campus was "thrown in free with the price of the 300 building lots by the owners of the land," only $33,000 of the $90,000 received for the 300 building lots sold went into the solitary building on the campus, and the only other expense was the improvement of the streets and sidewalks in the ten acres sold for residences. And at that, their contract called only for the improvement of the streets "running north and south." (Kemper's history of the county is authority for the sale of 300 lots at $300 each. Pp. 266-67.)

he was to be given title to the building. Two years later the venture failed. This was the first of five failures of the school [25] prior to 1918 when the X family bought in the property, with an appraised value of $400,000, for $35,000 in bankruptcy proceedings, and gave it to the State on condition that it be operated as a branch of the existing State Normal School.

The earlier study has been criticized by Middletown people for not making more of the college. In June, 1925, eighty students were graduated from the four-year course with the Bachelor's degree and 112 more completed the two-year course required of grade-school teachers in the state. Between 1919 and 1924, the summer enrollments had risen from 383 to 1,103. In 1924-25 the Normal School's physical plant was growing. It had added to its single gaunt old building, flanked by a dingy dormitory housing sixty students, a new $125,000 Science Build-

[25] The next chance to open the school came in response to an offer in 1901 from the United Brethren Church to turn it into a theological seminary. This plan fell through when no agreement could be reached on terms. In the same year the citizens of Middletown organized and tried to take over the school, but failed. In 1905 the school reopened as the Palmer Institute, and a new building was built on the strength of new financing that was apparently in sight; a $100,000 offer had been received from a wealthy New Yorker, Francis Palmer, contingent upon the raising of a matching amount from local citizens, but after the local money was raised the institute collapsed. Next, two professors opened in the building a combined "normal school and business college." A year or two later, and despite an enrollment of 350 winter students and 300 in the summer, this venture, too, failed, and the local citizens again got behind a new venture to conduct a normal school. This in turn failed after operating one year. An unsuccessful effort was made in 1909 to induce the State to take over the white elephant. In 1911 a contract was made with an educational promoter who brought together a struggling normal school from a near-by city, the National Manual Training Corporation of Plano, Ill., the [Middletown] Conservatory of Music, and the [State] Manual Training Company into an amalgamated school which reopened the doors of the building as the [Middletown] Normal Institute. This venture succeeded well enough in number of students—an enrollment of 800 being achieved—for the title to be transferred to the new company. Enrollment actually increased to 1,761 in the winter of 1916-17 and the graduating class to 100. But the school was again in financial difficulties. According to the local press, "Some say this [subsequent bankruptcy] might have been averted if the school had been in good standing with the public, but the losses that had been suffered by the people, together with the constant discouragement which always seemed to follow the reopening of the school doors, had robbed the school of this asset." In 1917 it failed; for a year more the school limped along under a bankruptcy receivership; and then in 1918 again closed its doors. At this point in 1918 the X brothers stepped in.

The above checkered record could probably be duplicated in scores of midland cities.

ing and was completing a large new gymnasium under a $250,000 gift from the X family. Businessmen were already beginning to figure the business value of the institution to the city at around a quarter of a million dollars a year.

Had Middletown been a "college town" in any observable sense in the fall of 1923 when the city was selected for study,[26] the study would not have been made there. Despite the rapid growth of the college, however, even in the spring of 1925 its impact on the town, other than its increment to local trade, was practically nil. It was an inconspicuous institution out in the edge of the cornfields, on the margin of the city's consciousness. It is the belief of the writers that local pride in the college today and the rapidity of its growth since 1924-25 distort Middletown people's recollection of its role ten years ago.[27]

Since the winter of 1924-25, however, through the initiative and large gifts of the X family, the Normal School has developed into an aggressive college which, in June, 1936, awarded twenty-two Master's degrees and 171 Bachelor's degrees, in addition to 141 two-year teaching certificates. A handsome $2,500,000 plant has developed on the site of the old property bought in for $35,000 in 1918, rivaling in attractiveness the best college and university campuses of the state, and the exclusive residential section of the city has swung from the East End westward to what the ambitious real-estate fraternity in this utterly flat prairie city hopefully call "University Heights." In the summer of 1936 nearly a thousand students were registered for each of its two summer sessions, and a local editor expressed the hope that "before too long this institution will be known as X State University, with a normal school merely one important department."

Today, the most generally expressed attitude in Middletown toward

[26] See the criteria used in selecting the city in *Middletown*, Ch. II, especially p. 7.

[27] A page of the earlier manuscript, cut in the necessary compression of the final revision, contained the following statement: "The growth of the local college is a matter of only the last half-dozen years. Not until 1924 did it secure a president of its own, apart from the other State Normal School, and begin to call itself a 'college.' It has not as yet developed sufficiently to affect the intellectual or artistic life of the city, but such an influence will doubtless begin to be felt in the near future. The establishment of a four-year college course has met with an immediate response locally and is adding to the college-going movement by reaching a class of students to whom the ability to live at home makes college attendance possible."

the college is one of outspoken and enthusiastic pride.[28] The faculty
and the college are penetrating constantly further into the city's life.
Businessmen hail the presence of a thousand students in the city
throughout the year, whose local spending is said according to a local
newspaper, perhaps over-optimistically, to aggregate $1,000,000 a year.
But on closer inspection, some elements of ambivalence still appear.
Local editorials still occasionally lament, as they did more frequently
in 1924-25, the fact that the city "does not appreciate" the college.
While the continued building program through the depression and
the inability of many able children to "go off" to college have swelled
local attendance and loyalty, there are numerous indications of an
attitude running all the way from apathy to sharp criticism. Remarks
such as the following by a recent male graduate undoubtedly reflect
in part a disillusionment as to the benefits of any college training on
the part of a generation unable to get jobs of the sort traditionally
associated with a college education: "X State College is a *joke* to Middletown. It's a lousy institution! What do they teach you out there?
They take Dos Passos off the shelves so you won't get polluted. Everybody out there's afraid of the shadow of a real idea!" With many,
particularly of the working class, this mood of apathy or resentment
is associated with the widespread ambivalence in the attitude of the
community toward the X family. Some resent the fact that "Now the
X's have control of education, too"; or the fact that a State institution
should bear the name of this family. The city is full of whispered
stories about the X family's interference in the running of the college: that one member of the family who is closely associated with
the D.A.R. blocked the staging of *Journey's End* by the college
dramatic group; that liberal outside lecturers may not be brought to
the college if the X's turn thumbs down. Still others allege that the
president is "just one more small-time politician," irrelevantly put in

[28] In June, 1935, an editorial called attention to the fact that "The X State
College has first-class college rating and has curricula and a faculty superior
to many educational institutions that rate as universities. The parents of high
school graduates everywhere should investigate the merits of X State before
sending this year's high-school-graduating sons and daughters to distant and
generally far more expensive colleges. A degree from X State is a mark of high
honor wherever the standing of this college is known, which is everywhere that
there is adequate knowledge of what the institution is doing educationally. . . .
That this college is rapidly coming into its own is indicated by the 321 graduates this year." Such pride in the superiority of the college has thus become an
additional rallying point for enhancing civic solidarity.

charge of a State educational institution to divert him from running for Congress. Like others of its civic symbols, the college elicits from Middletown a somewhat uneven loyalty.

Despite this present ambivalence, the college is destined to play a larger and larger part in local life. Chapter VII discusses its relation to the city's leisure. A further significant influence derives from the presence in the culture of a somewhat independent group of people whose business it is to maintain intellectual contact with a wider world than that of Middletown. The Federal Census shows an increase in the number of "College presidents and professors" in Middletown from seven men and two women in 1920 to twenty-nine men and twenty-one women in 1930. One of the problems of the Middletowns of the country, organized centripetally about the major concern with making their living, is resistance to new ideas from without that interfere with the smoothly gliding processes of their own living, an in-turned concentration on the local, the familiar, the habitual, in an era when the larger national culture is confronted with new issues and is restating some of its fundamental assumptions. And it is at this point that the fresh leaven of a college faculty becomes important —important both in its fortification and nourishing of a spirit of inquiry among the young, the ministers, the high-school teachers, and the isolated "lonely intellectuals" in Middletown's own population, and important as an outright originating agency. Just as Middletown's Y.M.C.A. reports that it is the boys who have been away to college who broach divergent ideas in the bickering groups around its soda fountain, so in a sense this faculty group represents the innovating stimulus of a "people from outside" to the entire Middletown culture. Thus the Globe Shakespeare Theatre company from London would probably not have been brought to Middletown from the Chicago Century of Progress if the college had not brought them; Engelbrecht, co-author of *Merchants of Death,* would not have been brought to Middletown in the winter of 1934-35 to say things about military armament that Middletown's D.A.R. and American Legion try to keep from being said in Middletown; and if it had not been for strong leadership in the social studies department in the college, the National Secretary of the Socialist Party would never have been brought to Middletown to speak in the winter of 1933-34. Middletown is uneasy about "radicalism out at the college"; the X family may keep an eye on their college and interfere from time to time; but "intellectual freedom" in a "college" in the United States still carries a traditional value far stronger than "intellectual freedom" in a high school, and the tether of the X State Teachers College faculty, though limited, is still longer than that of the high-school faculty and that of any Middletown minister of the three numerically largest churches. If the businessmen see in the presence of the college "a million dollars' worth of business a year" and the clubwomen "a fine cultural influence for the city," many public-school teachers and ministers look upon the college faculty as a powerful ally in trying to make Middletown extend its awareness and in keeping themselves intellectually alert. As one of the latter remarked fervently: "The college is the finest thing that's happened to the city! There are some people out there who speak my language. We lend books back and forth to each other and it helps to keep one intellectually fresh."

An important by-product of the growth of the college is the opening in 1929 in the West End of the city adjoining the campus of a handsome modern laboratory school operated by the college. This formidable new internal measuring stick imported into the Middletown public schools bids fair to affect fundamentally the qualitative side of local public-school education, while its new $300,000 plant, including all grades through the high school, sets a difficult standard for most of the rest of the city's school buildings, some of them fifty years old.[29]

[29] The assessed valuation per room of these buildings of varying ages and their contents (exclusive of site) in the winter of 1930-31 ranged all the way from $3,000 to $10,500 in the case of the elementary schools. The pressure of the new college experimental school fortifies the sharp protests of discriminating local teachers over the taking over by the public-school system of the basketball field house as a junior-high-school plant. The field house was built under private financing by a committee of local businessmen prior to the depression. It was primarily a tribute to the local enthusiasm for basketball, with the city's pride in its vocational education program represented in the plan by rooms surrounding the gymnasium intended to house a complete vocational education program. The bonds were forced widely throughout the city as an investment and as a matter of loyalty to the Bearcats, and at the same time heavy pressure was brought on all and sundry, including every schoolteacher, to buy five-year season tickets for $50; so that when the bottom dropped out and the 5 per cent interest on the bonds threatened to be defaulted, there was plenty of local sentiment to transfer the "white elephant," as the teachers call it, to the school system, despite the fact that the rooms formerly intended for the vocational education plant

As in the case of the college itself, this new laboratory school is subject to the cross-fire of conflicting local attitudes. Like any innovation which is set up to show veterans in the field how to improve their ways, it invites caustic comparison and criticism by Middletown. "But, Mother, aren't there *any* other good schools in [Middletown]?" asked one child after a few weeks under the confident staff of the laboratory school. Parents in other sections of town object to having some of their ablest teachers pulled out of their neighborhood schools to strengthen the experimental school staff; the school administration complains of the undue amount of worry and trouble the new school gives them because of constant criticisms from anxious parents who want "more discipline" or "Johnny taught to read earlier"; some able teachers feel that the newer methods are predicated upon small classes, and that if they are carried on in classes of thirty-five and forty, as must be the case if they are tried in other schools than the college experimental school, children actually lose by them; and these teachers also resent somewhat the atmosphere of pedagogical royalty built up in the new school around the requirement that only those with an M.A. degree shall teach there. But if some parents leave the district because of the school, more move in to gain the combined educational and social advantages of the West End; they may be critical of the actual practice of the new educational methods, but they like the idea of them. And veteran teachers, while they realize that superior teaching goes on independently of physical equipment or leadership, welcome the support of a school frankly committed to educational experiment.

The college laboratory school is giving new impetus to a tendency already under way in Middletown's schools, namely, the emphasis upon small classes and individual differences as over against mass educa-

are said by teachers to be poorly lighted and inappropriate for ordinary school classwork.

In passing, it is worth while to note that the names of Middletown's public schools afford clues both to the dates of the schools in some cases and, in all cases, to the values popularly associated with public buildings and with education in this culture: In the first group are buildings built in the administrations of Presidents Garfield, Harrison, McKinley, Theodore Roosevelt, and Wilson, and also a Blaine School; while in the second are Washington, Jefferson, and Lincoln among the patriot great, and James Whitcomb Riley, Longfellow, and Emerson. Of the fifteen schools, only three depart from the great tradition: Central High School, Stevenson School, and the new college school called after a locally known educator.

tion and conformity. In 1927-28 the Middletown schools embarked upon a ten-year program of school planning and reorganization. Taking off squarely from the platform of industrial "planning" ardently sponsored in those pre-New Deal days by the then Secretary of Commerce, and later President, Hoover, and commending the "many startling results" being accomplished by engineering intelligence applied to industrial problems, the Middletown school administrators pointed to the sweeping character of current social change, quoting Owen D. Young to the effect that "Our chief problem is no longer to adjust ourselves to a well-defined system, but to change"; they noted that "Municipal planning has not received as great attention as industrial planning, which no doubt accounts for much of its lack of progress in rendering an increased service with a decreased cost"; and they then installed a Research Department and began to plan. Central to this ten-year planning and reorganization program was the redefinition of the philosophy of education in Middletown, and central to the latter was the emphasis upon the individual child: [30]

"During the past few years of educational endeavor in [Middletown], the Board of Education and its school administrators . . . have faced the problem of selecting the educational philosophy on which to build. . . .

"The philosophy on which school authorities have attempted to build in [Middletown] may be made a bit clearer by first briefly contrasting it with that of the past. Our philosophy of education in America has been largely that of the pioneer. Prior to the last century, and during much of the nineteenth century, our philosophy was very largely nationalistic and aristocratic. We now believe in the education of the masses. We have spent too much time in transplanting to America the theories, practices, and educational traditions of European education.

"Educational tradition from Europe furnished us with much that is outworn and ineffective. There are still many disciples of aristocratic European traditions. From the beginning of time until recent years, world change has developed slowly. As a result, knowledge was traditionally handed down. Such a process became authoritative and the accepted basis of knowledge. Many held to such a traditional philosophy and advocated that to learn is basically acquisition and acceptance on authority.

"Ours is a different philosophy. It *advocates that the aim of education*

[30] The quotations in the paragraph above and the long quotation that follows are from a review of progress at the conclusion of the first five years of the ten-year plan. They are contained in the opening pages of a 105-page report on *Educational Planning in the [Middletown] Public Schools,* issued by the Department of Educational Research in 1933.

should be to enable every child to become a useful citizen, to develop his individual powers to the fullest extent of which he is capable, while at the same time engaged in useful and lifelike activities. . . . We believe in the doctrine of equal educational opportunity for every child to develop according to his abilities, interests, and aptitudes. [Italics ours.]

"In planning the educational work in [Middletown] in recent years, the Board of Education and school officials have tried to operate on the above basic philosophy of American Education. . . . The plan as at first laid out was to extend over a period of about ten years. The first five-year period has passed and it is the function of this Bulletin to briefly review what has been accomplished to date . . . and to look into the immediate future.

". . . While we do not desire [in the pages which follow in this Bulletin] to point to spectacular improvements, we do believe that the comparisons made will show a distinct advance from the practices of an earlier period. . . . The elements of the educational plan along which progress in varying degrees has been made, and upon which further thought and effort must be spent, are the following:

1. The personnel organization.
2. The gradual reorganization of the [Middletown] City Schools.
3. The reorganization and rearranging of curricular offerings in terms of pupil needs.
4. The revision of the courses of study and the development of technique of course-of-study construction.
5. The use of the appraisal and city-wide testing program.
6. Guidance program for counseling boys and girls of junior and senior high-school age.
7. The upgrading of teaching personnel.
8. Child accounting and holding power of the schools.
9. Budgetary procedure and the study of school costs and trends.
10. A survey of school sites.
11. Landscape plans for the school grounds.
12. A survey of school buildings."

Here speaks not the voice of the businessmen on Middletown's school board but that of the professional school of education, whose influence in the 1920's was pervading all American education and whose spirit had taken on flesh and fresh authority in Middletown in its own successful Teachers College.

In 1930 the Central High School adopted a new curriculum "devoted to the principle that the schools should fit the needs of the individual pupil instead of forcing the child to fit himself to the standard curriculum, as has been the practice in the past." Such radical changes in subjects taught, in methods of teaching, and in habits of teachers, as a literal putting into practice of such an educational credo involves, would require, according to some Middletown teachers, more knowledge of individual needs than at present exists, and more time to discover and meet these needs than administrators imagine. But, in response to this slogan, there is apparent today in the high school a slow diminution in the traditional emphasis upon factual courses and more emphasis upon exploratory work around main problems, supposedly closer to student needs. In chemistry, for example, individual supervised laboratory work is diminishing the role of class lectures. Mathematics is increasingly "shop math." There is, also, in the high school as in the grades, more grouping of students by ability, with more freedom and rapidity of progress for the more intelligent. Some of the abler children in the high school are receiving at the hands of unusual teachers a type of free-ranging training in social studies, wider than anything apparent in 1925, that is generally recognized in Middletown as answering these children's urgent questions and at the same time extending their horizon far beyond their local concerns.

This new emphasis upon the development of the individual student, coming at the same time as the new problems raised by the heavy increase in the high-school and college populations, has forced Middletown into a revaluation of the role of "an education." With the high school and even the college no longer serving as a screen sifting out the "scholars" from the "nonscholars" even as roughly as they did before the World War, and with secondary education become a mass experience, the feeling has grown that education must not only be good but must be good for something—to the individual and to society. Otherwise, a culture believing so firmly in things' "paying their way" and being "worth what they cost" finds it hard to justify the increased cost to the taxpayers of the delay in children's "settling down to work" and the encouragement of "children's wild ideas" which prolonged education entails. "Culture," in the literary sense, is a luxury to most of these hard-working folk whose children are now pressing into the schools, and they want something more tangible—a better job, the ability to earn more money—as at least one dependable outcome of "an education." As a partial answer to this problem, a "guidance program" has been inaugurated as a part of Middletown's new educational planning.

The chief aim of this guidance program, according to Middletown's

1933 Bulletin on *Educational Planning,* cited above, "is to assure every child the advantages of individualization, which have always been provided by the best teachers for the most fortunate children under the most favorable circumstances, and to improve these services." [31] Theoretically a combined social-, academic-, and vocational-guidance service, this work continues the old educational tradition by being strongest on the academic side. Every child, from grade 7 on, is seen by a counselor for ten minutes once each semester, with perhaps a quarter of the total being seen again during the year, there being one counselor for every eighty children in the junior high school and one for every 150 in the senior high school. A cumulative record for each student helps to give continuity to the process. The difficulties involved in incorporating into actual educational practices the aims of individual education set forth in the bulletin quoted from above are augmented by the fact that only ten minutes a semester are allowed for understanding and advising each child.

On the vocational side, the guidance work is as yet rudimentary, reflecting the general immaturity of the entire field of discovering vocational aptitudes. Middletown does little more at present, according to one of the high-school counselors, than to urge its girls to develop a "second-string" skill in home economics or nursing and its boys who are "good in mathematics" to "go in for engineering," to discourage flagrant misfits, and generally to urge everybody of normal intelligence to "go on to college." The guidance of students in their social problems, the head of the guidance service reports, "while decidedly secondary in emphasis, is demanding more and more attention."

Middletown's attitude toward the guidance program is uneven. Some parents regard it as just another educational frill costing the taxpayers money; and some teachers criticize it as "not getting anywhere," since it must inevitably use counselors not adequately equipped to diagnose and prescribe for individual needs. Meanwhile, the need of Middletown's youth for guidance was probably never so great. Individuals responsible for Middletown's educational policy explicitly recognize the fact that aims developed in educating "our" children must be modified for educating "their" children. The 1933 Bulletin on

[31] Mental tests, achievement tests, and elaborate "screens for selecting counselors" are among the measurements which Middletown employs in its program of "developing within the individual those skills, attitudes, and abilities which will enable him to make better educational and vocational adjustments."

Educational Planning, states that "one of the immediate factors which has precipitated the need of guidance more than any other is the recent rapid influx into our secondary schools. This has called for a variety of fundamental modifications not required in the more selective school." The multiplication of optional courses renders academic guidance more than ever before necessary. With South Side children crowding the high schools and subjected to social competition with children from other social environments, social guidance likewise clamors for formal recognition within the schools. The depression has, moreover, served to emphasize the passing of the old days, when society could believe with confident complacence that children mysteriously find their "callings" with the simplicity of water running down hill, and has thrust forward the need for vocational guidance. Confronted by this need for a threefold type of education, Middletown has made a move characteristic of a culture under strain. It has, for the most part, left the central educational train untouched and simply hitched on another boxcar called a "guidance program." And as noted above, the program in operation is as yet concerned primarily with academic guidance, leaving social guidance and job guidance largely untouched.

"Actually, with all our organized guidance machinery," commented one of Middletown's ablest teachers in close touch with this guidance work, "I don't believe it is as effective as the work we teachers used to do informally on our own in having children in our homes and in similar ways. We used to seem to have so much more time for students. Now everything is so organized and routinized; we teach more pupils and there is more pressure on our teaching and less time to see students. I suppose we must have missed many students in the old days, but we certainly had time to do a better job with many of them."

Middletown's ablest teachers are somewhat irked by much of the administrative clatter that has accompanied this research and administrative push since 1927. Some of them suggest that the plan is simply proposing what "the really good teachers here have been doing right along and not making any fuss about"; and they protest against the "endless reports, committees, and curriculum revisions" that it involves. "If we could only take a day off to teach!" exclaimed a teacher leaving the fifth special committee meeting in a week. Teachers in the high school expressed the belief that academic work continues "as poor as it was ten years ago," though they incline to blame this upon the crowding in of more students of marginal ability. A factual basis for this extenuating claim is afforded by an analysis by the schools of the 558 tenth-year pupils who entered the Central High School as sophomores in the fall of 1931, which showed 200 of the 558, or 36 per cent, as having Intelligence Quotient scores of 90 or less.[32]

The announced new emphasis of Middletown's schools on the "individual student" and "education for individual differences," however attenuated in actual practice, introduces sharp conflicts at this time when the local culture is putting renewed stress on elements that make for solidarity and unanimity.[33] Never before, save perhaps during the World War, has Middletown's business life been so centrally controlled as at present, and never before has this control system been in a mood to tolerate so little dissent. As noted in Chapter II in the discussion of Middletown's present attitude toward organized labor, the temper of the city is set to enforce group action to insure the city's future. Moreover, the depression has forced the community reluctantly to widen its recognition of common necessities rather than individual differences, and through its relief program to undertake some sort of planning for them.

Middletown, like every other society, lives by a relatively small and selected group of cultural clichés, bred of its experience and emotionally heavily loaded with moral affect. These are the underlying drumbeats of life in Middletown. They "make sense" and give the security of the familiar; and in times of strain they tend to stiffen and to become obligatory behavior. But a system of education committed to "education for individual differences" in however small a degree is not calculated to encourage the wholesale reliance on old symbols. Children encouraged to think are inclined to poke a finger through the paper wall and look in at the realities within. Sooner or later the schools' concept of "educating for individual differences" will again

[32] From *How Much Do Our Schools Cost the Taxpayer?* a bulletin of the Department of Educational Research of the Middletown Public Schools, issued in 1932.

An I.Q. of 90 is regarded by educators as at the lowest limit of the "normal intelligence" span on the scale, which "normal" span extends from score 90 to score 110. The actual range of these 558 students was from 65 to 128, with 56 per cent of the students in the "normal" range of 90 to 110, and 8 per cent between 110 and 128. Even those most skeptical of the I.Q. as a valuable measure of individual differences would regard this distribution as significant.

[33] See the discussion of civic loyalty and nationalism in Ch. XII.

be redefined. This concept, generated by the spirit of the teacher and diffused to Middletown as a formal "philosophy of education" by remote "philosophers" in university graduate schools of education, is no more consonant with certain dominant elements in Middletown at present than was the philosophy of Socrates with that of the Athens of his day. If, as seems not improbable, Middletown, in common with the rest of the nation, confronts a period of high taxes and depressed standard of living, with old latent issues sharpened by new and acute stresses involving more explicit definitions of aims, particularly in the dominant economic area, the same controls that are at present closing so firmly about "labor troubles" as a threat to "the life of the city" will close about the "philosophy" of the schools.[34] Even today students at the local college who get a reputation for being "radical" are reported not to have the backing of the institution in seeking positions. "Education for individual differences" will continue to mean tolerance as to the poet one reads, if any, and "majoring" in literature or science, but it may mean in the years that lie ahead, less than at any time in the history of the city, the right to be "different" as regards the broadening area of issues and activities which Middletown regards as central to its group welfare.

Like the curriculum, the teaching staff has been altered in response to two contradictory trends. On the one hand, the pressure of the outside yardstick has resulted in what the administrators call an "upgrading of the teaching personnel."[35] The school year 1931-32 saw 25.5 per cent of the teachers trained by five or more years of education beyond the high school, as against only 5.4 per cent in 1921-22 and 7.7 per cent in 1925-26; while, at the other end of the training scale, only 5.7 per cent had less than two years of training beyond the high school in 1931-32, as against 34.6 per cent in 1921-22 and 14.4 per cent in 1925-26. According to the printed statement issued by the schools in connection with these figures, "One of the outstanding accomplishments in the [Middletown] school system in the past ten years, especially since 1926, has been the almost revolutionary change in the professional standing of the instructional staff." This marked increase in

[34] See the news story of June, 1936, captioned " 'Fads' Will Give Way to Common-sense Plan [In Schools]," quoted below in this chapter, for a fulfillment of this prediction even before its publication.
[35] See Table 37 in Appendix III.

training is a direct result of two policies: the hitching of the salary scale, under the new educational program adopted in Middletown in 1927-28, to the factor of amount of education, which is sending Middletown teachers to summer school year after year to increase their salary rating, and the resulting raising of the minimum requirements for different grades of teachers as the general level of training rose. By 1933 the minimum training for the most elementary teacher was three years beyond high school, and in 1935 this minimum was further raised to a full four-year college course.[36]

It is a commentary both on the grip of the administrator's standards upon the teaching process and on the basic view of this culture as to what an education should be that good teachers are here assumed so largely to be made by the quantity of education they receive.[37] And this same emphasis upon quantitative efficiency has led to administrative insistence upon what is supposedly more efficient use of these better-trained teachers. If good teachers are a sound financial investment, "since better than three-fourths of all operating costs of the schools goes for teaching [and] poor teaching service is [therefore] one of the most extravagant and uneconomical things that could be allowed to continue in the schools," Middletown sees educational effi-

[36] The salary schedule adopted in April, 1935, carried the following stipulations:

1. The above schedule will be reached within a period of four years, or three if possible; meanwhile it will serve as a basis for estimating annual salaries.

2. The school board desires that teachers with less than the standard of training adopted for the system plan to add to their training as soon as possible.

3. Graduation from a four-year college course is required to teach in the elementary schools.

4. Graduation from a standard four-year college course is required for teaching in the junior high school, and the teacher must have specialized in the particular subject to be taught.

5. To teach in the high school, the teacher must in addition have either two years of experience, or one year of experience and a year of graduate work.

6. A Master's degree is required for supervisors or a supervisory principalship.

7. After reaching the age of sixty-six, a new contract will be issued for one year at a time, with provision for automatic retirement at age seventy.

8. No married women teachers will be employed.

[37] The American university and teachers college profit largely from the fees derived from this American quantitative attitude toward education, and enterprising university administrators have helped to fasten this tendency on American education by catering to it.

The mystic "four years" of college in our culture and the lack of prestige of the "two-year" college, as well as the "point system" in American collegiate education, are all phases of this American tendency to take its education in terms of its countable aspects.

ciency as achievable through hiring good teachers and making them teach more pupils. This line of reasoning has been apparent in the gradual pressure for a heavier pupil load per teacher. The emphasis of professional schools of education, in keeping with the desire for developing the individual child, has been in the direction of smaller classes. In 1889-90 the average per-teacher load in Middletown was fifty-eight pupils, and in the lower grades this went up to eighty. By 1923-24, this figure had dropped to thirty.[38] Under the pressure for "economy" and "efficiency" in the depression, the average rose to between thirty-five and thirty-six—and, as this is written in 1936, there is every indication that it will be forced even higher as Middletown's school board has announced its determination to "cut out extras" in the interest of the taxpayer. In the elementary schools classes of fifty and fifty-five are common today; and in the high school, where work is departmentalized, one teacher may be "educating for individual differences" 150 to 180 personalities in a day. Some of Middletown's administrators returned from the National Education Association convention in February, 1935, enthusiastic over the efficiency of "mass teaching," whereby there could be larger classes with the brighter pupils coaching the dull ones.

Not only has the depression aggravated acutely this clash between dollar efficiency and educational philosophy as regards pupil load per teacher, but teachers' salaries, already relatively low both in relation to other cities in Middletown's state and to other cities in the United States,[39] have been cut twice, by 10 and again by 5 per cent, in the

[38] See *Middletown,* p. 208.

[39] The following figures were published by the Board of Education in the pamphlet, *How Much Do Our Schools Cost the Taxpayer?* as evidence of the economical operation of the city's schools. These median salaries *antedate* the local salary cuts in the depression:

MEDIAN SALARIES IN 1930-31

Occupation	In 204 U.S. cities of 30,000 to 100,000 population (1)	In 19 cities in Middletown's state (2)	In Middletown (3)	Difference U. S. cities and Middletown (Col. 1 less 3) (4)	Difference state cities and Middletown (Col. 2 less 3) (5)
Sr. H. S. principal	.$4,281.00	$3,965.28	$3,400.00	$881.00	$565.28
Jr. H. S. principal	. 3,353.00	3,146.21	2,525.00	828.00	621.21
Elem. principal ...	2,646.00	2,441.88	2,325.00	321.00	116.88
Sr. H. S. teachers ..	2,111.00	2,046.99	1,762.50	348.50	284.49
Jr. H. S. teachers ..	1,860.00	1,763.04	1,611.11	248.89	151.93
Elem. teachers	1,609.00	1,572.55	1,500.93	108.07	71.62

The nineteen cities in Middletown's state referred to in the second and fifth

depression. Teacher morale has suffered seriously in the depression, notably that of women teachers, because there has been a tendency to grant to married men teachers salary increases above women's salaries.[40] In 1935, at the instigation of the local Teachers' Federation, a new city-wide salary schedule was approved by the school board, anticipating a return over a four-year period to the pre-depression salary level. This salary scale, when achieved, will create a salary range from $800 to a top of $2,065—the maximum for a teacher with five years of college training and fourteen or more years of experience being in an elementary school $1,775, in a junior high school $1,920, and in a senior high school $2,065.[41] The Chamber of Commerce led an attack on this new salary schedule in the summer of 1936 as part of its drive to reduce taxation, and, as this is being written, the Judge of the Circuit Court has ordered the teachers' salary list and the new salary schedule before the board of tax adjustment for reconsideration.[42]

The counter movements of rising pupil enrollments and slashed budgets appear in Table 38.[43] The total operating costs of Middletown's schools, after rising by 19 per cent between the school year 1925-26 and 1929-30, was driven down by 20 per cent from the 1929-30 level by 1932-33, and by 1935-36 had recovered only a quarter (27 per cent) of the loss since 1929-30. Cost per pupil fell from $86.21 in 1929-30

columns of figures are not selected, but include all cities graded down from the largest to the nineteenth in size. They comprise one city of the first class (250,000 and over); nine of the second class (35-250,000); eight of the third class (20-35,000); and one of the fourth class (10-20,000). Middletown was in 1930 ninth in size among these nineteen cities, placing it in the second class.

[40] At a "get-together" dinner of Middletown's men teachers in the spring of 1935, the school superintendent is said to have told the men "confidentially" that he was going to see that men were paid more than women. In response to the question, "How?" he is reported on good authority to have replied, "Well, by golly! I'll say that you do better work than the women."

[41] It is significant for teacher morale (and also significant as regards the status of the woman worker in Middletown) that women teachers do not believe that they will be allowed to reach these maximum salaries.

[42] Here one sees the familiar situation of a business culture slashing the social services in which it may believe, but in which it does not believe as much as in the goodness to business and to the city, in its competition for new industries, of a low tax rate. In a culture organized around competitive private business, all interpretations of the "public interest" that do not relate directly to this central pursuit occupy a vulnerable position and are the first to suffer in time of strain.

Middletown teachers feel that the community, including even the "better citizens," have "let education down" in the depression and that the future is very clouded and much less favorable than the outlook before the depression.

[43] See Appendix III for this table.

to $63.97 in 1933-34, and stood at virtually this figure in 1935-36. Meanwhile, against these failing budget totals, Middletown added 17.6 per cent more pupils between 1925-26 and 1929-30, and in 1935-36 the total was 33.0 per cent above 1925-26.

Here again one sees Middletown attempting to move in two opposed directions at once. It proclaims a new philosophy of "educating the individual" which admittedly depends upon teachers with exceptional insight and upon a small pupil load, and at the same time administrative thrift prompts it to reduce salaries and to use its better teachers as a device for increasing the pupil load. A culture thus busily stepping one step forward and one step back throws interesting light upon the "conservatism" and "resistance to change" that are such marked characteristics of every culture. Not only is the omnipresent retarding element of habit involved—and a "culture" is but the habits of a people—but in any complex culture different aims (*e.g.,* those of the businessmen on the school board and their hired administrators out to "make a record" with the taxpayers, as over against the aims of the teachers bent upon educating the young) may cancel each other out when they come to focus on a single issue.

One of Middletown's educational casualties due to depression economizing is its evening classes, formerly operated under the public schools. These classes were open to all persons over the age of sixteen not enrolled in the public day schools. They had tended in past years to enroll larger numbers in times when employment was temporarily down, and in the "bad" spring of 1925 they had an enrollment of 1,890.[44] In the flourishing winter of 1928-29 the enrollments were 753. In the first winter of the depression, 1929-30, the total rose to 993, though by the spring semester it had dropped to 450. In the winter of 1930-31 enrollments were only fifty; nine classes (including bookkeeping, shorthand, machine calculation, industrial chemistry, child development, parent education, and other homemaking courses) were dropped since minimum enrollments of fifteen per class were not achieved; and only four classes (applied electricity, drafting, machine-shop practice, and elementary typing) were continued. Following the winter of 1930-31, the evening school was abandoned entirely as an economy move. Apparently even the moderate course fees (all under

[44] See *Middletown.* p. 184.

$10) were too difficult for the community to meet in sufficient numbers, and the schools were anxious to be relieved of the financial cost.

In the fall of 1933 evening courses were reinaugurated under F.E.R.A. with no fees attached. During the winter of 1933-34, according to the County Emergency School Supervisor, "Almost the sole aim of these classes was to help the morale of the unemployed, which was very low. Some men and women came and worked hard at things they never expected to use, just to keep their minds off their troubles." During the winter of 1934-35 these classes totaled forty-six separate units, five in the morning, four in the afternoon, and thirty-seven in the evening, and they enrolled 400 men and 518 women, with an age range from sixteen to seventy-six years. The courses included a wide range, from straight vocational training to classes of fifty-nine in parent education, forty-four in mathematics, twenty in economics, two groups of sixty-seven and thirty-two respectively in the economic management of the household, and large enrollments in public speaking and dramatics. Of the 556 students enrolled in May, 1935, 227 were permanently employed, sixty temporarily employed, 180 were unemployed, and eighty-nine were on relief.

It is hard to appraise what these classes portend for the future. This F.E.R.A. work, though it is under the direction of the public-school system, straggles along as best it can under conditions which necessitate the use of only relief teachers of uneven training, with classes subject to summary closing as soon as a teacher gets "a real job." The local public-school system expects to resume its evening school when its budget permits, and the State hopes the present adult education program will become permanent. The eventual outcome may be a strengthened and broadened program of adult education in Middletown, though the odds are against this in the immediate future; for Middletown does not have the adult education habit very strongly, and the school board represents a control system to which educational innovations are at present largely unnecessary luxuries and adults are decidedly people who may be left to stand on their own feet in line with the "best American tradition."

According to the early American tradition the schools served as an extension and transmitter of the values upon which parents, teachers, religious and civic leaders were in substantial agreement. But during recent decades—as home, church, and community have each become in themselves areas of confused alternatives, and education has developed a professional point of view of its own, *of* the culture, but also somewhat *over against* the culture—it is not surprising that Middletown's schools have been becoming by quiet stages increasingly an area of conflict, an exposed focus of opposing trends in other social institutions, whose contradictions become more acute and threatening to Middletown as the shape and import of incipient immediate conflicts are magnified on the screen of the next generation.

There is conflict over the question of whose purposes the schools are supposedly fulfilling: Are these purposes those of the parent who wants education for *his* child in order that, through the acquisition of certain skills and knowledge or, more important, certain symbolic labels of an "educated person," he may achieve a larger measure of success than the parent himself has known? Or are they those of the citizen who wants, on the one hand, to have the fundamentals of community life, including its politico-economic mores, transmitted unchanged, and, on the other, to use the schools as an instrument of change sufficiently to bring any alien or backward children in the community up to these familiar standards? Or those of the teacher, with ideas derived from outside Middletown, loyal to a code of his own and obeying its philosophy? Or those of the taxpayers, businessmen, and school board members, whose chief emphasis is on "successful" and "progressive" schools, to be sure, but within the limits of a practical, sound, unextravagant, budget? Or are they the purposes of any one of the pressure groups who want to teach the children patriotism, health, thrift, character building, religion,—or any one of the other values more or less accepted by the community as a whole but become an emotionally weighted "cause" with one special group?

Each of these vested interests exerts its special pressure on the schools. Language teachers may resent the intrusion of a course in hygiene as a required subject in the high school, while grade geography teachers may protest the drive to merge geography and history. To some parents the college laboratory school represents "the solution," while others regard it, according to the local press, as "an expensive, dangerous laboratory in which children are used instead of chemicals"; some parents hail it as "developing reasoning," "broadening the child's field of thought," and "teaching things that will be of practical use," while others lament that it "has no discipline," "encourages children to do nothing but play," and that "my child has studied nothing but history and hasn't had a spelling lesson all year." If parents trained in another era are at sea as regards the present elaborate high-school curriculum, they still think they know what an "elementary education" should be and feel that they can insist upon "essentials" there.

To quote a veteran worker with Middletown's children, "Our parents are realizing the increasingly sharp divergence of their world and that of their children today as never before." And the parents' world strikes back! In many cases they attempt to use the schools as a means of holding the two worlds together. A high-school course in sociology has been dropped because of parental protest over the fact that problems of sex were discussed in class. Over the heads of Middletown teachers, trained according to standards wider than some of the mores of Middletown, hangs at all times the sword of parental conservatism and anxiety. This is rendered the more difficult because, in manners and morals as well as economics, politics, and religion, the local community contains taxpaying parents of widely varying personal standards. The teacher knows and the community knows that the children ranged in their seats are wise in matters not in the curriculum, and that many of these children are rebelliously clamoring for the right to raise questions and to be outspoken in the face of the official and parental restraints. As one teacher said, "I am facing a new problem nowadays: My pupils insist on raising questions I dare not let them discuss though my conscience demands that I not clamp down on their honest questions. The things they say continually keep me on pins and needles for fear some of them will go home and tell their parents. I have an uneasy furtive sense about it all."

Middletown's emphasis upon education for the community values of group solidarity and patriotism was noted in the 1925 study.[45] This concern, sharpened after the World War by America's realization of its closeness to the political turbulence of Europe and of the necessity for maintaining its own traditions, appears to have grown only slowly in Middletown in the latter years of the 1920's. American business in those years was prosperous and cocksure of its future and of the supremacy of the United States, and there was a sense of space and buoyant opportunity in the United States that made for latitude and tolerance. But the depression has again set the tide running strongly toward control of the schools "in the public interest." The restlessness and sense of "things being out of hand" that deepened as the depres-

[45] See *Middletown,* pp. 196-99 and 488-90.

sion ground its way through American life, forcing actions counter to some of the culture's deepest traditions, has prompted sharp renewal of the quietly tense struggle for control by two rival philosophies.

On the one hand, there is the belief, a natural outgrowth of the American individualistic and democratic tradition, that the schools should foster not only free inquiry but individual diversity, and that they best serve their communities when they discover, and equip the individual to use, his emotional and intellectual resources to the fullest extent, in however diverse ways. Although professional educators are still searching for ways in which this can be done, this philosophy has gained wide acceptance among them, and is in some cases used as a defensive bulwark against repressive forces. It inevitably runs counter to another philosophy, far more often found in human societies, namely, that the function of the educational system is the perpetuation of traditional ways of thought and behavior, the passing on of the cultural tradition, and, if need be, the securing of conformity by coercion. When the Middletown school board approved the "new philosophy" in its 1927 program, it was approving the first of these, and it was probably quite unaware of the element of defense of educational freedom against repression inherent in such new programs. When, therefore, some Middletown teachers saw in the breakdown of old ways under the weight of the depression an opportunity to meet new times with new education, involving more and franker discussion of current problems, they began to run a neck and neck race with various agencies of control in the community which were demanding more rigidity and conformity in the form of new compulsory courses and a closer scrutiny of the content taught.

Paradoxically, Middletown teachers whose opinions exhibit any variations from the dominant values of the community appear to be at present in the equivocal position of never having been so free from purely educational restraints and yet at the same time so dangerously in jeopardy from the community. Proponents of the occasional outstanding liberal teacher boast quietly of the fact that he or she "is teaching really fine, thought-provoking things that make an impression on the student's thinking," and they add that "so far" the teacher has "got by" despite the rumblings of occasional objectors.

This seeming tolerance of more contradictory extremes within the culture is a familiar aspect of a culture between two eras, gone adrift from its earlier anchors and in the process of being re-anchored by the competing groups in the culture. What one witnesses here is a common phenomenon met with in the course of social change. The adequacy of the old procedures comes gradually by imperceptible stages into question as experience and knowledge grow and conditions change. New elements in the culture, addressed to changed conditions, develop new philosophies, and different parts of the culture begin to operate along divergent and even in some cases contradictory lines. But the tendency of traditional control systems to overlook these subtle changes allows a wide measure of tolerance until some occurrence brings the conflict into the open and crystallizes the situation as a "public problem." Then the new elements favoring change, which have been growing bolder and more open in the pre-crisis weather of opinion which has included more and more open questioning, find themselves suddenly involved in a bitter process of "liquidation" by the aroused control system, provided the latter is still strong enough to enforce its will.

In Middletown the community pressure forces are mobilizing against dissent. Business knows what it wants. The patriotic groups know what they want. The D.A.R., always on a hair-trigger of watchfulness for "disloyalty," is reported to feel that both the high school and the college have "some pretty pink teachers"; and it is reported as characteristic of its activity that sons and daughters in the classrooms of suspected teachers have been enlisted to check up on the latters' teachings. When a social-science teacher in one of the high schools spoke favorably of joining the World Court, a local editorial warned that teachers ought to remember that the schools are supported by taxes. A State law, passed by the legislature in 1935 with the backing of the D.A.R., requires a new compulsory high-school course on the Federal Constitution. A local editor commented on this law in his column:

A rare opportunity for the public-school teachers of [this state] to instill patriotism into the minds of high-school pupils is given by the act of the 1935 State legislature which provides for the instruction of pupils in the national and State constitutions. Much depends, however, upon the attitude the teachers take toward such instruction and their enthusiasm for the subject, or the lack of such enthusiasm. The course will be mandatory beginning with the 1937 school year.

The conscientious teacher will explain in detail the meaning of our constitutions, how they came into being and the objects they are supposed to serve. She will show how it is the citizen's protection against various political theories, . . .

The same editor, writing of the Teachers' Oath bill in Massachusetts, said:

. . . a teacher in a public school or college is an officer of the government and all officers of the government are required to take such an oath from the President of the United States down to the township constable. Of course this thing could be carried too far. There is no such thing as compulsory patriotism. One cannot be made to love his country, but if he do not, he should not receive any compensation from it. The oath was designed as a method of weeding out of public service those who are not genuine Americans. . . .

Perhaps it is going a bit strong to require every school child to salute the flag, as is done in some places, even though the child may derive benefits from the government, for children's minds are immature or they would not be children, and if they are very young the salute at best would be automatic and perhaps meaningless. But the taking of the oath is based upon an entirely different premise—the premise that these teachers in public schools are officers and beneficiaries of the government, and if they are unwilling to subscribe to it they should get into some other business or profession where no oath is required.

It cannot be stated too often that these restrictions upon "freedom" in education imposed by the control agencies of Middletown are applied for what are regarded as the best interests of the culture. Middletown trusts education profoundly as a slogan—"I have never found a city economically sound which was not also educationally and spiritually sound," declared a popular speaker before the Lions Club—but it distrusts it at many points as an active reality. In its mellower moods Middletown likes to let its imagination run, and it praises education and envies the "educated man"; but in its more practical mood education must not be allowed to "get out of hand," and teachers are meager souls out of touch with life, the sort of people one can hire for the wages of a clerk in a retail store. At times Middletown can nod genially over such an editorial as the following in which the editor momentarily "let himself go":

Somewhere along the way the brightness [of our children] gets worn off and the eagerness gets dulled, and instead of faith there comes disillusionment, and year by year the world's follies and stupidities are repeated by a tribe of adults who are not recognizably better than their fathers and mothers. . . . The welfare of the world depends ultimately on the emergence of people who are wiser and kinder and in all ways better folk than we ourselves are.

And in the next breath the community applauds wholeheartedly a speaker who, drawing back in dismay from the prospect that "whosoever captures the mind of the child controls the beliefs of the next generation," asserted: "The education we give our children should be limited to those matters on which there is substantial agreement among educated men of serious purpose." Of the two points of view, the latter more cautious one is usually uppermost. It is hard for adult Middletown to tolerate in its children—of all persons—more "wisdom" than it has, and it easily assumes that "educated men of serious purpose" would "agree substantially" with the views sensible men of affairs in Middletown hold. And these men, beset by social change and perplexity, see no occasion for speeding up change through "unsettling" young minds; rather, to quote a speaker addressing the high-school seniors on the advantages of a college education, "College helps one to success, by which I mean poise, serenity, and kindness in the acceptance of routine living. It teaches the mechanism of endurance." Here speaks not the voice of "education for individual differences" to the end that past "follies and stupidities . . . repeated by a tribe of adults who are not recognizably better than their fathers and mothers" may be avoided, but the sober voice of the *status quo* urging the new generation to bear without murmuring the world handed on to them.

Progressive teachers in Middletown are greeting with mixed emotions the announcement, in the fall of 1936, that "[Middletown] Schools Will Stress Teaching of Information about Local Facts and History." The announcement reads:

[Middletown] schools will stress the teaching of information about Middletown this year. Study of the community will include industries of the city, with something of their history, evolution, products, processes of manufacture, and markets; utilities; police and fire protection offered; form and machinery of the city's government; and other important elements affecting intelligent citizenship in the community. An illustrated booklet containing such information probably will be printed in school printshops and distributed to children without charge.[46]

[46] The project subsequently grew to include a dozen separate pamphlets. It may or may not be significant, in view of the strength and tactics of the local

One may view this simply as a move in the direction of an education based upon the realities of daily life that surround the child and moving out from these to the study of the wider world of institutions. And one may also view this as a phase of the militantly defensive civic self-consciousness with which Middletown is emerging from the depression; as but another manifestation of the local control which is determined that there shall be no dissent in Middletown and that *our* town, *our* industries and public utilities, and *our* ways of doing things shall be accepted uncritically as right. There is much in the local scene to tempt one to this latter view.

The tightening of the conflict between the two philosophies of public education has resulted in a state of affairs in which mature, thoughtful, conscientious teachers not only fear what parents or organizations may say if they follow candidly the searching questions of their students, but in which a teacher discussing these problems with a colleague may interrupt the discussion by the apprehensive remark, "But I don't know whether I should discuss these things *even with you.*" To the outside observer bent on appraising the weight of the power systems in the community, there seems little doubt, in view of the preponderance of power on the traditional side in Middletown, as to the direction which the immediate resolution of the present ambivalence in Middletown's education will take. If conditions of national and local strain continue even moderately sharp, Middletown's forward-looking teachers will either "tone down" their teaching or conceivably be quietly removed.[47]

The temporary resolution of this conflict and the course of events in the immediate future are perhaps foreshadowed in a news story appearing in June, 1936:

public utilities noted at the close of Ch. IX, that the first pamphlets undertaken were devoted to electricity, to gas, and to water as they relate to the life of the city.

[47] See in this connection Harold Laski's review of the *Report of the Commission on the Social Studies* (*New Republic,* July 29, 1936) in which, after citing the conviction of members of the Commission that "The distance between the education a new America needs, and the education it is getting, is alarmingly wide," and that "If America is to make citizens capable of running, nay, of preserving, a democratic society, what is required is a basic, not a superficial, renovation of the whole system," he questions whether the kind of education advocated by the Commission is possible in a society organized as American society is at present.

"FADS" WILL GIVE WAY TO COMMON-SENSE PLAN

Sweeping changes will be made in [Middletown's] schools this year and next. Right now the school board is up in arms about teachers' salaries [under pressure from the Chamber of Commerce]. That's why the employment of personnel for the next school year, weeks overdue, was not carried through at the board's meeting Tuesday afternoon.

Salaries are only a part of the picture, however. Many so-called "educational fads" are doomed in favor of so-called "common-sense" methods. One of the major changes expected is limitation or elimination of the research department of the city school system. . . .

It is considered probable the board will insist next year on closer contact between the school administration and teachers. The board probably will appoint an assistant to the superintendent whose principal duty will be to visit classrooms personally to see results first hand. . . .

While the issue of these various conflicting pressures bearing on the schools is far from settled, it would appear:

That the things people in Middletown may want of education as persons are not identical with the things the community as a competitive unit in an industrial economy wants.

That the old tendency to relative identity of the wants of persons, homes, churches, and community exists today less than at any time in the past.

That many of the ideologies that are currently taught in the schools are in conflict with "common sense" assumptions by which Middletown lives from day to day.

That the schools of the city, after swinging out somewhat more freely in the 1920's on a course of their own, dictated by a philosophy of venturesome "education for individual differences," are being recaptured and harnessed bit by bit to the ends of a special type of unified culture.

That this culture which appears to be bending education to its special purposes is a culture dominated by a drive not for "individual differences" but for "community solidarity."

And that this community solidarity is being invoked primarily by the agencies of control under a philosophy which identifies community welfare with business welfare and sees solidarity as essential to the achievement of "business prosperity."

All of which, if this interpretation is correct, suggests a widening area of conflict in Middletown between the teacher and the educational administrator hired by the school board to "run" its schools; between school and community values; between parents who may want something other than docile conformity from the education of their children and the community bent upon achieving this solidarity; between the politico-economic pressure agencies and agencies for other types of pressure; and, above all, between the spirit of inquiring youth and the spirit of do-as-we-say-and-ask-no-questions.

The community places its greatest hope in its schools as instruments of "progress" when that progress is assumed to be a continuous straight-line development along the lines which Middletown understands and believes in: economic and material expansion under the familiar doctrine of "individual liberty." The community fears the schools as leading to change if this progress is along unknown and possibly "dangerous" lines which cannot be predicted and which may lead the young to ways unfamiliar to their fathers. It wants the schools to train more intelligent citizens, but it has a profound distrust of too much "cleverness" or novelty if applied to practical affairs. It wants character development but not to the point of raising ethical questions in regard to current group practices. Middletown has desired its schools to train its children for participation in the life of the community. But in a world in which the search for jobs has become—and may remain—more difficult than in the past, the schools must effectively delay this participation and become a place where adolescents and young adults may contentedly, and Middletown hopes fruitfully, spend their time as long as possible. This situation of prolonged schooling heightens the strains involved in the status of the young adult in Middletown,[48] and also conflicts with the pressure to force students ahead as rapidly as possible from grade to grade through school and off the school budget.[49]

The recapture of the educational system by agencies or community solidarity is facilitated not only by these ambivalences among parents and within different parts of the culture but also by the fact that the educators are themselves caught in the whirlpool of their own conflicting aims. Many of the external efficiencies proclaimed in the hundred-page bulletin, *Educational Planning in the* [*Middletown*] *Public Schools,* have been achieved at the expense of other alleged values of education. Despite the emphasis upon new imported "yard-

[48] See *Middletown*, pp. 140-41.

[49] In the first semester of the year 1933-34 there were "only 390 pupils who failed out of an enrollment of 7,618," a decline in failures hailed as an "improvement" which "means greatly reduced school costs."

sticks of efficiency," and even because of them, some of the more perspicacious teachers state, "Our schools are just drifting, without adequate leadership"; and "Our very efficiency is a serious liability. We live in such a clutter of 'revising the curriculum' and 'keeping records' that the teaching of the better teachers is suffering." The desire to achieve a standardized procedure widely acclaimed as desirable is frequently at sharp variance with the newly aroused sense of what education can mean in terms of individual development in actual present-day society.

Many of these conflicts are no doubt related to what Mr. Justice Brandeis has called in another connection "the curse of bigness." Middletown is now a city of nearly 50,000, handling a less and less selected group of children as compulsory school years lengthen and "everybody tries to go to college." As such it faces the necessity of more and more large-scale, routinized procedures; and there is no sector of our culture where the efficiency of large-scale routines is capable of being more antithetical to the spirit of the social function to be performed than in education. Likewise are such conflicts inevitable overtones, echoed in the sensitive reflector of the schools, of an era of change so rapid that it may be called a crisis era.

In such a period, it is natural for Middletown to attempt to resolve conflicts by grasping fixedly the points in its educational system which seem to offer the readiest means of measuring success and the greatest assurance of stability. And in the struggle between quantitative administrative efficiency and qualitative educational goals in an era of strain like the present, the big guns are all on the side of the heavily concentrated controls behind the former.

CHAPTER VII

Spending Leisure

Whatever may be affirmed or denied as to the economic basis of all human societies, Middletown clearly operates on the assumption that the roots of its living lie in the acquisition of money. The churches formally deny this, papers before its women's clubs and even occasional "inspirational" speakers before Rotary stress the primacy of the "higher things" of life, and one of the last things Middletown's formal training of the young stresses is how to "make money." But everywhere one runs upon the culture's commitment, implicit and explicit, to the necessity for and goodness of hard work in the acquisition of property. Not only do the leaders who "run the town" run it to "maintain prosperity" and "to attract new industries," but at many points, less formal than the operations of the business control group, one encounters this dominant commitment to the basic assumption of the primacy of economic interests, with all life built upon hard work for a livelihood, and with "success" in work—measured in dollars earned—as the goal and as the validation of the social utility of the individual's work. One hears the mayor declaim at a public dinner in the spring of 1929, "We have pride in our homes and elation in our schools, but the pulse of our city's life is in our industries." One reads in a business-class editorial that "While marrying for money alone is not advisable, there is probably nothing more important to domestic happiness in the world." And one hears in conversation the simple acceptance of his city by a workingman on the ground that "Of course we like [Middletown]; it's where we get our living."

The fabric of speech touching every aspect of activity sets forth the same philosophy of scarcity, of the need for hard work, of the value of success, and of money as the measure of success: The "good provider" is the "successful" family man; "It *pays* to send children to college"; "The church has made America prosperous. . . . Godliness is profitable even from a business standpoint"; "Jobs are the main issue. . . .

There is but one convincing argument for the average voter—one which appeals to his pocketbook"; "It is desirable to *spend* leisure *profitably*." Thus, not only does the community's activity center in getting a living, but the very symbols of group speech swing around economic values. The culture is repeating insistently that work is an inherently honorable thing by which other activities are measured; that no amount of labor is sufficient to wrest adequate sustenance from a niggardly environment; that group welfare is measured in terms of money prosperity; and that too much leisure for "the common man" is to be feared as deleterious to his character and retarding to the welfare of the whole group.[1]

Even within such an economically dominated scheme of things, however, one must distinguish at the outset the functional significance of leisure to the business class and to the working class. It is not irrelevant or by accident that businessmen in this culture are wont to speak of the "business game," and it is also not by accident that Middletown's machine operators and laborers do *not* talk of the "factory game." Business-class status in Middletown comes from the amount of money one makes, which in turn comes from the job one holds. The amount of money a businessman may make is theoretically unlimited at its upper end, and actually tends to reach in good times for a substantial number of businessmen into a local economic stratosphere which, though, for most of them, modest in terms of the "big" business world, is none the less remotely beyond the cruising range of Middletown's working-class men. Work, in this business-class universe, offers

[1] One of Middletown's most central cultural concepts, more deeply rooted historically even than such things as "Democracy" and "Christianity," is "Scarcity." It still conceives the central conflict and the grand adventure of its culture as that with man's oldest enemy: Scarcity. It has carried over intact the pre-Industrial Revolution emotional sanctions for the necessity for continuous hard work, the danger of too much leisure, and the essential moral goodness of individual striving to "get ahead" as the best way of doing one's personal bit toward the welfare of the group. It is characteristic that one feels at home in Middletown in reading a writer like Malthus. One might almost be listening to a speaker in a Middletown civic club when one reads in Chapter V of the *Essay on the Principle of Population* (1st ed., 1798): "Suppose that by a subscription of the rich, the eighteen pence a day which men earn now, was made up to five shillings. . . . [This] would make every man fancy himself comparatively rich, and able to indulge himself in many hours or days of leisure. This would give a strong and immediate check to productive industry; and in a short time, not only the nation would be poorer, but the lower classes themselves would be much more distressed than when they received only eighteen pence a day."

to the fortunate when business is zooming something of the element of exhilaration and adventure associated in our physically unprecarious culture with play activity: one's winnings depend upon one's drive, ingenuity, thrift, and skill, plus a substantial sporting element of luck.[2] It is conceivable that the lack of ingenuity exhibited by these men as regards their leisure is not unrelated to the fact that their ingenuity is so largely and absorbingly—at least in the case of the pace-setting leaders—focused elsewhere. On the other hand, the wives of the business class, gaining nowadays relatively little status from the arts of the housewife, throw themselves into leisure and have become the leisure-innovators of the culture. In this business-class world in which the job itself is so important to status and invites an endlessly "repaying" expenditure of energy, leisure among men is secondary to work: men work not to get leisure but to get money, to "get ahead," to "get up in the world." The resulting spectacle—of some of the ablest members of society, the men best educated, best "off" financially, and conceivably best able to live rich, many-sided lives, spending themselves unremittingly in work, denying themselves leisure and bending fine energies to the endless acquisition of the *means* of living a life they so often take insufficient leisure to live—is one factor leading certain contemporary psychiatrists to remark on the masochistic tendencies in our culture.[3] If the leisure of such men tends to be used instrumentally to further their primary business of getting ahead, it also becomes easy under the driving pressure of the "business game" for the business-class wife to make the leisure of the family contribute to her husband's business activity.

Facing this business-class world is that of the six to seven in ten of the city's population who compose the working class. They live in a world with an economic ceiling permanently and monotonously fixed at around $2,000 to $2,500. Nominally their economic ceiling is as high as that of the business class, but Middletown's workers

[2] It is not, of course, intended here to suggest that all Middletown's businessmen are equally preoccupied with business or equally able to profit from the business system. It is intended, however, to stress strongly the common morale which an economic order founded on centralized, privately controlled credit and characterized by opportunities for substantial private gain engenders in the "little fellows" as well as the "big shots" in the local business world. There is nothing in Middletown's culture more contagious than the chance to make a profit. See the discussion of "the Middletown spirit" in Ch. XII.

[3] This point is being developed by Dr. Karen Horney in a forthcoming book, and by Dr. Erich Fromm.

are apparently coming to believe in slowly increasing numbers that, as one of them expressed it, "That's just another one of the fairy tales the Chamber of Commerce feeds you." Status in the workingman's world, where skill is yielding to the machine and "getting ahead" is increasingly beyond the workers' reach, is not often derivable from the kind of job one does, or, with the blurring of the line between "skill" and "nonskill," from the difference between what one earns and what other workers earn.[4] You have a job—if you're lucky—and you work. If you are trying to send your children to college you may be working for that; but the depression has put a crimp in the claim of the 1920's that college educations for children of working-class parents are worth the sacrifices they cost. So you work. Someday you're going to die. Meanwhile, leisure assumes a simple, direct, and important place in your scheme of things: *it's* when you *live,* and you get all of it you can—here, now, and all the time.

Only by understanding this different focus upon leisure of the lives of those living north and south of the tracks can one appreciate the tenacity with which the workingman clings to his automobile. If the automobile is by now a habit with the business class, a comfortable, convenient, pleasant addition to the paraphernalia of living, it represents far more than this to the working class; for to the latter it gives the status which his job increasingly denies, and, more than any other possession or facility to which he has access, it symbolizes living, having a good time, the thing that keeps you working. And again, only by understanding how these two groups weigh the importance of work and leisure can one understand the exasperation of the business-man over the workingman's frequent preference for his car rather than for the slow, painful process of saving for the future.

In all that follows, therefore, it must be borne in mind that statements regarding "Middletown's leisure" are peculiarly open to error in that leisure tends to symbolize at certain vital points different things to the man who has a business and to the man who operates a machine.

In 1925 leisure was becoming more passive, more formal, more organized, more mechanized, and more commercialized.[5] And leisure was seemingly taking on, in those phases where it remained active,

[4] See the discussion in Ch. II of the relative rise between 1920 and 1930 in the share of Middletown's workers who are only "semiskilled."
[5] See *Middletown,* Chs. XVII-XIX.

more of the competitive emphasis so characteristic of this whole culture.

Since 1925 Middletown has been through two periods with widely different implications for leisure. The first was big with both the promise and reality of leisure—golf, mid-winter trips to Florida, and the vague hope in a few cases of "retiring" into that blessed land where "every day will be Sunday bye and bye" for the business class, and for the working class the tangible realities of automobiles, radio, and other tools for employing leisure. Then, swiftly, the second period, when enforced leisure drowned men with its once-coveted abundance, and its taste became sour and brackish. Today, Middletown is emerging from the doldrums of the depression more than ever in recent years committed to the goodness of work. Just as an editorial commented comfortably, when factory chimneys were again beginning to pour forth their soft black soot in the spring of 1935, "Nobody is complaining nowadays about the former 'smoke nuisance,'" so nobody today is wanting more time off from work. It is this feverish devotion to the goodness of work that gives added edge to the indignation of local businessmen over the proposal of the Roosevelt administration to continue its program of socialized devices for supporting men out of work. And it is, in part, this same sour background of too much leisure that prompts local workingmen to insist that they "don't want relief, but jobs."

Presumably, the present exaggerated emphasis upon work represents an overcompensation for the depression. What will be the permanent impression on the work-leisure complex in this culture left by the depression? Has Middletown learned anything permanently from the depression's blow to the prestige of business as a basis for a society's design for living, and from the sudden availability of unprecedented amounts of leisure? Has something of the honorific status traditionally associated with work extended to new possibilities in the use of leisure? Has the meaning of leisure to the business or the working class in any way been altered? Has it become to any less degree an extension of, or an alternative to, working activities in the orbit of getting a living, and acquired a more independent status of its own? Has the depression altered in any way the extent to which leisure is formal, passive, organized, a product shaped by the business and machine age?

One marked aspect of Middletown's leisure in 1935 is the innovations at both ends of the social scale. Whether as product of the prosperity era continued through the depression or of the growing size of the city, a significant new development is the emergence, noted at the close of Chapter III, of an upper class to whom certain leisure activities have value, not in relation to work, but quite independently as a symbol of status. This upper class, marked off from the less socially differentiated business class of 1925, includes the "horsey set" and the group of people interested in private aviation. Both of these new interests, as noted elsewhere, have been influenced by the turning aside of the second generation of the X-family men from exclusive attention to business and civic affairs to a more varied expression of their energies. Around these men have developed two exclusive riding clubs, with clubhouses, gaited horses, and an annual horse show begun in 1932 which today draws entries from all over the Middle West. Since golf is becoming, with a public eighteen-hole course as well as the Country Club course, everyman's game, and since the Country Club is becoming less exclusive, these riding clubs are becoming symbolic of "belonging" to the best set. Middletown's airport, opened in 1932 and run by a group of wealthy local men, has a plant far beyond the capacity of most cities of Middletown's size. Two licensed pilots are employed, an extensive rate card carries regular rates to points as remote as Washington, D. C., and because of its excellent facilities the station is one of only twenty-three throughout the United States where certain types of teaching are permitted. In addition to these public planes, several private planes were owned by local wealthy young men in 1935.[6] At the close of

[6] One can merely speculate as to what the presence of privately owned planes means to Middletown. Judging by the eagerness with which spectators throng the airport on a pleasant Sunday, flying has a strong hold on the popular imagination, particularly of the young. With each new thrilling invention of this sort, the imperatives in the psychological standard of living of a portion of the population increase. It is likely that the ownership of private planes by wealthy young men in town has done its bit to enhance the general sentiment among Middletown's sons as to the desirability of making money, and lots of it; while with Middletown's daughters it confirms the sentiment of the editor quoted above that "There is probably nothing more important to domestic happiness [than money]." A considerable part of the money-mindedness of this culture is related to the abundance of new interesting ways of spending money with which its technology has showered it in the last two generations. It is difficult for a man in such a culture to draw a line under his possessions at any point, summate them, and say, "Here I rest. I will strive to add no more." And the power of new inventions to reaffirm in the young of each generation the acquisitive patterns of their parents is not easily overstressed.

One may speculate, too, as to what it may mean to the working class to have the airplane come to town as a local reality in possession of the sons of the X

1934, the press reported that during the year planes owned by business-men and commercial flyers of Middletown flew an estimated 190,000 miles out of Middletown, averaging over 500 miles a day.

At the other end of the social scale, innovation was also apparent in 1935 in the increased public provision of leisure activities for masses of people. Here one is witnessing again the anomaly, noted in Chapter IV, of Middletown's expansion of its civic resources, thanks to the depression; for this extension of public recreation is directly due to the F.E.R.A. In the spring of 1925 Middletown had formed a Playground Association under the auspices of the Dynamo Club, and by the summer of that year two school playgrounds and one park were providing supervised play for more than 200 children a day, financed by the Community Fund. Under depression impetus this supervised play program has expanded until in the summer of 1936 it included nine play centers for older boys and girls and fifteen for smaller children, with a total of 9,883 in attendance during the first five days. In 1935 the attendance for the opening week was less than two-thirds of this number, and it was, accordingly, anticipated in 1936 that the attendance for the entire summer would surpass the 176,316 of 1935. Besides the usual array of softball and hardball games, track and field meets, volley ball, tennis, and other sports, the program included a hobby show, a doll show, a pet show, handicraft, singing, Junior Garden Club, paddle tennis tournaments, horseshoe meets, aquatic meets, and dramatics. Swimming in 1936 changed from the earlier program which "consisted chiefly in seeing that no one drowned" to a program of teaching swimming and lifesaving, with four expert instructors in addition to the lifeguards. Play programs for older children were on a full-time basis four days each week and half-time two other days, and those for younger children were on a half-time basis. Free programs for adults were in operation in three of the city's parks and in the high-school auditorium in the summers of 1935 and 1936. They included a series of public dances in the parks with both social dancing

family and others "across the tracks." Does it, for instance, increase their sense of class difference? The answer to such a question depends upon a number of factors. The rapid spread of automobiles and radios among all income levels may conceivably have lessened the sense of class difference. But does the man with an eight-year-old "Chevie" feel more *like* the man with a new Packard because both have a car, or more *unlike* him because of the disparity in the two cars? And does the ownership of an automobile make one tend to want an airplane more—or less?

and square dancing, talking movies, concerts by a specially trained orchestra of unemployed musicians, one-act plays, and a series of open-air "amateur-night" programs that drew large audiences.

Another leisure-time innovation, due to Federal emergency financing, is a spacious outdoor municipal swimming pool and surrounding park in the center of town constructed in 1934 on the site of a former unsightly city dump. This pool is heavily used by all classes of the population. All children attending the supervised playgrounds regularly are given free tickets to the pool three days a week.

Like other phases of deliberate social change in Middletown directly traceable to the depression, some of this public provision of leisure facilities, especially of those for adults, is likely to disappear with returning good times. Here, again, however, a bench mark has been set up. For the first time in its history, the community has asked, in effect: What are the human and physical resources for constructive play and leisure-time self-development in our midst? And how can we best utilize them for the welfare of the widest possible group of our people? Middletown has really set its parks to work. It has reversed precedent by throwing open certain facilities in its school plants for summer use. What this has amounted to is an effort to state *positively* the problem of leisure for the mass of Middletown's citizens.

In 1925 the trend toward increasing organization of leisure activities was apparent.[7] The old easy "dropping in" was giving way to more planned parties. This represents a permanent change, probably related in part to the growing size of the city. But in the depression, along with lessened expenditures for clothes and the increased age of its automobiles, many business-class adults of Middletown have cultivated more informality and less expenditure in their social life. There is less entertaining at the Country Club.[8] The following, from the Society

[7] See *Middletown*, p. 278 ff.

[8] A by-product of this depression curtailing of the use of the Country Club, involving memberships and golf as well as use of the dining room, has been the throwing open of the Country Club to a more catholic membership. The remark was frequently heard in 1935 that "Anybody with money enough to pay the dues can get into the Country Club now."

This decline in the prestige of the Country Club is also probably related to the rise of the narrow upper-class group mentioned elsewhere. Some of the people in the latter group have resigned from the Country Club. Their riding clubs have somewhat displaced the Country Club for buffet suppers and informal affairs limited to their own group.

column of a Middletown paper in June, 1935, sets the picture of this simpler entertaining:

Despite the extreme heat, there are parties and still more parties. Possibly one reason is that entertaining is becoming so easy since informality has become the keynote. Inviting guests for dinner a few years ago meant a formal meal. The time easily will be remembered when masculine and juvenile members of the household received glaring looks punctuated with lifted eyebrows when they forgot in the presence of guests and referred to the evening meal as "supper." But time has changed that. Smart [Middletown] folks are having buffet suppers, and many, as Mrs. X did last Saturday when she entertained for Miss M——, are having their suppers on porches. Screened-in porches are becoming the rendezvous for many social gatherings. Others are setting their tables under shade trees on their lawns or near their pools and flower gardens.

Speaking of buffet suppers, they are so ultrafashionable just now and are so easily prepared. A meat platter, often a variety of cold meats and cheese, a hot vegetable or salad used to garnish the meat or served from a large bowl, hot rolls or biscuits with preserves, relishes, a dessert, and a beverage are being served by many [Middletown] hostesses. The food is placed on the serving table and each guest is invited to "help themselves." Informality allows one to return even for a second helping of a favorite dish. No longer does the clever hostess try to plan unusual menus. Rather, she serves the old favorites which everyone is sure to like, which is after all the secret of having guests enjoy their food.

A prominent feature of this simpler entertaining, involving less use of away-from-home locations like the Country Club, has been the rediscovery by Middletown of its back yards. In the 1925 study the heavy loss of function of porch and back yard with the coming of the motor age was noted.[9] In 1935 four changes in Middletown's back yards were apparent: the development of back-yard grills for cooking *al fresco* picnic suppers; the coming of back-yard furniture, whereby back yards have been fitted up, as a local news note characterized it, "like outdoor living rooms"; the revival of back-yard vegetable gardens as a source of food supply;[10] and the development of a mild mania for flower

[9] See *Middletown,* pp. 94-95.

[10] Home preserving has returned to favor in the depression, primarily as a personal thrift move, but also because reports of booming depression business at the X plant, a national center for the production of fruit jars, imparted promptly to Middletown's housewives the sanctions of national precedent and local enthusiasm for standing over the boiling preserving kettle.

gardening. All of these were in the summer of 1935 subjects of local pride, friendly emulation, and status. One felt oneself closer to the Middletown of the 1880's than to that of 1925 in the quiet enthusiasm one met on every hand for "my delphiniums" and "the way we've fixed up the back yard." Here Middletown, including a good many of its men, has decidedly been finding new leisure-time values in the depression, which it may not entirely lose if and when the depression disappears.

Middletown is a flat, sprawled city without physical distinction, like hundreds of others in the corn belt, and with the added disadvantage of a malodorous "open cesspool" of a river winding through it. In 1925 the research staff had felt on the whole as did the editor of the local paper in the following printed comment in 1935:

In Middletown we have an almost utter absence of beautiful surroundings, unless you go out a bit. The business district is ugly except for the courthouse, and the county commissioners never try to increase the beauty of the surroundings there by parking the grounds. . . . Be away from Middletown a short time and in some city of great natural beauty as to its surroundings, and you inquire of yourself why you live in an utterly unbeautiful town. The reason is that you have a job there and you have friends there.

To be sure, the return to Middletown in 1935 was made in June, when any natural environment in this climate renders one somewhat giddy with its opulent loveliness. But as one passed along Middletown's streets in the long June twilight, with one's senses alert for changes as well as fixities in old familiar things, one felt keenly the physical presence of fragrant growing things. One quickly began to feel oneself an illiterate among one's friends who insisted upon taking one out to see "the garden"—not mere beans and tomatoes, but flowers in startling variety, some of them painstakingly gathered from remote places, and familiarly identified by their scientific names. A local branch of the Garden Club of America was organized in February, 1930, and this has given structure to the local enthusiasm, in the form of programs discussing gardening, garden parties, and an annual city-wide display in a South Side park to which families from every walk of life send their blooms in competition for prizes. Today, flower gardening has become a popular hobby and has contributed a new area of local achievement. People study one another's triumphs with friendly rivalry, and they show you "our garden" with the undisguised enthusiasm with which a young couple exhibits a new baby. While this new enthusiasm is more pronounced among the business class, where, as stated above, the presence of the Garden Club adds the starch of social organization and prestige, both working-class yards and their entries in the annual flower show attest the vitality of the movement all over the city. The very attractiveness of many working-class yards served to emphasize the stark discouragement of many other working-class homes where morale was gone.

The increase in easy, sympathetic "neighboring," reported by a number of business-class people as accompanying the depression, is probably not unrelated to this partial substitution of home living and inexpensive back-yard skills for the prevailing emphasis of the culture upon competitive possessions and spending.

Reading played a relatively larger part among Middletown's informal, unorganized leisure activities during the depression than before. The public library circulation figures [11] show in general that Middletown reads more books in bad times and fewer in good times. Circulation failed even to keep up with population growth in the busy years from 1925 through 1929, increasing by only 15 per cent during these four years while the population was growing by 25 per cent. With the depression, circulation jumped by 20 per cent above the 1929 total in the first year, 1930; 1931 surpassed 1930 by 24 per cent; 1932 rose 26 per cent above 1931; and the peak year, 1933, was 11 per cent above 1932. Combined, these gains show a total rise of 108 per cent between 1929 and the peak year of circulation, 1933, while the city's population rose by only 5 per cent to its peak in 1931-32, and in 1933 fell off to only 3 per cent above 1929. Stated in terms of per-capita circulation, the average number of books borrowed annually from the public library by each person of all ages within the city fell from 6.5 in 1925 to 6.0 in 1929, rose to 7.0 in 1930, to 8.5 in 1931, to 10.7 in 1932, and to 12.2, or more than double the 1929 average figure, in 1933. Cardholders rose by 17 per cent between 1929 and 1933, or three to five times as fast as the population increased, as more and more of the

[11] See Table 39 in Appendix III.

Middletown is not a book-buying city, though in this respect it is probably not different from other similar midland cities of its size. Book reading in Middletown means therefore, overwhelmingly, the reading of public-library books. There is not even a strong book-rental service in the city and this type of service again is performed by the "new book" rental library in the public library.

city's population turned to reading in the depression. By 1933 every cardholder was reading, on an average, twenty books a year, as against eleven in 1929. With the flicker of returning better times in 1934 circulation fell off slightly again, and this decline continued in 1935. The total drop in circulation by the end of 1935 was, however, only to 8 per cent below the total for the record year, 1933; and circulation in 1935 was still 92 per cent above that in 1929.

Part of this growth in reading was probably stimulated by the opening of two branch libraries since 1925, both located on the South Side, one of them opened in October, 1930, and the other in June, 1934. The major portion of their circulation simply replaced previous "extension" circulation and circulation through the main library, although some of it undoubtedly is new circulation stimulated by convenience of location. By far the greater part of the increased reading in Middletown is, however, undoubtedly traceable to the depression itself, with its accompaniment of new leisure.

A closer view of what the depression has done to adult reading alone may be had from Table 40,[12] which separates out the circulation of the adult department of Middletown's library and presents totals by fiction and nonfiction. These figures show an increase of 145 per cent in adult circulation between 1929 and 1933, as against the rise noted above of only 108 per cent in total circulation, including children's reading. The increases in each year over the preceding year were, in 1930, 35 per cent; in 1931, 25 per cent; in 1932, 30 per cent; and in 1933, 12 per cent. In 1934 total adult circulation fell off to slightly below the 1932 figure, and in 1935 it continued to decline. The drop from the 1933 peak by the close of 1935 was 20 per cent, though adult circulation in 1935 was still 96 per cent above the 1929 level. Adult reading, therefore, responded more markedly than did children's reading to depression conditions, rising more steeply and further with the onset of "bad times" and falling off more sharply with business recovery. The downward trend in circulation in 1934-35 was tending to repeat the pattern of the boom years 1926-29, when Table 39 shows that both per-capita and per-cardholder circulations were falling. It is too soon to gauge whether the depression experience will leave Middletown with a permanently sharply augmented level of book reading. It is significant, however, that circulation in 1935 was still nearly double that of 1929.

[12] See Appendix III for this table.

Adult nonfiction reading rose between 1929 and 1933, as shown in Table 40, at only 44 per cent of the rate of increase in fiction reading—by 72 per cent, as over against a gain of 163 per cent in fiction. This suggests that Middletown was turning relatively more heavily to the anodyne of fiction in the depression than to nonfiction, conventionally regarded in this culture as "serious" reading. The percentage of total adult reading that was nonfiction fell from 20.1 in 1929 to 14.2 in 1933, and in 1934 began to rise again. Between 1933 and the close of 1935 adult fiction fell off at twice the rate of adult nonfiction.

Shifts in the kinds of adult nonfiction reading may be of especial significance as a reflection of new interests, more time for old interests, and the temporary spurring forward of effort to understand the perplexing changes in Middletown's overturned world. The outstanding fact observable from an analysis of the circulation of different kinds of nonfiction in a sample month for the years 1925-35 [13] is that all types of books rose together to peaks in 1932 or 1933 and all fell off after 1933. The increases in Sociology (including Economics and Government), Science, Travel, and Biography are most striking, while History registered the least spectacular gain.

Although a growing share of adult Middletown's reading from 1929 through 1933 was fiction, it is significant that interest in nonfiction held up as well as it did. It suggests that for many of Middletown's six people in every ten who hold library cards the depression involved some genuine extension of interests. Footnote 1 in Chapter V cites the high percentage of "resigned" (48 per cent), "apathetic" (25 per cent), and "desperate" (11 per cent) families found by Lazarsfeld [14] in his study of an Austrian village after two years of acute depression. Middletown's plight in the depression did not begin to approach in seriousness that of Marienthal, where virtually the entire community had lost its livelihood. Marienthal represents a self-respecting village factory community living in complete depression, without hope of the return of its source of livelihood and with its whole situation several stages advanced beyond any depths which Middletown as a community reached. It is not unlikely, however, that, even in the face of Middletown's soaring reading totals, close inspection would reveal here and there in many of its homes on relief the beginnings of the

[13] See Table 41 in Appendix III.
[14] Op. cit., p. 50.

sort of apathy described in Marienthal in such passages as the following:

As we enter the community, the impression we get is that of drab uniformity [begins the chapter strikingly captioned *"Die müde Gemeinschaft"* ("The Weary Community")].

The most common attitude is one of apathetic, hopeless living-along, with the conviction that nothing can be done about unemployment, and with a relatively subdued state of mind only occasionally lightened by a momentary burst of cheer; the whole bound up with an obliviousness to the future, which does not even live on in fantasy. The attitude may best be described by the word resignation.

This all-pervasive let-down in people's morale [since 1929] is eloquently portrayed in some of the local institutions today [1931]. According to the leader of the little theater: "The greatest difference between former times and now is that the players lack enthusiasm. They can't keep their minds on it, and you have to urge them to participate. A few of our good actors have wandered away. Although everyone now has more time, no one has any longer the drive to go ahead."

Opposite the factory is the large park. Marienthalers were formerly very proud of it. On Sunday they turned out to sit on its benches that lined the paths with their carefully trimmed shrubberies and to stroll about. Now the park is overgrown; weeds flourish in the paths, and the lawns are gone. Although nearly everyone in Marienthal has time now in which he could tend the park, no one bothers with it.

More directly pertinent for our purposes here is the material in *Die Arbeitslosen von Marienthal* on the decline in reading:

The records of the Marienthal village library bear mute witness to the shrinkage in positive interests: Since 1929 [the last year before the sudden complete closing of the textile factory which was the community's sole means of support] loans of books by the library have decreased by 48.7 per cent—and this despite the fact that use of the library is now entirely free, whereas a charge was made formerly. At first, the number of readers simply fell off; but even the few who have remained loyal to the library now read less than formerly. The number of volumes per borrower fell from 3.2 in 1929 to 2.3 in 1930 and 1.6 in 1931. That this decline was due to a falling off in interest, rather than to the fact that local readers had exhausted the resources of the local collection of books, is strongly suggested by the fact that, shortly before the factory closed in 1929, the local collection had been considerably enlarged by the purchase of a library in a neighboring town.

It is not as simple a matter as is commonly supposed for the unemployed

person to shift his free time to other activities involving self-cultivation. . . .
The Marienthal folk voiced this situation over and over again in remarks
like the following: (Herr S——:) "I spend most of my time around home.
Since I have been unemployed, I have almost given up reading. One's attention just can't be held on the stuff." (Frau F——:) "I used to read a lot.
I knew most of the books in the library. But now I read less. Mein Gott,
there are too many other things to worry about now!"

. . . The area where [this alteration in institutions and in personal mo-
rale] is most clearly apparent is that of political behavior. The statement of
a leading local Socialist-party officer is characteristic of the general situation:
"I used to know the *Arbeiterzeitung* [15] by heart. Now I just glance at it
and then throw it away, although I have more time in which to read it." [16]

Many persons in Middletown may have hovered on the edge of such
a morass of helpless inactivity in the dark days of 1932-33. The marked
slowing up of the advances in the reading of nonfiction and to a lesser
extent of fiction in 1933 may reflect this creeping apathy; though the
artificial respiration pumped into Middletown by the New Deal may
also have been a factor causing the city to turn back from books toward
the "normal" pattern of somewhat less reading. Both the sharp rise in
nonfiction in 1932 and its abrupt slacking off in 1933 may be explained
in part by the following statement by a thoughtful local businessman:

"A lot of us tried to keep up and informed on these big issues early in
the depression and even when the 'bank holiday' and New Deal came. Big
things were happening that were upsetting us, our businesses, and a lot of
our ideas, and we wanted to try to understand them. I took a lot of books
out of the library and sat up nights reading them. But then we all began
to get scared. I waked up to the fact that my business was in immediate
danger. We small businessmen began to see that we had to save our own
necks. And so we stopped trying to understand the big issues and kind of
lost touch with them. They're too big for us anyway."

It seems not unlikely that many thoughtful people in Middletown
went through this personal cycle.

Clearly, Middletown's library has been filling a larger place in the
city's life during the depression, as an agency serving the people's leisure, providing morale-building interests, vital information, and, if we

---

[15] This is the official paper of the German-Austrian Social Democratic Party,
which "on account of its fuller attention to political issues and its generally high
intellectual level makes rather large demands upon the worker-reader."

[16] Here follow figures on the shrinkage in subscriptions to various newspapers
and a discussion of the waning of membership in political and other clubs.

are to believe a local editorial, providing an indispensable check to local radical tendencies. In May, 1933, when the fear of radicalism was at its height, this editorial commented on the closing of the public library in a neighboring city for reasons of economy, and added: "It cannot be doubted that the public libraries in Middletown have proved a safety valve for the insurgent spirits of thousands in Middletown. . . . The last public institution ever to be closed, except those which supply food and warmth and shelter to the needy, should be the public library."

Actually, however, the library has been carrying on its work under heavy pressure, due to a falling budget.[17] Informed local people regard it as weaker now than it was in 1925 and staffed with a younger, less well-trained, and more heavily overworked staff. As compared with the pre-depression period, the library of 1935, with two new branches to operate

—had doubled its circulation;
—had decreased its annual expenditures below any of the four depression years before 1934, and faced 1936 with a cut in the tax levy supporting it from a six-cent rate to five cents;
—was spending less for new books than it had in six of the preceding nine years;
—had a full-time staff, including the new branches, of ten persons, as compared with nine in the pre-depression years, although supplemented by untrained F.E.R.A. relief help;
—had the smallest salary budget of any year since 1926.

Magazine subscriptions and newsstand purchases have been cut in Middletown during the depression, and fewer periodicals in the home may account in part for the rise in certain types of public-library circulation. It has proved impossible to assemble adequate figures on periodical circulation trends in Middletown because records for past years are usually not available for single small cities. For such standard publications as the *Saturday Evening Post* and *Ladies' Home Journal*, however, for which figures are available, total subscription and newsstand circulation in Middletown dropped by 23 per cent by 1934 from a 1929 total of 1,701 in the case of the first, and by 31 per cent from a 1929 total of 1,947 in the case of the second. So wide is the range of periodicals and so varied their fortunes, that it is extremely difficult to generalize from figures for a limited number of them. For instance,

[17] See Table 42 in Appendix III.

the circulation of a growing new periodical like *Time* rose in Middletown, despite the depression, from 125 to 160 between 1929 and 1934; while the circulation of the *New Republic,* always small in Middletown, virtually disappeared between 1931 and 1934, only to rise steeply in 1936.[18] *Fortune,* again a growing new periodical, costing ten dollars a year and going into fifty-one of Middletown's wealthier homes in 1934, had almost trebled its circulation since its first year of publication, 1930. Likewise, the *New Yorker,* another relatively young periodical, increased its circulation from twenty to thirty-four between 1929 and 1934. On the other hand, *True Story* fell off by 1934 by 58 per cent from its 1930 total of 1,646.[19] It is perhaps in the magazines that depend heavily upon newsstand sales to medium- and low-income people that the depression has made the most consistently heavy cuts. According to a check of actual sales of the March issue for each year by the wholesale distributor of these periodicals in Middletown, newsstand sales of the following three groups of popular periodicals in Middletown have moved as follows:

NEWSSTAND SALES OF MARCH ISSUE IN MIDDLETOWN [20]

Year	Motion-picture group	Detective group	Western group
1931	1,120	1,020	1,960
1932	1,460	1,160	1,760
1933	940	840	1,120
1934	1,060	910	1,310
1935	1,140	980	1,470

Despite these declines of in the neighborhood of a third in 1933, one is impressed by the tenacity of cash sales of this "pain-killer" reading in the face of desperately hard times.

[18] The circulation of a "liberal" weekly like the *New Republic* in Middletown is in itself an interesting index to the temper of the community. In a population of roughly 47,000, with a college library, a central public library, two branch public libraries, and a college student population of nearly 1,000, the *New Republic* circulation was as follows: 1930, 5; 1931, 5; 1932, 0; 1933, 2; 1934, 1; 1935, 5; 1936, 14. The circulation of the *Nation* (not available for earlier years) was: 1934, 9; 1935, 6; 1936, 8.

[19] This drop by *True Story* occurred in spite of the lowering of its price from twenty-five to fifteen cents. How much of this drop is due to the depression, how much to the pressure of the Catholic Church against this type of magazine and some of the advertising it carries, how much to the competition of the radio, and how much to the fickle tides of reader loyalty in these romance magazines, it is impossible to say.

[20] In 1930 this dealer absorbed the business of his only competitor. Since sales by the latter are not obtainable, totals for years prior to 1931 are here omitted.

Some rough idea of the network of periodicals in Middletown's leisure in 1935 may be gained from the following total circulations, including subscriptions and newsstand sales, of a selected group of periodicals in that year (unless otherwise indicated) in Middletown's 12,500 homes:[21]

STATUS MAGAZINES OF THE UPPER CLASS

Esquire	105
Fortune	61
House and Garden	45
New Yorker	33
Vanity Fair	30
Vogue	37

[21] These circulation figures were collected by the Research Center of the University of Newark.

From the same source comes the following special tabulation, suggesting how representative Middletown is of cities of its size in this matter of periodical circulation: The circulations in 1935, where obtainable (and otherwise in 1934), of twenty-three representative periodicals in Middletown and in the ten cities in the United States nearest in size to the 1930 population of Middletown were secured. (All ten cities were within 1,000 above or below the population of Middletown.) The eleven cities were then ranked according to circulation of each individual periodical, and the city with the median circulation for each periodical thus secured. The average rank distance of each city from the series of twenty-three medians was then computed. If a city were to have the median circulation for each of the twenty-three periodicals, its average rank distance would be 0; and if a city were most remote of all eleven cities from the median in each of the twenty-three cases its average rank distance would be 5. A city with an average rank distance from the medians close to 0 would, therefore, be more typical of all eleven cities in its circulation of these twenty-three periodicals than one with an average rank distance close to 5. The results of this tabulation are as follows:

City	Av. dev'n from median	City	Av. dev'n from median
Middletown	1.59	Berwyn, Ill.	2.72
Aurora, Ill.	1.72	Portsmouth, Va.	2.94
Waterloo, Ia.	2.04	Elmira, N. Y.	3.26
Bay City, Mich.	2.22	Lexington, Ky.	3.44
Williamsport, Pa.	2.22	Clifton, N. J.	3.92
Stamford, Conn.	2.66		

This tabulation suggests that Middletown is indeed middle town in this respect among cities of its size.

Following are the publications used in making this computation: *American Magazine, Atlantic Monthly, Better Homes and Gardens, Christian Science Monitor, Collier's, Cosmopolitan, Esquire, Good Housekeeping, House and Garden, Liberty, Literary Digest, McCall's*, combined circulation of MacFadden's two detective magazines—*True Detective Mysteries* and *Master Detective, National Geographic, Pictorial Review, Popular Mechanics, Redbook, Saturday Evening Post, Time, True Story, Vanity Fair, Vogue*, and *Woman's Home Companion*.

SOLID BUSINESS-CLASS FAMILIES' READING

Atlantic Monthly (1934) 27
Harper's 52
Literary Digest 231
National Geographic 626
Time 170

FACTS AND ENTERTAINMENT FOR THE GREAT MIDDLE GROUP

American Magazine 1,599
Collier's 1,957
Cosmopolitan 759
Liberty (1934) 1,360
Redbook 380
Saturday Evening Post 1,286

FACTS AND ENTERTAINMENT FOR THE WIFE AND MOTHER

Good Housekeeping 1,123
Ladies' Home Journal 1,381
McCall's 1,205
Pictorial Review (1934) 780
Woman's Home Companion 2,075

OTHERS

Better Homes and Gardens (1934) 950
Popular Mechanics (1934) 340
True Story (1934) 697
Nation 6
New Republic 5

Movies occupy much the same large place in Middletown's leisure today that they did in 1925.[22] There are seven theaters today instead of the nine in 1925, but one of them, a resplendent new house with a decidedly "big-city" air, has the, for Middletown, entirely unprecedented seating capacity of 1,800. Three of the seven theaters are "first-run" houses (two of them catering more to the "white-collar" trade, and the other to the working class and farmers), three are "second-run," and the seventh follows a mixed policy. Attendance figures for the city could not be obtained, but the manager of the largest house, with an attendance of 14,000 a week, stated that "movies have been hit just like jewelry and other luxury trades." [23]

[22] See Middletown, pp. 263-69.

[23] This is probably an overstatement, as the declines in Middletown's movie attendance were undoubtedly nothing like the 85 per cent drop in local jewelry sales shown in Table 3. For the year 1933, the Census gives for the first time data on receipts of the "Places of amusement" (all of these being motion-picture

The movie ads of 1935 were interchangeable with those of 1925, including a liberal sprinkling of such captions as "You Can't Love a Married Man," "What's a baby between sweethearts—more or less?", and "Daring! Startling! True! Inflamed Passionate Youth Burned at the Altar of Ignorance and Desire." Middletown's movie interest was reflected in four front-page press stories with pictures and an editorial in quick succession in 1932 on "Jean Harlow Prostrate over Husband's Suicide." The local exhibitor in the largest theater believes there has been no relation between the depression and the taste of local movie-goers. The most discriminating local exhibitor, however, a graduate of an Eastern university and a man definitely interested now as in 1925 in bringing "good" films to Middletown, not only believes that the general level of films has been improved since 1925 but that local people have been more discriminating during the depression: "Having less money, they've shopped around the programs of the various houses before selecting a show. They have tended to rush for the good, worth-while pictures, the four-star hits, and to stay away from some of the others." [24] Audiences, according to the exhibitors, have been definitely wanting more pictures "on the happy side" in the depression. "They have wanted the movies more than ever to supply the lacks in their existence. The 'fairyland' type of picture has been more popular than ever—the type of picture that lifts people into a happy world of gaiety and evening clothes; and both our business people and working class have shied off serious and sad pictures—they have too much of that at home!" *Les Misérables* is reported to have been a "complete flop"; in addition to being a serious film, one exhibitor pointed out that it was also handicapped by the fact that Middletown didn't know how to pronounce it.

Saturday matinees for young children have become a marked feature of the movies. The morning paper reported in February, 1936:

houses) in Middletown. Their total receipts, $244,000, constituted an amount equal to 2.1 per cent of the total amount of sales in Middletown's retail stores in that year and 4.15 per cent of the total factory and retail payroll.

[24] Middletown is probably representative of other localities in the fact that, especially in the better-class houses, adult females predominate heavily in the audiences and, as one producer remarked, "set the type of picture that will 'go.'" In one of Middletown's better theaters, the audiences during the depression are estimated by its owner to have consisted of 60 per cent women over sixteen, 30 per cent males over sixteen, and 10 per cent children. The Middletown theater specializing in "thrill stuff for the farmers and working class," according to a local exhibitor, "draws mostly children."

Yesterday's children played at home on Saturdays in the family kitchen to be out of the way while mother cleaned the rest of the house. Today's attend the children's matinees at the local theaters [while] mother . . . is shopping, visiting, or playing bridge. . . . [Through a study by the two-year-old Motion Picture Council] it was learned that: The average attendance [at these children's matinees] varies from 1,000 to 1,400 children. . . . Tots as young as three years, accompanied by an older brother or sister, and adolescents of fifteen or sixteen represent the extremes of age groups; the age group between four and twelve numbered more than the one between twelve and sixteen, and the average age seemed to be from ten to twelve. . . .

Children wait for a half hour to two hours for the matinees. . . . Each child remained at least three hours, at least half of the children sat from five to six hours in the theater by remaining for the adult programs, while a few persisted for eleven hours until the theater closed for the night. . . . Films were "satisfactory," but no educational reels were offered during the period of observation. . . . They were exciting recreational films. The report did take exception to one of the adult features. This was "a murder-mystery drama featuring drinking, rowdiness and a series of horrible murders. . . ."

The report concludes: "Middletown is faced with the fact that the children's matinee draws more than 1,000 children every Saturday even on the coldest of winter days, and the summer attendance is by far larger."

If the older generation takes its movies as an anodyne, and small children as an exciting weekly event, adolescent Middletown goes to school to, as well as enjoying, the movies. Joan Crawford has her amateur counterparts in the high-school girls who stroll with brittle confidence in and out of "Barney's" soft-drink parlor, "clicking" with the "drugstore cowboys" at the tables; while the tongue-tied young male learns the art of the swift, confident comeback in the face of female confidence:

Scene in Barney's: A boy drinking a "coke" is joined by a girl.

Boy. "You see the Strand?" [*Joan Crawford in No More Ladies.*]
Girl. "Yes, it's swell!" [*They both light cigarettes.*]
Boy. "They were the best wisecracks I've heard in this town."
Girl. "Yea. Remember when he said—" [*then a repetition of the wisecrack*]
    [*The girl goes out, and soon the same boy is joined by another girl.*]
Boy. [*All over again*] "You been to the Strand?"
Girl. "Sure!"

Boy. "Ever heard such wonderful wisecracks?"

Girl. "They were *mar*-velous!"

Boy. "You remember when—" [*And out comes the wisecrack again, gaining more confidence of tone in the retelling.*]

If a comparative time count were available, it would probably be found that the area of leisure where change in time spent has been greatest since 1925 is listening to the radio. The earlier study of Middletown has been increasingly criticized in the last two or three years for "the small amount of attention paid to the radio." [25] This limited treatment was due to the then meager diffusion of the radio throughout the city. A rough sample check in 1924 revealed the presence of a radio in about one business-class home in eight and in one in sixteen among the working-class homes. By April, 1930, the Federal Census reported no less than 5,791 of Middletown's homes with radios, or 46 per cent of all the city's homes. This number has undoubtedly advanced very substantially since 1930, even despite the depression, with the general spread of cheap "midget" radios. According to a local man familiar with this situation, the manipulative outlet afforded by radio construction in 1924-25 has declined with the introduction of small cheap sets, and radio is now almost entirely a passive form of leisure in Middletown. It is likely that this inexpensive form of leisure, like the reading of free library books, has involved a relatively larger amount of time per radio during the depression; [26] and it is also possible that it has constituted a mild cohesive element in family life through the greater association of family members in this common activity within the home.

Middletown now has its own flourishing radio station which is part of the World Broadcasting System. Founded in 1926 as a one-man station carrying only three hours a week of broadcasting, the local station now has a full-time staff of fourteen and a fourteen-hour day of broadcasting. Local auditions, aggregating 300 to 500 a month, constantly winnow out local talent. The station stresses chatty, local programs—its slogan is: "The friendly spot on the dial"—for the increasing spread of radio ownership in Middletown to low-income families

[25] See *Middletown*, pp. 269-70.

[26] On the other hand, it is the experience of persons in close contact with families on relief that in a few families where morale is badly shattered the apathy mentioned earlier in this chapter extends in some cases even to listening to the radio.

has, according to the directors of the station, skewed taste more to the "popular" side. Four-fifths of local listeners were said in 1935 to prefer "popular" and "hillbilly" music. As many as 12,700 "fan letters" have been received in a single week commending these "hillbilly" programs, whereas local people who prefer symphonic music rarely send in "fan" mail. A commercial user recently received only four responses from an organ program, as against 246 from a "hillbilly" program. It is significant that no "fan" mail comes in from religious musical programs; and since the change to popular music on Sunday afternoons, the response to Sunday programs has been heavy, and the Sunday time is now completely sold out. Children's hours, with local juvenile performers, have been dropped, "because nobody but the families of the children who perform was interested."

The presence in Middletown of this local broadcasting station with membership in a national chain operates in two directions. Like the movies and the national press services in the local newspapers, it carries people away from localism and gives them direct access to the more popular stereotypes in the national life. It is this space-binding emphasis that probably helps to account for such new elements in Middletown today as the popularity of a highly sophisticated syndicated press column like Walter Winchell's "On Broadway," with its heavily localized New York lingo and subject matter. In the other direction, the local station operates to bind together an increasingly large and diversified city. A small city station has an especially heavy and direct financial stake in featuring local matters that will attract and hold local listeners against the pull of other stations. The station accordingly, early in its career, seized upon the local enthusiasm for basketball. The games of the high-school "Bearcats" are broadcast, with a heavy group of local commercial bidders for the advertising involved in sponsoring the programs, and this has helped very materially to build up the following of the station. Commencing in June, 1935, the station utilized the large auditorium of the Masonic Temple for the first local amateur program; the program was sponsored by the X family's department store and brought together within the auditorium the employees of the store and of their factory, while a host of friends listened in at home. The significance for the social cohesion of the city of this focusing of otherwise highly scattered citizens upon an evening of hilarious in-group enjoyment is potentially very great. In addition to such large programs, the station runs a steady stream of smaller local programs: a series of talks by professors at the local college, and talks by local ministers, clubwomen, and businessmen. These home-town programs tend to augment the "we" sense among all elements of a no longer small-town community.

If the word "auto" was writ large across Middletown's life in 1925,[27] this was even more apparent in 1935, despite six years of depression. One was immediately struck in walking the streets by the fact that filling stations have become in ten years one of the most prominent physical landmarks of the city; even between 1929 and 1933 the filling stations enumerated by the Census of Distribution increased from 41 to 70. Saturday-night parking now extends several blocks out from the main business streets into formerly deserted residential streets; and a traffic officer goes about marking the tires of cars parked on weekdays in the business section to enforce parking ordinances. In 1925 Middletown youngsters, driven from street play to the sidewalks, were protesting, "Where *can* I play?" but in 1935 they were retreating even from the sidewalks, and an editorial, headed "Sidewalk Play is Dangerous," said, "It is safe to say that children under the age of eight years should not be permitted to play upon sidewalks." [28] Many business-class people regard it as a scandal that some people on relief still manage to operate their cars. No formal effort has been made by the relief authorities to discourage car ownership and operation, and, as noted in Chapter IV, people on relief who own cars have been encouraged to use them in various ways to pick up small earnings. Even at the time of the labor-union fervor under N.R.A., local organizers tell one disgustedly, many Middletown workers were more interested in figuring out how to get a couple of gallons of gas for the car than they were in labor's effort to organize. While some workers lost their cars in the depression, the local sentiment, as heard over and over again, is that "People give up everything in the world but their car." According to a local banker, "The depression hasn't changed materially the value Middletown people set on home ownership, but *that's* not their primary desire, as the automobile always comes first." More hard-surfaced roads and faster cars mean an increased cruising range, and a local

[27] See *Middletown,* especially pp. 251-63.
[28] Middletown's county now has about 2,500 automobile accidents a year. One of the most insistent notes in the editorial columns of the afternoon paper in 1935 and 1936 was the editor's repeated protests against fast and reckless driving.

paper estimated in June, 1935, that "10,000 persons leave Middletown for other towns and resorts every fine Sunday."

In a further very significant sense the automobile was writ large over Middletown in 1935. For the Middletown of today is more dependent upon the automotive industry than was the Middletown of 1925. In 1928 General Motors, in addition to its Middletown plant making transmissions, moved in a large Delco-Remy unit, and a machine shop that was small in 1925 has changed hands and grown to large proportions manufacturing automotive parts. The local press hailed in March, 1934, the national settlement of the labor controversy in the automotive industry in terms of its crucial significance for Middletown: "3,000 Men Will Stay on Job," proclaimed the headlines. "The settlement affects directly more than 3,000 [Middletown] workmen and, including their families, perhaps 12,000 residents of the city." It then went on to list the five leading plants in the city dependent on the automotive industry. A year later, early in 1935, one of these, as noted in Chapter II, "passed its all-time employment peak," and in November of the same year it broke ground for a plant enlargement and again surpassed its employment record established in the spring; while the Delco-Remy plant also reached its highest production in its seven years in Middletown. To all of which must be added the major increment to the above newspaper list of a sixth plant with the return of the General Motors transmissions unit to the city in the spring of 1935; by June this plant was employing 800 men, with the prospect of early additions that, rumor had it, might run their force up toward 2,000. It is probably conservative to say that, by the close of 1935, half the factory workers in Middletown were producing for the automotive industry.[29] To a considerably greater extent than in 1925, Middletown's life is today derived from the automotive industry—and the city is aware of it to its marrow!

Car ownership in Middletown was one of the most depression-proof elements of the city's life in the years following 1929—far less vulnerable, apparently, than marriages, divorces, new babies, clothing, jewelry,

[29] The dependence of a city to such a large extent upon an industry in which production is as unstable as that of the automobile industry carries with it serious implications for the stability of Middletown's living. According to *Recent Social Trends* (p. 900), the index (in terms of cars, not dollars) of per-capita production of automobiles in the United States was as follows: 1919, 49.9; 1921, 44.2; 1923, 102.2; 1925, 100.0; 1927, 74.5; 1929, 115.4; and in 1930 production fell 38 per cent below 1929, and in 1931, 56 per cent below 1929.

and most other measurable things both large and small. Separate figures are not available for the city of Middletown,[30] as distinct from the
entire county, but the passenger-car registrations in Middletown's entire
county [31] not only registered scarcely any loss in the early years of the
depression but, both in numbers and in ratio to population, stood in
each of the years 1932-35 above the 1929 level.[32] Along with this tough
resistance of Middletown's habit of car owning to the depression undertow, went a drop of only 4 per cent in the dollar volume of gasoline
sales in Middletown between 1929 and 1933,[33] suggesting little curtailment in mileage of cars. That the pressure on Middletown's automobile budget was severe is shown by the fact that purchases of new cars
in Middletown's county, after rising from 1,885 in 1928 to 2,401 in
1929, were more than halved, to 1,162, in 1930; they virtually stood
at that figure in 1931, with 1,124 new purchases; they were halved
again in 1932, to 556, or only 29 per cent of the 1929 quantity; and in
1933 they began slowly to recover.[34] While, therefore, people were
riding in progressively older cars as the depression wore on, they
manifestly continued to ride.

All of which suggests that, since about 1920, the automobile has
come increasingly to occupy a place among Middletown's "musts" close
to food, clothing, and shelter.[35]

[30] A careful estimate from all available data suggests that, of the 13,533 passenger cars registered in Middletown's county at the close of 1934, approximately
9,000 were in Middletown. This suggests a rise to about one car for every 5.2
persons in the city from the one car to 6.1 persons at the close of 1923.

[31] See Table 43 in Appendix III.

[32] Table 43 shows that Middletown's state experienced a drop in passenger-car
registrations in every succeeding year from 1929 through 1933, with a total
falling off of 14 per cent over the four years. No explanation is at hand for the
fact that Middletown's passenger-car registrations show a 5 per cent gain in
1933 over 1929 (and a 10 per cent gain through 1932) while the state's cars
were falling off. The Commissioner of the State Bureau of Motor Vehicles is
unable to offer any explanation. It is barely possible that the point referred to
in n. *b* to Table 43, namely, that persons from other counties may, if they
choose, register their cars in Middletown, may be a factor, but it seems unlikely
that such an element of bias would suddenly have become so heavily significant
during the depression.

[33] See Ch. II and Table 3 in Appendix III.

[34] See Table 43 in Appendix III.
In 1923, 32 per cent of Middletown's cars were two or less years old, another
32 per cent three to five years old, and 36 per cent were more than five years
old. (See *Middletown,* p. 253.)

[35] The pounding impact upon the family's standard of living of the commercially manipulated pressure to buy new models is apparent from the following

No explicit data are at hand as to possible changes in the role of the automobile in the leisure life of Middletown in the depression. It is probable that there has been somewhat less random driving about on summer evenings to cool off and more staying home with the radio. One parent stated that since the whole family had been trying to use the car as little as possible there had been less trouble with the children over the use of the car. But the gasoline-consumption figures cited

whimsical comment by a local editor in February, 1929, after visiting the annual auto show staged by Middletown's automobile dealers: "I went to the auto show and came away greatly discouraged. . . . I was driving a car of much better quality than I can afford and only a year old; but, somehow, as I left the auto showroom the vehicle of which I had been proud seemed pitiable."

This is another example of the extent to which Middletown's life is caught in the grip and forced to do the will of the economic institutions by which it seeks its living. With the exception of women's clothing, at no point is this forcing pressure more apparent than in the deliberately instigated vogue of the annual new model of each make of automobile. But this institutionalized pattern of "deliberate obsolescence" is being extended continually to more and more of the things Middletown consumes. Paul Mazur describes this process graphically: "Wear alone made replacement too slow for the needs of American industry. And so . . . business elected a new god to take its place along with—or even before—the other household gods. Obsolescence was made supreme. . . . It could be created almost as fast as the turn of the calendar. . . . It is the degree to which the factor of obsolescence has been developed as an art or science of increasing consumer demand, and not the mere existence of obsolescence, that distinguishes the past few years. . . . It is a topsy-turvy world in which we are living, and the retailer is a willing party to the shortening style life of his products. Under his tutelage a year of style becomes first six months and then three months, and from materials, shapes, uses, and colors, he accepts new changes as often as he decides for obsolescence." (*Op. cit.*, pp. 92-97.)

Not only does this process tend to encourage in the consumer the pursuit of the new as an end in itself, but, once a pace is hit and an "annual model" habit established, it becomes difficult for industry itself to step out of the competitive merry-go-round it has fostered. This is clearly revealed in the predicament of the automobile industry in 1934: "With no overwhelming need for wholesale modernization, the industry would like to roll along for a while without any capital outlay. The cars themselves are good, already have everything a purchaser should want in the way of personal transportation. Just two things stand in the way of a truce on capital expenditures: efficiency and competition. Several manufacturers thought they had done enough *to make the prospects dissatisfied with their present cars and planned to bring out new models with noticeable but unimportant changes.* [Italics ours.] But competition, and the increasing necessity of trimming the last penny off every possible operation are forcing last-minute shifts. So the new models now being translated from paper to steel will have the traditionally radical differences. And the equipment makers . . . will get more business than they expected. And, one may add, the consumer will pay most of the bill." ("Detroit Spends to Save," *Business Week*, November 10, 1934.)

above suggest that these changes probably were not great, or were counterbalanced by wider use of the car over week ends or for other purposes.

The return of the bicycle to Middletown in the spring of 1935 probably represents little more than a high-school- and college-age fad. Ten years ago the bicycles which the research staff used for recreation evoked no end of merriment even from the youngsters, who were wont to call out, "Aw, why don't you get a car?" But in the spring of 1935, 300 bicycles were sold in Middletown, virtually all of them to people under twenty-one. The presence of the local college undoubtedly affected this fad, since the bicycle craze had struck the State University a hundred miles away the fall before.[36]

Dancing remains, as in 1925,[37] a prominent feature of the leisure and social life of Middletown people of all classes under thirty, with some following among the older group. It was a popular part of the F.E.R.A. amusement program provided free to the unemployed in the city's parks in the summers of 1935 and 1936. The depression stimulated an increase in the number of small, informal dance halls in connection with soft-drink parlors and bootleg beerhouses catering to the working class. In these places one could dance all evening to radio, phonograph, or piano for an expenditure of a few nickels for drinks. By the spring of 1932 their number had increased to such an extent that the police raided a number of them for operating without a license.

But while dancing is a popular and fairly constant recreational activity the year round for the young, bridge is adult business-class Middletown's way *par excellence* of "putting in an evening" with friends. On every hand one encountered statements that its vogue had increased notably since 1925 [38] and that there is today considerably more playing for money. The game is now an obligatory social skill

[36] The bicycle revival was a national phenomenon. In 1935, for the first time since 1899, the national production of bicycles passed the half-million mark. The production total of 639,439 in 1935 was 54 per cent of that in 1899. (See Census of Manufactures news release of September 5, 1936.)

[37] See *Middletown*, pp. 281-83.

[38] While bridge was common ten years ago, its hold on the city was not so strong but that Mah Jong could gain a decided temporary foothold as an alternative way of spending a social evening. It is dangerous to generalize about fads, but it seems decidedly less likely today, in view of the heavy commitment to bridge, that a counterpart of Mah Jong could achieve the vogue the latter did in 1925.

among the business class. It has increased markedly among high-school children, and has even reached down through the high school to children in the sixth grade. Leaders of local girls' work, such as the Girl Reserves, complain today of bridge as a definite hindrance to interesting girls in other activities. Bridge was very little played among the working class in 1925, but partly through the contagion of the younger group inoculated in high school, it is reported to be growing in popularity south of the tracks, spreading there first through the women's groups and then more slowly to a more resistant group of men, who prefer their pinochle and poker.

No one has analyzed the reason for the vogue of bridge in American life. It is conceivable that it never would have been anything but the sport of an esoteric few, had its growth depended entirely on the male world. Its development, however, has been primarily in the hands of women. It is the supreme hostess technique, supplying the best inexpensive guarantee our culture has discovered against a "dull evening" when friends "drop in." Social talking presents far more risks to a hostess, as it is a much more personal type of relationship liable to run on the rocks of monotony, vacuousness, gossip, or outright antagonisms. Middletown's business class shies off talk of a continuous sort addressed to a single subject or problem. It has in its genteel tradition, fostered by its women in their study clubs, certain vague canons as to "worth-while" things to discuss, and these also involve uneasy inhibitions as regards an evening of gossip and talking personalities. There is no tradition of facile talk for its own sake, for cleverness in such things tends to be confusing, and therefore annoying. "Worth-while" talk is accordingly "serious" talk, and most people have but a spotty fund of knowledge with which to carry on a prolonged conversation without becoming "heavy" or disputatious. All of this tends to make the effort to carry on an evening of talk overstrenuous and likely to be judged in the end as "not having got anywhere." Into this problematic situation has come bridge, the hostess' best friend and the universal social solvent: safe, orthodox, and fun. Men and women who are not interesting talkers can still be good bridge players. Most people's lives involve but a meager amount of sheer fun; they are busy and preoccupied and perplexed as to what to do to make living more fun. And most people, particularly men, in an urban culture crave more human contacts out of business hours with people they like in an atmosphere that liberates spontaneity. Neither the movies nor reading supply this sense of social participation. What bridge has done is to institutionalize fun-in-small-social-groups, at the same time that it is tending to drain serious talk from Middletown's leisure. It is an unparalleled device for an urban world that wants to avoid issues, to keep things impersonal, to enjoy people without laying oneself open or committing oneself to them, and to have fun in the process.

For Middletown's non-bridge-playing population there are pinochle, pedro, knock-rummy, and poker in the lodges and South Side homes, and, exclusively for the males, gambling in the poolrooms and cigar stores. The close connection between Middletown's commercialized gambling and its politics is described in Chapter IX. This situation is roughly familiar to every man in town, though the women are wont to think of "the awful places down on the Court House square and on South Walnut Street" as, like prostitution, just one of the unfortunate things that happen and that no one can do anything about. The location of the gambling houses has been the same for many years and their patronage continued strong throughout the depression. Local gambling is not usually a matter of big stakes and noisy scandals but, rather, one of the steady commercialized forms of leisure offered to the workingman of small income—a place to meet the boys, have a good time, and maybe pick up a little something on the side. When a cleanup drive occurred early in 1930, a local editor protested against the mayor's "interference with card playing in cigar stores for checks 'good on the house.' They should not be banned any more than women's bridge games. They play an important part in the social life of this factory city."

No description of the informal means of spending leisure since 1925 would be in focus without consideration of the larger place occupied by drinking. The earlier study has been criticized, with justification, for the fact that it failed to apprehend the amount of quiet drinking that went on in Middletown.[39] On every hand, the testimony in 1935 was that "There is much more drinking here now than ten years ago." To which one reliable person, in close touch with the high-school generation for the past fifteen years, added: "And there is much more 'passing out' in public now. Some people seem to regard it as the thing to do."

[39] See *Middletown*, p. 276, n. 8. This shortcoming, realized during the writing of the report, is acknowledged in a footnote to the earlier study.

Drinking by Middletown's business class in 1924-25 was not heavy or conspicuous. Only twice, in many evenings of dining with local people, was any liquor served to any of the five members of the research staff.[40] The X family had long thrown their resources heavily behind the Anti-Saloon League, did not to the best of the investigators' knowledge serve liquor to guests in their homes, and, owing largely to their influence, the Country Club had for some years prior to the Prohibition Act been an exception among the country clubs of the state in that it had operated at a loss rather than have a bar. It is probable that the X's quietly made up the deficit. The investigator was assured by one man in 1935 that there was, even in 1925, some drinking at the Country Club. "But," he added, "it was very much on the 'q.t.'" On the South Side there was much drinking of bootleg liquor and home-brew. Some people in all classes experimented with making wine.

Following 1925, things began to open up locally. According to a well-informed man:

"Drinking increased markedly here in 1927 and 1928, and by 1930 was heavy and open.[41] I may have been a little late in getting started, compared with some of the other men, but in the winter of '29-'30 I began like the rest taking it for granted and offering a drink as a matter of course to everyone coming to the house. This isn't so common now, and now I don't think of offering a drink as automatically as I used to. The earlier social compulsion has eased off. Drinking of the early-depression blatant sort has let up with repeal—though in the first days of repeal there were long lines standing at the store counters waiting to buy liquor."

During the late 1920's and early 1930's, sentiment was mounting against the Eighteenth Amendment. Young people motored out to outlying roadhouses in the early morning after dances and a number of rowdy fist fights resulted; and some parents began to urge that "things weren't so bad as this even when we had saloons." An occasional businessman got involved for having liquor transported through public carriers. Poison-liquor deaths were reported intermittently in the newspapers. In 1931 indignation ran high over the shooting and

[40] It is not intended here to imply that only two families in Middletown served liquor to guests in 1924-25. That, of course, could not have been the case. But when it was done, it was done very quietly among intimates, and liquor was in no sense the routine part of hospitality that it became later.
See n. 54 in Ch. V above.

[41] See this man's statement in Ch. V about "the collapse of public morals' locally with the coming of the depression.

killing by a local policeman of a prominent young Middletown athlete caught running beer. The papers in 1930 were announcing week after week: "Liquor Cases Keep Judge M—— Busy" and "Heavy Schedule for City Judge—15 Cases Set for Hearing—10 of Them Liquor Cases." An editorial in January, 1931, stated that "The average person objects to prohibition because of the high prices."

But the rising sentiment against prohibition encountered strong opposition from the evangelical section of the population, particularly from the women, many of whom had for years been devoted to the Anti-Saloon League cause. Middletown's papers still carry regular accounts of W.C.T.U. meetings under the heading "W.C.T.U. Notes," and in 1930 one of these groups adopted a resolution opposing the appearance of American women on the Senate floor against the prohibition amendment, and the women left the meeting promising "to pray for the amendment." When a medicinal liquor bill was before the State Legislature in 1931, a poll of the local doctors was taken and the afternoon paper announced that "Only 22 out of 42 [Middletown] doctors answered in the affirmative the question, 'Would you use whisky to save the life of a patient?' " [42] When the *Literary Digest* poll was taken in the spring of 1930, the 1,871 Middletown votes showed 46 per cent standing firm for enforcement, 24 per cent for repeal, and 30 per cent for modification. In 1931, Billy Sunday, speaking in the leading Baptist church, thundered to his hearers that "The arguments against prohibition are as weak as soup!"

In this tensely drawn situation, local speakeasies multiplied and flourished in their unostentatious, cautious way as repeal drew nearer. In April, 1933, the afternoon paper ran a story about the city's "speaks" which suggests the place they occupied in the leisure life of the city:

The very conditions [the strength of the W.C.T.U., Anti-Saloon League, and the churches] that made prohibition enforcement more vigorous in [this state] than perhaps in any other state, have molded local drinking houses into a veritable institution. Under such conditions, any great investment in a drinking establishment was not a thing to be seriously considered. To survive, those who sold drinks by the glass perforce had to avoid display of any kind. . . . These difficulties made [Middletown's] speakeasies what

[42] This sort of loosely worded question is open to various interpretations. It is cited here not primarily for the attitude of the medical profession which it suggests but as an indication of the way various groups in the community were drawn into the debate.

they are today—private homes to all appearances. . . . Virtually all of Middletown's liquor sellers live in unpretentious homes in the poorer sections of the city. . . . Most of these houses have no more than three rooms in which drinks are served. [Everybody is introduced by the host to everyone else present, the story went on to recount, with the result that] the shell of eternal suspicion which surrounds most persons in their business relations sloughs away when they enter the portals of the liquor houses. The atmosphere is one of genuine friendliness. . . . Except for the difference in the size of the houses, one Middletown drinking place can scarcely be distinguished from another. All have a front room furnished with overstuffed furniture. Conversation is sprightly, but somewhat subdued. Close harmony is banned unless the house is in a very isolated location. Each place has a regular clientele. Everyone knows everyone else. And the houses move to a new location every few weeks as a precaution.

The speakeasies, like their now legal successors in Middletown, the "taverns," performed a dual function: as a physical place of meeting new people, and, psychologically, as an environment conducive to spontaneous human association. The first of these is a relatively more acute need for the working class, who are more sparsely served than the business class in Middletown with institutions facilitating the meeting with and coming to know new people. It is easy for one with a business-class point of view to fail to realize the deterrents to human association, and the resulting isolation, loneliness, and even in some cases the mutual suspicion, that not infrequently characterize the lives of these working-class people. These deterrents are both physical and psychological, including shabby household furniture, too little money, no place to go and no money to go with, newness in a neighborhood, relatively fewer telephones than the business class for "telephone visiting," and the presence of family problems one does not want one's sharp-eyed, gossiping neighbors to know about.[43] The relatively high residential mobility of the working class—which accounts largely for the fact, shown in Table 21, that 42 per cent of Middletown's *renting* families were, early in 1935, living in homes which they had occupied less than one year, and 61 per cent in homes occupied by them less

[43] This social isolation was vividly brought out in many of the interviews with working-class families in 1925—*e.g.*, by the wife who exclaimed, "I'd go anywhere to get away from the house. I went to the store last night. I've been out of the house only twice in the three months since we moved here, both times to the store." (See *Middletown,* p. 310, for this and similar statements.) The decline in "neighboring," portrayed on pages 272-75 of the earlier study, further underscores the loneliness and even the fear of intimacy in many of these lives.

than two years, as over against 4 and 7 per cent respectively of the
owning families—aggravates this greater tendency of the working class
to become socially isolated. One has only to compare the way a working-class population leaves its church services in South Side churches,
lingering to talk in the aisles and on the steps, and the brisk dignity
with which the business class leave their Presbyterian Church, with
their heads full of plans for the afternoon, to sense some of this differential need for places and occasions of social meeting.[44]

In Middletown a difference between working class and business class
in this regard seems to lie in the fact that for the latter there is a
broader and longer stairway of contact institutions available. These
include neighborhood, church, and school contacts of one's children,
which are also available to the working class; and the lodge, which is
likewise available to both groups and relatively much more important
socially to the working class than to the business class; but, thereafter,
the facilities of the business class increase in number and widen in variety, while those of the working class largely peter out into such ragged
devices as "going uptown to the ten-cent store to meet people." Among
the business class, one goes on from neighborhood, church, and lodge

[44] The 1925 study pointed out the role of the church as a place of first meeting and of continued seeing of acquaintances in the case of both the business
class and the working class. (See *Middletown,* pp. 275-76 and 400-01.) It also
noted two other significant points: the tendency for the church to be used by
the business class as a first acquaintance maker somewhat more calculatingly
than by the working class, with an ensuing moving on to other institutional
agencies of social contact once the initial ice was broken through church acquaintance; and the tendency for business-class churches to be socially "colder"
than those of the working class. (See *Middletown,* pp. 275-76, including n. 5.)
  This whole question of the institutional acquaintance icebreakers available to
different income levels, occupational groups, activity groups (music, little theater, etc.), religious groups, neighborhoods, and temperaments in a community
is a problem that badly needs intensive comparative study. Removal from a
small town to Middletown or from Middletown to a metropolitan community,
for instance, involves for most people not possessed of outstanding wealth, personal attractiveness, or special skills an acute period of fumbling; the old institutions utilized in another setting for meeting people either are not duplicated
in the larger community, or operate differently (*e.g.,* they are "colder," recruit
their members on a different basis, etc.), or they stand at a different point in
the local hierarchy of social institutions (*e.g.,* a Methodist church in Middletown as against a Methodist church in New York City). If the metropolitan
community operates to enhance the number and variety of places (*e.g.,* night
clubs, dance halls, etc.) where people of certain sorts or of certain income levels
can meet strangers, it also tends to lower the prestige of, or to drop out completely, some institutions familiar to the population of a smaller community.

contacts to the wide array of member institutions in the Federate Club of Clubs, which are not for the most part markedly socially exclusive (and are even criticized by some of the "better" local women as being "too inclusive"), and which offer outlets for specialized interests in music, art, literature, and so on. For the men there are the half-dozen civic luncheon clubs. The local branch of the American Association of University Women beckons to all women college graduates. There are the D.A.R., Garden Club, Country Club, Chamber of Commerce and its Dynamo Club, the night clubs, formal dances throughout the winter, including some charity balls open to strangers, and a variety of other functions and institutions, including bridge playing. And it should be borne constantly in mind that, in the heavily organized social world of business-class women, if the woman gets to know people, the family does.[45]

Where a culture leaves the provision of such approved institutionalized places of social meeting and acquaintance to chance and to the accidents of individual initiative and financial resources, it is not surprising that the speakeasy and tavern, the latter often associated with an inexpensive place to dance, operate as an important agency for social acquaintance among those inadequately served by other means of contact.

On the psychological side, most urban people, particularly the less aggressive personalities, need the facilitation of spontaneity in social intercourse which an institutionalized agency of informality provides. The speakeasy and tavern, like bridge playing for the business class,

---

[45] Yet, despite all these aids, the fact should not be overlooked that a marginal group of business-class people feel socially lost in Middletown. This was vividly illustrated in the 1925 study in n. 5 on p. 276. Some of these people, like the couple there quoted, are the plain couples from small communities possessed of meager social graces. In view of the critically important role of the wife as the family's social entering wedge (see *Middletown*, pp. 116-17), a man who has married "the wrong kind of wife" may also be retarded.

As a postscript to all of the above, the question presents itself as to whether the preoccupation of Middletown's business class with bridge playing operates initially as a social door opener, and thereafter in the opposite direction. Bridge is *par excellence* a two-couple form of leisure, though of course bridge parties also spread the groups. The element of skill in the game and the new vogue of playing according to special systems tend to make like congregate with like, and, once having discovered another couple who "play a good hand," to cling tenaciously to them. It is conceivable that this tends to operate in the direction of a relatively higher degree of repetitive association of little cliques within cliques and the resulting curtailment of more miscellaneous associations.

help to institutionalize spontaneity. Here one sees a cityful of people, with little chance in their workaday lives to be directly personal in a spontaneous sense, finding out a way in their leisure to circumvent the strait-jacket set for them by their culture. The speakeasy and tavern mean being with people in a mood where one takes people on one's own terms and they take one in the same spirit; one can sit silent, or one can talk with a degree of animation and intensity that would make one feel silly and self-conscious in the more constrained environment of one's own parlor with one's neighbors about. In these informal places of conviviality one can be as spontaneous or silly as one pleases without needing to feel self-conscious about it. And an institution that can do this for people loaded with the sober constraints of convention, monotony, and fatigue is an institution for which people are apt to be willing to vote and to fight.[46]

So when it got "legal beer" in 1933, Middletown lost no time in celebrating. One banker, as noted in Chapter II, believes that the return of "legal beer" in April, 1933, with its heartening effect upon people's spirits, was a ponderable factor in the revival of local business. But the return of legal beer was just a curtain raiser, psychologically, to full repeal in December. The drinking by adults attending the high-school fraternity and sorority dances in the Christmas holidays of 1933 and 1934 is reported to have been "heavy and open." On New Year's Eve of 1933 the first night club with a "floor show" opened tentatively in Middletown's leading hotel, subject to continuance, the first advertisement stated, "if business warrants"; it was open three nights a week (Wednesday, Saturday *and Sunday*)[47] from nine to eleven, with a cover charge of thirty-five cents Wednesday and fifty-five cents Saturday and Sunday. Shortly thereafter the other two hotels

[46] See the discussion in Ch. XII of the ambivalence in people's values which is the outcome of such culturally generated restraints.

Men ordinarily turn to liquor in such a culture, not to get drunk but in order to ease themselves of enough of these conflicting outside pressures-to-conform to enable them to live for a few hours in a freer mood in which they are less fundamentally alone and constrained.

[47] The operation of a night club on Sunday evening in Middletown is a powerful acknowledgment of the lengths to which the secularization of the Sabbath has progressed. (See *Middletown,* p. 339, and also Index under "Secularization.") This would have been impossible in the Middletown of 1890, and it is doubtful whether local public opinion would have tolerated it in 1925. The nine-to-eleven hour suggests the modesty of the night life of the adults in an early-rising community in which the stores are open at 8 and 8:30 A.M.

also opened night clubs with floor shows. With liquor again legal, other aspects of local life associated with drinking began to come into the open. In the first week in January, 1934, an article on the women's page of the afternoon paper discussed the question, "Should children know their parents keep liquor?"—a problem that had troubled many parents' consciences.

Young Middletown has been put in a perplexing position as drinking has again come out into the open. Legal drinking is closely watched in the state, and legal dispensers are usually careful to avoid losing their expensive licenses by serving minors. But both minors and adults were wont prior to 1935 to be served by the speakeasies and roadhouses with few questions asked as to age. As a local man summed up the situation: "It's pretty hard on the minors. They can't get it now at the legal places and they can't get it at home; so they're still wangling any old thing they can get to drink anywhere they can get it." Middletown, in returning to its pre-prohibition condition which allowed adults to drink but barred persons under twenty-one, has not returned to the identical situation; for it now must cope with a flaunting of drinking by some adults at the children's own dances and elsewhere, and with a strong tradition among the high-school-age population approving drinking for people of their own age. Hip flasks have not been confined to adults during prohibition, few enterprising youngsters have been ignorant of where the family supply was cached, and drinking at high-school dances has been pronounced. In June, 1935, a beer and dance hall in the center of the business section—dirty, noisy, with a general atmosphere of drunken freedom between males and females, and with streetwalkers inside and hanging about outside —was one of the exciting dives in and out of which Middletown's young drifted. Many Middletown parents were worrying in 1935 over the "new problems repeal has brought."

There is some evidence of revived sentiment among many people for a return to more stringent liquor regulation. A lawyer declared emphatically in 1935: "I voted for repeal, but I certainly would vote the opposite way now! People are spending all their money on liquor and just running the thing into the ground." The women of the city seem in general never to have approved drinking and repeal as strongly as did the men. Generations in Middletown's state have been reared on the spectacle, held aloft by churches, Anti-Saloon League, W.C.T.U. and religious and secular campaigners like Billy Sunday and Carrie

Nation, of wives and children rendered ragged, hungry, and penniless by the excesses of males in that largely male institution, the saloon. And these sources of protest are today rapidly reforming their ranks. In June, 1935, the press quoted a local minister as predicting that "Prohibition will be back with the next legislature. If you don't think so, look at the graft in the liquor business. Nobody can be elected to the legislature from [this] county in 1936 and most other counties who does not favor prohibition again." [48] Local anti-liquor sentiment was strong enough so that the afternoon paper was in June, 1935, refusing advertising for hard liquor.

According to the local agent for a brewer, the working class drinks less hard liquor than does the business class at present because of its higher price.[49] Middletown's principal drink is beer, and local con-

[48] An editorial note in the fall of 1936, headed "Get Rid of Them, or Else—," stated:

"Unless the state and local alcoholic beverage boards get busy and cut out the licenses of two or three so-called taverns here, [Middletown] will 'go local option' with a bang, some of these days. If reports coming from 'wet' sources are correct, there are at least two 'joints' in [Middletown] that are more disgraceful than anything that was ever here in the old saloon days. The drys are probably displaying good strategy by doing nothing about them. They likely believe the situation eventually will become so putrid that everybody will be with them when they finally become ready to eliminate them.

"According to one who says he has been in the South Clark Street joints in Chicago in the old days and in those of Harlem and the East Side, New York City, 'You ain't seen nothin' yet, unless you have visited one of these [Middletown] emporiums.' He says shootings and stabbings are common enough, while ordinary fights take place almost nightly, these reaching their grand climax on Saturday nights. Unless these fights are fatal, which they seem not to have been thus far, they are passed off as of no consequence. We'll probably have to wait for a murder before cleaning them out."

[49] Beer was much more widely available in 1935 than hard liquor by the glass, for the simple reason that a beer license cost only $200 while a license to sell hard liquor cost $900, plus a $75 bond. Hence, remarked one of the newspapers in June, 1935, "There is no great rush here of applicants to sell hard liquor. Most of the 'boys' will be content with beer licenses." The State is seeking to keep a firm hand upon the sale of hard liquor. Not only is the retail license costly, but a wholesale hard-liquor license costs $2,800. The State allows no beer wholesaler to handle hard liquor. There were as yet no liquor wholesalers in Middletown in June, 1935, because of this high initial license cost.

Roadhouses outside the city, which during prohibition kept open after Middletown speakeasies closed at 1 A.M. and attracted much city trade, are no longer permitted by law. It was informally alleged locally that this discrimination in favor of the city is due to the bad reputation these roadhouses acquired, especially as rendezvous for the young prior to repeal, and that it also represents a move put over by city business people and politicians to hold this lucrative liquor business in the city. (This propensity for city businessmen to exploit

sumption has shifted heavily since 1933 from draught to bottled beer.[50] This shift marks growing consumption in the home, especially on Sunday when the "taverns" are closed, and, it is alleged, growing consumption by women.[51]

If liquor was a tension releaser in the depression, cigarette smoking was even more common and was noticeably more prevalent in 1935 than ten years before. This was especially marked among women, and restaurant service for women in 1935 invariably included an ash tray. This increase simply reflects the marked national increase in cigarette consumption. The index of national per-capita consumption, commencing with 67.8 in 1919 when 935 cigarettes per capita were consumed in the United States, rose as follows: 1921, 69.2; 1923, 88.0; 1925, 100.0; 1927, 103.8; 1929, 142.9; 1930, 149.2; and 1931, 147.3.[52]

As one passes from these unorganized ways of spending leisure— gardening in one's back yard, going to the movies, listening to the radio, driving about in one's car, or reading, playing bridge, or drinking—nothing about the organized life of Middletown at play strikes the returning investigator more forcibly than the hardy persistence of the city's club life.[53] Asked about any changes in local club life, a veteran Middletown woman exclaimed, "Goodness! we have more than ever."

In the humbler homes of the business class and all through the working class the same types of women's clubs, many of them the same clubs with the same names, thrive today as in 1925. The Jolly Club members still meet in one another's homes to play bunco for prizes of pillow covers and ash trays, while the notes in the "Society" columns of the press describing the meetings of the Silver Cloud Club,

the surrounding trading area for their own profit has been well described by Veblen in his chapter on "The Small Town" in *Absentee Ownership*.)

[50] A brewery which has supplied 40 per cent of Middletown's beer since the return of beer had monthly sales as follows in 1933 and 1934:

    1933: 1,200 "halves" (kegs); and 800 cases of bottled beer
    1934: 600-800 "halves" (kegs); and 2,000 cases of bottled beer

Consumption of half-cases doubled in 1934 over 1933.

[51] A press note in 1936 called attention to the fact that there are "several 'stag' bars in [Middletown]. The owners don't want women around. They say women create disturbances, 'mooch' drinks from men customers and buy little. But others cater to the women's trade."

[52] See *Recent Social Trends*, p. 897.

[53] See *Middletown*, p. 285 ff.

the All Star Pedro Club, the Friendship Club, the Why Not Club, the Sans Souci, the Kill Kare Club, the Moonlight Savings Club, and their scores of sister organizations suggest that this department of life, at least, has gone on its neighborly way despite the depression.

Uptown, their business-class sisters still go to the Federate Club of Clubs in its various departments. Here one still witnesses the most significant indigenous adult literary and artistic strain of the city in the meetings of the Conversation Club (organized in 1894), the Mary-Martha, the Entre Nous, the Martha Washington, the Philomathean, the Riverside Culture, the Round Table, and the other women's "study" clubs.[54]

In 1925 a slow shift was noted as taking place among these veteran study agencies, from the almost exclusive preoccupation with "literature" as the heart of things worth studying toward more active interest in the life of Middletown.[55] This trend, then apparent in comparison with the 1890's, has developed little further in the ten years since 1925. There is somewhat more attention paid to general world events; one "improves one's mind" on a fare somewhat less exclusively literary and artistic; but both current national issues and notably Middletown's own life are but thinly represented in the programs. With the exception of a series of four talks in one club in the winter of 1934-35 on various aspects of the New Deal by local male guest speakers from the college and high school, and an occasional paper in other clubs on such a topic as the Reforestation Camps or "Democracy under Strain," the depression has not appeared in the printed program announcements. Program papers and discussions fall chiefly into the following six classes: artistic and literary; historical; international affairs; travel and the ways of foreign countries; book reviews of novels, biographies, and outstanding recent nonfiction; and a wide miscellaneous group ranging from the Bible to astronomy, the "new Negro," and problems of the home.[56] On the whole, the topics of these last six years exhibit

[54] See *Middletown*, p. 287 ff.

[55] See *Middletown*, p. 290.

[56] It is the exception for programs for an entire year to be built around a single topic, though during the depression there have been two or three such programs by individual clubs on such topics as English History and Latin America. A rough idea of the range, as well as of the usual lack of sequence, of these programs from 1929 to 1935 is gained by setting down as they appear year after year, proceeding from club to club, the following representative topics: Mexico Today; The Physiology of Fear; New Russia; English As We Use It; Modern Poetry; Spain's Experiment; The New Negro; Alaska, A New Frontier;

somewhat less wrestling with recondite historical topics, less emphasis upon local patriotic subjects (including the poets, painters, scenery, and similar aspects of Middletown's state), less emphasis upon the Bible, and somewhat more emphasis upon international affairs and upon current books of the serious-popular type.

Middletown feels that the 1925 study painted, as one clubwoman expressed it, "a little too hard a picture of [Middletown's] intellectuals." The intelligent daughter of an educated and decidedly superior woman, in commenting on this local feeling, said:

"I think the picture is a little hard. The thing is that these women here have to be self-sufficient, with not much outside stimulus, so there is little talking back and forth about what they read and think. My mother belongs to a little group who are reading together such things as Hart Crane, E. E. Cummings, Gertrude Stein, and Vincent Sheean. They steer clear of most of the poets tinged with economic radicalism, but are well read on the symbolists. Yet I don't think they derive a great amount of personal satisfaction from their reading."

This last sentence may touch the core of the situation. As the business-class woman's role in the family has come to include less of the earlier unremitting dawn-to-dark toil, she has been forced, with less housework and fewer children to bear and rear, to find a socially and personally self-justifying role. The traditional attribution by this culture of finer sensibilities to women has prompted her to act as though she had wide and strong interests in the "finer things of life." This role assumption on her part has been accepted by the preoccupied males as giving some semblance of body to certain highly prized

Japan's Challenge; Astronomy; Parks of Our State; The Chaco War; Modern Drama; The Boston Tea Party; Is Christmas a Joy or Burden to You?; The Story of David and Jonathan; Leading Men of Science; Problems of Adolescence; Venetian Painters; Has the First Principle of the Declaration of Independence Become Obsolete? (review of E. D. Martin's *Liberty*); Our State's New Laws for Women; Gardens; Russia and International Relations; Television; Prewar America (review of Mark Sullivan's books); Latin America (year's program); Outstanding Books of the Past Year (year's program); Adult Education; Living Women of the English Nobility; Reforestation Camps; Our Navy; Emma Willard; Cathedrals of England; Birth Control and Sterilization; Charles and Wm. Beard's *American Leviathan;* George Washington; Modern Living and Its Changed Standards; The Huntington Library in Pasadena; Leisure in Family Life; Labor and Industry, the Consumer, the Farmer, and American Tariff Policy under the New Deal (a series of four addresses by outside speakers in one year before one club); Radio and Movies; The Understanding Parent; The History of the Violin; Famous Negroes; Women and Peace; Gandhi and India.

symbols of the culture such as "progress" and "culture" (in the artistic sense). The heavy concentration of "culture" in the refined, artistic sense in the female side of the community is the result. Actually, no population reared under our system of high-school education, including a wide diversity of temperaments and abilities, and aggregated into groups on a social rather than an interest basis, can have anything other than an uneven interest in being proficient in this—to Middletown in its daily concerns—largely symbolic world of "the finer things of life." It is no reflection on the business-class women of Middletown, thus herded into a stereotyped role for their sex, that their "study" clubs with their programs of reading "good" books and discussing "broadening" topics are earnestly pursued rather than reflecting the spontaneity of acute personal interests; and that the programs are scattered and casual rather than characterized by concentration of enthusiasm. The world of refined knowledge is today far too wide to be attacked successfully without the aid of the selective factor of interest in specific problems. It is unlikely that even half of the women in any of the city's study clubs read the foreign Associated Press dispatches in the local press with any consistency, care, or real interest. When such a club puts on a series of programs on "international affairs," it becomes for most of the members something of an intellectual *tour de force*. The following program of one study club for the winter of 1934-35 is a natural outgrowth of this sort of effort to reach for the cultural moon. Each member was assigned a country (other than the United States) and in successive meetings each reported for her country on the following: location and boundaries, legends, climate and seasons, population and language, music and sports, housing, war heroes, Christmas observance, economic prosperity, manners and customs, form of government, education, holidays and feasts, art and literature, exports and imports, its greatest social problem, religion.

The increasing participation of members of the faculty of the local college in the club life of the city bids fair to increase the range and vitality of discussion in the clubs. Both the Business and Professional Women's Club, which one alert newcomer to Middletown described as "by all odds the livest women's club in Middletown," and the local branch of the American Association of University Women have received new impetus since 1925 in the addition of members from the college faculty. The International Relations section of the latter club is supplying a point of view not only conspicuously lacking in this inland city but subtly discouraged by other bodies such as the D.A.R. and American Legion, which emphasize contrary and, to Middletown, more familiar tendencies. This section has pledged its support to disarmament, has voted a resolution urging the United States to enter the World Court, and has had leading teachers in the city address it repeatedly on such topics as "Regionalism and Recent Foreign Relations of the United States" and "The United States Senate and Foreign Relations." Both of these clubs have special reasons for the exceptional character of their programs: the first because it contains many of the ablest of the city's young professional and business women, a group of individuals sufficiently isolated in the prevailing pattern of Middletown's married, non-working, business-class women to make these club meetings a matter of more than incidental significance in their lives; [57] and the second because of its somewhat homogeneous, educated membership and because, unlike the Federate Club of Clubs, it receives strong stimulus and help in program-making from the energetic national headquarters of the Association.

The men's civic clubs continue much as they were in 1925.[58] They are in Middletown essentially prosperity clubs, thriving best when they float on the tide of general civic enthusiasm. Like Middletown's churches, they seek to build morale through a solidarity achieved by the reiteration of familiar slogans and the avoidance of divisive issues. During the depression they have continued, with one exception, to meet and to listen to speeches, but they have not as organizations shared in any concerted way in the solution of the city's urgent civic problems. The Dynamo Club,[59] the Monday-noon group of young businessmen members of the Chamber of Commerce, succumbed in the depression but was in process of revival late in 1935. Rotary carries, if anything, more prestige than formerly, and at least one leading businessman noted by the investigator has left another and less powerful club to enter Rotary's charmed tent. To the disgust of some local men, Rotary is becoming hereditary with the crowding of sons of

[57] Another element that is probably operative in this group of Business and Professional Women is the fact that, as a minority group toward whom the complacent male world of Middletown is unconsciously somewhat patronizing, they are quietly determined to make good, to show what women can do, and not to be, as one woman expressed it, "just another backslapping civic club."

[58] See *Middletown*, pp. 301-06.

[59] See *Middletown*, p. 303.

members into its increasingly elastic membership "classifications." [60] Rotary is less spontaneous and more self-aware than it was in 1925. No longer are guests greeted with the old informal " 'Lo, Bill," "Hi, Ed," and singing at the luncheons is now omitted. But if Rotary is growing more sophisticated and self-conscious, the other civic clubs still strike the authentic spontaneous note of 1925—songs and all.

One got some sense, however, of these men's civic club meetings as seeming tired, like a ritual too long performed, although too few of them could be attended in the briefer study in 1935 to make this anything more than a very tentative opinion. It is a significant new aspect of Rotary's meetings that certain of the younger members are now wont to congregate around one or two of the rear tables and, as one of them phrased it, "pass *sotto voce* cracks to each other on some of the tripe handed out by the speakers." This may conceivably mean that the orthodoxies of the older men are losing some of their sanctity with the younger set who take Rotary not as a fellowship but as mere "good business." Elsewhere is quoted the statement by a businessman of forty that the youngest group of men who are winning through the handicaps of the depression seem "more hard-boiled" than the older men. It may be that this younger wave of successful men, their ranks thinned by the depression, facing a difficult future with the sense of having missed, owing to their immaturity, the big "killings" of the 1920's, are developing a *Realpolitik* of their own stripped of even the mellowing rituals of their seniors.

In June, 1936, when a Lions Club was organized in Middletown, an editor commented: "That makes six men's civic clubs here, exclusive of the Chamber of Commerce. . . . Also two women's clubs of the same character—Altrusa and Business and Professional Women's. . . . If all were one club, what a power it could be in the city!"

Lodges, to quote one prominent local lodgeman, "have been shot to hell by the depression." The Elks have gone through bankruptcy, lost their expensive clubhouse, and now occupy an inconspicuous upstairs room over a store. While the lodges still struggle on, they appear for the most part to have even less vitality than in 1925. [61] The Masons' colossal million-dollar "temple," constructed in 1925 and now increasingly handicapped by the fact that its auditorium must compete with

[60] There are no less than five members of the X family in Rotary, although they all work in the family's glass plant.
[61] See *Middletown*, pp. 306-09.

the drift of concerts and lectures to the college auditorium, is regarded locally as an appalling white elephant, but it will probably continue to be carried by the business leaders out of sheer civic pride. It would appear that business-class membership in other lodges is doomed. The situation is quite different with the working-class lodges, since they perform a more necessary social function in the lives of working-class men and their wives. For the working class, deprived of Country Club and many other institutionalized social occasions, such as the sorority dances open to the business class, the lodges with their card tables, beer bars, and dances afford a place of meeting one's fellows and belonging that men so situated do not easily give up; and these working-class lodges were reported in 1936 to be "coming back strongly."

Public lectures, one of the old leisure-time stand-bys of Middletown but waning in popularity even in 1925,[62] have almost disappeared during the depression as a town-sponsored type of entertainment. The local Chautauqua has shriveled up completely and will never return,[63] but more important for the leisure of the city is the disappearance of the citizen-sponsored winter "lyceum"[64] and the attenuation of the sporadic lectures brought to town under the sponsorship of local clubs. A trickle of speakers such as Commander Byrd and Count Luckner have been brought to the city even during the depression by local organizations seeking to raise money, but in the main the latter are coming to regard concerts as more reliable moneymakers. The decline in local sponsorship of lectures is doubtless due in part to the radio, but even more to the fact that the college has so largely taken over this function. At present the college conducts a lyceum offering a wider array of speakers than Middletown's own citizens were able to bring

[62] See *Middletown*, pp. 226-29.
[63] See *Middletown*, p. 229.
There has been a heavy decline during the depression in "lectures" by itinerant "Professors" of "practical psychology," "mystic psychology" and the like. (See *Middletown*, pp. 298-99.) The sort of thing represented by the following advertisement in a local paper in April, 1929, virtually disappeared in the depression, along with the large-space ads of doctors with alleged "spiritual healing" powers (see *Middletown*, pp. 439-41):

"Free Lecture
Mystic Psychology—Numeral Pholosophy [sic]
by Dr. Alber Christy, Pasadena, Cal."

[64] See *Middletown*, p. 220.

to town in 1924-25. The students provide the attendance backlog, and local citizens fill in the rest of the needed ticket purchasers to make the lyceum pay its way. This transfer of lecture sponsorship to the college represents, however, another step in the process spoken of locally as "the transfer of the center of Middletown's intellectual and artistic life to the college campus."

The situation as regards artistic forms of recreation in Middletown since 1925 involves changes both in the kinds of activities and in the locus of sponsorship as between town and gown. A notable addition is the organization in 1931 of an amateur Civic Theater, presenting four or five plays a winter and regarded locally as a highly prized addition to the city's artistic and leisure resources. Middletown may owe this innovation in part to the stimulation of the local college dramatic club, the Spotlight Club, some of whose members graduate into its ranks; in part the development stems from the general growth of the little-theater movement throughout the country; and it is perhaps also attributable to the constant example of the movies, which have quickened in the popular imagination the sense that many of us might engage in this glamorous business of acting if we only tried. In any event, there are now two little-theater groups, one at the college and the other citizen-sponsored, presenting a type of recreational outlet extinct in Middletown in 1925 save for the Dramatic Club in the high school. In the main the Civic Theater is a strictly business-class affair, with a member of the X family as president, but it is significant of the social catholicity of the search for artistic talent in the small community that the present director of the theater, a graduate of the local college, is the son of a molder in a local foundry. The father is militantly active in the Middletown labor movement.

Participation in the presentation of plays has spread to the unemployed during the depression through the inauguration as part of the F.E.R.A. recreation program of the production of groups of one-act plays presented in the high-school auditorium. This, like many of the depression extensions of customary practice in Middletown, will almost surely disappear with the return to "normalcy."

At other points the college is stimulating the artistic activities of the city through its leadership. Local initiative in the field of art had declined from the 1890's to a point in 1925 where, aside from the art work in the public schools, "art" meant the reading of papers in women's clubs and the bringing to the city of occasional lectures and exhibitions of paintings by state artists.[65] One of the moving spirits in Middletown's art life for some years, aside from art teachers in the public schools, has been one of the wives in the older generation of the X family, who has traveled widely and owns a valuable collection of etchings, paintings, and other art objects. With the development by the family of the local college, this family civic interest in art development for Middletown has been transferred to the college. In 1935 a handsome Arts Building was being completed at the college on P.W.A. funds and a substantial contribution by the husband of this member of the X family. Today, this dignified building, with its workrooms, auditorium, and an exhibition hall housing a permanent exhibition of the art treasures of several members of the X family and other excellent occasional exhibitions brought to the city, is the most conspicuous manifestation of the art life of Middletown. Concomitantly with this development at the college, and probably stimulated by it to some extent, a small group of business-class people have recently taken to painting and have held exhibitions at the college. In the fall of 1935 two of these women who had visited the art center at Dayton, Ohio, opened a small workshop studio in a skylighted room in the home of one of them where two mornings a week a small class of women and children fifteen years old and above paint and sketch under their instruction. A woman in close touch with these artistic interests in Middletown summarizes the developments in recent years as follows:

"There has been a marked increase in interest in painting here in the past ten years. The inauguration some ten years ago of an annual January exhibition at Marshall Field's in Chicago of the work of painters from our state has been important in arousing and fostering interest in painting. Two local men, one of them a teacher at the college and the other living on a farm near here, have pictures there each year, and one of our local women also had a painting exhibited there one year. The art gallery at the college has also been a major stimulus. All classes of our citizens go out there Sunday after Sunday to enjoy the really fine exhibitions in that beautiful setting, and the enthusiasm of the general public is surprising. Our county exhibitions held at the college are rather pitiful, save for the work of about six or eight people, but these exhibitions are helping all sorts of people to realize that it is possible and delightful to attempt something creative."

[65] See *Middletown,* pp. 248-50.

At five points the musical life [66] of Middletown has been rendered, temporarily at least, stronger in the depression. The women's Matinee Musicale has strengthened somewhat its study and recital programs by its own members. Its student section, which died out in 1924, was revived in 1932; and in 1935 its membership included a senior section of adult women numbering 103, a student section of seventy high-school-age children of both sexes, and a junior section of one hundred younger children. A second development in the depression is the increase in popularity of all types of music—vocal and instrumental—in the high school. The advent of F.E.R.A. group music lessons at twenty-five cents an hour has also tended to strengthen musical participation among those of high-school age and younger. A fourth development has been the revival of chorus choirs, which were noted in 1925 as disappearing in business-class churches. In 1931 the Presbyterian Church introduced a chorus choir, followed by the leading Baptist and Methodist churches in 1932. Some local people believe that this revival of chorus singing is not primarily an economy move growing out of the depression but reflects a revival of popular taste for massed music stimulated by the radio. This view is supported by the fact that, even before the depression, the Matinee Musicale organized a women's chorus which has continued to be popular and has even traveled to Chicago to sing. A final development apparent in the depression is the increased number of local orchestras, bands, amateur radio programs, and community singing events. The Federate Club of Clubs now has a women's orchestra, and there is a F.E.R.A. orchestra and a Municipal Band.

Along with this increase in musical participation in the depression, one must also note that in the sponsorship of local concerts, as in art and public lectures, though not to so great a degree, the city has been becoming slowly more dependent upon the college. Before the depression and until 1933, the Civic Music Association, a nation-wide movement, was sponsored locally by the women of the Matinee Musicale. Concert-going is a decidedly marginal activity for perhaps two-thirds of the thousand people who were combed out of the homes of Middletown by these women for each of the winter series of four or five concerts which usually packed the Masonic Temple to its capacity of 1,000 to 1,100. The winter series of concerts was in 1934-35 run by the college, although occasional artists like Rachmaninoff continue to be

[66] See *Middletown,* pp. 242-48.

brought in sporadically by the Business and Professional Women's Club, the De Molays, and other organizations for money-raising purposes.

While this centralization in the college of the sponsorship of Middletown's contacts with the outside world of lectures, art, and music tends to involve greater regularity and more sustained quality of programs, it also probably involves a step in the direction of loss of autonomous concern for such matters, so common among the citizens of large urban units. As is pointed out in Chapter IX below, Middletown, in common with the larger national culture, has paid little attention to the question of what types of activities thrive best under centralized and what ones under diffused organization. It is possible that activities involving the more subtle aspects of personal cultivation, in areas which the preoccupation of the culture with business tend to relegate to a marginal position, need the highly personalized sponsorship of a widely diffused group of interested individuals. In the case of lectures, art, and music in Middletown, the removal to any considerable extent of the local generating center for these types of leisure from the persons of the city to an impersonal It, the college, along with the holding of these affairs out on the campus at one extreme edge of the city rather than downtown in the geographical center, may involve in time a slow attenuation of interest.

The organization of leisure has reached down further into the younger age groups since 1925. The urban child's out-of-school life appears to be swinging through a cycle: from close domination by parents in chores about home; [67] to a period of relatively fewer chores in more convenient dwellings with smaller yards to be cared for, [68] in which the child's leisure was largely unorganized and depended upon neighborhood play; to the present increasing organization, not by parents and home, but by a variety of "youth" agencies. This last phase of increasing organization has been growing steadily since the 1925 study was made. Supervised and organized play for children in summer, first begun in 1925 in a very tentative way on three playgrounds,

[67] See the school regulation of fifty years ago quoted in the earlier study (p. 211): "Pupils shall not be permitted to remain on the school grounds after dismissal. The teachers shall often remind the pupils that their first duty when dismissed is to proceed quietly and directly home to render all needed assistance to their parents."

[68] See *Middletown*, p. 94.

has developed into a city-wide system for both older and younger children. The Boy Scout movement has grown, and each city school now has its Girl Reserves. The Y.W.C.A., with its new building and enlarged staff, offers a much more heavily organized program of leisure to the girls of the city, while the Y.M.C.A. boys' program, formerly conducted *en masse* save for the school Bible classes, has now been organized into smaller Pioneering and Citizenship groups.[69] Organized extra-curricular activities in the high school not only continue unabated but have actually increased somewhat.

No discussion of organized leisure in Middletown can overlook the "Bearcats," a generic term for all of the Central High School teams, but meaning in Middletown the basketball team. In 1925 this hybrid animal came close to being "Magic [Middletown's]" official emblem,[70] and in 1931, despite the depression, the citizens gave gold watches to the basketball team when it exalted the city by winning the state championship. The depression years have apparently pulled some of the Bearcats' teeth, and there is some question as to whether basketball will ever regain its former frenzied preeminence. Local citizens tell one today that "Basketball isn't so prominent as it was," and some even go so far as to say that it is "just like any other fad." In addition to the factor of the cost of tickets to a population trimming its financial sails in a depression, four factors appear to be involved in the shrinkage of this civic symbol. The city overdid itself in the late 1920's when, emulating other cities and towns of the state, a group of loyal businessmen built for the team a basketball stadium seating 9,000, incurring thereby an obligation over the next fourteen years of $347,000. Those were the days when being a successful basketball coach had made a Middletown teacher successively high-school principal and then school superintendent. The citizens' committee, riding this high tide of enthusiasm, forced the stadium bonds heavily on the citizens, including the city schoolteachers, as an investment, and in addition no less than 675 loyal citizens undertook to pay $50 apiece for five-year admission tickets. During the depression this field house, as noted in Chapter VI, has become a financial white elephant which the city

[69] In 1934 the Y.M.C.A. offered the boys of the city ten different organized recreational outlets, claiming to reach 2,493 different boys during the year through these activities. In addition there were various social activities such as an annual Father and Son banquet, a Christmas party, and so on.
[70] See *Middletown*, pp. 284 and 485.

schools have had to take over and operate as a junior high school, despite its patent unfitness for such use. The whole affair has left a sour taste in the mouths of a good many people. A second reason for the sobered attitude toward basketball is the radio broadcasting of Bearcat games since 1930. This has made itself felt at the box office, and, to counteract the tendency to enjoy the games at home, exhortations in the press have proclaimed: "You owe it to our Bearcat team [to attend home games]. And you owe it to [Middletown]. It's all for [Middletown], our home, our city!" A third factor is the development of teams at the new high school opened in the fall of 1929 as part of the college laboratory school, in the junior high schools, and at the college. All of these have tended to divide somewhat the loyalty that, ten years ago, headed up exclusively in the Central High School team. As one citizen remarked, "The Bearcats no longer occupy the whole stage." A final important factor has been the marked development of a varied program of intramural sports in the schools. In 1931 there were 150 to 200 boys on all athletic squads at the Central High School, but by 1935 the number had increased to 400 to 500. In 1931 there were thirty-three boys playing football in the three upper high-school grades, and by 1935 this had increased to seventy-seven. In addition to the four sports —basketball, football, track, and baseball—of 1925, there are now tennis, golf, wrestling, cross country, volleyball, softball, and even horseshoe teams, with informal leagues through the several junior and two senior high schools of the city. This broadening of the participation base with more students active has meant less symbolic participation as spectators by "drugstore" athletes lounging about the downtown soft-drink hangouts. Another outgrowth was the sharp curtailment in 1935 of the number of Central High School " 'Pep' Chapels," which in 1925 were used to work up student delirium before all home games.

What a people does with its leisure, like the way it trains its young, affords a sensitive index to its values. What do the changes in the leisure of Middletown over these ten years suggest by way of answer to the questions posed at the outset of this chapter? What significance do such changes as have been noted have for the future of these people? The changes have involved in the main intensifications and diminutions of existing trends and very few radical departures. Over the long view it will probably be found that the socialization of leisure facilities, both participant and spectator, under the emergency F.E.R.A. program will have been the most significant departure of these ten years. Here one has witnessed a community attempting to state the problem of public recreation positively. Some of this extended work as it touches children will probably continue, since schools, Y.M.C.A., and Playground Association exist as already going agencies interested in furthering certain aspects of this work. It is, however, very unlikely that this individualistic culture will regard it as worth its while to carry on the adult program, once the emergency and supporting Federal funds have passed.

Next, perhaps, in significance is the return of beer and other alcoholic beverages to a legal, non-furtive status in the leisure of the city. The significance of this is perhaps greater in the lives of the working class than of the business class, for reasons noted above.

From other changes in Middletown's leisure, such as the doubling of library reading in the depression, little permanent residue will probably continue, as the city was already in 1935 headed toward a less unusual level of activity in this respect. Here and there, innovations learned under the jarring dislocations of habit in the depression—such, for instance, as the growth of interest in flower gardens—will continue. But the summary balance sheet of Middletown's four years of prosperous growth and six years of depression experience suggests decidedly that the community has not discovered with the help of its "new leisure" new designs for living. In the overwhelming majority of cases, the community has simply in the fat years bought more of the same kinds of leisure, and in the lean years made what curtailments it was forced to make and just marked time pending the return of the time when it could resume the doing of the familiar things.

Middletown's work-leisure pattern in the depression is perhaps best epitomized by the action of its retailers, who met the chance to increase leisure as business fell off by actually increasing the number of hours they kept their stores open. In other words, here is a community bound into service to moneymaking. Its deepest traditions emphasize hard work as the key to overcoming obstacles. It has been said that the Industrial Revolution gave the Western world a choice among more children, more leisure, or a rising standard of living. It chose the last—and technological advances and modern merchandising have seen to it that there has been no wavering in this choice. To such a culture, the depression has operated not as a call to adventure in developing new fruitful ways of "living," but simply as a deplorable interruption of the dominant work pattern. Wherever possible, men have met it by applying the old universal solvent for any type of difficulty and have worked harder; and where this has not been possible, they have fumed and created personal devils to denounce—"Wall Street speculators," "international financiers," "the people in Washington." Men kept their stores open longer, allegedly because, as some claim, "the Jews and the chain stores started it," but in part because latent within their skins and writ large all over their institutions is the master formula: Work = Money; Money Buys Leisure; Nonwork = Loss of Opportunity to Make Money, and Therefore Loss of Opportunity to Buy Leisure. It is thus that a pecuniary culture transmutes even leisure into its own terms. And in 1935 Middletown was rushing eagerly back to work, hailing the end of its unfortunate accident of depression leisure.

CHAPTER VIII

Religion

T HE EARLIER study of Middletown noted religious beliefs and practices as the most slowly changing of all the life activities of the people.[1] As habits of thought and action had changed in other areas of Middletown's life in the thirty-five years since the days of the pre-gas-boom village of the 1880's, religion had largely stood its ground. The religious institutions of the culture, even more sharply than "democracy" and the "Constitution" in the political sphere and the family in yet a third sphere, represent to Middletown permanence in the face of surrounding change. As the gap has widened between that large portion of Middletown's religious beliefs which are based upon a body of specific purported historical occurrences and the workaday habits of thought of the city's contemporary secular life, religion has operated increasingly behind a front of symbolic language and ritual.[2] Although there was wide variation from individual to individual, the dominant impression the research staff gained in a year and a half of attendance at Middletown's religious services and of talking with individuals in 1924-25 was that of an unalert acceptance,[3] punctuated periodically in the less socially sophisticated churches by bursts of religious energy during a revival.

The return to Middletown in 1935 offered, therefore, an interesting possibility to the research staff. The city had been shaken for nearly six years by a catastrophe involving not only people's values but, in the case of many, their very existence. Unlike most socially generated catastrophes, in this case virtually nobody in the community had been cushioned against the blow; the great knife of the depression had cut down impartially through the entire population, cleaving open the lives and hopes of rich as well as poor. The experience had been more nearly universal than any prolonged recent emotional experience in the city's history; it had approached in its elemental shock the pri-

[1] See *Middletown*, pp. 497 and 403-04.
[2] See *Middletown*, pp. 405-06.
[3] See *Middletown*, Ch. XXIII.

mary experiences of birth and death.[4] During this period, presumably, every institution in the community capable of giving hope and guidance, as well as material assistance, has had to reinventory its resources and to stretch its functions to the limits of its capacity. Traditionally, religion has been chief among the institutions giving both spiritual and material sustenance, though in recent years this role has narrowed largely to the giving of spiritual aid as the secular charities have increasingly taken over material succor.[5] The question the new situation of stress invited in 1935 was whether organized religion had grown in its significance in the city's life. Had its symbols floated down nearer to urgent day-by-day reality? Had its agencies of expression, the churches, changed or added to their functions? Would the element of lethargy of 1925 be less apparent?

The first indication of change in Middletown's religious institutions since 1925 struck one almost as one got off the train. In the heart of the downtown section of the city two imposing new stone churches have replaced rusty brick buildings that dated back to the gas-boom days of the 1880's.[6] One of these churches is a $350,000 plant including a $30,000 organ. In the outlying sections of the city three other new churches were completed during the early years of the depression at expenditures ranging from $16,000 to $70,000. All of these churches represent boom-time planning of the late 1920's.[7]

[4] The emotional experience of wartime solidarity in a common cause was different in that it involved a positive build-up of community morale, not its destruction; and it offered a superabundance of opportunities for tension release in socially highly approved activity.

[5] See *Middletown,* pp. 462-63 and Ch. IV above.

[6] In Middletown's culture a stone church carries more prestige than a brick church, symbolizing as it does durability and differentness from the secular city built of brick and wood.

[7] Easy money, denominational rivalry, and crusading preachers coincided with the obvious obsolescence of much local church property in producing this church-building boom. At least three other churches began to build but were caught by the depression; they succeeded only in putting in foundation and basement, roofed the latter over, and now worship in these dugouts. Both ministers who drove through the building campaigns for the two large downtown churches have since left, one of them under fire. One of these churches lost some members over the cost of the new church; there had been unhappy incidents due to the overprompt filing of pledge claims against estates of members who had died, and "after a long struggle the church succeeded in getting rid of the minister who had carried through the building campaign." One feels a none too thinly veiled social coercion in the notice in the calendar of this church that the "Honor Roll will be published early in July. Please try to pay your pledge. PLAN TO HAVE YOUR NAME ON THE HONOR ROLL."

The number of local congregations meeting in some sort of building or room every Sunday—sixty-five in number in 1935, and representing twenty-two denominations—has grown since 1925 roughly in step with the growth in population. The single Catholic Church in the old East End of town has opened a second building (one of the uncompleted basements mentioned in note 7) in the western district, adjoining the college; but in the main the additional congregations added since 1925 are the marginal groups somewhat deplored by the older denominations, two-thirds of the additions being among the one-third of the denominations falling in the general classification of Spiritualist, Holiness, Apostolic Faith Assembly, and so on.

Outwardly, therefore, in these more ponderable aspects religion in Middletown shows change since 1925, evidence that religion in some way means enough to people so that they spend their money to build churches.

But the sense of expectancy over possible new vitality to be found here in the religious sector of the culture evaporated as one began again to attend church services and to read the sermons reprinted in the Monday-morning newspaper. Here, scattered through the pews, is the same serious and numerically sparse Gideon's band—two-thirds or more of them women, and few of them under thirty—with the same stark ring of empty pews "down front." The audiences seem older than formerly and, especially in the business-class churches, persons between fifteen and twenty-five years of age seem fewer, although this is only an impression.[8] It is June, to be sure, a "bad time for church attendance," but the investigator had lived two other Junes in Middletown ten years before. The minister in a leading business-class church announces: "I shall preach during June and July on the great conditionals. The sermons will be short. They will, of course [with a reassuring smile], be practical. The text this morning is 'Whosoever would save his life, let him take up his cross and follow me.'" Then follows the sermon, the gist of which is:

The secret of a happy life is a cross. A cross is a blessing. [The minister pauses here, and then with fiery emphasis:] The absence of a blessing is a curse. [Then quietly and persuasively:] Until a person crosses his selfishness with a wider goal, he is lost.

[8] See *Middletown,* pp. 358-59.

To the observer it recalls many similar settings ten years earlier in Middletown: The earnest minister employing the familiar symbolic phrases, the prevailingly gray heads tilted slightly to one side in respectful attentiveness. Then the closing hymn, sung doggedly and rather raggedly by people who do not seem to enjoy hearing themselves sing, "O Jesus, I have promised to serve thee to the end." And the final subdued neighborliness of the greetings as the congregation files out.

In the working-class churches there was the same preponderance of gray-haired persons, and even fewer men, in part because the X glass plant was running on a seven-day schedule. But religion here seemed, as in 1925,[9] a more reciprocal experience between leader and congregation. The impression of the people's just "sitting and taking it" was less marked; nor did one get such a sense of earnestness channeled by custom and blunted by propriety as in the business-class churches. In one of these churches the minister, a man who knows the lives of his flock beyond the polite formalities of the parlor, spoke as one of "us men in overalls" to "you molders and machinists who have to keep your machines in production." And the "Yes's" and "That's right's" of his audience accompanied his thought.

Sermon topics in 1935 are interchangeable with those of a decade ago. Congregations listen to discourses on "An Unchangeable God in an Unchangeable World," "Lifting High Our Banners," "Shearing the Black Sheep," "The Iron That Swam," "Transformation by Beholding," "When All Else Fails," "God in the Commonplace," "God's Challenge," "Take Time to be Holy," "Fishers of Men," and so on, week after week.[10] And each Monday Middletown reads headlines declaring "Thirst for Spirit Exists in Every Man," or "Devil Dangles Temptations," or "Misery Is Only Reward of Sin," followed in each case by a half-column or more of summary and quotation, prepared by the minister from his sermon of the day before, in such form as the two following:[11]

[9] See *Middletown*, pp. 329 and 390.
[10] See *Middletown*, pp. 372-77.
[11] Reference is made in Ch. VII to the emphasis by certain students of the psychological aspects of American culture on the "masochistic tendency" in this culture. If the denial of life in the pursuit of "success" through "hard work" is one of the commonest current manifestations of this tendency, the Christian religion is its philosophical core. It has given certain words such as "pleasure," "idleness," "impulse," "sex," and "the human body" disreputable fringes of

"One who can lift his eyes beyond the horizon of practicalities and prece-dents and give himself to visions which ought to be realized, has spiritual vision," the Rev. —— said in his sermon . . . yesterday morning.

"It seems fantasy or folly, when Paul, interpreting the Christian attitude declares, 'We look not at things which are seen, but at the things which are not seen.' . . . But the blindest of all men are those who see only with their physical eyes. There are myriads of things not yet pigeonholed by science or catalogued in our philosophies; we may think we know the rose as we tear its petals off, but until one has seen, acknowledged, the subtle appeal of its beauty and mystery one has no real acquaintance with the flower.

"Charmed as we may be by the rustle of greenbacks or the chink of shekels in hand, deep within our hearts we know with infallible persuasion, that he is rich and he alone, who has wisdom, love, patience, who possesses friends, who creates kindly thoughts, whose life abounds with simple joy. . . . 'The earth is the Lord's' and He gives it to those who have eyes to see; real possession is entirely a matter of appreciation.

"The man who is proud of being practical tells us we waste our time, our energy and nerve power in stopping to think of ideal things; he says we must take the world as we find it, forgetting how fair and poetic it came to our hands, and how bleak and ugly we are like to leave it if driven by our always assertive greed. To him, trees are merely lumber, and he never sees the poem which Kilmer saw for all of us; grass and flowers to him are forms of hay for the market; bird songs, for him spell poultry in some form: wind and waters suggest commercial energy; and so the world has many who are so busy making things as to have no time for enjoying anything that is made. The insistent word, the loud spoken word of prac-tical lives is 'dollars,' and to most of those reiterating, manipulating the word and its ways, it may seem foolish to admire and answer to the thrill of the finer human passions: Alas for the man who never sees the light of heaven in another's tear, nor hears the brush of angels' wings when men and women fly to the aid of their fellows. . . .

"Foolish and unlearned a man may be, ignorant of the wise conclusions of the philosophers who have looked into all mysteries with their lanterns, but in every man there is a thirst after the things of the spirit which found exemplification in the Galilean life. Humanity in toto is hungry for the life that is more than things, the life of the spirit. People neglect the spiritual

---

connotation, while it has set such watchdog concepts as "sin," "temptation," "lust," and "perdition" over the lives of men. And it has sought to make the pattern of postponement and the patient "bearing of" present "burdens" sov-ereign among the ruling values of men, dislocating attention from "the world" to "the sweet bye and bye," a "hereafter" when men will "put off this corrup-tion" and "all things will be made perfect."

at the peril of their all. So anxious are the many to run life's present race, that they refuse time for him who rides in the chariot to drink of the water of life; yet the body is the chariot and the soul is the rider; the most practical common sense demands that we feed the inner places of our lives, the heart that has so long thirsted and hungered for love, for things too deep for words, for things that cannot be quoted in dollars."

Using as his text Matt. 4: 8-9, Dr. —— said: "God will change human nature, but he leaves to man to change human society. The devil wants to turn our virtues into vices, wants to turn our prayers into presumptions, wants to turn our religion into blasphemy. No worth of character deters him. He would take the little child from its mother's breast and make it an imp of his own.

"Jesus could have made sport of his three temptations to which the devil subjected him and could have made the devil look like a mere passing fancy, but that would not have solved the woes of the world. Satan has told people to let a snake bite them to prove the miraculous. That is not God's way. The redeemed life is the greatest proof of his power. Satan always ascends to the highest that he may bring you to the lowest.

"This great arch enemy plays his best cards. The first was to appeal to the appetite and immediate necessity. He came in the spirit of benevolence. He declared his own weakness by calling on the Christ to perform the miracle. This temptation was subtle and scheming, but the Master answered it with the scriptures, 'Man shall not live by bread alone.' Here we see the devil recognized both the human and divine side of Christ. He knew the Christ was capable of temptation. But the rest of us would not have had the power that Jesus had. He was hungry, grievously hungry. He made victory a thing to be fought for. He made it worth while to live and conquer. . . . [Here followed similar discussions of the second and third temptations in the same Biblical scene.]

"The devil takes advantage of us when we are off guard. In pleasure and business. He took advantage of Joseph when he was in the house of Potiphar. How easily he could have gone the devil's way and have missed all the jail life. But he chose the right. The devil told David to give it up, he had sinned; the devil told Job to curse God and die. He told Daniel, 'You had better stop that prayer life and be a little more careful, if you do not want to be in the lions' den.' Told the worthy Hebrew children to fall down and worship the great image and they would stand high in the king's course.

"So he goes on fooling and deceiving life. The devil takes advantage of circumstances. Our sorrows, trials, and reverses. If we stand these trials and temptations we are made stronger for tomorrow's conflicts."

Since the outward forms of religion are seemingly so unchanged, as much effort as possible was made within the time available to discover whether the depression has affected the inner feeling of Middletown people as regards religion. Have they been turning privately, if not publicly, to religion with greater frequency and depth of devotion? That those closest to local religious life have hoped for some such change is suggested by the following statement which served as the keynote to a Middletown rally of Sunday-school superintendents in 1932: "A great religious awakening follows each depression: What are we going to do about it? How can we increase attendance and develop leadership for Sunday school and mission work?" The very raising of these questions as relating to a future event suggests, perhaps, that there had been no marked upsurge up to that time. The following comments to the investigator in 1935 serve to answer the question further:

Comment by a thoughtful minister, an exceptionally discriminating religious leader of some ten years' local residence: "The depression has brought a resurgence of earnest religious fundamentalism among the weaker working-class sects on the South Side [12]—probably due in part to the number of casual workers that have drifted in from the Southern Mountains—but the uptown churches have seen little similar revival of interest."

Comment by the energetic pastor of one of the larger working-class churches, associated with one of the large denominations: "There has been some turning to religion during the depression, but it has been very slight and not permanent. Despite my constant visiting and an annual survey I make of all families in my district, there has been very little increase in church attendance and even less increase in religious interest on the South Side. There has been no increase at all in the children's interest."

Comment by the minister of one of the smaller and more primitive sects composed entirely of working-class people: "There has been only a very small turning to religion during the depression. My church has grown from 40 to 200 during the past four or five years as it is one of only two churches of our denomination and draws working people from all over the city. Our people live in great uncertainty as to whether they'll be working next week. There hasn't been much deepening of their aims and values except that their aims have shortened because of their constant economic uncertainty.

[12] See the statement above that two-thirds of the new congregations added since 1925 have been in the one-third of the denominations comprising this type of sect.

I expect that when prosperity returns people will probably turn away from the church again—just as the Old Testament predicts."

Comment by an unemployed factory worker: "I and a few other men I know have got interested in going to church because we didn't have any money to go anywhere else. Then we got interested in the teachings and activities and stuck. I guess we'll drift away again when things pick up."

Comment by another workingman: "I don't go to church because the church ought to have something to meet the needs of laboring men, and the laborers feel that the administration of churches is in the hands of wealth." [13]

A physician closely in touch with many phases of Middletown life seemed to sum up the situation with considerable accuracy when he said:

"There is no wave of religious feeling in [Middletown] in the depression, despite the prediction of the ministerial profession that the depression would bring the people closer to God. The churches, although they constantly point to their yearly membership growth, are conscious of the fact that they are slowly slipping. The average [Middletown] citizen has very definite religious beliefs, but for the most part they are a kind of automatic part of the scheme of inherited things and not anything he uses particularly in his daily life. And the depression hasn't changed this."

It is possibly indicative of the apparently negligible effect of the depression as a quickening factor in local religious life that the bottom has dropped out of the revival movement which flourished in 1925; [14] though other social changes are undoubtedly operative here also. According to a prominent minister: "The business-class churches are slowly giving up the revival idea. The last one, tried as a union effort in the spring of 1930, almost died on our hands. We used the big high-school basketball auditorium. The revival was billed as a great drive to regenerate Middletown. Toward the end of the four weeks it became very difficult to get attendance. I don't think these churches have much stomach for trying it again." [15] There has been a meager

---

[13] Isolated comments like these last two by workingmen signify very little, of course, in the absence of any check on their representativeness. They are included here simply as throwing further light on the statements of the ministers.

[14] See *Middletown,* pp. 378-81.

[15] A local "Committee of 100" was organized with the president of the college as chairman. The revival was billed as "a new Crusade, commemorating the 1900th anniversary of Pentecost, to bring a spiritual uplift to the city." Local

sprinkling of revivals in individual working-class churches during the depression, with the usual meetings "for men only" at which the revivalist speaks on "the trio of evils—women, wine, and gambling," while his wife talks to the women on "Why you should not get a divorce." In August, 1935, a girl evangelist "who has been preaching since she was 14" conducted a revival in a working-class church with the aid of a director of music who "was once leading tenor in the Boston Grand Opera Company . . . where he sang leading roles in *Il Trovatore* and *The Bohemian Girl.*" The evangelist's sermon subjects included "Thrills," "Choosing Sides," "The First Mortgage," "Beyond Sunset," "America's Greatest Need," "Evolution—Man or Monkey?" Such a series of meetings still arouses some response in a working-class church. But, on the whole, if the number of revivals is any index of religious interest in the depression, there has been a marked recession.[16]

As religion has come to involve heavy plant overhead at home and larger denominational overheads in the foreign-mission field, it has fallen more and more susceptible to the competitive strains of the economy in the midst of which it operates. This tendency has been sharply increased by the depression. The earlier study noted the large measure of spontaneous interdenominational attendance in Middletown's churches of fifty years ago [17] and the decline in this by 1925. At the latter date "Christian fellowship" among these competing vested interests in the "giving power" of the local public had so far declined that the largest Methodist church, situated on a central downtown corner, denied the use of its kitchen and basement to a small working-class church in its own denomination for a money-raising church supper.[18] Both congregations needed money for their respective build-

business firms joined in taking full-page space in a local paper urging attendance under the caption, "Have you heard A—— [the revivalist]?"

[16] See *Middletown,* pp. 378-81.

Possibly the depression has disclosed incidentally one of the major functions of the revival. Billed as religious revivals, they are, if successful, moneymakers. As such, they are extremely useful preliminaries to a building campaign or in liquidating a debt, since they not only draw attendance from other denominations and thus tap new and ordinarily jealously guarded sources of contributions but they also whip up the home congregation to a mood of more liberal giving. The elaborate revival described in the 1925 study was a deliberate preliminary to the building of a new $350,000 church building.

[17] See *Middletown,* pp. 333-34.

[18] See *Middletown,* p. 334, n. 4.

ing campaigns. Just prior to the depression many individual churches overextended their standard of living, with the result that all churches have been forced to be intent upon keeping themselves financially intact in the face of the ravages of the depression upon local giving. Summer "union services" by the uptown churches have ceased and each minister now "cares for his own." In 1931, union services during the annual January "week of prayer" were given up, and each church conducted such services as it chose. "The depression has seen a loss in cooperation among our churches," commented a leading minister. "The Ministerial Association [19] is *just dead wood*. It has done nothing about the depression. Some of the leading ministers in town do not even bother to go." [20]

The children of Middletown appear to have continued in what a local minister calls "their irresponsible way," despite the depression. As a group, their awareness of religious values does not appear to have increased. A "Boy Survey" sponsored by Middletown's Optimist Club, one of the men's civic clubs, in the fall of 1929, showed 39 per cent of the boys in Middletown and its county from eight to sixteen years old inclusive to be church members.[21] These figures afford no gauge of the trend, but should be seen against the strong local feeling that every child "should" belong to the church. Some rude evidence of trend is afforded by the statement of a high-school teacher, known in 1925 as today as particularly close to the high-school students: "Children are growing farther and farther from religion." A group of three

[19] See *Middletown*, pp. 351-54.

[20] Verbal support was given by the Ministerial Association in 1930 to the mayor in his attempt to "clean up" the city's gambling and vice, and resolutions were adopted against such things as Sunday golf; but both singly and collectively Middletown churches have continued to play a placid role, to the disappointment of those who feel, to quote from a local sermon, that "The church should not be the watchdog of righteousness but the builder of righteousness."

[21] This study was directed by a student at the college and data were secured through questionnaires distributed to their pupils by the principals of county and city schools. The study is based on a sample of 3,771 boys, including approximately three-quarters of the boys in the county in each year from eight to fifteen inclusive and roughly a third of the county's boys sixteen years old. (Middletown's own total population was, in 1930, 69 per cent of that of the county.) Slightly under 30 per cent of the eight-year-olds were church members, and of the ten-year-olds 40 per cent were members; this latter figure held until ages fifteen and sixteen when it rose to 45 per cent. (The 1925 study reported, on the basis of a study in Middletown's state, that "Children 'join the church' for the most part between the ages of nine and seventeen. Slightly over half of all members join before they are sixteen." See *Middletown*, p. 355.)

business-class men of about thirty commented: "As small boys one of us was an acolyte and won prizes in Bible class; and all of us pumped the organ and amused ourselves during the sermon by carving our names on the organ. Now none of the three of us goes to church. Not many people under thirty-five go to church—none that we know. It's mostly just the same older crowd that keeps on going."

Y.M.C.A. and Y.W.C.A. continue as active agencies, with more changes apparent in the program of the latter than of the former. With the completion of the new Y.W.C.A. building since 1925, the girls of Middletown now have their own swimming pool and recreation building supervised by a specialized staff of professional leaders.[22] There are Y.W.C.A. classes in ballroom, ballet, and tap dancing, including a "toddlers' class" for the three-to-four-year-olds and a "tiny tots' class" for the five-to-six-year-olds. Another shift in the Y.W.C.A. is the admission of Negroes to the building for occasional Negro dances.[23] Both agencies have suffered membership losses in the depression, with some curtailment of personnel. Both continue their Bible classes in the public schools,[24] with an annual enrollment now risen to 2,500 to 3,000 children of each sex, and Middletown has still been able to boast in recent years that its Y.M.C.A. "leads the world in Bible-class attendance."

A local college boy said of the strongly religious emphasis of the Y.M.C.A.: "All they have to offer on why Christianity is the truth is that it has lasted so long." Then he added a remark that seemingly epitomizes the attitude of Middletown, "I believe these things [Christianity], but they don't take a big place in my life." An editorial in 1934 said: "So far as youth is concerned, we may as well admit that any formalism in religion is out of the picture."

The association of churches with the secular social hierarchy of the community is today as strongly entrenched as in 1925 on the high-

[22] The new Y.W.C.A. building also provides a much-needed community center for adult women's meetings, comparable to the Chamber of Commerce Building and Y.M.C.A. for men's meetings. The roster of meetings of outside groups in the Y.W.C.A. for a single representative busy week in April included the following: *Monday:* Art League, Friendship Club, Woman's Club; *Tuesday:* Book Club, and a class party for the eighth-graders in the local Catholic school; *Thursday:* County Federation of Women's Clubs; *Friday:* Junior-senior reception of the high school of one of the small towns in the county; *Saturday:* Potluck supper of the Mildred Birt Sunday-school class (of one of the churches). In addition, the various school Girl Reserve units used the building for a number of meetings, including one mother-daughter program.

[23] See *Middletown,* p. 479.

[24] See *Middletown,* pp. 396-98.

school level. In certain prominent business-class churches girls' Sunday-school classes, led by socially prominent women, have become social sifting devices for the tightly competitive girls' club life in high school. As one business-class daughter of sixteen remarked: "There are special cliques in high school according to what Sunday school you go to. This means mostly, though, kids like us. The poorer kids are separated off, no matter what church they go to." The social emphasis of the most prominent of these Sunday-school classes, that in the Presbyterian Church, is enhanced by such class affairs as stylishly appointed luncheons at the Country Club.

In ministering to material, as to spiritual, needs, the church does not appear to have extended its function during the depression years. The main body of churches has continued to accept the fact that care for the unable has become secularized in the office of the township trustee, the Social Service Bureau, and the Community Fund; individual church members are strong supporters of these agencies, but the churches as organizations accept the role of spiritual agents rather than leaders or organizers of group care for the needy.[25]

The two exceptions to this position among Middletown's religious groups are the Salvation Army and the Middletown Mission, both of which have been notably active in direct relief work. The former, supported in part by the Community Fund, initiated the systematic feeding of hot lunches to school children on the South Side, and this work was subsequently taken over and extended by the Social Service Bureau. The mission, as noted in Chapter IV, was opened in the late fall of 1930 by a vigorous ex-bartender converted by Billy Sunday. By the close of 1935 it had served 228,935 meals to the destitute, had given 135,250 gallons of milk to needy families, and had furnished "clothing, stoves, and spiritual advice to thousands." [26]

Meanwhile, the secularization of the Sabbath [27] continues. The new municipal swimming pool, open every day, including Sunday, from

[25] See *Middletown*, pp. 462-63.

[26] The clash between this attitude of modern, organized, centralized charity and the older attitude of religiously motivated "giving with the heart" is discussed near the close of Ch. IV. It reveals an interesting type of conflict in points of view that occurs frequently in the course of social change, in which both factions are probably right in their contentions, and the difference between them is one involved in reasoning from assumptions derived from two different eras.

[27] See *Middletown*, pp. 339-41.

10 A.M. to 10 P.M., is heavily patronized by the younger set on Sundays; the upper-class smart-set climaxes its annual horse show on Sunday, and horseback riding is popular every Sunday morning. As pointed out earlier, the local radio station reports that it received no fan mail when it had a Sunday-afternoon program of religious music, but since it substituted popular music the response has been heavy, and its Sunday time is completely sold out. In 1931 the local ministers sought ineffectively to stop Sunday golf. It is further indicative of the slow glacial pressure of what Middletown still calls with apprehension "the Continental Sunday" that the minister of the city's largest church abandoned his Sunday-evening service in the latter part of the 1920's, although this church has resumed them under the subsequent minister. The automobile continues to lead among the secularizing factors; a local paper estimates that 10,000 persons leave Middletown by automobile for other towns and resorts every fine Sunday.

"There is less attendance at church than when you were here before," commented a Middletown professional man, "partly due to less interest, and partly because people drive more and are always out on the road. There are better roads now, and people can go more places at longer distances by starting before morning church and coming home too late for the evening service. But the opinion among Protestant and Jewish ministers here is that such lessened interest is the temporary recession found in all activities which move in waves, and that the pendulum will swing back soon."

A further secularization of Middletown's other institutions since 1925 is apparent in the effort to divorce religion and politics through a bill passed by the State House of Representatives in 1931 prohibiting any person or organization from sending questionnaires to candidates concerning their moral, religious, or legislative opinions, and forbidding candidates from answering such inquiries.

The role of Middletown's preachers as interpreters of the Permanent to a world of Change appears to have become even more difficult by 1935 than it was in 1925.[28] There is some evidence, despite the reported increase in "fundamentalism" during the depression among some of

---

[28] This is suggested as a nation-wide trend by an announcement by the national Federal Council of Churches in the spring of 1936 that a "preaching mission" was to be organized to visit the leading cities of the United States in order to strengthen the basic faith of Protestant ministers and laymen. This sort of move possibly suggests a recognition of troubled morale among ministers.

See *Middletown*, pp. 344-53, for a discussion of the status of Middletown's preachers in the community.

the more primitive South Side sects, that the older denominations have yielded to the pressure of events by becoming doctrinally less demanding. A local editor remarked, in the course of a conversation with the investigator: "All churches in town, save a few denominations like the Seventh Day Adventists, are more liberal today than in 1925. Any of them will take you in today no matter what you believe doctrinally." One minister attributes what he regards as the more liberal attitude of the churches today largely to the influence of the leaven of new minds brought to Middletown through the growth of the local college. In one church at least, that of a small doctrinally liberal denomination, one hears today religion awake and on the march. In preaching on "Christianity as the Spiritual Contribution to the Adjustment of Individual and Group Differences" in 1935, the minister of this church spoke out in words usually unfamiliar in Middletown's churches:

"We hear much in these times about a 'planned society.' Some talk as if this were something really new and also dangerous. The reason we are afraid of such plans is that they might not be in accord with our plans. We want strict regulations for our competitors and a free hand for ourselves. We want to plan our own businesses and force our competitors into chaos. . . .

"What is there wrong about a plan? Lack of a definite plan has always been the stumbling block to progress. Is there anything wrong about planning for the day when men can get employment and maintain their self-respect? Is a man unpatriotic who thinks we ought to have a plan to end poverty? We have a tuberculosis society. What is its purpose but to make plans to eliminate this dreadful disease and see that they are carried out. Society needs some intelligent planning, the planning that will stop group strife that makes poverty, war, hatred, jealousies, and the state of mind that destroys us."

This minister and two others are regarded by local people—somewhat dubiously—as "very progressive." But when one turns from such exceptional figures to the preaching of the more usual type, it is the continuities with 1925 that impress one most: the same "message" (mild and dignified on the North Side and more strenuous south of the tracks) with its heavy reliance upon old theological terminology and its avoidance of locally controversial issues.

The ministers are themselves harried, overworked, perplexed that religion has not vindicated itself more in the depression. Some have sought to minimize the depression, as in the sermon in 1932 which the press headlined on Monday morning "Depression Held Only a Small Thing," while others have preached troubled sermons on "Is the Church Becoming Antiquated?" and "Has the Church Lost Its Hold on the Community?" In this last sermon the minister deplored the fact that "There is too much of the spirit of tolerating the church." One sees the same anxious effort of the minister to be a "good fellow" and yet a Christian observed in 1925, as when one of them who is fond of hunting spoke before a men's civic-club luncheon on "the positive relationship between big-game hunting and character building." Middletown's ministers, less immediately identified personally than are their congregations with the united front of ideas of the local business world, tend in many cases to see "the other side" in social questions. But they, too, are branches of the central trunk of Middletown's life, and one finds them for the most part preaching what Middletown already believes in such matters. The following remark to the investigator by the pastor of a church deep in the South Side exhibits the wistful ambivalence of some of these religious leaders:

"It is clearly unfair to have people piling up their millions all the time when the worker gets so little. Huey Long has the right idea—'Share the wealth.' However, I'm against socialism because, of course, people must have profits as an incentive to invest their money, and since all people are not of equal ability they should not be made equal by the state."

The fact appears to be that religion, like education in Middletown, is torn by conflicts as to what its function is and whose values it shall serve, and the depression has aggravated this situation acutely. Its historical loyalty is explicitly defined by its Bible and denominational creeds. Emotionally, this literal loyalty is deeply bitten into the lives of people in the pews, yet in the operative aspects of living it lives chiefly as a much bandied-about symbol. Emotionally, Middletown feels with the editor of its afternoon paper when he wrote in 1932: "Take away from the ordinary people—and who is not one of them essentially?—their religion and you have destroyed about everything that is worth while in their characters." To Middletown, there is no cause for dissent when a local physician says in addressing Rotary that "There is no reason for our dying except that God has us here as an experiment"; or when one reads on the bulletin board of a business-class church the reminder: "Keep your appointment with God"; or over the pulpit of a working-class church: "He is coming. Are you ready?" But when this world of religious values cuts athwart Middletown's labor problem, or the city's devotion to such more immediate symbols as those identified with "patriotism," people's reactions are almost unvaryingly determined by their loyalty to these more immediate things rather than to the religious symbols.

A striking example of this occurred on the Sunday evening before election in November, 1936, when the minister of the largest church in the city preached on the subject, "Burning Issues," devoting his sermon to an exposition of why he intended to vote for Roosevelt. In announcing his intention at the morning service, the minister is reported to have said that his evening sermon would be frankly political and might cost him his position in Middletown. "Most of his congregation" are reported on good authority to have been "as mad as hornets" after the evening service. Rumors began to fly about that he was "mentally unbalanced," that while he was a "brilliant man, he has done a number of unaccountable things," that he "intends consulting a doctor in the East about his condition," that the church Board had met "to call in the bishop to remove him," and so on.[29] The three following sharp press comments, appearing on successive days following the minister's sermon, reflect Middletown's attitude toward such a mingling of religion and public affairs:

We hear that a minister here made a highly impolitic speech in his church Sunday, and greatly aroused his congregation. Didn't even take the trouble to investigate the story. Just hope it was untrue. The quickest way for a preacher to get "in bad" is by mixing politics and pulpiteering, although, of course, he has the same right as anybody else to play politics outside of the church.

A mystery: Why any minister of the gospel would make a political speech in his pulpit. One may have a kind of sympathy for anybody who bursts out on such matters, but he could not have much respect for his judgment.

[29] It is of interest that these charges of being "mentally unbalanced" are identical with the charges not infrequently heard regarding President Roosevelt from Middletown businessmen in 1935. Both cases reflect the emotional intensity with which many beliefs are held in Middletown as "things no sane man would doubt." And when someone dares to doubt them, the explanation for his action lies ready at hand.

It is said that the minister here who made a political speech from his pulpit last Sunday has not heard the last of it by any means; that indignant members of the church are preparing to carry the matter further.

Middletown does not stop to think what a religion is. It accepts the word automatically as synonymous with Christianity, and other religions are, therefore, by definition "wrong" or at best "inferior." So, in the main, those Middletown ministers who are not content to preach the literal "Word" straddle uneasily the widening gulf between the theologically defined Changeless [30] and the obviously Changing.

The role of religion in Middletown's culture as symbolizing the Permanent is at once its greatest strength and greatest weakness. The Catholics, Jews, and Episcopalians, who stress rituals somewhat more and rely less upon the "sermon," *i.e.,* a verbalized message, maintain a liaison between the permanent and the immediate with more dignity and less apparent sense of uneasiness than do most of the Protestant churches. The latter are on their plane of greatest reality and ease with their attending members when they remain on the ground of applied ethics, and they fall away rapidly in psychological contact when they must verbalize about their system of historical theology. While, theoretically, the very prevalence of rapid change in Middletown's culture would seem to enhance the potential role of an institution charged with the task of sifting out and identifying the elements of permanence in the current preoccupation with flux, the rigidity of religion in clinging to its theological verbal stereotypes inherited from an era in the remote past, increasingly unreal to Middletown, tends to introduce barriers to the performance of this very function. The gap between religion's verbalizing and Middletown life has become so wide that the entire institution of religion has tended to be put on the defensive; and the acceptance of a defensive role has tended to mean that it is timid in jeopardizing its foothold in the culture by espousing unpopular causes, when they appear in the economic order, in questions of world peace, and in the elements of contradiction in local institutions.

As a result, Middletown's churches appear to be forever bartering the opportunity for leadership in the area of change for the right to continue a shadowy leadership in the Changeless, as the church defines the latter. On almost every issue where controversy waxes hot

[30] See *Middletown,* pp. 405-06.

in Middletown's current world, the local churches take over the causes and symbols of the local business control group. Outstanding, is the almost complete merging of the two areas of religion and patriotism. Over and over again one hears this booming note:

Address by the president of the local college: "Christianity is the cradle of American democracy."

Sermon in a local church: "Communism is an empty threat to America. Christianity is an easy winner when people demonstrate the loftier values of life."

Lincoln's birthday sermon: "Lincoln was sent by God to save the nation as clearly as Christ was sent to save the race."

Public statement by Middletown minister after a minister in his denomination, the president of a college in the state, had made a speech favoring internationalism, disarmament, and social justice: "He is a disgrace to Methodism."

Editorial on "The Church Loyal" in the local press replying to a widely publicized statement by Bishop Jones that the United States has two religions—nationalism and that of its churches—and that it is impossible for a man to worship at both altars: "The involvement of the church in national and international political affairs is deplorable. A leader who advocates the entrance of the United States into the League of Nations or World Court is *not* representing the greater part of the church membership. . . . Church leaders who are pacifists represent only the Socialists and I.W.W.'s, not the 20,000,000 patriotic church members of the nation. This nation is safe only so long as the Christian church stands fast for our native land and her ideals before all others, and for her defense if need be against all others. . . . Whenever the time comes when the flag cannot consistently be displayed in schools and churches, then the end of religion will be at hand."

To the youth of Middletown the church holds up Middletown's own aggressive image. In the address at a Boy Scout father-son dinner in one of the leading churches the boys were told: "Men of strong mental development, able to maintain organizations already instituted, are the aim of the Boy Scout movement."

To such controversial issues as internationalism, disarmament, pacifism, labor organization, social planning in the interest of the masses and the redistribution of wealth, civil liberty, the amendment of the Constitution, socialized medicine, and birth control, the great majority of the churches of Middletown present the negative face of the community, or are silent, or talk such generalities that their position is equivocal.[31]

When the church does venture into controversial matters, its recommendations assume the vague character of the resolution of the state Sunday-school Convention when it met in Middletown in 1931, that "Men of business and wealth be urged to break down this era of frozen confidence and put into circulation the food and wealth of our nation so that we do not starve in the midst of plenty."

The preceding discussion has concerned principally the overwhelmingly dominant evangelical Protestant pattern of Middletown.[32] The Catholic Church pursued in 1935 the same quiet, resolute, inconspicuous course as in 1925. It is not involved in local politics[33] or any other public aspects of Middletown's life. The Christian Scientists are still represented by a single church, and the Jewish synagogue still continues a small congregation. The latter group appears to be somewhat stronger than in 1925,[34] though it is a very inconspicuous factor in Middletown.

In concluding this brief treatment of religion in Middletown the caveat of the earlier study[35] cannot be too strongly repeated. Such data as the above do not exhaust the meaning of religious symbols and practices to the people of Middletown.

[31] At the time of the Federal Council of Churches' 1931 statement in favor of birth control, a local paper interviewed leading local ministers. Nine refused to be quoted; one approved "because it is the voice of science"; another (Episcopalian) approved because of the endorsement of the Lambeth Conference of the Anglican church; another approved for the mentally deficient and criminally inclined; while another stated that it "would be another liquor problem. Its knowledge would be abused."

[32] The extremely small Catholic population of Middletown is fairly accurately revealed by the fact that the city had in 1931-32 only 2.9 per cent of its enumerated children of school age in its lone parochial school. Middletown stood in this respect nineteenth among the nineteen first-, second-, and third-class cities of the state, there being only two other cities with less than 5 per cent, and the range being from 2.9 to 24.2.

[33] The leading Methodist church continued in 1925 to be the "political church" of Middletown. It was stated on good authority, for instance, that "the president of the school board had been unable to get rid of a high-school principal because he could not buck [this] church."

[34] The appearance in the papers since 1925 of a joint advertisement of twenty-five business houses announcing their closing for Yom Kippur is an innovation suggesting the growth in coherence of Middletown's Jews.

[35] See *Middletown*, p. 390.

To one seeking to view religion as the thing it attempts to be in Middletown—*i.e.,* the agency forcing into consciousness the necessary links between experience and meaning and thus sifting and bringing into coherence and focus the values of the culture—there is the constant desire to discover what meanings the experiences of "going to church" and listening to these sermons have for Middletown beyond what appears to the outside observer. It is impossible completely to capture the full meaning to Middletown of such familiar phrases as "Prepare To Meet Thy God," or "The Heavenly Father's Love." Furthermore, here—more perhaps than at any other point in the culture—it is difficult to speak of Middletown as a unity. A culture is in its more dominant patterns simply a series of modal, *i.e.,* most frequently present, ways of thinking and acting by the individuals who are the carriers of the culture; and every type of behavior exhibits atypical behavior of more than and less than the central or modal type. Certain individuals in Middletown privately reject all religious forms, even including the preaching and singing and praying of the Presbyterians and the rituals and prayers of the small group of Episcopalians; and the latter two groups in turn tend to feel that the immersing Baptists and the vocal Methodists are "somehow different" and "less refined" than themselves; while all four tend to be somewhat pained by the ardor of the Seventh Day Adventists and Spiritualists. These last feel that the uptown churches are cold and lack spirituality. Many people in Middletown smile when they read in the morning paper:

Message Circle—A light message circle for the benefit of the National Psychic Church will be held at 8 o'clock this evening at [a private residence on the South Side]. Two mediums will be in charge.

Much closer to the central feeling of Middletown is the simple statement to the investigator by an elderly carpenter:

"There has been some kind of staying power during these hard times. I have faith in it, as I've always had faith in it. Don't believe, though, that I mean that I can give up my own effort. What is true is that *there is something controlling things for good.* Someday I've walked down a street and there was a job—what else can it be?"

To some Middletown people the church represents only "an institution one ought to support as a civic duty, as one pays one's taxes."

Some of Middletown's people undoubtedly felt self-conscious when a leading church organized in 1930 "block parties to get our members into each other's homes and better acquainted." On the other hand, others welcome the role of the churches in bringing people together.[36] They turn out eagerly for the "Penny Suppers," [37] and they feel grateful and "homey" when a working-class church announces for the following Sunday as a depression "get-together" device that the pastor and men are to wear their work clothes and the women their house dresses. To many Middletown people religion and the church give the reassurance so urgently needed; as they sit in church the perplexities of a too-perplexing world are resolved; their universe is once more made whole.

While Middletown people represent, therefore, a very wide range of interpretations of the role of religion—from the impersonally taken institution that is "good for" the other fellow and for society in general, to the highly personal source of strength and courage— one thing everybody in Middletown has in common: insecurity in the face of a complicated world. In this last may lie a clew to the willingness of the dominant portion of the population to accept uncritically as certainties, as fixed points, the fundamental assertions of Christianity as to the existence of God, His being on the side of the "right," the divinity of Jesus, and the promise of a life hereafter. So great is the individual human being's need for security that it may be that most people are incapable of tolerating change and uncertainty in all sectors of life at once; and, if their culture exposes them to stress and uncertainty at many points, they may not only tolerate but welcome the security of extreme fixity and changelessness elsewhere in their lives. They may even embrace what Vernon Lee has called "vital lies" if they afford this modicum of psychological security. In short, certain allegedly unchangeable aspects of Middletown's culture (*e.g.,* its religion, its democratic forms, and its Constitution) may operate to a considerable extent as emotionally needed counterweights to change; if the pace of business inexorably forces change and constant adaptation, if one's future is beset with uncertainties, if one's children insist

[36] See the discussion of this in Ch. VII.

[37] This is a form of depression "social" at which the women of the church furnished the food gratis which was sold at a penny a dish; a small bazaar sold towels, handkerchiefs, pillowcases, etc., made and donated by the women; simple entertainment was provided; and the proceeds of the whole went to the church.

upon stepping in tune with a brave new world of their own, and if the realities of local politics are chronically imperfect, the more blindly may one be impelled from within to insist that *some* parts of one's universe are perfect and built upon the eternal rock. And when Middletown's culture assimilates its religious and its patriotic values, this may reflect not a sense of their rational compatibility but, again, the spasmodic emotional need to extend the area of felt stability under its feet.

Thus, under the wrenching impact of a prolonged experience like the depression, religion may oscillate like the needle of a compass seeking the pole pull of people's greatest need for reassurance. Among many meagerly educated people on the South Side, the needle may swing back to what they have been told since infancy is the unfailing Rock of Ages, and the gap between what the intellectual world may call "religion" and "reality" may increase with a popular huddling back to fundamentalism; while with many businessfolk religion may be allowed to become less insistently dogmatic theologically, the "sword" of penetration which it is traditionally assumed to bring into people's allegiances may be sheathed, and its full weight may swing behind the moral condemnation of radicalism and the emotionally craved bolstering of the *status quo*. The vagueness met with everywhere in Middletown as to what "religion" *is,* other than a set of traditional beliefs, prepares the way for such ready oscillations in the interpretation of its role.

When Middletown's religious life is viewed in this way, comment on its "lack of independence of point of view" and its "conservatism" becomes irrelevant; for to Middletown the role of religion is not to raise troublesome questions and to force attention to disparities between values and current practice. And, if the experience of going to church can make the people in the pews feel that "The depression is only a small thing," or that "Communism is an empty threat to Christian America," or that "There is something controlling things for good," the emotional impact and function of these assurances are too obvious to be questioned by Middletown.

The predicament of institutions like the church and the school which may seek to alter Middletown's dominant values is further heightened by the pervasive instrumentalism that characterizes Middletown's culture. This instrumentalism is the hidden side of the bright banner of Progress under which this culture lives. Men immersed in rapid movement are not given to moods of contemplation as to goals. A culture devoted through all its history, as in the case of the American people, to horizontal expansion does not tend to consolidate at any given time or place and send down deep roots. Preoccupation with the *next* thing precludes more than rule-of-thumb appraisal of the now present *this* thing. In a pecuniary culture politically committed to the minimizing of class lines there tend to be relatively few plateaus of sheltered "arrival." Democracy under private capitalism has shaved off the edges of these plateaus and the whole population moves, according to the ethos of our culture, endlessly and breathlessly up one long un-broken sandy slope of acquisition. The sense of psychological "arrival" is minimized by the fact that—unlike a country like England where one can look about at other members, *e.g.,* of the "lower middle class," appraise one's own position, and say with some show of contentment that "What we've got is pretty good for the likes of us"—from every point on the unbroken incline one can look ahead and see others with more than one has oneself. And the spirit of the culture tells one to hurry to catch up with those ahead. Such a culture, dominated by mass instrumentalism in all its institutions, is not without its moments of "failure of nerve." There are aberrant individuals such as teachers and preachers who point to the prevalent confusion of means and ends—and these irritating interruptions occasionally give people a *mauvais quart d'heure,* because along with "progress," "wealth," "get-ting ahead," Middletown also has other symbols such as "religion," "righteousness," "loving one's neighbor as oneself," "social justice," and "wisdom." Actually, these interrupting agencies such as church and school that nominally stress ends rather than means are tolerated by the culture as saving ornaments and psychological guarantees of its progress. By a subtle psychological transfer, they are regarded as sym-bols *of* its progress. The "finer things of life" are not all in the future, but are supported by us here and now. Look, we have religion, educa-tion, and the arts in our midst. Someday we will all have time for them. And yet the very pressure of the enveloping instrumentalism does something to these institutions devoted to the ends of living. They themselves do not escape it: going to church becomes a kind of moral life-insurance policy and one's children go to school and college so that they can get a better job and know the right people. Bit by bit in a culture devoted to movement and progress these permanent things of life become themselves adjuncts to the central business of getting ahead, dependent symbols about the central acquisitive symbols of the community's life. And so progress recaptures and confines its own children.

Said a leading minister, speaking to Kiwanis: "In the old days people went to preachers for consolation, information, and inspiration. They still come to us for consolation, but go to newspapers for information and inspiration." This expresses succinctly the apparent role of religion in Middletown as an emotionally stabilizing agent, relinquishing to other agencies leadership in the defining of values.

CHAPTER IX

The Machinery of Government

MIDDLETOWN has added to its police system since 1925 two police matrons, radio squad cars, tear gas, and machine guns; there are new traffic lights at some intersections, and downtown parking time limits; a motorized sweeper cleans the streets; a new City Hall provides more spacious quarters for the leisurely business of running the city; the Republicans are at the moment "out" and the Democrats are "in"; the mayor's salary is $3,400 instead of the former $3,000; the city budget (not including schools) dropped from $385,275 in 1925 to $362,879 in 1935, its assessed valuation from $60,000,000 to $40,000,000, and the combined tax rate rose from $2.66 for 1925 and $2.68 for 1929 to $3.10 for 1935. But, save for such minor shifts, the machinery of local government—barricaded behind some of the most rigid sanctions of this culture—has almost stood still, while the city's economic life has swung to its greatest heights and depths. An informed local citizen greeted the investigator on his return in 1935 with the statement: "Whatever changes you may find elsewhere in Middletown, you will find that our politics and government are the same crooked old shell game."

A bird's-eye view of what this "game" is and how it has worked since 1925 has been presented briefly by a nonpartisan local analyst of the city's affairs as follows: [1]

Five phases of life in [Middletown] are discussed in the book [Middletown] under the heading of Community Activities. . . . The description of each seems to be fair and adequate, and that of local government perhaps too lenient rather than too severe.

The [Middletown] of 1934 was "governed" under the same antiquated plan described by the Lynds. . . . Popular ignorance of real technical issues encouraged continued indifference, and that, in turn, the dominance of one or the other of the political machines. Many prominent business and pro-

---

[1] The local source of this written statement may not be disclosed. It was based both upon familiarity with local conditions and upon careful study of available records.

fessional men had by 1934 become more active than previously in civic affairs, but they shied from participation in politics, or were easily eliminated by the machines.[2] National and State Governments had taken over most of the purely political issues, so local candidates, too smart to befuddle the popular mind with highly technical administrative problems, conducted campaigns on the vague issues of putting honesty into government, running out the gamblers, getting more Federal money poured into [Middletown], wrecking the contractor's trust, and beautifying the city. Once the vital issue of utilities ownership came near being the subject of a special election, but an injunction halted the proceedings.

The pendulum had swung from the Republican monopoly of 1924 to a Democratic regime. . . . A Democratic candidate for mayor in the 1934 campaign had held the office previously and had already served his penitentiary sentence, so he rated as machine candidate No. 1, defeated the incumbent in the primary, and was swept into office in the general Democratic landslide of that year. . . . A local editor concluded that the previous administration should at least be given credit for rounding off some of the street corners.

In the past ten years of "enlightened" city government, there have been a few minor innovations. The city has undertaken, more or less spasmodically, the supervision of park recreation and other amusements, has instituted a modern radio and scout-car system, and has employed one and later two police matrons. Since 1924 there had been further agitation for a more modern plan of city government, but it has not again become a referendum issue. There was one encouraging aspect of the election of 1934: The young Republicans sought a candidate from among the younger businessmen of the city, and one without strong party ties. But the man they backed was badly defeated by the machine in the primary.

The returning visitor does not even rub his eyes, so familiar are the old civic issues: some people still want the railroad tracks that bisect the city elevated to remove the grade crossings, and the railroads and other people who own factories with sidings on this railroad continue to block the move; there is still trouble over the tendency of the impartial jury wheel to turn out the names of the needy favorites of

[2] Another commentator bears out this point in a written communication: "It was true [in 1925] as the text of *Middletown* seems to imply, that the educated classes in [Middletown] failed to supply the guiding ideas of the city and did not serve in any advisory capacity or assist in making opinions for the city; such today is certainly not wholly the case. More and more, the trained groups are either being pulled in or are injecting their influence into the city's affairs. [See Chs. III and IV.] *This is true perhaps in every field but with the possible exception of local politics.*" [Italics ours.]

those in power; the nine city fathers, balloting on a tight issue, could still in June, 1935, when they voted on a new member of the school board, perform the miracle of finding ten votes in the box; Middletown wives still complain of the "smoke nuisance," though the depression has softened somewhat this chronic complaint, as there is at the moment a very lenient attitude toward factories able to operate at all, smoke or no smoke; the city health officer still tries to bring local milk up to the standards legally required by the State Board of Health, and the council still resists the move;[3] the headlines still carry such news as "Mayor Indicted by Federal Grand Jury"; North Side candidates still run as ardent partisans of the South Side; the old battle to construct a sewage-disposal plant that will take the stench out of the river and "make White River white" still drags along, to the gloomy prediction of the press that "it will probably not be solved until the year 2000."

Here, too, awaiting the observer is the same type of person serving as city official, the man whom the inner business control group ignore economically and socially and use politically. The newly elected mayor in 1935 was the man whose last term as mayor had been terminated fifteen years before by a sentence to the Federal penitentiary for fraud,[4] and with his duties as mayor he still carries on his private medical practice, with the aid of advertisements in the press.

And again one meets in the homes, business offices, and civic clubs the same blend of alternating exasperation and cynical apathy regarding the local civic administration that pervaded Middletown in 1924-25. And back of it all is the constant play of interested "deals" whereby the controls of the local *Realpolitik* are made to work in the interest of private interests or private interpretations of the public interest.

Beneath the alternating exasperation and apathy of the voters lies, however, a comfortable philosophy concerning these things which "makes sense" out of them. Central to it are the convictions that no people anywhere are better governed than are Americans, that such weaknesses as appear are not due so much to the institutions as to the inevitable failings of well-meaning but "poor, weak human nature," and that in government, as in the rest of the culture, progress is inevitable. This comfortable philosophy cushions the jarring disparities between the American scheme of things and the realities of local

[3] See Ch. XI.
[4] See *Middletown,* p. 422, n. 9.

politics, for one need not worry too much over failures if one is en-dowed with the best available facilities and things are inevitably getting better and better.

If the matter were pushed further into details and a Middletown citizen were asked what the government of his city is expected to do, his answer would probably run somewhat in this wise: Any city the size of Middletown must have a government, first of all to keep order —including everything from the suppression of crimes to the enforce-ment of contracts; then to provide certain safeguards to health such as pure water and waste disposal; to provide a good educational sys-tem; and generally to promote conditions likely to encourage home ownership and to make the city prosperous and a good place to live in. The informant might go on to add, if he is what is known locally as "pink," certain governmental activities which to many of the "better" people are somewhat marginal: the provision of recreational facilities at public expense, possibly the public ownership of certain public utilities, and the care for the needy when their necessity passes a cer-tain point—though he would not be very definite about this last.

If the questioner asked by what means the government performs these various functions, the answer would stress such symbols as "democracy," the "two-party system," the "will of the majority," "pub-lic service by elected representatives of the people," and "general welfare."

There is no area of Middletown's life, save religion, where symbol is more admittedly and patently divorced from reality than in govern-ment, and no area where the functioning of an institution is more enmeshed in undercover intrigue and personalities. All of which makes it peculiarly difficult to show clearly the relationship between the means of government and the ends they allegedly serve. This relationship will perhaps appear most clearly in the analysis of three phases of city government: the office of mayor, the major civic problem of securing a modern sewage system, and the treatment of crime.

Ordinarily the machinery controlling Middletown's office of mayor, like the rest of its governmental machinery, operates behind the scenes, with only a chronic rumble of minor protest in the open. But the mechanisms of control come somewhat more into the open in an occasional brawling civic scene when the controls have slipped mo-mentarily and a maverick candidate rides into power. This last had happened in the fall of 1929, when the editor of the local Democratic weekly, a man who had never run for local political office before, had ridden into the mayor's office on a South Side plurality of 1,349, polling what was until that time the greatest number of votes any man had ever polled for mayor. In the Democratic primary in 1929 he had defeated the regular Democratic party candidate for mayor and, against the united opposition of both regular parties, he took office in January, 1930, pledged to honest contract letting—a sore spot enlisting the support of the small Middletown taxpayer—and to a cleanup of local vice, gambling, and liquor, all long associated with local politics. He was regarded by many people as more honest, if more tactless, than the run of Middletown's officeholders; he had a record as a fearless fighter who had attracted national attention by his single-handed fight against the Ku Klux Klan when it had come into power in Middletown in 1924; [5]

[5] To some Americans this man, George R. Dale, was the best-known citizen of Middletown. When he died at the age of sixty-seven in March, 1936, the Associated Press obituary commanded space of half a column or more in the press of New York, Chicago, and other cities. Dale was a "white-haired little man with the seat worn out of his pants" who for twenty years had edited a local Democratic weekly. Always fearless, he rose to national prominence when, almost single-handed, he fought the Ku Klux Klan which ruled the state and city in the mid-1920's.

The Klan tried repeatedly to "get" him. Klansmen jostled him off the sidewalk in Middletown's business section; the lady Klanswomen, known as the Kamilias, are reported to have spit on him on the streets; Klansmen waylaid him three times, beating him and twice attempting to shoot him. Charges were made in the Federal Court that two of Middletown's policemen in the Klan administration had conspired to kill him. Dale repeatedly pilloried a local Klan judge in the columns of his paper, charging jury fixing and that crime was allowed to run rampant in Middletown because of the judge's Klan connections. (This judge taught the largest adult Bible class in the city in Middletown's leading Methodist church, "the big political church in town.") The judge ordered Dale's paper off the streets and eventually had the editor convicted on a contempt charge and sentenced to pay a $500 fine and serve six months in jail. Dale charged that his arrest was a straight case of Klan "fixing" and appealed the case four times. When the United States Supreme Court finally refused to pass on the question, Dale was pardoned by the governor. The case attracted nation-wide attention and brought to the editor's support nationally known lawyers like Samuel Untermeyer because of a celebrated decision by the State Supreme Court that "the truth is no defense" in a contempt case.

Between 1926 and 1929, while the case was under appeal, Klan pressure deprived Dale's little sheet of city, county, and state official advertising, its only advertising support; it was temporarily moved over the line into a town in the next state, where it continued to fire broadside after broadside at Middletown's Klan. At the point when, with no money for legal defense, he and his wife and seven children were reduced to the verge of starvation, the New York *World*

and he was a man long familiar, as an opposition editor, with the details of local politics, and possessed of a habit of "speaking his mind" bluntly.

Typical of this forthrightness was his clash with the judge elected with him on his ticket. During his campaign he had asked the candidate for police judge, a man not of his own picking, to get out of the race. To this publicly made request, the candidate for judge is reported to have explained that, while he did not expect to win, his purpose in running was to embarrass the head of the municipal ticket as much as possible. The judge was subsequently swept into office with the new mayor. The latter promptly cleaned out the old police force, and within six weeks the new force presented to the judge 103 arrested men charged with handling liquor. Only three of the 103 were jailed. Disgusted, the mayor ordered the police to take no more cases before the judge, announcing in his paper, "I've quarantined the judge." It was partly this directness and tactlessness which involved him from

came to Dale's aid with a campaign among its readers for a dollar fund for his defense.

Slowly the tide turned against the Klan in the state, and other papers began to widen the breaches begun by Dale. One governor went to the Federal penitentiary; another avoided prosecution on bribery charges by pleading the statute of limitations; the Grand Dragon of the state Klan and a number of his lieutenants were sentenced; the mayor of the state capital was removed from office, and the chairman of the State Republican Committee was convicted; and the Middletown Circuit Judge who had originally sentenced Dale was impeached before the State Legislature and escaped removal from office by two votes.

As out-of-town praise of Dale's courageous fight rolled in, the local attitude began to change. Middletown's Rotary Club phoned to ask if Dale would address them, which request he declined and, turning from the phone to a friend, commented dryly: "At last, I have arrived." At the next gubernatorial election, running as an Independent Democrat and without funds or endorsements of any kind, he polled 58,000 votes.

An article in the *American Mercury* for August, 1930, recounts numerous stories about Dale's administrative tactics during the early months of his term as mayor of Middletown, which began in January of that year. Direct, shrewd, tactless, honest, no worshiper of anybody's sacred cow, without party backing and dependent upon building up and holding a new backing, Dale's administration was, to quote a local editorial in 1933, "constantly in hot water, antagonizing everybody." The statement by the editor that "His nearly complete failure in administering the city's affairs . . . may be ascribed almost wholly to his lack of judgment and misconception of his own ability" represents the judgment of a culture living by compromise and indirection regarding the frank, often mistaken efforts of a lifelong crusader forced by temperament and circumstances to "go it alone." The life of George Dale provides an interesting commentary on the culture in which he lived: it could not use him and he could not use it

the outset in endless squabbles with his city council [6] which his enemies pointed to as evidence of his inefficiency.

His administration showed a quixotic disregard for "playing ball," "making deals," and political "face saving." As an outspoken, independent, lone-dog candidate unpopular with the businessmen, he entered office lacking the possibility of calling upon local men of ability to help him. A local editorial at the time of his death stated:

The very fact that he was no "pussyfooter" won the reluctant but generally secret admiration of those who decried his methods and even denounced his motives. . . . If you are an average citizen, you probably opposed many of the things for which George Dale stood, and because he had the special faculty of exciting prejudices against himself and his works by his utter lack of diplomacy, you may have declared in your exasperation at times, that he was never right about anything. And there you would have been wrong, for he was right about many things. As we look back coolly upon his administration as mayor of [Middletown] since he left that office, we are able to say among other favorable things that it was devoid of extravagance at a time when extravagance was common among public officers; that the city's affairs generally were cared for with efficiency. And there is nothing more important than these in the administration of any public chief executive. And whether you were a partisan of George Dale or an enemy, you give him credit today, at a time when it will do him no good whatever, for courage—a courage that was reckless at times, but nevertheless, courage in a day when too many men and women are prone to say, "On the one hand, but, again, on the other."

According to a newspaperman: "After he had been in office awhile, [Middletown] was closed up tight as a drum. He was effective against graft, but he had a weak crowd to work with, the city's businessmen were against him, and he could not get along with any of them." The

[6] When a local editorial taunted him with not getting along with his council and urged him and the council to "put their feet under the same table," the mayor retorted dryly, "If we all put our feet under the same table there wouldn't be room for anyone else's feet."

The newly elected mayor of a neighboring city warned this Middletown mayor in the fall of 1929 after the election that the latter had made a big mistake in not having run a personal slate of councilmen. "You won't get any cooperation at all," he warned, "while my men will do anything I say." To which Middletown's mayor replied, "Wait till your councilmen realize that they've been *elected* and that you can't fire them." "And," Middletown's mayor told the investigator, "sure enough, within six months A——'s mayor was purple in the face over a jam with his council: they had tried to get him to come along with them on a grafting city coal contract."

local political "regulars" warned him that they would "get" him within three months.

When the attack came, it is significant that it was on no central public issue in a local political scene chronically replete with varied types of graft and corruption dear to both parties, but on the eloquently righteous charge that the mayor had caused a gallon of whisky to be transported to the State Democratic Convention.

This use of a charge extraneous to the central cluster of conventional civic corruptions as a device by the pot to call the kettle black is an interesting instance of the oblique crabwise tactics of pressure politics. The Eighteenth Amendment offered corrupt politics an effective neutral fence from behind which to do its sniping without attracting attention to itself. How popular this righteous prohibition charge became as a device to "get" the political opposition is reflected in the following editorial from the Middletown evening paper of April 17, 1933:

The mayors of [Middletown] and M—— [a near-by city] are under indictment and the mayor of A—— [another near-by city], who was indicted and who was supposed to have resigned last January, is free of his indictments and demanding his job back. These three cities are within a few miles of each other and all have virtually the same class of population. More or less directly, alleged violations of the prohibition laws had to do with the charges against all three mayors.[7]

When, therefore, Middletown found itself in 1930 with a stubborn mayor it could not intimidate on its hands, the world of political "fixing" turned to its familiar weapons. Indictments were secured before a Federal grand jury in March, 1932, against the mayor, his chief of police, and nine policemen alleged to have been involved in the transport of the gallon of liquor. The case was appealed and, while on appeal before the Federal Supreme Court, was terminated in December, 1933, by a Presidential pardon. The pardon took specific notice of perjury by witnesses against the mayor during the trial.

[7] In January, 1929, a similar convenient use of a liquor charge at the heart of Middletown's political corruption center, the alliance between politics and road-building graft, brought streamer headlines in the press: "Resignation of Road Boss Asked." In this case, according to the press, a Republican county highway superintendent had originally been "asked" by the Democratic highway commissioners to resign "because the Board of Commissioners was Democratic." He had refused and court charges were subsequently brought against him for "intoxication, possession and transportation of liquor, inefficiency in office, and misuse of county property." He was later acquitted on the liquor charge.

When it appeared that the proposed ouster would be delayed by the mayor's appeal to the higher courts, his opponents in Middletown countered with two new moves. First, the city council, in September, 1932, claiming the authority of a State law making any person sentenced to six months or more in a Federal prison ineligible to hold office, voted the mayor's office vacant and elected a successor. It is significant that the man proposed to succeed him is now city controller under the succeeding "regular" Democratic administration. Of this ouster move a paper in the state capital said:

Once more the forces that do not thrive under honest government are after Mayor Dale of [Middletown]. This time the city council attempts to replace him with a member who, during the Federal court trial, was named as the paymaster for the unofficial agents who secured evidence against [the mayor]."

Meanwhile, the "regular" local newspapers began speaking of the mayor, while the case was still on appeal, as "former mayor Dale" and "Dale, who claims to be mayor." The whole case was subsequently thrown out late in 1932 by the Superior Court, and the mayor pro tem never took office.

Stalled thus by the appeal of the liquor charge and by the defeat of this effort to declare the mayor's office vacant, the "regulars" came back in January, 1933, with still a third wave of attack. The mayor, city attorney, city controller, and the fire-department secretary were indicted on twenty-six, twenty-six, eight, and eighteen counts respectively for conspiracy to coerce public employees. The charge involved the collection of "voluntary contributions" from employees on the city payroll for a legal "defense fund" for the indicted mayor. Here, again, the mayor had done, as a man of no private means and with no established party or business financial backing behind him, a thing so commonly practiced in Middletown party politics as ordinarily not even to excite comment or question.[8] By July, 1933, these indictments, too,

[8] Usually, however, the true purpose of these shakedowns is not stated so openly. Thus the press announced some weeks before the mayor elected in the fall of 1934 took office that he would organize a Two Per Cent Club whereby all city employees would "voluntarily donate" that share of their salary to local relief. When he took office the plan was at once changed as noted in the following announcement:

"WELFARE CLUB IS ORGANIZED

"POLITICAL WORK ALSO PART OF NEW ORGANIZATION

"Functioning both as a political and a welfare organization, the [Middletown] County Democratic Club was formed Thursday. [There followed here the names

were thrown out by the courts, and the mayor's opponents, defeated on three attempts to oust him, turned to see that he was not re-elected in 1934—which they succeeded in doing.[9]

It is a significant commentary upon the disparity that commonly exists in Middletown between the private ends of the professional politicians and the public needs of the community that this prolonged

of the officers of the new club, with the city controller—the man referred to above as cited under oath as 'paymaster' in the effort to 'get' the preceding mayor—as secretary-treasurer.]

"Modeled after the [State] Democratic Club, sponsored by Governor M——, the new organization, which replaces the Two Per Cent Club, will carry on welfare work primarily. . . .

"Other objects announced are that the club will 'advance the principles of government advocated by Thomas Jefferson; promote the election of officers devoted to Democracy, and encourage cordial relations among the followers of the Jeffersonian theory; and will uphold the present state and national administration.' The organization is sponsored by the mayor." [Italics ours.]

[The announcement then went on to publish the "nine classifications of members, with dues fixed in correspondence with the salaries and wages earned." These "dues" were graded up from $1.00 a month for city employees earning less than $75 a month to $6.00 a month for those earning $300 and over.]

The political aims of this club were loudly disguised under the announcement of the setting up of a city Social Welfare Department, consisting only of the volunteer services of a "publicity director" to "investigate conditions" (the publicity director being a wealthy local woman interested in charity and with a useful record of enlisting wide popular support for pet charities she publicizes in the press); of welfare work by the two police matrons who distribute old clothing, etc., collected by the city; and a gift of $35 a month from the fund toward the amortization of the $3,800 mortgage on a home for forty old men set up by the local Gospel Mission. As a symbol of the mayor's solicitude for the workingman, this charity, very popular with the working class, was a good vote-catching cause for the mayor to back with a flourish, especially as the $420 a year it would cost would not seriously impair the "more than $5,000" the assessment is alleged to net annually.

[9] It is characteristic that within six months of the beginning of the brave new reform administration of his successor as mayor in 1935, the afternoon paper was lamenting the new mayor's readiness to make friends and his optimistic belief that "money grows on bushes."
The mayor defeated for re-election in 1934 attributes his defeat to the fact that "I didn't want to make promises. [Middletown] people feel that it's a damned mean cuss who won't make promises. But [the candidate who defeated me] promised everybody everything: promised labor he'd treat them right, assured capital he was their man, promised poor people jobs, told the Negro voters he would build a new firehouse in their district completely manned by Negro firemen—and so on. He loaded up all the city departments on the strength of these promises—and is now having to fire them for lack of money, doing so with the air of "You see, boys, I did my durnedest." In the fall of 1935, its first year in office, as noted later in the present chapter, the new administration was skipping paydays.

factional attack by the political "outs" upon the "ins" occurred during years when the city was wallowing along skuppers-under in the midst of the unprecedented need for united civic action in the depression.

In June, 1935, the city's political business was again proceeding as usual. The present mayor, a "regular" Democrat, is said to be in the predicament of having his earlier conviction to the Federal penitentiary hanging like a sword of Damocles over his head, because of the State law making it illegal for a man who has served a Federal sentence of more than six months to hold public office. To this fact is attributed by some his shift from being in his earlier term a "people's candidate" to his present greater pliancy to the wishes of local business. The mayor was "playing ball"; business was behind him—though, as always, as a cat is behind a mouse; an energetic young member of the X family, as noted above, had become the local Democratic leader, so that local business sat astride both parties; the city's financing was going forward through "regular" channels, and the mayor was not forced, as his predecessor had been on one occasion when local banking control blocked him, to peddle the city's bonds personally in Chicago.

The professional politician in a city like Middletown occupies in reality a position somewhat apart. He is not ordinarily a person accepted in the inner councils of the business class, and yet he must work with it in order "to get anywhere." And, on the other hand, the business class have, as noted in Chapter III, little respect for local politics and politicians, viewing them as a necessary evil which business supports and controls only enough to insure cooperation in certain necessary matters. As a result, even in a business-sponsored administration like that which took office in 1935, squabbles between the city hall and the Chamber of Commerce arise from time to time. The opposition of the new mayor to the relief commissary, noted in Chapter IV, is a case in point. Another is the action of the mayor in forcing the Chamber of Commerce to side with him in a W.P.A. project favored by Middletown's working class before he would approve the pet project of the business class (opposed by the South Side) for an intercepting sewer.

In the midsummer of 1935 came the first jolt to local harmony under the new administration, when the citizens were confronted with a proposed civil city tax rate of $1.62. The Republican mayor elected in 1925 gave the city a city tax rate of 98 cents on an assessed valuation of $60,000,000; and under his Democratic successor, the vigorous editor who took office in 1930, the rate had fallen steadily to 89 cents in his last year, 1934, despite a drop to $40,000,000 in the city's assessed valuation. Only after a closely marshaled attack by the Real Estate Board and Chamber of Commerce was the 1936 rate subsequently forced back down to 98 cents.[10] Another jolt came in the early fall when the city was forced to pass paydays and some of the extra employees taken

[10] Nothing better illustrates the managed helplessness of the small citizen not organized into a Real Estate Board or other compact pressure group than does the procedure at the public hearing on this tax rate. Questions were asked as to why the police force had been enlarged, and the questions were evaded by the city controller. Two different citizens expressed the belief that if the "controller, clerk, and mayor would stay on the job expenses would be cut down." (The mayor continues to operate his office as a practicing physician. The controller is referred to locally as the "czar" of the local transportation system; he was reported in the summer of 1935 to be dickering with a group of other "insiders" to void existing franchises and set up a private corporation with a local bus monopoly; he is reported to have a personal stake in the newly organized municipal baseball team and he himself sells pop under the grandstand when business is brisk.) The controller pleaded in answer that he is "working ten to twelve to fourteen hours a day in his office." Another citizen cited a near-by city "which has built a modern sewage system and equals [Middletown] in other respects and still has lowered its tax rate to 51 cents." The controller replied that the city in question owns its own electric-light plant— only to be met with a chorus of, "Why doesn't [Middletown] own its utilities?" And so the meeting trickled on to its bickering end.

On the day following the public hearing, the president of the largest building and loan company was quoted in the press under the headline, "Says Taxpayers Were Insulted—Public Protests Ignored," in part as follows: "After the public hearing was concluded and the council convened, the ordinances were read so rapidly none of us could tell anything about them. There was absolutely no discussion of budget items. Everything was cut and dried before we arrived and we might as well have stayed home. The council, particularly the chairman, failed to give its attention to what was said by the taxpayers, and gave no practical consideration at all to the protests made against a higher tax rate. Those attending constituted a very representative group of taxpayers. The councilmen may have thought they were putting something over on that crowd; if so, they are badly mistaken."

When the rate was eventually reduced to the more familiar figure of 98 cents after the pressure had been applied, a local editorial commented with cynical resignation that those on the inside knew all the time that the proposed rate of $1.62 was considerably above what they would get, that it was submitted merely for bargaining purposes, and that the final rate of 98 cents on an increased assessment value actually gave them "about what they wished":

"While the rate remains the same," the editorial continued, "it applies to nearly a million dollars of increased property valuations and, therefore, the actual total to be paid in taxes next year will amount to many thousands of dollars more than were paid this year. . . .

"It is a serious error to place on boards [like the tax-adjustment board] a

on by the new administration in January began to be dropped.[11] But these are only the everyday headaches in Middletown's municipal life.

A further factor in the apparent discrepancy between what Middletown wants its government as represented in the office of mayor to do and what actually gets done appears in the following comments:

Thus it may be said that back of nearly all the candidacies of those who wish to be mayor of Middletown for the next four years is some private and selfish interest; the voters being in the main ignorant of these ties may easily be deceived. It is all very depressing. What are we going to do about

---

majority that represents the tax spenders. One such member would be enough. One does not permit a judge to preside in a case in which he is the defendant. That analogy may not be perfect but it's pretty good. This board, too, was handicapped by not having before it the detailed figures of proposed expenditures for comparison with these detailed expenditures of several past years. . . . As it was, the board a good deal of the time was like a child playing in the dark. "And the public officeholders—not all of them but a good many of them— played the same old game they always play. They submitted estimates of expenses far above their needs and far above anything they expected to receive in order that when the cutting was completed they would still have more than they ought to have. . . ."

[11] This enforced thinning of the ranks of the mayor's appointees was jubilantly hailed by his predecessor in the following editorial in his paper:

"TOO MUCH HIRED HELP

"Reckless overloading of city departments with employees has resulted in the inevitable. The engineer's office was loaded up with seven employees. . . . Monday three were fired. They were told money had got scarce. It was discovered at the end of the first six months there was only $1,400 left to pay salaries for the next six months. The three deputies [assisting the City Engineer] who flourish where but one grew in the last administration, wonder what is going to happen next. They do not need to make a blueprint and train the compass on the doodad to divide $1,400 by four. The engineer's budget for 1936 is in the neighborhood of $12,000, about twice the amount allotted for that office in the five previous years. High-priced harmony may help out the discharged employees the first of next January, but five months is a long time between snacks.

"And down in the police department much uneasiness prevails. The [preceding mayor's] administration managed to worry along with thirty-nine cops, but the new regime raised it to sixty-seven. They are all good policemen who contribute two per cent of their salaries every payday, along with firemen and other employees, to some great common undisclosed cause. But it takes money to pay a standing army. The 1935 police budget is fast nearing depletion and the forced retirement of a few battalions will result. . . .

"The privates are rapidly being discharged because of a scarcity of funds and shortly, unless the miracle of the loaves and fishes repeats itself, there will be nobody but the commissioned officers left to rake the leaves in the parks and push the brooms in the streets and alleys."

it? My guess is: nothing. The average voter does not know and he does not even suspect what is going on. (*Editorial, February, 1933.*)

"Politics here have been 'grab what you can and the devil take the hindmost.' The fellow who can promise the most gets elected and there have been plenty of promises." (*Unprinted comment by a local newspaperman, June, 1935.*)

One of these "private and selfish interests" is involved in the alleged long-time tie-up between local politics and the paving, road-building, and contracting interests in the city and county.[12] The editor who won a surprise victory and became mayor in 1930 had for years shown up this alliance in his paper and had run on a platform pledging him to break up the local "contracting trust." His election was accordingly an affront to a vested interest. One of his first acts after taking office was the cancellation of $300,000 of new street contracts signed by his predecessor just prior to the latter's going out of office, and the making of new contracts at a reported saving of thirty-five cents a square foot. In November, 1936, a gravel bid was thrown out at the last moment because the county attorney insisted that the legal advertisement for the bids had been illegal in that it had narrowed the field so arbitrarily as to have "eliminated competitive bidding."

A second "interest" of great political importance for the mayor and city government is connected with gambling. Gambling has a long tradition in Middletown associated with the best city administrations. Periodically the city reads in its papers such stories as the following from the morning paper in August, 1935:

POLICE CLAMP DOWN THE LID ON GAMBLING
HALF DOZEN ESTABLISHMENTS CLOSED BY ORDER

In a "surprise" move which was none too surprising to those within slingshot range of the situation, all alleged gambling establishments within the city limits were closed by police order Tuesday and last night. The police lid, descending quietly but quite firmly, squeezed out of operation a half-dozen establishments, and the casualties included one horse-racing book, numerous short-card games, one crap game, and innumerable tip books. The places where gambling is said to have flourished were dark and deserted last night, but they were not the only places to feel the police clamp. A number of local beer establishments and pool halls which had

---

[12] See *Middletown*, p. 423.

offered for sale the all-too-popular tip tickets were ordered to remove all books from their counters and shelves.

The sudden close-up order was brought about, those close to the "inside" said, because of the rather loud fashion in which a new alleged gambling place began operations. This establishment, opened a few days ago on South Walnut Street, got off on the wrong foot when one of its chief operators stated publicly that if his place was not allowed to run, then none of the other —— —— places would have their doors open twenty-four hours. This statement, it was said, became even more unwise when city police officials allegedly discovered that *all five of the brighter lights of the new business house were antagonistic to the administration.* [Italics ours.]

Police Chief M——, asked last night to disclose the reason for the clamping of the lid, declined to make a statement, calling the action of his department "routine business."

The broad implications here of a friendly understanding between the administration and the usual group of friendly gambling houses is clear. The earlier prison sentence of the present mayor was based upon an alleged misuse of the mails to defraud in a gambling scheme connected with a fake prize fight. In commenting on the "clamping down of the lid" in August, 1935, the local weekly edited by the ex-mayor captioned an editorial dryly:

THE FAMOUS LID

It is announced [ran the editorial] that local gamblers were told they would either have to stop operations or be arrested and that they all quit. The [morning paper] published the story Friday morning. It was not stated who gave the order—the mayor, the chief of police, the president of the board of safety, or the vice squad. It was stated that some gamblers, not in good standing, decided to open up. Whether the others quit by request or organized a sympathetic strike is not certain. . . .

Nobody ought to get excited though about hearing of wholesale gambling and other petty crimes in [Middletown]. A year ago last spring both political parties here nominated candidates for mayor who had distinguished themselves while in office before by especial consideration to the gambling fraternity. Apparently majorities of both parties voted for bigger and better gamblers, and now that they have got them, why worry? Let the people rule, say we.

Another editorial in 1935 in this same weekly paper stated in connection with a discussion of the prevalence of whispering campaigns in Middletown:

When I was elected mayor in 1929 . . . one story whispered from house to house was to the effect that a bunch of Chicago gamblers, headed by —— and ——, put $15,000 in my campaign kitty and that I had agreed, in the event of my election, to oust the current short-card fraternity and put Chicago in charge of gambling concessions then held by local talent.

Early in this mayor's term of office, too, the city had gone through another of its lid-clamping gestures. Nine days after he took office in January, 1930, the headlines announced, "Police Head Says 'Dives' Are Closed," followed by a police warning against their reopening. All through January of that year the battle continued: "[Mayor] Wars on Cigar-store Card Games—Cleanup Campaign Is Instituted." Those operating the card-game houses promptly took the matter to court, and by the middle of the month the headlines announced: "Legal War on Card Playing Looms Here," followed a week later by the announcement: "Judge M—— Holds Card Playing Is Legal—Mayor Says He Will Continue to Arrest Men Playing Cards in Cigar Stores." Meanwhile, the press had carried the announcement that "The administration's ban on card playing in cigar stores is said to be causing a revival of pool and billiard playing." Although, as noted in Chapter V, this mayor's drive against prostitution and gambling relaxed after its first year, one still read in the papers in November, 1931, near the end of his second year in office, "The mayor denies that sixteen out of eighteen penny machines confiscated by the police about a month ago are back in use."

What one is witnessing in Middletown's gambling is a continuing, institutionalized form of leisure closely linked with local politics. The poolrooms and cigar-store card rooms are virtually the political clubs of the city, run by local politicians or by men closely associated with them. The inner business group may meet and make their decisions as regards local politics in quite another setting, but it is here in these shabby smoke-filled poolrooms and cigar stores, supplemented by the working-class lodges, that the small-time political lieutenants maintain their grip on the working-class voters year in and year out. The periodic "lid clampings" usually represent either or both of two things: a gesture to public sentiment in a heavily evangelical town and/or a much more realistic move to keep the local gambling world safe for the administration in power as a source of funds for political fence building and as centers for political contact and organization. It is significant that these cleanups tend to come early in each administration. This represents a gesture in the direction of fulfilling the omnipresent campaign pledge to "clean up the town," and it also represents a realistic whipping into line of any recalcitrant unfriendly members of this politically useful group. The new mayor in 1930 had come in through a political upset, and *his* cleanup was aimed in part at showing the "boys" running the pool and cigar gambling houses who was boss and forcing into line with *him* a group of men affiliated with the rival political crowd just driven from office.[13] The 1935 cleanup, conducted by a mayor already "one of the boys" by reason of his past record, was probably aimed at warding off noisy, outside, unfriendly interests who were trying to "muscle in" on the tidy local gambling concession.

Middletown's political and gambling worlds seethe quietly beneath the outward surface of the city's life over these problems of the protection of gambling and vice. The local faction in favor maintains its inside advantage against local rivals, while both the "ins" and "outs" are apt to unite to block the invasion of the local field by outsiders. Typical of the unproved allegations which one picks up about the streets is the following cheap handbill, broadcast in 1936. It was signed by "The People's Friend" and probably emanated from a disgruntled "out" in the local underworld:

PROTECTED VICE CONDITIONS IN [MIDDLETOWN] EXPOSED

> As they have existed for the past two years and now exist with the full knowledge and consent of the Mayor, the Board of Safety, Chief of Police, the Police and Prosecuting Attorney.

Vice and gambling are in complete control of the city.

[Middletown's] Police and Board of Safety, . . . although they have been appealed to repeatedly, absolutely refuse to do anything to take any steps to stop this flow of Vice. The joints running under the jurisdiction and paid protection of [certain officials of the city specified by official designation] are the —— cigar store located at —— Street, operated and owned by A——. Another joint operated by the gambling chain is the store owned and operated by C—— located in the very heart of the city upstairs on

[13] It is, however, unfair to load all of this mayor's motive for his cleanup upon his personal political realism. As stated above, he was an eccentric, a combination of old-fashioned outspoken idealist and hard-headed realist. An editorial in another paper commented in the midst of his cleanup in January, 1930, that "Mayor Dale is in earnest about cleaning up the big gambling and booze joints."

the northeast corner of —— and —— Streets. The third joint belonging to this chain of gamblers is located at —— Street, and is operated by B——.

Employed at the A—— joint is A——, defeated candidate for [public office. He] is the brother of A——, owner and operator of the joint, which runs under the paid protection of our local police. A——, the proprietor of this said joint is a brother-in-law of Councilman ——. Young Walter A—— (a minor) is also employed at this joint. A——'s son, Jim A——, is using sucker money to broaden his education at the University of ——. Incidentally the A—— family is cleaning plenty of sucker money from their chain of gambling joints to educate several other A——s.

The A—— joint is located directly opposite the Court House, which houses our Prosecutor and Sheriff. Upstairs above the cigar store we find a race-horse bookmaker, with special ticker service. Bud B—— operates the horse book. B—— formerly lived in a beautiful $25,000 Westwood home. So far as can be learned, his name has never appeared on any factory payroll, nor has he ever been known to have been in any legitimate business. This horse-book business has been pretty soft for Bud, but we don't know of any of the boys that play the outside of the race-horse game who ever did live in Westwood. When the suckers don't play the ponies in sufficient numbers to satisfy A—— and B——, they send out their "riding baliff" [sic] Henry D——, on his trusty bicycle. He carries his race form sheet with him, together with some hot tips, direct from the track, and entices suckers both rich and poor to give him a bet. One of his most distinguished customers is Z—— [a school athletic coach], and [athletic] fans swear and declare that the success or failure of [his teams] is controlled by his success with ponies. . . .

Then not last nor least is the big poker game, right upstairs with the horse bookie. If it's not one gamble, it's another. This game is in charge of E—— and C——, and can anyone ever remember of any one of these eminent Knights of the Greencloth doing any manual labor? Each Thursday night is Smoker Night. They feed the sucker a 10¢ free lunch and take his last cent over the green cloth and leave a helpless wife and unfortunate children to get along the best they can.

Then comes the real steal, "crooked jackpot tip books." These books are so crooked that the sucker has absolutely no chance whatsoever of winning. These books are outlawed and banned in almost every state in the Union and every city of the states. The proprietor has a code to go by. He sometimes lets an outsider win a jackpot, but it is a very, very rare occasion. The proprietor knows the exact book the jackpot is in and knows exactly where the ticket is located on the book that will win the tip and the jackpot. This joint sells as many as 250 of these crooked books in one day, which makes the house a profit of hundreds of dollars. Some men spend their entire week's wages to win a jackpot, but very seldom are they successful.

IT IS THE WOMEN AND CHILDREN WHO SUFFER FROM THE FATHERS' LOSSES AT THESE GAMBLING JOINTS, and many complaints have gone into the Police Dept., Prosecutor, and Sheriff, and the answer is always the same: "Come up and file charges and we will arrest them." [The authorities have] refused point blank time and again to accept affidavits against our chain gamblers when unimpeachable evidence was laid in their laps. Why is it necessary for a defenseless woman to expose herself to the humiliation and contact with a gang of gamblers, so she might preserve the husband's wages for the necessities of life, for her children and herself?

It is the duty of our Police Dept. to rid the city of all this Vice regardless of who is doing it or whomever it affects. A——, head of the gambling chain, and [a certain police officer] are bosom friends. They go fishing, hunting, and drinking together, and only recently returned from a big trip out of town, where they spent several days hunting together. There were also other city officials on this trip. Looks like it would be rather embarrassing for friend [police officer] to have to arrest friend A——. A—— and B—— were arrested during the last grand jury investigation for owning and operating a gambling house, and poor B—— was allowed to plead guilty for gambling, and was subsequently assessed a small fine. In a recent term of court, [a local official specified by name] comes to the rescue of A——, king of the gambling chain, and moves the court for the following reason: That said A—— was jointly indicted with B—— in said cause for keeping a building and room for gambling; that said B—— has pled guilty and I believe there is not sufficient evidence to convict A——, and therefore ask the court to dismiss said cause against said A——. This is what we call a [public official] performing in behalf of the gamblers.

The administration took office Jan. 1, 1935. A——, at that time, was operating a gambling house full blast. The Grand Jury was called soon after it took office, but A—— continued to gamble all the time the Grand Jury was in session. Feeling secure that the protection of [the police, including] his old hunting partner, would immune him from being indicated by the Grand Jury, A—— holds the lease on the building, has the beer license, and is the owner of the establishment from top to bottom. Knowing these facts, why did the officials permit B—— to plead guilty and exonerate an accomplice who was equally guilty? A—— also sells beer in this gambling joint. [Officials have] acknowledged that they knew all this gambling was going on. One of them even acknowledged he entered the A—— establishment to get a check cashed and had to wade through tip tickets to get to the counter. Despite these facts and although the officials have the power, they have never once yet called for a Grand Jury to clean up the deplorable conditions that exist in our city.

The Grand Jury has been drawn and now is the time for them to be called into session. Not only investigate these deplorable conditions, but investigate why our Board of Safety, our Police Dept. and other law enforcement officials do not take steps to curb this flow of crime when they know it is going on and who is doing it. We demand an immediate calling of the Grand Jury and we will furnish the honorable body dozens of responsible witnesses who can and will testify that children of school age are permitted to frequent these places and are losing there money by gambling. Please watch for my next issue of VICE CONDITIONS IN [MIDDLETOWN] which will be published at a later date.[14]

Like gambling, beer has been seized upon by Middletown's politicians as a valuable source of power, patronage, and perhaps profit. The candid weekly paper described this situation as follows:

THE BEER BARONS

The sale of beer and more potent intoxicants has been legalized by State law, but the law will quickly become obnoxious and will be repealed if the State does not protect honest dealers against any "squeeze play" attempted in any unit of local government.

One of the three local wholesale distributors is said to have the city-administration blessing, and the power of suggestion, and possibly stronger urging, has been put to work to force vulnerable retailers to patronize that particular distributor. For instance, a representative of that particular wholesaler entered a local "tavern" recently. "Well," he remarked, "you are fixed fine here, with a baseball ticker, blackboard, and everything." And then he walked out. That was real salesmanship. The proprietor of the place ordered some of his beer. "He didn't have to write down on my blackboard what he meant," said the wise retailer. "What he really meant was that I'd better buy in the right place or get bobbed. I don't like it but I ain't lookin' for no trouble."

One wholesale dealer had the exclusive agency for a particular brand of beer. Without notice the brewery gave the agency to the "administration" distributor, and the word was soon spread among the retailers what kind of beer they had better buy if they wanted to get along easy like, without

[14] It is not intended here to underwrite the details of such a popular arraignment. Some of the individuals may be innocent of the charges made. For obvious reasons, all names have been changed in reprinting the above. The significant point to note is that conditions of the types here described are endemic in the political life of Middletown.

friction. Other retailers with applications for license pending do not hesitate to say that they have been told that they must buy of so and so if they
want to get their licenses. . . . Something will bust loose if this practice
continues.

Further evidence of this political tie-up appeared in the protests of a
local tavern keeper over the denial to him by the State Alcoholic Beverage Commission of a renewal of his license in the summer of 1935.
According to this proprietor, as quoted in the local afternoon paper,
he had been singled out at the instigation of the local politicians as the
only applicant in the county to be denied a license:

"The [Middletown] city administration did it. The local Democratic
machine has been trying to 'get' me, and it has succeeded—at least temporarily. It served virtual public announcement of its intentions when it had
police 'pinch' my little pin punchboards several weeks ago when at the same
time the big baseball-tip boards and other punchboards are running wide
open all over town—and are still running without the slightest police interference. When these people announced that they would 'get' me, I said they
were not big enough to do it, but I guess I took in too much territory. It
seems they were big enough. Then, too, the local wholesalers of beer were
pretty mad at me. I have not bought any beer of them for six months. Instead I have been buying it directly from the brewery more cheaply than
the [Middletown] wholesalers could sell it to me. I understand arrangements are already under way to lease the room on which I now have a
lease. If I were to give up the lease, another saloon would be operating
there within six weeks." A—— [the proprietor] asserted that several other
taverns have been licensed here whose reputations are far worse than that
of [his tavern] and he named them and gave his reasons for the statement.[15]

All these perplexities surrounding the work of its elected officers
suggest a conflict between the things Middletown wants its government to do and what is actually accomplished under the rituals according to which it carries on the processes of government. This same con-

[15] A large section of local public opinion undoubtedly favored the denial of
a renewal of license to this tavern. It is the heavily frequented "dive" in the
center of the business section described above and had been in operation a year
at the time its license was denied. Its central location and notoriety may have
been factors in local pressure to deny its license, but it is probable that other
factors such as those cited above were also involved, as Middletown has a habit
of tolerating houses of prostitution, gambling places, and other things which the
more fastidious local people regard as "nuisances" easily if those in charge do
the proper things.

flict appears further in the chronic predicament involved in trying to get adequate city sewage disposal.

Middletown wants a clean and healthy city. It has largely, though not entirely, left behind an age in which privies and wells stood side by side in back yards and garbage ripened at the mercy of sun and wind, but in 1935 it still dumped its sewage along with the excrement of a packing house and the waste of other industries into the convenient river that meanders in wide loops across the city. For the X family, who built their row of mansions along the river before White River had ceased entirely to be white, it is literally true that in midsummer when the wind is from the river they must keep their front windows closed; while to many lesser folk the stench and mosquitoes are a perennial hot-weather problem. One paper remarked: "[Middletown] should provide a good opening for a clothes-pin factory. The clothes-pins could be worn on their noses by [Middletown] residents during the hot weather so long as they tolerate the cesspool misnamed White River in its present noxious condition." The Izaak Walton League laments the absence of fishing, nobody uses the river for pleasure, and the farmers below the city have a difficult problem with their grazing herds in pastures bordering the river. In terms of standards of health, comfort, real-estate valuation, and civic self-respect which Middletown sets for itself, it would seem that it wants to move on to a more modern stage of civic sewage disposal. There has in fact been agitation for such a modernization of its sewage disposal for twenty years. By early 1930 the whole problem had reached the point where there were suits pending against the city by farmers in the county for river pollution; and the Chief Engineer of the State had declared, to quote the summary of his decision in a local editorial, that "[Middletown] either must build an intercepting sewer and sewage-disposal plant now or do it later, and, if later, probably pay in addition heavy damages to individuals and possibly to whole communities whose property and health have been affected by the contamination of the stream here."

The oldest controversial factor in this situation derives from the fact that the river incontinently loops its way through the North Side of the city. Strive as local reformers will to insist that it is for the good of the entire city to clean up White River, the working class on the South Side, through their councilmen, view the cost of the proposed new sewage system—about $1,100,000—as none of their affair. They are still paying for a faulty South Side sewer laid under the present mayor in his earlier administration, and they resent the alleged efforts of the wealthier North Side to tax them for a new sewer which "will benefit primarily the few rich people uptown who own property along the river." Thus Middletown's working class easily personalizes the situation and sees it as an affair of the millionaire X family rather than as a community matter.[16]

Another deterrent to action on such a big project arises from the fact that Middletown's political world is one in which it is natural for the press to announce in a matter-of-fact way whenever the city changes mayors such items as the following:

Plum Tree to Be Shaken Monday.[17]

Office seekers and those looking for political favors for their friends and relatives continued today to flock in numbers to the City Hall.

Mayor Starts Administration Off with Entirely New Police Force.[18]

New Mayor Places Third Relative on City Payroll.

Turnover in City Hall Offices Complete; Only Two Persons Left Over from [Republican] Administration, and Those Just Temporary.

Under such institutional arrangements somebody will, it is assumed, be likely to make a "neat personal pile" out of a contract of upwards of $1,000,000, and no political faction can quite bear to see any

---

[16] The same North Side *vs.* South Side opposition appeared when, after a wealthy citizen offered to donate to the city the land for a local airport in 1930, the city council failed to pass an ordinance authorizing a necessary $125,000 bond issue to develop this municipal airport. Here again the interest of the younger generation of the X's in aviation was a potent reason for the South Side's unwillingness to be taxed for an airport.

[17] These items are all from the papers of the first ten days of January, 1930, but they can be duplicated in the opening days of any change in local party control. (See *Middletown*, pp. 423-24.)

A variant on this was introduced during the period of the earlier study when the Ku Klux Klan waxed strong throughout the political forces of the city and Klansmen and their wives were substituted in wholesale fashion for mere Republicans or Democrats on the appointive offices and boards at the command of local politicians.

[18] This note in the press was followed three days later by the headlines: "Window-breaking Epidemic—An Effort to Embarrass New Police Force," followed by a statement that the "Vandalism was aimed at showing resentment of [the new Democratic mayor's] ousting of [his Republican predecessor's] police department."

other have the plunder. Furthermore, the controlling business group has a deep and genuine conviction that if a maverick Democratic administration not under its control happens to get into power, as it did in 1930, there will certainly be more mismanagement and graft than if a "regular" administration has the contract letting in its hands. Again, when councilmen are elected and not appointed (and removable) by the mayor, there is further chance of conflict as to just who shall be "in" on the business of contract letting; [19] and question also arises, as it did in January, 1930, as to whether the job should be done under the board of works or under a sanitary commission.

Into this twenty-year-old stalemate had come an order of the State Board of Health in January, 1930, that the city should make immediate provision for such disposal of its sewage as would clean up the river. Again, a year later, the State Board of Health forwarded a demand for action. The administration, faced with a million-dollar project in the midst of the depression, was locked in a political checkmate between the administrative and the legislative branches of the city government and was unable to act; and some of the mayor's opponents even taunted him with being devoid of civic pride. When, in 1933, Federal funds began to be available for such civic projects, the city hired an expert from Cleveland to draw plans and the mayor announced his intention of seeking funds from Washington. At this point, according to the mayor's statement, an attorney for the X family approached the mayor to tell him to come down and consult with one of the X's or he would have no chance of getting a Federal grant. The mayor, as he told the story, "told [the attorney] to go to hell and to take [X] with him," got on a train for Washington, and returned with a grant of $1,060,000 from Secretary Ickes.[20] The faction opposing the sewer project, including the "regular" Democratic candidate being put forward for mayor in the fall of 1934 and the X's attorney referred to above,[21] are alleged to have connived with the city council to block

[19] Over this issue the press reported within the first week of the new administration in 1930: "Mayor Jolted Twice by New Council."

[20] This mayor stood almost alone as a man of any prominence in Middletown who was openly anti-X family. His paper consistently opposed their power in the city. In recounting this incident to a member of the research staff, he made it quite clear that it was a part of his code to "make no deals with the [X's]." His death in the spring of 1936 removed almost the only clear note of dissent from the present pattern of control.

[21] This man became city attorney and a member of the boards of safety and public works under the new city administration voted in in the fall of 1934.

acceptance of the Federal grant. Reference to this "deal" is commonly heard in Middletown and was specifically charged in print by one of the city's independent citizens.[22] The State representative of the P.W.A. has been quoted in print in Middletown as saying in 1934 that "Some irresponsible from Middletown came to the state capital and assured him that 'We will block this sewer project until [the present mayor's] term of office expires,' and that 'The mayor plans to get $40,000 for himself out of the deal.'" According to the printed statement of the man who was mayor at the time, "These [local] people, some of them 'highly important' individuals, secretly gummed the works and the council refused to pass the necessary ordinance of acceptance of the government loan."[23]

The Washington offer of funds was canceled in September, 1934— to the disgust of many bewildered citizens and of the afternoon paper, which insisted that the problem of securing decent sewage disposal had got beyond the point of being tolerated as a political football. Under the new mayor in 1935, the city drew up a proposal for a $1,126,000 project, $66,000 more than the project under the preceding administration, and promptly went eagerly hat-in-hand again to Washington. In late October, 1935, a local editor lamented that the "sewer project lies unapproved in Washington. . . . Too, [Middletown] is in the uncomfortable position of asking the Federal government to do something the latter once agreed to do, only to be turned down by the city council. . . . Having passed up one offer of government help, it would not be a necessarily unsafe bet that if [Middletown] is to have the interceptor [sewer] and plant she will have to find a way to build it out of her own funds. . . . The city is too nearly broke to consider an adequate bond issue for this purpose—or any purpose."

[22] This man, independently well off, is the son of an old Middletown family and maintains his home there, though he spends much time out of the city. He is independent, keen, and somewhat of a local "character." His home is adjacent to the river and the new sewer has been a personal hobby—so much so that he paid out of his own pocket to have preliminary surveys made early in the depression leading to the bringing in of the Cleveland engineering firm in 1933 to draft the detailed plan for the sewer and sewage-disposal plant.

[23] A final clew to the blocking of the original 1934 Federal grant and the 1935 reapproval of the plan by the new city administration at a $66,000 increase in cost may lie in the sole change in the plan in 1935, which removed the site of the proposed sewage-disposal plant a mile further west of town. This shift, according to the local press, "would provide for the future development of a section west of Middletown now being developed." This is the section in which the new subdivisions have been pushing westward into the cornfields.

The citizens themselves do not understand the pressure factors be-hind this situation, any more than they understand the backstage dick-ering that increased their police force so sharply when General Motors moved back to town. They are puzzled by this spectacle of public-spirited citizens and elected representatives of the people blocking in 1934 a project long recognized as highly desirable for public health and comfort, and then turning about a year later and seeking feverishly to carry through the project themselves. They wonder, too, that, after campaigning on the South Side in the fall of 1934 on the appeal that the proposal was too extravagantly budgeted,[24] the new administration proceeded to sponsor a plan to cost $66,000 more. Again, a campaign device used (by the administration voted in in the fall of 1934 against the then concluding administration) to inflame Southsiders was the whipping up of an old South Side antagonism to sewers in general, by reviving the very sore point of the defective South Side sewer built by the city some years before; and yet, citizens who stop to think recall that the contract for this earlier sewer, for which a later city adminis-tration subsequently sued the contractors because of its faulty con-struction,[25] had actually been let under a previous administration of the same mayor who in 1934 used the iniquities and extravagance of the earlier sewer as an argument to secure South Side votes.[26]

At length, in 1936, the regular Democratic mayor, unimpeded either by his city council or by the business group, secured a Federal grant of $340,000 (one-third of the amount secured by his predecessor and ve-toed by the council) and, with a city appropriation of $180,000, a part

[24] "Woeful cries and tears were shed for the South Side by politicians who sought votes last year for their coming campaign. . . . No tears are being shed for the South Side now." (Democratic weekly, September 6, 1935.)

[25] *Middletown* quotes the following from a local newspaper in 1924: "City loses $101,800 suit. Sewer found defective after it was accepted by the board of works and the contractors had been released from their obligations. Bricks and brickbats used instead of cement in interstices." (P. 424.)

[26] The Democratic weekly reported these tactics as follows on August 30, 1935: "One of the favorite arguments used [in the 1934 campaign] was made by 'professional' Southsiders, whose only interest in the South Side sewer is to inflame voting fever by referring to the South Side sewer and pleading in behalf of citizens who have paid for a defective sewer and were to be required to pay for another. It seems to have been forgotten, or purposely overlooked, that the South Side sewer was projected and the contract let by the [present mayor's] previous administration, and that one of the flock of deputies now employed by the city was the city engineer at that time. 'Professional' Southsiders who live north of the railroad forget so easily, after accomplishing their political desires."

of the original sewer plan was undertaken as a W.P.A. project. As this is written, in the early fall of 1936, the city is still dickering hopefully with the Federal authorities to secure funds to complete the second section of the sewer and to build the sewage-disposal plant included in the original proposal.[27]

One of the things Middletown expects its city government, so constituted and so functioning, to do is to prevent, or at least to control, crime. It would appear from the police records that the varying conditions of the years of boom and depression may have had little if any more effect upon the prevalence of what Middletown chooses to call "crime"—*i.e.,* the things for which it arrests people—than the fact of whether each successive city administration was in its "new-broom" or "old-broom" phase. The full effects of the depression upon tendencies to violate group codes are, however, too subtle for appraisal as yet. Total annual arrests appear to have exhibited a fairly constant rate of 33 to 38 per 1,000 of population during the years immediately preceding the depression; they increased sharply in 1930 and 1931 to 49 and 44 respectively, fell off abruptly to 25 in 1932, and then climbed back until in 1934 and in the first five months of 1935, they were again running somewhat above the pre-depression ratio.[28]

This sharp increase in 1930 suggests a genuine depression impact of the sort one might superficially expect in hard times; but the halving of the 1930 rate in the difficult year 1932 and the relatively low rate in 1933 throw this hypothesis in doubt. One factor in this drop in 1932 may be the increasing acceptance by the community as the depression wore on of the necessity for providing public relief to the able-bodied, thereby lessening somewhat their need to beg, borrow, or steal. But this hardly accounts entirely for the decline after 1930 and 1931. The causes of these sharp fluctuations in arrests probably lie in part at least elsewhere than in the obvious factor of the immediate pressure of the depression on the population. In a small, neighborly city like Middletown where crime tends to be home grown rather than perpetrated by the type of roving criminal which congregates in large cities, there was possibly some tendency for the police to be lenient regarding certain types of small first offenses during the bad years 1932-33; though

[27] See the discussion of this and other W.P.A. projects in Ch. IV.
[28] See Table 44 in Appendix III.

the city was, as noted below, intensely excited over the prospect of bank banditry in these years, and police pressure against certain more serious crimes probably actually increased. Another and even more important factor influencing this fluctuation in arrests concerns the ebb and flow in local politics. As usual, the municipal campaign of 1929 had featured the pledge to "clean up the town," and since the winning candidate was unusually energetic about it, Middletown was shortly "closed up tight as a drum." But, as noted earlier, the mayor experienced difficulty in getting the city judge to convict the cases brought to court and temporarily "quarantined the judge" in 1930 by ordering the police to make no more arrests on liquor charges. Under these circumstances, according to a press reporter covering the city hall and courthouse for his paper, "After the first big drive, enthusiasm for reforming the city waned, to pick up again in the campaign year, 1934. The two years 1932-33 were an 'in between' period of the mayor's administration." Unfortunately, detailed police records are not available for years prior to 1931, but arrests in each of the years, 1931-34, for sex offenses, for gambling, and for liquor charges [29] appear to corroborate this suggestion of sharp fluctuations in administrative zeal. Arrests for all sex offenses dropped from sixty in 1931 [30] to nine in 1932, and to two in 1933; for gambling and keeping a gambling house, from 108 in 1931 to eighteen in 1932; for liquor offenses, from 661 in 1931 to 356 in 1932, and 270 in 1933, though these rose again sharply to 469 in 1934.[31] Arrests for motor-vehicle offenses suggest the same erratic shifts in police alertness, dropping from 156 in 1931 to 57 in 1932, rising again to 118 in 1933, and falling off to 46 in 1934.

The annual totals of arrests on charges more directly associated with property and violent assaults upon persons—forgery, issuing fraudulent

[29] See Table 45 in Appendix III.

[30] Though figures are not available, arrests for sex and liquor offenses were probably even higher in 1930, the first year of the new mayor's "reform administration."

[31] There is little evidence of any abatement in gambling or in the volume of illegal sex activity during the worst of the depression. Money was scarce, but more women were on the streets looking for "pickups" for even twenty-five cents and half a dollar, while the pressure to augment small sums in the local small-stake gambling games was great. In the case of liquor, as noted in Ch. V, there is reported to have been a sharp increase in drinking locally in 1930-31, characterized as accompanying "a general loosening of public morals." This may have influenced the high total of sex offenses somewhat, although the great bulk of the sex arrests in 1930 and 1931 were in cases involving prostitution

checks, arson, petit larceny, burglary and grand larceny, carrying deadly weapons, and murder and homicide—remain fairly constant and show small evidence of a local crime wave generated by the depression. The outstanding exception is that of arrests for petit larceny, which rose from 67 in 1931 to 80 in 1932, to 112 in 1933, and then dropped sharply to 50 in 1934. The "burglary, banditry, robbery, housebreaking and grand larceny" group dropped slowly from 26 in 1931 to 16 in 1934. Arrests for issuing fraudulent checks dropped away from 12 in 1931 to 1 in each of the years 1933 and 1934. The heavy program of public relief from 1931 on undoubtedly operated to hold down these crimes against property and persons.

During the four and a half years from January, 1931, to June, 1935, juvenile arrests remained low and did not fluctuate as much as adult arrests, as shown by the following figures:

Year	Total arrests	Adult arrests	Juvenile arrests
1931	2,134	2,049	85
1932	1,183	1,113	70
1933	1,398	1,320	78
1934	1,837	1,756	81
1935 (first 5 mos.)	900	865	35

These relatively low totals of juveniles arrested do not exhibit the actual situation which has been troubling many in the community, if we are to believe those in touch with Middletown's youth. The principal of the large South Side junior high school was quoted in Chapter IV as saying, "Our boys at the —— Junior High School did a good deal of stealing during this last winter [1934-35], and the ominous thing has been the increasing extent to which they seem to feel that it is O.K. if they can get away with it." Testimony of this sort suggests that, despite the fall in petit larceny arrests in 1934 and the standstill of juvenile arrests over the four years, there may be in process a subtle shift in morale among the young not revealed by the figures for juvenile arrests.

The sex ratio of offenders exhibited little change. The percentages of females, both white and Negro, were high in 1931, owing largely to the campaign against prostitution, and the percentages of males were correspondingly lower in the same year than in any of the following years. The facts that Negroes, comprising only 5.7 per cent of Middletown's population in 1930 and almost entirely confined to the low income group, constituted throughout approximately 17 per cent

of the persons arrested, and that Negro males, in nearly all cases engaged in unskilled marginal jobs, rose slowly but steadily in percentage
of arrests as the depression progressed, suggest an apparently growing
economic pressure in the case of those at the very bottom of the
social and economic scale.[32]

Middletown's state was the home of Dillinger and the scene of a
number of his daring crimes. From 1931 on, the city became highly
excited over banditry, as neighboring cities and villages experienced
bank holdups. A County Vigilantes Society was organized to protect
the banks early in 1932, and in the fall of 1933, eight-column headlines shouted, "[Middletown] Acts as Outlaws Run Wild: Blockading
of Streets is Urged by [Chief of Police]." Out of this scare came, early
in 1934, the appropriation of funds for five police radio squad cars and
three motorcycles, and headlines informed all and sundry of "Modern
War School for Our Police: Machine Gun and Bomb Technique
Taught." In a press statement in 1935 the police attributed the decrease
in various forms of robbery, which "have been averaging two or three
a day, to the greater mobility of the police in these speedy squad cars."
While increasing the police force is not ordinarily regarded by experts
as a major deterrent to crime,[33] the deterring effect of such mechanized
policing in a small city like Middletown is probably real. For in a
small, peaceable, native-born population like Middletown's there tend
to be few hardened habitual criminals; big-city criminals may occasionally use the Middletowns as a quiet hideaway, but they are not
likely to stay in cities of this size and "work" them repeatedly, because
of the greater ease with which they can become known. Furthermore,
the research staff, fresh from New York with its omnipresent policemen, was struck by the inconspicuousness of Middletown policemen;
there was one officer who directed traffic at a crowded corner opposite

---

[32] The percentage distributions of persons arrested, by sex, and by whites and
Negroes, are as follows:

Year	Total Arrests	Whites Males	Females	Negroes Males	Females	Total
1931	2,134	74.3	8.7	12.9	4.1	100.0
1932	1,183	79.5	4.9	13.8	1.8	100.0
1933	1,398	79.6	4.7	14.1	1.6	100.0
1934	1,837	77.6	5.2	15.0	2.2	100.0
1935 (first 5 mos.)...	900	78.9	4.0	15.7	1.4	100.0

[33] See *Middletown*, p. 428, n. 16.

a bank and another was engaged in going the rounds of the business section to check up on over-long parking; but one usually walked through a mile of shady residential streets anywhere about town without encountering a policeman. Most of Middletown's crimes against property are "small-time" affairs. Negroes steal chickens, hungry men hold up small groceries (sometimes, according to press reports, even apologizing to the owner for taking the $30 from his till), and boys rob coal sheds. To people of this sort the possibility of having squad cars concentrated upon an isolated spot in five minutes by telephone probably represents a genuine deterrent.

Under pressure from both sides—fear of a "crime wave" on the one hand, and, on the other, an enhanced sense of the straits in which the unemployed have found themselves in the depression—the judicial machinery in Middletown has wavered. Sentences have tended to be heavy; for instance, a ten-year sentence was given to an unemployed youngster for holding up a grocery for $75, and one to ten years to two Negroes for stealing forty chickens.[34] But this tendency to "put down crime" by heavy sentences has been offset occasionally by judicial waverings in the other direction. Thus we see the judge in one case sentencing an unemployed father of six children to a $20 fine and thirty days in jail for stealing coal in midwinter, and then stepping out of character to express to the court his regret that the sentence had to be imposed. As the State institutions became more and more crowded during the depression and taxpayers more clamorous over costs, the local judge of the Juvenile Court hit upon the plan of taking juvenile offenders on a threat tour of the reformatory and then turning them loose on probation. The press announced that the judge had "saved $11,000 of taxpayers' money on thirty-one such cases by this procedure in 1931." If judges in adult cases have, in the main, tended to press home high sentences, they have apparently done this in the face of some increase in resistance on the part of the common folk who compose juries, for a prosecuting attorney protested to a civic

[34] While the research staff was in Middletown the press carried a prominent story from another county in the state on the sentencing of two boys, aged fourteen and seventeen, to ninety-nine years each for handcuffing with his own handcuffs a sheriff who had just arrested them for stealing an automobile. A bit of grim hilarity ensued a few days later when the State prison refused to admit them because of their tender age, and the State reform school likewise refused on the legal ground that it could not receive boys with ninety-nine-year sentences. The sentence had subsequently to be reduced.

club during the depression that jurors were getting more apathetic about "doing their duty, and law enforcement is thereby rendered harder."

In this whole matter of crime and its treatment Middletown is today, as in 1925,[35] working with an equipment of institutions encased in a rigid legal and ideological framework generated by sentiments of right and wrong that have tended to be all blacks and whites. The city still states its crime problem negatively as a thing to be kept down and checkmated. And the close connection between the handling of crime and the prevailing political system operates as a heavy check against any tendency to re-view crime in its relation to factors wider than the waywardness of the individual.

Through such a jungle of equities and connivings, public pledges and private deals, Middletown does its civic work, with "good will," "civic spirit," "private gain," and "we're not as crooked as they are" claims and charges inextricably intermixed. Middletown businessmen who seek to lessen the wastes of the civic administrative system believe themselves to be working for the public good, and those who seek to break the grip of the North Side on local affairs believe just as sincerely that they are trying to save the mass of the city's population from exploitation. If much of the roast pig is lost in the burning down of the house or if an undue share of the carcass goes to the politicians and their allies, this is regarded as simply inevitable and in the nature of things.

Valuable chunks of the pig may even become diverted from the mass of ordinary citizens who represent that vague concept "the public interest" to one or another of the extra-ordinary citizens who happen by accident or design to stand in with local officialdom, as suggested by such incidents as the following. An "ordinary" citizen in Middletown considered buying a home on a dusty unimproved street outside the city limits on the western edge of town, and he asked the officials in charge whether it was planned to surface the street. The reply was that no information of that sort could be given out in advance, whereupon he dropped the matter. "Within six weeks," he reports, "an agent of the X's bought that house and others near by and the government began to surface the street," over the possibly

[35] See *Middletown*, pp. 427-34.

captious protests of taxpayers in other parts of town that "it was a real-estate deal of the millionaires." In the Westwood real-estate development the streets were paved by the city under an agreement, according to the editor who was then mayor, whereby the cost would be repaid by direct assessment on adjoining property. After the work was completed the assessments were never collected, and subsequently, he alleged, the city taxpayers paid the bill.

The same ambiguous relationship between the private citizen and his government appears in the sudden increase of the city police force in 1935 from the usual thirty-nine to upwards of sixty, despite the greater mobility of the force afforded by radio cars.[36] In Chapter II is reported the alleged pledge of the city administration to local industry in 1935 that "There will be no labor trouble in [Middletown]." This assurance synchronized with the removal of the Toledo General Motors plant to Middletown, following the Toledo strike in the spring of 1935. It also synchronized with the 50 per cent increase in Middletown policemen. To Middletown taxpayers, particularly to the working class, confronted by a request to increase the police department's budget from $83,255 to $124,182, again to quote from a local editorial, "You've got to know a lot of politics even to begin to figure out what it all means."

All these things irk Middletown, as the following press comments show:

[Middletown] is receiving the kind of advertising she does not appreciate. Yet we cannot say we do not deserve it. Whatever may be wrong in this community where so much also is right lies squarely and bawlingly on the doorstep of the voters. (*October, 1932.*)

NO COMMUNITY COURAGE HERE

One great trouble with the [Middletown] civic situation . . . is that the average [Middletown] citizen does not have the common ordinary courage that would make a better situation out of an almost intolerable one. . . . (*October, 1932.*)

[36] A State law seeks to protect local taxpayers by limiting the permissible size of the notoriously politically controlled city police forces in the state to one policeman for every 1,000 of the population. This would place Middletown's maximum at forty-seven, and as late as 1934 the city had only thirty-nine policemen. This State-fixed ratio was set before the advent of squad cars, and, according to a local press statement, "Most cities estimate a squad car as equal to 13 to 14 foot policemen."

The city council, as it is constituted in [Middletown], nearly always is a feeble thing. It is tottery and weak. Usually a few quite worth-while men are named, but they are in a painful minority. But we should remember that such a situation is indicative of the mental state of the voters. The situation of the council and mayor ordinarily would be laughable if it were not so tragic. (*January, 1933.*)

[Middletown] citizens [are] pretty badly discouraged by three years of fighting and brawling in the city administration and by the community's failure to accomplish the things that it should have accomplished. . . . (*January, 1933.*)

The average taxpayer when this subject [of taxes] is mentioned wears an air of complete defeatism. He has been robbed all his life by those in public office and he fears he always will be and that there is nothing to do about it, although there is plenty he could do if he would cease sobbing and get into action. This average taxpayer looks down his nose when he should be looking through the tax spenders' heads to see the greed that's in them; he holds up his hands in lamentation when he should be doubling up his fists to deal stout blows; he bellows after he has been robbed but doesn't even whisper while the robbery is going on. (*September, 1935.*)

Occasionally Middletown thinks down below this continuous splutter of protest and asks why it should be run by councilmen paid $250 a year, a mayor paid $3,400, a controller paid $2,400, a treasurer paid $720, a city attorney paid $2,100, a street commissioner paid $1,800, and whether such things as these are related to the prevalence of local graft: [37]

The cheapest investment Middletown could make right now would be in a mayor worth $20,000 to $25,000 a year and who would be paid that sum. (*February, 1933.*)

The law as it now stands permits [Middletown] to pay its mayor a salary of little more than $3,000 to run its $60,000,000 corporate business. That leaves the community only with the vague hope that somebody who is capable of carrying on the city's affairs in a businesslike manner could be induced, from patriotic motives, to sacrifice himself for a job and then run the chance of being defeated. And "sacrifice" is the right word. One capable of handling this situation would have to subject himself to mud slinging, vilification, and misrepresentation by opponents. . . . The people of [Mid-

[37] See *Middletown*, p. 421.

dletown] appear to be pretty tired of what has been going on here. (*February, 1933.*)

WHO WILL MAKE THE SACRIFICE?

The incessant question that is put up by interested persons when the subject of intolerable civic conditions is brought up is, "Who is going to do anything about it?" And that is wholly puzzling. There never seems to be anything like a concentrated source of authority in behalf of the public. There is nobody working at the job of looking after the people's interests. Thus we know that we should elect a competent mayor of [Middletown] and an intelligent city council, but who, exactly, is going to work unselfishly at the job of nominating and finally electing men of that kind this year. One who wishes to be mayor will step out and spend his time and money to bring about his nomination and election, but there is no people's lobby to defeat him if he happens to be the wrong sort. One who wishes to be mayor of [Middletown] should not be made mayor. But who is to prevent him from being nominated and elected? . . . Men who are competent cannot afford to take the job, as a rule. (*February, 1933.*)

In its political life Middletown swings round and round in a vicious circle. Its stereotypes regarding official integrity as well as official remuneration were laid down in an era when being a "public servant" carried far more prestige than it does today. In the simpler sort of community for which American political institutions and ideas of public service were devised, the gap between the remuneration of a mayor or judge and that of the businessman and corporation lawyer usually tended to be far narrower than it is today, and prestige was not rooted so exclusively in money. Today, the rewards of enterprise in business have increased far beyond those of the honest public servant. This has operated to sift a different type of man into municipal office— in Middletown the business hanger-on. Obviously, as the citizen taxpayer goes through Middletown's city hall and sees these officials "at work" with their feet on their desks, the latter strike him as paid about what they are worth. And in an institutional world in which the drive of the taxpayer is to keep costs down, and in which it is a basic part of the code that "Nobody pays more for a thing than it is worth," it does not seem justifiable to raise municipal salaries. And so the self-perpetuating system swings helplessly around in its deeply-worn ruts.

Writ large throughout the chapter in the 1925 study on "The Machinery of Government" was the pervading sense that local politics is losing its gusto to Middletown. One got a sense of the smaller city of the 1880's as having been confronted with fewer distracting choices, of its having lived a more neighborly life at a slower tempo, with the business of the city a thing which one belonged to and which belonged to one, a matter of personal comprehension and more active personal discussion and participation. Perhaps this romanticizes what citizenship felt like to the citizen of Middletown in the 1880's. But certainly there can be no doubt about the pervading popular attitude today: apathy, alternating with indignant frustration. Schooled in the tradition that citizenship is a duty and that people get the kind of government they want if they only want it enough; confronted by the obligation to assume through the ballot responsibility for matters increasingly large and complicated and about the technical details of which he knows less and less; with the disparity between management personnel in business and in government becoming constantly more obvious; with a sense of civic obligation constantly frustrated by the tawdriness of this close-up view of democratic institutions in action in a capitalist culture and by the sense of the impotence of the individual voter— with these divergent pullings and haulings within his skin, the hard-beset citizen tends to turn his back on the local political mess. And he salves his tension over the resulting split within his personality over his role as citizen by occasional bursts of irritated voting *against* things and persons.

Middletown is today immune to the small cultural shocks of chronic graft and inefficiency in its public offices. Nothing short of a major breakdown is likely to amplify the steady "knock" in its municipal engine to proportions likely to prompt its citizens to "do something about it." Its citizens are, after all, primarily concerned with getting a good living, and only very incidentally and instrumentally as occasion arises concerned with citizenship. The relief problems of the depression, along with the example of Federal planning, may have come close to providing shock and stimulus sufficient to instigate fresh scrutiny of the city's machinery of government. But the frantic resistance of local business leaders to administrative innovation in Washington under the New Deal has carried over to the local scene as a wet blanket over any proposal to change the "fundamentals of the American system of local government." And the uproar over the efforts to "get" the independent mayor served further to divert attention from fundamental changes, by forcing attention to a personalized devil and away from the conflicts within the institutions themselves.

Early in the depression, as noted in Chapter IV, relief had been a pork barrel on which some politicians and their friends and relatives throve. A citizens' committee appointed by the business leaders had developed the commissary plan—not without its business benefits to certain firms "in the hands of the bankers"—and forced a considerable degree of coordination between tax relief and the professional staff of the Social Service Bureau. This enforced control over relief never ceased to irk the politicians. The mayor elected in the fall of 1934 capitalized as a vote-catching device on the South Side the complaints of the poor against the commissary, and pledged himself to do everything in his power to abolish it and turn relief back to orders upon private groceries. Whether this represented merely the common local practice of "making different campaign promises uptown and downtown" is not known. But it is significant that a man, reputed to be "honest," refused in January, 1935, to assume the office of township trustee after a post-election clash over the commissary with the mayor and the other members of his official family. He gave no reason save his disinclination "to take over an office and have a continuous wrangle with outsiders over how to run it." An editorial stated in connection with this action on his part that "The law governing the distribution of poor relief by the trustee is very plain and sets forth how he can be removed from office for his failure to cooperate." A local politician stated unequivocally to the investigator that the man in question would not take office because he feared he would be "framed by the politicians." One can read various interpretations into this situation. It may represent an honest difference in official opinion as to the worth of the commissary, as noted in the discussion of the abandonment of the commissary in Chapter IV. In 1936 direct relief returned entirely to the township trustee, and the Social Service Bureau withdrew its professional supervision. The net result is that politics appears to have returned in Middletown to "business as usual."

But if Middletown is apathetic about its local politics, it still rises magnificently to the quadrennial symbolism of national elections. Here, in the more remote field of national public affairs, the irritating discrepancies in, and the fly-specked condition of, political "democracy." "the will of the people," "the supremacy of the American two-party system," and "public service" fade; and the banners of citizenship retain much of their original glamor.[38] These symbols stiffen one's latent Republican or Democratic biases into sources of personal emotional conviction and consequent support to one's divided civic personality. Every fourth year comes this cleansing opportunity to shake off the mundane aspects of citizenship, to join in the affirmation of a great faith, and to merge oneself in the crusade for a world to be saved.

A significant insight into the political temper of Middletown, as well as a suggestion of the kind of stuff with which any third-party movement has to reckon in American life, is gained from the national presidential vote in Middletown's county shown in Table 46.[39] Here one sees the almost complete grip of the two-party system on the imagination of these midland folk. In 1924, 95.4 per cent of the votes were for the Republican and Democratic candidates, 3.3 per cent for La Follette, and only 1.3 per cent for all other candidates; in 1928, 99.5 per cent were for the two old parties; in 1932, 98.1 per cent; and in 1936, 99.2 per cent. There almost literally are no other parties, as shown by the very thin scattering of these minority votes, though it is impossible to know how much tampering with the votes for minority parties occurs in the course of counting the ballots. This last is undoubtedly an insignificant factor in the total, and the heavy concentration on the old familiar parties affords eloquent testimony to the repugnance to innovations in areas involving old allegiances that is so markedly characteristic of Middletown's life. The fact that even the working-class precincts exhibit this same pattern of resistance to political aberrations is consistent with both the conservative, small-farm background of many of these people and with their general apathy toward labor organization and radicalism noted in Chapters II and XII. It is indicative of this last that the state A. F. of L., meeting in Middletown in September, 1935, voted down a resolution endorsing the formation of a labor party by twenty to one. Radical parties are strongly disliked by this culture, as the votes indicate. A veteran labor man, one of the few radicals in Middletown, commented, "A few of

[38] The word "government" carries an honorable connotation to Middletown, while the word "politics" has a strong flavor of chicanery associated with it. Middletown tends to assimilate the honorable qualities of "government" to the national scene and to bestow the negative connotations of "politics" upon its local administrations.

[39] See Appendix III for this table. The population of Middletown comprised in 1930 69 per cent of the population of the county.

us are socialists. Even if we wanted to, as very few do, we would not be communists, because the Communist Party can't be on the state ticket, the trade unionists have no use for it, and you can't get over a lot of other things for labor if you brand yourself as too radical."

The closing of the jaws of public opinion upon radical political parties appears in the passing by the State Legislature of the following act, approved on March 15, 1935:

An act concerning political parties and prohibiting certain political parties from appearing on or having the names of their candidates printed on the ballot used at elections.

SECTION 1. BE IT ENACTED BY THE GENERAL ASSEMBLY OF THE STATE, That no political party shall be recognized and given a place on or have the names of its candidates printed on the ballot used at any election which advocates the overthrow, by force or violence, of the local, state or national government, or which advocates, or carries on, a program of sedition or of treason, by radio, speech or press. Any party which is in existence at the time of the passage of this act, or which shall have had a ticket on the ballot one or more times prior to any election, and which does not advocate any of the doctrines the advocacy of which is prohibited by this act, shall insert a plank in its platform that it does not advocate any of the doctrines prohibited by this act. No newly organized political party shall be permitted on or to have the names of its candidates printed on the ballot used at any election until it has filed an affidavit, by its officers, under oath, that it does not advocate the overthrow of local, state or national government by force or violence, and that it is not affiliated in any way with any political party or organization, or subdivision of any organization, which does advocate such a policy by radio, speech or press. The affidavit herein provided for shall be filed with the board of election commissioners of the state or the county or city or town having charge of the printing of the ballot on which such ticket is to appear. The board of election commissioners with which such affidavit is filed shall make such investigations as it may deem necessary to determine the character and nature of the political doctrines of such proposed new party, and if the board is of the opinion that such proposed new party advocates doctrines which are in violation of the provisions of this act, or is affiliated in any way with any political party which advocates such doctrines the board shall not permit such ticket on the ballot.

A member of the State Board of Election Commissioners commented as follows on this act, in a letter to the writers under date of July 29, 1936:

"I presume that it was thought that this Act would prevent the Communist Party from qualifying.

"However, you will notice that if an existing political party states in its platform that it does not advocate any doctrine prohibited by the Act, or if a new political party submits an affidavit of its officers that it does not advocate any such doctrine, it may be entitled to a place upon the ballot. There is no provision by which a party which was in existence at the time of the passage of this Act can be kept off the ballot if it adopts the above required statements in its platform. There is a provision that as to a new political party, even if it submits affidavits of its officers, yet the Board of Election Commissioners after investigation may deny the new party a place on the ballot, if the Board is of the opinion that it does advocate the prohibited doctrines.

"Since the Communist party was in existence at the time of the adoption of this Act, it would seem that it would be entitled to a place upon the ballot if it inserts the required plank in its platform.

"I have no knowledge as to whether such party either has, or proposes to adopt, such a plank."

Business-class Middletown fears any tendency on the part of labor to enter politics, either by massing its vote behind a single one of the older parties or by putting forward a new party. During the summer and fall of 1936, the labor majority in Middletown's population was constantly encouraged to split itself up among *all* the parties, with no central political philosophy as a class. When, in August, 1936, the Central Labor Union planned to invite in a prominent Roosevelt backer to deliver its Labor Day address, businessmen viewed this with apprehension. A local editorial argued with labor, in terms of its own welfare, as follows:

The [Middletown] Central Labor Union, formerly the [Middletown] Trades Council, always, until now, has prided itself upon keeping out of politics, but apparently it would have as a speaker here, Labor Day, somebody prominent in the Roosevelt-for-President Club—whatever that is. Union labor has advanced itself to its present position by abjuring partisan politics. That has been especially true in [Middletown]. Does it now wish to alienate many of its former friends by dabbling into it? A strip that is easily torn is harder to mend. . . . It looks like local union laborites are being misdirected, but union men here who have the best interests of the cause of unionism at heart would better step their feet upon some of their aspiring leaders with political proclivities, who may prove to be, on close analysis, really job hunters. . . . The advance to better conditions union labor has made has been by using ALL political parties to their advantage, not by endorsing any one of them.

No precinct within the city of Middletown returned more than 4 per cent of its total votes for Norman Thomas, the Socialist presidential candidate, in 1932, although the highest La Follette vote in any precinct in 1924 climbed to 12 per cent. In 1936 no precinct returned more than nine-tenths of one per cent of its vote for the Socialist and Communist presidential candidates combined; and the precinct showing the largest relative vote for the Union candidate (Lemke) returned less than 2 per cent of its total vote for that candidate. The ingrained Republicanism of Middletown in its national vote, in contrast to its frequently Democratic municipal vote, is reflected in the facts that only two out of the city's thirty precincts went Democratic in their votes for president in 1924; one out of the thirty-two precincts in 1928; and only 13 out of the thirty-two in 1932. Immediately prior to the 1936 election local Republicans were reassuring themselves by recalling that their county has "always been rock-ribbed Republican and it was the only one of the ninety-two counties in the state to go all the way Republican in the Democratic landslide year, 1932." In the 1936 election, despite this record, Middletown's county returned a 57.3 per cent majority for Roosevelt, and Middletown itself 59.1, and twenty-five of the city's thirty-two precincts went Democratic.

If one attempts a rough classification of Middletown's thirty-two precincts by whether they are business-class or working-class neighborhoods, the city's presidential vote in 1936 breaks up as follows:

Type of neighborhood	No. of precincts	Total no. of votes	Per cent of total Roosevelt-Landon votes for Roosevelt	No. of votes for candidate of		
				Union Party	Socialist Party	Communist Party
Working class	14	9,186	68.8	41	16	4
Largely working class but mixed	4	3,188	65.0	20	5	2
Negro [40]	3	1,953	63.4	14	3	0
Largely business class but mixed	5	3,483	52.8	21	13	1
Business class	9	6,960	46.8	54	17	3
Total	32	22,817		136	51	10

[40] Negro precincts fall in the "Largely working class but mixed" group. They are here shown separately to indicate how Middletown's Negroes voted.

The cleft between business class and working class in their votes for the two major candidates here stands out clearly. The size of the Roosevelt vote even in the business-class neighborhoods suggests, however, an important check on the tendency to speak of the business class as though its members think and act alike on important matters. The following appraisal by a responsible local newspaperman throws further light on the nature of this division among Middletown's business class:

"Big business, of course, was solidly for Landon, but there were many small businessmen for Roosevelt. [A local Democratic city official] thinks small businessmen were 50-50. I think there was a substantial majority for Landon. However, I know of several merchants who were Roosevelt men. Many people in that classification were strong for the Republican state candidates, but favored Roosevelt. The luncheon-club personnel I have encountered at their meetings were almost solidly rabid Republicans, except schoolteachers."

The line of division between the city's big-business industrialists and the merchants and small businessmen corroborates the point made in Chapter XII regarding class lines within Middletown's population.

In the 1924 campaign the press—and then as now "the press" meant the two militantly Republican papers, as there is no other in town save the small Democratic weekly—applied the thumbscrews directly to Middletown in terms of the voter's job and family safety: "A vote for Coolidge is merely a vote for your own safety. You will vote tomorrow for or against your job." [41] In 1932 the same pressure was ground home repeatedly by such statements as the following from a front-page editorial:

A vote for President Hoover is a vote to retain your job if you have one and for getting a job if you haven't; it is a vote to retain your business if you have one; it is a vote for an opportunity to keep your home or farm if it is in financial distress. . . . Does any employee of the [two leading factories] imagine he could possibly have a job there or that these two factories could operate, except that their workers would have to submit to a wage of a few cents a day, unless [Hoover's high tariff policy is continued]?

The 1936 election witnessed perhaps the strongest effort in the city's history by the local big businessmen (industrialists and bankers) to stampede local opinion in behalf of a single presidential candidate.

[41] See *Middletown*, p. 416.

These men own Middletown's jobs and they largely own Middletown's press; and they made use of both sources of pressure—though not to the point of excluding summaries of President Roosevelt's speeches from the latter. The one important channel of communication which they could not control was the national radio networks, which brought "the other side" before local voters, notably in President Roosevelt's own speeches.[42] The pressure in the factories is reported to have been heavy and direct, as suggested by the following post-election communication from a reliable and informed source:

"Local factories tried to exert a lot of pressure on their employees—so much so that in some cases they overreached themselves and succeeded in rousing the ire of many men and creating additional Democratic votes. The X glass plant practically forced employees to wear Landon buttons. The men wore the buttons at the factory, took them off outside the plant, and voted for Roosevelt. I know two of these workers who became so infuriated that they changed their allegiance even from Roosevelt and voted for more radical candidates.

"The worst offender probably was the local General Motors transmission plant. ——, the head of the plant, skated close to violating the law. He carried the campaign openly into the shop and was later reprimanded by his superiors for going too far.

" 'Landon and higher wages' was the theme of the attack, with the Social Security Act as the principal weapon.[43] Much literature was dis-

[42] With both local papers heavily Republican, the customarily "rock-ribbed Republican" vote of Middletown in presidential elections is the more understandable. Without minimizing in any respect the landslide nature of the 1936 election and the presence of economic issues antedating the tightening of local newspaper pressure on the voters in the summer and fall of 1936, it is interesting to speculate on what Roosevelt's 59.1 per cent majority might have been had not the radio channel been kept open to local voters.

See in this connection n. 5 in Ch. X.
[43] Following is the slip inserted in the pay envelopes of local factory workers regarding the Social Security Act:

"To Answer Questions Which Have Been Asked In Connection With Federal and State Taxes On Payrolls, Here Are Some of the Facts:

"A Federal law taxing payrolls was approved by the President on August 14, 1935, and a State law taxing them was approved by the Governor on March 18, 1936. Under these laws this Company has paid a tax on every check you have received since last March.

"Beginning next January the Company will be required by these laws to deduct for taxes approximately 2 per cent (1.9 per cent) from all pay checks. If these laws remain unchanged the amount that must be deducted from your pay check will reach approximately 4 per cent during the next few years. Under

tributed through the factories, stressing deductions from pay under the Act. There was no mention of any benefits ever to accrue to the worker, and there was much talk of the probable folding up of the scheme with loss of money to everyone and of its effects in making pay rises impossible. Apparently many of our workers decided that if the industrialists were so set against the program it must be a bad thing for employers and a good thing for employees—and voted accordingly.

"There are a lot of bewildered business and industrial faces around here. The industrialists, while stepping up production and (some of them) raising wages, are predicting freely a bad crash in the not distant future."

In the press the early campaign appeals were the ones familiar in previous elections, stressing the identity of Republican administrations, high tariffs, and prosperity:

The important thing about this election is to vote against inflation, against having a $30 a week salary with a buying power of $10.

JOBS ARE THE MAIN ISSUE!

Of course a 12-year-old child knows that you can't give jobs to Americans by giving them to foreigners, as we are now doing under the bland beneficence of Mr. Roosevelt's reciprocal trade treaties. . . . We are "selling out" our workingmen, our farmers, our manufacturers.

There was much talk of "Landon, the careful Kansan." [44] Daniel Webster was quoted in his appeal: "Let us then stand by the Constitution as it is, and by our country as it is." The "courage and patriotism" of Al Smith, who was anathema to Middletown in 1928, was praised in connection with his denunciation of Roosevelt and the New Dealers as persons who welcome "even a Communist with wire whiskers and a torch in his hand": "But Al Smith could not be for Roosevelt and for America at the same time, so he chose America. A man cannot ride two horses going in opposite directions at once."

When the social-security issue was injected into the campaign, the press dotted its pages with emphatic capitals:

Remember, too, that this so-called "social security law," unless it is amended or repealed, does not make it certain what you will get, if any-

---

these same laws this Company must also pay additional taxes on all money that it spends for payrolls, and these additional taxes will amount to approximately 6 per cent of the money spent for payrolls in the next few years."

[44] See the discussion in n. 22 of Ch. XII of the adroitness with which these appeals for Landon were couched in terms dear to the middle-of-the-road mood of Middletown.

thing, in return for what you pay, although if you live long enough you MAY get something.

You can only be sure that YOU WILL HAVE TO BEGIN PAYING THIS TAX, AMOUNTING TO A SUBSTANTIAL REDUCTION IN YOUR WAGES OR SALARY BE-GINNING NEXT JANUARY 1, AND THAT THE PAYROLL TAX FOR THE SAME PUR-POSE LEVIED UPON YOUR EMPLOYER IS LIKELY TO PREVENT HIS RAISING YOUR INCOME, THUS LEAVING YOU IN A FINANCIAL RUT FOR A LONG TIME TO COME.

When you receive your pay check after January 1 and note that one per cent has been deducted without any assurance that you will EVER GET ANY OF IT BACK, and that the same thing will happen to you every pay day . . . you may not be exactly happy but, cheer up—it soon will be worse. By 1949 your contribution will be three per cent of your salary or wages.

And remember, NO TAX COLLECTOR WILL VISIT YOU TO GET THIS MONEY. IT IS REQUIRED BY LAW THAT YOUR EMPLOYER TAKE IT OUT OF YOUR PAY ENVELOPE AND TURN IT OVER TO THE TAX COLLECTOR.

SWELL CHANCE YOU HAVE OF EVER GETTING A "RAISE" IN YOUR PAY WITH YOUR EMPLOYER'S BEING THUS "SOAKED" BY THIS NEW TAX. . . .

YOU WILL RECEIVE NO RELIEF FROM THIS BURDEN IF ROOSEVELT IS RE-ELECTED.

GOVERNOR LANDON HAS PROMISED TO GIVE RELIEF IF HE IS ELECTED.

The damping down almost to extinction of this flaming party ardor as one turns from national politics to Middletown's election of its own local officials is a social phenomenon that will bear watching. As a local press editorial observes, "Middletown people are Republican or Demo-cratic nationally, but party ties bind them loosely, when at all, in local affairs." Not only does this represent a change from the Middletown of the 1880's, when a man who was a Republican or a Democrat nationally tended to stand staunchly by the same party locally, but it also probably suggests the presence of a profound social change in process in the meaning of political symbols to Middletown.[45]

As one comes downward from national politics through state politics

[45] An editorial comment on election afternoon in 1936 notes both this long-term trend toward the dulling of the personal urgency of election issues and also the unusual degree of local tension that characterized the 1936 election in Middle-town:

"Who remembers when on the night before election there was a series of fights around the courthouse square that kept the policemen busy? And election days when in certain precincts it was a foregone conclusion there would be fist fights if not more serious altercations? Mostly the partisans take it out in verbal argument, nowadays, but feeling is so tense there is more of a chance for diffi-culty today than at any election time recently."

to local politics, the honorific, emotionally weighted symbols become dimmer and fewer, one votes less as a burning patriot and more as a person performing a necessary but rather dull routine responsibility. Platforms become even vaguer, and the same paper quoted above as clamoring in November, 1932, that grass would grow in the streets if the Republican party was not elected had commented calmly after the conventions in June, 1932, that "The chief difference between the Republican and Democratic state platforms this year is that the Democratic one is briefer"; and in June, 1934, before the local mayoralty election, "Nobody would know from observation that a city campaign presumably is on in Middletown. Almost nobody talks politics and probably that situation will continue until cooler weather begins."

So far has this blurring of party significance in local issues gone that today, as in 1924,[46] some of the business leaders in town—numbering among them many of the very men who stress hardest party differences in national politics and who oppose impersonal "planning" so bitterly in Washington—favor the obliteration of party lines in local government and the substitution of a city manager. "The truth is," commented a recent editorial characteristic of this point of view, "that political parties have come to mean little of late years in local elections. . . . [Middletown] is strongly Republican in national affairs, but five times in comparatively recent years she has elected Democratic mayors." The editorial went on to note the similarity between efficient administration in business and in government and pointed out that the city-manager system means simply that one manages a municipality with the same absence of irrelevant tomtom beating that exists in a well-run business.[47] In the fall of 1936 this same editor stated roundly:

I'd like to have the chance, just once before I die, of voting for somebody to take charge of public business in the city who would be named not because he was a Democrat or a Republican, but because he knew how to run the city in a business-like way.

[46] See *Middletown*, p. 427.
[47] From the point of view of the strategy of social change one wonders whether the advocates of planning and administrative efficiency in national administration might do well to put relatively more of their weight behind the growth of the city-manager system in the small and medium-sized cities of the country; for, if Middletown's experience is characteristic, it is here that the encrusted political symbols appear to be disintegrating fastest and that some willingness to take a matter-of-fact, unemotional attitude toward governmental administration appears most clearly.

There is at least a possibility that by the time another city campaign rolls around, a commission-manager form of government may be authorized. . . . In 1921 [Middletown] had the chance to adopt such a system. At that time I was bitterly opposed to it and personally campaigned all over town, in the company of both Democratic and Republican politicians, against it. We wanted the federal system of government to continue in the cities. We won by a ratio of something like two to one. And I have had to apologize since for my attitude. If that question should ever come up again I'd be found standing rigidly with those who believe politics should have nothing to do with the conduct of our local affairs.

A key to the understanding of this contrasting intensity of Middletown's adherence to party symbols in national politics and relative disregard of them in local politics may lie in the following: Political parties have become associated nationally with the *earning* of people's living—hence the clamor about "voting to safeguard your job," and the idea in the heads of many Middletown businessmen concerning the "unsoundness" of the Democratic party; whereas local politics have traditionally concerned only the *spending* of income, and, at that, only of that small fraction of one's income that goes into taxes.[48] The typical central issue in Middletown's local campaigns is not "assuring the continuance of prosperity" but "economy," "keeping taxes down." In an economy which has inherited its system of ideas from a pre-industrial-revolution world of "scarcity," and which today still sees its welfare as dependent only upon the productive side of its economic equation, it is natural that national politics should thus center around questions of the significance of parties and candidates for one's ability to *earn* dollars. And it is likewise natural that, with such crucial things as "tariffs" and "prosperity" lying outside the sphere of influence of Middletown's mayor and councilmen, theirs should be the lesser task of helping the taxpayer to *save* pennies.

[48] It is difficult to overstress the power of the popular stereotype as to what the "tax rate" "should" be in the local voter's mind. Local taxes are compact and aggregated into a single annual figure. The taxpayer tends to think not of positive things for his local government to do, but rather to feel that the important thing is to hold the rate down. The fact that it is a *rate* and not a total budget disguises shifts in the latter as assessed valuations change. The rate is the crucial thing to him. Middletown feels that the combined local rate is "right" when it is under $3.00 and protests loudly when it goes above that. For years the rate has run mainly between $2.50 and $3.00: 1890, $2.86; 1900, $2.62; 1910, $3.34; 1920, $2.22; 1921, $2.66; 1922, $2.70; 1923, $2.70; 1924, $2.66; 1925, $2.58; 1926, $2.42; 1927, $2.60; 1928, $2.68; 1929, $2.94; 1930, $2.94; 1931, $2.72; 1932, $3.07; 1933, $3.39; 1934, $3.10.

But, a countertrend may be in process locally: As noted in Chapter II, the depression has accentuated Middletown's already strong sense of its dependence upon its industries, and, more important still, has crystallized a strong conviction among Middletown's business class that the city must act as a unit to maintain such competitive industrial advantage as it can over other centers of production. The first fruits of this are the mayor's public announcement in 1935 that "There will be no labor trouble here," the assurance to General Motors of open-shop conditions, and the increase in the police force to safeguard what amounts to a municipal open-shop policy. Such things have been long familiar in company-owned towns in the steel-production districts, but in this openly avowed form they are somewhat new to Middletown.[49] Though Middletown's voters are not generally aware of this closer new alignment of the local municipal administration behind the maintenance of productive interests in the community, such policies bid fair in time to restore a positive quality to fading local political symbols.

The New Deal phase of the depression commencing in 1933 has at least opened the way to incipient change that may hold seeds of the future. In a culture habitually more than 95 per cent Republican and Democratic, the basic attitudes of citizens toward the national government do not tend to reveal strong cleavages along class lines. But the more active role of the Federal government since 1933, coupled with the fact that some resulting legislation has been of benefit to workers, has introduced a potential line of division in outlook upon Washington that may become significant, if indeed it has not already become so in the results of the 1936 election. Middletown's business class feels bitterly that the Federal government has ceased to play *for*

[49] A somewhat similar economic determination of politics exists today in acute form in Middletown's state. The southern part of the state has become in recent years an increasing economic burden. There has been some discussion of taking over large areas of its meager marginal farm land as state forests in order to save the costs of schools and other services to a sparse and often backward population. In contrast, the northern part of the state has within a generation come to contain, in addition to many other industrial cities, a city that is today the country's largest steel center. The state, like Middletown, has, therefore, an increasingly large and obvious financial stake in keeping its political administration behind its source of income. As this is written (1936), a dispatch from Washington states that Middletown's state's governor is "a sincere labor hater" and that this state and Alabama stand together in "the undoubted hostility of the [state] administration" to the drive of the Committee for Industrial Organization to organize the steel workers.

"us" and is playing *against* "us." There is the disappointment and resentment of insiders in a profitable and comfortable venture suddenly deprived of the margin of advantage so long occupied as to have come to appear "normal and just." Their natural reaction is to seek to "turn out the government" and to restore the *status quo ante* in Washington. On the other hand, conversations with Middletown's workers in June, 1935, indicated that events in Washington following March, 1933, have kindled the first faint awareness among some of them that a "government," instead of being simply a miscellaneous ally of everybody in general, may actually be able to do things *for* "us," even if need be *against* "them." There are plenty of indications of working-class disappointment and disgust over such things as the collapse of collective bargaining under N.R.A.; but, nevertheless, the initiative in providing relief and some measure of social security in chronically exposed areas of working-class life is coming in tangible form from Washington; and some of Middletown's workers are contrasting such concrete facts with the clamor of local business leaders that such Federal spending cease. In this situation, the sprawled inertness of Middletown working-class opinion—as over against the more vocal and coherent opinion of the business class—may conceivably take shape slowly in a self-conscious sharpening of class lines. But neither class morale, sources of information, nor personal leadership for such a development is apparent at present among Middletown's working class. Much depends upon whether "good times" return in as beguiling a form as they wore in the 1920's. If they do, the deeper pattern of political loyalty to the old symbols, plus the willingness of these individual working-class atoms to dance to any tune that will give them an automobile and "show them a good time," will transform their momentary position in the political limelight under the New Deal and in the election of 1936 into only a vaguely remembered bench mark. For today, as in 1924, the Middletown voter is not a political self-starter, and Elihu Root's advice, widely heralded in Middletown at the time of the 1924 election, still applies: "All you have got to do is to wake them up, have someone take the head of the crowd and march them. Tell them where to go, whether Democrats or Republicans, I do not care . . . and the organizers . . . will welcome them and set them to work." [50]

[50] See *Middletown*, p. 426.

As was noted in connection with the spending of leisure, Middletown, like the rest of America, has paid little attention to the types of activity that thrive best under centralized and those that thrive best under diffused organization. The tradition that everything possible should be left to the initiative and diffused control of individuals is unequivocal. At certain points the culture has frozen the definition of the relative spheres of centralized and of more diffused authorities, as in the Federal Constitution. The dominant business section of the culture has likewise inherited a sacred tradition of "individual initiative," "free competition," and "the small businessman" which is officially braced strongly against all forms of centralization; though, under cover of this orthodoxy, there has for three generations been an increasing departure nationally in the direction of greater centralization in such matters as "trusts," "holding companies," "price fixing," "administered prices," and the other familiar accompaniments of centralized economic control. But, in general, Middletown accepts the fact that the individual does nearly everything for himself, while the city, State, and Federal governments care for only a scattering of commonplace things; and people in general do not stop to question this traditional allocation of functions, or whether it actually operates as it is theoretically supposed to operate.

Middletown businessmen look with apprehension upon the enlargement of the scope of Federal administrative powers since 1933. Their ingrained philosophy of government is that where things cannot be left to the individual citizen they should be cared for as isolated problems by local governmental units wherever possible. Otherwise "things will get out of hand." As over against Federal relief, Middletown urges, in the words of a local editorial, "Let's take care of our own." No good, these people feel, can come from a system that scrambles up jurisdictions and substitutes remote central administration for local responsibility. "Other people," so runs the argument, "can never spend our money as wisely and economically as we can." Thus, in the midst of the scramble for Federal funds, Middletown could look upon the money it managed to get from Washington as but a partial repayment for taxes drained from the state by a bloated and misguided Federal government. This point of view was expressed in the following editorial in 1936:

Think the good ole Federal gov'ment has been mighty liberal in its spending of money on [our state]? Then ponder how liberal [we people in this state] have been with the good ole gov'ment. Last year taxpayers of [this state] contributed more than $68,000,000 to the Federal funds and in return received less than $42,000,000. In other words our own taxpayers could have done for the state what the Federal government did and had $26,000,000 remaining in the state's "kitty." The money contributed by the citizens of [our state] to Washington was derived largely from individual income taxes, corporation taxes and taxes on beer and distilled spirits. The money returned was distributed among 22 kinds of projects.

It is for this reason it is important for any given community to "git while the gittin's good," and not because it necessarily approves all of the vast expenditures that are being made. If we are not permitted to spend all of our own money, then it appears necessary to grab as much of it as possible and let it go at that until such time as the spending orgy is officially ended.

The time is not so far past when some Middletown citizens who had no children protested their enforced payment of taxes to support expensive schools for other people's children. Today many local citizens are scandalized by the thought that the Federal government is using the money of Middletown people to do things for people in other communities, states, and remote corners of the nation. Local thought resists stubbornly the proposition that more and more problems are part of a widespread institutional system and may not be coped with successfully by the individual citizen or, at most, by the local community. Yet as Middletown has learned to grasp eagerly at outside funds as an aid in meeting its relief problem, it has unconsciously been breaching the psychological walls that mark off *its* life, *its* administrative boundaries, and *its* fiscal problems from those of the wider culture. In this respect the depression has involved a significant move in the direction of social change in this area of localism and individual competence.

At yet another point Middletown has been questioning the proper sphere of governmental activity. Since 1925, the issue of the public ownership of Middletown's local utilities has arisen on two occasions. Its outcome epitomizes some of the deeper biases of Middletown's culture, including the differential control by interested business and by "the public" over matters that lie in the limbo of "the public interest," and the panicky popular skepticism as regards anything run by Middletown's city government. The mayor who was swept into office in 1930 by a surprise victory had campaigned on a pledge of municipal ownership of local public utilities, but nothing came of this plank in his platform in the hurly-burly of the succeeding five years. Meanwhile, a small Public Ownership League, composed of socially and economically unimportant people and sponsored by a former Ku Klux Klan organizer, was formed and began to agitate for the public ownership of the water, gas, and electric plants. When the movement reached the point where popular support had resulted in the scheduling of a special vote on the issue in the spring of 1934, the local utilities opened fire. Large-space newspaper advertisements pounded away at the voters:

Do you know that it will cost the people over $10,000,000 to buy the utilities in [Middletown]?

The public utilities are [Middletown's] biggest single taxpayer. On election day vote "No" on the scheme to load the city with this huge debt.

107 employees anxious to serve you. We work, live, and spend our dollars in [Middletown]. Thirty of us own our homes here and we want to remain here. Our company is more than meters, mains, and boilers. It is human.

The local press, itself not without an obvious advertising stake in the continued private ownership of industries characterized by such liberal spending for "public relations," had epitomized Middletown's deep skepticism as regards the extension of public administration when it had repeatedly said:

The history of such things [as the municipal ownership of utilities] is that neither a city, state nor national government is able to operate a utility as economically as a private concern can do it, and the result when such attempts have been made almost invariably has been waste and added expense to the citizens. . . . It has been proved so many hundred times, too, that politics and public ownership of public utilities do not mix, that the very suggestion that a city go into this kind of business is frightening. Let the shoemaker stick to his last.

Most municipal experiments in the operation of public utilities have been failures and most of them will continue to be until public ownership and operation can be divorced from politics.[51]

[51] It is perhaps a commentary on the extent to which advertising pressure can influence the editorial point of view in the midst of an acute local campaign like this that the same editor who wrote these paragraphs wrote in the fall of 1936, after the 1934 campaign was no longer an acute issue, the following editorial

Looking backward down the years at some of the city administrations Middletown has had, a thinking person is inclined to hesitate before jumping body and boots into municipal ownership of public utilities. Politicians are congenitally unadapted to the management of important business, especially business of so highly technical a kind as that of the public utilities. As a rule they cannot even manage their own private business successfully. Now this is not an argument against the public ownership of utilities— merely a statement of the [Middletown] situation. If [Middletown] had the city management form of government . . . or, if [Middletown's] population were business-minded rather than political-minded, then public ownership would have a better chance of success than it would have under the present conditions.

To arguments such as these the Public Ownership League rejoined:

[Middletown] is surrounded by towns such as [naming fourteen near-by cities and towns], all told 188 towns and cities in [this state] that are operating THEIR OWN UTILITIES at a great PROFIT. A—— [a city twenty miles distant] has cleared more than $250,000 on their electric light plant for years, and averaged $68,000 clear each year on their water company. R—— [another city near by] clears about $300,000 each year. And all of these plants have lower rates than [Middletown] under private ownership.

About $600,000 per year, in profit, in our three utilities is sent to Chicago and New York to pay dividends on heavily watered stock and to pay unjust, unfair, and high salaries to officials not earning their money. How long will this continue? Just as long as WE PERMIT IT.

But a few days before the election the whole business was comfortably disposed of by a permanent injunction against the election, secured by the local utilities from the Superior Court, "on the theory," as summarized in the press, "that the electrical and gas companies here have vested rights in franchises that remove them from being subject to the municipal ownership law in [this state]." [52] And so well have the

note lauding the saving to taxpayers in an adjacent city of Middletown's size through municipal ownership of local utilities:

"[Middletown's] civil city tax rate for 1937, as proposed, is $1.05; that of A——, a city of comparable size, is 22 cents and of this 17 cents is for retirement of bonds and payment of interest. But for old indebtedness, A—— would be a taxless town in 1937, according to the *Bulletin* there. The city government of A—— has been operated without a general tax fund levy during the last four years. Reason? Profits from the municipal light and power plant."

[52] On the eve of the special election on the utilities question and prior to the granting of the injunction, the question was put to the editor of one of Middletown's dailies: "How does the town stand on the question?" He replied, "My

agencies of public opinion done their work and so strong is the stench of New Deal interference with private business in the nostrils of Middletown's leading businessmen, that most of the latter have greeted the saving action of the court as a relief from further possible political trouble.

For over all Middletown's sins of political omission and commission rests the comforting conviction: "But time will cure all things." "Whatsoever things are good" will all come in time, and meanwhile the "middle-of-the-road" policy is best. The outlook of a Spengler that anticipates "the decline of the west" is foreign to the mood of Christian, American Middletown. So Middletown jogs along in its civic affairs, riding uneasily with one foot on the back of each of the ill-gaited horses of Democratic Symbol and Urgent Reality. As an observer watches team and rider, questions inevitably arise as to how long the two horses will continue within leg-stretch of each other, how rapid the pace of change must become and how obvious the disparity needs be between symbols and reality before Middletown may cease to believe in inevitable progress—and what may happen then within the lives of these busy, hopeful people?

guess is the vote would be about half and half. Probably the advocates of municipal ownership would have won a month ago. But the companies have been handing out some powerful propaganda." (From "Middletown—Ten Years After," *Business Week*, June 2, 1934.)

CHAPTER X

Getting Information: The Press

"It seems to me the newspapers should have brought this [referring to a local civic problem brought before Middletown in a letter to the editor] up a long time ago, for after all that is the duty of the newspapers. . . . I would like to see someone start a campaign for absolute honesty and open dealing with problems. . . . I could ask questions all night to which I can get no answer and which should be cleared up. I think this is the job of the newspapers. It has to be done by someone not dependent on a job for a living." (*Communication in the "Letters to the Editor" column of Middletown's afternoon paper, 1933.*)

"Mr. ——, some day you may need money from my bank to carry on your business, and your credit is not so good that you can afford to tell me what to do about the Community Fund." (*Reported remark by a Middletown banker to a critic of his actions in connection with the Community Fund.*)

"USE OF NEWSPAPERS REFLECTS IN SALES

"One of the oldest users of newspaper advertising, SSS Tonic, continued to advertise in the newspapers during the depression, and their advertising manager reports that their faith was fully justified in that, with the turn in conditions, their 1934 sales to date show an immediate jump of 34 per cent and are still climbing. . . . The SSS formula has been in use for more than 100 years, and has been nationally advertised, almost exclusively, in newspapers for the past 68 years." (*News item in Middletown paper, 1934.*)

"The average voter does not know and he does not even suspect what is going on. That is pathetic, but it is true. [Then followed the statement that the press is helpless] because you can't get affidavits." (*Editorial comment on corruption in politics in Middletown's afternoon paper, 1933.*)

"The [Middletown morning paper] is still struggling against its mixed emotions. One minute it overcomes its artificial instinct to say everything is all right and busts loose with the truth, and then in its next subsides into docility. The [paper] has real newspaper writers of ability . . . if these men and women were given free rein to paint the picture as they see it.

But great interests own and control the [paper]." (*Editorial in the local Democratic weekly, 1935.*)

In these varying comments one gets the predicament of Middletown's press: obligated on one side by a tradition of a "free press" with the high obligation to report all the news, and by the community's traditional expectation of "fearless" leadership from it; confined on another side by the financial controls over Middletown and by its own dependence upon commercial advertising for the bulk of its financial support; bound on yet another side by the fact that, save for the struggling local weekly, its editors do not own their own papers but are hired men; and curbed finally by the omnipresent fear of libel in a culture that knows well the arts of using the courts to protect vested interests and reputations. Within the narrow quadrangle formed by these four high bounding walls Middletown's "press" must contrive to operate—which means to build its circulation and to get advertising.

One dropped back into reading the Middletown papers in 1935 with the sense of picking up a familiar story where one had left off. There is still the morning paper, belonging to a chain including a powerful paper in the state capital in which the X family owns an interest; the more independent afternoon paper; and the belligerently independent little weekly, a personal organ of its old-style independent owner and editor, kept alive by the fact that as the sole Democratic local paper it can legally claim the routine public advertising of the city's official notices.[1] It is only the first two papers that local people refer to when they speak of "our newspapers"—and, since the death of the owner and editor of the weekly in the spring of 1936, despite the effort of his widow to continue its publication, the morning and afternoon papers have become more nearly in fact Middletown's only newspapers.

In the spring of 1934, when labor organization under N.R.A. was at its peak in Middletown, a labor weekly, the *Labor Record,* began publication in Middletown as a tabloid-size, eight-page sheet. Backed by the Middletown Central Labor Union and carrying the complete International Labor News Service, it ran the following "Platform" at its masthead:

To encourage the principle and practice of conciliation and arbitration in the settlement of differences between capital and labor as a first line of defense.

[1] See the characterization of this editor in n. 5 in Ch. IX.

To maintain and establish the right of every worker to select representatives of his own choosing.

To build up organizations where all worthy members can participate in the discussion of those practical problems, upon the solution of which depends the welfare of the workers.

To foster clean politics in our community and support labor's friends of any political party.

To support a program for public ownership of natural monopolies.

To cooperate in all movements looking to the public welfare of our city and vicinity; supporting the principle of home trade and home labor.

This paper called upon Middletown's workers to "appreciate anew that they gain little in 'playing' politics with party organizations. . . . The only result is the double cross after you have paid the price of admission." The *Labor Record* lived five issues and then passed on and became only a remembered part of Middletown labor's N.R.A. fiasco.

The morning paper appears virtually to have stood still since 1925, being as regularly Republican, pro-business, anti-labor, and discreet as ever in its editorial columns about the things behind the local news. The afternoon paper, meanwhile, has assumed the local lead as the more independent, alert, and active of the two papers.

In 1936 Arthur Brisbane's "Today" still edified Middletown at its breakfast; Dorothy Dix's face, ageless as Lydia Pinkham's, smiles benignly at the head of a column indistinguishable from its 1925 predecessor; and Edgar Guest's "Just Folks" still "sends folks smiling down the street." Foreign news continues, inevitably, brief and uneven as compared with the news of a large metropolitan daily with its staff of foreign correspondents. Patent-medicine advertisements still pepper the pages,[2] as well as advertisements of doctors not recognized by the medical profession, making large promises of cures, and advertisements of "Madame Claire, Palmist." The papers claim that they scrutinize such advertisements more carefully than in 1925, and certainly these advertisements are fewer in number, but, if one may judge from those that are accepted, it is the depression rather than stricter censorship that is primarily responsible for the diminution in their number.

The outstanding innovation in Middletown's newspapers is the increased share of signed syndicated features from Washington and New York in the news columns. Whereas Brisbane's column and David Lawrence's dispatches were the sole features of this sort in the politico-

[2] See Ch. XI and *Middletown*, pp. 437-41.

economic field in 1925, Middletown read in its morning paper in 1935 Brisbane's "Today," Drew Pearson and Robert Allen's "Daily Washington Merry-Go-Round," Will Rogers' daily paragraph, Leslie Eichel's "World at a Glance," and Kirke Simpson's "A Washington Bystander"; while the evening paper in 1935 had also entered this field with Walter Lippmann's "Today and Tomorrow," "The National Whirligig," Paul Mallon's Washington dispatches, and Frank Kent's "The Great Game of Politics." Syndicated columns of a nonpolitical sort include, in the morning paper, O. O. McIntyre's "New York Day by Day," Logan Clendening's "Diet and Health," Dorothy Dix's column on love and marriage problems, a beauty column by Gladys Glad, Edgar Guest's "Just Folks," Alex Morrison's "Golf Facts," and a "Now You Know" column of Ripleyesque strange facts; and in the afternoon paper, Dr. Fishbein's "Our Health," A. E. Wiggam's "Let's Explore Your Mind," Walter Winchell's "On Broadway," Emily Post on etiquette, a beauty column, a "Strange As It Seems" column, another on "Bringing Up Children," and a trailing array of other features on marriage, contract bridge, styles, recipes, and sports.

No actual recount of the allocation of space in Middletown's papers was made in 1935.[3] The following summary analysis was prepared independently by a responsible graduate of the local college on the basis of a space count of two sample issues of the afternoon paper (those for July 12 and December 29, 1934):

About one-third of the space in each issue was devoted to advertisements,[4] and the remainder to news, features, and pictures. Purely local news occupied only from one-tenth to one-fifth of the total page space, and in each case about half of the local news could be readily identified as having come from publicity agents and organization secretaries. In other words, the bulk of the space was devoted to "canned" features and standardized news sent in over the wire, while the local reporters divided their time between news gathering and the revision and copying of "dope" handed them by local publicity-seeking groups and businesses.

The significance of the one important change shown by this count as well as by observation—the increased amount of signed, syndicated material, especially political columns from Washington—appears to

[3] See *Middletown,* pp. 472-73.
[4] The decline in advertising from the larger proportion found in the 1923 space count, referred to in the preceding footnote, is probably due largely to the depression, which curtailed advertising generally.

be great. Middletown believes itself to be getting today a "better" news service through these signed columns. As one of the local editors commented, "These signed features insure more information from 'the other point of view,' that is, both sides of a question." Certainly Middletown today reads in its papers more of this semi-editorialized information from the East. Actually, however, this increment appeared to involve in 1935 not so much a counterbalance to the editorial point of view of these two Republican papers as an intensification of that point of view; for both the newspaper columnists and the radio commentators (such men as Edwin C. Hill and Boake Carter) were engaged in the main in opposing the same things in Washington which Middletown businessmen and their newspapers oppose. This coincidence may be regarded as merely fortuitous and temporary; but a matter-of-fact viewing of the institutions of the culture suggests that in a society in which private business is the dominant institution, and in which press and radio are themselves private businesses and draw the great bulk of their support from other private businesses, rather than from readers and listeners,[5] and a political commentator is paid in proportion to his

[5] The following communication in December, 1936, from the circulation head of a nationally known newspaper (whose name we are not at liberty to print) reveals the "normal" sources of newspaper income:

"Replying to your letter regarding the percentage of advertising and circulation revenue, I can tell you confidentially that our figure for 1935 ran 66⅔ and 33⅓, or roughly 70-30. Much depends upon the price of the newspaper. For example, on the Pacific Coast a price of five cents per copy would somewhat upset a general average of 70-30. Abnormal circulations such as the New York *Daily News* would also offset this. By and large, however, I would say that 70-30 is normal, although in 1936 some newspapers, including our own, with increased advertising rates and increased lineage will not conform so closely."

In ordinary times a successful periodical such as *Good Housekeeping* also derives roughly two out of every three dollars of its income from advertising and only one dollar from subscriptions. It is this relationship between circulation and advertising that enables a periodical such as the *Saturday Evening Post* to sell for five cents a magazine whose editorial, manufacturing, and distributing costs aggregate thirty-five to forty cents per copy sold.

Political speeches over the radio are an exception to the general doctrine that privately owned media of communication may be controlled in their content according to the caprice of the owner. It is an interesting commentary on the growth of institutions and the emergence of awareness of problems as "affected with public interest" that the radio operates under Federal control, whereas the older institution, the newspaper, is not subject to such regulation in such matters as its right to accept or to exclude news. In a city like Middletown, where both dailies are committed to the same political party, the earlier assumption that each community will tend to have an "opposition" newspaper breaks down completely. The fact that the heavy majority of American newspapers

ability to write comment that the owners of newspapers and broadcasting systems and their advertisers like, the coincidence is neither fortuitous nor temporary. In other words, information in this culture tends to reach the public largely "with the compliments of" business; and in a culture committed to moneymaking and to the basic doctrine of the *quid pro quo,* of "paying for what you get and getting what you pay for," this tends often to cost Middletown precisely what the editor quoted above feels these syndicated politico-economic news columns provide, *i.e.,* "the other point of view."

The presence of more syndicated material in Middletown's papers is working further—hand in hand with movies, radio, nation-wide fashion services, automobile mobility, imported standards in education, Federal-sponsored relief policies, and many other aspects of its culture —to make Middletown identify itself with the wider America that surrounds it. This tendency is somewhat opposed to the intense localism, pride in Middletown as "the finest place in the world," in Middletown's state, in the state's artists and poets, that was observed in 1925 as so characteristic of this culture,[6] as well as to the increased economic localism so urgently apparent in 1935. There has always been a tendency in Middletown's press and folk talk to play up the town and small city in contrast to the metropolitan big city. Outside the realm of finance and public affairs, the news selected for printing from a center like New York still tends to encourage local people somewhat in this belief in the "unnaturalness" of big-city life in contrast to their own. In June, 1935, the editor of the afternoon paper took repeated occasion to congratulate Middletown that it did not live in the treeless apartment world of New York where there is no place for children and dogs to play. And the New Yorker temporarily in Middletown is continually running upon featured dispatches from New York that he would have missed entirely in his New York paper, such as "Baby's Body, Pinned to Bed by Stiletto, Found in New York." There seemed to be, however, a noticeable increase by 1935 in the tendency to take over and absorb the "smart" ways of the more gaudy world outside.

sided with big business interests in actively backing the campaign of Governor Landon in 1936 suggests that this clash between symbol and reality, between the newspaper as a public agency for the dissemination of necessary information and the newspaper as a privately-owned business venture, is in no sense peculiar to Middletown.

[6] See *Middletown,* pp. 484-88; also the close of Ch. IX and Ch. XII in the present study.

Perhaps the most striking innovation in this respect is the appearance of Walter Winchell's "On Broadway" as one of Magic Middletown's "most popular syndicated features," according to the circulation department of the paper which runs it. Here Middletown reads in the smart Winchellese *patois* that "Miriam Hopkins is worried because a vengeful man is threatening her in a messy suit" or "What two famous socially listed married duos on the Long Island North Shore have swapped mates for the summer?" or that "Kay McCarthy's new low license plates spell a naughty word." Only thirty-three Middletown families were taking the *New Yorker* in 1935, but the fact that enough of the nearly 9,000 of Middletown's 12,500 families who read the afternoon paper should enjoy Winchellisms to make it a highly desirable local press feature is abundant evidence of the rate at which the small city is losing its isolation under the cultural drenching of movies, radio, and other agencies of sophistication. And, in this connection, the deliberate drive of these agencies should be noted to build up their following by stressing the note that small-town folk are essentially indistinguishable from big city folk.[7]

What one appears to be witnessing in all of the above is a struggle between the old pride in localism, in being Middletown, and the opposed pride in being *en rapport* with the "newest," the "smartest," the "most approved by the right people in the big outside world." Nor is this as simple a matter as it appears to be on the surface—as simple, that is, as substituting silk stockings for cotton, or princess style for low waist line. Mankind everywhere has a deep-seated emotional need

[7] This closer binding of Main Street to Fifth Avenue and Broadway in the past two decades, not only through such media as motion pictures and radio, but, also, through such institutions as the chain-store and nation-wide distributive systems, is epitomized by the women's fashion world. A generation ago the high styles of Fifth Avenue one year tended to become the high styles of Fourteenth Street (a working-class shopping section of New York) and of the Main Streets the following year. Today, the popular fashions—the "hot numbers" as the trade calls them—of New York's exclusive stores and of Hollywood's "four-star hits" are copied in cheaper price lines within a fortnight and are relayed by fast express (and even by airplane in the case of leading stores in the larger inland cities) to the Middletowns of the country. Such low-price chains as the W. T. Grant Stores play an important part in this process. Even in the case of the large mail-order firms like Montgomery Ward and Sears, Roebuck serving low-income and farm women, the lag of six to seven months between the selection of styles by the buyers and the appearance of their semi-annual catalogues has become so serious as to hamper their sales of dresses other than house dresses. (See the investigator's chapter on "The People as Consumers" in Vol. II of *Recent Social Trends* for a further discussion of this point.)

to feel itself not peripheral and marginal but central in the scheme of things. The strengths of democracy as a political and social system and of Middletown's cosmology and religion lie in their acknowledgment of this fundamental need of the individual to "belong" to his world. Middletown people call their city "Magic Middletown" as one of the symbols that keeps life resilient—just as expatriate Wisconsin dry-land farmers in Wyoming sing feelingly "Out Where the West Begins" and wax eloquent about the plains' sunsets: "You don't get them like that back East!" Living as Middletown does today with an unprecedented number of space-binding agencies that bring to it contact with the habits and possessions of authoritative people who "belong" in the wider national culture, Middletown is shifting its centers of "belonging" at a number of specific points to conform to these more distant centers of prestige.

If the multiplication of these syndicated columns of news comment from Washington grows in part from the increase in speed, urgency, and complexity of the moves of the Federal government in the depression; if the popular taste for them in Middletown represents at once the desire of local citizens to "keep up" with these fateful developments in Washington and also the growing demand for authoritative, "inside," shorthand information; a net result has been to dwarf still further than in 1925 the role and authority of Middletown's own newspapermen. Their comments on national issues have lost authority in the face of the semi-editorial news and comment in the political "features" from Washington. A Middletown editor confessed this growing helplessness of the lone local commentator on the news and his dependence upon the outside editorial specialists who write the syndicated columns when he said: "The issues the country faces are so complex and so many that we local newspapermen can't possibly devote adequate space to them." [8] The function of the newspaperman in the

_____

[8] The newspaperman shares this predicament with the individual citizen in our current world. A too-little-considered aspect of our current culture is the extent to which in all sectors of living problems have grown in complexity far beyond their former proportions. It is less tolerable today than a century ago to subsume the problems of living under simple blanket formulas. As localism has dwindled and science and technology have invaded field after field, simple activities—all the way from nutrition and child rearing to making goods and carrying on international relations—have become complex matters defying even the experts at many points. "Science," the "growth of knowledge," and "progress" have caused disturbing questions to sprout where fewer choices were

small city is thus becoming more and more that of the collector of local news. And, thus forced back into the local scene, the newspaper-man confronts a high-tension area of local personalities, banking sources of the credit by which his newspaper operates, pressure groups, and threats of libel suits. In the face of this situation, the editorial page of Middletown's morning paper has become even more colorless and noncommittal than it was in 1925. The editor of the afternoon paper has extricated himself somewhat from the pressure for colorless safety on the editorial page by building up since 1928 a first-page personal column of signed comment—a feature (like the position held by Bris-bane in the morning paper) in which, under guise of whimsical chitchat, he manages occasionally to drop in a paragraph about the news behind Middletown's news that escapes the more cautious editing of the rest of the paper. In thus retreating behind the privilege of the old-time editor to be "a bit of a local character," he is reviving the salty personal journalism that the ever-narrowing constraints surround-ing modern journalism tend to cramp. But one has only to turn to the slashing captions and text of the local opposition weekly, almost devoid of advertising save for its legal advertisements of public business, to glimpse what the earlier personal journalism really was, and the gap between it and editing a modern newspaper.

Middletown's press, like its pulpit, has largely surrendered its tradi-tional role of leader; both have bartered their peculiar rights to pro-claim sharply dissident truths for the right to be well supported by the reigning economy. And as a result, in the central areas of business, national politics, and civic pride they tend to reflect the point of view convenient to the purposes of this dominant core of business interests, while on lesser issues both press and pulpit tend largely to assume the neutral, middle-of-the-road tone so characteristic of Middletown's life.[9] And this passivity in most issues, involving as it does the tendency to refute an issue by a slogan rather than by acute analysis, involves the local press in constant unresolved dilemmas. One of these was

recognized before. This has put at many points in our institutional life strains upon the human agents in the culture never anticipated when these institu-tional frameworks were erected in an earlier era.

[9] Since the sources of this universal toning down of contrasting colors in Middletown's thought and action are wider than merely local conditions, one can probably say that this neutral quality is in no sense peculiar to Middletown but something it shares with all cautious, thrifty, "progressive" middle-class America.

sharply pointed out by the editor of the Democratic weekly in the fol-lowing editorial:

PULLING BOTH WAYS

[Middletown's] two Republican daily newspapers get their metaphors all mixed up. Loyalty to the grand old party compels them both daily to assail the recovery plan of President Roosevelt as being "grossly extravagant," and in the same breath to urge that [Middletown] go the limit in securing allotments for needed improvements.

They prove by the logic of canned editorials that government money spent here for needed public works and relief for the unemployed is ruin-ing the country, but they are contributing to the national catastrophe by constantly urging and demanding application for government money for the welfare of [Middletown].

If they were honest in their belief that the New Deal is all wrong, they would urge that [Middletown] should refuse to accept unconstitutional money for any purpose whatever. . . .

Likewise, in such matters as the relative interests of local capital and labor the papers face an uneasy dilemma. Approximately seven persons in ten in Middletown are in the working class and only three in ten in the business class; but the operation of a profitable newspaper de-pends upon securing at one and the same time maximum circulation from the working class and maximum advertising and credit from the business class. This issue is for the moment being successfully avoided by two slogans: "Civic Unity" and "Radicalism Is Un-American." When strikes threaten, editorials take the ground of "public interest" and urge persuasively, as noted in Chapter II, that "It is the public that suffers in the long run through strikes, lockouts, and other inter-ferences with industry"; and when a strike goes ahead and occurs any-way, the editorials call for "an immediate settlement of the present difficulties before they threaten the town's progress and its consequent prosperity further." As one local man commented in 1935, "The atti-tude of our local papers toward labor is not at all subtle." [10] Labor's

[10] See the discussion in Ch. II of the activities of the Middletown press and radio station in June, 1935, when Dillon came to Middletown to attempt to organize the General Motors workers. In this connection the emphasis of head-lines, also noted in Ch. II, should be borne in mind: "Ohio Union Chief Sent to Prison," "Chicago Unions Seized by Gangsters," "Kentucky Labor Leader Convicted," "Radicals and Police Battle in Chicago," "Workers Fight Union Control—Steel Company Employer Says [at Senate hearing on Wagner bill] Men Satisfied," "Bloodshed and Rioting Mark California Strike—One Killed, Policemen Are Beaten."

"atrocities" tend fairly consistently to be featured on page one, and its equities and victories to be played down and relegated to an inside page. In the next breath, editorials tend to brush over the rough edges of the situation by urging, "It is pretty sad to relate that labor costs are down, but a man out of work would rather work for low wages than not to work at all. However, pay as good wages as you can. Don't grind down any men who do your work."

"Radicalism," as noted in Chapter II, is neither a congenial concept nor a channeled mood of Middletown workers, and the press struggles to encourage this local abhorrence. The term is used broadly as a generic term including "Reds," "Russian Godlessness," "Pacifists," "Socialists," and "Communists." In June, 1935, on the same day that the New York *Times* captioned its story of the third-party convention in Chicago, "'Third Party' Men Hunt for Leaders," Middletown read of the same convention under headlines giving the convention a to-Middletown fantastic twist: "Radicals Promise $5,000 Income to Every Family." When a front-page picture is shown of police or troops "mussing up" strikers, the caption is likely to feature the word "Radicals," so that the picture portrays the forces of law and order putting down an un-American, anarchistic brute threat from the underworld—and this makes sense to Middletown, even to most of the workers.

In view of the dilemma of local editors, it is interesting that the "Letters to the Editor" sections of both papers are more outspoken than either news columns or editorials. In April, 1933, a slashing three-column attack upon the administration of the local Community Fund by a prominent local woman asked questions and raised problems right and left. The afternoon paper printed it under the comparatively mild caption "[Middletown] Charity Worker Sees Community Fund Flaws —Mrs. —— Believes 'Deadwood' Is Hampering Work of City's Welfare Agencies"—but it printed it.[11] It is significant that the editor who

[11] This woman is, to the best of the investigator's knowledge, the only person of wealth in Middletown who is openly critical of Middletown's business hegemony. Formerly an independent professional woman, she became a Middletown wife in 1911 when she married into the one wealthy family of local manufactures who have always stood somewhat apart from Middletown's central control group centering around the X family. Her life in Middletown typifies that of the outsider, particularly the married woman outsider, in such a culture— tied to the city by her husband's business, too wealthy to be ignored, too energetic and restless to conform, alternately speaking her mind and championing lone charities, and able to "get away from it all" by long periods of travel. Soon after she came to Middletown she turned her energies to running a regular

printed this letter is reported on good authority to have been summoned to the office of a banker who had given much time to the Community Fund to "give an account of himself." [12] This letter, the outstanding protest of its kind in recent years, evoked other letters—some of endorsement, and others, signed "Hopeful Henrietta" and "Optimistic Oscar," calling for a truce in this business of "forever denouncing people and things." The fact that the papers do print such communications represents not only "good journalism," in that it elicits popular interest, but also a break in the ordinarily solid editorial front. It is conceivable that peppery letters of this sort are not unwelcome to an editorial staff themselves unable to print all that they suspect or know to be going on in the community. The fact that editorial comment ordinarily evokes few letters but that a frank letter of this sort unlooses a flow of local communications affords a commentary on the gap between a local newspaper as a formal business venture and as an institution seeking primarily to evoke local thinking and to focus opinion upon problems close to a given public.

It was pointed out in the 1925 study that in Middletown, grown large and dependent upon the institutionalized dissemination of news necessary for a citizen, it rests upon the accidents of whim and the purse of the citizen whether the latter ever reads a paper.[13] As Table 47 [14] shows, Middletown's approximately 12,500 families were receiving

column about "The McNutt Family" in the morning paper, taking off some of the foibles of local people in the kindly colloquialisms of common folk. Then she turned her ready pen to publicizing local winter relief, building up an annual drive for local charity that became for several years a local institution. This last was revived in the depression as an important pre-Christmas drive that swelled the Christmas of Middletown's poor and left large surpluses over for later distribution. All through the depression she was the champion of the poor against the shortcomings of the local relief system. In 1935, as noted in Ch. IV, she was responsible for the opening of a home for forty old men by a local Gospel Mission.

[12] The editor of a small-city paper is in the anomalous position of being both freer and more constrained than is the editor of a large-city paper. He is freer in that the lines of policy that dictate his sheet's relations to the complex world of business through the sensitive medium of the advertising office are less defined in advance and peremptory, and his editorials are less likely to be closely scrutinized by the watchful eyes of the lucrative national advertisers. And he is more constrained by reason of the editor's being known personally by local businessmen who feel free to "jump down his throat" on the phone or hale him before them, as in the case above, when the paper displeases. He is too close to his public to be taken as impersonally as the editor of a metropolitan paper.

[13] See *Middletown*, p. 471.

[14] See Appendix III for this table.

in 1929 roughly 10,000 copies of the Middletown morning paper and 8,500 copies of the evening paper. By 1933, against a rise of 1,000 in the city's population, the city circulation of the morning paper had fallen off by 22 per cent and that of the afternoon paper by 16 per cent. In 1933, with a rise in Middletown's total families from about 12,200 to 12,500 since 1929, the city was receiving about 3,500 less papers daily. The morning paper had dropped from a coverage of roughly 80 per cent of the city's families to 60, and the afternoon paper from 70 to 55. It is impossible to tell how much of this drop entailed the discontinuance of only one paper by families formerly taking both papers. While this was undoubtedly a real factor, there is still the strong probability of a genuine increase in the number of families who could afford or who were interested in no paper at all. It is significant that this shrinkage occurred in 1933, when the large innovations under the New Deal might have been expected to increase the number of newspapers read, had people been financially able to buy them. It is a commentary on this culture that, during a fateful year like 1933 when sweeping changes in national policy—necessitating ultimately the judgments of every adult as voter—were being made with unusual rapidity, the "normal" course of events was for fewer citizens than usual to be regularly informed as to what was occurring.

It is probably among the working-class groups actually unemployed, on relief, or threatened with going on relief that the bulk of the families going entirely without papers occurred. While this was probably due primarily to sheer lack of money among a population with roughly 3,000 of its 12,500 families on relief, the element of apathy which Lazarsfeld found in his study of the unemployed in Marienthal was undoubtedly incipiently present in many instances. As noted in the discussion of reading in the depression in Chapter VII, prolonged unemployment in Marienthal resulted in a sag in interest in politics and a sharp decline in the reading of news; the characteristic comment of the unemployed dwellers in this "tired community," as regards reading as well as politics, the local little theater, and other activities, was "One just can't keep one's thoughts on things any more!"

The reading of out-of-town papers has suffered more than local papers. Table 47 shows that the Middletown circulation of the Sunday edition of the six out-of-town papers with the largest circulation in Middletown dropped more than 50 per cent from 1929 to 1933.

Secondary to the newspaper, but still significant as purveyors of news to Middletown, are the radio [15] and national periodical. The former has advanced in importance as a medium of news since 1925, and especially during the depression, with the entry of radio into the daily news-dissemination field, though its time devoted to news broadcasts is still relatively limited. Not only has radio ownership in Middletown increased greatly since 1925,[16] but people have clung tenaciously to their radios in the depression.

Periodical circulation has fallen during the depression, as noted in Chapter VII. In general it is Middletown's business class alone that gets current news (as distinct from recreation) from periodicals. There were among Middletown's roughly 12,500 families in 1935 combined newsstand and subscription sales of only 170 copies a week of *Time*, and of 231 copies of the *Literary Digest*. Such media as *Collier's*, *Liberty*, and the *Saturday Evening Post*, primarily bought for entertainment but also containing some editorials and news articles, have wider circulations, the 1935 weekly totals of the three above-named being respectively 1,957, 1,360, and 1,286.[17]

The uneven diffusion of these media of information throughout Middletown, when coupled with the relative thinness of the coverage of the world's news noted above,[18] raises interesting questions in view of the democratic assumptions on which Middletown's political practices are based. Two of the most fundamental assumptions of this culture concern the vesting of essential power in the millions of adults who vote and the basic equality of each adult when he goes to the polls. Both assumptions imply a universe of issues compassable by the rank and file of the electorate and equal facilities available to all for comprehending and forming judgments about these issues. But what

[15] There are perhaps sound grounds for saying that in the 1936 election the radio was a more important channel of national political news to Middletown than were the local newspapers. (See n. 5 above.)

[16] See Ch. VII.

[17] See *Middletown*, p. 240, for the sharp differences in the numbers and kinds of periodicals going into the homes of the city's business class and working class in 1925.

[18] Verbatim reports of critically essential documents and decisions in international and even in national affairs scarcely ever reach Middletown through its channels of information. What Middletown usually reads is a summarized summary extracting phrases, sentences, and paragraphs from the original, and the editorialized comments of various somebodies on the original.

one appears to be witnessing in Middletown is something like the following: The multiplicity and complexity of the issues confronting the citizen have been increasing much more rapidly, especially since the World War, than has the coverage of these issues by the services of information in the press and elsewhere to the mass of Middletown citizens. The culture, in its official ideologies, does not recognize this change in the relative adequacy of the information served to cover the magnitude and intricacy of the issues involved; nor does it recognize any political significance in the differential coverage by a New York *Times* and a Middletown *Star*. The official line of thought is simple: things happen, or are about to happen; anyone can if he only takes the trouble know all about them; it is the citizen's duty to inform himself and ignorance on his part is no defense. If, however, the brute fact remains that the gap between issues and their comprehension is widening, democratic institutions would appear to be subject to further acute strain. This strain will be met by Middletown in the familiar manner by invoking the traditional symbols, which process, like looking through the "wrong" end of a telescope, reduces a formidable mountain to the manageable proportions of a molehill. And as the issues press for prompt and forthright action, those elements in the culture with more information, more perspective on the issues, and more power of money and propaganda may chafe under the dragging unawareness and "uncooperativeness" of their brethren in the Middletowns, and may spend their money to invoke symbols useful in persuading Middletown to jump through the appropriate hoops. And herein one glimpses once more the possible seeds of an eventual coercive control which in Europe today goes under the name of fascism.

CHAPTER XI

Keeping Healthy

As in certain other phases of its life, Middletown's chief innovations[1] in caring for health during this decade have come at the two ends of the economic scale: the important addition of the new hospital, an outright gift from the X family, during the boom years, and the extension of free health service to the needy under the impact of the depression.[2]

With the opening of the new hospital in the early fall of 1929, Middletown has moved from a lagging position as regards hospital plant to one well beyond that of most cities of its size. What such a large modern institution means to the health of the city is suggested by the fact that the number of trained nurses at the city's command increased six times as rapidly as the population between 1920 and the spring of 1930. The development of the hospital as an active research center, with skilled research personnel imported from outside the city, has the enthusiastic cooperation of the abler local doctors and will in time probably affect markedly the morale of the entire profession in Middletown. The city now receives several times the number of laboratory diagnoses it received in the early 1920's.

The habit of hospital treatment was growing slowly in Middletown

[1] A minor change affecting the entire city was the adoption of a new plumbing code. Following the passage of a State law in 1926 requiring modern plumbing codes in local municipalities, Middletown passed an ordinance in conformity with the new law. In January, 1930, the local press called attention to the fact that these stricter plumbing requirements "have resulted in a reduction in the number of cases of sickness per 1,000 of [Middletown's] population during the past two years, as revealed by the Report of the State Board of Health." According to a local plumber, "The new code is enforced right to the letter. It requires waste lines run on a proper angle, with necessary cleanouts and all fixtures properly vented and trapped. This means a lot less of the small leaks that used to make sewer gas. The strictness of the code actually works out with us so that fewer people can now afford this more expensive plumbing." (See Table 25, which shows 13.4 per cent of Middletown's residential units in January, 1935, as without running water, and Table 28 which shows 18.5 per cent of the units as still using back-yard privies.)

[2] See Ch. IV for the discussion of the relation of this to other phases of relief.

388

in the early 1920's, though sharply limited by the cramped facilities and indifferent reputation of the antiquated fifty-three-bed building.[3] During the late 1920's the sharp rise in hospital admissions [4] was probably stimulated in part by the approaching completion of the new hospital begun in 1927. Between 1925 and 1928 total admissions increased by 64 per cent, while the city's population grew by only 14 per cent. Even during the early years of the depression, use of the hospital continued to increase. In 1930, the first full year of operation in the new hospital, the number of admissions was more than twice that in 1925 and 31 per cent above 1928. The total continued to climb in 1931, fell off to its depression "low" in 1932 [5]—though in the worst year of the depression the total stood above that of all years prior to 1930—mounted slowly in 1933-34, and only in 1935 passed the record previous total of admissions in 1931.

Owing to frequent changes in classification of cases between 1929 and 1934, shifts in types of cases cannot be shown, save for obstetrical cases. The decided rise in hospital deliveries affords one of the most sensitive indices of what modern hospital facilities have meant to Middletown.[6] Total hospital obstetrical cases increased by 33 per cent between 1925 and 1928, and rose in 1930 and 1931, despite the depression, to 83 and 87 per cent, respectively, above 1928. While total hospital admissions fell off by 15 per cent between 1931 and 1932, obstetrical cases still managed to rise by 7 per cent. The sharp gains in hospital deliveries during the years 1928-30 were flattened off to a plateau in 1932-34, but the total number virtually held its own, despite the fact that Middletown's birth rate declined by 16 per cent between 1929 and 1933; and in 1935 the number of hospital deliveries rebounded 29 per cent above the highest preceding year, while total hospital admissions surpassed the best previous year by only 8 per cent. Live births in Middletown's hospital totaled only 11.7 per cent of total live births in the city in 1925 and 14.7 per cent in 1928; but in 1930 they were 25.0 per cent; in 1931, 24.6 per cent; in 1932, 24.9 per cent; in 1933, 29.5

[3] See *Middletown,* p. 453.

[4] See Table 48 in Appendix III.

[5] July, 1932, was the hospital's lowest depression month, when the average daily number of patients dropped from the eighty-nine of 1931 to only sixty-five, following the heavy blow to local morale involved in the removal of the General Motors plant from Middletown.

[6] See Table 49 in Appendix III.

per cent; in 1934, 28.6 per cent; and in 1935, 38.5 per cent.[7] Use of the hospital for obstetrical cases thus proved somewhat depression-proof, although it is even today largely a business-class habit.[8]

The pressure of hard times is reflected in Table 50,[9] which shows a drop by 1933, even from the depression year 1931, of 45 per cent in number of patients who could afford a private room. Despite returning confidence in 1935, when total admissions were 8 per cent above 1931, Middletown was still opening its pocketbooks for the luxury of private rooms cautiously, and there were still 27 per cent fewer users of private rooms than in 1931. Deprived of this more lucrative patronage and having an inadequate endowment to carry the strains of the depression, the hospital has had a difficult time, and its potential service to the community has suffered. Despite efficient administration, the modest number of free cases the hospital could afford fell off by a third between 1931 and 1933. The number of admissions to the hospital unable to pay privately for services and handled as charity cases under public and private funds declined, as shown in Table 50, by 21 per cent between 1931 and 1932; though the larger use of public funds for relief hospitalization reduced the lag in succeeding years, as compared with 1931, to 6, 14, and 12 per cent respectively in the three years 1933-35. According to the head of the hospital, people who have come to the hospital during the worst of the depression have been sicker, and it is the frequently optional type of operation—such as female abdominal repairs, hernias, appendectomies—that has been postponed.

With all its modern hospital plant, Middletown is reported to be, even in less difficult times than the years 1929-35, somewhat "hospital poor." A few citizens are critical of the X family for not setting up an adequate endowment for the hospital when they gave it to Middletown. As one of them stated this in writing, "Not all of the X monumental structures have adequate endowments for maintenance. The hospital, Masonic Temple, Y.M.C.A., and Y.W.C.A., for example, with all their splendid equipment, have high operating costs. As a result, these organizations are sometimes burdensome financially to

---

[7] Hospital totals of live births are available only from 1931. The above percentages for preceding years were secured by deducting eight stillbirths (the average for the five years 1931-35) from the total of obstetrical admissions to the hospital. This takes no account of twins. The percentages are, however, correct to within a few decimals.

[8] See *Middletown,* pp. 453-54.

[9] See Appendix III for this table.

their members and to the community at large, and in some cases their humanitarian service is crippled by too much emphasis on ability to pay." What one is here witnessing is a familiar experience where private munificence has equipped a community with facilities beyond the community's immediate customary rate of use and financial support. It involves the dilemma of social change stimulated by private will rather than arising from public awareness of need: change casually generated by circumstances tends to lag in adequacy of adjustment to need; but suddenly superimposed change frequently necessitates a waiting period of cramped administration until the community learns how to use and to support its suddenly expanded facilities.

The depression, coinciding with the opening of the new hospital, has simply aggravated this situation. As a result, Middletown's hospital still tends to be, as in 1925, "too expensive for the poor"—though the last half of the 1925 quotation "and not good enough for the rich," no longer applies.[10]

Parenthetically, if one takes a longer view of the correlation between available money and access to adequate health services in Middletown, one receives a disconcerting reminder of the chronic burden of avoidable health disabilities which is "normal" under our culture, particularly in cities like Middletown where the hospital conducts no outpatient clinic and free services are available through public and private charity only for the most desperately ill and indigent.[11]

The postponing effect of bad times has apparently been particularly marked in the area of dental care. Local dentists state that there has been widespread deferral of dental work, particularly among the working class. The testimony of one dentist is typical of the statements by others:

"In the depression my working-class patients have tended to delay about two years longer in coming in, and then the tooth has become so bad that there is nothing left to do but to extract it. Relatively more of my practice in the depression has been this sort of emergency work, as compared with the preventive work I did formerly. My business-class patients have delayed longer, too, but they tend more often to catch a tooth when it can still be filled. Business-class women have taken better care of their teeth than their husbands. I don't do as much bridge work for either men or women, but

[10] See *Middletown*, p. 453.
[11] See *Middletown*, pp. 443-45 and 454-55.

men particularly tend to avoid replacing a lost tooth unless their work is of a nature requiring contacts with the public."

While the new hospital was offering widely extended facilities for medical care for those who could afford to pay for them, the depression was forcing the health needs of those who could not afford to pay upon the attention of the community. And the city took unprecedented steps toward meeting them as a routine civic service.[12] These innovations took the form of extensive free medical services at the expense of the taxpayers and of an extension of free health services to needy school children, not all of them from families on relief, involving free milk, cod-liver oil, and in some cases hot lunches.

In providing for this care of health at public expense the township trustee was spending by 1932 the following amounts:

Hospital care	$22,351
Dentists	1,140
Doctors	26,022
Medical supplies	311
Burials	2,281
Total	$52,105

This rate of expenditure was totally unprecedented for Middletown.[13] While itemized expenditures for the pre-depression period are not available, some idea of the increase may be gained from the fact that the above total represents two and one-half times the total expenditures by the township trustee in the last pre-depression year, 1928, *for all kinds of poor relief.* In 1932 this sum of $52,105 paid out for public health relief represented only 21 per cent of total payments for poor relief by the township trustee.

In addition to provision by the city for the health of the unable during the depression, private charities extended their services. The same group of Community Fund health agencies that existed in 1925 continued in 1935. Additions to their services were few, but these agencies have stretched their facilities to the limits of their financial resources. The county Anti-Tuberculosis Association, in addition to maintaining its weekly chest clinic, has added a periodic sinus clinic— both receiving the donated services of the County Medical Society

[12] See Ch. IV.
[13] The above figures do not include health expenditures by Middletown's privately financed charities under the Community Fund. (See Ch. IV.)

members serving in rotation, and operating under the stipulation of the doctors that no one shall be served who is not too poor to pay privately for the service.

The Visiting Nurse Association has grown in the volume of its work, as indicated by the following totals:

	Number of nurses	Number of visits
1925	6	4,722
1930	11	21,800 [14]
1934	8	16,519 [15]

In addition to its nursing, the Association added in the depression a child-welfare service that includes two monthly half-day free baby clinics, one for white children and the other for Negro children, and a weekly child welfare nonmedical service. The baby clinics are open only to persons too poor to pay a doctor, and in 1935 they reached 224 white and 76 Negro children.[16] The nonmedical work, involving both home visiting by nurses and group conferences in the Association's attractive rooms, represents a small but probably important beginning in Middletown of the "child-development" program which has made rapid strides in the United States since the World War. The Association, in cooperation with the Parent-Teacher Association, the Public School Health Department, as well as the Medical Society, inaugurated in 1935 a midsummer diphtheria immunization clinic for children entering the first grade in September from homes too poor to be able to pay for examination by their family physician.[17]

[14] The increase in 1930 is due in part to the taking over in that and subsequent years of the nursing work formerly carried on by the County Anti-Tuberculosis Association.

[15] These visits in 1934 reached a total of 3,410 patients.

[16] This new work for children began locally in 1931 under the combined sponsorship of The Child Welfare Department of the State Board of Health, the local American Legion Auxiliary, and the County Anti-Tuberculosis Association. When the State Board withdrew, the Visiting Nurse Association took over the work.

[17] The growth of the Visiting Nurse Association in Middletown reflects the slow process by which a community's habits change in such matters as health care. The local Association was started in 1916 by the women of the Federate Club of Clubs. It had only two nurses at the outset and its work involved only nursing. Ten years later it was still overwhelmingly a straight charitable service for the most needy, and only 6 per cent of its budget came from persons able to pay the small fees charged where such charge is warranted. The depression and the growing habit of utilizing skilled nursing service have extended the work of the Association somewhat above the bottom of the income scale, with the result that in 1935, despite the enlarged educational program for which no charge is made, 35 per cent of the budget came from fees from patients.

Use of the venereal clinic has apparently correlated roughly inversely with local business conditions; during the prosperous last half of the 1920's its number of treatments declined somewhat, and during the depression they have increased sharply. According to the doctor in charge, the depression increase is related to more prostitution during the depression, to more referrals of cases by local doctors who unload unprofitable cases on the free clinic, and to the growing volume of doubtful or unsuspected cases located as the habit has grown among the medical men of making Wassermann tests in doubtful cases. When times are good, on the other hand, according to the head of the clinic, men are employed and find it inconvenient to come to the clinic at its fixed hours, and more of them can afford to patronize private doctors.

The annual health inspections of school children under the health department of the public schools have been curtailed somewhat since 1930 in the number of children covered.[18]

The citizens' committee set up as a depression emergency move in the late fall of 1932 to plan relief health services made the following recommendations: [19]

We believe, all problems considered, that the following program represents the most adequate solution:

(1) Ambulatory patients should be handled through an out-patient department established in connection with the hospital. The services of this out-patient department should be limited to (a) patients going through the Social Service Bureau and then approved by the township for poor relief, and (b) township patients in the hospital discharged to the out-patient department.

(2) Patients who must have home visits should be handled by the present system [of payment to physicians by the township trustee]. Some physicians may be expected to keep more adequate records of diagnosis and treatment.

[18] In the fall of 1935, all new children entering the school system for the first time and all children in Grades 1, 2, 3, 5, 7B, and 9A were examined. The examinations of each child are made by three local doctors: a general practitioner, a nose and throat specialist, and a dentist. The examinations are very rapid, covering, according to a school principal, approximately 150 children in an hour.

[19] From the *Report of the Committee Appointed at a Joint Meeting of the Directors of the Community Fund and the Relief Agencies to Study the Problem of Relief of Distress in Center Township,* February 7, 1933.

Other recommendations of this committee are discussed in Ch. IV.

(3) Cost: In this emergency we believe the cost to the township should be about as follows:

    (a) The hospital should furnish room, clerical service, and nursing service for the clinic at a nominal cost.

    (b) Professional services should be rendered gratuitously in the out-patient department.

    (c) Drugs, bandages, etc. should be furnished at actual cost.

We believe this solution is most satisfactory because:

(1) The establishment of an out-patient department for indigent ambulatory patients seems to be in line with the best practice in any community that is a well-defined medical center as Middletown is ambitious to be.

(2) There is made available to the indigent the value that comes from clinical diagnosis and records, and yet this system preserves for the patient the privilege of choice of physicians for home illness.

(3) This plan is more economical than the present plan, as an out-patient department can be operated much cheaper per quarter than the $2,490 spent in the first three months for office visits.

But nothing came of the central proposal for an out-patient department at the hospital, and the city and township continued to distribute ambulatory cases among the doctors of the city on a regular fee basis paid by the township trustee.

In the midst of these various innovations and proposals, the attitude of the majority of Middletown's doctors regarding private practice and public-health facilities remains substantially that described in 1925.[20] All proposals to develop clinical facilities of whatever type in Middletown still operate within the strait jacket of insistence by the majority of the local medical profession that nothing shall be done to make Middletown healthier that jeopardizes the position of the doctors. When a birth-control clinic was tentatively proposed by one of the younger doctors during the depression, local doctors as a group could not be interested. "Middletown doctors won't stand for a birth-control clinic," said a local person who is directly and professionally qualified to speak. "Even when any other sort of clinic is suggested, they rise up in arms. They think a free clinic would get the population too used to free care." When the free out-patient clinic at the hospital was proposed, as noted above, as a move to reduce the cost of relief medical

[20] See *Middletown*, pp. 443-44 and 451.

care to the city, the recommendation was favorably received by the hospital, but the Medical Society called a special meeting and passed a resolution condemning the proposal, which successfully blocked further action. This action was taken against the active protest of a minority of Middletown's physicians. A communication to the afternoon paper in May, 1933, by the head of a small good-government league in Middletown,[21] summarizes the situation. The sixty-eight members of the medical profession were split on the issue into a small minority who favored the establishment of such clinical facilities and a majority who opposed it; and the communication suggests the possible presence of the same sort of political favoritism in the handling of public relief payments to some doctors that is alleged to have existed in the case of certain grocers.[22] The communication reads:

It certainly is not just a coincidence that about five or six doctors in the city of [Middletown] happen to get most of the business out of the [township] trustee's office, in the face of the fact that I have had calls at my office from numerous doctors wanting to know why they have been discriminated against. It certainly is no coincidence that about eleven or twelve of the leading physicians of the city called me into conference with them and indicated that it was their desire to give their services to the poor. They also indicated that they had made a strenuous effort to establish a clinic at the hospital, which would easily have saved this township around $20,000 last year for doctoring the poor alone. It certainly is no coincidence that those doctors who are receiving most of this money out of the poor fund are the very ones who have fought the clinic, and finally in desperation offered to cut fees in two, which they have done since the first of April, in order to retain this fee system over the protests of many of the reputable physicians in their own organization.

The action of the majority in blocking the proposal for a relief clinic at the hospital is in keeping with the fact that when one of the ablest of the city's young doctors read a paper recently before the State Medical Association urging the profession to cooperate with rather than to fight socialized medicine, many of his local colleagues called him a "wild man" for making the proposal. Confronted with the opportunity for professional leadership, most of the doctors have elected to follow

---

[21] This is the organization which agitated for the special election on the public ownership of Middletown's utilities in 1934, as described in Ch. IX.

[22] See the findings by the emergency citizens' committee on relief costs, quoted in Ch. IV, regarding the apparently dishonest juggling of payments for office and home visits by certain doctors under the relief system.

the competitive pattern of the culture.[23] Meanwhile, however, the ground has been shifting under their feet and they occupy an ambivalent position. As noted in Chapter IV, they have been receiving during the depression considerable sums directly from tax funds for care of a large relief population, and they have fought to maintain this source of income. In so doing, they have invited the first serious public acknowledgment in the history of the city that "two or three full-time township physicians" on the public payroll "is the most economical plan possible" for caring for public medical relief.[24] Although the committee of leading businessmen who drafted this report drew back from the radical step of recommending this procedure, here again a precedent has been established to which public opinion may revert in the future and which the local medical profession may find itself forced in time to follow.

In such a world, in which sickness and money are so closely related and the institutional world encourages self-help, it is not surprising that patent medicines flourish today as in 1925. Middletown papers still carry doctors' advertisements of the "NO knife, NO pain, NO drugs, NO danger, and NO high rates" sort [25] and patent-medicine advertisements [26] promising:

Stomach ulcer, gas pains, indigestion victims, why suffer? For quick relief get a free sample of Ugda, a doctor's prescription at [the largest drugstore in the city].

or

Old Mohawk Indian Tonic . . . regularly $1.00 a bottle but 49 cents upon presentation of this ad. Limited 3 to a customer. We also guarantee

[23] In so doing, they afford but another instance of the lethargy and prevailing helplessness of local cultural agencies to originate forthright departures from accepted practice noted in n. 28 below.

For an excellent treatment of the contemporary professional man's ambivalent position in seeking to "serve two masters," see Mr. Justice Stone's address at the dedication of the new University of Michigan Law Quadrangle, reprinted in the *Harvard Law Review* for November, 1934, under the title "The Public Influence of the Bar."

[24] This statement appeared in the report cited in n. 19 above and is quoted in full in Ch. IV.

[25] See *Middletown*, pp. 439-42.

As stated in *Middletown* (p. 441, n. 5) some of Middletown's advertising doctors boast of their earnings. One of these men, who had started as a poor boy, committed suicide in 1933, leaving an estate announced in the daily press as totaling $300,000 but which, according to a local banker, ran well in excess of that amount.

[26] See *Middletown*, pp. 437-39.

to refund full purchase price to any person who is not satisfied that the medicine is worth at least ten times what he paid for it. Within 12 hours Old Mohawk Indian Tonic will drive poisons from your system as black as any ink that ever came from a bottle. . . . This makes you less liable to appendicitis, rheumatism, and other dangerous diseases.

The local press claims to be stricter in its censorship of all such advertisements than it was in 1925, but the only difference apparent to the investigator was a decrease in number and the use of smaller space. This decline in number and size of advertisements has been characteristic of all advertising in the depression.

Some indication of the decline in sales of patent medicines is afforded by the following statement in 1935 by the manager of a local drugstore, known before the depression according to a local druggist as "one of the best patent-medicine stores in the state":

"At the bottom of the depression our sales of patent medicines fell to about one-third of their pre-depression volume. Now they've climbed back to about one-half. Just take Lydia Pinkham's Vegetable Compound: we used to sell four to five dozen bottles a week, and now it runs to only one to one and a half dozen. Listerine we used to sell so fast that we had to pile it up on the floor behind the counter. Scott's Emulsion and things like that we used to carry in quantities, but we now only stock a case or so of a dozen bottles at a time."

While it is impossible to isolate drugs from the large volume of other sales by drugstores or to control the factor of changes in the price level, patent-medicine sales undoubtedly figure heavily in the drop in dollar volume of drugstore sales in Middletown, from $874,000 in 1929 to $470,000 in 1933, recorded by the United States Census of Retail Distribution.

If the foregoing presents some of the dilemmas in the private care of health in Middletown, the peculiar dilemmas in the public care of health appear in the persistence into 1935 of many of the problems which vexed the city ten years before. The public pulling and hauling over its noisome sewage problem has been described in Chapter IX. The effort to insure pure milk to the city presents the same predicament that it did in 1925: [27] the local health officer, with the backing of the State Public Health authorities, recurrently points out local inade-

[27] See *Middletown,* p. 450.

quacies, and the local city council refuses to pass recommended ordinances. In 1930 the city council killed two proposed ordinances that sought to bring local milk into line with State Board of Health requirements by requiring the pasteurizing of milk sold in the city. A State inspection in the summer of 1935 pronounced the local situation "serious" and revealed nine of Middletown's twenty milk supplies to be below the standard set by the State Board of Health—the bacteria count in one dairy being 8,100,000 per cubic centimeter, when the maximum safe count set by the State is 100,000. In the face of this report and the refusal of the city council to act, the city health officer reported himself helpless to correct the situation in the absence of a satisfactory milk ordinance, and the local press warned, "Boil your milk before giving it to babies." [28]

This milk situation, whereby dairies are tolerated with bacterial counts ranging from 2,400 to 8,100,000, is probably one of the factors involved in Middletown's high infant-mortality rate.[29] In most recent years the city's infant death rate has been markedly higher than that of the state as a whole and also than the rate of the state's urban population.

In such public-health problems, aside from the partial sewer project

[28] Proponents of centralized governmental authority and planning can find strong support for their case in the chronic stalemates over such elementary health matters in Middletown. It is not too much to say that the great majority of local social changes that Middletown's culture ultimately regards as "constructive" are not locally generated but are diffused to Middletown, against the pressure of local inertia and resistance, from outside agencies. (See n. 1 in the present chapter, and also *Middletown,* p. 457.) The immediacies of local vested interests tend to be too strong, in matters where changes will not patently serve some powerful local group's financial interest, to make change congenial. Local power groups are too closely deadlocked in the struggle to maintain immediate advantages to be hospitable to "long-term planning" or "scientifically drafted standards." It is normal to such locally pot-bound cultural units to look upon many things as "right in principle" but "locally impractical."

Pure milk is a case in point: Middletown people all accept the desirability of pure milk as too obvious to need debating. And yet as a community Middletown has been powerless to effect such a simple change as the passing of a modern milk ordinance. Early in 1935 the State passed legislation setting up a State Milk Control Board with power to fix prices and to license dealers. This right to license dealers was upheld by the Superior Court of the State in July, 1935. If, on appeal, it remains unchallenged, this licensing provision will probably affect the Middletown situation, as, *e.g.,* one local dealer announced in June, 1935, his installation of a pasteurizing system in compliance with the State Board's requirements.

[29] See Table 51 in Appendix III.

under Federal financing, Middletown has not changed its ways during the boom and depression years.

The health costs of a great depression to a community are not things that ordinarily lie on the surface. Virtually no one in Middletown has actually starved to death in the depression, and the slowly cumulating debits of rachitic children, abscessed teeth, and tuberculosis are readily overlooked in this go-as-you-please culture in which the onus for keeping healthy is placed traditionally on the individual. One indication of the health cost of the depression may be apparent in the fact that the county Anti-Tuberculosis Association carried 1618 active cases into 1935, which is 200 more than it carried into 1934 and 400 more than it carried into 1933. As against 272 new cases taken on by the association in 1933, 481 were added in 1934. This may suggest a reversal of the trend which has reduced the county's tuberculosis death rate per 100,000 of population from 102 in 1924 to 47 in 1933. Another indication of the health debit of the depression appears in a news story in September, 1935, on the findings of the doctors in their annual fall inspection of school children:

Last year supplementary feeding programs in [Middletown] schools were abandoned, except for the giving of milk and cod-liver oil late in the school year. Wednesday morning school medical inspectors saw the results. On their routine inspection at Roosevelt School, the doctors found that the majority of the pupils are anaemic, especially in the lower grades. There is but one major reason for that condition, the doctors are convinced: The children aren't getting enough food at home, particularly the costlier items such as milk and butter.

Wherever they go, the doctors see reflected in the health of pupils the economic conditions of the school districts. At Wilson Elementary School, for example, they found children in excellent health. This they attribute to increased employment in that part of the city and the increased use of garden produce during the summer, many residents in that part of town having space for large gardens. At Roosevelt School, the worst school they have found from the standpoint of under-nutrition and anaemia, they point out that the neighborhood depended largely on the old Republic Iron and Steel plant, one of the first to close down and still inoperative except for one small department.

Middletown is not aware of having learned any permanent lessons regarding public and private health since 1929, or since 1925. Social health services have been extended at some points. Those minor extensions under the private charity agencies will remain; such changes as free milk, lunches, and cod-liver oil for school children will probably be abandoned; and the large-scale provision of free medical care at tax expense will certainly be abandoned at the earliest possible moment. The city's leaders intend to shrink health services, like all other community emergency activities, back to "normal" (*i.e.*, pre-depression practices) as rapidly as possible. If, therefore, one contents oneself with looking out upon the problem of public and private health through Middletown's own eyes, one must conclude that, aside from the new hospital and the extension of the work of the Visiting Nurse Association, Middletown stands today substantially where it stood in 1925. In a more subtle sense, the fact that chronic lacks have been amplified by the depression to proportions compelling public attention and direct though temporary adaptations of local practices to obvious needs may, here as elsewhere in the city's life, have sown the seed of eventual major social change.

CHAPTER XII

"The Middletown Spirit"

ONE CANNOT talk about "what Middletown thinks" or "feels" or "is" without a large amount of distortion. As many qualifications must be noted in speaking of a "typical" Middletown citizen as in speaking of Middletown as a "typical" American inland city. Some of these qualifications, distinguishing attitudes of different racial groups, business class and working class, men and women, parents and children, as well as differing attitudes of individuals, have been noted in the preceding pages, and others will be discussed in this chapter.

And yet, Middletown can be lived in and described only because of the presence of large elements of repetition and coherence in the culture. As one moves about the city one encounters in the city government, in the church, the press, and the civic clubs, and in the folk talk on the streets and about family dinner tables points of view so familiar and so commonly taken for granted that they represent the intellectual and emotional shorthands of understanding and agreement among a large share of the people. These are the things that one does and feels and says so naturally that mentioning them in Middletown implies an "of course." Individual differences at these points have become rubbed away, and thought and sentiment pass from person to person like smooth familiar coins which everyone accepts and no one examines with fresh eyes. Just as surely, too, there are other things that one does not ordinarily say or think or do. Around these patterns of customary acceptance and rejection certain types of personality develop. Those persons who most nearly exemplify the local stereotypes thrive, are "successful," and "belong"; while dropping away behind them are others who embody less adequately the values by which Middletown lives, down to the community misfits who live meagerly in the shadow of frustration and unpopularity. These latter deviant types often labor under pressures and lack of support in Middletown which they might not experience in other communities—larger communities, communities harboring a wider range of types, where one's life does not lie so open to one's neighbors or where one's dissident ideas or actions are not taken so personally as threats to one's neighbors' accepted ways of life, or even where certain types which are out of the ordinary in Middletown are normal rather than deviant.

It is the purpose of this chapter to attempt to uncover the patterns of life and of personality which are of the "of-course" type accepted by the mass of Middletown people, as well as modifications of these patterns among different groups in the population during the span of the last ten years.

These accepted regularities in Middletown tend to appear in each significant area of living. They tend also to form a design of some rough continuity,[1] so that if one picks up the life of a Middletown citizen anywhere throughout the web, one can go on familiarly throughout the rest of the pattern without meeting many unexpected knots. This is what gives some rough unity to Middletown culture, and enables one to speak, as did the title of the local newspaper editorial set at the head of this chapter, of "the [Middletown] spirit." This by no means implies that in carrying on its daily operations of living Middletown acts necessarily according to these values which it affirms. Often quite the contrary is the case. But these are the values *in the name of which* it acts, the symbols which can be counted upon to secure emotional response, the banners under which it marches.

The following suggest the rough pattern of things Middletown is *for* and *against*—in short, its values.

By and large Middletown believes:

In being honest.
In being kind.[2]

[1] See *Middletown,* pp. 492-93.
[2] A favorite quotation from Ella Wheeler Wilcox still appears in Middletown's club programs:

> "So many gods, so many creeds,
> So many paths that wind and wind,
> While just the art of being kind,
> Is all the sad world needs."

A resident of twenty-five years in Middletown, describing the launching of the first Christmas campaign for helping the poor some years ago, writes: "Within three days the [newspaper] office was so piled with contributions that the reporters couldn't find their desks. Middletown people may have no culture, but when appealed to in the right way there is no limit to their sympathy."

In being friendly,[3] a "good neighbor," and a "good fellow." [4]

In being loyal, and a "booster, not a knocker."

In being successful.

In being an average man. "Practically all of us realize that we are common men, and we are prone to distrust and hate those whom we regard as uncommon." [5]

In having character as more important than "having brains."

In being simple and unpretentious and never "putting on airs" or being a snob.[6]

In prizing all things that are common and "real" and "wholesome." "There are beauties at your own doorstep comparable to those you find on long journeys."

[3] Willis Fisher presents an excellent picture of the mellow friendliness of the small community in the Middle West in his chapter, "Small-Town Middle-Westerner," in *Who Owns America?*, edited by Herbert Agar and Allen Tate. (Boston; Houghton Mifflin, 1936.)

[4] The quoted words and phrases scattered through this list of things Middletown believes are from local editorials, club programs, civic-club and other addresses and papers, and from conversations. All are included because, in the experience of the writers, they represent widely-held Middletown attitudes. For the sake of brevity, the many sources are not always identified in this long listing.

[5] Middletown business people for the most part think of themselves as being a city of "small businessmen" and make a virtue of it. A note of editorial comment in November, 1935, stated: "Several persons were asked how many people in [Middletown] in their opinion have a weekly income of $100 or better, and the top estimate was 1,000. Most of them believed half that number would be more nearly correct. A few thought 200 would be about right. The right answer probably is somewhere between these last two extremes."

[6] Such "folksy" jingles as the following in Edgar Guest's daily "Just Folks" in Middletown's morning paper evoke a comforting chuckle of agreement at the breakfast table:

> My overcoat, when winds blow cold,
>   Is stout enough to keep me warm,
> This year it will be three years old
>   And sag a trifle round my form,
> But what of that? I shall not freeze
>   Nor feel the weather more than they
> Who bought their garments overseas
>   At prices I could never pay;
> Comparisons are relative
>   When everything is said and done,
> Though on a lesser plain I live,
>   I get my share of honest fun.
> My friends are neither rich nor great,
>   But I am fond of them, and they
> Are fond of me, I dare to state.
>   What more can pomp and fortune say?

In having "common sense."

In being "sound" and "steady."

In being a good sport and making friends with one's opponents. "It doesn't help to harbor grudges." [7]

In being courageous and good-natured in the face of trouble and "making friends with one's luck." [8]

In being, when in doubt, like other people.

In adhering, when problems arise, to tried practices that have "worked" in the past.

That "progress is the law of life," and therefore:

That evolution in society is "from the base and inferior to the beautiful and good."

That, since "progress means growth," increasing size indicates progress. In this connection Middletown tends to emphasize quantitative rather than qualitative changes, and absolute rather than relative numbers or size.

That "the natural and orderly processes of progress" should be followed.

That change is slow, and abrupt changes or the speeding up of changes through planning or revolutions is unnatural.

That "radicals" ("reds," "communists," "socialists," "atheists"—the terms are fairly interchangeable in Middletown) want to inter-

[7] Elections evoke this prevalent mood of friendly and good-natured acceptance of victory or defeat in characteristic form. The day after the 1936 election an editorial in the local Republican press remarked simply: "After an election we must get together and support everybody who has been elected. In [Middletown] this thing does not hurt at all, because those who were elected are our own folks, regardless of politics."

Another editorial stated that anyone wishing to protest the 1936 election could do so before November 15, and added, "But you don't contest earthquakes and landslides." The same editor commented in his column on an attorney who was looking for a community in which to hang out his shingle, who described himself as "an honest lawyer and a Republican": "He was told by a friend, 'It doesn't make any difference where you go, for if you are an honest lawyer you will have no competition, and if you are a Republican the game laws will protect you.' "

[8] Despite Middletown's general faith in the forward movement of things in America, its personal goals tend to be moderate, and adversity is not a total stranger when it visits most of these families. Under the brave exterior of confidence, a common mood is that "It isn't a good thing to expect too much of life."

fere with things and "wreck American civilization." "We condemn agitators who masquerade under the ideals guaranteed by our Constitution. We demand the deportation of alien Communists and Anarchists."

That "in the end those who follow the middle course prove to be the wisest. It's better to stick close to the middle of the road, to move slowly, and to avoid extremes."

That evils are inevitably present at many points but will largely cure themselves. "In the end all things will mend."

That no one can solve all his problems, and consequently it is a good rule not to dwell on them too much and not to worry. "It's better to avoid worry and to expect that things will come out all right." "The pendulum will swing back soon."

That good will solves most problems.

That optimism on our part helps the orderly forces making for progress. "The year 1936 will be a banner year because people believe it will be."

That within this process the individual must fend for himself and will in the long run get what he deserves, and therefore:

That character, honesty, and ability will tell.

That one should be enterprising; one should try to get ahead of one's fellows, but not "in an underhand way."

That one should be practical and efficient.

That one should be hard-working and persevering. "Hard work is the key to success." "Until a man has his family financially established, he should not go in for frills and isms."

That one should be thrifty and "deny oneself" reasonably. "If a man will not learn to save his own money, nobody will save for him."

That a man owes it to himself, to his family, and to society to "succeed."

That "the school of hard knocks is a good teacher," and one should learn to "grin and bear" temporary setbacks. "It took an early defeat to turn many a man into a success." "After all, hardship never hurts anyone who has the stuff in him."

That social welfare, in Middletown and elsewhere, is the result of the two preceding factors working together—the natural law of progress and the individual law of initiative, hard work, and thrift —and therefore:

That any interference with either of the two is undesirable. "The Lord helps him who helps himself." "Congress," an editorial remarked sarcastically, "is now preparing for farm relief, while the wise farmer is out in the field relieving himself."

That society should not coddle the man who does not work hard and save, for if a man does not "get on" it is his own fault. "There is no such thing as a 'youth problem.' It is up to every boy and girl to solve his own problem in his own way."

That "the strongest and best should survive, for that is the law of nature, after all."

That people should have community spirit.

That they should be loyal, placing *their* family, *their* community,[9] *their* state, and *their* nation first. "The best American foreign policy is any policy that places America first." "America first is merely common sense."

That "American ways" are better than "foreign ways."

That "big-city life" is inferior to Middletown life and undesirable.[10] "Saturday-night crowds on [Middletown] streets," comments an editorial, "are radiantly clean as to person and clothes. . . . Saturday-night shopping becomes a holiday affair after they have bathed and put on their best garments at home. . . . [Middletown] is still a 'Saturday-night town,' and if big cities call us 'hicks' for that reason, let 'em."

That most foreigners are "inferior." "There is something to this Japanese menace. Let's have no argument about it, but just send those Japs back where they came from."

[9] A recently arrived new resident in Middletown remarked: "Beauty in any form seems to be conspicuous by its absence, and yet seemingly intelligent people praise the town as the most desirable possible place in which to live."

[10] There is in Middletown's press an undertone of disparagement of New York and other big cities, as noted in Ch. X. A shrewd observer of long residence in the city, describing her first years there, says: "I was quite unconscious at first of the fact that people from New York and other big cities are looked on with suspicion."

That Negroes are inferior.

That individual Jews may be all right but that as a race one doesn't care to mix too much with them.

That Middletown will always grow bigger and better.

That the fact that people live together in Middletown makes them a unit with common interests, and they should, therefore, all work together.

That American business will always lead the world. "Here in the United States, as nowhere else in the world, the little business and the big business exist side by side and are a testimonial to the soundness of the American way of life."

That the small businessman is the backbone of American business. "In no country in the world are there so many opportunities open to the little fellow as in the United States. . . . These small businesses are succeeding . . . because they meet a public need." "A wise [Middletown] banker once said: 'I like to patronize a peanut stand because you only have one man to deal with and his only business is to sell peanuts.'"

That economic conditions are the result of a natural order which cannot be changed by man-made laws. "Henry Ford says that wages ought to be higher and goods cheaper. We agree with this, and let us add that we think it ought to be cooler in the summer and warmer in winter." [11]

That depressions are regrettable but nevertheless a normal aspect of business. "Nothing can be done to stop depressions. It's just like a person who feels good one day and rotten the next."

That business can run its own affairs best and the government

[11] The above is from a Middletown editorial comment of January, 1930. Another editorial states: "It never is safe to tamper with natural laws—and that of supply and demand is one of them. So to a student of economics or even one who is not a student but has some slight knowledge of them, such schemes as 'pools' and holding companies for grains have slight appeal because, essentially, they are attempting to do something by sheer economic pressure that natural causes and their inevitable results cannot sustain. Of course this sounds like rank heresy to those who believe, notwithstanding the long history of failure, that man-made laws really are of some consequence when opposed to Nature-made ones."

And still another comment in the same vein: "The advancing price of farm products [is] not due to any kind of legislation, but to natural causes which are always responsible for prices whether high or low."

should keep its hands off business. "All these big schemes for planning by experts brought to Washington won't work."

That every man for himself is the right and necessary law of the business world, "tempered, of course, with judgment and fair dealing."

That competition is what makes progress and has made the United States great.

That the chance to grow rich is necessary to keep initiative alive. "Young folks today are seeking material advantage, which is just exactly what all of us have been seeking all our lives."

That "men won't work if they don't have to." "Work isn't fun. None of us would do a lick of work if he didn't have to."

That the poor-boy-to-president way is the American way to get ahead.

That ordinarily any man willing to work can get a job.[12]

That a man "really gets what is coming to him in the United States."

That "any man who is willing to work hard and to be thrifty and improve his spare time can get to the top. That's the American way, and it's as true today as it ever was."

That it is a man's own fault if he is dependent in old age.

That the reason wages are not higher is because industry cannot afford to pay them. "Employers want to pay as high wages as they can, and they can be counted on to do so just as soon as they are able."

That the rich are, by and large, more intelligent and industrious than the poor. "That's why they are where they are."

That the captains of industry are social benefactors because they create employment. "Where'd all our jobs be if it wasn't for them?"

That capital is simply the accumulated savings of these people with foresight.

That if you "make it too easy" for the unemployed and people like that they will impose on you.

That nobody is really starving in the depression.

That capital and labor are partners and have basically the same interests. "It is a safe bet that if the average worker and employer could sit down calmly together and discuss their differences, a

---

[12] This, like some of the other assumptions regarding economic matters in this section, is a commoner business-class than working-class point of view.

great deal more would be done to solve their difficulties than will be accomplished by politics or by extremists on either side."

That "the open shop is the American way."

That labor organization is unwise and un-American in that it takes away the worker's freedom and initiative, puts him under the control of outsiders, and seeks to point a gun at the head of business. "We wouldn't mind so much if our own people here would form their own unions without any of these outsiders coming in to stir up trouble."

That strikes are due to troublemakers' leading American workers astray.

That Middletown people should shop in Middletown. "Buy where you earn your money."

That the family is a sacred institution and the fundamental institution of our society.

That the monogamous family is the outcome of evolution from lower forms of life and is the final, divinely ordained form.

That sex was "given" to man for purposes of procreation, not for personal enjoyment.

That sexual relations before or outside of marriage are immoral.

That "men should behave like men, and women like women."

That women are better ("purer") than men.

That a married woman's place is first of all in the home, and any other activities should be secondary to "making a good home for her husband and children."

That men are more practical and efficient than women.

That most women cannot be expected to understand public problems as well as men.

That men tend to be tactless in personal relations and women are "better at such things."

That everybody loves children, and a woman who does not want children is "unnatural."

That married people owe it to society to have children.

That it is normal for parents to want their children to be "better off," to "have an easier time," than they themselves have had.

That childhood should be a happy time, "for after that, one's problems and worries begin." "Everyone with a drop of humanitarian blood believes that children are entitled to every possible happiness."

That parents should "give up things for their children," but "should maintain discipline and not spoil them."

That it is pleasant and desirable to "do things as a family."

That fathers do not understand children as well as mothers do.

That children should think on essential matters as their parents do.

That young people are often rebellious ("have queer ideas") but they "get over these things and settle down."

That home ownership is a good thing for the family and also makes for good citizenship.

That schools should teach the facts of past experience about which "sound, intelligent people agree."

That it is dangerous to acquaint children with points of view that question "the fundamentals."

That an education should be "practical," but at the same time, it is chiefly important as "broadening" one.

That too much education and contact with books and big ideas unfits a person for practical life.

That a college education is "a good thing."

But that a college man is no better than a non-college man and is likely to be less practical, and that college men must learn "life" to counteract their concentration on theory.

That girls who do not plan to be teachers do not ordinarily need as much education as boys.

That "you forget most of the things you learn in school." "Looking back over the years, it seems to me that at least half of the friends of my schoolday youth who have made good were dumbunnies. . . . Anyway they could not pile up points for honors unless it was an honor to sit someplace between the middle and the foot of the class."

That schoolteachers are usually people who couldn't make good in business.

That teaching school, particularly in the lower grades, is women's business.

That schools nowadays go in for too many frills.

That leisure is a fine thing, but work comes first.

That "all of us hope we'll get to the place sometime where we can work less and have more time to play."

But that it is wrong for a man to retire when he is still able to work. "What will he do with all his time?"

That having a hobby is "all very well if a person has time for that sort of thing and it doesn't interfere with his job."

That "red-blooded" physical sports are more normal recreations for a man than art, music, and literature.

That "culture and things like that" are more the business of women than of men.

That leisure is something you spend with people and a person is "queer" who enjoys solitary leisure.

That a person doesn't want to spend his leisure doing "heavy" things or things that remind him of the "unpleasant" side of life. "There are enough hard things in real life—books and plays should have a pleasant ending that leaves you feeling better."

But that leisure should be spent in wholesomely "worth-while" things and not be just idle or frivolous.

That it is better to be appreciative than discriminating. "If a person knows too much or is too critical it makes him a kill-joy or a snob not able to enjoy the things most people enjoy."

That anything widely acclaimed is pretty apt to be good; it is safer to trust the taste and judgment of the common man in most things rather than that of the specialist.

That Middletown wants to keep abreast of the good new things in the arts and literature, but it is not interested in anything freakish.

That "being artistic doesn't justify being immoral."

That smoking and drinking are more appropriate leisure activities for men than for women.

That it is more appropriate for well-to-do people to have automobiles and radios and to spend money on liquor than for poor people.

That it is a good thing for everyone to enjoy the fine, simple pleasures of life.[13]

[13] Characteristic is the article which first appeared in the editor's personal column, *Comment,* on the first page of the afternoon paper in 1933. In response to many requests, it has been reprinted every year since then:

"WHEN THERE MAY NEVER BE ANOTHER?"

"I hate to sleep, these summer nights. I may never have another summer, and this one is fleeting as a bird on wing. I only have this summer hour, this sum-

That "we folks out here dislike in our social life formality, society manners, delicate food, and the effete things of rich Eastern people."

That the American democratic form of government is the final and ideal form of government.

That the Constitution should not be fundamentally changed.

That Americans are the freest people in the world.

That America will always be the land of opportunity and the greatest and richest country in the world.

That England is the finest country in Europe.

That Washington and Lincoln were the greatest Americans. (Edison is sometimes linked with these two as the third great American.)

That only unpatriotic dreamers would think of changing the form of government that was "good enough for" Washington and Lincoln.[14]

That socialism, communism, and fascism are disreputable and un-American.

That socialists and communists believe in dividing up existing wealth on a per-capita basis. "This is unworkable because within a year a comparatively few able persons would have the money again."

mer minute, but today summer is mine, if I will take it—summer with verdant grass dew-besprent in the early morning and birds at dawn singing their matin songs; summer with the glory of its sunsets of mackerel and gold as night approaches; summer with its mellow moons and its chirpings and plaintive calls of little wild creatures from out the dark. . . .

"And so I like to crowd into life in summer time all the hours that I can summon. Hot winds may sweep across the land, but they are summer winds and betimes they cool; flitting insects may annoy, but they express the life that is of summer's essence; the sun may beat down upon us, but it is summer's sun that makes the flowers to give us their radiance, the trees to rear their leaf-crowned heads in majesty against the cerulean blue and shadow in fine traceries the white fleece of the clouds.

"Sleep? In summer? When there may never be another?"

[14] Middletown is wont to invoke old leaders against new leaders who threaten to leave the "safe and tried middle of the road." Such innovations as its Revolutionary founding fathers and the other heroes in its pantheon stood for are forgotten; their revolts were but the orderly work of natural progress; their conservatism was their essential contribution as persons. Thus, a recent editorial on "Lincoln the Conservative" urges that "Lincoln's name has been taken in vain by radicals. . . . He was a political fundamentalist and knew his Constitution" and did not believe in "tearing out the foundations of government in the attempt to rebuilt it on the blueprints of Utopians. . . . He kept the middle of the road."

That radicalism makes for the destruction of the church and family, looseness of morals, and the stifling of individual initiative.

That only foreigners and long-haired troublemakers are radicals.

That the voters, in the main, really control the operation of the American government.

That newspapers give citizens "the facts."

That the two-party system is the "American way."

That it does not pay to throw away one's vote on a minority party.

That government ownership is inefficient and more costly than private enterprise.

That the government should leave things to private initiative. "More business in government and less government in business." (Events since 1933 have been causing large numbers of people in the lower income brackets in Middletown to question this formerly widely held assumption, though the upper income brackets hold to it as tenaciously as ever.)

That high tariffs are desirable. "Secretary Hull's tariff policy is putting the American producer in the city and in the country in competition with the peasant and serf in Europe and Asia."

That taxes should be kept down.

That our government should leave Europe and the rest of the world alone.

That the United States should have large military and naval defenses to protect itself, but should not mix in European wars.

That pacifism is disreputable and un-American. "We're militaristic rather than pacifist out here—though of course we don't want wars."

That many public problems are too big for the voter to solve but that Congress can solve them.

That "experts" just "gum up" the working of democracy.

That national problems can be solved by "letting nature take its course" or by passing laws.

That problems such as corruption in public office can be largely solved by electing better men to office.

That local problems such as crime can be ameliorated by putting people in jail and by imposing heavier sentences.

That, human nature being what it is, there will always be some graft in government but that despite this we are the best-governed nation in the world.

That organizations such as the American Legion and the D.A.R. represent a high order of Americanism.

That because of "poor, weak human nature" there will always be some people too lazy to work, too spendthrift to save, too short-sighted to plan. "Doesn't the Bible prove this when it says, 'The poor ye have always with you'?"

That charity will always be necessary. "For you wouldn't let a dog starve."

That in a real emergency anyone with any human feeling will "share his shirt with an unfortunate who needs it." [15]

But that a "government dole" on a large scale is an entirely different thing from charity to an individual, and that "a paternalistic system which prescribes an exact method of aiding our unfortunate brothers and sisters is demoralizing."

That idleness and thriftlessness are only encouraged by making charity too easy.

That it "undermines a man's character" for him to get what he doesn't earn.

That it is a fine thing for rich people to be philanthropic.

[15] This mood of human kindliness to people in distress is met with everywhere in the talk of Middletown. It is conspicuously met with among the people who protest most loudly against public relief. One may suspect that the indignation of many of Middletown's business class over the existence of such a broad policy of public relief as has existed in the depression derives in part from their knowledge that they, in common with people generally in Middletown, have this deep, neighborly attitude towards "anyone really in dire need." It is significant of the contradictions into which Middletown's thought and emotions run in matters involving the specific single cases of need and generalized policies for handling need as a social problem that the same editor, quoted in Ch. IV as writing in his paper that there are so many down-and-outers on relief in Middletown that it would be a boon to everyone if a plague would come and wipe them all out, also sprinkles his column with such mellow human comment as the following:

"Do you know how much the average waitress is being paid in [Middletown]? Neither do I, but it's something scandalous. They are expected to remain virtuous on eight dollars a week. Your tip might help a bit."

"He slithered into the restaurant early in the morning. He was not so old in years as he was in appearance. . . . The world had beaten him down. He was unlovely to behold, as degenerate age always is. . . . 'I'd like to have a cup of coffee,' he said, and his glance was sidewise. He fumbled about for a nickel and finally laid it on the counter. 'We don't charge for coffee today,' said the waitress. I hope she won't be fired. I hope she has a chair in Heaven."

That recipients of charity should be grateful.

That relief from public funds during the depression is a purely emergency matter to be abandoned as soon as possible, and that it is unthinkable for the United States to have anything resembling a permanent "dole."

That things like unemployment insurance are unnecessary because "in ordinary times any man willing to work can get a job"; and that they are demoralizing both to the recipient and to the businessman taxed to support them.

That Christianity is the final form of religion and all other religions are inferior to it.

But that what you believe is not so important as the kind of person you are.

That nobody would want to live in a community without churches, and everybody should, therefore, support the churches.

That churchgoing is sometimes a kind of nuisance, one of the things you do as a duty, but that the habit of churchgoing is a good thing and makes people better.

That there isn't much difference any longer between the different Protestant denominations.

But that Protestantism is superior to Catholicism.

That having a Pope is un-American and a Catholic should not be elected President of the United States.

That Jesus is the Son of God and what he said is true for all time.

That Jesus was the most perfect man who ever lived.

That God exists and runs the universe.

That there is a "hereafter." "It is unthinkable that people should just die and that be the end." [16]

That God cannot be expected to intercede in the small things of life.

[16] The related belief in reward or punishment after death is less bluntly held by Middletown's Presbyterians, Episcopalians, Universalists, and Friends, who are for the most part business-class folk, than by other denominations. Emotionally, a vague, uneasy belief in a hereafter where there will be some sort of accounting lingers deep in the lives of a very large share of Middletown's population. It is characteristic of a culture sure of its rightness in the best of all possible nations that the pleasant idea of "immortality" is strong while the idea of "punishment" is receding.

but that through faith and prayer one may rely upon His assistance in the most important concerns of life.[17]

That preachers are rather impractical people who wouldn't be likely to make really good in business.[18]

That I wouldn't want my son to go into the ministry.[19]

That preachers should stick to religion and not try to talk about business, public affairs, and other things "they don't know anything about."

Middletown is *against* the reverse of the things it is for. These need not be listed here, but they may be summarized by saying that Middletown is *against:*

Any strikingly divergent type of personality, especially the non-optimist, the non-joiner, the unfriendly person, and the pretentious person.[20]

Any striking innovations in art, ideas, literature, though it tolerates these more if they are spectacular, episodic intrusions from without than if they are practiced within Middletown.

[17] Middletown people vary widely in the literalness of their belief in prayer. In general, women believe in it more than men and the South Side more than the North Side. While only the women in a South Side church might ordinarily pledge themselves to pray for a piece of legislation, as did one group in the case of the Eighteenth Amendment, in times of great personal or familial emergency even many businessmen will admit to close friends that they "prayed" over it. "Not," as one of them explained, "that I exactly thought it would make any difference, but my wife was so sick I just wasn't going to leave any stone unturned."

[18] This is the male attitude. Women tend to accept the minister more on the latter's own terms.

[19] This again is more a male attitude. Women would be more apt to feel secret pride in a son in the ministry.

[20] In a poem by a local poet entitled "Middletown," in a column headed "Our Own Poets" in the local press in 1935, the following lines occur:

> "There she lies, by fear prostrated
> Fear of doing aught unusual,
> Fear of thinking, fear of doubting,
> Fear of frankness, fear of gossip,
> Fear of those in higher places,
> Fear of those who are the lowly,
> Fear of herself and others
> Fearing 'twill be known she's fearing."

Any striking innovations in government, religion, education, the family.

Centralized government, bureaucracy, large-scale planning by government. "It's impossible to plan on a large scale. There are too many factors involved. It is best to leave it to individuals, who are likely to take a more normal or more natural course."

Anything that curtails money making.

Anybody who criticizes any fundamental institution.

People engaged in thinking about or working for change: social planners, intellectuals, professors, highbrows, radicals, Russians, pacifists, anybody who knows too much.

Foreigners, internationalists, and international bankers.

People who are not patriots—for city, state, and nation.

Non-Protestants, Jews, Negroes—as "not quite our sort."

People who stress the importance of sex, including those who favor the general dissemination of information about birth control.

People who buy things, do things, live in ways not customary for one of that income level.

Frills, notions, and anything fancy.

People and things that are fragile or sensitive rather than robust.

Forty years ago Lord Bryce said of the United States:

Let us then . . . endeavor to discover what are now the salient intellectual features of the mass of the native population in the United States.

As there is much difference of opinion regarding them, I present with diffidence the following list:

1. A desire to be abreast of the best thought and work of the world everywhere, to have every form of literature and art adequately represented, and excellent of its kind, so that America shall be felt to hold her own among the nations.

2. A fondness for bold and striking effects, a preference for large generalizations and theories which have an air of completeness.

3. An absence among the multitude of refined taste, with a disposition to be attracted rather by brilliance than by delicacy of workmanship; a want of mellowness and inadequate perception of the difference between first-rate work in a quiet style and mere flatness.

4. Little respect for canons or traditions, accompanied by the notion that new conditions must of necessity produce new ideas.

5. An undervaluing of special knowledge or experience, except in applied science and in commerce, an idea that an able man can do one thing pretty much as well as another, as Dr. Johnson thought that if he had taken to politics he would have been as distinguished therein as he was in tragic poetry.

6. An admiration for literary or scientific eminence, an enthusiasm for anything that can be called genius, with an over-readiness also to discover it.

7. A love of intellectual novelties.

8. An intellectual impatience, and desire for quick and patent results.

9. An over-valuing of the judgments of the multitude; a disposition to judge by newspaper "success" work which has not been produced with a view to such success.

10. A tendency to mistake bigness for greatness.[21]

Many of the characteristics which Lord Bryce points out will be seen to be similar to those noted above in connection with the things Middletown is for and against. The most striking difference lies in the emphasis Americans placed, according to Lord Bryce, on the adventurous and the new in contrast to the emphasis Middletown now places on the tried and the safe. If both observations are correct, it raises the interesting question as to whether Americans have put less emphasis on new experience and more on security as their pioneer background has receded further into the past and as conflicts between symbols and the necessities of life have been sharpened. Or the divergences may suggest the question as to whether Middletown exhibits certain characteristics of the small, inland American community, while Lord Bryce was generalizing more from the larger cities where "lion-hunting" and the pursuit of "genius," "intellectual novelties," and "distinguished foreigners" is better developed. Certainly Middletown would have been awed and elated had a Lord Bryce come to lecture there in the nineties—or today—and would have turned out in heavy numbers to hear him, but had Lord Bryce come to live in Middletown he would have made the community uncomfortable.

The design for living of an accepted Middletown businessman would look something like the following: He embodies the central beliefs and qualities recognized locally as desirable and American. He is es-

21 James Bryce, *The American Commonwealth* (New York; Macmillan, 1897), Vol. II, pp. 760-61.

sentially moderate, a middle-of-the-roader.[22] He may have some unusual traits or abilities—a hobby, private enthusiasms for cultivated
things most Middletown men know little about—provided they are not
too exceptional and do not "distort" him. He must be active in trying
to "get on" in the world. The quality of his life is measured in terms
of tangible success, achievement, "something to show for it," ability
to "produce the goods," but this success is mistrusted unless it is won
by hard work, common sense, and careful planning. Hard work is

[22] It was not by accident that, following Landon's nomination by the Republicans for President in June, 1936, he began to be sold to Middletown through the
following slogan-appeals dear to Middletown's heart. Full-page headlines proclaimed:

"LANDON, THE CAREFUL KANSAN

"Yes, It's True Alf Landon as a Boy Swam a Two-mile Lake,
But He Didn't Take Any Chances—
He Had Sense Enough to Be Followed by a Comrade in a Boat!"

Then followed such sure-fire symbols as the following:
A picture of his mother, "descended of fighting pioneer stock."
A picture of the First Methodist Church in Marietta, Ohio, "where the growing Alf Landon attended Sunday School." [Methodist Church membership is
the best religious aid a Middletown candidate can have.]
A picture of the boy *and his dog,* with a caption saying that the candidate
was "recalled by playmates as 'quiet, easy to know and likeable.' "
Then a "Thumbnailing Landon's Life" summary featured in heavy type and
including such common-denominator traits as these:

"MARRIED: Twice. First wife died. [No divorce or scandal.]
"CHILDREN: Three [a family man].
"BELONGS TO: Methodist Church [a religious man], Phi Gamma Delta, Phi
Delta Phi, Masons, Odd Fellows, Elks [a joiner and regular fellow, "one
of us"; these lodges include both Middletown's business-class and working-
class lodges], American Legion [a veteran and patriot].
"HE IS: Five feet nine [a good average height—no giant and no runt]. Black-
haired, but beginning to gray [youth and energy touched with sobriety].
About 170 pounds in weight. Brown-eyed.
"HE LIKES: Pipe-smoking and old hats. [A plain fellow without pretentions,
who likes his comfort like the rest of us.] Fishing and horseback riding.
[A love for dogs, horses and fishing is good political bait in Middletown.]
Bridge. [Spends his leisure "like we do" and not always being serious
like Roosevelt's Brain Trust.] Baseball and football. Ministers [again a
religious man who likes God-fearing associates]. Reading [a thoughtful
man]."

Then began the life history of the man who "embodies all the best traits of
the respectable prairie citizen who 'has done right well by himself.' " [The success note—this man can be no dunderhead, because he has made money.]
These are psychologically sound terms in which to "sell" a candidate to Middletown, and the fact that they were inadequate suggests the force of other
factors, involving economic security, which outweighed personal appeal.

more valued than "living by one's wits," common sense more than theory. He is the kind of person to whom many things may be "all right in theory, but not in practice." He should be married, have children, and be a church member, a lodge man (though he need not go often to church or lodge meetings), and a member of a civic club, and be active in the Community Fund drive and other civic activities. He is a person who is practical and positive, not a dreamer or questioner; one who is genial, friendly, "one of us." And he must share Middletown's essential civic loyalty and optimism.

For a Middletown woman the measurable kind of success is somewhat less coercive and success lies in a different sphere. Her success as wife and mother is measured in terms of her husband and children. She may be quiet and unaggressive socially and interested primarily in her family; but she should have some interest in club work, church work, social life, and philanthropy, be responsive to other people and to good causes, and helpful and friendly. In her case, too, there are certain desirable negative emphases, toning her down to the "womanly" type and to a position secondary to that of men; a woman should not be too intelligent, too witty, too aggressive and independent, too critical, or too different. She should not want a career, and should not compete with men, but rather back them up. The woman who markedly infringes any of these taboos may have both men and her own sex arrayed against her.[23]

Special conditions, including the possession of certain qualities in outstanding degree, may lift the local taboo on many things Middletown objects to in people. By all odds, the chief among these taboo-lifters is business success. A pecuniary culture, that buys its way step by step through life, identifies the achievement of business success (which in this culture means the "making" of money) with the creation of general welfare. Deep in the pioneer past and in the more recent farm past of Middletown people, work meant the production of things needed for immediate use in the universal struggle against scarcity—such things as food, clothing, and shelter. Since no man grew or made all the things he needed, his neighbor's work was necessary to him as it contributed to the common store of badly needed goods under a system of division of labor. Thus the habits of life and thought under a handicraft system tended to build the enterprise of the individual rather solidly into the joint social enterprise. As private business has

[23] See Ch. V.

superseded this pattern of reciprocal work, money has come to stand for goods; the contiguous "making" of money by many private businessmen is, by a simple transfer in thought, still regarded as cooperative work; and the older idea has been carried over in the form of the belief that acquisition of money means not only the production of wealth but, as under earlier conditions, the production of *common* wealth, *i.e.,* welfare. This carrying over into modern times of the identification of work, the creation of socially needed goods, money "making," and the common welfare results in the businessman's being looked upon today "as the putative producer of whatever wealth he acquires. By force of this sophistication the acquisition of property by any person is held to be not only expedient to the owner, but meritorious as an action serving the common good." [24]

As, therefore, the chief contributor to the community's welfare, the successful businessman in Middletown elicits from his fellow citizens wholehearted praise, as well as envy and emulation. Since Middletown's values are regarded as leading to "success," it follows easily that those who are successful must obviously have these values to have become successful. So, by this subtle and largely unconscious process, Middletown imputes to the successful businessman the possession—again "of course"—of the qualities of being "hard-working," "practical," "sound," "honest," "kindly," "efficient," "enterprising," "thrifty," and so on through the city's other values.[25]

[24] Thorstein Veblen, *The Theory of Business Enterprise* (New York; Viking Press, 1904), p. 291.
The line of argument in the above paragraph follows closely that of Veblen at this point.
[25] It is this confusion of the ideal (its values) and the real (its businessmen) that presents to Middletown's schools and churches their most acute problem. They are supposed to be "free" agencies whose role is to hold before a preoccupied community the richest values in the past and present experience of the culture and to help it to a continuously new creative discovery of rich values. But they find Middletown's powers of valuing heavily mortgaged in advance to the things that make for business success; not through caprice, but through the sheer emotional need to find the thing which one spends one's life in pursuing "good," coherent, important, and inclusive enough of one's values to warrant one's spending one's life on it. Human beings do not readily tolerate wide splits in their field of values. Under the pressure of this heavy emotional need, if values from outside the business system—*e.g.,* those put forward by religion and education—diverge in emphasis from those of the dominant field of "practical" life, the pull is overpoweringly in the direction of restating these deviant interpretations in terms of customary practice. And if they prove stubborn to restatement, the tendency of the culture is to ignore them or even to suppress them. In this situation lies an explanation for the prevalent "capture" of Middle-

If, then, the successful businessman, who has thus been made the realistic carrier and justifier of the community's values, elects to ignore any of the community's virtues, the weight of the many other virtues imputed to him by reason of his business success makes it easy to overlook or to excuse the exceptions. He may be more socially exclusive, cold, abrupt, dictatorial, or cynical than a less successful person can afford to be—and still meet with a large measure of community tolerance and even active approval.[26] It is in the reconciliation of its values that cluster around "forcefulness," "enterprise," "shrewdness," and "power" (the qualities particularly important in gaining competitive

town's education and religion by the business ideologies of the city and the resulting secondary position of both, save as redeeming symbols, in local life.

It is in the subordinate world of Middletown's women that the deviant ideals tend to live, in so far as they live outside the walls of the church and the school. The very facts of the relatively much heavier preoccupation of Middletown's women with outside values, in their study clubs and in their role as major carriers of "culture" in the refined sense, and of their much closer preoccupation with the long shadow of present values in the lives of their children tend to keep alive in them the "other world" of values. There lies before the investigator as this is written a statement from a responsible Middletown source quoting two prominent business-class wives in sharp dissent from their husbands on an important matter of local welfare. Both of these women are reported as saying, in effect, "My husband is boss in our family on such matters and I can't do a thing with him." This sort of thing suggests that the merging of the two worlds of value may be much more complete in the case of Middletown's men than of its women, and that the latter may suffer from tensions generated by this partial splitting of personality more than do the men. Within the privacy of Middletown's homes wives, "yoked to an unbeliever" in some of their deeper values, may be struggling to thwart the pressures of a husband molded perforce by another set of ideals. The men themselves confess in their easier moods that women are "finer," "purer," "more sensitive" than men—but Middletown's dominant world is the world of men.

[26] An instance of this ability of Middletown to find its necessary values under the hard and somewhat ruthless externals of a life that exhibited power of sorts in its midst is exhibited by the following editorial note on the occasion of the death of a local lawyer, public utility executive, and politician:

"So into the shadows has gone ———. It can be said fairly of him, I think, that he had a concealed tenderness of character. By that I mean that while occasionally his exterior appeared hard, especially to those with whom he disagreed, beneath the surface of him there was no hardness and much charity. . . . During much of his life he was 'the big boss' in local Republican politics, and he was not an 'easy boss' either. He expected service from those connected with him and he got it. He once was compared by an unfriendly newspaper to Mark Hanna. . . . The one little incident that he was about the first person to visit me in the case of my serious illness, although we had been factional opponents at least half of the time since I was a kid, seemed to me to be rather indicative of his character and important. . . . He lived usefully all his days. He was not an encumbrance upon anybody."

mastery in business), and of those associated with "kindness," "friendliness," "considerateness" (the "lovable" qualities), that Middletown has most frequently to make allowances for the failure of its successful businessman ideal to be the complete embodiment of all its ideals. This is done in part by the attribution of certain qualities such as "brusqueness" to men in general; in part by excusing a lack of interest in other people or in the arts of leisure by the fact that a "big man" is "naturally" too busy to do everything; and in part through attributing certain harsh qualities to the unavoidable nature of business, *e.g.,* a banker must be cold to appeals for leniency "because he is handling other people's money." Even such a rudimentary demand by Middletown as that for "honesty," is modified somewhat to allow for the customary exigencies of business and political practice. Certain sorts of misrepresentation—in advertising, retailing, floating an issue of securities, presenting corporate statements, legal matters such as a lawyer's *ex parte* pleading, political platforms, campaign speeches, and so on through all the things to which the philosophy of *caveat emptor* and "each for himself and God for all of us as the elephant said as he danced among the chickens" applies—have become conventionalized by the culture as part of the accepted fabric of custom in successful business or politics. In such cases the departures from "honesty" have been ritualized and conventionalized to enable customary practices to continue without too great a strain on the values which these practices undercut. But in the case of the man who in his private, personal dealings resorts to the "dishonesty" of misrepresentation, no such exculpating public ritual exists, and the judgment of the community is direct and severe. Similarly, "consideration" and "unselfishness" are hardly to be expected of a successful man in his strictly business relations, but they are demanded of anyone whom Middletown honors in his personal relations out of business hours.

Not many people in Middletown are successful in business or profession in outstanding degree. Lacking this, the others may yet thrive in local esteem if they are especially warm, friendly individuals, or if they are particularly helpful in civic matters. Certain other personality characteristics, either frowned upon or unusual in Middletown's eyes, may also be accepted if they do not challenge too directly the traits of activity, honesty, kindness, desire for success, loyalty, and moderation. A person may be a somewhat solitary person, a scholar, an artist, a person of reflection rather than of activity, provided that he does not thereby set himself up as superior to his neighbors, or display his interests too blatantly, or question any of Middletown's essential loyalties. Or even greater extremes of certain of these traits may be accepted provided they do not appear in more than one or two individuals. It may confer a certain rather exciting distinction upon a town to have one or two persons who are not striving for anything, who are indifferent to business or professional success, and who prefer working with music or flowers or collecting rare books. Even one professional cynic or one radical or scoffer or atheist or an extremist of almost any kind can be a town oddity or pet, but many of them would corrupt the youth and upset the fundamentals.

Some of these tolerated exceptions are patently in direct conflict with the community's basic values. As such, they are cells of potential social change, as was noted in Chapter II in discussing the group of dissident young spirits who, instead of scattering to larger cities, have been forced by the depression to remain in Middletown. If the United States faces a prolonged period of depressed opportunity for its people to move about over the country to find jobs, one of the characteristics of small-city life will decline, namely, the tendency in the expanding United States of the past for local communities to throw off centrifugally their deviant members. People who were too radical, too unconventional, too artistic, too little imbued with community loyalties, too different in any respect to be happy in and accepted by the Middletowns have been thrown off to the Chicagos, the Clevelands, the New Yorks. Middletown may be facing a future in which it can less easily keep a united front in its morale by shedding its inconvenient dissenters. The "frontier," of the once glamorous West and of the big city, is less readily absorbing them. As noted above, a few cultural deviants or "strangers"—Negroes, Jews, "odd" personalities, "unconventional" people, "radicals," and so on—tend to be tolerated, but as the number increases they may become a "problem" and mild antipathies may crystallize into antagonism.[27] With these aberrant temperaments and

[27] J. L. Moreno has demonstrated this experimentally in his work at the Hudson School for Girls, a New York State correctional institution. The girls are grouped by houses with six or eight in a house. Moreno has found that one Negro girl can be inserted in a white group with little or no racial resentment appearing on the part of the white girls, but when the number of Negroes in a house group is increased antagonism increases at a more rapid rate than the mere addition of a second or third Negro girl would seem superficially to warrant.

personalities backed up within Middletown, the local mores will have in some manner to accommodate them, or it will try to suppress them. Middletown may face in the future more occasions to mass its resources to "put down" various cells of dissent, for the city is too small to overlook large centers of dissent as can a metropolitan city.

A study is much needed of the shifts in tolerance in a city like Middletown and the conditions of their occurrence. Tolerance is not a general trait but specific, occurring in a specific situation or type of situation, and subject therefore to erratic manifestations from situation to situation. Middletown's own experience over time seems to be somewhat as follows:

Tolerance in religious matters has increased markedly in recent decades.

Economic tolerance—*e.g.,* toward deviant economic theories, labor organization, and so on—has diminished.

The press has assumed an outwardly more urbane and tolerant air at the same time that the sources of news and the editing of the news have come more markedly under the influence of the single, peremptory point of view represented by its business world.

Its educational tolerance has increased in the scope of things studied and the leeway accorded the individual student of real ability, but, as noted in Chapter VI, this tolerance is increasingly likely to be curtailed by the growing awareness by the city leaders that they must control the things taught to the young.

Its political tolerance has probably increased in so far as party lines mean less in the administration of the city; but its tolerance has apparently decreased in regard to national politics. Here again appears the enhanced recognition of the stake of business in national politics.

The growth of the city and its increased communication with the outside culture have brought it into contact with a greater variety of ways of living differing from its own, and thus have encouraged more tolerance of certain types of unfamiliar people and manners—movie actresses, wealthy people who live expensively, freer sex ideas, women who paint their faces, modern art, the bachelor girl, and so on. But at the same time the growing awaresnss of the complexity of the choices it must make in every department of living has tended to make Middletown huddle back defensively away from innovation and toward being "like other people," "playing safe," "being regular," "voting the good-fellow ticket straight."[28] In crisis situations, security is more valued by Middletown than new experience. To some extent it may be said that the old active tolerance, bred of mutual respect and zest for adventure in a brave new world yet to conquer, has given way to a defensive tolerance which allows dissent only where it must or where the thing tolerated is of no consequence.[29]

The heightening of insecurity during the depression has brought with it greater insistence upon conformity and a sharpening of latent issues. A central conflict in this culture was thus rendered more acute, namely, that mentioned above in the discussion of the successful businessman between the power-dominance-aggression values of the business world and the affectional-lovable-human values of family and interpersonal life.[30] Middletown is emerging from the worst of the depression, as noted in Chapter II, scarred by fear—fear of economic in-

---

[28] See *Middletown*, pp. 492-94.

[29] An elderly citizen contrasts vividly the cautiousness with which substantial Middletown men today express any doubt regarding the rightness of Republican party policy with "the way we used to go at it hammer and tongs as we walked back and forth from home to office." It was noted in the 1925 study (p. 300 f.) that forums of free discussion like the Ethical Society of the 1890's, where men freely debated such topics as atheism, find no place in respectable business circles today.

A point worth noting in this connection is the loss of intellectual leadership and independence by Middletown's doctors and lawyers. Some of Middletown's most ruggedly independent thinkers in 1890 were the local doctors, judges, and lawyers. These men less often speak their minds; they have become to a greater extent intellectually colorless, and are sticking to their last making money, like the rest of Middletown's businessmen.

[30] It is important to note the strains which current cultural demands for dominance and aggression create in the individual personality. The pursuit of "success," particularly in the business world where the males of the culture struggle, involves the acceptance of a heavy burden of disciplines and constraints. Most people, as a result, spend most of their time doing things in which they are not particularly interested, at a tempo which is not their own but dictated by the system. As Lawrence K. Frank has pointed out, to be "businesslike" means in our present culture to be *"im*personal." This is but one of the false faces that the culture forces men to wear. Everywhere one is confronted by the demand that one be "on time," act "like a man," hide one's emotions, talk and appear "successful," be "energetic," "sure of oneself," and so on indefinitely through the stereotypes of being "regular." Along with this channeling of individual bent and temperament that the "success pattern" imposes upon many businessmen must be noted in the case of the workingman the major constraints of inactivity due to recurrent unemployment and to being "bottom dog" in a culture which habitually stresses and glorifies the traits and possessions of its "top dogs." (For a brief suggestion as to how these constraints in the male world affect the accompanying women's world, see the second paragraph in n. 25 above.)

security, fear of governmental dominance, of organized labor, of losing factories and livelihood to other hungry cities. This is fertile soil for *Schrecklichkeit*. If personal and community security continue to be in serious jeopardy, not only the gentler values but values fertile for growth—*e.g.,* hospitality to new experience—may find themselves held in the iron grip of "practical" need. And the necessity for keeping things going, keeping the system at work, may relegate to a position of secondary concern questions of how it is done.

One of Middletown's values that has been heightened in the last ten years is its intense nationalism and acceptance of the United States and its institutions as superior to the rest of the world. Middletown's stereotype for "foreigners" is that they are "queer" or even "backward." The postwar turmoil in Europe, augmented by the facts that foreign nations "don't pay their [war] debts" and that "the international bankers" helped "get us into this depression mess," has left Middletown in the 1930's acutely intolerant of the world beyond the Atlantic and Pacific Oceans.

A summary of this position, representative of dominant group feeling, appeared editorially in the afternoon paper in January, 1932:

A GOOD PROGRAM FOR 1932

1. Keep the nation in a respectable position of defense.
2. Put the unemployed to work by enacting economic defenses such as a high tariff.
3. Drop the job of saving Europe from itself and tackle the job of saving America for ourselves.
4. Stir up a revival of old-fashioned patriotism and religion and get away from some of the fads and follies that have mussed up our national thinking.

More than ever, Middletown today wants to believe in America's ability to solve her own problems. "Some people still mistakenly think that conditions in Europe have something to do with America's coming out of the depression," said another editorial. Or again, "We must return to the old, sturdy, clean, upstanding America, the America that faced disaster unafraid and that went forward with the Bible and the flag."

Local patriotic organizations, even more vigorously than a decade ago, fan this in-group national feeling. The D.A.R. appears to be more active than in 1925 in its militant "safeguarding" of local patriotic sentiment, and it has organized a C.A.R. (Children of the American Revolution) branch. It is said to maintain a "close and continuous dictatorship" over the local Girl Scouts. The American Legion likewise appears to be more active. It maintains a large clubhouse, the "Château," in one of the spacious old residences, and it conducted in November, 1935, "the largest Armistice Day celebration in [Middletown] since World War hostilities ceased seventeen years ago."

Nowhere does this tendency to "protect ourselves from people whose ways are not ours" appear more clearly than in the treatment of Russia in the daily press. Russia is the arch-symbol of ways that are different: economic change, dictatorship, radicalism, immorality, an all-round threat to Middletown's own cultural security. Over and over one recurrent note with scarcely any mitigation is struck in the press: the monstrous tyranny of this communist state and its recurring failures:

Recognition of the Soviets [said an editorial in 1933 when American recognition of Soviet Russia was pending] merely means bringing additional troubles upon ourselves as the same course has brought trouble to other nations and most forcibly and often to Great Britain. Stalin and his crew cannot be dealt with as we deal with other rulers, for they do not recognize the common rules of honesty and of honor by which most governments are guided.

With monotonous regularity the headlines and news columns feature such things as the following:

Soviets Order Men into Slavery.
Russia Mourns under Tyranny.
Russians Kill Their Pets.
Russian Trade-union Officials Caught Trying to Revive Roman Orgies in Moscow.
Moscow Plans Civil War in the United States.

The Soviets are deadly foes of those who are educated beyond their fellows.

Lack of strong opposition leadership is probably the only thing that has prevented a serious revolt ere this. Foreign observers say that in time another revolution is certain and that "millions of Russians await 'der Tag.'"

After reading such reiterated rejection of Soviet Russia in Middletown's morning and evening papers throughout the eight years for

which these papers were covered in this restudy, it was novel to read a
first-page story in the afternoon paper in June, 1936, headed, "Russians
Get Vote, Freedom of the Press; New Constitution Will Restore Liberties." The news story under the headlines reported the new Russian
constitution with no adverse overtones. On the following day the leading editorial gave a clew to this favorable treatment. It read in part:

BEGINNING OF FREEDOM IN RUSSIA?

The announcement from Russia that the nation soon will have a constitution, a parliament, the secret ballot and liberty of speech and of press,
is a little hard to believe. The average American must think there is some
catch to it somewhere . . . but if the Soviet Republics even make a small
beginning toward granting liberty to the masses, that is encouraging.

Nobody need believe Russia will turn from Communism to a capitalistic
state overnight, nor that she will replace military coercion by an actually
democratic government in a day or a year, but her leaders have shown they
are susceptible to changes when they find their own plans unworkable or
when other plans are better. All these things give rise to the hope that
some day, not too many years away, the Russian people will gain at least
a respectable measure of freedom.

In other words, here was the prodigal son seeing the light and acknowl-
edging that "the American way is best, after all." And when he has
time to wash, shave, and think things over he may eventually be re-
habilitated and achieve a measure of the freedom all Americans have.[31]

The same vigorous repudiation, colored by fear, carries over directly
to the treatment of domestic "radicalism." A local manufacturer, elected
president of Rotary a week later, brought Rotary to its feet in April,
1933, with a speech reported as follows in the local press:

[31] Middletown's news treatment of fascist Germany and Italy is in general
negative and disapproving, but one is not impressed in the relatively meager
news carried on these countries by as much emphasis upon "shockers" as in the
case of Russia. This is probably related to the facts that political tyranny is what
Middletown expects of foreign nations and therefore is not "news"; the ethos
of fascism is more complicated and less readily understood by Middletown than
is the "simple black and white of communism"; and communism is news in
Middletown because it constitutes an open and confessed denial of Middletown's
reigning system of capitalism, and the need is accordingly great for Middletown
to prove it wrong.

THE RED FOG

Communism Is a Grave Menace
Revolt Feared; Propaganda Is Being
Spread Gradually

"Most Americans are living in a red fog and don't realize it. The Communist propaganda now being spread in the United States and directed from Moscow is the most demoralizing the world has known. One hundred and seventy organizations in the United States under one guise or another are promoting the propaganda," according to John U—— in a talk before the Rotary Club yesterday.

"Although it is established that there are but 2,000 paid-up Communists in the United States and the party got only 100,000 votes at the last election, that does not mean anything. Most of the Communists here are foreigners and are not entitled to vote. Also, a majority is not needed to cause a revolution. There were only 40,000 Communists in Russia when the Red revolution occurred."

Mr. U—— named the so-called Unemployed Councils as instruments of Communist propaganda: "This propaganda is being carried on here in [Middletown] by the Unemployed Council. I will not say that the local organization has direct connections, but knowingly or unknowingly it is carrying on the Communist doctrines.

"We are getting pretty close to Communism right now in Washington. We have known, out-and-out liberals in the government. The farm program they are putting through is nothing but the Russian system. Things are being done in the name of emergency which we will have to pay for.

"Effective propaganda," the speaker went on to report, "is being spread through colleges, universities, and high schools by the League for Industrial Democracy, for instance in Columbia University and DePauw University, and these propagandists have been successful.

"Socialism and Communism are half-brothers. Socialism is the vestibule to Communism. The Communists are opposed to private ownership. To them a capitalist is anyone who believes in owning even a dog. Production for use and not for profit is the academic way they express their belief.

"Our economic system has made our country the best in the last 150 years, and it will again if permitted to remain."

In news reporting in the Middletown press during the depression one hears the steady drumfire of similar attack upon radicalism:

Under a date line from the state capital: Army of Reds to Wage War: Vicious Communist Publications and Literature Have Been Circulated Here.

Under a Chicago date line: Reveal Plot for Red Uprising.

Under a North Carolina date line: Reds Spread Poison in South. . .
Communists with queer-sounding names. . . .

And along with these go editorials suggesting the next step:

Aliens Should Be Registered.

Squelch Demonstrators.

OUST THE UNDESIRABLES

Most Americans will approve the program urged by the Improved
Order of Red Men to rid the United States of undesirable aliens. The 250
lodges of the organization in our state have indorsed the national crusade.

The editor who wrote the editorial quoted above welcoming the
bestowal of civil liberties on the Russian people commented in his column four days earlier:

Some officers of labor unions, Communists and Socialists, backed by the
Civil Liberties Union, are protesting to the Governor and to Vigo County
authorities that union organizers have been kidnapped and deported from
Terre Haute by policemen there without warrant, the officers saying the
men whom they ran out of town are "agitators." *The backing of the Civil
Liberties Union makes the case of the allegedly deported men suspicious.*
[Italics ours.]

He then went on to condemn the removal of the men from the city
without warrants. The significant point here is Middletown's tendency
to regard civil liberty as an absolute, something all Americans practice,
while the intervention and very existence of a Civil Liberties Union is
an impertinent denial of American institutions.

A characteristic editorial in 1932, headed "Peons, Peasants, Coolies,
or Men," warned local labor pointedly:

If industry is made unprofitable, no money is going to be invested in it.
[And, the editorial continued, as it becomes unprofitable, less men will be
employed and wages will be cut.] Every political radical believes in tearing
down our now inadequate defenses that protect Americans from sharing
the common lot of peasants and peons.

"Communists, socialists, internationalists are all brothers under the
skin," asserts another editorial. And local patriots are, as this is written,
demanding the resignation of a college president in the state for his
professed internationalism. Commenting on reported radicalism in this

college, another editorial strikes a characteristic Middletown note: "We will never get a better social order at the hands of people who talk about socialism, pacifism, and internationalism but who won't do their bit to 'brighten up the corner where you live.'"

One is impressed by the blanket acceptance of the "Red fog" rumor by local people of all groups. A school principal in a working-class district spoke to the investigator over the luncheon table of his having been approached by an out-of-town group to start a new boys' organization in his school as a local branch of the Boys' Club of America. He had refused "because I suspect it of having a political tie-up." Whereupon, the third man at the table, a college graduate and man of local standing, inquired guardedly. "Do you mean it was being paid for by this Russian money?" [32]

A local man in close touch with the youth of the city stated: "Our college boys are bringing back radicalism to [Middletown]. The head of our Y.M.C.A. is scared to death of it and tells the boys they can't talk radicalism in the building, but you ought to hear the fellows talking around the 'Y' soda fountain!" There is a small group at the local college who sometimes embarrass speakers by pointed heckling. Officially, the college is against radicalism, as noted elsewhere. Its chief donor and head of its board of trustees was guardedly described by a businessman as "the chief local radical head-hunter." The college lyceum course is reported to be carefully supervised, but the college Y.M.C.A. brings occasional liberal speakers to the campus.

In the main, however, the "united front" against radicalism is solidly maintained in Middletown. Radical young men have been warned by employment managers that they will "see to it that you never get a job in this town." As a local professional man remarked cautiously, "This town is a closed corporation. You're either in or you're out. If you are known as a radical there is no chance of getting a job unless it is with some out-of-town concern."

In such a "closed corporation" the maintenance of civic integrity and pride has grown in importance even since 1925. As Middletown faces the strains of outside competition its confidence in what it has and is must be stepped up to meet the strain. Middletown wants inveterately to believe in itself, and it loses no opportunity to reaffirm its faith in

[32] See the discussion later in the present chapter of the extent to which business class and working class share the same beliefs and fears.

itself. It enjoys reading editorials on "When You Are 'Just a Small-town Man,'" cataloguing the "lot of grief the small-town man escapes." It likes to read in its paper, that "Most of the failures in life are due to the acceptance of alien measures of value and the neglect of near-at-hand inspiration." It rationalizes the fact that most of its children go to small colleges by telling itself that it likes them to go to small colleges because, as one of its papers recently phrased it, "Small colleges give something besides the ability to feel at home in evening clothes." [33] When possible, unfavorable factors are turned inside out in quest of a silver lining. Thus an editorial in 1932 expressed satisfaction that "Although the average salary of Middletown teachers is below the average of first-, second-, and third-class cities, and although the tax rate for school purposes is lower than the average, the quality and efficiency of teaching here is far above the average."

Middletown exhibits today an advanced philosophy of Mercantilism. The depression has made the "Buy in Middletown" slogan more prevalent than ever, just as it has increased the Mercantilist emphasis in national economies. "Keep that $15,000,000 annually coming to Middletown factories. Consider where your pay check comes from and on what it depends," is the frequent type of reminder in the press, and Middletown is nursing its trading area more sedulously against the larger cities at the other end of the smooth new ribbons of concrete that radiate out from it. Even Middletown's police got the spirit and in

---

[33] Occasionally, a local person breaks through Middletown's official "front," as did the well-to-do wife who exclaimed in private conversation, "This is just a twenty-five-cent town!"

It is significant that one tends to get both the most extravagant eulogies and the most cynical disparagement of Middletown from its women rather than from its men, and also more criticism from persons of both sexes between eighteen and thirty than from older persons. From the women who, from long habituation and (or) lack of desire to diverge from the stereotyped role of the Middletown married woman, have thoroughly accepted Middletown, one hears in their club papers and in private conversation ardent endorsements of "our city" and "our state." From wives imported from larger cities and from business-class wives who want other contacts or a career and feel themselves frustrated by the local pattern (as described toward the close of Chapter V), one may hear a dissonant note of rebellion against what they call Middletown's "complacency" and "provincialism."

As in so many other phases of Middletown's life, the preoccupation of the males with the practical affairs of earning a living makes them more or less automatic local boosters and more gray and neutral than the women in matters that do not concern their jobs. The restlessness of some of the wives is regarded by some men as due to "their thinking too much."

1936 announced cut-rate "dollar fines" for any out-of-town infringers picked up by them on one of the local merchants' "dollar days."

The acute focusing of local thought upon bettering Middletown's trade advantage is well illustrated in the type of suggestions as to "How to Make Middletown Better" put forward by citizens, both men and women, in a series of eighteen afternoon and evening conferences conducted by the Chamber of Commerce as part of the city's recovery of morale in the fall of 1935. While perhaps some allowance should be made for the unconsciously biasing effect of the auspices under which the conferences were held, no effort was made to hold suggestions down to the immediately practical or to things solely within the scope of the several standing committees of the Chamber of Commerce. The list of suggestions for bettering the city was taken down in shorthand and, when analyzed, gives impressive evidence of the extent to which the civic desiderata in the forefront of Middletown citizens' minds have to do with surface booster tactics. In a city living by dollars and the attraction of dollars to the city, it is not surprising that concerted thought as to how to "better" the city should result in the following group of suggestions, in descending order of frequency:

1. *Improve Traffic Conditions*

107 suggestions, including provide better parking facilities in the business section; widen streets; get through-highways routed through the city, and (not from a retailer) *don't* get through-highways routed through the city; develop more police courtesy.

2. *Improve Middletown's Physical Appearance*

57 suggestions, including have better lighted streets; buy up run-down homes and demolish them ("We should be able to take visitors any place in the city"); keep streets cleaner; cut weeds; clean up the river and the courthouse.

3. *Improve Chamber of Commerce*

43 suggestions, including "The Chamber of Commerce should work closely with the city administration and try to get leading officials to join"; "The Chamber should coordinate the civic clubs and arrange to centralize their work around some general scheme of things"; "The Chamber and the Real Estate Board Should Cooperate"; "The Chamber should see that one committee does not work to reduce taxes and another work to increase them"; get its members interested in its work; "The Chamber or the civic clubs should pick out a few things and see that they are done rather than talk so much about it."

4. *Improve Middletown's Economic Assets*

33 suggestions, including reduce taxes; retailers should try harder to attract new business; prosecute non-licensed peddlers; help small industries more; push campaign to "Buy where you earn your wages"; "Do anything to bring money to [Middletown]."

5. *Publicize Middletown's Attractions*

21 suggestions, including advertise city; publicize the college; point out local historic spots; put up billboards reading "You'll Like [Middletown]"; capitalize on book, *Middletown.*

6. *City Government*

16 suggestions, including pass a milk-regulation ordinance; create more parks and playgrounds; adopt the city-manager plan; enforce better cleaning and sterilizing of containers in soda fountains; do not cut school budget; "Good businessmen around the city should look after the city instead of leaving it to politicians."

7. *Miscellaneous*

8 suggestions, including show more friendliness to newcomers; do something about housing, as "families coming to town cannot find good places to live"; abolish noisy radios up and down the streets and whistling by trains passing through town. To this group should probably be added the cynical comment by one person: "I could say something about many conditions, but it wouldn't get us anywhere."

While the obvious keynote of the above is "Do anything to bring money to Middletown," and the underlying assumption is "If we can only make Middletown bigger, it will be a better town"—the familiar identification of "progress" and "bigness" noted earlier—other points are significant. Here one sees a community in which the tradition is that if everybody just goes along being honest, working hard, and being a "good citizen," good things will grow more or less spontaneously; this old keynote was struck by one of the conferees in the above meetings who advised, "Just continue with the good work of the past and everyone will be pleased." The growth of values, the things Middletown is "for," has gone along in the past with little or no city planning. Middletown has three agencies nominally interested in planning broadly for the welfare of the entire city: its city government, its civic clubs, and its churches. As regards the first, the city is disillusioned as to its ability to plan impartially for the city's good. Even on such a rudimentary engineering matter as the routing of highways the community feels that, as one speaker expressed it in these conferences, "We will never be able to do much about routing highways as there is too much politics involved." The churches, ostensibly the planning agency for the city's "higher" values, have been warned by their financial supporters to "stick to religion and keep out of practical issues"; they constitute an internally competitive and outwardly timid array of disparate units with no concerted program for the city.[34] The civic clubs, again, representing as they do many conflicting local interests in their membership, keep scrupulously off fellow members' toes, stress "fellowship," compete as clubs against each other for prestige, sponsor occasional non-controversial individual ventures for the "good" of the city—e.g., Kiwanis' award of annual medals to the best boy and girl students in the senior class of the high school—and, for the rest, as one of the conferees quoted above phrased it simply, "talk about" doing things.[35]

[34] See Ch. VIII and the summary of the programs of the Ministerial Association in *Middletown,* pp. 351-54.

[35] The newspapers, too, should perhaps be mentioned as agencies of community planning, though the pressure on the independence of Middletown's press, noted in Ch. X, tends to reduce this independence to the vanishing point on serious controversial issues. Middletown's morning paper contents itself largely with a colorless type of comment on local affairs as they occur. The afternoon paper, with its more personal type of editing, occasionally espouses isolated local causes. During the depression it appraised Middletown against a list of civic "assets and liabilities" presented by Ernest Elmo Calkins in the *Rotarian* (the national organ of the Rotary Club). After listing the "assets" ("tree-lined streets, pleasing parks, good public schools, free public library," etc.) and noting that Middletown lacks the assets of "a modern sewage-disposal plant and beautiful surroundings" listed by Calkins, the editorial noted the following local "liabilities that prevent a city from becoming a model of its kind": "Too many filling stations on best corners, unsightly public [courthouse] square, little concern for historical monuments, unsightly or obnoxious stream through the town, burning of soft coal, too many streets badly paved, poor milk inspection or poor ordinance governing it, too many barrooms, college not sufficiently appreciated by the town."

The year 1936 witnessed, for the first time in Middletown's experience, the publication by a local paper of an extended "platform" for the improvement of the city. Its appearance is a direct result of the program of local public works stimulated by Federal emergency funds. Day after day in August, 1936, the following appeared at the top of the editorial column of the afternoon paper:

[MIDDLETOWN] *PRESS* PLATFORM FOR [MIDDLETOWN]
AND [ITS] COUNTY

Construction of a city sewage-disposal plant and a southside intercepting sewer.
The White and Mississinewa rivers, Buck Creek and all other streams freed of ALL pollution, not just SOME pollution.
Every important county road dust-proofed.
A competent city forester.
Rigid civil-service examinations for all policemen and firemen, conducted by

Down from these nominally impartial, city-wide agencies of planning for the "good" of the city straggle a long list of widely diverse groups which see the good of the city in terms of certain special interests: the Chamber of Commerce would make Middletown "better" by making business, principally manufacturing, "better"; the Merchants' Association works for civic progress through stimulating more retail trade; the bankers and inner coterie of businessmen manipulate the credit resources and bring pressure to bear for certain things they regard as "good business" for the city; the Real Estate Board fights to "keep taxes down" on the simple theory that "taxes are always too high," despite the possibility put forward by two of the conferees in the Chamber of Commerce 1935 conference on "How to Make Middletown Better" that "higher taxes might be a good investment for the city if the money were properly spent"; the Medical Society fights to maintain individual practice of medicine as "for the best interests of Middletown"; the public utilities carry on propaganda to secure a permanent court injunction against Middletown's "working against its own best interests" by holding a public referendum on the public ownership of utilities; the D.A.R. and American Legion seek to make Middletown patriotic; the Teachers Federation would improve it by helping teacher status; the Public Ownership League by opposing the utilities; and so on through agencies big and small.

Middletown's traditions are all against centralization of planning and control in public affairs. An editorial in 1936 quoted Glenn Frank approvingly for his "denunciation of centralized power as a stepping-stone to Old World autocracy"; then followed the familiar phrases: "The words of Jefferson on individual initiative and those of Franklin on economy and thrift . . . ," ". . . true liberalism always advocated

a nonpartisan or bipartisan commission, appointments to be made according to grades and without regard to politics, and terms of office to end only because of misconduct or disability.

More playgrounds for children.

Completion of the boulevard system.

Dams in White River through and near [Middletown] when all waste is removed, to make the stream navigable to small pleasure boats and to provide free swimming pools.

Completion of the bay [for boating and swimming] in White River opposite McCulloch Park.

An amusement park on the edge of town or not far outside, preferably along a body of water.

Impound a great body of water southeast of town to be used by [Middletown] in case of a drouth emergency.

the freest expression of individual effort and enterprise that is consistent with sound public policy," and ". . . we will resolve political elements [fused into centralized power by the New Deal] into their proper spheres." And yet, the most significant aspect of the holding of the above conferences by the Chamber of Commerce in 1935 was the tacit recognition that the city's value-forming agencies should be coordinated and led; that, as one of the conferees remarked, "[Middletown] doesn't get together on propositions but could get somewhere if everyone worked together." Despite itself and its traditions, Middletown is slowly moving, under pressure from the competitive world around it, toward the liquidation of the traditional right to "go as you please" in matters importantly affecting the public interest; and toward the closer coordination of city government, civic clubs, and other value-carrying and -forming agencies under its business agencies to present a united front to the world.[36]

The closer merging of the values of "business enterprise" and "loyalty" helps somewhat to retard the widening of the gap between Middletown's "power" values (enterprise, shrewdness, dominance, success) and its "lovable" values (friendliness, kindliness, gentleness) noted above. By making "loyalty" and "good business" synonymous, much the same simplification of life occurs as when Puritan doctrine identified the service of God with the profitable pursuit of one's "vocation" in conformity to the canons of the market place.[37] In both cases one is being worthy and helpful at the same time that one is being strong. Such identifications of basically opposite values may be expected to occur increasingly in the Middletown of the future as people struggle to allay the tensions engendered by values that pull urgently in two directions at once. But the acuteness of the city's conflicts will probably tend to mean that the "power" values will *assimilate and use* the

[36] It is not meant to imply that it is contemplated that all of this shall be done at once. Most Middletown people probably regard the conferences at the Chamber of Commerce simply as the sensible extension of the practice of keeping alert to suggestions for bettering the city which has always been a part of the Chamber's job. The thing suggested above is that such step-by-step procedures are consonant with other trends in Middletown toward centralization of the city's philosophy and its power agencies, and that under the domination of the pecuniary aims of business they point in a direction significant for the future of Middletown's institutions.

[37] See R. H. Tawney's *Religion and the Rise of Capitalism* (New York; Harcourt, Brace, 1926).

other values; the process of identification will hardly tend to work in the reverse direction.

It is difficult to assess what the depression has done to Middletown's prized value of "friendliness," for the evidence is equivocal. There is no personal trait—unless it be honesty—of which Middletown is prouder than of its friendliness. And no one who has lived among these people, as did the research staff in 1924-25 and again in 1935, can doubt for a moment the continued strength of this friendliness; it is a warm, spontaneous expression that easily overcomes even the handicap of one's being an outside observer who has said frank things in print about the community. Beyond the crowded four- or five-block business section, people on the streets greet strange passers-by with a friendly smile or even a neighborly "Howd' do?" If one steps into a store out of the rain one may be invited to "Have a chair. Take off your raincoat," and be engaged in friendly conversation. Waitresses still greet one with a smile and receive one's order with a "You bet!" or "All rightee!" On the city's buses passengers talk with the driver, crane their necks to watch the changes in traffic lights, and call out their findings helpfully to him. A postman with a heavy bag stops to help a very small boy cumbersomely trying to sweep a sidewalk, saying, "Here, son, you're going at that backwards. Let me show you how." One reads on the front page of the paper a feature story of a businessman from Middletown's state, grown rich and moved to New York:

GREAT BUSINESS MOVED FROM NEW YORK BACK TO [MIDDLETOWN'S STATE]

Henry ——, internationally known contractor, sitting in a luxurious suite in his New York hotel, with everything money could buy, suddenly asked his wife, "If I should die, who would be my pallbearers? Just my business associates." So he decided to move his business back to his home town.

Some Middletown people are inclined to believe that the depression has made people more friendly and helpful. "A lot of our people in all classes were on a high-horse in 1928-29," commented one man. "They were riding high, running around a lot, and generally trying to elbow their way ahead." Another said, "A lot of people have come back down to earth during the depression. There has been less pretentiousness in dress and things like that. People have put their diamonds in safety-deposit boxes because they don't have the face to wear them nowadays. Nobody has been buying clothes."

But, as over against this "coming down off high horses," the depression appears to have introduced new areas of social wariness and defensiveness and to have sharpened the harsh edge of human meanness that frequently tends to appear in personal transactions involving dollars. People tell you in low tones of how so and so broke his word and squeezed so and so to the wall in the depression. One woman commented that some of Middletown's wives "have been as cold-blooded as the men, eagerly moving up into the desirable homes which some of their acquaintances have been forced out of by foreclosures." As one prominent businessman with a ready but noncommittal smile summed up the situation, "People are friendly and kindly, but in many things, especially those involving the making and spending of money, they play safe and suspect they'll be gypped." One bumped into this wariness about being "gypped" much more frequently than in 1925. "There's no doubt," commented a small businessman, "that people are less friendly in Middletown than they were; they make less effort to know you and they are less willing to give you a break." Another man, who has come to Middletown in the depression to assume a responsible post, characterized Middletown as "cold to outsiders": "They invite you vaguely to come to the Country Club and then never do anything about it. They're a stand-offish, cliquey bunch." More than one person pointed to the growing divisive, "inner circle" quality within Rotary, whereby nepotism and in-group favoritism are reported to play a more prominent role today in membership additions to this dominant club.[38] One member of a prominent civic club spoke bitterly of the way his fellow club members had "faded out" on him during the depression: "I went to my fellow members, men who had known me for years, had seen me building up my business and working my head off for [Middletown]. I couldn't get a penny. Who was it came to me? It was [the Russian Jewish junk-dealer quoted on pp. 407-08 of *Middletown*], a man treated patronizingly by [Middletown's] moguls. He said to me, 'I guess you need some money. Here's $500.' He just reached in his pocket and pulled it out. He didn't want any note; wouldn't take one, and just said, 'I know you.' Then our family doctor helped, and also [a young man in a small manufacturing plant in town]. But not one single member of —— [the civic club]."

[38] See the discussion of this in Ch. VII.

The Middletown of 1935, while tolerant of many things such as clothing and externals, struck the investigator as having greater difficulty in taking a positive view of human nature and its potentialities and as striking more frequently a note of wary cynicism about people's actions and motives. One was told of many little meannesses. Of how, for instance, the Business and Professional Women's Club had held a benefit bridge at the Masonic Temple attended by "the most representative people; and at the end of the evening thirty to forty decks of cards borrowed by the Club for the occasion were missing." [39]

No precise trial balance of these gains and losses in friendly helpfulness can be attempted.[40] The cases of generosity by certain individuals mingle with the turning of the cold shoulder. Middletown is a bigger city than it was in 1925 and it is easier for mutual avoidance in a city of nearly 50,000 to prevent the healing of deep scars to personality. The continuing fear to which Middletown businessmen confessed in 1935 does not create a social atmosphere conducive to large generosities.

Among Middletown's working class, it is not unlikely that the psychological defenses associated with being on relief and the isolating tendencies deriving from increased residential mobility, noted in Chap-

[39] Other instances of this sort related to the investigator may not be mentioned because of the danger of identifying the individuals involved.

[40] Lazarsfeld's conclusions from his study of the Austrian village, Marienthal (*op. cit.,* pp. 39-40), are equally equivocal. "In the opinion of several officials, the balance of friendly and unfriendly attitudes has remained essentially as before."

He calls attention to one interesting type of meanness prevalent among those on relief in Marienthal which suggests a serious break in community morale under conditions of prolonged unemployment: "The decline from the higher cultural level of political differences to the more primitive level of personal spite can almost be demonstrated factually. We allude here to the anonymous notices posted in public places against those picking up prohibited casual earnings while on relief. Punishment therefor is often long-term withdrawal of relief. Usually these notes are a reaction to a change in the amount of relief received by the person scribbling the notice, or an act of personal animosity. Here is a typical notice of this sort: 'The Local Industrial Commission is hereby notified that [name given] is working for a farmer while receiving unemployment relief; that he also raises chickens and rabbits; and that his wife also is on relief. In other cases relief is at once withdrawn when one earns something on the side. Those not in need of it are drawing down unemployment relief; and the others may starve.'" In recent years the following number of notices by Marienthalers against fellow Marienthalers were posted:

	Number of notices	Number of notices which were unwarranted
1928-29 (pre-depression)	9	3
1930-31 (depression)	28	21

ter V, have increased the isolation and suspicion of neighbors observed among a number of working-class families in 1925.[41] People under pressure seek easement through such devices as the setting up of a scapegoat. Middletown's working class fell easy prey to the Klan propaganda in 1923-25, and their religious beliefs readily made Catholicism an issue that split the city's outward solidarity. As this is written, in the summer of 1936, comes the hint of the formation of a new organization in Middletown "based upon prejudice."[42] Nerves too long frayed by unemployment and the humiliation of relief may again be finding a way to punish one's neighbor for the wrongs one's institutional world has done to one.

Thus, in its relations to outside groups—other nations, other cities— and perhaps in relations among individuals within the city, Middletown seems recently to have been building its fences higher. The city is more antagonistic to outside groups; individuals in the city are seemingly more wary of each other; need of protection and security is more emphasized.

One of the questions of most concern to the research staff in returning to the city after ten years was whether the same thing is true of various groups within the city: whether they have drawn closer together, or whether they face each other with hostile or uncomprehending eyes across wider barriers. The staff attempted to discover what cohering and what divisive experiences the city has gone through since 1925, and whether the outcome has been a more united or a more split city.[43] The types of personality and the values discussed at the outset of this chapter were described as generally unchallenged by the city as a whole. And yet, since they were derived frequently from the press,

[41] See *Middletown,* pp. 272-73.

[42] This hint comes in the form of the following paragraph in the column of Comment by the Editor in the afternoon paper: "[Middletown] was settled largely in her early days by Methodists, 'Campbellites' and Baptists and 'sprinklings' of other Protestant denominations and Catholics. And they lived together amicably and in spite of occasional denominational rivalry that found chief expression in the size of the 'revival meetings' each church was able to put on. Then about ten years ago along came the Klan movement that set brother against brother and disturbed the community. But [Middletown] recovered from that, too, in time. Now the story is around that some other kind of 'funny' organization is being formed, based upon prejudice of some kind or other. But maybe that part of the story is just a myth and the organization has some legitimate object."

[43] See *Middletown,* pp. 478-84.

from articulate leaders of opinion, from *expressed* opinion, it is evident that they are most clearly the symbols of the business class, who have most access to channels of expression. To what extent are they accepted by the entire city? Is there any less general acceptance of these beliefs than ten years ago, and are the groups within the city more differentiated by separate ways of thinking and feeling and new awareness of difference?

Even in analyzing the folkways of the smaller city of 1925 it was necessary at many points to discuss separately the business class and the working class. As in 1925, these classes are today marked off in terms of income, which in turn tends to follow type of occupation, *i.e.,* whether one works with one's hands at things (the working class) or with promotional and service techniques addressed to *people* (business class).[44] Repeatedly the question was put to a great variety of local people as to whether the business class and the working class, the North Side and the South Side, have drawn closer together or moved further apart during these years.

Middletown's business class doesn't know the answer to this question. A local editor, reared in the city, commented, "Middletown never was much of a unity. I don't know whether the gaps have increased or not." Business people know that labor got "troublesome" in 1933-34, and, as pointed out in Chapter II, they are determined that this sort of thing shall not happen again. But, in answer to the direct question as to whether the distance between business people and workers has widened, their answers ranged all the way from, "No, I don't think so. We don't have differences of that kind here. We treat our workers right and they aren't made to feel different," to "Yes, decidedly. The people up here on the North Side don't know those people down there exist any more." Business people seemed uneasy in the face of such a question, and one got a distinct impression that they do not like to think of "classes" and feel happier in ignoring the possibility of their existence. And tradition aids them in thus disregarding such distinctions, for, according to the "American way," even the workingman with a wife and four children and eighteen dollars in his Saturday pay envelope is on his way to becoming, if not a millionaire, at least independent and secure in his old age. Or, if he isn't, it is because he is lacking in initiative or thrift or industry and is therefore simply getting what he deserves—which is in itself a vindication of the tradition.

[44] See *Middletown,* p. 22.

In line with this tradition is the deliberate effort of the business-class agencies of opinion to emphasize unity rather than points of difference in the city. The newspapers, as observed in Chapter X, minimize differences in their effort to spread the idea that the community is just one big happy family. This belief is fostered through the control of virtually all of the channels of local communication:

[Middletown] possesses some peculiar advantages as an industrial center [commented an editorial on the occasion of the civic dinner in honor of the return of General Motors in June, 1935]. The community is almost devoid of industrial or business strife. Her citizens are peaceful and get along pretty well together most of the time, there is nearly a complete absence of political and social radicalism, and the classes mingle pretty well in a friendly spirit of cooperation.

As an all-around town for purposes of pleasurable living, education, culture, and business, it stands high among cities of its class. It is not a Venice, a modern Athens, a Pittsburgh, a Chicago, or a New York, but it has many of the good qualities of all of these cities and lacks most of their bad qualities. As St. Paul said of his home town, one living here might say, "I am a citizen of no mean city."

As one open-shop automobile-parts plant to another (to quote a full-page advertisement by another automotive plant greeting the return of General Motors): "[Middletown] is a good town to live in! A good town to work in!" This happy, "constructive" note is very characteristic. In 1932, the high-school dean proposed that high-school girls wear a simple uniform "in order to eliminate class distinctions in high school and to place the poor on an equal footing with the rich"—a proposal addressed to a problem that distresses many South Side girls acutely (some of them to the point of withdrawing from high school), many parents of all classes, and high-school teachers sensitive to conditions affecting personality.[45] But the evening paper promptly shuddered editorially at such regimentation and denial of democratic prin-

[45] This problem of competitive dressing by high-school girls is of long standing. See such statements by parents in the 1925 study (p. 162) as, "No girl can wear cotton stockings to high school"; "The dresses girls wear to school now used to be considered party dresses. My daughter would consider herself terribly abused if she had to wear the same dress to school two successive days"; and the wail of the thirteen-year-old girl whose mother dressed her in gingham and lisle hose, "Mother, I am just an object of mercy!" The problem has become more acute in the depression. High-school clothing standards have been toned down somewhat, but the clothing of the poorer girls has deteriorated more than that of the well-to-do, thereby widening the contrasts.

ciples, taking the high ground that "The purpose of the educational system is to build personality by stimulating thought rather than to force students to accept ideas unthinkingly"; and it then shunted off the whole problem by announcing cheerfully that "Little distinction is found today between rich and poor dress in so far as high-school girls are concerned. The only difference is in taste." In 1935 the same editor commented with satisfaction in his column, ". . . naturally [factory girls] cannot indulge in the feminine furbelows of some other working girls, which is too bad. But in the evenings, the work day over, they cannot be distinguished in appearance from the clerks, bookkeepers, and other 'white collar' workers. The American melting pot does a better job of melting women than men."

In August, 1936, this denial of class differences was made still more explicit in two local editorials:

THE MIDDLE CLASS RULES AMERICA

We hear talk about the supposed ferocity of the revolution in Spain. . . . There is one reason why a revolution of the kind now existent in Spain is improbable in the United States under our present economic and social system. . . . Spain has no middle class, but is divided into the extremes of aristocratic wealth and working-class poverty. . . .

The United States never was a feudal nation. . . . As a result, while some became very rich and others very poor, the sovereign authority rested with a great middle class, whom we like to term the typical Americans. They were the people whose ideal of life was to own a home, and rear and educate a family in the fear of the Lord and in obedience to law. It is from the children of these middle-class families that our industrial and political leaders have come. They have been neither revolutionists nor class baiters. They have held the government on an even keel. That is why the radicals have hated them so—the Reds well know that this middle class is the great obstacle to revolution.

So long as the United States eschews class division and maintains this great middle-class America, we shall be free of such troubles as now beset unhappy Spain. But once we permit the middle class to be destroyed by taxation or other form of confiscation, giving us only class consciousness instead, then we may expect bitterness and hatred, even revolution, to take the place of the American ideals of free government.

NEARLY ALL ARE IN "WORKING CLASS"

Sometimes we hear from a platform orator, generally one who is running for office, that he is the friend of the "workingman." Perhaps it would be just as well to pause and inquire, just who is this "American workingman," anyhow, and how did he get that way? . . .

In the United States . . . every man has worked who had the ambition and the opportunity to do so. There has been no class of idle rich. The average industrialist has put in as many hours as the salaried man or wage earner, and he often points with pride to the number of jobs he has been able to afford for others through the effort of his own thrift, intelligence, and industry.

Abraham Lincoln put it well when he said: "There is no permanent class of hired laborers amongst us. Twenty-five years ago I was a hired laborer. The hired laborer of yesterday labors on his own account today, and will hire others to labor for him tomorrow."

Here is embodied the true American principle of progress. It is in recognition of such a principle that we have builded the greatest economic empire ever known to man, in a little more than a century and a half.

Work has never been looked upon in America as degrading, but as the means to better things for the individual and his family. . . .

The great danger is that an attempt at redistribution of wealth through increasingly high taxes, will only end in poverty and misery for all, as has been the case in Russia. But there is another danger which is just as great—a danger that the United States will become a nation of class-conscious haters. Such a condition will spell the end of American prosperity and American progress.

Another editorial, in November, 1936, stated:

The welfare of the masses cannot be bettered through class division and struggle. . . . Capital has a responsibility and must have labor, but labor has as great a responsibility and must have capital, which makes its position possible. The two working honestly together can spell progress. The two pulling apart can spell revolution and destruction.

Middletown's working class, likewise, does not, for the most part, spend its time thinking of itself as different from the people on the North Side. In the main it has followed the same symbols, trying intermittently, as work allows, to affirm them as loudly as does the business class, and to narrow the gap between symbol and reality. It, like the business class, is busy living, manipulating the poker chips at its command, and trying to get more. Its drives are largely those of the business class: both are caught up in the tradition of a rising standard of living and lured by the enticements of salesmanship; and the modern merchandising device of "price-lining," coupled with installment selling, enables the workingman to have many things that "look like" the possessions seen in the "nice" store windows uptown and in the movies.[46] Class ideologies are foreign to Middletown's working class, and, without identifying oneself as a member of one class as over against another, one lives along, in the pursuit of what plums one can contrive to get in one's porridge. A large majority in any population are so intent on the immediately next succeeding moves that, like the Abbé Siéyès when asked what he did during the French Revolution, the recapitulation of any stretch of living for them may be largely comprehended within the words, "I lived." Here, in this ability to exist ahead, in season and out, with a job or without, one is dealing with a thing that underlies the large degree of unconsciousness as to class that was such a marked characteristic of Middletown's working class even in the sixth year of a great depression.

The absence of strong working-class leadership and of distinctive symbols and organizations has been noted in Chapter II. The local working class, fresh from the farm and untainted by a foreign element with the stereotyped slogans of large-city radicalism, "will listen to a speaker who criticizes the bankers or the X family, but if you try to talk to them about scrapping the Constitution they just walk out on you. You can't persuade our working people here to real radicalism." Lacking leadership and symbols, Middletown workers have little sense of direction, save up the now largely symbolic "ladder of success." [47] With no place to go save where other people are going, local labor leaders are constantly being drawn into minor posts in the local political machines, where their labor identification becomes blurred. The

[46] An interesting problem inviting students of psychological standards of living is the location in our American culture of areas of desire to be "like" and to be "different" from others. As a proposition worth testing the following is here thrown out for consideration: People on the lower-income rungs do not want to be "different," but, instead, to imitate as closely as possible the regularizing, identifying habits of those with money. There is security in being like others. What is popularly called the "middle class" is an area of the population in the main bent, like the "lower" class, upon being "regular," and frequently under even more pressure than the latter to be so. The innovations of the "middle class" are highly stylized, safe copies in the main of an "upper-class" innovation. It is only among the wealthy that one tends to see innovation boldly embraced, not to identify one with others but to distinguish one *from* others. "Differentness" is feared by people of small income and sought by those with large incomes—though every generalization of this sort must be used cautiously. Very little study has been given as yet to the location of these areas of conformity and deviation.

[47] See the discussion of the attenuation of this "ladder" of opportunity and success at the close of Ch. II.

aggressive young president of Middletown's Central Labor Union in 1925 was subsequently appointed City Building Commissioner and, failing of reappointment in the next administration, has drifted completely away from the labor movement and is now a traveling man selling automatic ventilators. Another officer was appointed to the same post in January, 1935, "and about a dozen others of our union men were trying for the same job," according to a local labor leader. "Many union men want steady jobs as policemen and firemen. Some of them try to get elected councilmen or to county jobs. Another of our officers has a minor Republican appointment. All these things work to take the edge off organized labor here."

Even in the program of the short-lived labor paper published by the Central Labor Union at the height of the labor organizing fervor in the spring of 1934, the policy advocated was that of "conciliation and arbitration in the settlement of differences between capital and labor." No talk of a "class struggle" was involved.

In a word, what Middletown's business class wants is to be let alone to run its own business, and what the working class wants is a job so that it can pay the rent, own a car, and go to the movies. As a small businessman—one of the two private individuals in Middletown in 1934 (including students at the college) who subscribed to the *New Republic*—remarked: "These workers here don't want to 'steal the works,' but just to have a job, security, and the chance to bring up their kids and have some fun. If the employing crowd here could just realize that and act accordingly toward their men, it'd be worth money to them." Like most other people, Middletown folk don't want to have to think too much. They reluctantly ask "Why?" And the occasional persons who do keep their questions to themselves. A leading lawyer remarked, "We can't solve all these problems. They're too big for us. We've our own problems, and we send men to Congress to try to solve the big problems." Occupied with personal immediacies, Middletown generalizes the succession of daily experiences with difficulty. To most of its people, of whatever group, "class differences" and "class consciousness" are vague, unfamiliar, and, if recognized, unpleasant and sinister terms. And above all, Middletown people avoid questioning the assumed adequacy of the reigning system under which they live. It is much less troublesome and more congenial to attribute troubles to personal devils. Thus, in commenting on the unrest in France in 1936, a local editorial noted simply that conditions there are attributable "mainly to machinations of politicians rather than to capitalism." By the same process any talk about "class differences," a "class struggle," and similar unpleasant things is attributed to "reckless outside trouble-makers." Officially, Middletown scoffs at the "class struggle." "Remnants of that notion [of the class struggle] are still with us," said a local editorial in 1935. "Indeed, many people do not realize that that theory has been exploded once and for all." And a local pundit, in a "guest editorial" in one of the papers, voiced the conviction commonly held by Middletown businessmen that "As a scheme for society and as a plan for the government of a state, *Das Kapital* is a flop. . . . For a quarter of a century [Marx and his followers] wisecracked against the existing order, and then disappeared as a social force."

And yet—despite the fact that tradition, inertia, and intent combine to blur any potential class differences, indications of a sharpening of awareness of some class lines continually break through tendencies to bury them.

Businessmen frequently forget in conversation their formal denials of the separate existence of a working class; they tend to speak of it as a group apart, people who are "different from us." From a number of business-class persons one picked up impatient characterizations of the working class as having a high percentage of "intellectually inferior" members. Characteristic, too, is the impatient remark of a local real-estate man on "the impossibility of inculcating any aesthetic values in people like that. Why, give 'em a brand-new house, and in a few months it'll look like a pigstye." One intelligent man said, "It seems to me that the working class are different here from any other place. They are more incapable, stupid—just a crummy lot, biologically inferior, with a lot of these dopes from Kentucky and Tennessee. They never do anything." Another man, protesting to the investigator against the treatment of the monotony of certain types of jobs in the 1925 study, exclaimed, "Those people aren't like us! They *love* that kind of job. Why, there isn't anything there in those fellows to begin with."

Of interest, also, is the statement of a real-estate man: "The biggest fruit and vegetable market in town is located just south of the tracks. It used to have a branch on the North Side but closed it to save overhead. But now they've found that North Side women, even in their cars, won't come across the tracks to shop." Farmers and working-class folk take possession of the business district Saturday afternoon and evening, and the remark of one woman member of an old business-class family represents an attitude which, though by no means general, may nevertheless be significant: "Did you ever see such a sight as the Saturday evening crowd on Walnut Street? I never walk down there Saturday evening. It makes you feel like a three-penny piece. It's so cheap. I don't like it any time after noon Saturday."

This sort of talk was heard somewhat in Middletown in 1925, and it combined with the somewhat different rhythms of their days,[48] their different work, and different command of income to mark off the one group from the other. But the impression was clear in the investigator's mind at the end of the field work in 1935 that the line between working class and business class, though vague and blurred still, is more apparent than it was ten years before. Business-class nerves are raw from the strain of the depression, social legislation, and the endorsement of labor organization under the New Deal. Business-class control over the city has tightened, and the determination to run an open-shop town has increased. Business doesn't intend to tolerate any funny business from labor. Local editorials reiterate that "capital and labor are partners," but to Middletown that means that the working class does well to dance to the tune that the business class pipes. In a frank discussion of conditions of local labor around the table at one of the smaller business-class luncheon clubs, there was general agreement from the dozen or so men present that the "partnership of capital and labor" doesn't offer much hope to workingmen at present, and that the working class in Middletown realizes more keenly than ten years ago that it is not going to get anywhere—"that it is just a cog in a great big wheel." As a businessman interested in the labor situation summarized the situation, "To say that Middletown has a class consciousness, in the sense of a class-conscious proletariat, would be, of course, sheer nonsense, but out of the depression there is unquestionably emerging the first faint outlines of local labor solidarity."

From conversations with the South Siders themselves one got still more keenly an occasional awareness not of definitely antagonistic interests but of growing social distance, and in some cases the definite voicing of the question, "Where is this going to lead us?"

This apparently arises not from any formulated theory of divergent class interests or of an "exploited" working class, but from the fact that workers feel that in one situation after another they find themselves on the opposite side of the fence from the business class and

[48] See *Middletown*, p. 53.

pulling in an opposite direction. The contrasts have been rubbed in in the homes whose juniors must run the gantlet of high-school life. The alert principal of the large junior high school on the South Side replied to the question as to whether class consciousness between North and South Sides is growing with the following concrete instances:

"I have noticed two things recently: Our parents have been coming to me urging that we have our own senior high school down on the South Side, 'so that our children won't have to go up to Central High School where they don't like it—the dressing, clubs, and social contrasts.'

"And the second thing I've run against in urging our boys to keep their records clear so that they'll be eligible for the Central High School Bearcat basketball team. They say to me: 'Mr. ——, you *know* we don't have a chance to make teams up there against the North Side boys.' And that's true—they *are* handicapped."

The Central High School, today as in 1925, is split up into competitive social groups. The general status of the South Side students appears to have been further handicapped in the depression, however, by the presence among their number of an increasing number of marginal persons who are going on into high school because they cannot get jobs.[49] One teacher described them as "soggy intellectually and socially and usually nonparticipants in high-school life." A new phenomenon today is the fact that, according to a high-school graduate of 1934, some boys and girls now no longer dare brave the front door of the high school "with the steps crowded with richer students looking you over," but go around to the side entrance. There is possible significance in the pride with which some South Siders pointed to the extension of chain grocery stores to the part of the main shopping street lying south of the railroad tracks, saying, "Now we don't have to go up there to shop so much."

With all this freshly in mind, one went down across the railroad tracks and stood at the gate of the General Motors plant watching the men come off the job in the afternoon: Here was a horde of men heavily on the young side, walking rapidly toward the parking space for employees' cars, laughing and talking in groups of twos and threes about baseball, exclaiming, "Boy! I'm goin' home and have a steak"; or "What's the weather goin' to do Sunday? We wanta drive up to the lakes." The whole feel of the scene was on the easy, resilient

[49] See Ch. VI and the discussion of job scarcity for persons under twenty-one n Ch. II.

side. Here was no crew of helots or men cowed into furtiveness. Half an hour later, as one walked the tree-shaded streets, one saw these men mowing the lawn, painting the garage, playing "catch" with a small son, and smoking a pipe over the evening paper on the front porch.

Perhaps it was because it was June; part of it undoubtedly was because these men had jobs again after the long layoff; part of it was probably due to the general optimism in the air locally. But something else was undoubtedly present, too, to account for these contradictory elements in these workingmen. Actually, both a deep concern over their insecurity and an almost happy-go-lucky indifference exist together inside the skins of Middletown workers. The very presence of the former probably helps to create the latter as an emotional defense enabling the sequence of big and little incidents of daily living to make a tolerable degree of sense.

But one must go deeper to understand the inertias, the lack of solidarity, the concern with present immediacies, the easy contentments, the happy-go-lucky quality, that baffle labor organizers and make Middletown an industrialists' happy hunting ground. The Middletown workingman is American born of American parents. He lives on a Middle Western farm, has moved in from the farm, or his father's family moved to town from a farm. He is thus close to the network of habits of thought engendered by the isolated, self-contained enterprise of farming. One local worker caught up the resistance of these American farm and ex-farm dwellers to labor-union efforts in the succinct statement: "Shucks! fellows from Selma and De Soto [outlying hamlets] can't be organized." This Middletown worker has not lived in a large city where he lost contact with the earth; even his single-family house has a yard, shade trees, and often flowers. This means that he feels he "belongs" on the earth and in this Middletown culture to an extent not so likely to be true among large-city workers living in impersonal flats off the ground. He has not worked with masses of big-city men, many of them foreign born, where he has lost his personal identity and learned to substitute as symbols of his "belonging" the traditions and ideologies of massed proletarians concerning the "class struggle" and similar amalgamating concepts. He is an individualist in an individualistic culture, and he owns some kind of an auto instead of riding other people's streetcars and buses. He has or he wants a job—being "on the county" is a calamity to him—and he is bent primarily on getting ahead under his own steam and ingenuity, like a "good American," even though he is apparently increasingly in a twilight zone of doubt as to whether he can actually get ahead. In his bleak moments of doubt or of sobering advancing age, there are still his "kids going to high school" to keep up the illusion or reality of progress in his life. He doubts, and he also hopes vaguely—and meanwhile he continues to live. This man, with his feet on the ground, jerked about disconcertingly by "good" and "bad" times, lives in the South Side subculture of similarly placed working people, in which one learns to tolerate, as normal, kinds of discontinuities that would upset his brothers north of the tracks. Like the Eskimos under the Arctic Circle, one learns to stabilize one's life on a chancy plane of circumstances.

To such a man, class solidarity and unionization are emotionally foreign, and when tension and opportunity do mount to the point of inducing him to join a union, he is apt to want quick action, or his union becomes just another thing that bothers him needlessly as he patiently seeks to knit a living out of the scant threads at his command.[50]

The Middletown worker may be licked by the economic order now —and now—and now—in the endless series of each day's immediate issues; but the only generalizations about life that his culture has taught him concern *tomorrow,* and "tomorrow" according to the American formula always means "progress," getting closer to whatever it is that one craves. Save for a few veteran socialists who knew Gene Debs, there is not chronically present in Middletown the type of generalization of living that pulls down tomorrow's hope to the dead level of today's frustrations and finds a permanent cause of labor's stalemate in the man-made elements of a capitalist economy. Like the business class, Middletown labor is prone to recognize its disabilities only when they become especially acute, and to take good and bad alike as "in the nature of things," and more due to the inscrutabilities of the cosmic order than to man-generated causes. In the absence of a hard-bitten, tenaciously held system of rationalizations of labor's place in a capitalist economy, Middletown labor in characteristic American fashion lacks any driving sense of class consciousness. It has no dynamic symbols for itself as *over against* the business class; but it has been

[50] See in Ch. II the discussion of the impatience of Middletown's workers during the period of labor organization under N.R.A. when organization did not result immediately in strikes and wage rises.

taught by press, by school, by church, and by tradition to accept, as its own, watered versions of the official business-class symbols. The investigator sensed in the sore, defeated South Side of 1935 more doubts, more sense of being "permanently licked" as a group, of the emptiness of business-class hopes *for them,* a little more feeling of being a permanent group apart, than he sensed in 1925. But all these doubts and incipient tendencies to class consciousness must operate in the face of the strong, clear note of hope so conspicuous in the culture.

In connection with this incipient drawing apart of business class and working class, two other significant tendencies should be noted here. One is the emergence, as pointed out in earlier chapters, of a small, self-conscious upper class from the earlier more democratic situation, in which the few wealthy families tended to avoid ostentation and to merge themselves in the general business class. The presence of this group is tending to focus some of the conflicts in values discussed early in the present chapter. Middletown's new upper class tends to cultivate the unusual rather than always the homely middle-of-the-road things; it plays more than its parents did, and its play is more sporty and expensive; it reads the *New Yorker, Esquire,* and *Fortune;* it enjoys swank with just a touch of laughing at itself for doing so; its children go to Eastern schools; it can talk about New York's "Rainbow Room" and the "Sert Room" from first-hand knowledge; it opens its garage doors by an electric button; and it laughs at Eddie Guest and takes Rotary casually. Middletown's top sliver of families who constitute this emerging upper class are neither lazy, undemocratic, immoral, nor blatantly "different"; but their ways of living may as time goes on bring out into the open some of the alternatives to Middletown's traditional values which have hitherto existed locally only in occasional exceptional individuals. Furthermore, the very existence in the community of their riding clubs, airplanes, and expansive new homes in the correct Westwood section heightens the contrasts with the working class and makes it more difficult to maintain the symbols of the unified city, in which each is simply on a different rung of the same ladder with the top accessible to all.

The other tendency, accompanying the drawing away of the top group of the business class into a nascent "upper class," is the apparently clearer demarcation of another and larger group of families at the lower end of the business class as a Middletown "middle class." These are the "small" white-collar folk—struggling manufacturers with no particular future, the smaller retailers and tradespeople, salesmen, officeholders, schoolteachers, and many of the growing group of hired professional assistants noted in Chapter II. These minor white-collar people are beginning to realize as the city grows larger that they definitely do not belong with the small new upper class and that even in relation to the central bloc of substantial business people they are hangers-on rather than of their number. They are courted by this more successful group when a membership drive for the Chamber of Commerce is on or when a Community Fund has to be raised. But their contacts are intermittent and on terms which the more important businessfolk elect. The depression has brought home to all Middletown businessmen the extreme degree to which extension of credit depends upon the "Yes" or "No" of a few individuals; but whereas the more "well-fixed" business and professional folk can rub elbows socially with such central sources of power, the white-collar small fry are, more today than in 1925, out of easy reach of these power controls. And these dependent persons seemed to the investigator to be more sharply aware of their dependent position, below both the upper class and the bloc of influential business people who jointly prescribe the city's central values.

Few people in Middletown are articulate about this. From a few persons in this group one gleaned statements like the following:

"I'm one of these people getting along comfortably by working hard but definitely set apart from that crowd out in Westwood. I believe Middletown's middle class is waking up to the fact that it is being used by those in power for their own ends; and we are giving up some of our faith that we belong with the wealthy and that if we will only stick with them here they'll make us rich along with them." (*A businessman with a small independent business of his own.*)

"Classes certainly are drawing apart here. Many of the lower business class are beginning to realize that they are permanently blocked and won't go any further. Some men who were making good modest livings before the depression, belonging to the less prominent civic clubs, and generally feeling themselves as 'one of the boys,' now feel uneasy and self-conscious and not so sure that they 'belong.'" (*A man from this group with a degree from the local college.*)

Undoubtedly this crystallizing of a "middle class" somewhat apart from Middletown's dominant business class is not an entirely new tendency. There were in 1925, as today, plenty of sober business-class folk who were "outsiders" and cheerfully accepted themselves as such. It is the impression of the investigator, however, based upon frankly tenuous data and brief observation, that this trend toward the separating out of a middle class is definitely increasing in Middletown.

It is interesting to view these current changes in Middletown against Lewis Corey's conclusions in his *The Crisis of the Middle Class*.[51] Corey characterizes the American middle class today as "a split personality." The split he sees is between the "old" middle class of small-scale manufacturers and merchants, and a "new" middle class of salaried employees of big business; and it is the emergence of big business which has thus split the middle class.

This is a broad frame over which to stretch Middletown's modest canvas, but the attempt shows up certain elements both of similarity and of difference. Middletown's traditions are all those of what Mr. Corey calls the "old" middle class. Its history and native bent are those of a city of neighborly small middle-class businessmen living in not unfriendly community with a working class assumed to be on its way to working up to become members of this easy, competent, independent "old" middle class. The absence of an "upper" class in 1925 prompted the classification of all Middletown's business and professional people together as a single middle-class group called the "business class," with only the "working class" below them.[52] And this essentially middle-class quality still applies to the city today. In the national drama Middletown represents in its present struggle to maintain itself the struggle of an "old" middle-class town to hold its own against other "old" middle-class towns like itself, and also against the pressure of encroaching "big business."

At the present stage in local development, big business has come into Middletown in the form of General Motors (two units), Borg-Warner, and Owens-Illinois. Middletown sees in the continuance of these big-business units in the city the most spectacular symbol and guarantee of its continued livelihood, at the same time that some members of the business population sporadically resent the hustling domination by big business that accompanies the blessing of its presence. The outstanding native "big-business" unit, the great X plant, which grew up as "old" middle-class small enterprise, has through civic-spirited local ownership

[51] New York; Covici-Friede, 1935.
[52] See *Middletown*, pp. 22-24, especially the last paragraph of n. 3 on p. 23.

and management obscured its actual coming of age as a bigger and different kind of unit; but it now belongs definitely with these outside big units in Middletown's big-business bloc. In 1935 it was these big-business units—and other hoped-for additions [53]—that dominated the city's imagination as regards its civic future.

In this situation, Middletown's formerly largely undifferentiated, middle-class business world appears, as suggested in the preceding pages, to be slowly and unconsciously drawing apart into three groups: The smallest but most powerful group around the X family continues to operate the city but has oriented its interests and planning closely around those of outside big business. This upper class includes the leading industrialists and the inner group of banking and business interests. A second group, the town's old backbone of smaller independent manufacturers, its independent merchants, and its real-estate and independent professional people, such as doctors and lawyers other than corporation lawyers, holds its own as best it can, insisting that *it* still is Middletown—although the clashes of the Real Estate Board and of the retail Merchants' Association with the Chamber of Commerce reflect the lack of unity between the "old" middle-class points of view of the two former bodies and that of the Chamber of Commerce with its bent to the big-business side. In general, this old middle-class group welcomes the prosperity brought to *its* city by big business, at the same time that, as just noted, it draws back from the domination of *its* affairs involved.

Below these two groups is the group characterized above as Middletown's newly forming middle class—not in Corey's sense, for in his sense Middletown's entire business population except the very small emerging upper class is middle class, but as the middle class within Middletown's own developing class lines.

According to this line of analysis, then, one may discern in Middletown the following groups:

1. A very small top group of the "old" middle class is becoming an upper class, consisting of wealthy local manufacturers, bankers, the local head managers of one or two of the national corporations with units in

[53] In 1935 the press announced guardedly that two other unnamed large national plants were considering moving into Middletown, implying that those few influential local men who knew about such things were consummating big things for the city. This sort of news has an electric effect on Middletown and tends to bind the city emotionally closer to the inside group of powerful bankers and manufacturers who can wield these magic wands.

Middletown, and a few well-to-do dependents of all the above, including one or two outstanding lawyers. (This class is largely identical with the group referred to throughout as the business control group and also with the group setting new and expensive standards in use of leisure.)

2. Below this first group is to be found a larger but still relatively small group, consisting of established smaller manufacturers, merchants, and professional folk (Middletown's outstanding "old" middle-class members in Corey's sense) and also of most of the better-paid salaried dependents of the city's big-business interests (the "new" middle class of the favored administrative caste within Corey's scheme). These two elements in Group 2 constitute socially a unity but, in their economic interests, often represent somewhat divergent elements; for while all of Group 2 tends to follow the lead of the upper class (Group 1 above), the salaried dependents of Group 1 do so unreservedly, while the "old" middle class of native small manufacturers, professional people, and substantial retailers seeks occasionally to assert its independent identity as the "real" Middletown, and it even at times offers resistance of an overt or passive sort to occasional moves by the dominant big-business interests that "run" the Chamber of Commerce.[54] On important matters, however, this native "old" middle-class element may usually be counted upon to huddle close toward Group 1. In critical decisions Groups 1 and 2 still tend to constitute in Middletown a single group.

3. Below Groups 1 and 2 come those who have been identified above as Middletown's own middle class in purely locally relative terms: the minor employed professionals, the very small retailers and entrepreneurs, clerks, clerical workers, small salesmen, civil servants—the people who will never quite manage to be social peers of Group 2 and who lack the constant easy contacts with Group 1 which characterizes Group 2.[55]

4. Close to Group 3 might be discerned an aristocracy of local labor: trusted foremen, building trades craftsmen of long standing, and the pick of the city's experienced highly skilled machinists of the sort who send their children to the local college as a matter of course.

5. On a fifth level would stand the numerically overwhelmingly dominant group of the working class; these are the semiskilled or unskilled

[54] One will even pick up, for instance, in private conversation with some of these men strong endorsement of the right of labor to organize, along with such statements as, "They"—the people in control of local industry—"ought to give our people here a right to live better." Outwardly, however, these men "go along," as they are thoroughly aware of the dependence of the town on the "theys" who control its industrial fate. Some of these people diverged from the solid Landon vote of Group 1 in 1936 and voted for Roosevelt.

[55] Groups 1, 2, and 3 all fall under the general classification, "business class," as employed throughout the present study and in the earlier one. Likewise, Groups 4, 5, and 6 all fall in the "working class."

workers, including machine operatives, truckmen, laborers, the mass of wage earners.

6. Below Group 5 one should indicate the ragged bottom margin, comprising some "poor whites" from the Kentucky, Tennessee, and West Virginia mountains, and in general the type of white worker who lives in the ramshackle, unpainted cottages on the outlying unpaved streets. These are the unskilled workers who cannot even boast of that last prop to the job status of the unskilled: regular employment when a given plant is operating.

Psychologically, Groups 1, 2, and 3 cling together as businessfolk, over against Groups 4, 5, and 6. Mr. Corey suggests that in time the lower-salaried middle class (Group 3 above) must come to recognize its lost condition and to throw in its lot with the working-class groups below it *against* the world of 1 and 2. The actual amount of income of this group and its narrowing economic opportunities, pointed out in Chapter II, would suggest that this might conceivably be the case in Middletown. But there are no signs of such a shift in psychological alignment, though there is chronically more sympathy in Group 3 than in Groups 1 and 2 for the position of labor, and it exhibited more tendency, like labor, to vote for Roosevelt rather than for Landon. The people in Group 3, for the most part, think of themselves as part of the business class and cling hard to their status as white-collar folk—perhaps the harder because of their slowly growing sense of uneasiness as to their isolation—and they would be startled by Mr. Corey's suggestion. There is observable, however, a somewhat different quality in the psychological adhesions between Groups 1 and 2 and between these two and Group 3, and socially they are drawing apart. The psychological tie between Groups 1 and 2 is real and spontaneous, whereas that between these two and Group 3 is more tenuous; it consists in a neighborly tolerance on the one hand and, on the other, in the *desire* of Group 3 to hold its status as part of the business group—to live on the North Side, to go to business-class churches, to join business-class lodges, to belong to business-class women's clubs, and even, in the case of the men, to join one of the less conspicuous men's civic clubs.

If the nascent "class" system of "Magic [Middletown]" appears to follow somewhat the above lines, Middletown itself will turn away from any such picture of the fissures and gullies across the surface of its social life. It is far more congenial to the mood of the city, proud of its traditions of democratic equality, to think of the lines of cleavage within its social system as based not upon class differences but rather upon the entirely spontaneous and completely individual and personal predilections of the 12,500 families who compose its population. Persons in Groups 1 and 2 even express impatience over the fact that various groups of inconspicuous folk keep breaking off from the central big-business drive of the Chamber of Commerce and setting up bitter little pressure groups to try to protect their interests. These things are regarded as "disloyal," as "stirring up dissensions," and as the work of "troublemakers." Thus the dominant business group is annoyed by the organization among the schoolteachers of a Teachers' Federation to fight, in Middletown and at the state capital, against business pressure groups bent on hammering down teachers' salaries along with the tax rate; it also objects to the teachers' "mixing in politics" by endorsing a Democratic candidate for governor. Much more congenial to Middletown than such emphases on differences within itself is the harmonizing, friendly proposal made in jest in a local editorial to start a "Patched Pants Club, to be composed only of men who in their youth were forced because of poverty to wear patched trousers to school." Such a proposal brings a warm sense of neighborliness back to the hearts of parents who are worried because their daughter is excluded from the recently organized Junior Cotillion, and to those who must look from a wistful distance at the new homes of the wealthy springing up in the exclusive Westwood subdivision.

No other divisions in the community, except the paramount Negro-white cleavage noted below, compare in importance with those along economic lines. Certain other divisions are, however, worth noting briefly.

Membership in an "old family" carries some prestige—more so in the women's world than in the men's world—but only the usual element of habit and familiarity in association operates to slow up the acceptance of any economically and personally eligible outsider. Associations such as the women's clubs and churches get used to the presence of old familiar family names and faces, and some business-class newcomers consider Middletown slow in accepting them.[56] But "family"

---

[56] See *Middletown* (p. 480, n. 3) regarding the two sets of cards given to the new minister in the Episcopal Church when he came to Middletown, "the pink ones inscribed with the names of members of long standing and the yellow ones with the names of 'new people in town who might work in well later.' Some of these 'new people,' he discovered, had been in the church for ten years."

is not usually in Middletown a conspicuous source of social division.

Religious affiliation in a doctrinal sense within the Protestant sects is, if anything, less of an element of cohesion and division in Middletown today than formerly. Even as compared with 1925, Middletown cares less nowadays *what* people believe. As the essentially passive church takes its color from and is used by the forces in the community, however, the class identification of various churches tends to increase with the slowly defining class differences in the city, and nominal membership in the socially "right" churches is still an important device for identifying oneself socially. The social stigma upon being a Catholic is ordinarily small, though furtively apparent, in Middletown. This difference was abnormally exaggerated among the working class in 1923-25 by the local Klan agitation, and the latter has left some scar tissue. Being a Catholic appears, on confessedly slight evidence, to establish somewhat more of a social barrier among all classes today than in pre-Klan times, despite increasing doctrinal tolerance. Middletown's heightened nationalism and suspicion of internationalism, and the related increased identification of religion and patriotism noted earlier in the present chapter, make Middletown slightly impatient of the need of anybody to have a religion tied up to an international headquarters; and the close identification of Rome with the distrusted welter of European political and economic chaos makes Middletown draw back the more. There is at present no "Catholic issue" in Middletown, but the fuel for such a local fire lies all about in the habits of thought and feeling of the city.

The Jewish population of Middletown is so small as to be numerically negligible. It has increased slightly in size since 1925, and it now advertises cooperatively the closing of its stores on religious holidays, which is, perhaps, an evidence of its growing coherence as a group. Jews in Middletown are quietly on the defensive, as suggested by the fact that the "chief message" of the feast of Purim is announced in the press as lying "in its representation of the triumph of the Jewish people over blind anti-Semitism"; but their defensiveness is generated more by conditions outside Middletown than within. There is frank social discrimination at critical points such as membership in Rotary, but in general it is mild, and the facts that the Jewish group is so small, is made up of small merchants, and does not force the issue on the city make the local Jewish issue slight. Here again, however, as in the case of the Catholics, the issue is tinder ready for kindling if and as Middletown wants a bonfire to burn a scapegoat. If the issue grows acute, it may be sharpened primarily by the local merchants, who were already in 1935 blaming the lengthening of retail-store hours upon "the Jews and the chain stores." And any move for an emotional purge of irritating "outside elements" will find strong backing among the more evangelical Protestant element both north and south of the tracks to whom the brief Klan experience of 1923-25 offered an exciting Roman holiday.

The cleft between the white and the Negro populations of Middletown is the deepest and mostly blindly followed line of division in the community. The 5.7 per cent of Middletown's population who are Negroes live in two sections of the city: the principal one on the northeastern outskirts is fairly solidly Negro-inhabited, but in the other, to the south of it, a poor class of whites and Negroes are mingled fairly indiscriminately along certain outlying, poorly paved or unpaved streets. Active resentment of Negroes is largely confined to Middletown's working class, who face some competition from Negroes for jobs, and who have their residential neighborhoods abutting on or actually invaded by them. Business-class Middletown tolerates the Negro population complacently as a convenient instrument for getting certain types of dirty work done for low wages. According to the head of Middletown's local branch of the State Employment Service office, "Negro labor in Middletown has fairly steady employment at the harder, meaner type of job in certain of Middletown's factories, as hod carriers and similar unskilled labor in the building trades, on road gangs, and, in exceptional cases where a Negro's character is above question, as janitors. But the only thing a Negro man can do beyond that is a long step up from there to the professional class serving his own race. There are no intermediate steps—a Negro cannot, for instance, become a machinist." An officer in a large automobile plant stated simply, "We don't have any Negroes at all. It's degrading to a white man to have Negroes doing the same type of work."

To white Middletown, Negroes occupy the menial position they do because they are "inferior." When it read in its papers of "the discharge of the only Negro cadet at West Point," the inference was obvious: Negroes are inferior. And when Roland Hayes sang in Middletown it was his "genius" that prompted the press to comment somewhat patronizingly, "Genius destroys color lines and wipes out racial distinctions. . . . His skin may be black but his voice has something of the divine spark." And always there is the stigma of imputed greater criminality (their percentage of total local arrests runs around three times the per cent they constitute of the total population) and immorality. Here, as in most other cases, Middletown sees little relation between a culture and the behavior of its members, for the tradition of "free will" and "self-help" is too strong in its thinking. Middletown shuddered and felt confirmed in its views when two Negro boys were lynched in a near-by city; and when in June, 1931, a colored man was arrested in Middletown in connection with robbery and the death of a white woman, feeling ran so high that he was transferred to a jail in the next town to avoid mob violence.

Meanwhile, local residents report that "real gains" have been made by Middletown's Negroes in the past decade. Their political strength was sufficiently strong in 1934 so that the present mayor promised the Negro community a firehouse in their district manned by Negro firemen. (Incidentally, in the year and a half since his election nothing had been done about materializing this pledge—thereby confirming the comment in the local weekly that the Negroes "would do well to get even a doghouse, and at that they'd have to furnish the dog!") There are more organizations among Middletown Negroes today. References appear in the press to the organization by the "Colored Y.M.C.A." of "Colored 'Y' Clubs" in three Middletown schools; to the "Colored Y.M.C.A. Glee Club"; to the "Colored Elks' sponsoring of an oratorical contest"; to "the colored division in Middletown's American Legion"; and to the organization of a colored women's auxiliary of the Red Cross for emergency relief service. In 1934 a series of talks on Negro problems by Negro leaders was given in the Central High School and the talks were fully reported in the press. It is significant that the auditorium of the new X-donated Y.W.C.A. building is now thrown open on certain evenings during the winter for Negro dances.

White business-class Middletown carries magnanimously its "white man's burden." It encourages "good works" among its dependent black population. It even shares at times the resentment of local Negroes over some of the unfair condemnation under which they suffer. As an editorial commented encouragingly in 1934:

Colored people quite rightly protest against members of their race being forced to carry more than their share of the burden of crimes committed here and elsewhere. It is not so well known as it might be that there is a strong uplift movement among the leaders of the colored race here which is having generous support and which is given a setback when unwonted accusations are made against local Negroes, as has been the case more than once. . . . Those who are working in the community for the betterment of the colored population and for a better understanding between the races deserve encouragement.

But Middletown's Negroes, for all their bettered leadership and organization, occupy a more exposed position today than before the depression. They are the most marginal population in Middletown. It may have been true in the past that, as a Middletown employer remarked, "Our Negroes work for the most part at jobs where there is little or no competition from whites. They apply for certain jobs and whites apply for the others"; but in a world of too few jobs [57] such tentative color lines will tend to vanish. And the Negro, always suspect to the whites in a crisis, will tend to receive the full brunt of white resentment as the whites seek to wrest their jobs from them. The angry race resentments set roaring by the Klan in Middletown only ten years ago can again be made to blaze out in Middletown's South Side almost overnight.

In all the preceding discussion of attitudes and cleavages in the Middletown of the 1930's little has been said of the imponderable influence of the growing size of the city. In Chapter II it was pointed out that sheer size of an American urban unit tends to influence the pattern of vocational opportunities, particularly the availability of new and unusual types of work. In many other respects this factor of physical size must influence the character of a city's living, despite the manifest uniformities of American life.

Middletown has grown by more than a quarter since 1925, and is now a city of almost 50,000. In 1935 the investigator had constantly the sense as he moved about the city that it had somehow "grown up" in a material sense since 1925 and become less of a "big town" and more of a city. Such impressions are obviously based upon external indices and can be misleading, particularly when external features are paid for by Federal relief funds and private philanthropy. Among these signs of growth were, in somewhat descending order, the greatly

[57] See the discussion of the slowly failing number of available jobs in Middletown in the 1920's near the close of Ch. II.

augmented college group of buildings, the new hospital, the impressive new residential development near by, the beginning of the dredging of the river and construction of new bridges and a parked boulevard along its banks, the spacious airport, the municipal swimming pool— and thence on down through such smaller things as brighter store fronts on the main shopping street, traffic lights, radio police cars, and similar changes. To be sure, underneath these externals, Middletown felt at point after point utterly familiar. But the net feeling of "growing up" persisted. It was striking, for instance, in driving around the city with a lifelong resident to find him unable to identify the occupants of certain pretentious new homes, obviously belonging to people of much more than average means. This loss of contact did not feel like Middletown!

We know as yet so little of what it means for a city to pass from even the 15-20,000 to the 50,000 class that it is difficult to appraise the implications of smaller shifts, in this case that from a city of 36,500 in 1925 to 47,000 in 1935. As size increases, one may hazard the postulates that such changes as the following tend to occur in American urban units:

People tend to lose each other in the community-wide acquaintance sense.

One may know more people by sight, at the same time that one probably knows a smaller percentage of the total. But this will probably differ to the extent that people in the upper income levels—with their Country Club, Women's Club, Chamber of Commerce, and similar city-wide organized means of meeting each other—may tend to know by sight or to speak to more people than the low-income people who tend to participate in fewer of these city-wide organizations and to live relatively more within a neighborhood. It is apparently the case that business-class children tend to know more of the larger high-school population of today than do working-class children.

Acquaintance and association become more selective.

Formal social organization, involving repeating association with the same people, tends to replace informal contact and informal organization; and this tends to occur more rapidly among the upper social class than among those low in the social scale, and thus to crystallize more rapidly among the former a sense of class solidarity.

One's sense of "belonging" intimately to the entire social group probably tends to decrease with the increased size of the city, with a resulting tendency to a lower average participation in local movements of various kinds. This again probably tends to be more true of the low and low-middle income people than of the upper-income people; since, as a city grows, it tends to increase the number of its organizations by adding new charities (*e.g.,* a child-welfare clinic) and organizations (*e.g.,* local branches of the League of Women Voters, Garden Club, Association of University Women, etc.) run by the same heavily overlapping small upper-income group. One got the impression in 1935 that at least the women of the upper-income group in Middletown were busier with more committee and board meetings in 1935 than in 1925, and that among the men the same selected group of individuals were called upon repeatedly to carry as committee and board members the brunt of its organizational life.

With growing size, the number of persons who really lead and control local life tends to increase numerically, but at a slower rate than the population grows. This tends toward a concentration of control in the hands of a relatively smaller percentage of the total population; and this in turn operates to increase the sense of divisions within the group and of class lines as between the leaders and controllers and their immediate associates and, over against them, the large group of the manipulated and led.

Progressively as one comes down the social scale, the chance of becoming a lost individual, untied in any active sense to community-wide life and values, increases. One "lives in" a town, "makes one's money there," is part of its "available labor supply," rather than necessarily being an integral part of the town.

One insensibly becomes a citizen of a wider world as a larger city tends to develop a more metropolitan emphasis in its press, as its stores become more sensitive to the "latest New York styles," and as better-known speakers can be imported for civic clubs, and so on. One may hazard again the guess that this trend toward less localism tends to affect upper-income folkways somewhat more markedly than those of the lower-income people— though differences in this respect based upon income are probably less today than ever before, due to the heavily democratic character of the movies, radio, periodicals, and other mass media which import the outside world.

Residential areas tend to become more segregated and homogeneous. Such externals as where one lives become more important as placing one in the larger and less familiar population. This factor of residence has apparently played a definite role, as noted elsewhere, in the crystallizing of an upper-class neighborhood and class sense in Middletown's West End, replacing the less homogeneous East End of ten years ago where big and little homes ran along together.

And, related to the preceding, personal means of placing one in the group, involving considerations of the kind of person one is, yield to more quickly determinable, shorthand symbols, notably what one owns. This illustrates Veblen's point [58] of the paramount importance of "conspicuous consumption" as an identifying device in a community grown too big for more subtle means of appraisal. This would suggest the tendency, as a community grows, for its citizens to put relatively more of their possessions "on their backs," into cars, and other seeable goods.

And, in order to renew the semblance of unity in such a city of many human units tied to local residence chiefly by the accident of job tenure, those at the top who want united action must increasingly invoke gross emotional symbols of a non-selective sort by which masses can be swayed. And, with the fiber of community life rendered flabby by the presence of many untied persons, the ideologies and symbols that move the community tend to be generated at the top and to be imposed on those below, rather than rising spontaneously from the soil of community life.

All such postulates as the above regarding the relation of growing size in a population unit to the ties between the individual and community are offered very tentatively, since they lie for the most part in the no man's land beyond the front edge of what social science as yet knows. They certainly do not apply to all communities, and there may be stages of growth, such as the extreme of the metropolitan community, where some of them may not hold. They seem, however, to offer useful clews as to how the variable of numerical population size may be playing its part in the changes apparent in "the Middletown spirit."

One of the most sensitive approaches to the values and "spirit" of a culture is to be had through scrutiny of the way in which the culture, including its various subgroups, orientates itself with regard to the concept, "the future"—as over against "the past" and "the present." Every culture instills, whether by intent or inadvertently, some rationale of time into its members, and this tends in the case of a given culture to constitute a normal pattern of attitudes and behavior, around which individuals, age groups, and sexes may exhibit variations. In some cultures the past lies heavy upon the present as a golden age from which the society reluctantly recedes, while in others the past is an imperfect thing to be forgotten. Again, the present may largely dominate living. Or the present may assume the instrumental aspect of a transition stage to a more or less remote future when life "will be

[58] See *The Theory of the Leisure Class* (New York: Macmillan, 1899).

better." A wide variety of experiences may help to determine the direction toward which a culture bends its members' gaze.

In the main Middletown's culture teaches its members to live *at* the future rather than *in* the present or past. The culture has acquired its projective outlook on the future from a number of sources: from its very location in a northern climate where a long winter follows the season of crops and the earth's yield varies so that cautious husbanding of its output has until recent generations been necessary; from the Christian eschatology; from the stern Puritan emphasis upon "developing" one's character through careful, thrifty stewardship; from the spirit of private capitalism with its stamp of authority upon individualism and an endlessly growing acquisitiveness; from the frontier tradition under which one was in process of building, ever building, tomorrow out of a crude present; from the validating nineteenth-century doctrine of evolution; and, more recently, from the hypnotizing promise of more and more things tomorrow which its machine technologies and rising standard of living offer.[59] The very growth of Middletown within two generations from a drowsing county-seat town to a city of nearly 50,000, "the metropolis" of the eastern section of its state, is to Middletown tangible evidence of the fact that "tomorrow will be better." "Progress"; "growing" wealth, power, character; improvement; "bigger and better" everything; "a competence in old age"—these are some of the symbols that live daily in the skins of Middletown folk, lifting their gaze ahead. If politics is corrupt, it will "get better"; if one is poor, one can work hard and grow richer; if times are "bad," they will improve; if one is ignorant one can "improve one's mind."

[59] Contrast this striving, accumulating society, always pulling up stakes from the present in the hope of striking it rich in the future, with the following picture of another type of culture, situated in a climate where nature is opulent the year round and life focuses without strain on the present. "Economic conditions in Manua [Samoa]," says Margaret Mead, "must be understood against a background of economic plenty. Only in hard times of great disaster, such as the destruction of crops and houses by a hurricane, is there poverty in the group. No one lives below a comfortable subsistence level; all have sufficient food and clothing and shelter. The large descent groups take care of temporary disasters to any of their members. The old, the imbecile, the blind, the sick, are easily provided for. Conditions approximate to those in a prosperous farming district in summer, when the gardens are bearing and a few more mouths to feed made very little difference. In Samoa there is no winter, no lean season, no period when scrimping and saving are necessary." (*Social Organization in Manua*. Bernice P. Bishop Museum Bulletin 76, Honolulu, 1930, p. 65.)

So, at point after point, Middletown is habituated to leaning the ragged present into the achievable future.

Within this deep belief in everyone's getting ahead together, and consistently bolstering it, is the optimistic faith that there is "a power not ourselves" that will bring things right. This arises not only from a belief in Matthew Arnold's God—and with many people, especially south of the tracks, in the more definite and meticulously watchful God of Luther and Calvin—but even more perhaps from an ingrained belief in an Order of Nature exemplified to these folk in the past development and "manifest destiny" of America. When things get "a bit out of hand" and the lines to past precedent are fractured by new situations, the instant apprehension of an essentially conservative but hopeful community is wont to be at once capped and blunted by the assurance that things will come out all right—for "America cannot fail." Thus, as a Labor Day editorial commented in the face of the mounting unemployment in the fall of 1932, "Although several hundred men in Middletown are wishing today that they could labor, in the end all things will mend."

According to the editorial on "The [Middletown] Spirit," in February, 1931, Middletown's philosophy is one of "conservative optimism." "The [Middletown] citizen," the editorial states, "believes in himself and his community; he takes temporary troubles and defeat as temporary and not permanent; and when in moments of discouragement he is tempted to think that progress has stopped, he recalls that [Middletown] has always gone forward and it is reasonable to suppose it always will."

One of the questions with which the research staff returned to Middletown was: What has the depression done to this faith of Middletown in the future? Are people living in terms of a longer future or has the future been telescoping back into the present? Are people insisting harder than ever upon "the will to believe" in the old symbols of their personal and collective manifest destiny, or are they becoming more pessimistic or cynical? Questions of this magnitude invite more detailed and extended analysis than the limits of the present study allowed. But even in a brief time certain clews could be secured.

The concept, "the future," involves two things to Middletown: a congeries of large symbols, slogans, values, and beliefs, floating high and clear above the daily realities of life; and up and down the shady streets, inside the homes, offices, and bare factories, a network of small plans, hopes, and guesses. In the boom years of the late 1920's, the sky of symbols, slogans, and personal dreams moved perceptibly closer to daily life—here was the old truth gloriously reaffirmed, for the future *was* meaning progress, and progress was meaning that Americans were the most favored people on "God's footstool," while all the rest of the world was laboring in bitterness and disappointment.

What has apparently happened during the depression is that the distance between the symbolic universe of belief and the pragmatic universe of everyday action has widened. They have again floated abruptly apart, and so far apart as to demand of Middletown *either* that it apply its customary formula and blindly deny that the gap has actually widened, or at least regard it as merely a temporary interruption; *or* that it revise this high-floating world of symbols, restating it in humbler and less hopeful terms so as to re-locate it closer to everyday reality; *or* that it accept as normal the fact of living in an enhanced state of tension because of the unwonted permanent remoteness of the two planes.

This symbolic ceiling over Middletown is largely set and defined for the city nowadays by its business class. The chance for the mass of the population to "go up in the world" to affluence and independence appears to be shrinking noticeably. It so happens, however, that those who still retain the best chance to rise in the world, to skim the cream from the economy, also control the press, the radio, the movies, and the other formal media of diffusion of attitudes and opinions. They are thus in a position—in the kind of urban world suggested above, containing an increasing group of untied residents who do not contribute materially to the native ideologies of the folk—to tell the cityful of people largely living off the skimmed milk of the economy what to believe.

One may read into the tenacious persistence with which those who thus define the sky above Middletown make it gaudy with symbols of "Progress," "Opportunity," and the "Bigger and Better" a canny realization of the need to "put on a good show" to reassure the groundlings and render them amenable. Middletown's press reflects the awareness of this necessity to "doctor up" the morale of the rank and file; but, as remarked above, Middletown's "class consciousness" is as yet rudimentary, and only in times of threatened labor trouble or political upheaval do those at the top bear down hard. Actually, it is the emotional need for hopes and expectations by the business class at present, quite as much as the need of the working class, that renders necessary this sedulous devotion to a star-spangled future. For while nearly every family in Middletown has met reverses of sorts in the depression, for a considerably greater proportion of the working class these reverses have not been the novel experience they have been to the business class. The latter do not have so much habituation to living close to sudden shattering changes like unemployment, and their personal identifications with the big-symbol world of "Progress" and "Opportunity" have been in the past more continuous and confident. The welter of choices and decisions that make up human living in a price-organized culture—such decisions as What shall we plan to do? When can we do it? Do we dare count on it? How long ahead can we plan? Will tomorrow support the decisions of today?—these things tend to be fitted over two somewhat different patterns of time-relationship between "today" and "tomorrow" in the case of the business class and of the working class; and they present a somewhat different aspect to the two groups. For Middletown's business class, the sheer fact of having any job at all which has gone on with a large measure of continuity has probably been much less important in the depression—or one might better say that its importance has been more easily forgotten and taken for granted—than for the working class. Long-term planning of one's family economy, on the other hand, involving *less* psychological readiness to accept life as a barehanded struggle with discontinuous realities week after week and a *more* elaborately conceived and institutionalized set of hopes and expectations of the future, has probably been more marked in the past experience of the business class, taken as a whole. Such a remark as the following is perhaps a significant confirmation of this point. The alert principal of the large junior high school in the heart of the working-class district was asked about evidences of the effects of the depression on the morale of people in his district, and he replied: "None, in particular. Our people down here aren't hollering about the depression as much as the middle- and upper-income groups on the North Side. To those North Side people the depression has meant losing things they had or had wanted. Our people down here have always lived closer to poverty and emergency. They have seemed to adjust to the depression pretty well, taking their small amount available from relief agencies for food and managing to live on it somehow."

While the working class has shared, in its role as minor partner, many of the basic experiences and emotional convictions of this American culture, it is the business class that has tended more often to live in terms of a deliberately anticipated long future—involving the building up of an estate or of an industry over half a lifetime, and financial provision for one's old age and for one's children—while for the working class the future has of necessity been more compressed to "next month" or "this year." It is natural, therefore, that the business-class leaders should have been insisting in 1935 with determined intensity upon the continued nearness of the old symbolic ceiling, and that they should have been resisting efforts, whether by Washington with its program for taxing the rich or otherwise, at a restatement of these symbols in humbler terms more consonant with the experiences of the depression years.

And reaffirming the doctrine of opportunity, without alteration in spirit or detail, appears to be precisely what the more influential members of business-class Middletown were busily doing in 1935-36. They were doing this largely by denying any real shift in the relative applicability of symbol to reality and by creating a personal devil in the form of the Roosevelt administration. These people were convincing themselves, with the aid of such things as the *Saturday Evening Post's* articles in 1935 dating the beginning of recovery in the summer of 1932,[60] that they would already have been on the march long since toward the businessman's New Jerusalem, thanks to "natural forces," had it not been for the meddling Roosevelt administration which seeks to "ruin the country." This, then, is the "official" Middletown attitude as set by its business leaders and the press: the future is intact, and all that is wrong is the Roosevelt administration in Washington, and we'll go right ahead garnering our American heritage as soon as ever we can turn them out of office. That so many of the lesser business folk actually voted for Roosevelt in 1936,[61] in the face of the bitter solidarity of the city's leaders and the press, suggests the extent to which Middletown's middle class may be drawing apart from the upper class in this respect and viewing their future in more sober and less confident terms. It is possible that they view a future involving deliberate changes in the traditional open-handed rules of the game—changes curbing the freedom of big business—not only with

[60] William Starr Myers and Walter Newton, "The Origins of the Banking Panic of March 4, 1933," *Saturday Evening Post,* June 8, 15, 22, and 29, 1935.
[61] See the analysis of the 1936 presidential vote in the closing pages of Ch. IX.

less hostility than do the more successful, but in the guise of increasingly useful defenses of their own exposed position as economic small-fry.

The press has liked during the depression to paint in rosy colors the optimism of even those hardest hit. Human-interest stories have appeared under such captions as "Destitute, Perhaps Hungry, Still They Look to the Future." The inquiring reporter then goes on to recount an interview with three unemployed men and states that "All have reasons to be thankful."

In fact, as part of this insistence upon the unimpaired future, Middletown's business class is even inclined to talk a good deal about the "benefits" of the depression. "It's done us a lot of good—brought us down to earth—cleaned out a lot of foolish values. We're in better shape than ever to move ahead—and, boy, are we set to go!" exclaimed one businessman, and this hopeful sentiment was reechoed in one form or another repeatedly. "This Depression Has Its Points" was the caption of a local editorial:

Great spiritual values have come out of the depression. . . . Many a family that has lost its car has found its soul. . . . Nerves are not so jaded. Bodies are better rested, and though fine foods are not so plentiful, digestion is better. . . . Churches have been gaining . . . because some who were once members of golf clubs can no longer afford to play.

In the pit of the depression, in January, 1933, when even business-class Middletown's time-span was temporarily narrowed down to the anxious effort to save oneself today, this rejection of all effort to redefine "the future" was expressed by another editorial as follows:

For human life, after all, is made up mostly of a series of little guesses about the most immediate future. We never look ahead much beyond the ends of our noses. It simply isn't possible. If we can get through next month's difficulties, the year after next—and all eternity thereafter, for that matter—can take care of itself.

This, sometimes, makes serious thinkers despair of us. We seem blind and heedless, incapable of vision. But we can't, in the very nature of things, be anything else. We have today's job to do, and tomorrow's to worry about—and we haven't time for anything else. We have to live in the present.

This same note was struck in a conversation with a dozen men around the luncheon table. At the close of a discussion as to "how long the future feels" to them, one of them expressed it as follows, with the others nodding assent:

"Every one of us is busy in the depression asking, 'What's this mean for *me*—now?' That's why we aren't wasting much time trying to dope out causes or to look away ahead into the future. Each of us is on his own special hot spot, and we want to get off! No one wants to think of uncertainties in the future, so we whoop it up over General Motors' coming back to town and take maybe too simple a view of the depression and its causes. We think this is just a dip in business. The curve will naturally turn up soon again, as it always has in the past. Deep down inside we're all scared as hell, but we tell each other we aren't—and that makes us feel better.

"Even workingmen aren't speculating much. They just want to get their jobs back so that they can know where next week's pay is coming from and buy a car. But they seem to have learned *this* much: they're not rushing to buy houses and tie themselves up with debts, because they have a darned lively sense now of how easily a plant can be moved in and out of a town."

One got the impression in talking to Middletown's workingmen, however, that, while they are inarticulate and not pondering causes, they are not coming out of the depression clinging to the old symbols of future arrival as securely as are many in the business class. To many of them whose hopes have been hammered thin by unemployment and the necessity of living on relief, these older symbols have floated off so far as to be largely out of sight and only real in so far as dull, automatic habits keep them meagerly alive. Many of these people struck one as having pulled in their personal future to the point where it has little existence beyond the drab struggle just to keep alive. By many of them, the future is resisted as a threat rather than fondled as a hope; though one always hastens to rein in a statement of this sort in view of the obvious toughness of human hope as one saw it in June, 1935, busily painting the porch and watering the lawn in the more comfortable South Side homes. The director of the State Employment Service office commented: "These men are a lot less confident and flip. They're worried. And they are going back to work in the mood of eating a lot of dirt just to hold on to their jobs." Right now Middletown workers aren't pyramiding life into any long future, but doggedly fighting for a mere toehold of immediate security. In this respect they appear to differ rather markedly from the business class. An observant man from a family on the margin between business and working class wrote on request the following summary of his impression as to how Middletown is looking at the "future":

"During the depression, the working classes have become more pessimistic in relation to the traditional formula of work, save, success. The impression seems to be growing that no matter what you do you will eventually find yourself in a *cul de sac*. I think that a brief period of prosperity would again inculcate the philosophy of economic individualism in the mass of people, but there is growing unquestionably a deep-seated mistrust in the present way of doing things. I talked recently with a young man who said: 'I can't see much ahead of me except work—if I ever get any.' Another told me, 'My father is a good man. He has worked hard and saved what he could, but where did it get him?' I know of course that you could have duplicated these expressions ten years ago, but the trend is distinctly away from the old way of thinking."

One of the ablest of the local ministers summed up the situation by saying: "I think the American dream has been dimmed considerably for a lot of our people by the depression."

"Saving" ranks with "hard work," in the central Middletown tradition, as one of the two joint keystones of the arch of a man's "future." The doctrine is unequivocal: saving, not living up to the feather-edge of one's income, is a fundamental mark of "character" and essential to "self-respect." In this association in Middletown's mind of "thrift," "hard work," and "character" one touches the nerve center within the individual on which Middletown believes all respectable living depends. As pointed out at the beginning of this chapter in the listing of the things in which Middletown believes, the well-nigh universal business-class explanation heard in Middletown of why the poor are poor is that "They don't work hard and they don't save." Since both an era of boom-time "killings" and an era of financial collapse, especially when the latter is coupled with talk of inflation, constitute direct assaults upon the careful spirit of "A penny saved is a penny earned," one of the questions that interested the research staff in returning to Middletown was: Have boom and depression worked any change in Middletown's fundamental faith in saving?

The bare bones of the changes in Middletown's available funds are presented in Appendix II and its accompanying chart showing the movement of deposits in Middletown's banks and building-and-loan associations by year from 1925 through 1935. The consolidated deposits in all these institutions rose between January, 1925, and the peak in January, 1929, at a rate nearly 75 per cent more rapid than the growth of the city's population. Consolidated deposits stood at the latter date 42 per cent above their total at the beginning of 1925; and they fell off at their lowest depression point to only 5 per cent above 1925. Deposits in the city's building and loans rose by 85 per cent in the good years, and it was not until the beginning of 1935 that they reached their depression "low," 33 per cent above 1925, and leveled off. The share of the city's total deposits that was in building and loans rose from 37 per cent at the beginning of 1925 to 54 per cent on July 1, 1933, and by the close of 1935 had receded to 39 per cent. It is significant of the uncertainty of the small saver as to what to do with his hard-saved money that postal savings deposits rose from only $9,011 at the close of 1928 to $27,798 at the close of 1930, and then began a march to a peak total of $438,780 at the end of 1935. All of the above figures, however, involving as they do both corporate and private funds, while affording a valuable summary view of the institutional aspects of saving in Middletown, reflect but little of the intense drama within the lives of Middletown's individual savers.

Confusion has been introduced into Middletown's thrift pattern at a number of points. Thrift is an essentially conservative doctrine built of, by, and for the common man, the little fellow who lays by small sums on the theory that "Many a mickle makes a muckle." Saving is, according to the traditions of the culture, a hard, denying affair, a thing that "hurts"; and the maintenance of morale in such a process depends largely upon there being no "exceptions"—no people who "crash the gate" without paying the price. In Middletown there have been relatively few such gate-crashers. Even the X family, Middletown likes to think, began poor and "worked and saved for what they got." But the liquid fire of speculation in the bull markets of the 1920's burned its way into Middletown as the big-city investment houses and the banks cultivated the small investor. Stories got about as to how "So-and-so cleaned up a thousand dollars in three weeks playing the market." That's a lot of money to Middletown, and "easy money" like that left saving at the rate of five or even twenty-five dollars a month a bit down in the mouth. There apparently *was* another way even for Middletown folk to get ahead without this everlasting scrimping!

Concurrently with the spread of market speculation, and even dating

back to the beginning of the 1920's, was the equally irresistible install-
ment-selling drive put on by American business after the World War
as part of its high-pressure campaign to manipulate desire and move
goods.[62] This operated subtly to diminish the old Middletown sentiment that there is something reckless and disreputable about buying
things other than a home before one can "pay cash" for them. Here
was the second blow to thrift; you could actually enjoy an automobile,
a radio, a vacuum cleaner, a piece of jewelry, a fur coat *while* you
saved the money to pay for it. This made saving seem much less painful, and dislocated its old temporal antecedence to enjoyment; and this
last, by telescoping the future into the present, largely eviscerated the
classical theory as to the motivation of abstinence. There was still old
age to look out for, but there was a growing tendency in the 1920's
to carry that as a fixed charge through life insurance, thus removing
saving for one's old age somewhat from the category of endless nickel
pinching toward an indefinite future sum.

Middletown's realization of the confusion that has been injected into
this emotionally heavily buttressed area of saving by the new gospel
of free spending is reflected in the following editorial warning in
July, 1935:

Our parents and grandparents taught their sons that the good things of
life come through work, ability, and saving. Now children are being taught
that the less work the better, that one who is without skill has the same
right to the fruits of the earth as the man of high intelligence, and that
spending for spending's sake alone is a virtue and thrift is a vice. . . . Is it
not about time for the American people to go back to that common
sense which for a century and a half has served them well enough to
build a nation that is the envy of all others?

When the depression struck, it set up two counter moods as regards
saving in Middletown. "How has the depression made you people feel
about saving?" local people were repeatedly asked by the research staff
in 1935. The answers tended to cluster around two extreme poles: On
the one hand were those who said, "Never again! You sweat and deny
yourself, and make what you think are good safe investments, and
then—pfft! it goes up in smoke through no fault of your own"; and
at the other extreme, "We were all damned fools in the 1920's! We

[62] See *Middletown,* pp. 46 and 82, and Index under "Installment buying." See
also n. 73 and n. 108 in Ch. II of the present study, and n. 35 in Ch. VII.

thought we had the world by the tail and forgot the old truths that 'a nickel saved is a nickel made.' I'm never again going to be caught the way I was in this crash. From now on I'm going to live away within my income and you bet I'll save! I don't know where I'll keep my savings, but I'll keep 'em all right!"

Early in the depression further confusion was imparted to the philosophy of thrift by the advocacy by President Hoover and other prominent persons of a diametrically opposed doctrine. At the same time that Middletown's banks were conducting their customary annual "Thrift Weeks" to encourage private thrift as the keystone of one's personal economy, the country was deluged with the counter doctrine that *spending* was the keystone of the national economy. "Spending Will Win the War against Depression" clamored a local editorial. Hard-pressed Middletown wavered between the two stools, one labeled in effect, "Saving—the Private Man's Only Safeguard," and the other "Spending—the Nation's Hope." The city was not stampeded by the new gospel, but further uncertainty was introduced into its philosophy of thrift as it was thus asked to face, even though temporarily, the fundamental contradiction between the needs of the individual and the needs of private business under modern technology and the control of production by private capital.

Rising Federal taxes, while directly affecting in any serious way only a fragment of Middletown's population, have been played up by the press as confiscatory and destructive until these, too, have been made to look to Middletown like discouragements to thrift. One hears over and over in Middletown the exclamation by businessmen, "What's the use of saving? The government will only take it away from you!" A leading local editorial in June, 1935, asked, "Why Not All Quit Saving?" After reciting recently enacted taxes, the editorial concluded:

What inducement is there for an individual who has worked and saved money to invest it in an undertaking that would employ labor? Why run the risk?

The American people are hardy. They are pioneers. They are energetic. They want to do things. But the mounting trend in taxation and the confiscatory inheritance taxes which destroy lifetime savings may break the heart of private initiative and enterprise.

It will be a grim crop the taxgatherer reaps as he starts harvesting the estate taxes of America. He may gather one good crop from each family, but, in his greed, it looks as if he would fail to leave enough seed to pro-vide "profitable" income from inheritance taxes in the future.

Inflation talk, accompanying fear of high taxes, has added a des-perate poison to the cup of thrift. And along with everything else has come a floundering uncertainty as to what to do with one's money even if one saved it. Here, to Middletown, is the last futility of thrift. A businessman remarked:

"The greatest impression made on the middle-income people of Middle-town during the depression was the growing feeling of the insecurity of future investments due to national governmental policies. Stocks and bonds are now very uncertain. Some are becoming interested in investing in commodity exchange and in warehouse receipts. Where can a fellow put his money to have old-age security?"

Some Middletown people, as noted in Chapter V, were eagerly buying up farms as investments early in 1935. "They are not fooled much," com-mented a local editor in June, 1936, "about this theory that 'all wealth comes from the soil.' Stocks and bonds have blown up on them and real-estate hasn't amounted to much for several years, but they have no place to invest money that will bring them over 3 per cent, and then the State and Federal governments take part of that away from them, so they are again talking in terms of apartment houses, little and big farms, home owning, and such." The editor then went on to recite the long list of woes of the man who invests in real estate, and con-cluded his recital as follows:

How should [Middletown] people invest their money? Best advice I can give on this subject is the same I gave to a young man living in a distant city who said he had a few thousand dollars he wished to invest "safely," and asked what to do. To his letter I replied this: "If I had a million dollars this minute I would not know how to invest even one dollar of it safely—except by spending it in having some fun before further inflation attacks us and makes money more nearly worthless than it is now. Don't be thrifty. If you become a pauper the government will gladly support you."

Here again Middletown faces both ways. Tied emotionally through generations of tradition to regarding saving as the way to confront the future, it rocks restlessly in a world that also says to it, "Don't be thrifty. Have what fun you can while you can and trust to luck for the future." Bankers complain of the "loosening of public morality as regards the sacredness of debts." As one of them phrased it:

"There's been a widespread demoralization here of the sense of responsibility. It dates from the first statement by President Roosevelt that small home owners and farmers would not lose their homes. People began right away to expect the building loans to let their debts slide. They began coming into the banks asking to compromise their debts. This H.O.L.C. stuff didn't help either! Everybody got the idea it'd be fine to have two years' relief from payments. We told 'em it was intended only for people *in extremis.* So what'd they do? They went home and began letting their payments slide, and then came back to us when they were really in hot water! Will Rogers didn't help any when he said it was a good idea for people to forgive their debts so that everybody could start clean again. And [the editor of our afternoon paper] helped the thing along by calling attention approvingly to the ancient Jewish custom of forgiving all debts every twenty years. When that sort of ground-fire starts running through a community, it's hard to stop it. Even now, in 1935, this crazy expectation on people's part is holding over to a considerable extent."

Today both attitudes, the "I'll never save again! What's the use!" and the "I'll save harder than ever," are present in Middletown. In the main, the latter appears stubbornly intact with most of the population, and even somewhat enhanced. The following qualifying generalizations are hazarded tentatively on the basis of the information it has been possible to gather:

There was some agreement among Middletown people of all sorts with whom the matter was discussed that the "spend-it-if-you-have-it" attitude is more prevalent among the young than among the old.

The following remark by a veteran carpenter is characteristic of comments heard in conversation with the older workers: "One of the lasting changes made by the depression is that it has shown people they can't live beyond their earnings. It's taught us frugality. If you'd've told me six years ago my family would have to live on what we're living on today, I'd have said you were crazy. But we've learned our lesson!"

The "spend-it-if-you-have-it" attitude was more prevalent in 1935 among the working class as they were again getting employment than among the business class. This may have been merely temporary, reflecting the greater depletion of physical equipment among these people during the depression. The head of a large building-and-loan association commented in June, 1935, when employment was rising and a marked recovery spirit pervaded Middletown: "Our deposits are increasing again, but chiefly from our white-collar accounts who are cashing bonds. The thing I miss in the picture is the workingmen's deposits. They are absent so far. I don't know whether they are just paying their debts, fixing up their homes, buying cars, or what." As noted in Chapter IV, Middletown's skilled workers have clung with especial tenacity to the idea of getting off relief and back to "regular" work. It is unlikely that these people have relaxed to any extent their habits of work and saving. Among the little-skilled groups, however, futility, coupled with the experience of government relief, may have bred a more casual attitude toward the future, though no definite evidence of this is at hand. The presence of such an attitude would depend, in part, on whether the psychological goals of these people are felt by them to have been permanently lost or whether they still regard them as merely postponed.

Business-class people are going in heavily for annuities and other forms of conservative saving. Among even those business people who have been hardest hit, the dogged attitude persists, as expressed by one man: "I'm starting all over, just as I started twenty years ago. I lost all my money in the crash, mostly invested in bank stock.[63] I don't even have a car or telephone. The only thing I have saved is my office equipment. And a few years ago I was worth a few thousand dollars. But I'll come back!"

At least two groups in Middletown have been giving more thought to the future since the depression. Parents and educators are deeply concerned about the future of the next generation, and young people between eighteen and thirty are asking questions of the future rather than taking it for granted. A press account in April, 1936, quotes the president of the college as saying: "How are we to teach thrift to those who have lost everything? Why teach youth to rise early when there are no jobs to go to? Why teach honesty when it has been reduced to a legal technicality?" The editorial comment continues, "He was speaking of the problems that confront educators. Solomon had no

[63] Middletown people, particularly working people, are coming out of the depression with an enhanced suspicion of banks, though the public guarantee by the X family in 1933 that it would stand behind Middletown's banks has carried over somewhat as a reassuring factor. As stated in Ch. II, it was a novel public heresy for Middletown to have the editor of one of its papers say during the depression in his column: "Far be it from this column to laud banks unduly. In general, its opinion of them is not so high." And, though in 1935 the mild local hostility to banks was easing, one could still read in the editor's column of Comment, following a human-interest story of a local businessman wiped out by the depression: "He will come back, but when he does, don't even try to sell him or even give him any bank stock."

such questions to answer. . . . Today's schoolteacher must be wiser than Solomon."

What Shall We Do with Our Children? [asks another editorial in 1935.] There is something tragic, heartbreaking about their plight. A speaker at a Kiwanis Club luncheon the other day asked this question, and he confessed he could not answer it. What these boys and girls wish is to find their niches in the world. . . . And just now there is nothing for them to do. This is a situation that was virtually unknown to the older generation. . . .

"I just feel that I am not wanted," said a boy recently out of Central High School. "I know what I want to do, but there is no opening for me, and I cannot even get work at things that I do not care about. It is pretty tough on a kid to get up of a morning and look forward to a day of idleness. I go to the library and read and then I go home for my lunch. Then I take a spurt and start out hunting for a job, any kind of a job. It is the same thing day after day. I was an honor student in school, but that does not get me anything. I have a girl, too. Gone with her since we were kids in the grades. . . . She doesn't kick about it and keeps me bucked up, but we are both missing the fun we ought to be having while we're young. But I could stand all this if only I could see an end to it. . . . What am I going to do with myself?"

Another comment in the editor's column reveals the clashes between parents, reared in an era of "opportunity" and unable to understand this depression world, and their boys unable to get jobs:

A high-school graduate came in yesterday to say that a sentence or so in this column, about parents who fail to understand that boys cannot always get jobs immediately after leaving school, told his own story to his father. "Dad keeps throwing up to me all he has done for me, and that has been a good deal," admitted the boy. "He has put me through high school. Knowing that my schooldays would be over soon, I started out six months ago to try to land a job, and I still haven't any. Father has thought it was all my fault, because he has never been out of work a day in his whole life if he wished to work. I showed him that clipping from your column and I think it helped. But I am not going to be dependent upon him a minute longer than I can get away from it, even if I have to take to the road."

But, Lord, the problems of these young people that ought to be solved and are not being solved and that leave older people dazed and utterly bewildered! Take the case of a girl graduate of X State Teachers College. She wishes to be a teacher in the public schools and she is qualified, but she has been informed, quite truthfully, that the normal colleges are turning out every year thousands more graduates than can possibly find jobs. So, she said, "Here I am prepared to do something worth while and my services are not wanted."

As late as November, 1936, in the midst of much talk of returning prosperity, the same note continued in press comments: "—always the recurring question, 'How are we going to get jobs?' Nothing else apparently is of much importance to the boys and girls of [Middletown] or anywhere."

And parents, watching their children, are asking uneasily, "What are our children thinking?" Middletown parents do not like their children to think different thoughts, to diverge from the parental pattern other than through achieving larger successes. These worried parents continue to send their children through high school and, in many cases at extreme sacrifice, to college. "There are no jobs," they tell one, "and they'd better be in school than running the streets." But one gathers that that part of the American dream which equates "education" and "bettering one's future" has evaporated in some households.[64] Some working-class people are even letting go that most tenaciously held part of the American ideology touching the future: the belief that "Somewhere on ahead our children can achieve the things we have dreamed of and couldn't get for ourselves." As jobs return to Middletown—if they do—one suspects that the youth in Middletown working-class homes may have to fight harder with their families than they did in the booming 1920's for the chance to "get a college education."

Among the younger generation, one can find everything from smoldering rebellion to a determined success pattern that outdoes that of their elders when young. "Our younger businessmen who do have jobs are harder than nails, harder boiled than the older generation," commented a successful businessman in his forties. "They know they've *got* to be good, and they're not taking any chances by giving anyone else an unnecessary break. They're fighting for every advantage and holding on to it like a vise when they get it." Another businessman described the sober determination among the still younger business-class youth as follows: "Our younger generation still believe

[64] See the discussion of college education in Ch. VI, and also that of the apparently growing employment vacuum confronting would-be workers of ages eighteen to twenty in Middletown in Ch. II.

there's a ladder to climb to a future, though they realize it's a tougher ladder. On the whole, those who are not yet out of school and kicking around hunting jobs are still optimistic."

It is largely the working-class children still in school and in the age group out of school in their late teens and early twenties who present disillusionment and rebellion. A high-school teacher remarked: "Our working-class children know there is a depression all right! And they worry about it—not only as it hits their own future but as a family problem they must help face." The youngsters out of school fall into three groups: those who have contrived to find jobs not devoid of a future of sorts; those who have taken jobs away below their expectations, offering neither present satisfactions nor future hopes; and a third large crowd without jobs. The latter again, according to one of the staff of the Y.M.C.A., are made up of two groups: "Those who keep looking, and the others who, after getting thrown down in try after try for a job, give up and come in here to the Y. to play checkers."

One picks up frequent references to a growing apathy among some of the young. In part it appears to be a defense mechanism. "I feel stupid not being able to get a job," said one boy, "and I've just got to pretend I don't care." With others it is no pretense: "Young people in their twenties," commented a working-class boy, a graduate of the college employed in delivering parcels, "are just accepting the fact of a lower station in life and not struggling any longer. They're some of them going right on marrying and accepting financial difficulties and no future as part of what they've got to expect from now on, or they're turning to escapes—the auto, gambling, drink, anything that'll make them feel less lost." "They're just getting used to the idea of there being no job," commented another high-school teacher, "and there isn't much explosiveness." A few of the boys who have been at the college, in touch with the restless liberal minority on the campus, are frankly though quietly in revolt against "the system." One such boy, a clean-cut graduate of the local high school and college, now employed at ten dollars a week in a local business, remarked to the investigator with quiet bitterness: "Our group feel we're thoroughly stopped. There's just no future for our generation. I'd like to get out of town, but, hell! where'd I go? I don't want to become a bum in one of these transient camps. I'm working quietly for socialism; it won't come in my lifetime, but it'll come some time."

It is no new thing for the youth of the small city to want to "get out of town" and to move on to larger cities. This psychological desire seemed more prevalent in 1935 than a decade ago, but the outward flow had ceased and the tide was even reversed. Early in the depression, many of them had tried to leave, most of them to return later after beating the streets of larger cities looking for jobs or trying to sell Fuller brushes. As the depression has worn on, while the desire to migrate has increased, the nearer side of the road has also come to look more attractive to some. For the most part, young Middletown is just "sticking around." And yet the repetitiveness of this familiar round of life among neighbors may become acutely distasteful if either of man's great peacetime anodynes for routine—marriage and work— are denied him. This is precisely the predicament of many of these Middletown youngsters in their twenties. They have no work and some of them feel they cannot marry, despite the heavy tradition of early marriage in Middletown; and it is not merely the hoped-for chance of a job that beckons them away but the outward thrust of too much spare time seeing the same small group of people over and over and doing the same thing day after day. The element of repetition is always high in the small community. One social set of half-a-dozen couples in Middletown, disliking the clichés of the larger business-class social life, are trying to develop their own social life. They have jobs and some of them are married, but after visiting round and round and "getting all talked out, there's been nothing for us to do but to take to drink."

Middletown likes to solve all these depressing things by the thought that "The pendulum will swing back soon." It seems probable, however, that as more and more of the city's dissident young are backed up within Middletown in a possible period of more or less chronic job stringency, the city will have to accommodate relatively more of these diverging minority groups, and small city life may become a more diversified thing. Against the possible thrust of such a broadened base of young dissenters, however, the slow aging of the entire population should be borne in mind. Middletown, in common with the rest of the country, is having fewer children and the average age of its people is rising. The conservative weight of the growing share of its population over forty will tend to offset some at least of the mounting restlessness of the young.

CHAPTER XIII

Middletown Faces Both Ways

THE PRECEDING chapters have sought to make explicit the elements of permanence and of change in Middletown as the city has met with four types of experience peculiarly conducive to cultural change: sudden and great strain on its institutions, widespread dislocation of individual habits, pressure for change from the larger culture surrounding it, and at some points the actual implementing from without of a changed line of action. These ten years of boom and depression might be expected to leave permanent marks on the culture.

The boom experiences were not essentially different in kind from those Middletown had known before: optimism, growth, making money—these things are in the city's main stream of tradition. Such an experience as climbing to the very verge of the long-expected population of 50,000 contained elements of novelty and has, despite the depression, left a permanent deposit in the city in the form of increased self-regard. The prosperity of the fat years, while sharpening the disappointments of the depression, also remains today in Middletown in the form of enhanced personal goals and glimpsed new psychological standards of living for many of its citizens. The fact that Middletown does not regard the depression as in any sense "its own fault," or even the fault of the economy by which it lives, makes it easy for the city to think of the confusion following 1929 as "just a bad bump in the road," one of those inevitable occurrences that spoil things temporarily but do not last. The gold-rush scramble back to confidence which the research staff witnessed in 1935 was the inevitable result of such a rationale of the depression. Middletown was in effect saying, albeit soberly and decidedly anxiously: "It's all over, thank God! And now we'll get after all those things we were planning for ourselves in 1928-29!" In a culture built on money, the experience of better homes, better cars, winter vacations in Florida, and better educated children dies hard; and while some people's hopes, especially among the work

487

ing class, have been mashed out permanently by the depression, the influential business group who determine the wave length of Middletown's articulate hopes are today busily broadcasting the good news that everything is all right again.

The depression experiences contained more outright novelty than did the years 1925-29:

A city exultantly preoccupied with the question, "How fast can we make even more money?" was startled by being forced to shift its central concern for a period of years to the stark question, "Can we manage to keep alive?"

A city living excitedly *at* a future which all signs promised would be golden lived for a while *in* the present with its exigent demands.

A city living by the faith that everyone can and should support himself lived through a period of years in which it had to confess that at least temporarily a quarter of its population could not get work.

A city intensely opposed to society's caring for able-bodied people has taxed itself to support for an indefinitely long period one in every four of its families.

A city that has chronically done without many manifestly needed civic improvements, on the philosophy that it does no good to hunt up and plan desirable things to do because there isn't any money to pay for them, has lived for a time in a world in which not money but ability to plan and carry out progress was the limiting factor.

A city built around the theory of local autonomy has lived in a world experiencing rapid centralization of administrative authority and marked innovations in the interference by these centralized agencies in local affairs.

A city that lives by the thought that it is one big cooperating family has had the experience of a wholesale effort by its working class to organize against its business class under sponsorship from Washington.

A city committed to faith in education as the key to its children's future has had to see many of its college-trained sons and daughters idle, and to face the question as to what education is really "worth."

A city devoted to the doctrine that "Work comes first," to an extent that has made many of its citizens scarcely able to play, has faced the presence of enforced leisure and heard people talk of "the new leisure." Civicly, the community has begun to state positively the problem of the leisure of the mass of its people, and to make wider provision for popular leisure pursuits.

A city still accustomed to having its young assume largely the values of their parents has had to listen to an increasing number of its young speak of the world of their parents as a botched mess.

A city in which the "future" has always been painted in terms of its gayer-hued hopes has been forced to add to its pigments the somber dark tones of its fears.

Experiences such as these partake in their cumulative effect of the crisis quality of a serious illness, when life's customary busy immediacies drop away and one lies helplessly confronting oneself, reviewing the past, and asking abrupt question of the future. What has Middletown learned from its crisis and partial convalescence?

Chapter I stated some of the larger questions of this sort which the research staff took to Middletown in June, 1935. The broad answer to these questions is that basically the texture of Middletown's culture has not changed. Those members of the research staff who had expected to find sharp differences in group alignments within the city, in ways of thinking, or feeling, or carrying on the multifarious daily necessities of life, found little to support their hypotheses. Middletown is overwhelmingly living by the values by which it lived in 1925; and the chief additions are defensive, negative elaborations of already existing values, such as, among the business class, intense suspicion of centralizing tendencies in government, of the interference of social legislation with business, of labor troubles, and of radicalism. Among the working class, tenuous and confused new positive values are apparent in such a thing as the aroused conception of the possible role of government in bolstering the exposed position of labor by social legislation, including direct relief for the unemployed. But, aside from these, no major new symbols or ideologies of a positive sort have developed as conspicuous rallying points. Leadership in the community has not shifted in kind, but has become more concentrated in the same central group observed in 1925. The different rates of change pointed out in the earlier study as occurring in the different areas of living have not altered materially:[1] economic activities have set the pace and determined the cadence of these years, though the changes have not differed in kind over these ten years anything like so sharply as during the thirty-five-year period covered in the earlier study; in

[1] See *Middletown*, p. 497.

terms of actual rate of change and radical quality of innovation, the institutions concerned with care for the unable leaped into the lead during the depression, although Middletown likes to regard the changes in this area as "purely emergency and temporary" in character; education, leisure, and the relations among family members have exhibited some changes; while the city's local government and religion have remained as before most resistant of all its institutions to change.

With the exception of the widespread innovations in caring for the unemployed, which by 1936 were already contracting their scope, a map of Middletown's culture shows today much the same contours as before; no wholly new hills and valleys appear save in this "temporary" provision for the unemployed and the resulting new public works; the configuration is the same. Even the fault lines which appear today and show signs of developing into major fissures within the community were faintly visible in 1925. In the main, a Rip Van Winkle, fallen asleep in 1925 while addressing Rotary or the Central Labor Union, could have awakened in 1935 and gone right on with his interrupted address to the same people with much the same ideas.

Such changes as are going forward in Middletown are disguised by the thick blubber of custom that envelops the city's life. The city is uneasily conscious of many twinges down under the surface, but it resembles the person who insists on denying and disregarding unpleasant physical symptoms on the theory that everything *must* be all right, and that if anything really is wrong it may cure itself without leading to a major operation. The conflicts under the surface in Middletown are not so much new as more insistent, more difficult to avoid, harder to smooth over. Many of these latent conflicts, aggravated by the depression and now working themselves toward the surface of the city's life, have been pointed out in the preceding pages: conflicts among values hitherto held as compatible; conflicts among institutions —economic and political, economic and educational and religious, economic and familial; conflicts among groups in the community breaking through the symbols of the unified city; conflicts between deep-rooted ideas of individual and collective responsibility; conflicts, above all, between symbols and present reality.

The physical and personal continuities of life are relatively great in the small community, and the average dweller in such a community probably has a sense of "belonging" that is qualitatively somewhat different from that of the big-city dweller. The institutions in the small city tend to be familiar and, with the help of many assumptions of long standing as to how they are linked together and operate, a quality of simplicity is imparted to them in the minds of local people. By assuming continuities and similarities, this simplicity is interpreted outward to include "American life" and "American institutions."

One of the major elements of conflict imparted by the depression to Middletown has been the injection of a new sense of the inescapable complexity of this assumedly simple world. As indicated earlier, the more alert Middletown people met the depression with an earnest desire to "understand" it—only to be thrown back later, in many instances, with a sense that it was "too big" for them and that all they could do was to try to stick to their jobs and save their own skins. One suspects that for the first time in their lives many Middletown people have awakened, in the depression, from a sense of being at home in a familiar world to the shock of living as an atom in a universe dangerously too big and blindly out of hand. With the falling away of literal belief in the teachings of religion in recent decades, many Middletown folk have met a similar shock, as the simpler universe of fifty years ago has broken up into a vastly complicated physical order; but, there, they have been able to retain the shadowy sense of their universe's being in beneficent control by the common expedient of believing themselves to live in a world of unresolved duality, in which one goes about one's daily affairs without thought of religion but relies vaguely on the ultimates in life being somehow divinely "in hand." In the economic order, however, it is harder for Middletown to brush aside the shock by living thus on two largely unconnected levels, for the economic out-of-handness is too urgently threatening to daily living.

So Middletown tries to forget and to disregard the growing disparities in the midst of which it lives. Its adult population has, through its socially gay youth and busy adult life, resisted the patient scrutiny of problems and the teasing out of their less obvious antecedents and implications. As a local man remarked in 1924 in commenting on the pressure of modern living, "We've lost the ability to ponder over life. We're too busy." And, if in the boom days Middletown was "too busy" to ponder, it was too worried to do so in the depression. It is quite characteristic, for instance, that, as one woman remarked in 1935, "We never get down to talking about things like the coming of fascism. The only time we ever talk about any of those things is when we comment on a radio program." Rather than ponder such things, Middletown prefers either to sloganize or to personalize its problems. And the more the disparities have forced themselves to attention, the more things have seemed "too big" and "out of hand," the more Middletown has inclined to heed the wisdom of sticking to one's private business[2] and letting the uncomfortable "big problems" alone save for a few encompassing familiar slogans. Where Middletown cannot avoid these big problems and must on occasion present at least the semblance of a balance in this system of nonbalancing intellectual bookkeeping, it is resorting increasingly to the suppression of detailed entries and to the presentation of only the alleged totals.

One frequently gets a sense of people's being afraid to let their opinions become sharp. They believe in "peace, but—." They believe in "fairness to labor, but—." In "freedom of speech, but—." In "democracy, but—." In "freedom of the press, but—." This is in part related to the increased apprehensiveness that one feels everywhere in Middletown: fear on the part of teachers of the D.A.R. and the Chamber of Commerce; fear by businessmen of high taxes and public ownership of utilities and of the Roosevelt administration; fear by laborers of joining unions lest they lose their jobs; fear by office-holders wanting honest government of being framed by the politicians; fear by everyone to show one's hand, or to speak out.

But this process of avoiding issues goes on less and less fluently. With a widening gap between symbol and practice in the most immediate concerns of living, there are more forced choices as to where one's emphasis is to be placed. Middletown wants to be adventurous and to embrace new ideas and practices, but it also desperately needs security, and in this conflict both businessmen and workingmen appear to be clinging largely to tried sources of security rather than venturing out into the untried. Middletown people want to be kind, friendly, expansive, loyal to each other, to make real the idea of a friendly city working together for common ends; but, in a business world where one is struggling for self-preservation, or for power and prestige as a

[2] Middletown receives ample encouragement in this congenial resolution of its problems. It read, for instance, on page one, column one, of its morning paper the following eloquent sermon by Arthur Brisbane on the prize fighter, Gene Tunney: " 'Seest thou a man diligent in his business, he shall stand before kings.' Tunney was diligent in HIS BUSINESS, learned to know it thoroughly and now stands before kings, at least money kings. It is very important to know one thing thoroughly."

supposed means to self-preservation, warm personal relations, like the more fastidious sorts of integrity, may tend to become a luxury and be crowded to the wall. If necessary, one dispenses with affection. People want to continue to live hopefully and adventurously into the future, but if the future becomes too hazardous they look steadily toward the known past.[3]

On the surface, then, Middletown is meeting such present issues and present situations as it cannot escape by attempting to revert to the old formulas: we must always believe that things are good and that they will be better, and we must stress their hopeful rather than their pessimistic aspects. This leads to the stating of such social problems as may arise defensively and negatively [4]—rather than to engaging in a positive program for social analysis and reconstruction. It is still true in 1936 that, to Middletown, such things as poverty or a depression are simply exceptions to a normally good state of affairs; and anything that goes wrong is the fault of some individuals (or, collectively, of "human nature") rather than anything amiss with the organization and functioning of the culture. The system is fundamentally right and only the persons wrong; the cures must be changes in personal attitudes, not in the institutions themselves. Among these personal cures for its social woes are the following six basic qualities needed for a better world outlined in a local address: "faith, service, cooperation, the Golden Rule, optimism, and character." "The typical citizen," says an editorial approvingly, "discounts the benefits of the political and economic New Deal and says that common sense is the answer to the depression. . . . He thinks hard work is the depression cure." Or again, "If profits are low, it is still possible to get a good deal of

[3] As pointed out in Chs. II and XII, Middletown's working class appears today to be less sure of many of the old values than is the business class; but in Middletown they have developed no ideology of their own, and they lack security on any basis of their own, such as labor organization. Hence, doubtful and uncertain, they tend to straggle after the wealthier, pace-setting fellow citizens in their affirmations of established values in the midst of confusion.

[4] See the discussion of the handling of the relief problem in Ch. IV.

In keeping with this tendency to state its problems defensively and negatively, Middletown tends to avoid facing the implications of differences between its practices and those of other communities by recourse to the easy extenuations that "Our situation is different," or that a given problem "is just one of the peculiar problems that *our* community has always had to cope with." Such reasoning allows local practice to continue its course along the smooth grooves of past custom.

enjoyment by doing the best possible under adverse circumstances and by taking pride in our work."

This marked tendency in Middletown's thought and feeling to see the place where remedial change is needed in individual people and not in its institutions helps to ease its tension over local political corruption and other shortcomings in the midst of which it lives. Its faith in the ultimate quality and final perfection of its institutions is thus left intact, and its Christian emphasis upon the need to spur on weak and faltering human nature to that perfecting of itself "which all history proves to be slowly taking place" makes the individual shoulder the whole burden of blame. Over and over again one sees Middletown following this line of reasoning. Thus, for instance, the reason Middletown's business class is unable to see any sense in such a concept as "class differences" is that it recognizes no relevant basis for "classes" in the institutional system. And it does not recognize them because, according to its way of viewing things, "getting ahead" is a personal matter. The institutions are there, fixed and final in their major aspects, and the individual must struggle to make them work and to be more worthy of them. Once one gets this point of view, Middletown's rationale of "the rich" as "social benefactors," and of "the iniquity of the New Deal" becomes apparent. One can see why Middletown feels the rightness of recent editorials in its press such as the following:

LET'S GIVE THE RICH A REST

It is popular just now to assail the wealthy, and unpopular to defend them, and yet most of the economic progress that America has made would have been impossible had this not always been a land of opportunity for those who wish to make money without undue restrictions upon their gains. . . . Thousands of boys reared in poverty have become millionaires through their own ability, through their unbridled ambitions, and in becoming so have supplied occupations and the comforts of life to many times the number of thousands who have acquired the millions.

Instead of laying all our troubles upon those who have had the talent and the brains to become wealthy, why not each of us assume our share of responsibility for the economic situation of the nation?

MONEY-MAKING THE BIG INCENTIVE

The way to make both the poor man and the rich man poorer is to tax wealth so greatly that it loses its incentive to produce. . . .

ON THE "SOCKING" OF THE RICH

Who remembers when the American boy was taught he had as good an opportunity to become wealthy as the town's richest man had at the same age? And when the rich, while perhaps they were envied by others, were thought worthy of emulation? When riches were not considered a disgrace but an honor, and millions would have died rather than accept charity?

Now the demagogues, the social outcasts, the unsuccessful, the lazy, the ambitionless, the ignorant all join in a swelling chorus in denunciation of those who by their work and ability have acquired more of the world's goods than others have been able to obtain, making no distinction between the wealth that has come by reason of intelligence, hard work, and thrift and that which has been obtained through trickery and fraud. . . . So we preach the doctrine of "socking" the rich, because the majority of us are not rich and are not likely ever to be rich, since the majority have not the ability, even given the opportunity, to acquire great wealth.

But without great accumulations of centralized capital America today would be almost wholly a nation of farmers, instead of being divided between agriculture and industry. Except for centralized capital, how could great factories be constructed, great buildings be erected, hospitals built and maintained, vast charities be supported, scientific investigations be made, and the results of such investigations given free to the world!

To men holding the philosophy these editorials reveal, efforts in Washington or elsewhere to make changes in *institutions* by which men live constitute a misguided assault on the one source of strength and progress within a nation, namely, the personal drive within the individual to accumulate wealth and to "better himself." "Progress," according to this philosophy, is a by-product of the pursuit of wealth.

The essentially instrumental character of Middletown's living noted earlier—namely, its emphasis upon the "future," "saving," "trying to get somewhere in life," and so on, as over against the present quality of living—tends to augment its tension over emerging conflicts. This sort of instrumental living puts a heavy premium upon assumed simplicity and reliability in the underlying institutional system. One can hardly live confidently *at* the future unless one assumes a guaranteed highway; if one assumes the broad, sure highway, one need not concern oneself too much over dusty inadequacies in the present, because the road mounts surely just around the next bend; but if one questions the very existence of a sure highway "as some radicals and long-haired thinkers do," then what is to become of all the virtues of fortitude and hard work! A culture thus committed to instrumental living tends, because emotionally it so badly needs to do so, to do with its present difficulties along the road precisely what Middletown has tended to do with the depression, *i.e.,* to regard it as just an unduly stiff bit in the road. And only with great difficulty or as a result of prolonged discouragement will it do what a minority of Middletown's working class are beginning to do—ask whether the road is really leading anywhere, whether after all it is the best possible road, or even whether the present isn't a good time and place to recognize one's difficulties and to begin to face them.

Loudly as Middletown affirms and reaffirms all its hopeful, ameliorative beliefs, the "Down here under our vests we're scared to death" note was heard again and again in 1935 when business-class or working-class people were talking unofficially. Some of its tensions it had been unable to overlook, to sloganize away, or to brush aside as merely personal frailties subject to correction as men become "better." The long pull of the depression had even prompted occasional rare questions as to whether the system itself was as sound as Middletown liked to believe. An editorial in mid-1933 on "Machines and the Human Equation" had stated:

We have been making society mechanical instead of making machinery social. We have to humanize our mechanized industries by putting human values above material values and the real welfare of all above the false welfare of the few. . . . What is needed here is social engineering.

An even bolder editorial (in the afternoon paper—it could hardly have appeared in the morning paper) about the same time, remarking on the suicide of an unemployed man, had said under the unfamiliar caption, "The Right to Live by Work":

Why should anybody wipe himself out of existence because he has no money? Have we set up some kind of a false standard of value? . . . Someday and somehow, finally, we are going to straighten these things out. You may call the new order by anything you please, but it is coming. The inherent right of every man and woman who is willing to do his part to maintain reasonable social conditions, which means to live decently, cannot be gainsaid by any system. That is basic. Let us not fool ourselves by thinking the old systems are to be continued indefinitely. . . . The right of a willing man to work and live by his labor is paramount. There is nothing else important.

Although the official front had recovered its flawless exterior by 1935, Middletown people knew that they had been living for a while in a world that made more natural the raising of such questions. The acute concerns of the depression were dropping somewhat behind, but over the contours of the city stood out the bench marks of depression experience. And Middletown was afraid, even as it whooped things up over "the return of prosperity"; and perhaps it whooped things up the more just because it was afraid.

Week after week during 1935 the outside radio was bringing in talks by men like Father Coughlin and Huey Long. Over the air came into the cottages and even into many business-class homes points of view not allowed to appear in a favorable light in the local press. "I'm surprised," commented a businessman, "at the number of intelligent people who listen to Father Coughlin and believe he talks sense. Curiously, too, people don't seem to resent his being a Catholic." Down at Pop Alexander's South Side beer hall men talked freely and favorably of Father Coughlin, and some South Side families had his emblems in their homes. On the South Side, too, Huey Long's slogan, "Share the wealth," elicited loyalty. Some working people expressed their willingness to "follow any kind of man who stands for that." [5]

As this goes to press, Middletown has just come through what many of its people regarded as the most critical national election within the memory of anyone now living in the city. The weight of frightened hope with which the city's leading businessmen backed Landon to defeat Roosevelt was almost literally beyond exaggeration—and, even more than in previous elections, the employers were prepared to go to

[5] Huey Long did not have as good a standing in Middletown as Father Coughlin. "People don't trust him and his power is waning here," remarked a businessman in 1935. "People here dislike him morally, and they hold against him that rowdy fistfight down at the Sands Point Casino on Long Island." Another businessman put it even more bluntly: "[Middletown] thinks Huey Long rough and crude and a damned fool. Strange as it may seem, this community puts some emphasis on dignity. [Middletown] likes a smooth politician—even south of the tracks."

The Townsend plan was not being discussed in Middletown at the time of the field work. Lemke, as Table 46 shows, polled in 1936 but 187 votes in Middletown's entire county.

great lengths to contrive to make their employees "vote right." [6] To these businessfolk this particular election was a holy crusade; if Landon and the Republican party had won, a cool, cleansing sponge, they felt, would have wiped out all their nightmare memories of four years of New Deal flaunting of American ideals and security.

With its characteristic proclivity for resolving issues into stark blacks and whites and personalizing each within the manageable compass of a devil or a savior, business leaders in Middletown see in Roosevelt all that they are against, the personified denial of all their wants and of all the virtues of the pioneer tradition. There is infinitely more than "campaign talk" behind an editorial like the following appearing in June, 1936; these Middletown businessmen think their backs are squarely against the wall:

TO PREACH HATRED OF THE RICH

"To preach hatred of the rich man as such [said Theodore Roosevelt] . . . is *to seek to mislead and inflame to madness honest men whose lives are hard and who have not the kind of mental training which will permit them to appreciate the danger in the doctrines preached.* All this is to commit a crime against the body politic and to be false to every worthy principle and tradition of American national life."

In the New Deal lexicon, anybody who has been industrious enough to accumulate two dollars to clink against each other, who has been thrifty enough to save some money for the inevitable rainy day, who has acquired wealth in order that he might employ it to give jobs to others seems to have become, per se, a dangerous character who should be suppressed. . . . Franklin D. Roosevelt, chief of the New Dealers, is asking that the only persons who can give private jobs and keep business going be mulcted of the means for doing the very thing the President is thunderously demanding. . . .

Theodore Roosevelt realized the necessity of the existence of capital if the American people are to prosper. . . . *He did not seek to inflame the masses against the very men upon whom, finally, the prosperity of all the people depended in so large part.*

Theodore Roosevelt regarded rich men and corporations as custodians of

[6] See *Middletown*, pp. 415-16, and also Ch. IX above. As noted in Ch. IX, these efforts to influence votes actually overreached themselves, stirred up suspicion and resentment, and ended in many cases by creating votes for Roosevelt. Middletown even began to joke about the situation. Humorous stories flew about town, *e.g.*, about the man down at the X plant who broke his leg falling over the pile of Landon buttons discarded by the men outside the plant door.

wealth, most of whom possessed the special business skill needed—with some government supervision, to be sure—to keep the ship of state upon an even economic keel. He did not think that college professors were skilled enough to take over business.

Theodore Roosevelt, with a sincere love of his fellows in all walks of life and with the ardent wish to promote the welfare of the lowliest as well as the highest in the social scale, nevertheless was a practical man. . . . He thought straight. There was no warp nor crook in his logic.

And with what disgust would he have observed the attempt today to array class against class, to make fine theories take the place of sensible practices! [Italics ours.]

In the view of Middletown's business leaders, there has been "an insane man in the White House," with "our best mindless thinkers advising him." The bitterness of speeches before civic clubs and of statements in the casual conversations of businessmen, and the monotonous, shrill efforts by the two daily papers to mobilize local public opinion greatly surpass the quieter conservatism met with in 1925:

"We businessmen here aren't just a bunch of tories," commented a local banker heatedly, "but we're scared to death that a lot of reckless political wild men will take everything away from us. We believe in change and know it's going on. We believe in looking ahead, but we don't believe in trying to do it all at once. It'll take two or three hundred years to get the perfect state. Change is slow and big changes won't come in our lifetime, so meanwhile we intend to go ahead and not worry too much about what these changes will be or ought to be.

"And we *know* politics. Have you seen our Congressman? You can size *him* up by just looking at him! Look [pulling a sheet from his desk], here's an application of the brother of our Negro janitor for a C.C.C. job. The boy's a graduate of Tuskegee. See here, the first four recommendations he has to send in on the back of this application are his district leader, then two more local politicians, and finally his state political boss. We businessmen see this rotten political business everywhere, in all these alphabet organizations in [Middletown]; the word comes down the line from Washington—it's just party politics.

"We've no faith in Roosevelt—his angel wings and smiling words cover up a worse political machine than Hoover ever had. He isn't honest—he talks one way and acts another. He has no courage—or rather courage at the wrong time. He isn't fit to be President and can't hold a candle to Hoover. I've been reading the articles in the *Saturday Evening Post* [7] about

[7] These are the articles referred to in n. 60 in Ch. XII.

the depression, and they're right—I know from our banking connections with New York and Chicago.

"Sure we need planning. But these bright boys that jam Washington don't know their stuff. Who's a big enough man to plan? We businessmen are afraid of bureaucrats and planners. I've walked through Washington offices, and I never saw so much loafing in a business office. Now a business outfit like the American Telephone and Telegraph Company plans, but what do *they* do? They don't rush into experiments all over. They try an experiment in a single state. And look at the controls they have over them! Their common stockholders control them, and if they don't make money, they're turned out. But government employees don't have to make money.

"All these big plans they're making in Washington look well, read well—but they just won't work. They're Utopian, and we don't live and try to do business in a Utopia! By what God-given right do these fellows in Washington think they can do a job so big? It's the very immensity of national planning that makes it impossible. The old law of supply and demand can't be repealed or amended. It applies to labor and to materials, raw and finished. Roosevelt's like a general who sits at the top and hands down orders from man to man till they get to the privates sweating under a sixty-pound pack—and he's the fellow that carries out the order.

"You can't make the world all planned and soft. The strongest and best survive—that's the law of nature after all—always has been and always will be."

From this vision of catastrophe, Middletown's business leaders turned back terrified to "the old ways—the American way" embodied in "Landon, the Careful Kansan." Here Middletown saw its own "middle-of-the-road" image reflected reassuringly back to it. As the following somewhat careful, because pre-nomination, editorial in early June of 1936 indicates, here was a man who, business-class Middletown was prepared to believe, thinks and feels as it does:

ESTIMATE OF "ALF" LANDON

"Alf" Landon is without any important political career behind him. He is not especially attractive of personality, his radio voice is poor, he never has accomplished big things in any given line of thought and endeavor, his qualities of statesmanship are yet to be discovered, his knowledge of economics is uncertain, . . . but the people seem to believe he is utterly honest. Given utter honesty, other things appear unimportant.

Maybe "Alf" Landon is not a statesman. . . . Maybe he knows more about drilling an oil well in wildcat territory and striking it lucky than he knows about the proper sartorial accouterment for our ambassador to the Court of St. James. . . . But the people of the United States, beyond doubt, have the conception that he is "square" in a time of many governmental intrigues: that he has common sense with which to combat the subtleties of the theories advanced by the professorial bloc at Washington. . . . Maybe we should be gradually settling down to this business of having common sense in government, and maybe "Alf" Landon is the new prophet. . . .

Landon has two advantages as a candidate. One of them is that he has a very short record in public service and, therefore, is little known. The other is that he speaks the language of the common people. If there is a third it is . . . that he has the common sense that is the inheritance of those who live in the Midwestern prairies.

Even on the eve of the election, leaders in Middletown's business class hoped for victory. On October 28, one of the X brothers announced that "Defeatism is gone. . . . We go into the closing days of the campaign determined to achieve our goal of true American government . . . as opposed to radicalism, waste, and dictatorial powers." The day before election, a long editorial warned Middletown solemnly:

BUT IT COULD HAPPEN HERE

One who goes to the polls Tuesday should do so with a feeling of the solemn obligation that rests upon him and with thankfulness in his heart that THUS FAR he still has a privilege that is denied to most of the peoples of the earth—the privilege to play his part in government. In spite of attempts at regimenting about everybody in America in the last three and a half years, the voter is still free to cast his ballot as he sees fit.

A dictatorship may come to America, as it has come to other nations; our freedom may be destroyed or greatly limited. . . .

A good deal has been said in this campaign as to whether we Americans are to retain the American plan of government—a plan that has been more successful than any that ever has been tried. Under it the United States grew great and rich and prosperous. The plan contemplates the restoration of good times UNDER THE LAWS OF FREEDOM AND INDIVIDUAL ENTERPRISE. That is the path we have taken down the years, and it has been a good path. The plan has not been perfect, of course, for no plan of government is that, nor is one ever likely to be that has to take into account human frailties and human proneness to err. But we can say of it truthfully that it has proved to be the BEST PLAN any nation ever has tried. . . .

"It can't happen here?" . . .

THIS THING COULD NOT HAVE HAPPENED TO GERMANY—BUT IT DID HAPPEN. [Here followed a recital of the plight of Italy and Russia.] Nor do we know from week to week what may happen to France now that Communism has become so powerful a factor there.

So it is no idle fear that comes to us in America that we, too, some day may suffer the fate of these other nations from which the last vestige of liberty has departed. Nor can we quiet ourselves by the thought that the American plan of government will continue.

The way tomorrow's election goes may have a great deal to do with the maintenance of this American plan of government unsullied.

IT CAN HAPPEN HERE!

It is difficult to say what Middletown's 59 per cent majority for Roosevelt in 1936 means. The local press is inclined to take it philosophically as one of those occasional blind acts of nature; editorially the vote is spoken of as an "avalanche" and an "earthquake." Despite the city's long record of Republican majorities, most of Middletown looks upon the quadrennial national election as it does upon a horse race: in all such things occasional upsets will occur, in the nature of things. The easy tolerance of these people is great, their ability to adjust and to "make the best of" situations almost unlimited. There are grounds, therefore, for brushing aside the local result of the 1936 election as of little permanent significance. Certainly it does not signify the presence of "radicalism" or of a desire for drastic change. The vote for minority, left-wing parties through the entire county was less than 1 per cent of the total. Implicit in the vote were all of the following in varying degrees: a belief that things were at least better in 1936 than they had been four years before, the experience of positive relief aid from Washington, a vague feeling on the part of the numerical majority who constitute the working class that a government may be something than can operate on *their* side in *their* behalf, reaction against the forceful tactics of business leaders in the campaign, and in some cases the settling of scores "against the X family" and their dominance in local affairs.

To an unparalleled extent the election of 1936 probably represented to Middletown people the chance to do something for personal security. And it is the different views of different sections of Middletown's population as to where security lies *for them* that gives to this election such significance as it may prove in future to have had. Despite the tendency of Middletown folk to look upon presidential elections good-naturedly as "a bit of excitement, after which we all settle down again and resume whatever we were doing before," a definite sense of local "class differences" has been generated by the election by reason of its acute depression background, the activity of the Federal government in helping to meet local problems, and the resulting diverging class views as to where security for individuals in different strata of the population lies.

As noted elsewhere, there is but little evidence of the emergence in Middletown of any clear sense of class solidarity among the working people. Likewise, the fifty-fifty vote of the middle-class folk of small income reveals their ambivalence, though, again, it is possibly significant of their growing uneasiness as to where *their* security lies that so many of them refused to side with the big-business group on the unusually acute issues presented by the campaign.

For the more coherent group of business leaders, however, the situation is far otherwise. One sees here a financially and socially dominant group of leaders of the city, men who usually dominate the opinion of the city in terms of the public interest as they interpret it, groggy and ill-tempered with seven years of denied hope, and now thwarted in the hope that was to end fear and the need for hope. They confront a city in which the usually docile six to seven in every ten in the population who make up the working class have "gotten out of hand" and asserted their numerical predominance. These earnest, hard-working, able businessmen read in their afternoon paper the post-election comment by the editor:

I talked with the manager of a great industry not long ago who put it this way: "The big hogs are letting the little pigs up to the trough. They know that if they don't they'll all be little pigs pretty soon, for the big hogs will be butchered."

Faced with the necessity to "endure four more years of Roosevelt," it is likely that these men will adopt a definite policy of putting on the brakes at every possible point to prevent things they dislike from happening.[8] Their purposes are being clearly stated in post-election editorials:

[8] The temper of these leaders in Middletown and the role they desire to play in the modest sphere of their influence are somewhat akin to those of Stanley Baldwin as the leader of the National Government in England, as described by John Strachey:

"One of his supporters once said that Mr. Baldwin's achievements were always

The best bulwark of defense for American institutions continues to be the courts, especially the Supreme Court of the United States.

If the President seeks to attain such N.R.A. objectives as limitations on working hours, wage boosts, and improved working conditions there would be conflict.

If President Roosevelt moves to the right or if big business the country over contrives a working alliance with him, Middletown's business leaders will "go along." Should the present tension continue unabated, the mood of men of power and ability such as these may conceivably lead to explosive action. Middletown does not ordinarily do things suddenly. Its mood is cautious. It does not tend to initiate change. But it will line up overnight behind a widely diverging *fait accompli* if the latter suits its deep emotional need for security.

At the moment, Middletown looks equally askance at both fascism and communism. Both are foreign, authoritarian, and intensely distasteful. "All that stands between communism and fascism and what the United States has," declared a speaker before Rotary, "is a little paper ballot. The ballot is the only heritage left us by the men who fought in the Revolutionary War. Whenever one of the fundamental liberties is taken away it leaves an open road to the forces of communism and fascism." "Fascism is as violent and dictatorial as Bolshevism," said an editorial in March, 1932. "It means revolution just as surely as Bolshevism does; it is just as false to the common man's rights." In bracing its feet against "centralized government," "bureaucracy," and the "great danger that by over-generosity [government relief] we shall impoverish the thoughts and lives of thousands who would otherwise have been independent of mind," Middletown is simply voicing its conviction that, as expressed in a local editorial, "When bureaucracy and bloc control destroy representative govern-

negative; that he had spent his political life almost exclusively in *stopping* things from being done. It is true; for Mr. Baldwin knows that the limits of profitable action in Britain are becoming narrower and narrower. The strength of the British Empire is still enormous, but it is almost wholly defensive strength. He realizes instinctively that almost anything that anybody *does* will only make matters worse. He is the perfect statesman for an empire in decline; he is forever stopping things. He, in effect, attempts to stop the decline, and if he does not wholly deceive himself into believing that he can do that, he can at any rate, he knows, prevent it being immeasurably accelerated by the foolish actions of others." John Strachey, *The Coming Struggle for Power*. Chapter XV, "An Empire on the Defensive: The Role of Mr. Baldwin." (New York; Covici, Friede, 1933.)

ment, fascism may be just around the corner, or something even worse. When the individual arrives at the point where the government must become his guardian we have bureaucracy in full bloom. Then, with the failure of bureaucracy, despotism invariably follows."

During the 1936 campaign the local press reprinted Roger Babson's predictions that:

The chances are 50-50 that the United States will go Fascist when the next depression comes.

There is the possibility that the coming national election may be the last one for many years.

An editorial late in November, 1936, headed "Fascist Movement in the U. S.," after reviewing the evidence presented by "a writer of considerable prominence and of thorough reliability" that "a Fascist movement of importance is now under way in the United States," concluded:

The picture as painted seems almost fantastic, but it is possible that while all the furore has been going on about communism, another equally subversive force has been at work to undermine American institutions. But if the people are informed in time about what is going on they should have no difficulty in suppressing this movement as well as that of the communists.

There is no place in America either for communists or fascists. One is as bad as the other. Both are not only un-American, but anti-American.

But, averse as Middletown is to any sort of dictatorial control, what its business leaders want even more than political democracy is what they regard as conditions essential to their resumption of money-making. And those who do the more conspicuous money-making are probably prepared to yield a good many other things to the kind of regime that will flash for them the green "Go" light. These men recognize the power of the strong man, the man with power, and being successful in business is one long apprenticeship at adjusting to stronger men than oneself. They do not fear such a man, providing he is on their side.

If Middletown's press lumps fascism with communism as "undesirable and un-American," it also carries a significant trickle of editorial comment that leans, perhaps unconsciously, toward the "strong man" of "the right sort."

Why shouldn't the average man who has little personality of his own use discretion and attach himself to men who are now what he would like to be? [asked an editorial in 1932.] If this strong man is a conservative with a well-lined nest and conviction that all who advocate change or disturbing of dividends should be jailed or deported, those who follow him are a little off the middle of the road too, but they're not as bad as the radicals.

A year before, when, in the midst of Chicago's municipal confusion, a Chicago businessman suggested that the businessmen of that city take over the running of the city, a Middletown editorial, under the caption "Business Steps into Politics," asserted:

When misrule continues too long, business will assume the dictatorship. And it, at least, will give us efficiency and economy.

An editorial in 1932 proclaimed:

WANTED—A RULING CLASS THAT WILL RULE

We are disgusted because the ruling class doesn't rule. . . . [The class that will rule] need not be the rapidly diminishing wealthy class, of course. It may be any class that possesses vision, sanity, and a sincere wish for the public welfare.

In conversations with businessmen in 1935, one gained a strong sense of their desire for "a leader"—one of their own sort. They cannot move without a leader, because "things are too big," but they know how to follow. One such man remarked in conversation: "Individualism has made a sorry mess of things. The government in its try in the New Deal has made a mess of things. So, what? Hitler and Mussolini may be wrong, but *we've* been wrong, too, so far. What we need is a capable leader." Increasingly, these men see a choice between "radicalism" and a something-that-will-put-down-radicalism. They think of the latter as an "American," a "patriotic" movement, and of the struggle between the two forces as a struggle to "save democracy." "Communism Is Spreading Here" was the headline late in 1936 over an address by the national director of Americanism for the American Legion, sponsored by the public affairs committee of the Y.M.C.A. "We cannot close our eyes," said an editorial, "upon the fact that communism, especially, has been making some inroads in America, with the backing of Moscow. As a natural offset to this we may see fascist demonstrations before long." And while the editorial reflects the mood of Middletown in urging that both movements should be uprooted "as noxious weeds," such an editorial as the following, probably concurred in wholeheartedly by every member of Rotary and the other men's civic clubs, leaves little doubt as to which of the two movements is more "noxious," and as to which direction Middletown's official thought will take if events warrant:

LEGION OF PEACE AND PATRIOTISM

There are few finer expressions of patriotism than are to be found in the preamble to the [American] Legion's constitution:

"For God and Country, we associated ourselves together for the following purposes: . . . To COMBAT THE AUTOCRACY OF BOTH THE CLASSES AND THE MASSES . . ."

In these days when the nations of the old world are torn by the strife of communism on the one hand and fascism with its dictatorship on the other, with democracy there fighting for its very existence; in these days when we know that in this country, too, radicalism has added greatly to its strength, and subversive forces are actively at work to undermine and destroy our own government, it is good to know that there is such an organization as the American Legion standing foursquare for the preservation of those democratic principles that are America.

These veterans offered their lives for the maintenance of the basic laws that hundreds of thousands in this country are seeking by subtle ways, and often openly, to overthrow. But so long as the American Legion and kindred organizations declare it to be their purpose "to uphold and defend the Constitution," and "to foster and perpetuate a one-hundred-per-cent Americanism," as they promise, the people of this nation will know that, whatever may happen, they have a staunch force and strong of heart manning the outer breastworks, and that there will be no surrender of our sacred institutions of government without a struggle.

The American Legion and the other patriotic organizations have enlisted for a fight that may come sooner than they now realize.

At this moment we have the spectacle of one of the country's important newspapers [the Seattle *Post-Intelligencer*] being prevented from publication by a mob led by a handful of communists, in spite of the fact that the workers on this paper have no grievance and are anxious to continue in their jobs.

Only the other day communists, with banners proclaiming their allegiance to a party that would overthrow our government by force, were successful in closing by mob action a factory not far from [Middletown], in spite of the fact that 450 of the 500 workers there wished to continue in their jobs and declared their relations with their employers were satisfactory.

So the communist terror in this country is a real thing—not a ghost in a bush, and such organizations as the American Legion have their work cut out for them to destroy Red Russianism in America before it has the chance to destroy the rest of us.

In the American's Creed adopted by the Legion, it is declared to be the duty of a patriot to defend his country "AGAINST ALL ENEMIES," which means the enemies from within, just now, rather more than the enemies from without, for the former are more immediately menacing. . . .

The returning tide of business in 1935-36 has only served to heighten Middletown's impatience with the things beyond its control that hamper its return to buoyant prosperity. It is, under the surface, worried, sore, and frustrated. The frankest statement of civic pessimism and emotional bankruptcy the writers have ever read in the public press of Middletown (other than in the habitually caustic Democratic weekly) appeared in the personal column of the editor of the afternoon paper in January, 1936. Here one actually reads the sort of thing one heard in close privacy in 1935. It represents in part a somewhat whimsical editorial frankness, but also a stark candor rare in public admissions by business-class Middletown and capable of becoming highly explosive if it spreads. It happens to deal more immediately with local issues, but the mood that generates it easily leaps geographical boundaries. After reciting certain hoped-for local civic improvements, the editor said:

YOU JUST ARE NOT GOING TO GET ANY OF THE THINGS NOW THAT YOU HAVE BEEN PROMISED. Don't kid yourself about this. It just isn't in the cards. You'll have the river stinking as noisomely next summer as ever before; you'll be driving in and out of town over the same roads you always have driven; you will see the men working along the river banks and bed without accomplishing much of any importance—and all the rest of it. So don't deceive yourself.

Naturally comes the question of readers of this column, if any, Why? The story is too long and too complicated to tell, but the reasons have their roots in selfishness, inefficiency, ignorance, lack of concentration, politics, and THE LACK OF ONE SINGLE ORGANIZATION WHOLEHEARTEDLY DEVOTED TO THE INTERESTS OF THE PEOPLE WHO LIVE IN THIS COMMUNITY. One capable person at the head of [Middletown's] affairs could straighten out all the tangles in a week. We have a lot of civic organizations in [Middletown] like the Kiwanis Club, the Exchange Club, the Rotary Club, the Dynamo Club, and others, which gather for the purpose of eating once a week and which pride themselves on performing certain small services, whereas if they were to unite and have some real program, they could bring about most of the things that are of vital interest to [Middletown.] But what do they do? Living in a city that is far less civilized than many in China where, at least, they have a program to take the sewage out of canals and streams, our civic clubs applaud themselves because they have sponsored something like a farm program, or they have folks tell them funny stories, and always they applaud any movement for the public welfare, applause being easy and inexpensive, and then go back to their jobs. . . .

I am getting very tired of all this hypocrisy of those who say they are trying to do things for [Middletown]. . . . I'd say they are trying not to do things for [Middletown] but to DO [Middletown]. . . .

[MIDDLETOWN] IS LACKING IN INTELLIGENT LEADERSHIP.

If I have put this thought over I have done a little something, but it won't amount to anything in action. I know that. It's all so terribly hopeless, this situation of the mass mind. . . .

Here speaks the voice of a culture seeing itself, despite its surface optimism, as conceivably in a *cul de sac*. It is not inconceivable that such a society of individuals who feel themselves floundering might go over like a row of cards and vent its pent-up anxiety in a mighty whoop of affirmation, if the right individual came along and gave it the right assurance in symbolic patriotic phrases. The working class, unorganized and devoid of symbols of its own, in 1924 served as a keyboard on which Klan organizers played *fortissimo* on the keys of patriotism and religion. In 1932 an ex-Klan leader started an abortive brown-shirt movement, with meetings replete with the fascist salute and other trimmings. If, when, and as the right strong man emerges— if he can emerge in a country as geographically diffuse as the United States—one wonders if Middletown's response from both business class and working class will not be positive and favorable. For unless there is a sharp rise in working-class solidarity in the interim, this Middletown working class, nurtured on business-class symbols, and despite its rebellious Roosevelt vote in 1936, may be expected to follow patiently and even optimistically any bright flag a middle-class strong man waves.

It seems not impossible that, unless this sense shared by business class and working class alike of being a wanderer in a world too big for one is lulled by returning prosperity, or unless the working class develops more cohesion of its own, the way may be paved for an acceptance of a type of control that will manhandle life deliberately and coercively at certain points to the end of rescuing a semblance of control over these all-important economic institutions. At the moment, Middletown businessmen are bitterly opposed to "bureaucracy" and to "centralized control," but it is at least possible that this opposition in the name of traditional *laissez-faire* freedom would recede in the face of a seizure of power carefully engineered as *by* the business class and *for* the business class and publicized in the name of Americanism and prosperity.

While such contingencies are possible, more likely is continued adherence of sorts to Middletown's customary middle-of-the-road course. If labor organization and other forms of "radicalism" become sufficiently insistent, compromises will be made, the "middle of the road" will be relocated somewhat to the left; the new path will in time become familiar and the "American way." Compromise and expediency rule Middletown's course. At point after point—in its handling of relief, in city government, in its dealings with dissent—it deals with present situations simply as it must, using the old words. Marked shifts in national policy would change this. Strong impact from more explosive centers would change it. But, in the absence of such inescapable pressures, Middletown itself is likely to continue its course of reluctant adaptation and expediency into the future.

In viewing this sober, hopeful, well-meaning city, caught in its institutional conflicts, caught between past and future, and not knowing which way to move, one recalls now and again Tawney's characterization of the ruling class in Europe after the French Revolution: ". . . they walked reluctantly backwards into the future, lest a worse thing should befall them." [9]

[9] R. H. Tawney, *Equality* (London; Allen and Unwin, 1931), p. 127.

"The people learn, unlearn, learn,
  a builder, a wrecker, a builder again, . . ."

" 'Precisely who and what is the people?' "

"Hope is a tattered flag and a dream out of time.

. . . .

Hope is an echo, hope ties itself yonder, yonder."

"In the darkness with a great bundle of grief
    the people march.
In the night, and overhead a shovel of stars for
    keeps, the people march:
                        'Where to? what next?' "

Carl Sandburg, *The People, Yes.* (New York; Harcourt, Brace, 1936.)

APPENDICES

APPENDIX I

The Size of the City: 1925-1935

Middletown had in 1920 a population of 36,524, and on April 1, 1930, when the Federal Census was taken, this total had risen to 46,548. There is strong reason for believing, as will be shown below, that this increase occurred after 1925. There is also reason for suspecting, if Middletown resembled other farm-recruited urban populations, that this sharp gain in the boom years may have been followed by a leveling off or even by a loss in population in the chaotic years following 1929, when the marginal population still retaining ties with the surrounding rural area returned to the farm and other workers, especially those unencumbered by children in school, scattered over the cities of the Middle West in search of jobs.

Intercensal population estimates for local units in a period of rapid expansion or contraction of business represent a "confusion of tongues." Nobody knows with any precision exactly what happens to the population total in any given intercensal year. Middletown itself in 1929 was estimating its population as 62,000 for the following year, 1930. The Federal Bureau of the Census has estimated Middletown's population as of July 1 of each year as follows:

Year	Population	Year	Population
1920	36,715	1927	40,494
1921	37,097	1928	40,877
1922	37,479	1929	41,260
1923	37,862	1930	46,643
1924	38,245	1931	47,025
1925	38,628	1932	47,407
1926	40,111	1933	47,790

But these estimates are confessedly based on a general national formula and do not take account of current local data reflecting peculiar local conditions.

Local figures on total users of city water and gas obviously reflect in part population changes. But Tables 25 and 30 [1] show that such elementary services are not universal in Middletown homes. There was undoubtedly a more rapid rate of installation during the boom years, and some of the

[1] See Appendix III for these tables.

shrinkage in the depression is traceable to inability to pay for the services and their consequent temporary suspension rather than entirely to removals from the city. There were also during the 1920's some extensions of service to outlying streets. Such figures on the use of public utilities also miss the important depression phenomenon of families' doubling up in the same quarters.[2]

In each year Middletown births exceeded deaths by 300 to 400:

Year	Excess of births over deaths	Year	Excess of births over deaths
1925	344	1931	350
1926	298	1932	340
1927	375	1933	275
1928	272	1934	271
1929	413	1935	329
1930	442		

This factor alone accounts for a theoretical net gain of 3,709 persons over these eleven years. But these figures again tell only a fragment of the picture in dramatic years like these characterized by relatively heavy migrations into and out of the city.

The local index probably most to be trusted is the total number of children in Grades 1-6 of Middletown's schools. These are years of compulsory schooling prior to the junior high school. Even these figures, however, are somewhat unsatisfactory as a basis for estimating population in a period of rapid expansion or contraction; for they disguise four variables in the situation, as noted in a footnote to the table at the end of this appendix, one of the most important of which is the probably greater mobility of single persons and childless couples into and out of an industrial city in times of rapid increases and declines in employment. The estimates in the table just referred to have sought to take account of these factors.

[2] Total users of water and gas were as follows:

Year	Total active users of city water	Total gas meters in service
1925	7,184	6,761
1926	7,646	7,038
1927	8,456	7,327
1928	8,992	7,853
1929	9,602	8,228
1930	9,816	9,094
1931	9,622	8,161
1932	9,142	7,659
1933	9,213	6,999
1934	9,405	7,297
1935	9,513	....

Middletown appears to have lost population in the early 1920's and not to have returned to the 1920 figure of about 36,500 until 1923-25. The entire 27 per cent gain in population between 1920 and 1930 appears to have come after 1925. As noted in Chapter II, the city did not feel the depression sharply at first, and the population passed the Census figure of 46,548 in 1930 by 1,500 in the succeeding year, dropped off to 46,500 in 1933, and recovered slightly to 47,000 in 1934-35.

The ten years under study have, accordingly, been years of marked growth succeeded by a virtual stoppage of growth.

The following table presents the year-by-year population estimates employed throughout the study:

ESTIMATED POPULATION OF MIDDLETOWN, BY YEAR: 1920-1935

Year	Total enrollment Grades 1-6 [a]	Index of local industrial employment [b].	Estimated population as of June 1 [c]
1920	4,580	"Good"	36,524 [d]
1921	4,490	"Poor"	35,500
1922	4,314	"Fair"	34,500
1923	4,466	"Good"	36,500
1924	4,492	"Fair"	37,000 [e]
1925	4,379	78.2	36,500
1926	4,372	100.0	37,000
1927	4,794	82.4	40,500
1928	4,834	99.3	41,500
1929	5,249	108.8	45,500
1930	5,336	77.0	46,548 [d]
1931	5,542	82.0	48,000
1932	5,626	60.1	48,000
1933	5,480	50.2	46,500
1934	5,532	58.3	47,000
1935	5,493	84.9	47,000

[a] Enrollment figures for Grades 1-6 in the one Catholic parochial school are not available. A flat 200 has been added to the public school total for each year to cover these Catholic pupils.

Annual enrollment totals are taken in the first week in June at the close of the school year. Enrollment for 1920, e.g., represents, therefore, enrollment for the school year 1919-20.

No separate figures are available for the number of pupils enrolled in the city schools from outside the corporate limits, but according to the Director of Research in the city school system, "Practically all children coming to the city schools from outside the corporation line are in grades above Grade 7."

[b] The numerical index of local employment was compiled by a local bank, commencing with 1925. (See Table 2 in Appendix III.) The words here used to characterize the years 1920-24 have been checked by the official responsible for the subsequent numerical index.

[c] A major problem in calculating these estimates was the adjustment of the changing ratio of this school population to total population: In 1920 the ratio

APPENDICES

between the June 1 school enrollment figures and the January 1 Census total was
1:8.0, whereas that between the June 1, 1930, school enrollment and the April 1,
1930, Census was 1:8.7. The difference between the ratios at the two ends
of the ten-year period is probably related to the following four factors, possibly
in the descending order named: (1) the greater mobility of single workers and
married workers without children, who were probably drawn into Middletown
in the period of growth following 1926 in relatively greater numbers than were
adults with children in school, and who also probably tend to drift out of town
first when unemployment rises; (2) the increasing promotion rate, which has
tended to push the children on through the schools with less retardations; (3)
the "bump" in the ratio created by the drop in births caused by the war, especially births in 1919, though this was partially compensated for by the ensuing
postwar rise in 1921; and (4) the slow secular trend toward less births.

The following ratios were accordingly employed: For 1920, 1:8.0; 1921, 1:7.9;
1922, 1:8.0; 1923-24, 1:8.2; 1925, 1:8.3; 1926-27, 1:8.5; 1928, 1:8.6; 1929-31, 1:8.7;
1932-34, 1:8.5; 1935, 1:8.6. The best that can be said for these is that they represent an effort to weigh the elements that were apparently involved.

d The Census figures are used for these two years, without attempting to estimate the shifts between the Census dates and the dates of the school enumera-
tions.

e In the 1924-25 study (see *Middletown,* p. 510) a population estimate of
38,000 was given for 1924. This estimate was based upon enrollments for Grades
1-8, a less reliable base than Grades 1-6, used in the present study. In 1935 a re-
check of the earlier figures originally received from the school offices for 1920
revealed an error of 332 in the original total compiled by the schools for that
year. The 1920 enrollment should have been 5,643 instead of 5,311. This corrected total, compared with 5,651 for 1924 suggests a more nearly stationary
population since 1920 than was indicated by the earlier estimate of 38,000.

Middletown's Banking Institutions in Boom and Depression

In view of the central importance of Middletown's institutions concerned with savings and banking in the events of the past decade, this special appendix covering outstanding developments in Middletown's banks and building-and-loan institutions over the years 1925-35, inclusive, is here included as a footnote to the general study. The chart on page 520 shows the movement of deposits in all of Middletown's financial institutions by year. This chart should be interpreted in the light of the following chronological sequence of events:

Middletown had in 1925 a population of 36,500; in 1929, 45,500; and in 1935, 47,000. (Population totals for all intervening years are given in the table in Appendix I.)

Middletown had in 1925 five banks, including two national banks, one large trust company (these three constituting the chief banking institutions), two smaller state banks (one a trust company), and four building-and-loan associations. It entered the depression with the same line-up. On March 29, 1930, one of the state banks closed, and the second closed on April 19, 1930. At the close of 1929 these two banks had carried deposits of $362,636 and $1,000,065, respectively, or approximately 13.8 per cent of total money on deposit in Middletown. The first of these banks was not in the clearing house and was allowed to fail. It subsequently paid out 86.5 per cent to its depositors. The other bank was taken over by the clearing-house banks and its depositors were paid in full immediately. On October 1, 1930, two of the four building-and-loan associations merged, leaving three, which number continued through 1935.[1]

At the time of the "bank holiday" in early March, 1933, one of the two major banks, a long-established national bank, failed to reopen and was quietly "merged" with the remaining bank and trust company. From 1933 through 1935 Middletown had one national bank, one trust company, independent but closely affiliated, and the three building-and-loan associations noted above.

[1] The deposits of these failed and merged institutions are all carried in the totals in the accompanying chart for the years in which they operated.

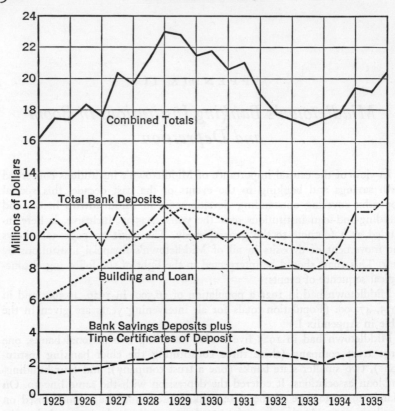

Deposits in Middletown's Banks and Building and Loan Associations, by Year: 1925-1935

Consolidated deposits in all institutions rose by 42.2 per cent between January 1, 1925, and January 1, 1929, as against a rise of 24.7 per cent in the city's population. Building-and-loan deposits accounted for 75.2 per cent of this rise, gaining by 85.5 per cent.

In the six months, January 1–June 30, 1929, total deposits fell off very slightly, though the building and loans continued to register a rise totaling $510,800 in these six months, after which they, too, declined.

Middletown's deposits showed the following shifts in percentage distribution over the pre-depression and depression period:

Type of account	Jan. 1, 1925	July 1, 1929	July 1, 1933	Jan. 1, 1936
Deposits carried in bank checking accounts	53.8	36.1	32.3	48.5
Deposits carried in bank saving deposit accounts and time certificates of deposit	9.1	12.7	13.7	12.9
Deposits carried in building and loans	37.1	51.2	54.0	38.6
Total	100.0	100.0	100.0	100.0

Following is the chronological picture of events influencing the movements of the several curves representing deposits of different types in the chart:

Pre-depression

Rates of interest:
Bank savings and time deposit accounts: 4 per cent.
Building and loan: 6 per cent.
A service charge was introduced on bank checking accounts at the rate of 50 cents a month, January 1, 1928.
The second of the national banks opened a savings department on January 1, 1929.

1930

First state bank failed, March 29.
Second state bank failed, April 19.
Two of the city's four building and loans merged on October 1.

1931

Metered service charge introduced by both banks and the trust company on checking accounts, July 1.[2]
The General Motors plant and another older plant closed in the first half of the year. A local banker comments regarding the closing of the former: "This was a resounding blow to the whole town. The sharp decline in bank deposits in the second half of 1931 was accelerated by the closing of these two plants."

[2] The Middletown Clearing House Association was the first in the state to introduce this metered service. This was still operating in 1935, as follows:

Average balances	Basic monthly charge	Checks free per month
Under $100	$1.00	10
$100-199	.50	10
$200-299	None	10
$300-399	None	15
$400-499	None	20

Extra checks were charged at the rate of 5 cents each.
For accounts averaging $500 and over, interest was calculated on a predicated earning; and charges were deducted at the rate of 1 cent per local check deposited, 3 cents per out-of-town check deposited, 5 cents for check or payroll order drawn, 5 cents for each deposit in excess of 50 per month, and for cost of check imprinting and exchange charges for drafts.

The bank interest rate on savings and time deposits dropped from 4 per cent to 3 per cent on November 1.

1932

The building-and-loan interest rate dropped from 6 to 5 per cent on July 1.

1933

On February 27, prior to the "bank holiday," when widespread hoarding threatened a currency shortage, a guarantee was publicly made by the X family that they knew the depositors' interests to be safe and with that knowledge they guaranteed: "To see to it that sufficient cash means are provided to take care of [Middletown's] banking requirements in this emergency." [3] This so tempered the uneasiness of the public that no currency was ever called for by the banks outside of their own resources.

One national bank failed to reopen after the "bank holiday" in March; its deposits were taken over by the remaining national bank and the trust company without loss to depositors.

In the first half of 1933 a State tax of one-fourth of 1 per cent on deposits superseded the general property tax.

The building-and-loan interest rate was lowered to 4 per cent on July 1.

1934

Federal Deposit Insurance became effective on amounts up to $2,500 on January 1, and was raised to cover amounts up to $5,000 on July 1.

A local branch of the Federal Savings and Loan Association was chartered on February 16. This was operated in connection with one of the old building and loans, which transferred all its assets to it on April 1, 1935.

The bank interest rate on savings and time deposits was lowered on July 1 to 2.5 per cent on deposits up to $5,000 and to 1.5 per cent over that amount.

1935

The bank interest rate on savings and time deposits was lowered on January 1 to 2.5 per cent on accounts up to $2,500 and 1 per cent beyond that amount. It was lowered further in March to 2 per cent on accounts up to $1,000, .5 per cent on accounts of $1,000 to $5,000, and no interest on amounts over $5,000.

The return of General Motors and a sharp revival of public confidence occurred in the late spring.

The following further comment in writing by the president of the trust company, as of December 31, 1935, amplifies this picture:

Level of total deposits shown in accompanying chart: The line of total bank deposits, in the chart, which includes the savings and time money, requires some comment. One's first impression is that, in common with both other lines, the bottom shows a shrinkage of about 34 per cent from the $12 million peak. I would suggest that it might be more soundly considered that up to the middle of 1931 the peaks above $10 million represented excessive boom conditions. If this is true, it would then indicate that our present high level will decrease with the return of the more active employment of idle funds on deposit.

[3] See Ch. III.

Relation of interest rate to total of savings deposits in building and loan companies and banks and to time certificates of deposits in banks: The rate paid has been a secondary consideration in the minds of the depositors for the past three years. The main point involved is the adjustment of their understanding of the proper functions of a building and loan—that is, that it cannot pay money on demand and keep it working fully enough to pay a high rate of dividend.

The building and loans had been able to pay 6 per cent dividends because of the rapid and steady accession of fresh money left with them. The minute that condition stopped, they had a hard time to satisfy their customers, who had been trained to expect cash on demand.

Effect of Federal deposit insurance: You will note the sharp rise in total bank deposits following this "insurance." You may be tempted to assume that public confidence was a large element in restoring our deposits. I think it fair to say that it is a factor with some uncertain portion of the public, whose deposits would necessarily be in the lower brackets. Analysis in February, 1934, showed that the 67.5 per cent of all active accounts [in our trust company] which are in the brackets up to $300 accounted for only 8.5 per cent of our total deposits. Analysis last month [November, 1935] showed the same brackets as 57.2 per cent of our total accounts and 2.8 per cent of our total deposits in dollars.

Change in number of checking accounts: It is impossible to measure changes in the number of checking accounts because of the different policies in dealing with dormant accounts, hundreds of which have been eliminated by the application of an annual maintenance charge in the past five years. In the period covered by the chart, for example, our trust company's checking accounts ranged from 1,674 at the beginning of 1925, to 1523 at the end of 1930, and 988 at the end of 1931; at the end of 1932 we showed 434 active and 256 dormant accounts; in 1933, 548 active and 167 dormant; in 1934, 634 active and 222 dormant; and in 1935, 800 active and 114 dormant. The average daily balance for the two past half-years has increased from $812,000 in 1934 to $1,051,000 in the first half of 1935, and $1,294,000 in the second half of 1935.

Change in number of savings accounts: The change in savings accounts in our trust company ranges from 2,330 at the beginning of 1925 to 3,514 at the beginning of 1930 and 3,500 at the beginning of 1931. The beginning of 1932 showed 3,373, of which 2,584 were active. During the period enumerated, our average daily balance in savings ranged from $550,000 in 1925 to just under $600,000 in 1929. A peak of $633,000 was reached at one point in 1929, and, thereafter, the curve was steadily down to $428,000 in 1932. The number of active accounts, beginning with 1932, are as follows: 1932, 2,584; 1933, 2,230; 1934, 3,778; 1935, 3,416. The sudden increase of 1,548 in 1934 is, of course, due to the taking over of the time deposits of the national bank merged with our trust company and the remaining national bank at the time of the bank holiday in 1933. The amount of deposits, too, increased to a daily average of better than $1,050,000, and our trust company is ending 1935 with a daily average of $1,161,139.

I assume that the above indication of decline in numbers would be a fair average picture for all institutions in the city, as our chart of total deposits in our trust company over this period was fairly steady, and my personal investigation showed the gradual exhaustion of many individual accounts, with little decrease in total numbers.

General comment: Throughout the picture runs the "booming" and decline of the individual institutions. The later years reflect the general lack of public confidence, and, distinct from that, the change in the understanding by the public of the status of their shares in the building and loans—that is, they found out they were not deposits subject to withdrawal when wanted.

The closing of the two small state banks in 1930 and the conversion of the deposits in the national bank that failed to reopen after the "bank holiday" in 1933 do not seem to have affected the general picture. The closing of the first two rather restored public confidence temporarily. The liquidation of the national bank came at a time when, seemingly, nothing more could be lost.

The building-and-loan situation is reflected in the following index numbers for business at the close of each year from 1925 through 1935 for the largest institution of this type in Middletown:

Year ending December 31	Number of savings accounts (1926 = 6,156)	Number of loan accounts (1926 = 2,403)
1925	90.3	88.6
1926	100.0	100.0
1927	100.7	105.5
1928	110.4	112.6
1929	120.4	127.9
1930	116.4	128.8
1931	123.4	125.5
1932	115.4	122.4
1933	107.2	117.4
1934	89.8	95.6
1935	88.5	96.6

The sharp shifts in the dollar volume of loans on property by this institution are shown in Table 22 in Appendix III. According to the head of this building-and-loan association, October, 1932 (when local taxes were due), was the peak of withdrawals. At that time the association began restricting withdrawals to from twenty-five to fifty dollars per week per account, depending on the size of the account. By the time of the "bank holiday" in March, 1933, withdrawals were restricted to five dollars per account. From then on, loans were heavily restricted; but in January, 1935, loans were resumed, letters were sent to all those refused loans earlier, "and about one-third of these came in and borrowed."

One other element, not included in the chart accompanying this Appendix, belongs in the picture as a minor but increasingly important element in Middletown's savings from 1925 on. This is postal-savings deposits, which totaled as follows as of the close of each indicated year:

Year	Total at close of year	Year	Total at close of year
1925	$ 6,844	1931	$104,768
1926	7,428	1932	186,340
1927	7,171	1933	321,024
1928	9,011	1934	409,863
1929	10,700	1935	438,780
1930	27,798		

APPENDIX III

Tables

LIST OF TABLES

13. PER CENT OF TOTAL DIVORCES IN MIDDLETOWN'S COUNTY GRANTED TO HUSBANDS, BY YEAR: 1925-1935.

14. MEDIAN SIZE OF PRIVATE FAMILIES IN MIDDLETOWN, IN THE URBAN EAST NORTH CENTRAL STATES, AND IN THE URBAN UNITED STATES, BY NATIVE WHITE, FOREIGN-BORN WHITE, AND NEGRO: 1930.

15. NUMBER OF RELATED PERSONS IN MIDDLETOWN PRIVATE FAMILIES AND IN THE NATIVE WHITE FAMILIES OF THE URBAN UNITED STATES: 1930.

16. NUMBER OF CHILDREN UNDER 21 YEARS IN MIDDLETOWN PRIVATE FAMILIES: 1930.

17. BIRTHS IN MIDDLETOWN, WITH INDEX OF LOCAL INDUSTRIAL EMPLOY-MENT, BY YEAR: 1925-1935.

18. NUMBER AND COST OF NEW DWELLINGS IN MIDDLETOWN, AND INDEX NUMBERS OF COST OF NEW DWELLINGS IN MIDDLETOWN AND IN 257 CITIES OF THE UNITED STATES, BY YEAR: 1926-1935.

19. AGE OF MIDDLETOWN'S RESIDENTIAL STRUCTURES, FOR SINGLE FAMILY DETACHED AND FOR ALL OTHER TYPES: 1935.

20. NUMBER OF DWELLING UNITS IN MIDDLETOWN, BY TYPE OF STRUCTURE: 1935.

21. OCCUPIED RESIDENTIAL UNITS IN MIDDLETOWN, BY LENGTH OF OCCU-PANCY BY PRESENT OCCUPANT, FOR OWNED AND RENTED: 1935.

22. INDEX NUMBERS OF NUMBER AND DOLLAR VOLUME OF LOANS ON REAL ESTATE BY A LEADING MIDDLETOWN BUILDING-AND-LOAN ASSOCIATION, BY YEAR: 1924-1934.

23. RENTED DWELLING UNITS IN MIDDLETOWN, BY AMOUNT OF RENTAL, IN APRIL, 1930, AND IN JANUARY-MARCH, 1935.

24. PERSONS PER ROOM IN MIDDLETOWN, BY DWELLING UNITS OCCUPIED BY OWNERS AND BY RENTERS: 1935.

25. DWELLING UNITS IN MIDDLETOWN BY TYPE OF WATER SUPPLY IN HOUSE, FOR OWNED BY VALUE, FOR RENTED BY RENTAL, AND FOR TOTAL: 1935.

26. DWELLING UNITS IN MIDDLETOWN BY NUMBER OF BATHING UNITS AND BY NUMBER OF FAMILIES USING EACH, FOR OWNED BY VALUE, FOR RENTED BY RENTAL, AND FOR TOTAL: 1935.

27. DWELLING UNITS IN MIDDLETOWN BY TYPE OF REFRIGERATION, FOR OWNED BY VALUE, FOR RENTED BY RENTAL, AND FOR TOTAL: 1935.

28. DWELLING UNITS IN MIDDLETOWN BY NUMBER AND TYPE OF TOILETS AND NUMBER OF FAMILIES USING EACH, FOR OWNED BY VALUE, FOR RENTED BY RENTAL, AND FOR TOTAL: 1935.

29. DWELLING UNITS IN MIDDLETOWN BY TYPE OF ARTIFICIAL LIGHTING, FOR OWNED BY VALUE, FOR RENTED BY RENTAL, AND FOR TOTAL: 1935.

30. DWELLING UNITS IN MIDDLETOWN BY TYPE OF COOKING FACILITIES, FOR OWNED BY VALUE, FOR RENTED BY RENTAL, AND FOR TOTAL: 1935.

31. DWELLING UNITS IN MIDDLETOWN BY TYPE OF HEATING, FOR OWNED BY VALUE, FOR RENTED BY RENTAL, AND FOR TOTAL: 1935.

32. INDEX NUMBERS OF TOTAL DOLLAR VOLUME OF BUSINESS BY A LEADING MIDDLETOWN COMMERCIAL LAUNDRY, BY YEAR: 1923-1934.

33. NUMBER OF TELEPHONE INSTRUMENTS IN USE IN MIDDLETOWN AND SIX-MILE SURROUNDING RADIUS, BY YEAR: 1925-1936.

34. INDEX NUMBERS OF SCHOOL ENROLLMENT IN MIDDLETOWN, BY ELEMENTARY AND BY HIGH SCHOOL, BY YEAR: 1928-1935.

35. NUMBER OF MIDDLETOWN HIGH-SCHOOL GRADUATES AND NUMBER AND PER CENT SEEKING ENTRY TO COLLEGE, BY YEAR: 1929-1934.

36. PROPORTION OF GRADUATES OF MIDDLETOWN HIGH SCHOOL WHO WERE BOYS: 1910-1936.

37. DISTRIBUTION OF ALL MIDDLETOWN PUBLIC-SCHOOL TEACHERS BY YEARS OF PROFESSIONAL TRAINING, FOR 1921-1922, 1925-1926, AND 1931-1932.

38. ENROLLMENT, STAFF, AND OPERATING EXPENDITURES BY TOTAL AND PER PUPIL IN MIDDLETOWN SCHOOLS, BY YEAR: 1925-1936.

39. PUBLIC-LIBRARY CIRCULATION AND CARDHOLDERS IN MIDDLETOWN, BY YEAR: 1925-1935.

40. ADULT CIRCULATION OF MIDDLETOWN PUBLIC LIBRARY, BY FICTION AND NONFICTION, BY YEAR: 1928-1935.

41. ADULT CIRCULATION OF MIDDLETOWN CENTRAL PUBLIC LIBRARY BY CLASS OF BOOK, FOR MONTH OF MARCH, BY YEAR: 1925-1935.

42. CIRCULATION, EXPENDITURES BY KIND, AND SIZE OF STAFF OF MIDDLETOWN PUBLIC LIBRARY, BY YEAR: 1926-1935.

43. PASSENGER AUTOMOBILE REGISTRATIONS IN MIDDLETOWN'S COUNTY AND STATE, AND NEW CAR PURCHASES IN THE COUNTY, BY YEAR: 1925-1935.

44. ARRESTS IN MIDDLETOWN PER 1,000 OF POPULATION, BY YEAR: 1926-1935.

45. ARRESTS FOR SELECTED TYPES OF OFFENSES IN MIDDLETOWN, BY YEAR: 1931-1934.

46. TOTAL VOTE CAST IN MIDDLETOWN'S COUNTY IN PRESIDENTIAL ELECTIONS OF 1924, 1928, 1932, AND 1936, BY PARTY.

TABLE I: MIDDLETOWN'S MANUFACTURING ACTIVITY, 1925-1933, AND RETAIL
ACTIVITY, 1929 AND 1933

(From the United States Census of Manufactures and Census of
Distribution)

	1925	1927	1929	1931	1933
Estimated population	36,500	40,500	45,500	48,000	46,500
Manufacturing					
Number of establishments *a*	99	105	105	97	80
Average number of wage earners	6,853	7,738	10,269	7,364	5,461
Wages (in thousands) *b*...	$9,153	$10,228	$13,456	$7,940	$4,513
Value of products (in thousands) *b*	$41,254	$52,381	$65,752	$46,270	$28,621
Retail c					
Number of stores	......	......	610	......	648
Net sales (in thousands) *b*.	......	......	$26,999	......	$11,585
Average number full-time employees	......	......	2,298	......	1,343
Average number part-time employees	......	......	462	......	460
Total payroll, including part-time (in thousands) *b*	......	......	$3,087	......	$1,370
Part-time payroll (in thousands)	......	......	$101	......	$127

a These industries include those doing $5,000 or more of business in the indicated year. A press summary in January, 1930, listed the following numbers of new industries coming to town in each year since 1925: "In 1926, four units; 1927, eight units; 1928, nine units; 1929, nine units." This gross increment of thirty units is five times the small Census net increase. Most of the additions were, therefore, either doing less than $5,000 of business by 1929, had failed, or had replaced other small units that failed.

The 1935 Census of Manufactures is not available for Middletown as this goes to press. Totals for the state are, however, available. The latter show the following trends for Middletown's state, when the figures are reduced to index numbers, with 1929 as the base:

	1929	1933	1935
Number of establishments	100.0	66.5	77.6
Av. no. of wage earners	100.0	63.2	80.3
Wages	100.0	41.1	63.0
Value of products	100.0	41.0	65.3

b All comparative dollar figures are undeflated and therefore influenced by the changing price level. The following index numbers of wholesale prices, constructed by the National Bureau of Economic Research, suggest the degree of correction necessary following 1929, when large changes occurred in the price level. The separate index numbers for total durable goods are included because Middletown's industrial output is so heavily concentrated in consumers' and producers' durable goods. The Bureau's cost of living index (constructed from the U. S. Bureau of Labor Statistics' semi-annual index of the cost of living of industrial workers) is also presented for its bearing on payroll figures in the above table:

	Index numbers of—			
Year	Consumers' goods total	Producers' goods total	Durable goods total	Cost of living
1929	100.0	100.0	100.0	100.0
1930	93.3	88.5	93.0	97.9
1931	80.7	73.2	84.6	89.5
1932	70.8	64.9	78.8	80.8
1933	71.2	68.4	81.0	76.2
1934	79.6	78.6	87.6	78.8
1935	84.4	83.0	87.0	81.1

c The Retail Census was not taken prior to 1929.

TABLE 2: INDEX NUMBERS OF EMPLOYMENT IN A REPRESENTATIVE GROUP
OF MIDDLETOWN INDUSTRIES AND OF TOTAL INDUSTRIAL EMPLOYMENT
IN THE UNITED STATES, BY YEAR: 1925-1935

Year	*Index numbers of average number on payroll*	
	Middletown [a] *(1926 av. no. of 4,386 = 100)*	*United States* [b] *(1926 = 100)*
1925	78.2	98.2
1926	100.0	100.0
1927	82.4	97.7
1928	99.3	97.7
1929	108.8	103.6
1930	77.0	90.4
1931	82.0	76.5
1932	60.1	63.3
1933	50.2	68.2
1934	58.3	77.9
1935	84.9 [c]	81.2

[a] This index was constructed by the leading local bank for its use, along with payroll wage totals, building-construction permits, and similar business data, in gauging local business conditions. It includes a varying total of six to eight plants "some big, some of moderate size, and diversified as to kind of business," representing, according to the officer in charge of compiling it, approximately 50 per cent of Middletown's industrial payrolls up to 1929 and about 40 per cent thereafter.

Inasmuch as only plants in actual operation are included by the bank in this sample, the extent of the city's actual decline in industrial employment experienced in periods of economic recession tends to be understated in the index. Furthermore, the degree to which the data are representative of operating plants has varied. In constructing the index, four or five of the largest plants in the city are included throughout. However, as a large new plant such as the Delco-Remy battery unit of General Motors came to Middletown it was added in 1928 to the base used on the index; and when a plant like the General Motors transmissions unit was withdrawn from Middletown it was dropped from the index. Thus not only do the data refer only to operating units but even their representativeness of such plants varies somewhat. In addition, the nature of the more prominent plants included in the index, *e.g.,* the heavy representation of Middletown's automotive groups, is such that the index may possibly tend to rise over-rapidly in times of business prosperity and to lag unduly when business falters, as compared with the remainder of Middletown's industrial enterprises.

Interpretations of the above table ought, therefore, to be tempered by the realization that employment gains and peaks are adequately pictured, while reductions tend to be underestimated, perhaps increasingly with the extent of the decline, as such slowing up is accompanied by plant failures and removals.

b Based on the index of the U. S. Bureau of Labor Statistics. The base has here been shifted to 1926 by recalculating the index, using the Bureau's index of 101.2 for 1926 (based on the three-year average of 1923-25) as 100.

c The sharpness of the recovery in the latter part of 1935 is reflected by the fact that as late as June 1, 1935, when the research staff was in Middletown, the index had risen only to 62.0.

TABLE 3: NUMBER OF RETAIL STORES IN MIDDLETOWN AND NET SALES IN
DOLLARS (UNDEFLATED), BY KIND OF STORE, 1929 AND 1933 [a]

(From the United States Census of Distribution) [b]

Type of store	1929		1933		Per cent decline in dollar volume
	Number of stores	Net sales (in 000's)	Number of stores	Net sales (in 000's)	
Estimated population	45,500		46,500		
Food	209	$6,548	210	$3,311	49.4
Candy and confectionery......	*14*	*217*	*11*	*66*	69.6
Eating places	65	1,061	84	393	63.0
Drug	20	874	20	470	46.2
Furniture, household, radio	23	1,734	19	536	69.1
Furniture	*7*	*952*	*6*	*342*	64.1
Radio and music	*11*	*657*	*2*	*c*	
Apparel, including shoes	55	2,680	49	1,015	62.1
Men's and boys' clothing, furnishings	*15*	*1,053*	*11*	*349*	66.9
Women's ready to wear specialty (apparel and accessories)	*9*	*511*	*10*	*269*	47.3
Shoes	*16*	*609*	*13*	*300*	50.7
General merchandise	16	3,186	10	1,751	45.0
Department stores	*5*	*2,150*	*4*	*1,191*	44.6
Variety (5¢, 10¢ to $1.00).......	6	795	4	489	38.5
Jewelry	10	348	4	52	85.1
Automotive (excluding filling stations)	49	4,740	66	1,186	75.0
Motor vehicle	*21*	*4,036*	*15*	*877*	78.3
Garage and repair	*14*	*262*	*40*	*120*	54.2
Accessories, tires, batteries.....	*14*	*442*	*11*	*189*	57.2
Filling stations	41	1,128	70	1,087	3.6
Lumber, building, hardware.....	46	2,512	37	557	77.8
Lumber and building materials	*14*	*1,453*	*11*	*263*	81.9
All other [d]	70	1,393	83	1,279	8.2
Total	610	26,999	648	11,585	57.1

[a] The classification of stores by types employed in this table is the one used by the Census of Distribution. Care should be taken in reading this table to allow for the variety of goods sold in a given type of store. Thus, drugstores sell many things other than drugs, including food and a variety of small articles; the general merchandise stores overlap apparel and other fields; filling stations sell accessories, as do garages, and the latter sell gas.

The subclassifications employed—e.g., "Candy and confectionery" under the general type "Food"—are selected and not exhaustive. Many subclassifications had to be omitted because comparable totals for them were not available for both 1929 and 1933. It is particularly unfortunate that comparable figures on more types of clothing stores were not available.

Changes in the price level given in note *b* of Table 1 should be borne in mind in reading this table. A separate index for foods is not there included. The Bureau of Labor Statistics index of the average retail cost of forty-two foods in the United States, using 1913 as 100.0, moved as follows: 1925, 157.4; 1927, 155.4; 1929, 156.7; 1931, 121.3; 1933, 99.7.

b Some of the figures presented in this table are not included in the published Census reports but were made available for this study by the Census.

c Dollar sales in these two stores are withheld by the Census to avoid the risk of disclosing confidential data on individual establishments.

d This miscellaneous group includes the Census types "Farmers' Supplies and Country General" and "Other Stores."

TABLE 4: BANK DEPOSITS AND DEBITS IN MIDDLETOWN, NUMBER OF BUILD-
ING PERMITS, AND ESTIMATED VALUE OF BUILDINGS CONSTRUCTED,
BY YEAR: 1925-1935

Year	Bank deposits as of January 1 [a] (in 000's)	Bank debits as of January 1 [a] (in 000's)	Number of building permits	Estimated value of construction (in 000's)
1925	$16,200	$147,369	770	$1,478 [c]
1926	17,500	163,677	1,810	1,883
1927	17,700	166,579	2,074	2,444
1928	19,700	188,693	2,265	2,306
1929	23,000	200,750	2,237	1,778
1930	21,500	161,046	1,223	445
1931	20,600	133,480	937	350
1932	19,100	86,637	526	128
1933	17,400	74,568	451	111
1934	17,400	93,502	537 [b]	708
1935	19,500	128,424	1,251	650

[a] Includes building and loans as well as banks. See Appendix II for a more detailed treatment of these deposit figures in relation to savings.

[b] What these depression building permits represent in terms of actual types of work may be seen from the following breakdown by kind for 1934:

New dwellings	8	New private garages	58
New factory units	3	Repairs and alterations	449
New public buildings	3	Miscellaneous	8
New gas and service stations	8		
		Total	537

The virtual cessation of new residential construction is particularly noteworthy. For permits for new residential construction by year, 1926-35, see Table 18.

[c] 1925 was a moderately poor business year locally. The dollar total for this year was high because it includes expensive new buildings for a leading bank, the Y.W.C.A., and a new City Hall.

TABLE 5: CHANGES IN NUMBER OF MIDDLETOWN'S TOTAL GAINFULLY
EMPLOYED,[a] BY MAJOR FIELDS OF WORK: 1920-1930

(From the United States Census)

Occupation	Number of gainful workers		Per cent change	Per cent distribution of 2,986 gainfully employed added 1920-30
	1920	1930		
Total	16,150	19,136	+18.5	100.0
Agriculture	120	165	+37.5	1.5
Extraction of minerals...	34	21	−38.2	..
Manufacturing and mechanical industries ...	9,086	9,811	+8.0	24.4
Transportation and communication	1,007	1,456	+44.6	14.5
Trade	2,181	2,776	+27.1	19.9
Public service	193	278	+44.0	2.9
Professional service	892	1,388	+55.6	16.6
Domestic and personal service	1,358	1,714	+26.1	11.9
Clerical	1,279	1,526	+19.3	8.3

[a] The term "gainful workers" in Census usage includes all persons who usually follow a gainful occupation, although they may not have been employed when the census was taken.

TABLE 6: CHANGES IN THE NUMBER OF MIDDLETOWN'S POPULATION AND IN THE PROPORTION GAINFULLY EMPLOYED,[a]
BY SEX AND BY BROAD AGE GROUPS: 1920-1930

(From the United States Census)

Sex and age groups	1920			1930			Per cent change: 1920-1930		
	(1) Number in group	(2) Number in group gainfully employed	(3) Per cent of group gainfully employed	(4) Number in group	(5) Number in group gainfully employed	(6) Per cent of group gainfully employed	(7) Number in group	(8) Number in group gainfully employed	(9) Per cent of group gainfully employed (col. 3 less col. 6, over col. 3)
MALES 10 and over	15,361	12,737	82.9	19,301	15,188	78.6	+25.6	+19.2	−5.2
10 and under 20	3,180	1,219	38.3	3,705	707	19.1	+16.4	−42.0	−50.1
20 and over	12,181	11,518	94.7	15,596	14,481	92.8	+28.1	+25.6	−2.0
FEMALES 10 and over	14,827	3,413	23.0	18,828	3,948	21.0	+26.9	+15.7	−8.7
10 and under 20	3,221	767	23.8	3,628	409	11.3	+12.6	−46.7	−52.5
20 and over	11,606	2,646	22.8	15,200	3,539	23.3	+31.0	+33.8	+2.1
TOTAL 10 and over	30,188	16,150	53.5	38,129	19,136	50.2	+26.2	+18.5	−6.1
10 and under 20	6,470	1,986	30.5	7,333	1,116	15.2	+13.2	−43.8	−50.2
20 and over	23,718	14,164	59.7	30,796	18,020	58.5	+29.9	+27.1	−2.0

[a] The term "gainful workers" in Census usage includes all persons who usually follow a gainful occupation, although they may not have been employed when the census was taken.

TABLE 7: DISTRIBUTION OF MIDDLETOWN'S GAINFULLY EMPLOYED,[a] BY SEX
FOR NARROW AGE GROUPS IN 1920 AND IN 1930

(From the United States Census)

Age group	Males gainfully employed				Females gainfully employed			
	1920		1930		1920		1930	
	Number	Per cent	Number	Per cent	Number	Per cent	Number	Per cent
10-13	35	.27	1	.01	3	.09	1	.03
14-15	147	1.16	7	.05	69	2.02	2	.05
16-17	465	3.65	179	1.18	335	9.82	79	2.00
18-19	572	4.49	520	3.42	360	10.55	327	8.28
20-24	1,535	12.04	2,100	13.83	679	19.89	882	22.34
25-44	5,830	45.77	7,318	48.18	1,320	38.69	1,800	45.59
45-64	3,507	27.54	4,323	28.46	567	16.62	780	19.76
65 and over	600	4.72	740	4.87	71	2.06	76	1.92
Unknown	46	.36	0	0	9	.26	1	.03
Total	12,737	100.00	15,188	100.00	3,413	100.00	3,948	100.00

[a] The term "gainful workers" in Census usage includes all persons who usually follow a gainful occupation, although they may not have been employed when the census was taken.

TABLE 8: THE SHARE OF MIDDLETOWN CHILDREN OF AGES 14-19 IN SCHOOL, GAINFULLY EMPLOYED, AND IDLE: 1930

Age	(1) Estimated population	(2) Estimated number of children in school [a]	(3) Total gainfully employed [b]	(4) Total children not in school or employed (col. 1 less 2 and 3)	(5) Per cent of total children not in school or employed
14	720	680	} 9	86	5.9
15	735	680			
16	750	590	} 258	277	18.3
17	765	390			
18	780	320	} 847	333	21.1
19	795	75			

[a] These are children enrolled in the spring of 1930 in Grades 8-12 inclusive, plus estimated totals, based on Table 35, of the number attending college and taking nurses' training, etc. Age and grade do not correspond in all cases, but it is assumed that the errors in either direction are roughly compensating. The pressure in the schools, noted in Ch. VI, to decrease school costs per pupil has resulted in a distinct lessening in retardation since 1925.

[b] From Table 7. These totals may be slightly lower than in a "normal" year, owing to the fact that the 1930 Census was taken on April 1, after 6 months of the depression. That portion of Middletown's children who completed their schooling in June, 1929, may have carried forward to April, 1930, a group larger than usual of children *never* gainfully employed. This would only have affected children who waited to get jobs until after the summer of 1929 was over. In many cases, however, those not regularly employed were able to get jobs for brief periods prior to April 1, 1930, and would in all likelihood have been enumerated as "usually" gainfully employed at those temporarily held jobs.

TABLE 9: CHANGES IN NUMBER OF MIDDLETOWN'S GAINFULLY EMPLOYED,[a]
BY SEX AND BY MAJOR FIELDS OF WORK: 1920-1930

(From the United States Census)

| Occupation | Number gainfully employed | | | | Per cent change 1920-30 | |
| | 1920 | | 1930 | | | |
	Male	Female	Male	Female	Male	Female
Total	12,737	3,413	15,188	3,948	+19.2	+15.7
Agriculture	119	1	164	2	+37.8	......
Extraction of minerals...	34	0	21	0	−38.2	......
Manufacturing and mechanical industries.....	8,117	969	8,931	880	+10.0	−9.3
Transportation and communication	896	111	1,333	123	+48.8	+10.8
Trade	1,712	469	2,267	509	+32.4	+8.5
Public service...........	191	2	270	8	+41.4	......
Professional service......	524	368	797	591	+52.1	+60.6
Domestic and personal service	482	876	690	1,024	+43.2	+16.9
Clerical occupations......	662	617	715	811	+8.0	+31.4

[a] The term "gainful workers" in Census usage includes all persons who usually follow a gainful occupation, although they may not have been employed when the census was taken.

TABLE 10: EXPENDITURES FOR DIRECT RELIEF IN MIDDLETOWN'S TOWNSHIP,[a]
FROM COMMUNITY FUND, AND FROM TAX FUNDS, BY YEAR: 1928-1935 [b]

Year	Direct relief expenditures from—		Total
	Community Fund [c]	Public tax funds, including bond issues [d]	
1928	$17,872	$ 21,214	$ 39,086
1929	21,754	25,436	47,190
1930	50,145	45,076 [e]	95,221
1931	48,504	158,604	207,108
1932	37,129	293,091	330,220
1933	35,941	304,483	340,424
1934	27,847	156,858	184,705
1935	25,186	148,186	173,372

[a] The 1930 Census recorded 95.1 per cent of the population of Middletown's township as within the city of Middletown.

[b] It is a striking commentary on Middletown's municipal housekeeping that nobody in the city, including public officials, bankers, Chamber of Commerce, and persons professionally in charge of the administration of private charity under the Community Fund, has an accurate record of total local relief expenditures year by year in the depression. The totals here presented are believed to be substantially correct, on the basis of repeated checking of all available sources. The following comment on the above table, by a man long in close touch with local welfare work and the best local source of data on such matters, should, however, be noted: "To add to the confusion [in attempting to reach accurate local totals], the director of the Social Service Bureau tells me that she has no record whatever of State and Federal funds used to pay bills sent to [the State capital] with the Social Service Bureau's O.K. and paid by outside check. This is probably covered in the second paragraph of your footnote d to your table." (See below.)

[c] The figures for the years 1928-32 are from the *Report of the Committee Appointed at a Joint Meeting of the Directors of the Community Fund and the Relief Agencies to Study the Problem of Relief of Distress in Center Township,* issued February 7, 1933. These totals, according to the *Report,* cover direct material relief, exclusive of administrative costs, by the five of the twelve Community Fund agencies giving such relief. These agencies are the Social Service Bureau, Visiting Nurse Association, Red Cross, Jewish Welfare, and Salvation Army. The great bulk of the increase between 1928 and 1930 falls in the allotment to the Social Service Bureau, whose total allotment for relief and administration from the Community Fund rose from $7,362 in 1928 to $34,900 in 1930. Of these total relief expenditures, the following amounts were for relief nursing under the Visiting Nurse Association: 1928, $12,748; 1929, $14,531; 1930, $16,586; 1931, $18,588; 1932, $16,088.

The figures for the years 1933-35 include the following estimates for relief nursing expenditures: 1933, $16,000; 1934, $15,000; 1935, $14,000.

[d] In addition to expenditures from current taxes, these totals include expendi-

tures from special poor relief bond issues during 1932-33 by the township totaling $216,750, and direct relief expenditures by the Federal government of $115,512 in 1933, $38,740 in 1934, and $21,424 in 1935.

These totals do not include Federal outlays under C.W.A., F.E.R.A., and W.P.A. C.W.A. started in Middletown on November 15, 1933, with an outlay of $6,700 the first week. By mid-January, 1934, its expenditures were at the rate of $33,500 a week. This rate declined gradually to May 1, 1934, when F.E.R.A. began. The weekly payroll under the latter ran at times as high as $16-17,000, and even in June, 1935, was $9-11,000.

e This total for 1930 covers only eleven months. According to the source of these figures, this was "due to culpable neglect on the part of one of the deputies." According to the *Report* of the citizens' committee cited in the first paragraph of n. *c* above, the total for the entire year was $72,804. Since all other figures given in the *Report* for the years 1928-32 check substantially with those secured for the present study from the best available sources, it seems likely that the figure of $45,076 in the table above should be raised substantially for the full year.

TABLE II: SUICIDES IN MIDDLETOWN'S COUNTY AND STATE, BY YEAR:
1924-1935

Year	Number of suicides in county	Number of suicides in state	Estimated population of county a	Number of suicides in county per 1,000 of population
1924	13	406	57,000	.23
1925	18	443	56,200	.32
1926	15	434	56,900	.26
1927	12	487	60,400	.20
1928	24	539	61,900	.39
1929	12	524	65,900	.18
1930	34	649	67,300	.51
1931	6	668	68,600	.09
1932	13	646	68,600	.19
1933	21	689	67,400	.31
1934	18	605	68,100	.26
1935	16	524	68,100	.23

a *These estimated rates are rough and must be used tentatively.* Middletown's estimated population is given in Appendix I, and these estimates themselves, while based upon the best available data, are necessarily rough and subject to inaccuracy. No figures are available for the population of Middletown's county in intercensal years. In 1920 the city's population was 65 per cent of that of the entire county, and in April, 1930, 69 per cent. The county population estimates here have been secured by arbitrarily assuming that the 65:100 ratio still held for 1925-26, when the city's population still stood at the 1920 level; that it was 67:100 in 1927-28, when the population of Middletown increased by 4,000; and 69:100 in the years 1929-34.

TABLE 12: MARRIAGES AND DIVORCES IN MIDDLETOWN'S COUNTY, BY DECADE,
1890-1920, AND BY YEAR, 1925-1935

Year	Marriages in Middletown's county		Divorces in Middletown's county		Per cent divorces constituted of marriages [e]	Index of industrial employment in Middletown [f]
	Number	Number per 1,000 of total population [b]	Number [c]	Number per 1,000 of total population [d]		
1890	283	9.4	30	1.0	10.6	....
1900	631	12.7	117	2.4	18.5	....
1910	557	10.8	147	2.9	26.4	....
1920	798 [a]	14.1	261	4.7	32.7 [a]	....
1925	651	11.6	280	5.0	43.0	78.2
1926	690	12.1	245	4.3	35.5	100.0
1927	616	10.2	298	4.9	48.4	82.4
1928	728	11.8	336	5.4	46.2	99.3
1929	753	11.4	281	4.3	37.4	108.8
1930	546	8.1	255	3.8	46.7	77.0
1931	549	8.0	276	4.0	50.3	82.0
1932	478	7.0	218	3.2	45.6	60.1
1933	512	7.6	207	3.1	40.4	50.2
1934	661	9.7	259	3.8	39.2	58.3
1935	720	10.6	330	4.8	45.8	84.9

[a] Marriages were unduly high in 1920 because of marriages of returning soldiers. The totals for 1919 and 1921 were 672 and 625 respectively. Had the 1920 marriages stood at the average of the 1929 and 1921 totals, the marriage rate per 1,000 of population would have been 11.5, and the per cent divorces constituted of marriages in 1920 would have been in the neighborhood of 40 instead of 32.7.

[b] The population of Middletown constituted 69 per cent of the population of the county in 1930. See n. a under Table 11 for the method of figuring the population of Middletown's county for the intercensal years. The fact that Middletown's population for the intercensal years is estimated, combined with the necessity for estimating the county's population from these estimates for the city, introduces an unavoidable element of error here. Any errors that may exist for a given year are, however, believed to be small.

The crude marriage rate per 1,000 of total population for the United States as a whole was as follows:

1925—10.3	1928— 9.9	1932— 7.9
1926—10.3	1929—10.1	1933— 9.7
1927—10.2	1930— 9.1	1934—11.2
	1931— 8.5	

[c] For the three years, 1925, 1928, and 1929, Federal Census Bureau totals of divorces in Middletown's county fall 17, 8, and 19, respectively, below those published in the Statistical Report of the Clerk of the Circuit, Superior, and Criminal

Courts issued by the State Legislative Bureau. This problem is here resolved as was the 1923 discrepancy (see *Middletown*, p. 521) by assuming, on the advice of the State official in charge of compiling these statistics, that the Federal figures may not include the returns from both the circuit and superior court of the county for which their respective clerks make separate reports. The State figures are accordingly followed here.

d See paragraph one of n. *b* above.

The crude divorce rate per 1,000 of total population for the United States as a whole was as follows:

1890—0.53	1920—1.60	1930—1.56
1900—0.73	1925—1.52	1931—1.48
1910—0.90	1928—1.63	1932—1.28
1915—1.05	1929—1.66	

The collection of these statistics was discontinued by the Bureau of the Census at the close of 1932, as a result of the Economy Act of 1932. It had not been resumed by 1936. Figures available for eighteen states show a rise in crude divorce rate from 1.21 in 1932 to 1.66 in 1935.

e See *Middletown*, p. 521, Table XI, for divorces, marriages, and percentages of divorces to marriages for years 1889-95, 1905, and 1915-24.

f From Table 2.

TABLE 13: PER CENT OF TOTAL DIVORCES IN MIDDLETOWN'S COUNTY GRANTED TO HUSBANDS, BY YEAR: 1925-1935 [a]

Year	Per cent	Year	Per cent
1925	16.8	1930	20.4
1926	28.2	1931	18.1
1927	20.2	1932	15.1
1928	22.6	1933	39.6 [b]
1929	23.1	1934	17.8 [b]
		1935	8.2 [b]

[a] For the total number of divorces in each year see Table 12.

In the United States taken as a whole, the percentage of divorces granted to husbands has fallen as follows: In 1887-96 the average percentage was 34.2; in 1897-1906, 33.0; in 1916, 31.1; 1922, 32.0; 1923, 32.2; 1924, 31.5; 1925, 30.1; 1926, 29.5; 1927, 29.0; 1928, 28.6; 1929, 28.7; 1930, 27.7; 1931, 27.2; 1932, 26.5. (The collection of these statistics was discontinued by the Bureau of the Census at the close of 1932, as a result of the Economy Act of 1932. It had not been resumed by 1936.)

[b] The figures for divorces in Middletown's county for the years 1929-35 were rechecked by the Statistician for the State Department of Inspection and Supervision of Public Offices. In a letter under date of April 17, 1936, he stated: "There is a sharp divergency in the percentage of divorces granted to husbands in [Middletown's] county from that shown for the state as a whole. [The state percentages were 25.7 per cent in 1929; 25.9 per cent in 1930; 25.8 per cent in 1931; 21.7 per cent in 1932; 25.4 per cent in 1933; 24.6 per cent in 1934; and 25.0 per cent in 1935.] In fact, [Middletown's] decline since 1933 has been one of almost geometric proportions. I have carefully checked the reporting sources for these figures and it seems extremely unlikely that any error was made in reporting the marriages and divorces to this Department. The same official reported the statistics from 1932 to 1934; and there seems to be little likelihood that any error was made in 1935. I can think of no possible reason for the significant change in the percentage relationships for the past several years. While a new judge took office in the Superior Court on January 1, 1935, the percentage relationships under his term of office continued the same proportionate decline as for the previous two years; hence, I believe this matter to be of no effect. Moreover, the Circuit Court judge remains the same as in previous years."

TABLE 14: MEDIAN SIZE OF PRIVATE ^{a} FAMILIES IN MIDDLETOWN, IN THE
URBAN EAST NORTH CENTRAL STATES, AND IN THE URBAN UNITED
STATES, BY NATIVE WHITE, FOREIGN-BORN WHITE, AND NEGRO: 1930

(From the United States Census)

Type of family	Number of families in Middletown	Median size		
		Middletown	Urban families in	
			East North Central States ^{b}	United States
All families............	12,474	3.13	3.27	3.26
Native white..........	11,521	3.15	3.16	3.15
Foreign born white....	255	2.80	3.74	3.76
Negro	691	2.93	2.74	2.70
Other races............	7	....	....	....

^{a} The "private families" to which these medians pertain exclude "quasi-families" (e.g., in Middletown the 547 residents in twenty-four institutions, hotels, and boarding houses with more than ten lodgers, who in the customary "Census family" are counted as twenty-four families). Single persons, however, of which there are 763 in Middletown, and unrelated persons sharing quarters as partners are here included.

The identity of the median size of Middletown's native white families with that of all native white urban families in the United States should not blur one's awareness of the wide range of variations in median sizes that actually exists. The range for cities of 10,000 to 100,000 population in Middletown's state in 1930 was from 2.97 persons per native white family in a college town with few industries to 3.46 in an industrial community with many native white persons of foreign parentage. The Borough of Manhattan in New York City, on the other hand, a residential unit marked by a high percentage of one-person families and families without children, falls as low as 2.43 for the median size of its native white families.

^{b} Wisconsin, Michigan, Illinois, Indiana, and Ohio.

TABLE 15: NUMBER OF RELATED PERSONS IN MIDDLETOWN PRIVATE FAMILIES
AND IN THE NATIVE WHITE FAMILIES OF THE URBAN UNITED
STATES: 1930 [a]
(From the United States Census)

Number of related persons constituting family [b]	Number of families in Middletown	Per cent		
		Middletown families	Native white families of urban United States	Middletown families of two or more persons (11,711 families)
1	763	6.1	7.7	....
2	3,560	28.5	26.8	30.4
3	3,034	24.3	23.8	25.9
4	2,212	17.7	18.6	18.9
5	1,321	10.6	11.0	11.3
6	763	6.1	5.9	6.5
7	405	3.3	3.0	3.5
8	221	1.8	1.6	1.9
9	111	0.9	0.8	0.9
10	34	0.3	0.4	0.3
11	22	0.2	0.2	0.2
12 or more	28	0.2	0.1	0.2
Total	12,474	100.0	100.0	100.0

[a] The comparison between all Middletown families and the urban native white families of the United States is not precisely accurate. The Census does not break down Middletown's families by size according to racial and national backgrounds, but gives simply the above distribution of total families. The fact that only 7.6 per cent of Middletown's families are not native white, however, makes the comparison very close. As noted in Table 14, the median size of all Middletown's families is 3.13; of its native white families, 3.15; and of all native white families in the urban United States, 3.15.

[b] These family sizes include only persons permanently domiciled in a given dwelling unit. A grown son or daughter, e.g., permanently residing elsewhere, is not included. They also include single persons living alone and two unmarried persons sharing quarters as partners. See the first paragraph of n. a under Table 14.

TABLE 16: NUMBER OF CHILDREN UNDER 21 YEARS IN MIDDLETOWN PRIVATE
FAMILIES: 1930[a]

(From the United States Census)

Number of children in family	Number of families	Per cent
0 children under 21	5,458	43.8
1 child under 21	2,911	23.3
2 children under 21	1,985	15.9
3 children under 21	1,037	8.3
4 children under 21	534	4.3
5 children under 21	284	2.3
6 or more children under 21	265	2.1
Total	12,474	100.0

[a] These child groups include only children permanently domiciled in the family at the time of the Census.

This table does not mean, for instance, that 43.8 per cent of Middletown's married couples have no children. The Census was counting private households, not marriages. Included here, therefore, are single persons living alone but classed by the Census as "families"—aggregating one in seven of this childless group; also "unrelated persons sharing quarters as 'partners' "—an unspecified but probably small group; related persons living together but not husband and wife; and a sizable group of elderly households in which all children have come of age. All families are, however, "private families," according to the Census usage, *i.e.*, they do not include institutions. (See n. *a*, to Table 14.)

TABLE 17: BIRTHS IN MIDDLETOWN, WITH INDEX OF LOCAL INDUSTRIAL
EMPLOYMENT, BY YEAR: 1925-1935

Year	Number of births a	Birth rate per 1,000 of total population b	Index of local industrial employment for preceding year c
1925	819	22.4	. . .
1926	814	22.0	78.2
1927	899	22.2	100.0
1928	887	21.4	82.4
1929	997	21.9	99.3
1930	977	21.0	108.8
1931	922	19.2	77.0
1932	899	18.7	82.0
1933	857	18.4	60.1
1934	892	19.0	50.2
1935	922	19.6	58.3

a As noted in Table 49, hospital obstetrical cases, after rising but little in 1925-28, doubled after the opening of the new hospital in 1929. It is likely that Middletown, with its bettered hospital facilities, has been drawing relatively more obstetrical cases from its own and neighboring counties than was the case prior to 1929. These births from out-of-town, accordingly, probably swell the total of Middletown's births slightly more from 1929 on. Of the total increase in hospital cases (120 to 130 a year for 1930-34), probably not more than 25 a year represent this extra increment of out-of-town cases.

Excess of births over deaths by year is given in Appendix I.

b See table in Appendix I for the population of Middletown in each year.

c This index of local industrial employment is from Table 2. In order to relate it to the date of inception of pregnancy, the industrial index has here been moved forward by one year in each case: thus the index number 78.2 given for 1926 is actually the index for 1925, but is placed opposite 1926 births because most of the 1926 babies were conceived in 1925.

Since the amplitude of fluctuations in Middletown's industrial plants is larger than the fluctuations in total employment (including, e.g., trade, clerical, etc.) these figures for wage earners distort somewhat the economic condition of the population viewed as a whole.

TABLE 18: NUMBER AND COST OF NEW DWELLINGS IN MIDDLETOWN, AND
INDEX NUMBERS OF COST OF NEW DWELLINGS IN MIDDLETOWN AND
IN 257 CITIES OF THE UNITED STATES, BY YEAR: 1926-1935

Year	Population	Number of new dwellings	Estimated cost (in 000's)	Index of cost (1926 = 100)	
				Middletown	257 identical cities in the U. S. [a]
1926	37,000	270	$ 719	100.0	100.0
1927	40,000	317	1,120	155.8	84.5
1928	41,500	340	1,135	157.9	82.4
1929	45,500	313	903	125.6	63.4
1930	46,548	44	152	21.1	26.6
1931	48,000	34	76	10.6	18.9
1932	48,000	11	22	3.1	4.6
1933	46,500	11	30	5.6	4.0
1934	47,000	8	23	3.2	3.4
1935	47,000	44	99	13.8	...

[a] Figures for 257 cities are based on index numbers in the United States Bureau of Labor Statistics' *Monthly Labor Review* for April, 1935, p. 1084.

TABLE 19: AGE OF MIDDLETOWN'S RESIDENTIAL STRUCTURES, FOR SINGLE
FAMILY DETACHED AND FOR ALL OTHER TYPES: 1935

(From Middletown F.E.R.A. Real Property Inventory, 1935)

Age in years	Single family detached [a]	All others [b]	Total	
			Number	Per cent
0-4	107	10	117	1.1
5-9	823	27	850	7.7
10-14	926	39	965	8.7
15-19	743	25	768	6.9
20-29	1,508	92	1,600	14.5
30-39	1,960	211	2,171	19.7
40-49	1,775	302	2,077	18.8
50 and over	2,046	445	2,491	22.6
Total	9,888	1,151	11,039	100.0

[a] Single family detached structures constitute 89.6 per cent of the total.
[b] For composition of the types grouped under "All others," see Table 20.

TABLE 20: NUMBER OF DWELLING UNITS IN MIDDLETOWN, BY TYPE OF
STRUCTURE: 1935

(From Middletown F.E.R.A. Real Property Inventory, 1935)

Type of structure	Number of occupied dwelling units, excluding light-housekeeping	Number of occupied light-housekeeping units	Total occupied units		Number of vacant units [a]
			Number	Per cent	
Single-family detached	9,579	438	10,017	80.3	326
Single-family semi-detached and attached ..	946	27	973	7.8	100
2-family	459	20	479	3.8	32
3- and 4-family ..	145	5	150	1.2	12
Apartments	310	8	318	2.6	28
Flats over stores.	465	78	543	4.3	64
Total	11,904	576	12,480	100.0	562

[a] These vacancies existed at various times during January, February, or March, 1935, when the inventory was being made. They include a total of thirty-eight vacant light-housekeeping units: seventeen of them in single family detached structures, sixteen in flats over stores, three in single-family semi-detached and attached, and two in apartments.

TABLE 21: OCCUPIED RESIDENTIAL UNITS IN MIDDLETOWN, BY LENGTH OF
OCCUPANCY BY PRESENT OCCUPANT, FOR OWNED AND RENTED: 1935

(From Middletown F.E.R.A. Real Property Inventory, 1935)

Length of occupancy by present occupant	Owner-occupied		Tenant-occupied [a]	
	Number	Per cent	Number	Per cent
Less than 1 year	207	3.8	2,942	42.2
1 year	162	2.9	1,281	18.4
2 years	192	3.5	1,089	15.6
3-4 years	417	7.6	846	12.2
5-9 years	1,463	26.5	509	7.3
10-19 years	1,960	35.6	212	3.0
20 years and over	1,110	20.1	90	1.3
Total	5,511	100.0	6,969	100.0

[a] Includes 576 occupied light-housekeeping units.

TABLE 22: INDEX NUMBERS OF NUMBER AND DOLLAR VOLUME OF LOANS
ON REAL ESTATE BY A LEADING MIDDLETOWN BUILDING-AND-LOAN
ASSOCIATION, BY YEAR: 1924-1934

Year	Index numbers (1926 = 100)	
	Number of loans on property	Dollar total of loans on property
1924	78.4	78.5
1925	76.2	83.4
1926	100.0	100.0
1927	88.9	104.2
1928	106.7	129.4
1929	61.8	78.9
1930	28.7	31.4
1931	31.4	29.4
1932	3.9	4.4
1933	15.5	17.2
1934	14.1 [a]	10.4 [a]

[a] In the first five months of 1935 both number of loans and dollar total exceeded those for the entire year 1934.

TABLE 23: RENTED DWELLING UNITS IN MIDDLETOWN, BY AMOUNT OF
RENTAL IN APRIL, 1930, AND IN JANUARY-MARCH, 1935 [a]

(1930 Rentals from the United States Census and 1935 Rentals from
Middletown F.E.R.A. Real Property Inventory, 1935)

Monthly rent	April, 1930		January-March, 1935	
	Number	Per cent	Number [b]	Per cent
Under $15	603	10.0	3,386	53.0
$15-29	3,449	57.6	2,311	36.2
$30-49	1,540	25.7	565	8.8
$50-99	352	5.9	66	1.0
$100 and over	10	.2	1	0.0
Not reported [c]	38	.6	64	1.0
Total	5,992	100.0	6,393	100.0

Median Rent, 1930: $25.27
Median Rent, 1935: $14.45 [d]

[a] These figures are subject to some possible inaccuracy for purposes of comparison because of the different auspices under which the two counts were made. In each case, however, all homes were visited and the data gathered as part of an extended formal interview.

[b] 562 vacant units (38 of them light-housekeeping) and 576 occupied light-housekeeping units are here omitted in order to make the 1935 figures more nearly comparable to those of the 1930 Census. If the latter 576 are included in their appropriate rental groups the percentages are changed only in the decimal column, e.g., "Under $15" would become 53.1 per cent; $15-29, 36.6 per cent; $30-49, 8.3 per cent.

[c] In the 1935 survey these 64 cases are returned as "Special rent," with no amount given. It is here assumed that they involve the same types of cases as those returned by the Federal Census as "Not reported."

[d] Those paying less than $15 monthly fall into three uneven groups as follows: under $5, 108 families; $5 to $9.99, 1,137; $10 to $14.99, 2,141.

TABLE 24: PERSONS PER ROOM IN MIDDLETOWN, BY DWELLING UNITS
OCCUPIED BY OWNERS AND BY RENTERS: 1935 [a]

(From Middletown F.E.R.A. Real Property Inventory, 1935)

Persons per room	Number			Per cent		
	Owned dwelling units	Rented dwelling units	Total dwelling units	Owned dwelling units	Rented dwelling units	Total dwelling units
0-.50 ("Very spacious") [b]...	2,667	1,945	4,612	48.4	27.9	37.0
.51-.75 ("Spacious")	1,358	1,831	3,189	24.7	26.3	25.6
.76-1 ("Adequate")	1,044	1,917	2,961	18.9	27.5	23.7
1.01-2 ("Crowded")	416	1,184	1,600	7.5	17.0	12.8
2.01-3 ("Over-crowded")....	22	82	104	.4	1.2	.8
Over 3 ("Greatly over-crowded")	4	10	14	.1	.1	.1
Total	5,511	6,969	12,480	100.0	100.0	100.0

[a] This table omits the 562 vacant units.
[b] The characterization of each ratio of persons per room quoted in parentheses follows the usual nomenclatures used in the Government's Real Property Inventories.

TABLE 25: DWELLING UNITS ᵃ IN MIDDLETOWN BY TYPE OF WATER SUPPLY IN HOUSE, FOR OWNED BY VALUE, FOR RENTED BY RENTAL, AND FOR TOTAL: 1935

(From Middletown F.E.R.A. Real Property Inventory, 1935)

Type of water supply	Owner occupied					Rented ᶜ					Total ᶜ	
	Number	Value under $2,000		Value $2,000 and over		Number	Rent under $15		Rent $15 and over		Number	Per cent
		Number	Per cent	Number	Per cent		Number	Per cent	Number	Per cent		
No running water in house ᵇ	687	612	30.9	75	2.1	946	906	24.7	40	1.3	1,659	13.4
Cold water only	1,370	844	42.7	526	14.9	2,818	2,230	60.9	588	18.4	4,202	33.8
Hot and cold	3,454	523	26.4	2,931	83.0	3,084	526	14.4	2,558	80.3	6,567	52.8
Total	5,511	1,979	100.0	3,532	100.0	6,848	3,662	100.0	3,186	100.0	12,428	100.0

ᵃ The 524 vacant units are included, but the 614 light-housekeeping units (38 of them vacant) are omitted. Sixty-one of the light-housekeeping units were listed as having no running water, 200 cold only, and 353 hot and cold.
ᵇ Many units probably have a hydrant in the yard but no running water in the house. Figures for these homes are not available.
See n. 2 in Appendix I and n. d under Table 30 for the decline in users of city water during the depression.
ᶜ 69 rental units having "special rent" arrangements or for which rental was not reported are here omitted from the Rental columns but included in the final Total columns.

TABLE 26: DWELLING UNITS [a] IN MIDDLETOWN BY NUMBER OF BATHING UNITS AND BY NUMBER OF FAMILIES USING EACH, FOR OWNED BY VALUE, FOR RENTED BY RENTAL, AND FOR TOTAL: 1935

(From Middletown F.E.R.A. Real Property Inventory, 1935)

Type of bathing facility	Owner occupied					Rented [b]					Total [b]	
	Number	Value under $2,000		Value $2,000 and over		Number	Rent under $15		Rent $15 and over			
		Number	Per cent	Number	Per cent		Number	Per cent	Number	Per cent	Number	Per cent
None	1,647	1,268	64.1	379	10.7	3,288	2,945	73.5	343	10.0	4,976	38.1
1 or more baths used by 1 family	3,522	663	33.5	2,859	81.0	3,530	807	20.1	2,723	78.9	7,078	54.2
1 bath used by 2 or more families	328	47	2.4	281	8.0	560	225	5.6	335	9.7	893	6.9
2 baths used by 3 families	14	1	...	13	.3	78	30	.8	48	1.4	92	.8
Total	5,511	1,979	100.0	3,532	100.0	7,456	4,007	100.0	3,449	100.0	13,042	100.0

a Bathing facilities in vacant and light-housekeeping units are included.
b 75 rental units having "special rent" arrangement or for which rental was not reported are here omitted from the Rental columns but included in the final Total columns.

TABLE 27: DWELLING UNITS ᵃ IN MIDDLETOWN BY TYPE OF REFRIGERATION, FOR OWNED BY VALUE, FOR RENTED BY RENTAL, AND FOR TOTAL: 1935

(From Middletown F.E.R.A. Real Property Inventory, 1935)

Type of refrigeration	Owner occupied					Rented ᵇ					Total ᵇ	
	Number	Value under $2,000		Value $2,000 and over		Number	Rent under $15		Rent $15 and over		Number	Per cent
		Number	Per cent	Number	Per cent		Number	Per cent	Number	Per cent		
None	431	307	15.5	124	3.5	730	618	18.3	112	3.8	1,184	9.9
Ice	3,499	1,488	75.2	2,011	56.9	4,642	2,696	79.6	1,946	66.1	8,173	68.7
Mechanical	1,581	184	9.3	1,397	39.6	957	72	2.1	885	30.1	2,547	21.4
Total	5,511	1,979	100.0	3,532	100.0	6,329	3,386	100.0	2,943	100.0	11,904	100.0

ᵃ 524 vacant and 614 light-housekeeping units (38 of them vacant) are here omitted. In the case of the former, the type of refrigeration depends somewhat upon the occupant, though the survey shows 132 of these as having no provision for refrigeration at all, 468 ice refrigeration, and 14 mechanical. The light-housekeeping units, also omitted above, include 430 which had no refrigeration, 80 ice refrigeration, and 14 mechanical.
ᵇ 64 rental units having "special rent" arrangements or for which rental was not reported are here omitted from the Rental columns but included in the final Total columns.

TABLE 28: DWELLING UNITS [a] IN MIDDLETOWN BY NUMBER AND TYPE OF TOILETS AND NUMBER OF FAMILIES USING EACH, FOR OWNED BY VALUE, FOR RENTED BY RENTAL, AND FOR TOTAL: 1935

(From Middletown F.E.R.A. Real Property Inventory, 1935)

Type of toilet	Owner occupied					Rented [b]					Total [b]	
	Number	Value under $2,000		Value $2,000 and over		Number	Rent under $15		Rent $15 and over		Number	Per cent
		Number	Per cent	Number	Per cent		Number	Per cent	Number	Per cent		
Outdoor only	1,000	858	43.3	142	4.0	1,496	1,422	35.5	74	2.1	2,529	19.4
1 or more indoor used by one family	4,129	1,050	53.1	3,079	87.1	5,179	2,189	54.7	2,990	86.8	9,346	71.6
1 indoor used by 2 or more families..	354	71	3.6	283	8.1	629	315	7.8	314	9.1	986	7.6
2 indoor used by 3 or more families..	28	0	0	28	.8	152	81	2.0	71	2.0	181	1.4
Total	5,511	1,979	100.0	3,532	100.0	7,456	4,007	100.0	3,449	100.0	13,042	100.0

[a] Toilet facilities in vacant and light-housekeeping units are included.
[b] 75 rental units having "special rent" arrangements or for which rental was not reported are here omitted from the Rental columns but included in the final Total columns.

TABLE 29: DWELLING UNITS ^a IN MIDDLETOWN BY TYPE OF ARTIFICIAL LIGHTING, FOR OWNED BY VALUE, FOR RENTED BY RENTAL, AND FOR TOTAL: 1935

(From Middletown F.E.R.A. Real Property Inventory, 1935)

Type of lighting	Owner occupied					Rented ^b					Total ^b	
	Number	Value under $2,000		Value $2,000 and over		Number	Rent under $15		Rent $15 and over			
		Number	Per cent	Number	Per cent		Number	Per cent	Number	Per cent	Number	Per cent
Electricity	5,390	1,867	94.3	3,523	99.8	6,523	3,349	91.5	3,174	99.6	11,967	96.3
Gas	4	3	.2	1	0.	9	7	.2	2	.1	16	.1
Oil	117	109	5.5	8	.2	312	302	8.2	10	.3	443	3.6
Other	0	0	0	0	0	4	4	.1	0	0.	4	0
Total	5,511	1,979	100.0	3,532	100.0	6,848	3,662	100.0	3,186	100.0	12,428	100.0

^a 524 vacant units are included, but 614 light-housekeeping units (38 of them vacant) are omitted. 598 of the latter are electrically lighted, 1 by gas, and 15 by oil.
^b 69 rental units having "special rent" arrangements or for which rental was not reported are here omitted from the Rental columns but included in the final Total columns.

TABLE 30: DWELLING UNITS ^a IN MIDDLETOWN BY TYPE OF COOKING FACILITIES,^b FOR OWNED BY VALUE, FOR RENTED BY RENTAL, AND FOR TOTAL: 1935

(From Middletown F.E.R.A. Real Property Inventory, 1935)

Type of cooking equipment	Owner occupied					Rented ^c					Total ^c	
	Number	Value under $2,000		Value $2,000 and over		Number	Rent under $15		Rent $15 and over		Number	Per cent
		Number	Per cent	Number	Per cent		Number	Per cent	Number	Per cent		
Gas ^d............	3,820	852	40.9	2,968	82.5	3,541	969	25.6	2,572	79.2	7,390	57.8
Electricity	251	35	1.7	216	6.0	121	11	.3	110	3.4	374	2.9
Coal or wood	782	583	28.0	199	5.5	1,473	1,288	34.0	185	5.7	2,276	17.8
Oil or gasoline.....	829	613	29.4	216	6.0	1,898	1,518	40.1	380	11.7	2,744	21.5
Total	5,682	2,083	100.0	3,599	100.0	7,033	3,786	100.0	3,247	100.0	12,784	100.0

^a 524 vacant units are included, but 614 light-housekeeping units (38 of them vacant) are omitted. 414 of the latter had gas, 4 electricity, 50 coal or wood, and 154 kerosene or gasoline—8 of the 614 having more than one type.
^b 356 units had two types of cooking facility.
^c 69 rental units having "special rent" arrangements or for which rental was not reported are here omitted from the Rental columns but included in the final Total columns.
^d N. 2 in Appendix I shows that gas meters in service fell off 23 per cent between the high year, 1930, and the lowest depression year, 1933. This is more than three times the drop in city-water users, the latter declining by only 7 per cent.

TABLE 31: DWELLING UNITS *a* IN MIDDLETOWN BY TYPE OF HEATING, FOR OWNED BY VALUE, FOR RENTED BY RENTAL, AND FOR TOTAL: 1935

(From Middletown F.E.R.A. Real Property Inventory, 1935)

Type of heating equipment	Owner occupied					Rented b					Total b	
	Number	Value under $2,000		Value $2,000 and over		Number	Rent under $15		Rent $15 and over		Number	Per cent
		Number	Per cent	Number	Per cent		Number	Per cent	Number	Per cent		
Hot air	2,788	365	18.4	2,423	68.6	1,793	155	4.2	1,638	51.4	4,595	37.0
Steam	214	5	.3	209	5.9	513	28	.8	485	15.2	735	5.9
Hot water	115	9	.5	106	3.0	132	8	.2	124	3.9	248	2.0
Stove	2,385	1,595	80.5	790	22.4	4,408	3,470	94.8	938	29.5	6,839	55.0
Other	9	5	.3	4	.1	2	1	0	1	0	11	.1
Total	5,511	1,979	100.0	3,532	100.0	6,848	3,662	100.0	3,186	100.0	12,428	100.0

a 524 vacant units are included, but 614 light-housekeeping units (38 of them vacant) are omitted. 229 of the latter are heated by hot air, 112 by steam, 16 by hot water, 255 by stove, and 2 by other means.

b 69 rental units having "special rent" arrangements or for which rental was not reported are here omitted from the Rental columns but included in the final Total columns.

TABLE 32: INDEX NUMBERS OF TOTAL DOLLAR VOLUME OF BUSINESS BY A
LEADING MIDDLETOWN COMMERCIAL LAUNDRY, BY YEAR: 1923-1934 [a]

(1926=100.0)

Year	Index numbers	Year	Index numbers	Year	Index numbers
1923	82.1	1927	108.5	1931	97.9
1924	85.4	1928	123.0	1932	73.5
1925	84.8	1929	136.1	1933	53.5
1926	100.0	1930	109.2	1934	63.7

[a] It was not possible to correct the dollar volume of business either for changes in the dollar or for changes in the price of certain items involved.

TABLE 33: NUMBER OF TELEPHONE INSTRUMENTS IN USE IN MIDDLETOWN
AND SIX-MILE SURROUNDING RADIUS, BY YEAR: 1925-1936

Year	Number of telephone instruments [a]	Index numbers (1926 = 100)
1925	7,871	98.1
1926	8,027	100.0
1927	8,186	101.9
1928	8,730	108.7
1929	9,091	113.3
1930	8,931	111.3
1931	9,010	112.2
1932	7,256	90.4
1933	6,589	82.1
1934	6,860	85.5
1935	7,130	88.8
1936	7,809	97.3

[a] Includes all extensions from business and factory switchboards and in private residences.

The relative proportions of the instruments within and outside Middletown is suggested by the totals for 1936: 879 instruments (11.1 per cent of the total) were in 1936 outside the city limits 213 of them being in suburban homes and 666 in farms.

TABLE 34: INDEX NUMBERS OF SCHOOL ENROLLMENT IN MIDDLETOWN, BY ELEMENTARY AND BY HIGH SCHOOL, BY YEAR: 1928-1935 [a]

Year	Total population of city [b]	Total school enrollment in grades 1-12 [c] (June, 1929=8,483)	Enrollment in grades 1-8 (June, 1929 = 6,493)	Enrollment in grades 9-12 (June, 1929 = 1,990)	Per cent of total enrollment in grades 9-12
1928-29	100.0	100.0	100.0	100.0	23.4
1929-30	102.2	100.0	100.3	99.0	23.2
1930-31	105.4	106.0	104.0	112.9	25.0
1931-32	105.4	108.4	105.0	118.9	25.7
1932-33	102.1	107.3	103.1	121.0	26.5
1933-34	103.1	109.1	105.8	119.9	25.8
1934-35	103.1	109.1	106.6	117.0	25.2

[a] Middletown operates on the 6-3-3 plan. The division here is made by the grades 1-8 and 9-12 because eight years of schooling is the minimum required by law. Children between the ages of seven and sixteen are required by law to attend school, but a child over fourteen and under sixteen who has completed the eighth grade may withdraw, secure an employment certificate, and go to work. Enrollment by year in grades 1-6 is given in the Table at the close of Appendix I.

[b] Since school enrollments are taken at the close of the academic year, the population for the calendar year in which the second half of the academic year falls is here used, e.g., the 1929 population is used with the academic year 1928-29.

[c] Kindergarten is not here included. In 1928-29, 496 children were enrolled in kindergarten, and in each of the years 1929-30 through 1935-36 between 550 and 600.

Postgraduate students in the high school are also not included. During the depression these totaled 25 to 35 a year. By late October, 1935, only 15 were enrolled. The school director of research attributes this to the bettered economic conditions.

All enrollments are as of the first week of June at the close of the indicated school years.

TABLE 35: NUMBER OF MIDDLETOWN HIGH-SCHOOL GRADUATES AND NUMBER
AND PER CENT SEEKING ENTRY TO COLLEGE, BY YEAR: 1929-1934 [a]

Year	Total high-school graduates	Number of high-school graduates of indicated year with surnames A-M applying for college entry [b]			Estimated total applications for college entry from class [a]	Estimated per cent of total class applying
		In fall of same year they graduated from high school	In later years [c]	In all years to June, 1935		
1929	250	41	7	48	76	30
1930	302	68	10	78	124	41
1931	269	58	7	65	103	38
1932	362	43	8	51	81	22
1933	333	42	7	49	78	23
1934	391	35	8 [d]	43 [d]	68 [d]	17 [d]

[a] This is not a table of persons actually attending college but of persons who requested the high school to forward a transcript of their academic record to a college. These transcripts are required by all colleges. These data are used because they are the only form of record kept by the Middletown schools.

The individual student cards in the school offices, on which an entry is made when a transcript is sent to a college, were checked for all students in each year whose surnames begin with the letters A to M inclusive. Since Middletown's population is so heavily native American, the ratio of A-M's to N-Z's in the population was found by assuming that the space distribution in the phone book is representative. (Space listing the bunching of entries employing the names of the city, country, state, and United States, and also all multiple branch entries under a business entry were omitted.) That the resulting 63:37 ratio employed in calculating column six of this table is substantially correct is suggested by the fact that the total of 76 in 1929 is identical with the total of members of the high-school graduating class of 1929 announced by the schools to have been in college a year later.

[b] Persons having their records sent to secretarial schools and "business colleges" and to hospitals where they intended to take nurses' training are not here included. The last-named group (nurses' training), having their records sent to the Middletown hospital or to hospitals elsewhere, totaled 3 in 1929; 1 in 1930; 5 in 1931; 2 in 1932; and 1 in 1934.

[c] The check of high-school records on which this table is based was made in June, 1935. These totals for college applications are probably final for the high-school graduating classes of 1929-31 but those for the classes of 1932-33 may eventually have two or three additions. See n. d.

[d] The estimate of 8 later applications from the class of 1934 is a guessed extrapolation into the future. All of these 1934 figures should, therefore, be treated somewhat more tentatively than the others.

TABLE 36: PROPORTION OF GRADUATES OF MIDDLETOWN HIGH SCHOOL WHO
WERE BOYS: 1910-1936

Year	Number of high-school graduates	Percentage of boys among graduates	Year	Number of high-school graduates	Percentage of boys among graduates
1900	40	a	1928	268	50.7
1910	86	44.2	1929	250	46.4
1915	67	32.8	1930	302	49.0
1920	114	33.3	1931	269	49.4
1924	236	45.8	1932	362	47.8
1925	283	41.7	1933	333	49.3
1926	272	44.5	1934	391	48.3
1927	276	43.1	1935	300	48.7
			1936	403	49.9

a Not available.

TABLE 37: DISTRIBUTION OF ALL MIDDLETOWN PUBLIC-SCHOOL TEACHERS BY
YEARS OF PROFESSIONAL TRAINING, FOR 1921-22, 1925-26, AND 1931-32 [a]

Years of professional training beyond high school	School year		
	1921-22	1925-26	1931-32
Total number of teachers	250	298	282
Less than 2 years........	34.6 per cent	14.4 per cent	5.7 per cent
2-3 years................	19.6	33.9	13.5
3-4 years................	16.5	12.8	15.2
4-5 years................	23.9	31.2	40.1
5 years and over........	5.4	7.7	25.5
Total	100.0	100.0	100.0

a From *Educational Planning in the [Middletown] Public Schools,* Bulletin
88, Department of Educational Research, 1933, p. 44.

TABLE 38: ENROLLMENT, STAFF, AND OPERATING EXPENDITURES BY TOTAL AND PER PUPIL IN MIDDLETOWN SCHOOLS, BY YEAR: 1925-1936

School year	Total enrollment a	Number in teaching and administrative staff b	Total operating expenditures (in 000's) c	Cost per pupil d
1925-26	7,696	298	$654	$85.02
1926-27	8,172	298	650	79.54
1927-28	8,381	296	665	79.38
1928-29	8,979	292	688	76.61
1929-30	9,048	310	780	86.21
1930-31	9,597	309	761	79.26
1931-32	9,781	310	742	75.89
1932-33	9,675	298	623	64.41
1933-34	9,804	299	627	63.97
1934-35	9,822	301	643	65.45
1935-36	10,239	...	665	64.91

a Kindergarten enrollment is included. Hence totals differ from Table 34.

b These totals include classroom teachers, principals, supervisors, school nurses, and administrative officers in the Middletown system, and teachers and principal only in the college school. The size of the administrative, supervisory, and related staffs has grown since 1925 relative to teaching staff. The actual number of instructors was, e.g., in 1931-32, 282; and in 1932-33, 277, plus one half-time person. The low teaching load at the college experimental school, approximately 21.2 students per instructor throughout, has tended to make the above totals higher in all years after 1928 than would have been the case if the same pupils had been taught in classes of the same size as those in the other city schools.

c These figures include interest on indebtedness and all other operating expenditures except debt service and capital outlay. With the beginning of the school year 1929-30, the new college laboratory school was opened. It took over in the first year 402 of the city's pupils, and by 1934-35 its pupils had risen to 635. Its total operating budget was $67,500 in 1929-30 and in all succeeding years its operating budget ranged from $72,000 to $80,000. The Middletown school system paid 31 to 36 per cent of this total in each year and the State paid the remainder of the cost. The figures here presented also include the 64 to 69 per cent of the operating cost of this new school paid by the State. If the extra costs involved in operating this expensive school are eliminated and its students are carried simply at their pro rata cost in terms of the rest of Middletown's schools, the peak operating expenditures above, in 1929-30, would become approximately $745,000, and those for the lowest years, 1932-33, would shrink to approximately $580,000. This would represent a contraction of 20 to 25 per cent in total operating expenditures while the school population was increasing by 7 per cent.

d See n. c above. The high cost per pupil at the college school disguises somewhat the drop in average cost per pupil in all Middletown's schools after 1929-30. In 1929-30, with 402 pupils, the per pupil cost in the college school was $167.86; in 1934-35, with 635 pupils, the cost had fallen to $122.53. These figures are roughly double the per pupil costs in the rest of Middletown's schools.

TABLE 39: PUBLIC-LIBRARY CIRCULATION AND CARDHOLDERS IN MIDDLETOWN, BY YEAR: 1925-1935

Year	Population a	Library circulation	Per-capita circulation a	Number of cardholders b	Cardholders per 1,000 population a	Circulation per cardholder
1925	36,500	237,525	6.5	18,431	505	12.9
1926	37,000	243,276	6.6	20,136	544	12.1
1927	40,000	248,131	6.2	20,469	512	12.1
1928	41,500	259,240	6.2	21,551	519	12.0
1929	45,500	272,567	6.0	24,149	531	11.3
1930	46,548	327,791	7.0	25,850	555	12.7
1931	48,000	406,483	8.5	26,198	546	15.5
1932	48,000	511,960	10.7	28,306	590	18.1
1933	46,500	565,830	12.2	28,280	608	20.0
1934	47,000	532,807	11.3	28,215	600	18.9
1935	47,000	523,238	11.1	27,917	594	18.7

a All per-capita figures here are slightly high since the population figures employed are those for Middletown, whereas the library serves the entire township. The population of the city in 1930 was 95.1 per cent of that of the total township.

b The Public Library is used by some students at the college, situated about one and a half miles away. These student cardholders are included among the cardholders in this table. The library has kept a separate count of their numbers from 1928 to date, as follows:

1928—706	1931—636	1934—371
1929—711	1932—664	1935—418
1930—660	1933—497	

This student circulation distorts the picture of the reading done by Middletown's residents, though decreasingly since 1929 as the college library has bettered its collection of books. The almost halving of these student users by 1934 makes the contrast between Middletown's own reading in the 1920's and in 1933-34 the more striking.

TABLE 40: ADULT CIRCULATION *a* OF MIDDLETOWN PUBLIC LIBRARY, BY
FICTION AND NONFICTION, BY YEAR: 1928-1935

Year	Fiction		Nonfiction		Total		Per cent of total that is nonfiction
	Number	Index nos.	Number	Index nos.	Number	Index nos.	
1928	118,228	104	28,202	99	146,430	103	19.3
1929	113,248	100	28,527	100	141,775	100	20.1
1930	158,286	140	33,027	116	191,313	135	17.3
1931	201,510	178	37,096	130	238,606	168	15.5
1932	262,571	232	47,966	168	310,537	219	15.4
1933	297,878	263	49,160	172	347,038	245	14.2
1934	260,956	230	45,698	160	306,654	216	14.9
1935	234,879	207	44,048	154	278,927	197	15.8

a Includes combined circulation through central library, branches, and extension (book wagon, etc.).

TABLE 41: ADULT CIRCULATION OF MIDDLETOWN CENTRAL PUBLIC LIBRARY BY CLASS OF BOOK, FOR MONTH OF MARCH, BY YEAR: 1925-1935[a]

Class of book[b]	Av. circ'n in March '25 and '26	Av. circ'n in March '28 and '29	1930	1931	1932	1933	1934	1935
Philosophy	115	123	145	191	**218**	205	141	158
Religion ..	115	89	125	146	149	**218**	166	187
Sociology .	170	211	215	251	388	**447**	329	269
Philology .	12	8	17	24	**30**	17	17	10
Science ...	88	87	91	92	**205**	169	127	132
Useful arts	188	216	237	208	**358**	343	316	274
Fine arts..	271	288	330	412	509	**534**	391	350
Literature.	367	464	499	485	544	**693**	612	465
History ..	252	229	264	**344**	308	309	294	230
Travel ...	75	148	224	202	336	**440**	343	311
Biography.	148	186	249	251	394	**472**	361	293
Fiction ...	8,746	8,098	9,961	9,283	12,072	**14,548**	12,652	10,054

[a] Annual totals by kind of adult nonfiction read are not available. These figures are for the representative month of March throughout and include only books circulated from the main library building, omitting branches and extension.

The highest year for each classification appears in bold-face type.

Small differences from year to year on this single-month showing are not significant. The general trends, however, are significant.

[b] The classifications are those of the Dewey system by which the library keeps its records. This system is somewhat unsatisfactory for our purposes, since some of the categories are too inclusive; for instance, the category "Sociology" includes economics and government as well.

TABLE 42: CIRCULATION, EXPENDITURES BY KIND, AND SIZE OF STAFF OF
MIDDLETOWN PUBLIC LIBRARY, BY YEAR: 1926-1935 [a]

Year	Circulation	Total expenditures	Expenditures for new books and periodicals	Expenditures for salaries (excluding janitors)	Full-time persons on staff (excluding janitors) [c]
1926	243,276	$24,775	$ 5,690	$ 9,868	9
1927	248,131	27,631	6,603	12,458	9
1928	259,240	26,782	5,026	11,637	9
1929	272,567	24,053	5,734	11,632	9
1930	327,791	42,024 [b]	10,575	12,013	11
1931	406,483	33,754	9,037	13,155	11
1932	511,960	28,890	7,872	12,782	10
1933	565,830	25,291	5,248	12,533	9
1934	532,807	24,205	4,968	11,404	9
1935	523,238	24,521	5,372	11,200	10

[a] Middletown's library facilities consist of a central library (open daily from
9 A.M. to 9 P.M. and on Sundays from 2 to 5 P.M.); two branches (one open
three days a week from 12:30 to 8:30 and three days from 12:30 to 6, and the
other open two days from 12:30 to 8:30 and three days from 12:30 to 6); sixty-
one classroom libraries in ten city schools and seven in two township schools;
six adult stations in stores, factories, etc.; and a book wagon making fifty-two
trips a year over four routes in the township.

[b] In 1930 the building for a new branch was donated by private philanthropy,
but books and equipment had to be supplied from the library budget.

[c] In addition to the full-time staff, the library has used various part-time employees as pages. Prior to 1932 they were paid from petty cash at the rate of
20-30 cents an hour. From 1932 the library has had part-time workers as follows:
1932, 6; 1933, 6; 1934, 7, and 4 F.E.R.A.; 1935, 5, and 4 N.Y.A.

TABLE 43: PASSENGER AUTOMOBILE REGISTRATIONS IN MIDDLETOWN'S COUNTY AND STATE, AND NEW CAR PURCHASES IN THE COUNTY, BY YEAR: 1925-1935 [a]

Year	Number of cars registered in county [b]	Index of car registrations in county (1926 = 100)	Number of car registrations per 1,000 of population in county	Number of new cars sold in county	Number of cars registered in state [c]
1925	9,721	93.5	173	....	627,173
1926	10,395	100.0	183	....	663,540
1927	10,410	100.2	172	....	696,457
1928	12,032	115.7	195	1,885	718,173
1929	12,650	121.6	192	2,401	755,161
1930	12,034	116.7	179	1,162	733,792
1931	12,871	123.7	187	1,124	731,065
1932	13,892	133.6	202	556	673,490
1933	13,329	128.2	198	697	652,800
1934	13,533	130.2	199	1,091	679,578
1935	14,661	141.0	215	....	716,994

[a] From State Bureau of Motor Vehicles.

[b] A minor element of error may be latent in the registration totals in that they are totals for licenses issued through the county office. Persons from other counties may apply for their licenses at other than their own county offices. However, county lines are fairly sharply drawn, and nearly all matters of this kind tend to be handled in one's own county seat.

[c] The rapidity of the spread of passenger-car ownership in the state is reflected by the fact that their number more than doubled between 1920 and 1925, increasing from 294,338 to 627,173. In 1915 the total was only 96,615; and in 1905, not only passenger cars but all types of motor vehicles as well totaled only 4,253.

TABLE 44: ARRESTS IN MIDDLETOWN PER 1,000 OF POPULATION, BY YEAR: 1926-1935

Year	Number of arrests	Number of arrests per 1,000 of population	Year	Number of arrests	Number of arrests per 1,000 of population
1926	1,326	35.8	1931	2,134	44.5
1927	1,341	33.1	1932	1,183	24.6
1928	1,575	38.0	1933	1,398	30.1
1929	a	....	1934	1,837	39.1
1930	2,267	48.7	1935	a	....

a Total not available. Local police statistics are not kept by annual totals. Totals for 1931-34 were compiled from monthly figures. Prior to that press figures were used. It has proved impossible to elicit the 1935 total from the police department.

The press reports 2,111 arrests for 1936.

TABLE 45: ARRESTS FOR SELECTED TYPES OF OFFENSES IN MIDDLETOWN, BY YEAR: 1931-1934 a

Type of offense	1931	1932	1933	1934
All liquor offenses	661	356	270	469
All sex offenses	60	9	2	6
Gambling and keeping a gambling house	108	18	34	11
All motor vehicle offenses	156	57	118	46
Forgery	5	3	4	3
Issuing fraudulent checks	12	6	1	1
Arson	2	0	0	0
Petit larceny	67	80	112	50
Burglary, banditry, robbery, housebreaking, grand larceny	26	23	21	16
Murder, manslaughter, homicide, and shooting with intent	1	6	2	2
Carrying or drawing deadly weapon	12	6	7	15
All other offenses	1,024	619	827	1,218
Total	2,134	1,183	1,398	1,837

a Figures are not available prior to 1931.

TABLE 46: TOTAL VOTE CAST IN MIDDLETOWN'S COUNTY IN PRESIDENTIAL
ELECTIONS OF 1924, 1928, 1932, AND 1936, BY PARTY [a]

Party	1924		1928		1932		1936	
	Number	Per cent	Number	Per cent	Number	Per cent	Number	Per cent
Republican	14,411	61.8	19,102	68.8	15,939	52.0	14,207	42.4
Democrat	7,830	33.6	8,532	30.7	14,138	46.1	19,048	56.8
Socialist	.....	.....	54	.2	583	1.9	69	.2
Progressive ..... (La Follette) .	767	3.3	.....	.....	.....	.....	.....	.....
Socialist Labor ..	.....	.....	5	.....	.....	.....	.....	.....
Workers	33	.....	5	.....	.....	.....	.....	.....
Prohibition	299	1.3	72	.3	.....	.....	.....	.....
Communist	.....	.....	.....	.....	2	.....	16	.1
Union	.....	.....	.....	.....	.....	.....	187	.5
Total	23,340	100.0	27,770	100.0	30,662	100.0	33,527	100.0

[a] There is no way of knowing how much tampering with minority candidates' votes went on in the counting of votes or whether scattered votes for some of the minority parties were simply not counted.

The population of the county was 57,000 in 1924; 61,900 in 1928; and 68,600 in 1932. (See n. a under Table 11 for the basis of these estimated totals.) In 1930 Middletown's population was 69 per cent of the total for the county.

TABLE 47: INDEX NUMBERS OF AVERAGE DAILY CIRCULATION WITHIN MID-
DLETOWN OF MIDDLETOWN'S MORNING AND AFTERNOON PAPERS, AND
OF COMBINED SUNDAY CIRCULATION IN MIDDLETOWN OF SIX
LEADING OUT-OF-TOWN PAPERS, BY YEAR: 1929-1935

| Year | Middletown papers [a] | | Afternoon paper (1929: 8,478 copies = 100) | Combined circulation in Middletown of Sunday editions of six leading out-of-town papers (1929: 4,535 copies = 100) [b] |
| | Morning paper | | | |
	Daily (1929: 9,934 copies = 100)	Sunday (1929: 9,038 copies = 100)		
1929	100.0	100.0	100.0	100.0
1930	98.1	97.4	98.0	93.2
1931	95.0	93.0	97.1	79.4
1932	85.6	83.1	90.3	75.2
1933	78.5	76.5	84.1	47.9
1934	88.3	86.4	99.0	61.9
1935	95.7	92.1	106.0	64.3

[a] Figures for the two Middletown papers are national Audit Bureau of Circulation total average paid circulation figures for Middletown only, excluding county and other outside circulation.

[b] Figures for Sunday editions of out-of-town papers were supplied by the local news distributor. They cover actual sales, both delivered to homes and newsstand sales, for the second Sunday in March of each year. The six papers and their circulations in Middletown for 1929 and for 1933, respectively, are as follows: Chicago *Tribune:* 1,680 and 819; Chicago *Herald-Examiner:* 1,740 and 680; Cincinnati *Enquirer:* 340 and 187; Indianapolis *Star:* 370 and 246; Cleveland *Plain-Dealer:* 72 and 58; Detroit *News:* 333 and 182.

TABLE 48: TOTAL ADMISSIONS, AVERAGE PER DIEM NUMBER OF PATIENTS, AND
TOTAL PATIENT DAYS IN MIDDLETOWN'S HOSPITAL, BY YEAR, 1925-1935

Year	Admissions [b]	Average per diem number of patients	Total patient days [c]
1925	1,238	40	......
1926	1,475	47	......
1927	1,741	55	......
1928	2,029	58	......
1929 [a]	2,302	63	......
1930	2,664	79	......
1931	2,869	89	32,344
1932	2,446	81	29,452
1933	2,572	78	28,617
1934	2,798	91	33,347
1935	3,104	102	37,300

[a] The new hospital was opened and the old one closed on September 1, 1929.

[b] During these eleven years Middletown's population rose by nearly a third at the peak in 1931-32 and dropped off to about 26 per cent above the 1920-25 population in 1933-35. (See population totals by year at the close of Appendix I.) Hospital admissions should not, however, be compared solely with Middletown's own growth, since the new hospital has stimulated the bringing in of more patients from outside Middletown and even from near-by counties.

[c] Not available prior to 1931.

TABLE 49: TOTAL OBSTETRICAL CASES IN MIDDLETOWN'S HOSPITAL, BY YEAR:
1925-1936

Year	Number of obstetrical cases b	Year	Number of obstetrical cases b
1925	104	1931	258
1926	120	1932	276
1927	114	1933	274
1928	138	1934	273
1929 a	193	1935	376
1930	252	1936	477

a The new hospital opened on September 1, 1929.

b The gains here recorded following 1929 were registered in the face of a lowered birth rate. See Table 17 for the birth rate by year.

TABLE 50: NUMBER OF ADMISSIONS TO MIDDLETOWN'S HOSPITAL, BY TYPE
OF ROOM OCCUPIED AND BY WHETHER PAID FOR PRIVATELY OR BY
OTHER INDICATED AGENCIES, BY YEAR: 1931-1935 [a]

	1931	1932	1933	1934	1935
Total admissions	2,869	2,446	2,572	2,798	3,104
Type of room occupied [b]					
Private room	1,191	802	656	803	871
Semiprivate	246	213	187	232	248
Ward	1,205	1,207	1,476	1,508	1,630
Sources of payment					
Paying privately	2,099	1,838	1,845	2,136	2,424
Paid for by others	770	608	727	662	680
Public funds [c]	396	377	514	424	401
Local industries [d]	79	79	62	86	106
Private charitable endowment [e] .	198	81	88	63	114
Transient Service Bureau	0	0	0	14	9
Hospital (free cases)	97	71	63	75	50

[a] Owing to a change in the hospital head and a consequent change in record keeping, comparable data for years prior to 1931 are not available.

[b] Newborn infants omitted.

[c] Of these patients paid for by public funds, 63 to 78 per cent in each year were paid for by Middletown's township; 2 to 11 per cent by Middletown; 6 to 13 per cent by the county; and 11 to 19 per cent by individual townships other than Middletown's township.

[d] These are accident cases for which industry pays the cost because of liability under the Workmen's Compensation Act. Some industries carry insurance policies to cover these, while others pay their own costs at the rates set by the State Compensation Board.

[e] One of Middletown's early manufacturers, now dead, set up some years ago a small endowment for the hospitalization of the families of his former workers. (See *Middletown,* p. 71.) The fund is now used for payment for hospital services for the city's poor.

TABLE 51: INFANT DEATH RATE PER 1,000 BIRTHS IN MIDDLETOWN, IN ITS
STATE, AND IN THE URBAN POPULATION IN THE STATE, BY YEAR:
1929-1935 [a]

(From Annual Reports of the State Division of Public Health)

Unit	1929	1930	1931	1932	1933	1934	1935
Entire state	63	57	57	54	52	56	51
Urban population of state	67	61	60	58	56	61	56
Middletown	79	58	85	65	79	64	53

[a] The State publishes total deaths of persons of all ages only for Middletown's entire county. The county death rate, using the population estimates in Table 11 above, moved as follows:

Year	Total deaths in county	Number per 1,000 of total population
1925	703	12.5
1926	739	13.0
1927	726	12.0
1928	858	13.9
1929	832	12.6
1930	782	11.6
1931	806	11.7
1932	784	11.4
1933	783	11.6

These rates show the drop in the depression experienced elsewhere in the United States.

INDEX

581

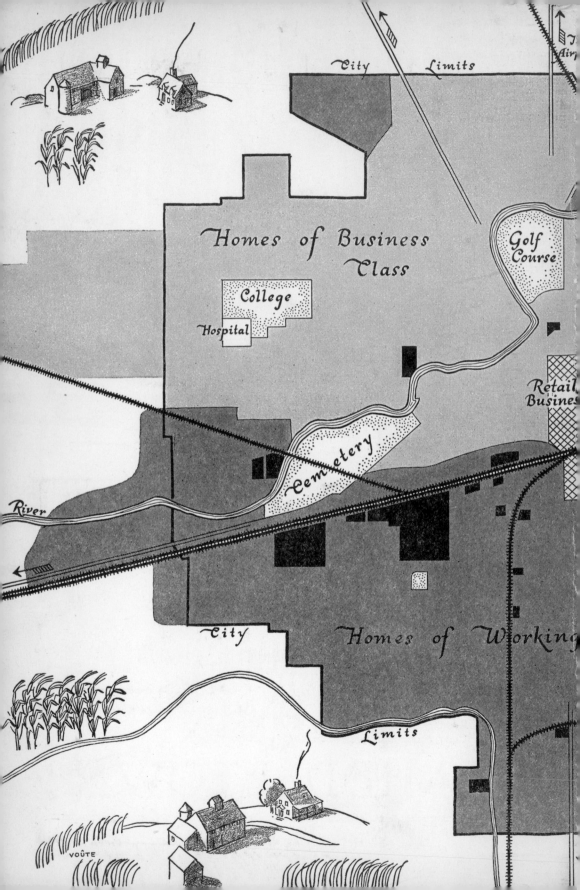

City Limits

Homes of Business Class

Golf Course

College

Hospital

Retail Business

Cemetery

River

City

Homes of Working

Limits

VOÛTE